10 How is the buying power of a teacher's salary affected by cost-of-living increases? (p. 38)

11 How has the increased recognition of student rights and responsibilities affectd the work of teachers? (pp. 52, 55, 58)

12 What are the rights of teachers to bargain collectively? What are the rights of teachers to strike? (pp. 64, 71, 72)

13 Are the projected increases in elementary and secondary schools great enough to offset the teacher surplus during the 1980s? (pp. 23, 30)

14 How does the so-called Buckley Amendment (the law regarding the privacy of student records) affect the practices of classroom teachers? (p. 60)

15 Is the trend toward concentrated teacher efforts for political action a prudent move for teacher organizations? (pp. 93, 225, 236)

16 What are the prospects for a merger of the NEA and the AFT? (p. 92)

17 Has there been a relationship of teacher power to teacher militancy? (p. 82)

18 To what extent is teching regarded as a profession? (pp. 4, 290, 293, 321, 494)

Society and the School

19 What values should public schools try to instill in pupils? (pp. 102, 148, 151, 290, 398)

20 What part should the public schools have in ameliorating America's race relations? (pp. 137, 138, 140, 321)

21 What can the public schools do about poverty in America? (pp. 135, 168)

22 What should the public schools do about school dropouts? (p. 142)

23 What is the responsibility of public schools in combating crime and delinquency? (p. 143)

24 What should the public schools do in combating sexism in our society? (pp. 59, 67, 141)

25 How can schools deal with drug abuse and environmental problems? (p. 146)

26 How do social values affect the function of today's school? (pp. 75, 102, 107, 109, 113, 118, 121, 127, 149, 152, 330)

27 What is the subculture of a school and how does a teacher cope with it? (pp. 117, 119, 123, 125, 128)

28 What changes in values have taken place in American society during the last three decades? (pp. 105, 108, 122, 123, 126, 150, 156, 292, 363)

29 What are the chief social needs that the federal government has supported financially by establishing a nationwide educational program? (pp. 160, 163, 164, 165, 433)

30 How can the schools address minority needs and concerns? (pp. 111, 115, 137, 158, 165, 166, 195, 196, 198, 202, 207, 209, 227)

31 Who should control American public education? (pp. 113, 176, 178, 180, 193, 202, 206, 208, 216, 220, 223, 226, 235, 257)

(Continued on Inside Back Cover)

Introduction to the Foundations
of American Education

Introduction to the Foundations of American Education

SIXTH EDITION

James A. Johnson
Northern Illinois University

Harold W. Collins
Northern Illinois University

Victor L. Dupuis
Pennsylvania State University

John H. Johansen
Northern Illinois University

ALLYN AND BACON, INC.
Boston ▪ London ▪ Sydney ▪ Toronto

Library of Congress Cataloging in Publication Data
Main entry under title:

Introduction to the foundations of American education.

    Includes bibliographies and indexes.
    1. Education—United States. 2. Educational
sociology—United States. I. Johnson, James Allen,
1932–
LA212.I57 1985   370'.973   84–18488
ISBN 0–205–08322–6

Printed in the United States of America.

10 9 8 7 6 5   90 89 88 87

Photo Credits
Pages 1, 104, 164, 371: Klemens Kalischer; page 11: Raimondo Borea/Art Resource, NY; pages 17, 159, 336, 399: David S. Strickler/THE PICTURE CUBE; pages 42, 449: photograph copyright Andrew Brilliant 1984; page 62: Laimute Druskis/Art Resource, NY; page 73: Owen Franken/Stock, Boston; page 91: Eric A. Roth/THE PICTURE CUBE; pages 93, 352: copyright Susan Lapides 1983; pages 98, 120: Kathryn Muus; page 129: © Elliot Varner Smith; pages 140, 172, 222, 250, 326, 392, 408: Alan Carey — The Image Works; page 145: Julie O'Neil/Stock, Boston; page 167: Charles Kennard/Stock, Boston; page 186: Frank Siteman/THE PICTURE CUBE; pages 194, 218, 384, 454, 493: Jerry Howard/Positive Images; page 203: Ellis Herwig/Stock, Boston; page 262: Ed Malitsky/THE PICTURE CUBE; page 310: The College Archives, Smith College, Northampton, Mass. 01063; pages 320, 432, 447: Rick Friedman/THE PICTURE CUBE; page 322: Andrew Sacks/Art Resource, NY; page 360: Eric Kroll/TAURUS PHOTOS, INC.; page 402: Margaret Thompson/THE PICTURE CUBE; page 426: Christopher Morrow/Stock, Boston; page 460: Robert V. Eckert, Jr./THE PICTURE CUBE; page 467: Don Rutledge/TAURUS PHOTOS, INC.; page 471: Frank Wing/Stock, Boston; page 478: (O'Connor) Sygma, (Ferraro) John Spragens, Jr./Picture Group; page 488: Margarite Bradley/Positive Images

Series editor: Susanne Canavan
Production administrator: Jane Schulman
Editorial production services: Barbara Willette
Designer: Patricia Torelli
Cover designer: Christy Rosso

Contents

Appendices

Preface

The foundations of American education constitute the basis of professional teacher education. By studying these foundations future teachers will learn to appreciate the proud heritage of the teaching profession and will begin to formulate a personal educational philosophy. Such a study also enlightens future teachers about the school's responsibilities to society and provides an understanding of school administrations and curricula. The sixth edition is divided into seven parts:

- Professional Aspects of Teaching
- School and Society
- Control, Organization, and Support of American Education
- Historical Foundations of Education
- Teaching Styles, Current Views, and Philosophical Concepts
- Program Purposes, Artifacts, and Practices
- American Education and the Future

The authors have also prepared a teaching aid for the instructor of foundations courses, *Resource Booklet and Overhead Transparency Masters,* that is correlated with this textbook.

In creating these materials we have kept in mind the problems that exist for instructors in the foundations of education; consequently, we have tried to construct a set of instructional materials that is comprehensive, interesting, and timesaving for both students and instructors.

Our intention was to make the contents of this book as direct and easy to understand as possible. Furthermore, we have tried to remove the foundations from the realm of theory and present them instead as useful tools for practicing educators.

We are indebted to the many people throughout the United States who have used the previous editions of this book and have provided valuable suggestions for this new edition.

I

Professional Aspects of Teaching

Teaching as a career continues to be an attractive choice for thousands of new graduates each year. As the job market begins to improve for prospective teachers in the mid-1980s, the number of college students selecting teacher preparation programs is expected to rise accordingly. In choosing a career the thoughtful undergraduate will consider all aspects of the working conditions associated with a particular area of employment. Students weighing teaching as a career usually seek information about what the average teacher is like, criticisms and expectations about teachers, teacher supply and demand, teacher salaries, legal aspects of teaching, teacher and student rights, professional liability, and teacher organizations.

Many recent articles in newspapers, magazines, and professional journals have focused on the negative aspects of teaching. The expression "teacher burnout" refers to thousands of thoughtful and dedicated teachers who are abandoning the profession. Teacher burnout is caused by the many problems that plague teachers, such as violence in the classroom, vandalism, disruptive students, inadequate salaries, interfering parents, oversized classes, and excessive paperwork. While the term "teacher burnout" most often pertains to experienced teachers who have left teaching, it is interesting to note that many beginning teachers leave teaching for the same reasons. For example, according to officials for the district and the local teachers' union, about 2,000 of New York City's 6,800 new teachers for the 1983–84 school year quit their jobs before March, often because of the difficult working conditions in the urban schools.

A host of recent reports and studies (see Appendix I) produced by various agencies, commissions, and foundations focus on other kinds of shortcomings of teaching. Several reports suggest that not enough academically able students are being attracted to teaching and that teacher preparation programs need substantial improvement. On the other hand, the February 22, 1984, issue of the *Education Week* newspaper listed two reports that found the quality of future teachers promising.

A survey of 5,000 students at 21 high schools in six states, sponsored by Texas Christian University, found that 9 percent of all college-bound seniors were "very interested" and 26 percent were "somewhat interested" in pursuing a career as a teacher.

Another survey, conducted at six colleges in Pennsylvania, suggests that education majors are as academically able as most of their college peers—a finding that contradicts the low rating given them by many educators on the basis of Scholastic Aptitude Test scores. . . .

The teacher-training programs most likely to be successful in attracting these students, the research suggests, are those that emphasize subject matter rather than methodology and provide early clinical experience.

While positive voices continue to speak in defense of our schools and teachers, the dissidents are more vocal. Given the preponderance of negative expressions regarding teachers and our schools, why would one bother to consider teaching as a chosen profession?

The authors do not suggest that teaching is an appropriate career choice for everyone. For those who possess the prerequisite commitment to education, adequate personal and social skills, and the basic ability to develop the technical skills a teaching career is an excellent choice. Teaching provides an opportunity to work with other college-educated persons, each committed to educating young people. Besides personal satisfaction, however, there are many other aspects of teaching that prospective teachers should consider.

While elementary and secondary public school enrollments have dropped considerably in the last decade, the whole of education represents one of the largest enterprises in the United States.

According to estimates provided by the Department of Education's National Center for Education Statistics, education was the primary activity of approximately 61.4 million Americans in the fall of 1984. Included in that total were 57.8 million students estimated to be enrolled in classes from kindergarten through graduate school.

The entire field of education continues to be one of the largest employment fields in the United States. In addition to the 3.3 million classroom teachers, about 300,000 other educators serve as superintendents, principals, supervisors, and other instructional staff members. When the noncertified support staff of secretaries, custodians, bus drivers, cafeteria employees, maintenance personnel, and others employed directly by the schools are included, the total number of employees rises considerably.

Teachers represent the foundation of the educational system. While the total number of persons qualified to teach continues to increase, the rate of increase has declined. Owing to the general teacher surplus during the late 1970s, the number of students preparing to teach has been steadily decreasing. It is estimated that the supply of new teacher graduates will exceed total demand for additional teachers through 1985. However, during the period 1986–1990, total demand for additional teachers will exceed the supply of new teachers. This reversal of the trend will improve the employment prospects for new teachers to the extent that some observers are forecasting a general teacher shortage beginning in 1985. While prospects for employment are improving, considerations related to salary and fringe benefits, the legal aspects of teaching, and membership in teacher organizations should also be reviewed carefully in considering teaching as a profession. For example, the impact of current inflation is unprecedented—particularly in the cost of such necessities as fuel, food, housing, and medical care. It has become increasingly more difficult for many teachers to provide a moderate standard of living for themselves and their families, since teacher salary increases have not kept pace with the inflation rate. These and related aspects of the teaching profession warrant early discussion in a book designed for the prospective teacher. Part I is intended to provide an awareness of some of the professional aspects of teaching. ■

1

Teaching: Demographics, Criticisms, Expectations

Focus Questions

- Has teaching as a career choice lost its appeal to many of the best college students? If so, why?
- Why do you want to become a teacher?
- In what ways are the educational expectations of our society being eroded by the so-called "rising tide of mediocrity"?
- Do you think public attitudes toward the teaching profession have changed? How? Why?

- Do you agree that states should encourage competency assessment of teachers before certification? Why? Why not? After certification?
- Merit pay plans for teachers are suggested as a means of rewarding the best teachers, yet merit pay plans have not worked well in the public schools. Why do you believe merit pay plans have not worked well when tried in the past? Will merit pay plans work now? Why or why not?

Key Terms and Concepts

Teacher demographics
National Commission on Excellence in Education
"Tide of mediocrity"
Competency-based certification
Competency assessment of teachers

Master teacher plans
Merit pay
Differential staffing
Career ladders for teachers
Tenure

What Would You Do?

You report to the preschool in-service workshop for teachers and discover that one of the discussion topics deals with the poor quality of beginning teachers. All teachers are urged to contribute their thoughts to the discussion.

As you begin your first year of teaching you find that parents and educators in your community expect increased discipline, higher standards for students, and more homework. At the same time your school is an open school. Many of the parents have few years of formal schooling, and the school philosophy has been to assign homework that can be completed during the day at school.

Education begins with teachers. Yet teaching seems to be losing its appeal for many of the best and brightest college students. In high school, many of the best students decide that they want to be teachers, but their relatives and friends soon convince them to change their minds. One student's mother kept reminding her of the relatively skimpy salaries teachers currently earn until the student changed to another major. Another student took computer science courses because his father thought that teachers were at the bottom of the social ladder. One said that none of her friends looked upon teaching as a worthwhile career, so she came to think of teaching as not noble enough and went into pharmacy instead. According to several recent reports on the shortcomings of American public schooling, teaching's lack of appeal for the brightest college students is one of the teaching profession's most worrisome problems.

Many articles on teaching, currently popular in newspapers, magazines, and professional education journals, concentrate on the negative aspects of teaching. The expression "teacher burnout" is commonly ascribed to thousands of thoughtful and dedicated teachers who are leaving the profession. Teacher burnout is caused by such problems as violence in the classroom, vandalism, inadequate salaries, involuntary transfers, interfering parents, oversized classes, and excessive paperwork. Even the best teachers cannot solve a child's problems, but many of them believe the public expects them to, and they give up teaching in despair.

Despite the more limited financial prospects, the deterioration of the American public's attitude toward teachers, and the problems caused by disruptive students, many of the best students conclude that they want to pursue careers in the classroom after all. The three students mentioned above discovered that they wanted personal fulfillment from their life's work more than they wanted material rewards. Each eventually chose to become a teacher. However, a growing body of evidence shows that such students are exceptions, rather than the rule, in America's more than 1200 teacher-training programs. Many teacher-training schools are beginning to look at ways to recruit the kind of people who would be inclined toward the positive aspects of teaching. The teaching profession has to become more attractive to good students.

Prospective teachers in the 1980s will see increased emphasis by national teacher organizations, state certification agencies, and local districts on improving the status of the profession, as well as on improving teacher salaries. Continued efforts to eliminate jobs teachers do that are not teaching—such as policing the rest rooms, hallways, and cafeterias—are important for upgrading the profession.

While teaching is not a wise career choice for all, teaching is a noble and rewarding profession for those who indeed seek personal fulfillment from their life's work. The first year of teaching is frequently the most frustrating year in a teacher's life. The experience of solving problems that deal with instruction, students, parents, administrators, and fellow teachers is of immeasurable value for future success.

> Many of those who stay in teaching, of course, go on to become excellent teachers. They become excellent, however, not as a result of the carefully thought out introduction into teaching. They excel because of their personal qualities and efforts. Indeed, they excel in spite of the manner in which they are introduced into the profession.[1]

Profile of the Public School Teacher

Although there is no single set of statistics on which to build a profile of the public school teacher, there are some average statistics on currently practicing teachers that are useful. They help one view the characteristics of the average teacher who belongs to teacher groups like those the beginning teacher will eventually join.

Table 1.1 presents average demographics about public school teachers during the 1982–83 school year. The average years of experience for all public school teachers was fifteen years, twelve of which were in the same

TABLE 1.1 *Public School Teacher Demographics, School Year 1982–83*

Item	All Teachers		Elementary		Secondary	
	1973	1983	1973	1983	1973	1983
Years of experience (mean)	11	15				
Years in present school system (mean)	8	12				
Average age of teachers	37	41	38	41	35	41
Sex						
Male	36%	33%				
Female	64%	67%				
Average number of pupils taught per day			27	24	133	117
Highest degree held						
Bachelor's	66%	52%				
Master's or six years	34%	48%				
Doctor's	(less than 1%)	(less than 1%)				
Average Salary (based on 9½-month contract)	$9,835	$20,531	$9,618	$20,205	$10,038	$21,052

Source: Adapted from *Teacher Opinion Poll: Demographic Highlights,* Research Memo, National Education Association, Washington, D.C., September 1983. Reprinted by permission.

school system. The average age of teachers, both elementary and secondary, was 41. In 1973, by comparison, the average age of elementary teachers was 38, and the average of secondary teachers was 35. In 1982–83, 67 percent of all public school teachers were women, and 33 percent were men. The elementary teacher taught 24 pupils during the day; the secondary teacher taught 117 pupils daily in five class periods. Fifty-two percent of all teachers had at least a bachelor's degree. The average salary for elementary teachers in 1982–83 was $20,205, and that for secondary teachers was $21,052. Table 1.1 compares the 1973 data with the 1983 data. The 1985 average salary for all teachers was $23,582.

The 1983 NEA Nationwide Teacher Opinion Poll also found that:

- Fifteen percent of the respondents report that they hold no memberships in national teachers' organizations. Of the 85 percent who are members of one or more teachers' organizations, 79 percent belong to the National Education Association, 8 percent belong to the American Federation of Teachers, and 4 percent belong to some other organization.
- More that three-fourths (77 percent) of all teachers are presently married. Of those not married, 10 percent have been previously married.
- The racial/ethnic composition of all teachers is 88 percent Caucasian, 8 percent black, 2 percent Chicano-Hispanic, 1 percent American Indian/Alaskan Native, and 1 percent Asian/Pacific Islander.
- Thirty-one percent of all teachers do not consider themselves to be affiliated with any political party. Two-thirds (68 percent) of the respondents classify themselves either as a Democrat (42 percent) or a Republican (26 percent). Less than 1 percent are affiliated with another political party.

Teachers were asked to rate various phrases that describe specific aspects of teaching. A scale of 1 to 10 was used with 6 to 10 indicating satisfaction and 1 to 5 indicating dissatisfaction.

A majority of respondents rated the following aspects of teaching in the 6 to 10 range, indicating relative satisfaction in these areas:

- The flexibility you have in deciding how to teach ....88 percent
- The personal fulfillment you get from teaching..................83 percent
- The support you receive from other teachers in your school.....80 percent
- The availability of up-to-date textbooks ....75 percent
- The support you receive from your principal ....74 percent
- The support available to you from teachers' organizations ......71 percent
- The time you spend supervising students outside of class........68 percent
- The availability of teaching supplies ....66 percent
- Student behavior in your class(es) ....66 percent
- The number of students in your class(es) ....65 percent
- The support you receive from the parents of your students......61 percent
- The procedures used for handling student
  misbehavior in your school ....55 percent
- The fringe benefits you receive.................................55 percent
- The time you spend on school work after working hours ....50 percent

A majority of respondents rated the following aspects of teaching in the 1 to 5 range, indicating relative dissatisfaction in these areas:

- The amount of time you spend on record keeping and clerical duties ....66 percent
- The salary you receive ....61 percent
- The treatment of education by the media in your community ...61 percent
- The amount of clerical help available to you from teacher aides or other support staff ....60 percent
- The quality of in-service education provided by your school system..52 percent

Several specific state or local efforts to maintain and expand a competent teaching force are supported by a majority of teachers. Specifically, 55 percent of the respondents support salary supplements to reward outstanding teachers, 46 percent support stipends to teachers in "critical shortage" areas such as science and mathematics, and 83 percent support differential salary schedules for teachers based on career stages such as beginning, professional, and master.

Commissions, Reports, Studies: Point

On August 26, 1981, U.S. Secretary of Education Terrel Bell created the National Commission on Excellence in Education. The Commission was directed to present a report on the quality of education in America to the people by April 1983. When it was released, the report, entitled *A Nation at Risk: The Imperative for Educational Reform,* hit the public schools like lightning. The introductory paragraph of the report stated:

> Our Nation is at risk. Our once unchallenged preeminence in commerce, industry, science, and technological innovation is being overtaken by competitors throughout the world. This report is concerned with only one of the many causes and dimensions of the problem, but it is the one that undergirds American prosperity, security, and civility. We report to the American people that while we can take justifiable pride in what our schools and colleges have historically accomplished and contributed to the United States and the well-being of its people, the educational foundations of our society are presently being eroded by a rising tide of mediocrity that threatens our very future as a Nation and a people. What was unimaginable a generation ago has begun to occur—others are matching and surpassing our educational attainments.

A Nation at Risk may indeed be the imperative for educational reform. Findings and recommendations are presented regarding content (curriculum), expectations (knowledge, abilities, and skills), time (in classroom and on homework), and teaching.

> The Commission found that not enough of the academically able students are being attracted to teaching, that teacher preparation programs need substantial improvement; that the professional working life of teachers is on the whole unacceptable; and that a serious shortage of teachers exists in key fields.

- Too many teachers are being drawn from the bottom quarter of graduating high school and college students.
- The teacher preparation curriculum is weighted heavily with courses in "educational methods" at the expense of courses in subjects to be taught. A survey of 1,350 institutions training teachers indicated that 41 percent of the time of elementary school teacher candidates is spent in education courses, which reduces the amount of time available for subject matter courses.
- The average salary after 12 years of teaching is only $17,000 per year, and many teachers are required to supplement their income with part-time and summer employment. In addition, individual teachers have little influence in such critical professional decisions as, for example, textbook selection.
- Despite widespread publicity about an overpopulation of teachers, severe shortages of certain kinds of teachers exist: in the fields of mathematics, science, and foreign languages; and among specialists in education for gifted and talented, language minority, and handicapped students.

The recommendation regarding teaching consists of seven parts. Each is intended to improve the preparation of teachers or to make teaching a more rewarding and respected profession. Each of the seven stands on its own and should not be considered solely as an implementing recommendation.

1. Persons preparing to teach should be required to meet high educational standards, to demonstrate an aptitude for teaching, and to demonstrate competence in an academic discipline. Colleges and universities offering teacher preparation programs should be judged by how well their graduates meet these criteria.
2. Salaries for the teaching profession should be increased and should be professionally competitive, market-sensitive, and performance-based. Salary, promotion, tenure, and retention decisions should be tied to an effective evaluation system that includes peer review so that superior teachers can be rewarded, average ones encouraged, and poor ones either improved or terminated.
3. School boards should adopt an 11-month contract for teachers. This would ensure time for curriculum and professional development, programs for students with special needs, and a more adequate level of teacher compensation.
4. School boards, administrators, and teachers should cooperate to develop career ladders for teachers that distinguish among the beginning instructor, the experienced teacher, and the master teacher.
5. Substantial nonschool personnel resources should be employed to help solve the immediate problem of the shortage of mathematics and science teachers. Qualified individuals including recent graduates with mathematics and science degrees, graduate students, and industrial and retired scientists could, with appropriate preparation, immediately begin teaching in these fields. A number of our leading science centers have the capacity to begin educating and retraining teachers immediately. Other areas of critical teacher need, such as English, must also be addressed.
6. Incentives, such as grants and loans, should be made available to attract outstanding students to the teaching profession, particularly in those areas of critical shortage.
7. Master teachers should be involved in designing teacher preparation programs and in supervising teachers during their probationary years.

In addition to the *A Nation at Risk* report, it seemed that hardly a week went by in mid-1983 without a new study of the nation's public schools. In May 1983 the College Board Report—*Academic Preparation for College: What Students Need to Know and Be Able to Do*—asserted that high school students who intend to go to college should master a comprehensive body of knowledge that includes six basic academic subjects: English, mathematics, science, social studies, foreign language, and the arts. This report was prepared as part of the Educational Equality Project, a ten-year effort to develop and implement a national standard for achievement in secondary education.

In August 1983 a report by the Carnegie Foundation for the Advancement of Teaching, entitled *High School: A Report on Secondary Education in America,* was published. This report may be the most thoughtful and specific of the batch of reports detailing the shortcomings of the American schools. In an introduction to the study, Ernest Boyer, president of the foundation, said that better teaching is essential if the current proposals for improving schools are to succeed. He also suggested that whatever is wrong with American public schools cannot be fixed without the help of those teachers already in the nation's classrooms, since most of them will be there for years to come. While visiting high schools throughout the country, Boyer and other researchers who worked on the report discovered that teachers are troubled not only about salaries but also about loss of status, bureaucratic pressure, negative public image, and the lack of recognition and rewards. To talk about recruiting better students into teaching without examining the current circumstances that discourage teachers is simply a diversion.

In August 1985 the Seventeenth Annual Gallup Poll of the Public's Attitude toward the Public Schools reported that Americans believe public schools to be better today than they have been in about a decade but are less willing to pay higher taxes to support them. In a survey analysis written shortly before his death in July 1984, pollster George H. Gallup said, "Americans are more favorably disposed toward the public school today than at any time in the past decade."

In large part, the poll reflected the growing campaign to improve public schools.

Commissions, Reports, Studies: Counterpoint

As expected, in late 1983, responses to the several reports on the American schools were highlighted by television, radio, newspapers, magazines, journals, teacher organizations, politicians, and other individuals. Most of the furor was about the Report of the National Commission on Excellence—*A Nation at Risk.* A professor at prestigious Georgetown University indicated that his students were bright enough to recognize the report of the commission for what it was: a scam. On the other side, Dr. Norman Francis, President of Xavier University in New Orleans, declared that the report "is a sound document prepared by serious educators."

With education a major issue in the 1984 presidential campaign, President Reagan maintained that the primary role in reconstructing education belongs to the states and school districts. He insisted that the challenges be met without a huge increase in federal spending. Democratic presidential candidate Walter Mondale and the country's two largest teacher unions (NEA and AFT) countered that the school rescue effort cannot succeed without a multibillion-dollar boost in congressional appropriations. U.S. Education Secretary Terrel Bell strongly defended President Reagan's education policies and accused the Democrats of being angry because the President had taken a position on an issue once thought to be the exclusive political province of Democratic candidates.

While President Reagan has claimed credit for helping to initiate reforms to improve the public schools, the Sixteenth Annual Gallup Poll of the Public's Attitude toward the Public Schools (August 1984) found that Americans believe that schools would be in better hands if Walter Mondale were president, since Ronald Reagan has pushed federal spending cuts in education. To the question "Which presidential candidate do you feel would be more likely to improve public education?", 42 percent said Mondale and 34 percent said Reagan; 24 percent had no opinion. The poll also said that Americans, by large margins, regard public education as more important to the nation's future than industrial strength or military might.

On May 11, 1984, following a year-long debate on education touched off by the *A Nation at Risk* report, the same commission issued a second report called *The Nation Responds*. This report declared that a tidal wave of school reform was improving public education. President Reagan cited *The Nation Responds* report to bolster the administration's position that educational change is underway without major new federal outlays. Some of the school improvement efforts by the states that were reported are as follows:

1. The number of state-level task forces appointed to study school reform had reached 275.
2. Thirty-five states have approved tougher graduation requirements, and thirteen others are considering similar action.
3. Twenty-one states are upgrading textbooks and instructional material.
4. Twenty-four states are examining master teacher or career ladder programs for teachers to pay superior instructors higher salaries. Six states have embarked on statewide or pilot programs.
5. Eight states have lengthened the school day, seven have lengthened the school year, and eighteen have mandated that more time during the school day be spent on instruction.
6. Five states have adopted more rigorous academic requirements for

participation in athletics and other extracurricular activities, and eight more are moving in this direction.

While the report also cites greater willingness by taxpayers to spend more on education once reform programs have been undertaken, some educators contend that none of these reforms gets to the heart of the school malaise. Unless some way is found to reinvigorate teachers and to radically reorganize schools so that teachers play an important role in policymaking, the spate of reforms being mandated by the state legislatures may prove to be as short-lived and ultimately inconsequential as the ones that were mandated after the Soviets won the race into space in the late 1950s.

   Teachers angrily reject the scapegoat role assigned to them by these kinds of reports. Charges by President Reagan and other politicians that many of the problems with education can be traced to inadequate teaching are strongly resented by teachers and their organizations. Most teachers insist that shortcomings in the schools are rooted in broader economic and

Quality education requires quality teachers.

social problems, including shrinking local taxes and the growing number of single-parent families. Much of the criticism leveled at teachers comes from people looking for an easy and inexpensive way of dealing with a very complicated issue.

"Tide of Mediocrity" Revisited

Sputnik, the first manufactured earth satellite, was launched into space by the Soviet Union on October 4, 1957. It was not until May 5, 1961, that Alan B. Shepard, Jr. became the first American in space. Shepard's flight in the space capsule *Freedom 7* lasted fifteen minutes and ended 300 miles out in the Atlantic Ocean from the launch pad at Cape Canaveral, Florida. By this time, Soviet Major Yuri Gagarin had orbited the earth in the world's first space trip on April 12, 1961. These space adventures highlighted the gap in space technology favoring the Soviet Union and brought forth charges of mediocrity in United States schools. It should be noted that most of the clamor during the late 1950s and 1960s for improving the schools was over the need for additional teachers, better facilities, and better student services; there was little castigation of teachers.

While the *Cooperative Research Program of 1954* had authorized the U.S. Commissioner of Education to enter into contracts with universities, colleges, and state education agencies for the conduct of educational research, Sputnik moved the federal government to take specific measures in providing funds for action. The *National Defense Education Act of 1958* provided monies for equipment and remodeling facilities for science, mathematics, and foreign language teaching; loans to students in institutions of higher learning; assistance for guidance, counseling, and testing services; and assistance for research in experimentation in the more effective use of television and other audiovisual media. The *Elementary and Secondary Education Act of 1965* enabled most school districts to qualify for funds to improve elementary and secondary education throughout the United States. The five titles of the Act provided for financial assistance for children of low-income families, library resources and instructional materials, supplemental educational centers and services, educational research and training, and grants to strengthen state departments of education. A myriad of other federal acts provided dollars for improvements in our schools.

During the 1960s and 1970s, schools grew in quality and size, enrollments burgeoned, economic advances were evident everywhere, the United States passed the Soviet Union in space technology, and faith had been restored in the public schools. Teaching was recognized as a noble career, and teacher salaries were given more attention than ever before. But were all these good signs merely cosmetic dressing for the longer-range failure of our schools? Was the infusion of dollars inadequate? What happened to the status of teaching? The plethora of commissions, reports, and studies of the early 1980s seems to place much of the responsibility for the most recent "tide of mediocrity" on teachers and their quality of preparation.

Competency-Based Teacher Certification

Public opinion polls show that the American public's attitude toward teachers deteriorated from 49 percent expressing a "great deal of confidence" in them in 1974 to only 29.8 percent in 1981. Much of this loss in confidence may be identified with studies showing that teacher competencies in the basic skill areas (three Rs) are well below the national averages for college graduates. This has given rise to the mandating of competency-based teacher certification provisions in many states. Figure 1.1 shows the twenty states that will have such provisions by 1985. With few exceptions, states with competency-based teacher certification were located across the southern tier of the country from coast to coast. In those states the competency tests utilized were the National Teacher Examinations or respective State Board of Education tests. Other states are expected to develop similar certification provisions.

Competency Assessment of Teachers

Figure 1.2 shows that 42 states are engaged in some stage of competency assessment of teachers. In addition to the 29 states with provisions for competency assessment of teachers, thirteen other states are planning to require such assessment. Only eight states indicate no activity in competency assessment programs for teachers. While it is true that plans for competency assessment of teachers seem to lend credence to the scapegoat role of teachers, the public demand for measurable teacher competency is reasonable.

One of the most active states in requiring all teachers to pass tests in reading, writing, mathematics, and specified subject areas is Arkansas, which has long been one of the poorest states with regard to educational expenditures. Governor Bill Clinton led the push for legislative reforms that will force all of the state's 24,000 teachers to pass basic competency tests or lose their jobs. Those who fail will be required to take more training; and if they cannot pass the tests by 1987, they will lose their jobs. While the 17,000-member Arkansas Education Association considers the tests offensive to a large majority of teachers, many parents and educators support the tests. A poll taken by a Little Rock television station found that 61 percent approved of teacher testing.[2]

Colleges of education are also getting in on the act. Many are requiring minimum competencies in the basic skill areas as measured by standardized achievement tests for admission in their teacher preparation pro-

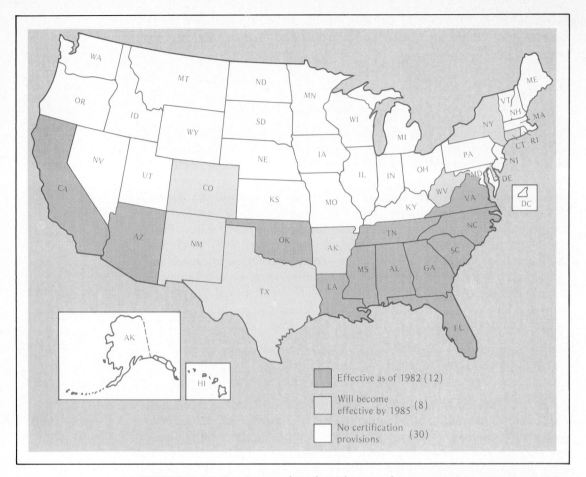

FIGURE 1.1 *Competency-based teacher certification provisions.* (*Source:* U.S. Department of Education, *The Condition of Education*, 1983 Edition, National Center for Education Statistics, Washington, D.C., p. 67.)

grams. Most of the reports that are critical of teacher preparation programs recommend that such entry standards be invoked by colleges and universities. Prospective teachers, as well as experienced teachers, should be challenged by such public expectations and work at whatever activity is available to fully satisfy such expectations. Further, prospective teachers are urged to check carefully the specifics of teacher certification and teacher assessment in the states where they choose to seek employment, since criteria vary considerably from state to state.

Career Opportunities in the Schools

Most of today's schools are complex organizations in which the expertise
5 of varied specialized educators is used during the day to serve the pupils'

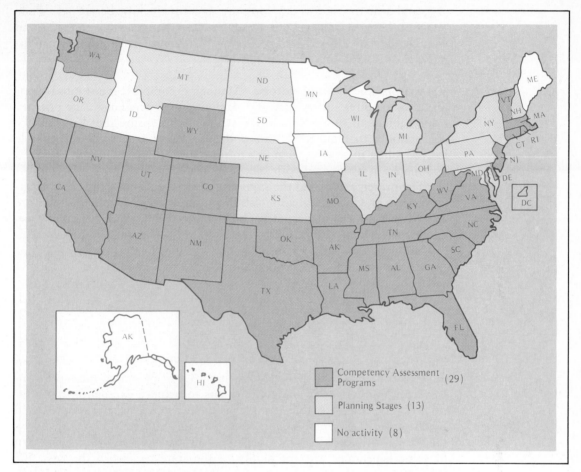

FIGURE 1.2   *Competency assessment of teachers.* (*Source:* Adapted from U.S. Department of Education, *The Condition of Education,* 1984 Edition, National Center for Education Statistics, Washington, D.C.)

educational needs. Many classroom teachers get additional training in or-der to qualify for the opportunities for new careers as educational spe-cialists, supervisors, and administrators.

Education Specialists.   The range of specialized occupations presents op-portunities for both prospective and regular classroom teachers to further their careers by more study of a specialized subject. Certified educational specialists work with the handicapped to overcome hearing, seeing, and speaking problems or with students who have other handicaps—physical, mental, or emotional. Specialists work as academic and vocational coun-selors, as librarians and learning resource directors, as teachers of students who have learning difficulties, and as teachers of bilingual students. Some schools are fortunate enough to have specialists to assist with music, fine arts, and athletics and to develop programs for the gifted students. While many of these specialists work mostly as classroom teachers, each has had enough additional preparation to qualify for a specialized teaching assignment.

Supervisors and Administrators.   Managing complex educational organizations requires supervisory and administrative personnel. The primary responsibility of supervisors in the schools is to ensure that high-quality instruction is maintained. To this end, supervisors are usually responsible for providing in-service programs to inform teachers about new methods and materials associated with successful teaching.

The principalship and the superintendency are among the most familiar careers in educational administration; other administrative careers are related to business management, school personnel, pupil personnel services, curriculum, and buildings and grounds. The various positions in educational administration usually provide the greatest opportunity for twelve-month employment and thus the greatest opportunity for higher salaries.

Master Teacher Plans

Merit pay, master teacher plans, differential staffing, career ladders—no matter what the label, the idea is turning out to be one of the more controversial ingredients in the states' plans to achieve excellence in education.[3] One of the first state efforts was the Master Teacher Plan proposed by Tennessee Governor Lamar Alexander in January 1983, followed by the Master Principal Plan in February 1983. Because the primary concern of some legislators was the ability of the state to absorb the cost, the original proposal was not enacted by the legislature. However, the Governor and the legislature did provide separate funding for the Interim Commission on Master Teacher-Administrator Certification to gather ideas on the criteria that might be used in a new teacher evaluation plan.

The Tennessee Master Teacher Plan illustrates the career ladder concept for teachers. Four career stages are identified in the plan: apprentice, professional, senior, and master teacher. Each stage would have a five-year licensing plan for renewal.

Apprentice and *professional* teachers would be paid according to existing scales. An apprentice could apply for a professional certificate at the end of the third, fourth, or fifth year of teaching. At the end of five years, having been regularly observed and evaluated by senior and master teachers, the principal, and supervisors, an apprentice would either become a professional teacher or lose certification. Professional teachers would be evaluated at least every five years with reviews of supervisors' and principal's evaluations, records of student performance, and observations made by master teachers.

Senior teachers would be in one of two categories: one category would continue with the regular 10-month contract with a 10 percent salary increase, and the second category would be placed on an extended 11-month contract with a 30 percent salary increase. Senior teachers would be expected to assume additional duties and responsibilities.

Master teachers would have a 10-, 11-, or 12-month contract with 15 percent, 35 percent, or 60 percent salary increases, respectively. A master teacher would need a minimum of five years experience as a senior teacher and would be required to have increased responsibilities.

Teacher unions are usually opposed to master teacher plans that would require teachers to renew their licenses periodically. Most states have tenure laws, which are intended to provide security for teachers in their positions. (See Chapter 3 for additional discussion of teacher tenure.) Master teacher plans would eliminate tenure as a permanent concept. The merit salary increases would threaten the salary schedule aspect, which is treasured by teacher unions. One wonders, however, if the teacher organizations are in tune with their members regarding master teacher plans. As cited earlier, when teachers were individually polled in the NEA Teacher Opinion Poll of 1983, 83 percent of the respondents supported differential salary schedules for teachers based on career stages such as beginning, professional, and master.

Good teachers never really stop learning.

Summary and Implications

We stress that teaching is not an appropriate career choice for everyone. For those who possess the prerequisites—commitment to education, good personal and social skills, and the ability to develop the technical skills— teaching could be a fine choice. It provides opportunities to work with other college-trained individuals committed to educating young people. Within the career itself, many avenues are available for teachers to specialize, to modify their orientation, and to pursue well-paying supervisory or administrative positions.

In 1983, several reports and studies called for the improvement of education in the American schools. Schools were pictured as being threatened by a rising tide of mediocrity resulting from poorly prepared teachers, low requirements in basic subjects, lack of money, and poor working conditions. New ideas for improving the schools included a longer school year; longer school days; more emphasis on basic academics; more math, science, and computer science; more discipline; more rigorous standards for teachers; and more involvement in schools by business, labor, members of professions, and community organizations. Most teacher organizations, which represent more than 2 million teachers, put aside the criticisms of education with the predictable reaction that more money was needed. On the other hand, other teacher organizations, such as the California CTA, supported and pushed for many reforms.

8   The average salary for teachers in 1983 was $20,531 with experience averaging 15 years. Employees in business and industry with comparable experience and training continue to be better paid. While teacher unions are generally opposed to merit pay plans, the general public, parents, teachers polled individually, business and industry personnel, and politicians believe that teachers should be evaluated and paid accordingly.

A national trend for certification of teachers is toward competency-based evaluations before licensure to teach. Some states require competency assessment of teachers whether or not the test results have any bearing on certification. Other states are developing plans for renewing the teacher certification every five years or so. Teachers who do not keep up on competencies in basic skills and in their teaching areas could have their certification revoked and thus lose their jobs. Several study commissions are engaged in reviewing data related to certification and evaluation of teachers. Colleges and universities are being urged to upgrade the quality of teacher preparation programs, including higher standards for student admission.

Implied from conditions and criticisms of education, especially for teaching, are increased expectations from parents, educators, and the American public. The fervor to improve the schools should bring about a significant change in the daily chores of the classroom teacher. Attention to increased discipline, higher standards for students, more homework, and longer school days and school years will enable teachers to spend more time doing what they are hired to do—teach.

As teaching positions become more available in the late 1980s, teacher salaries will increase to meet demand. Special incentives such as scholarship programs, tuition waivers, and stipends will be used to recruit high-quality students to teaching, especially in the areas of highest demand such as mathematics, science, and computer sciences. Teaching does provide one with personal fulfillment from one's daily work that cannot be measured in dollars. As increased attention is given to improve education in our schools, the teaching profession will improve in status, as well as in remuneration.

As with any choice of career, prospective teachers must understand the conditions, criticisms, and expectations associated with selecting teaching as a career.

DISCUSSION QUESTIONS

1. Reports and studies of American schools have inundated educators and policymakers with demands to improve the schools. In your opinion, what should teacher preparation programs do to upgrade their standards for admittance? What incentives could be available to attract more top-quality students to teaching? Should teachers be expected to pass competency-based tests in order to be certified?

2. Teachers in the U.S. public schools average 41 years of age, 15 years of experience, and 12 years in their school systems. What disadvantages does this imply for the beginning teachers? What advantages?

3. Make a checklist of the qualities of a good teacher. Of a poor teacher. Are there differences between elementary and secondary teachers? Between secondary and college teachers?

4. Over the years it has been a common belief that teaching offers job security. Does this belief have merit today? Why is job security a worthy consideration for making a career choice?

5. The most politically acceptable way to give more money to teachers is by merit pay or master teacher plans—assurances that good money would go to cherished good teachers. Discuss the pros and cons of merit pay.

SUPPLEMENTAL ACTIVITIES

1. Arrange for a panel of students to report on the National Commission on Excellence in Education report, *A Nation at Risk* (1983). Focus the discussion on the recommendations of the report about teaching.

2. Visit local schools (both elementary and secondary) for the purpose of determining the level of standards expected for English, social science, mathematics, science, computers, and foreign languages. How could the standards be raised above present levels? Were the teachers competent? Review as a class discussion.

3. Write to your state teachers' association for materials about teaching as a career. Ask about employment opportunities, working conditions, retirement benefits, and the like.

4. Arrange for a panel of teachers (elementary, secondary, college) to discuss with your class the woking life of today's teachers. Discuss problems that generate from school administrators.

5. Arrange for a panel of school administrators (elementary, secondary, college) to discuss with your class the working life of today's teachers. Discuss problems encountered with classroom teachers.

NOTES

1. Kevin Ryan, *Survival is Not Good Enough: Overcoming the Problems of Beginning Teachers* (Washington, D.C.: American Federation of Teachers, May 1983), p. 25.

2. Ellie McGrath, "No More Dragging Up the Rear," *Time* (December 26, 1983): 77.

3. Chris Pipho, "Merit Pay/Master Teacher Plans Attract Attention in the States," *Phi Delta Kappan* 65 (November 1983): 165.

BIBLIOGRAPHY

Boyer, Ernest. *High School: A Report on Secondary Education in America*. Princeton, N.J.: Carnegie Foundation for the Advancement of Teaching, 1983.

Gallup, George H. "Fifteen Annual Gallup Poll of the Public Attitudes Toward the Public Schools." *Phi Delta Kappan* 65 (September 1983): 33–47.

Howe, Harold, II. "Education Moves to Center Stage: An Overview of Recent Studies." *Phi Delta Kappan* 65 (November 1983): 167–172.

McGrath, Ellie. "The Bold Quest for Quality." *Time* (October 10, 1983): 58–66.

National Commission on Excellence in Education. *A Nation at Risk: The Imperative for Educational Reform*. Washington, D.C.: United States Department of Education, 1983.

Nationwide Teacher Opinion Poll 1983. Research Memo. Washington, D.C.: National Education Association, September 1983.

Opportunities Abroad for Teachers, 1980–81. Washington, D.C.: U.S. Government Printing Office (Stock Number 017-080-02041-6), 1979.

Ryan, Kevin. *Survival is Not Good Enough: Overcoming the Problems of Beginning Teachers*. Washington, D.C.: American Federation of Teachers, 1983.

Schuttenberg, Ernest M. "Preparing the Educated Teacher for the 21st Century." *Journal of Teacher Education* 34, no. 4 (July–August 1983): 14–17.

Today's Education (1983–84 Annual Edition). Washington, D.C.: Journal of the National Education Association, 1984.

2

Teacher Supply, Demand, Salaries

Focus Questions

- Since teachers have been considered poorly paid for their efforts in relation to the college preparation required for certification, what other aspects of teaching attract new teachers?
- Why are teachers reluctant to follow the general population shifts in the country? Shouldn't teachers move to where they are most needed?
- Illustrate the ways in which lower pupil-teacher ratios would aid classroom teachers. Are there some classes that would function just as well with larger numbers of students?
- How do you account for critical teacher shortages in chemistry, mathematics, physics, and data processing?
- Why is it that the beginning salary for teachers continues to be lower than the salary paid the beginner in business and industry? What needs to be done to correct this difference?

Key Terms and Concepts

Pupil-teacher ratio
Supply and demand
Differential pay
Salary schedules

Cost of living
Retirement incentives
Fringe benefits

What Would You Do?

During your first year of teaching you learn that teacher cutbacks in your district are made on the basis of seniority for most teachers. At the same time you learn that three or four additional courses in the sciences would qualify you to teach in the critically short science area. Your principal assures you that becoming qualified to teach science would serve you well in avoiding being laid off.

After your first year of teaching, your supervisor informs you that your yearly evaluation was highly satisfactory. At this time you are offered a position in private business at a modest raise in monthly salary. You then learn that your school will adopt a merit pay play within the next two years.

Unless more college students go into teaching, the nation may be faced with a teacher shortage in the late 1980s. This situation would sharply contrast with the large general oversupply of teachers that existed during the 1970s and that is expected to continue, at a reduced level, into the early 1980s. However, college students have responded to the large teacher surplus by enrolling in other fields of study. Since 1970 the percentage of new teacher graduates among bachelor's degree recipients dropped from 37 percent to only 12 percent in 1981. As a result, the supply of new teacher graduates has decreased from 284,000 to 159,000 over the same period.[1] The projections of new teacher graduates show an increase to 238,000 in 1990–91, representing about 26 percent of bachelor's degrees that year. This projection is based on the assumption that as the demand for additional teachers increases and as teachers' salaries improve during the 1980s, the proportion of college students preparing to teach will also increase.

The total demand for additional teachers includes those needed to allow for enrollment changes, for changes in pupil-teacher ratios, and for replacement of teachers leaving the profession. The cumulative demand for additional teachers fell from 896,000 in the five-year period 1971–1975 to 728,000 in the 1976–1980 period. As enrollment continues to decline, the demand for additional teachers is expected to continue to decrease. As a result, only 689,000 additional teachers are expected to be hired during 1981–1985. But in the late 1980s, as enrollments begin to increase, the demand for additional teachers will rise, resulting in the expected hiring of 983,000 teachers during 1986–1990. This represents an increase from 138,000 additional teachers hired each year (from 1981 to 1985) to 197,000 additional teachers each year (in the 1986–1990 period).

The supply of additional teachers consists of new teacher graduates and former teacher graduates who were not employed as teachers in the previous year. New teacher graduates are those graduates of institutions of higher education in a given year who are prepared to teach for the first time. Former teacher graduates are those who graduated in preceding years and are prepared to teach, but did not hold teaching positions in the previous year. Some of these former teacher graduates are former teachers; the remainder have never been employed as teachers.

For many years, teachers have been considered to be poorly paid for their efforts in relation to the college preparation required for certification. Such intangible rewards as the opportunity to work with students at every age level and professional status in the community were assumed to be attractive fringe benefits. As teacher organizations became increasingly powerful and militant, particularly during the 1960s, teachers began to demand increased salaries and other fringe benefits. Consequently, boards of education have since approved substantial increases in salaries and benefits.

Enrollment Projections

During the next decade, enrollment declines in elementary and secondary schools will end, and a gradual increase will begin as the 5- to 17-year-old population begins to increase in 1985. The enrollment increase is expected to continue into the 1990s, resulting in an enrollment boom that may surpass the peak levels of 1971. [13]

The enrollment rates for most of the school-age population (5- to 17-year-olds) are all close to 100 percent. Since school is compulsory to age 16 in most states, elementary enrollment closely reflects the 5- to 13-year-old population, and secondary enrollment tends to reflect the 14- to 17-year-old population. Enrollment in regular elementary and secondary schools decreased continuously from 51.3 million in 1971, its peak year, to 46.1 million in 1980 (Table 2.1). These enrollments continued decreasing until they reached a low point of 44.0 million in 1984. Then, as the 5- to 17-year-old population begins to increase, enrollment will also rise, gradually, to 46.7 million in 1990.

The character of education in the 1980s will be shaped to a large extent by the size of the population it serves. Between 1980 and 1990 the American population is expected to increase, and the age composition will be significantly different from that of the previous decade. By 1990 the median age is expected to be 32.8 years, almost five years older than the median age in 1970. This aging of the population is the result of several social trends that have had and will have a strong influence on the educational system in the United States.

While it is projected that enrollment will continue to decline in the early 1980s, it is also projected that pupil-teacher ratios will decline as well. The latter should offset the enrollment decrease and stabilize the problem of surplus teachers. In other words, more teachers will be needed for fewer students. The stabilization projected for the eighties will allow prospective teachers to feel more secure about entering the profession. It may be that some of the schools that were closed in the last few years will be opened to serve increased enrollments. On the other hand, school buildings are needed in those areas where the students live. If the majority of the new enrollments are in the Southwest region, for example, then job opportunities for new teachers will be best in the Southwest.

Supply of New Teachers

There is a lot of debate in educational circles over the nature and extent of the oversupply of teachers. Although the supply of beginning teachers has been declining dramatically, other factors related to teacher demand [6]

TABLE 2–1 *Enrollment in Regular Elementary and Secondary Day Schools, by Control and Organizational Level of Institution: 50 States and D.C., Fall 1970 to 1990 (in thousands)*

Year (fall)	Total Public and Private			Public			Private		
	K-12	Elementary	Secondary	K-12	Elementary	Secondary	K-12	Elementary	Secondary
1970	51,272	31,553	19,719	45,909	27,501	18,408	5,363	4,052	1,311
1971	51,281	31,588	19,693	46,081	27,688	18,393	5,200[1]	3,900	1,300
1972	50,744	31,023	19,721	45,744	27,323	18,421	5,000[1]	3,700	1,300
1973	50,430	30,135	20,295	45,429	26,435	18,995	5,000[1]	3,700	1,300
1974	50,053	30,082	19,971	45,053	26,382	18,671	5,000[1]	3,700	1,300
1975	49,791	29,340	20,451	44,791	25,640	19,151	5,000[1]	3,700	1,300
1976	49,484	29,255	20,229	44,317	25,430	18,887	5,167	3,825	1,342
1977	48,716	28,751	19,966	43,577	24,954	18,623	5,140	3,797	1,343
1978	47,636	28,749	18,887	42,550	25,017	17,534	5,085	3,732	1,353
1979	46,679	28,551	18,128	41,579	24,851	16,728	5,100[1]	3,700	1,400
1980	46,095[2]	27,987	18,108	40,995	24,287	16,708	5,100[1]	3,700	1,400
				Projected[3]					
1981	45,189	27,555	17,634	40,189	23,955	16,234	5,000	3,600	1,400
1982	44,544	27,286	17,258	39,544	23,686	15,858	5,000	3,600	1,400
1983	44,165	27,106	17,059	39,165	23,506	15,659	5,000	3,600	1,400
1984	44,039	27,113	16,926	39,039	23,513	15,526	5,000	3,600	1,400
1985	44,166	27,338	16,828	39,166	23,738	15,428	5,000	3,600	1,400
1986	44,556	27,936	16,620	39,456	24,236	15,220	5,100	3,700	1,400
1987	45,004	28,660	16,344	39,804	24,860	14,944	5,200	3,800	1,400
1988	45,358	29,389	15,969	40,158	25,589	14,569	5,200	3,800	1,400
1989	45,905	30,205	15,700	40,605	26,305	14,300	5,300	3,900	1,400
1990	46,667	31,022	15,645	41,267	27,022	14,245	5,400	4,000	1,400

[1]Estimated.

[2]Preliminary, private figures rounded to nearest 100,000.

[3]For methodological details, see Volume II of *Projections of Education Statistics to 1990–91.*

Note: Because of rounding, details may not add to totals.

Source: U.S. Department of Education, National Center for Education Statistics publications: (1) *Statistics of Public Elementary and Secondary Day Schools;* (2) Bulletin: *Selected Public and Private Elementary and Secondary Education Statistics,* October 23, 1979; (3) *Statistics of Nonpublic Elementary and Secondary School;* and (4) unpublished NCES tabulations; National Center for Education Statistics, Washington, D.C.

need to be analyzed. The increase in total school costs, which limits how much pupil-teacher ratios can be lowered, is another factor that impinges on the availability of teaching positions. Since employment opportunities in the business and industry areas have also decreased, the rate of teacher turnover has decreased; thus there are fewer openings for new teachers. The nature and extent of the teacher surplus for the years ahead will continue to be related to pupil-teacher ratio, teacher turnover, student enrollment, availability of new teachers, and general economic conditions. Continued development of early retirement incentive programs, and also the predicted increase in the birth rate for the mid-1980s, could conceivably turn the mid-1970s teacher surplus into a mid-1980s teacher shortage.

The supply of new teachers is usually derived from the graduates who have recently received a degree qualifying them to teach. While there will be a steady increase into the 1980s in the total number of graduates with bachelor's degrees, the number of degrees granted in education will continue to decline until the late 1980s. As was previously mentioned, the number of education degrees decreased from approximately 37 percent of all those graduating from college in 1970 to about 12 percent in 1981 (Figure 2.1). There are, however, some brighter possibilities. The projected demand for additional teachers in the late 1980s may result in better employment prospects and higher teacher salaries. Just as students reacted to the drop in demand by moving out of teacher preparation, so too are students projected to enter teacher training as the job market improves. Table 2.2 provides estimates of new teacher graduates compared with estimated demand for additional teachers from 1971 to 1990. It should be noted that 15–20 percent of new teacher graduates do not apply for teaching positions at all. That factor is not subtracted from the supply numbers in the table. With the projected demand during the late 1980s, the number of teacher graduates will increase beginning in 1986.

Classroom Teachers and Pupil-Teacher Ratios

Figure 2.2 and Table 2.3 show how many classroom teachers were in regular elementary and secondary day schools in the United States from 1970 to 1980—with projections through 1990.

The number of classroom teachers in public elementary schools increased from 1.13 million in 1970 to 1.19 million in 1980, primarily as a result of decreased pupil-teacher ratios. Although it is expected that enrollments in public elementary schools will continue to decrease through 1983, corresponding decreases in pupil-teacher ratios will probably offset the enrollment decreases; thus there should continue to be over 1.17 million public elementary teachers through 1984. It is expected that by 1985, the pupil-teacher ratio will have decreased to 19.6. This means that with

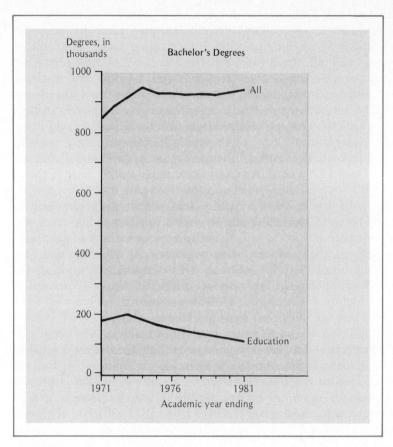

FIGURE 2.1 *Bachelor's degrees conferred in all disciplines and in education, 1971–1981. (Source:* U.S. Department of Education, *The Condition of Education,* 1983 Edition, National Center for Educational Statistics, Washington, D.C.)

increased enrollments considered, the classroom teachers in public elementary schools will begin to increase beginning in 1985.

The number of classroom teachers in public secondary schools increased from 927,000 in 1970 to over 1 million in 1975 as a result of approximately 1 million enrollment increases (14.6 million in 1970 to 15.6 million in 1978) and significant reductions in the pupil-teacher ratio. It is expected that for the next few years, the number of teachers in public secondary schools will increase slightly as enrollment remains somewhat stable and pupil-teacher ratios continue to decrease. Sharp enrollment drops expected in the early 1980s will be too large, however, to be offset by decreasing pupil-teacher ratios. As a result, the number of teachers in

TABLE 2.2 *Estimated Supply of New Teacher Graduates Compared to Estimated Total Demand for Additional Teachers: Fall 1971–1990*

Fall of Year	Estimated Supply of New Teacher Graduates,[1] in Thousands	Estimated Demand for Additional Teachers, in Thousands	Supply as Percent of Demand
1971	314	163	192.6
1972	317	189	167.7
1973	313	180	173.9
1974	279	178	156.7
1975	238	186	128.0
1971–1975	**1461**	**896**	163.1
1976	222	150	148.0
1977	194	181	107.2
1978	181	140	129.3
1979	163	126	129.4
1980	144	152	94.7
1976–1980	**904**	**749**	120.7
		Projected[2]	
1981	141	99	142.4
1982	139	108	128.7
1983	138	146	94.5
1984	138	142	97.2
1985	135	175	77.1
1981–1985	**691**	**670**	103.1
1986	156	187	83.4
1987	177	192	92.2
1988	197	189	104.2
1989	218	198	110.1
1990	238	217	109.7
1986–1990	**986**	**983**	100.3

[1]Estimates for 1971 through 1980 are from National Education Association, *Teacher Supply and Demand in Public Schools, 1980–81.*
[2]For methodological details, see Volume II of *Projections of Education Statistics to 1990–91.*
Source: U.S. Department of Education, *Projections of Education Statistics to 1990–91, Volume I,* 1982, and unpublished tabulations (December 1982), National Center for Education Statistics, Washington, D.C.

public secondary schools for 1990 are projected to be 893,000 (105,000 fewer than in 1980).

The number of classroom teachers in nonpublic elementary schools increased from 153,000 in 1970 to 187,000 in 1980, even though enrollment in these schools decreased by an estimated million students. The

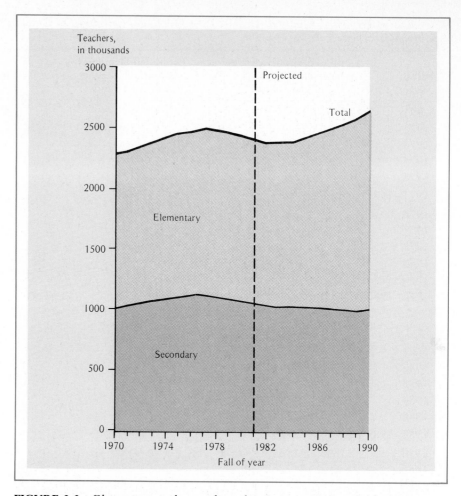

FIGURE 2.2 *Elementary and secondary classroom teachers. (Source:* U.S. Department of Education, *The Condition of Education,* 1983 Edition, National Center for Educational Statistics, Washington, D.C.)

number of teachers increased, since the large decrease in enrollment was more than offset by the sharp reduction in pupil-teacher ratios. It is expected that pupil-teacher ratios will continue to decrease while enrollments continue to rise in the nonpublic schools, causing an increase in the number of teachers in nonpublic elementary schools from 187,000 in 1980 to 214,000 in 1990.

The number of teachers in nonpublic secondary schools is projected to increase from 89,000 in 1980 to 95,000 in 1990. Future increases in the number of nonpublic school teachers will be attributable to reductions in pupil-teacher ratios and increased enrollments in nonpublic secondary schools.

TABLE 2.3 *Classroom Teachers in Elementary and Secondary Schools: Fall 1970–1990 (in thousands)*

Fall of year	Total			Public			Private		
	K–12	Elementary	Secondary	K–12	Elementary	Secondary	K–12	Elementary	Secondary
1970	2288	1281	1007	2055	1128	927	233	153	80
1971	2293	1263	1030	2063	1111	952	230[1]	152	78
1972	2334	1294	1040	2103	1140	963	231[1]	154	77
1973	2374	1309	1065	2138	1152	986	236[1]	157	79
1974	2410	1331	1079	2165	1167	998	245[1]	164	81
1975	2451	1352	1099	2196	1180	1,016	255[1]	172	83
1976	2454	1349	1105	2186	1166	1,020	269	183	85
1977	2488	1375	1113	2209	1185	1,024	278	190	89
1978	2478	1375	1103	2206	1190	1,016	273	185	87
1979	2456	1374	1082	2181	1188	993	275[1]	186	89
1980	2460	1373	1087	2184	1186	998	276	187	89
				Projected[2]					
1981	2411	1361	1050	2136	1178	958	275	183	92
1982	2374	1351	1018	2100	1168	931	275	183	92
1983	2377	1359	1018	2100	1175	925	277	184	93
1984	2376	1356	1020	2098	1171	927	278	185	93
1985	2408	1385	1023	2128	1199	929	280	186	94
1986	2450	1431	1019	2163	1238	925	287	193	94
1987	2495	1485	1010	2201	1285	916	294	200	94
1988	2534	1539	995	2238	1338	900	296	201	95
1989	2580	1596	984	2278	1389	889	302	207	95
1990	2642	1654	988	2333	1440	893	309	214	95

[1]Estimated.
[2]For methodological details, see Volume II of *Projections of Education Statistics to 1990–91*.
Note: Details may not add to totals because of rounding.
Source: U.S. Department of Education, *Projections of Education Statistics to 1990–91*, Vol. I, 1982, and unpublished tabulations (December 1982). National Center for Education Statistics, Washington, D.C.

Figure 2.3 compares the average pupil-teacher ratios in public and private schools for each state to the national average. For example, Utah, with the highest pupil-teacher ratio of 25 pupils per teacher in its public schools, had ten more pupils per teacher than Vermont, which had the lowest ratio. It should be noted that pupil-teacher ratios are usually computed by dividing the number of pupils in the school by the number of certified teachers on the entire staff, some of whom are not assigned to a classroom. Therefore the actual number of pupils per classroom is usually more than the pupil-teacher ratio for the school.

Teacher Demand

Although other factors undoubtedly help account for the current oversupply of teachers, four factors—new teachers entering the job market, near record total numbers of college graduates, restricted school budgets, and lower birth rates—probably account for most of the surplus. Population changes are expected to affect enrollments over the next decade. Increases in the nursery and kindergarten and in the elementary age groups are expected throughout the 1980s, while decreases are expected in the secondary and postsecondary age groups.

Although declining enrollment brings about a reduced demand for new teachers, the need for additional new teachers will continue so that lower pupil-teacher ratios can be accomplished and teacher turnover offset. Another consideraton related to the brighter prospects for teacher graduates by the mid-1980s is the continuing reduction in the number of students preparing for teaching careers. Figure 2.4 projects the decline of the supply of new teacher graduates through 1985, the total demand for additional teachers equaling the supply of graduates during the 1986–1990 period.

Studies made by the U.S. Commissioner of Labor Statistics suggest that supply and demand projections are always tenuous in our rapidly changing society and that the supply-demand relation is likely to be affected by many unpredictable adjustments. With labor supply constraints lifted, more communities may introduce or expand kindergartens, nursery schools, and curricula for the handicapped and the gifted. Also, as the supply of teachers improves, local school officials could take steps to improve the quality of education by hiring additional teachers to reduce class size and expand the scope of educational offerings.

Teacher organizations point out, however, that the teacher surplus would disappear quickly if our society wanted high-quality education strongly enough to pay the taxes necessary to support it. In other words, if the pupil-teacher ratio were to be lowered significantly through reduction in numbers of oversize classes and expansion in the availability of special education and vocational education programs, all the surplus

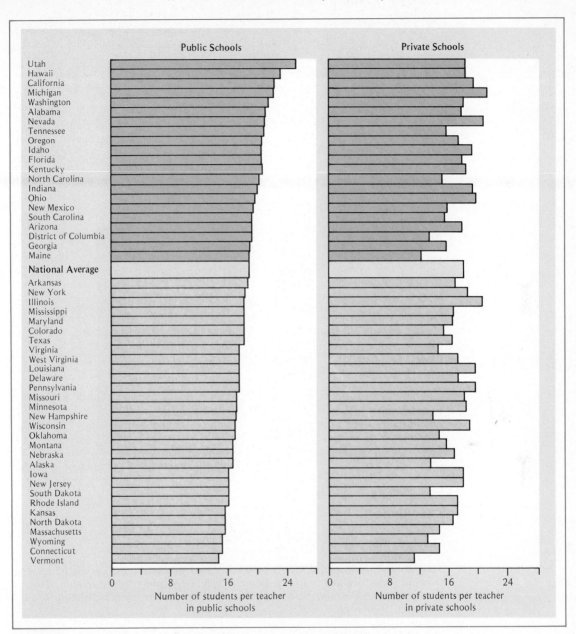

FIGURE 2.3 *Pupil-teacher ratios in public and private elementary and secondary schools.* (*Source:* U.S. Department of Education, *The Condition of Education,* 1983 Edition, National Center for Educational Statistics, Washington, D.C.)

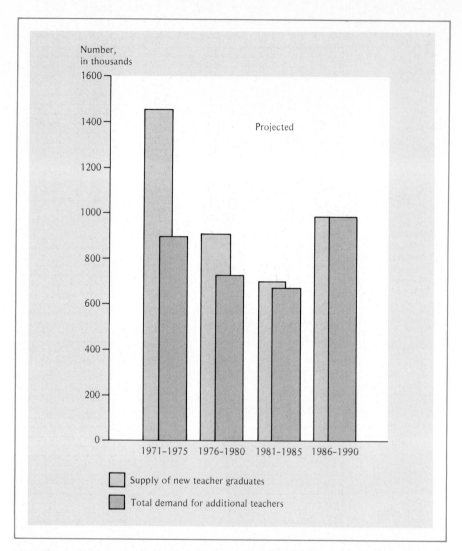

FIGURE 2.4 *Estimated supply of new teacher graduates and estimated total demand for additional teachers.* (*Source:* U.S. Department of Education, *The Condition of Education*, 1983 Edition, National Center for Educational Statistics, Washington, D.C.)

teachers would be needed to staff the schools. It is even conceivable that if such a trend were to become pronounced, and were not to be accompanied by a growth in the supply of qualified applicants, there would be a significant shortage of teachers by the mid-1980s. Unfortunately, most education practitioners believe that the average taxpayer probably will not pay for increases in their yearly tax assessments for an improved public school system.

The teacher surplus has several positive aspects. During the 1950s and 1960s, school districts had to hire many poorly prepared teachers, since fully certified teachers were few. The last eight years of surplus have made it possible for districts to hire fully certified teachers and to be selective in their choices. The recent oversupply of well-qualified teachers also has made it possible for school districts to replace substandard and provisionally certified teachers they have hired for most types of assignments. Another good thing about the teacher surplus is that it should provide some relief for colleges and universities that did not expand sufficiently during the years of teacher shortage to turn out enough teachers for the nation's classrooms. Many teacher educators hope that the end of the teacher shortage will let colleges and universities concentrate on producing fewer teachers of high quality, as opposed to mere large numbers.

Shortage and Surplus by Subject Area

ASCUS (Association of School, College and University Staffing) issued a research report in January 1983 that listed teacher shortages and teacher surpluses by subject area as indicated by placement directors in institutions of higher education producing over 70,000 new teachers. The placement directors ranked the subject areas on a continuum from considerable surplus to considerable shortage. Table 2.4 shows the areas of critical shortage to be chemistry, mathematics, physics, and data processing. Also reported as shortage areas were biology, special education, vocational agriculture, industrial arts, earth science, and speech pathology. The shortage areas were found to be in secondary education for the most part. Areas of surplus were art, elementary education, health, men's and women's physical education, social science, home economics, foreign languages, speech, and journalism.

College and university placement directors suggest that students planning to become teachers should be apprised of the fact that opportunity exists in practically any field for the top-quality graduate. For example, even though there is a good supply of teachers, far more graduates are employed in elementary education, English, and social studies than in areas that now have shortages. Thus high-quality candidates in some teaching areas having less demand are still likely to find a teaching position.

Also, the U.S. Department of Defense operates a school system for the children of American men and women in the armed services abroad. This school system, the United States Dependents School, is one of our nation's largest school systems, enrolling about 130,000 students in over 260 schools in 23 countries. The approximately 7500 teachers in this system come from every state in the union. Although not officially organized as an international education program, these U.S. Dependents Schools widen the chance for citizens of the United States and citizens of other nations to exchange cultural experiences.

TABLE 2.4   *Teacher Shortage/Surplus Index, as Perceived by Placement Directors*

	1984	1983	1982	1981	1980	1979	1976
Teaching fields with considerable teacher shortage (5.00–4.25)							
Mathematics	4.78	4.75	4.81	4.79	4.80	4.68	3.86
Science—Physics	4.45	4.46	4.41	4.56	4.28	4.36	4.04
Computer Programming	4.34	—	—	—	—	—	—
Science—Chemistry	4.25	4.30	4.13	4.42	4.18	4.09	3.72
Teaching fields with slight teacher shortage (4.24–3.45)							
Data Processing	4.18	4.36	3.86	—	—	—	—
Bilingual Education	4.04	3.83	4.13	4.10	4.21	4.32	—
Special Education—LD	3.98	4.09	4.20	4.47	4.48	4.50	4.00
Special Education—ED/PSA	3.84	4.08	3.98	4.22	4.36	4.22	3.42
Speech Pathology/Audio.	3.83	3.62	3.95	4.27	4.17	3.83	3.68
Special Education—Multi. Handi.	3.77	3.82	3.93	4.13	3.87	3.24	—
Special Education—Gifted	3.74	3.80	3.81	4.10	4.33	4.56	3.85
Science—Earth	3.70	3.80	3.89	4.08	3.64	3.82	3.44
Science—General	3.65	—	—	—	—	—	—
Special Education—MR	3.55	3.71	3.84	4.14	4.23	4.39	2.87
Industrial Arts	3.50	3.96	4.36	4.72	4.77	4.68	4.22
Special Education—Reading	3.48	3.39	3.73	4.21	4.23	4.27	3.96
Teaching fields with balanced supply and demand (3.44–2.65)							
Vocational Agriculture	3.44	4.02	4.36	4.46	4.73	4.67	4.06
Science—Biology	3.40	4.10	3.66	3.98	3.50	3.49	2.97
Nurse (school)	3.40	—	—	—	—	—	—
Library Science	3.30	3.09	3.12	3.31	3.58	4.26	—
Music—Instrumental	3.25	2.97	3.28	3.33	3.65	3.33	3.03
Language, Mod.—Spanish	3.18	2.77	2.68	2.95	3.34	2.88	2.47
English	3.13	2.90	3.21	3.37	3.51	2.78	2.05
Business	3.11	3.24	3.47	3.50	3.80	3.65	3.10

TABLE 2.4   *(Continued)*

	1984	1983	1982	1981	1980	1979	1976
Language, Mod.—German	3.08	2.51	2.48	2.58	2.70	2.17	2.03
Language, Mod.—French	3.00	2.59	2.49	2.58	2.68	2.49	2.15
Music—Vocal	3.00	2.89	2.95	3.06	3.32	2.97	3.00
Psychologist (school)	2.98	3.19	3.56	3.70	3.87	3.43	3.09
Counselor—Elementary	2.80	3.03	2.72	3.05	3.38	2.96	3.15
Speech	2.70	2.51	2.76	2.65	2.50	2.47	2.46
Counselor—Secondary	2.67	2.83	2.79	3.13	3.76	3.03	2.69
Teaching fields with slight surplus of teachers (2.64–1.85)							
Driver Education	2.61	2.94	2.77	2.87	2.98	3.06	2.44
Journalism	2.60	2.63	2.61	2.77	2.98	2.50	2.86
Home Economics	2.43	2.44	2.43	2.54	2.85	2.67	2.62
Social Worker (school)	2.33	2.27	2.34	—	—	—	—
Elementary—Intermediate	2.20	2.11	2.26	2.56	2.84	2.33	1.90
Elementary—Primary	2.13	2.11	2.02	2.24	2.77	2.19	1.78
Social Science	1.91	1.75	2.11	2.05	1.98	1.83	1.51
Health Education	1.90	1.76	1.90	2.24	2.17	2.16	2.27
Art	1.89	1.92	1.84	2.00	2.45	2.06	2.14
Teaching field with considerable surplus of teachers (1.84–1.00)							
Physical Education	1.61	1.54	1.72	1.80	1.82	1.67	1.74

5 = greatest demand, 1 = least demand.
Source: ASCUS Research Report, January 1984, Association of School, College and University Staffing, Madison, Wis. Reprinted by permission.

Opportunities for Americans to teach abroad are increasing. Teacher shortages in other nations, combined with a surplus of teachers in the United States, have heightened foreign employment. Recruiters from West Germany and Australia, for example, have visited many college and university campuses hoping to hire teachers from the United States.

A concise summary of opportunities for studying or teaching abroad can be found in *Educational and Cultural Exchange Opportunities,* a booklet published by the U.S. Department of State, Bureau of Educational and Cultural Affairs, Washington, D.C. 20520.[2]

Teacher Salaries

Increases in teacher salaries have never been unanimously supported by the taxpayers who support the schools. Many believe that teachers work only a few hours a day and have all the school holidays as paid vacations. Increasing numbers of defeated local school tax referenda show that taxpayers throughout the nation no longer are willing to pay additional taxes to provide higher teacher salaries. Also, legislative cutbacks at the state level reflect the general belief that the tax burden is already too high. The public schools will travel a rocky road during the 1980s, battling against spending restrictions.

Whether or not teachers are adequately paid will continue to be a subject of discussion for the taxpaying public. Teachers working through powerful teacher organizations will continue their efforts to upgrade salaries and other economic aspects of teaching. Taxpayers, governmental agencies that support schools, and others not in direct contact with the schools will probably continue to resist attempts to raise taxes in order to raise teacher salaries.

As general economic conditions improved during the past few years, teachers' salaries rose somewhat. Table 2.5 shows the rise in average annual salaries of public school instructional staff across the United States and for each of the states from 1966–67 to 1982–83. During the sixteen-year period the average pay rose from $7,129 to $20,531 (188% increase). The change in instructional salaries from 1967 to 1983 exceeded 100 percent in every state. Alaska (376 percent), New York (252 percent), Hawaii (248 percent), and Wyoming (237 percent) showed the greatest change in instructional salaries. Mississippi (100 percent), Arkansas (113 percent), and Vermont (115 percent) showed the least change in instructional salaries.

TABLE 2.5 *Average Salaries of Instructional Staff, 1966–67 and 1982–83*

State	1966–67		1982–83		Purchasing Power in 1967 Dollars
	Amount	*Rank*	*Amount*	*Rank*	
U.S. average	$7,129	—	$20,531	—	$6,769
Alabama	5,800	42	17,850	36	5,885
Alaska	9,392	1	33,953	1	11,195
Arizona	7,430	15	18,849	28	6,215
Arkansas	5,113	48	15,176	49	5,004
California	9,000	2	23,555	6	7,766
Colorado	6,824	22	21,500	14	7,089
Connecticut	7,959	4	20,300	21	6,693
Delaware	7,804	6	20,665	18	6,813
Florida	7,085	18	18,538	31	6,112
Georgia	6,075	36	17,412	42	5,741
Hawaii	7,910	5	24,796	3	8,175

TABLE 2.5 *(Continued)*

State	1966–67		1982–83		Purchasing Power in 1967 Dollars
	Amount	*Rank*	*Amount*	*Rank*	
Idaho	6,012	38	17,549	39	5,786
Illinois	7,525	14	22,618	10	7,457
Indiana	7,663	8	20,067	22	6,616
Iowa	6,531	28	18,709	29	6,168
Kansas	6,270	32	18,299	34	6,033
Kentucky	5,680	45	18,400	32	6,067
Louisiana	6,598	27	19,265	26	6,352
Maine	5,950	39	15,772	45	5,200
Maryland	7,547	13	22,786	9	7,513
Massachusetts	7,550	12	19,000	27	6,264
Michigan	7,650	9	23,965	5	7,901
Minnesota	7,050	19	22,296	12	7,351
Mississippi	4,707	50	14,285	50	4,710
Missouri	6,307	30	17,726	38	5,844
Montana	6,300	31	19,463	25	6,417
Nebraska	5,800	42	17,412	41	5,741
Nevada	7,786	7	20,944	16	6,905
New Hampshire	6,207	33	15,353	47	5,062
New Jersey	7,647	10	21,642	13	7,136
New Mexico	6,740	25	20,600	19	6,792
New York	8,500	3	25,100	2	8,276
North Carolina	5,869	41	17,836	37	5,881
North Dakota	5,515	46	18,390	33	6,063
Ohio	6,782	23	20,360	20	6,713
Oklahoma	6,103	35	18,110	35	5,971
Oregon	7,274	16	22,334	11	7,364
Pennsylvania	7,181	17	21,000	15	6,924
Rhode Island	6,975	20	23,175	8	7,641
South Carolina	5,421	47	16,380	44	5,401
South Dakota	5,000	49	15,595	46	5,142
Tennessee	5,755	44	17,425	40	5,745
Texas	6,075	36	19,500	24	6,429
Utah	6,780	24	19,677	23	6,488
Vermont	6,200	34	15,338	48	5,057
Virginia	6,342	29	18,707	30	6,168
Washington	7,597	11	23,413	7	7,719
West Virginia	5,917	40	17,370	43	5,727
Wisconsin	6,954	21	20,940	17	6,904
Wyoming	6,635	26	24,000	4	7,913

Source: Adapted from *Estimates of School Statistics, 1967–68*, p. 30, and *Estimates of School Statistics, 1982–83*, Research Division, National Education Association, Washington, D.C., p. 35. Reprinted by permission.

Cost of Living

Despite steadily climbing salaries, teachers entered the 1980s with less buying power than they had sixteen years ago, as illustrated in Table 2.5. While the average teacher salary rose 188 percent above the 1966–67 school year salary of $7,129, the 1982–83 salary had a purchasing power of only $6,769 in 1966–67 dollars. The result is a net loss of $360 in real income for the average teacher over the sixteen-year period. The net loss is much greater for teachers in states where the average salary is less than the national average. In Mississippi, for example, the 1982–83 average salary of $14,285 had a purchasing power of only $4,710 in 1966–67 dollars. Teachers' salaries in only thirteen states kept up with the cost of living to provide the equivalent purchasing power in 1982–83 to the 1966–67 salaries.

In the last few years, teachers' buying power has been particularly hard hit as the cost of living has been much greater than the increases in salary. During the downturn of the general economy in the early 1980s, teacher salaries, as well as those of other workers, did not increase sufficiently to offset the cost of living increases.

No one ever entered teaching expecting to get rich, of course, but the rapidly rising costs of such necessities as fuel, food, housing, and medical care make it difficult for many teachers to provide even a moderate standard of living for themselves and their families. Consequently, thousands of teachers have lowered their living standards, turned to second and even third jobs to make ends meet, and in many cases have left the profession entirely to pursue better-paying work.

Table 2.6 lists the average salary for beginning teachers by geographic regions of the United States. The states for each of the nine regions are as follows:

Region 1 Washington, Oregon, Idaho
Region 2 California, Nevada, Utah, Arizona
Region 3 Montana, Wyoming, Colorado, New Mexico
Region 4 North Dakota, South Dakota, Minnesota, Iowa, Nebraska, Kansas, Missouri
Region 5 Oklahoma, Arkansas, Texas, Louisiana
Region 6 Kentucky, West Virginia, Virginia, Tennessee, North Carolina, South Carolina, Mississippi, Alabama, Georgia, Florida
Region 7 Wisconsin, Illinois, Michigan, Indiana, Ohio
Region 8 New York, Pennsylvania, New Jersey, Maryland, Delaware, District of Columbia
Region 9 Maine, Vermont, New Hampshire, Massachusetts, Rhode Island, Connecticut

It should be noted that while in some cases the averages were based upon limited salary data, the data do provide an overview of salaries paid beginning teachers across the United States.

TABLE 2.6   *Average Salary for Beginning Teachers by Geographic Regions*

		Special Education		Elementary/Secondary	
		Bachelor's	*Masters*	*Bachelor's*	*Masters*
Region 1	1981–82	12,651	13,750	12,410	13,417
	1982–83	13,275	14,500	13,038	14,250
	1983–84	13,607	15,400	13,806	15,000
Region 2	1981–82	12,505	13,510	12,505	13,510
	1982–83	13,000	14,922	13,707	14,772
	1983–84	13,900	15,723	14,375	15,665
Region 3	1981–82	14,157	15,389	13,742	15,475
	1982–83	15,061	16,550	14,421	15,700
	1983–84	14,681	16,917	14,345	16,313
Region 4	1981–82	13,291	15,438	12,758	14,883
	1982–83	12,789	—	12,051	—
	1983–84	13,914	15,659	13,144	15,345
Region 5	1981–82	11,792	12,503	11,175	11,725
	1982–83	12,903	13,813	12,642	13,302
	1983–84	13,090	14,335	12,815	14,114
Region 6	1981–82	12,078	13,396	11,496	12,567
	1982–83	11,750	12,750	12,000	12,750
	1983–84	13,875	15,225	13,480	14,725
Region 7	1981–82	12,503	13,958	12,090	14,040
	1982–83	13,213	15,477	12,890	15,054
	1983–84	14,140	15,475	13,328	14,825
Region 8	1981–82	11,875	12,500	11,875	12,500
	1982–83	12,875	13,875	12,875	13,875
	1983–84	13,333	14,500	13,250	14,500
Region 9	1981–82	10,000	11,100	10,332	11,100
	1982–83	10,500	11,750	10,365	11,000
	1983–84	11,667	13,233	11,369	13,233
Alaska	1981–82	22,000	25,000	22,000	25,000
	1982–83	22,000	25,000	22,000	25,000
	1983–84	—	—	—	—
Hawaii	1981–82	13,271	14,245	13,271	14,245
	1982–83	14,598	15,669	14,598	15,669
	1983–84	14,589	15,669	14,598	15,669

The above average salary for beginning teachers are from data furnished by survey respondents. The averages in some cases are based upon limited salary input, thus reliability is not assured.

Regions are coded as follows: Alaska, Hawaii, 1-Northwest, 2-West, 3-Rocky Mountain, 4-Great Plains/Midwest, 5-South Central, 6-Southeast, 7-Great Lakes, 8-Middle Atlantic, 9-Northeast.

— indicates data were not available.

Source: James N. Akin, *Average Salary Reports,* January 1984, Association for School, College and University Staffing, Madison, Wis. Reprinted by permission.

Salary—Teachers Versus Private Industry

The beginning salary of a teacher with a bachelor's degree continues to be much lower than the average salary paid to a beginner with a bachelor's degree in most other fields of work. In the academic year 1983–84 the average salary for a beginning teacher with a bachelor's degree was esti-

[8]

mated to be $14,349 for a typical work period of nine and a half months. This salary adjusted to a twelve-month basis to compare with other fields would have been $18,120 (Table 2.7), while beginning salaries for bachelor's degree graduates in other fields who were hired by business and industry ranged from $19,344 for liberal arts majors to $26,844 for engineers.

The problem extends beyond beginning teachers' salaries. The disparity over time between salaries of teachers and those in other white collar occupations is revealed when one examines average salaries paid which include employees at advanced stages of their careers. Figure 2.5 illustrates that the relatively low position of teachers' salaries continues over time. Most of the recent reports on the quality of education in the United States call for higher standards for teacher preparation coupled with sizable increases in salary for both beginning and experienced teachers. However, it is naive to think that teacher salaries will become equal to salaries paid to comparably prepared employees in business and industry in the near future.

Opportunities for Women

A factor that bears upon the availability of competent, qualified teachers for all subject areas, but that is not mentioned often, is the ever-increasing opportunities for women in business and industry, as well as in other areas

TABLE 2.7 *Salary Comparisons of Beginning Teachers and Bachelor's Degree Graduates in Other Fields—1983 and 1984 Classes*

Field	Average Starting Salary (1983)	Average Starting Salary (1984)	Percent Increase
Engineering	$25,944	$26,844	3.5
Computer Science	23,490	24,864	5.8
Chemistry	23,508	24,192	2.9
Math/Statistics	20,664	22,416	8.5
Other fields	22,212	23,136	4.2
Accounting	19,452	20,172	3.7
Economics/Finance	19,584	20,484	4.6
Business Administration	19,128	19,416	1.5
Sales/Marketing	18,828	19,620	4.2
Liberal Arts	18,564	19,344	4.2
Teachers*	17,100 (est.)	18,120 (est.)	6.0

*The mean bachelor's degree minimum average salary for teachers for 1984 was estimated to be $14,349, or $1510 per month computed on a 9.5-month contract. Salary adjusted to 12 months to compare to other fields (12 × $1510 = $18,120).
Source: Adapted from Victor R. Lindquist, *The Northwestern Endicott Report,* Northwestern University, Evanston, Ill., 1984. Reprinted by permission.

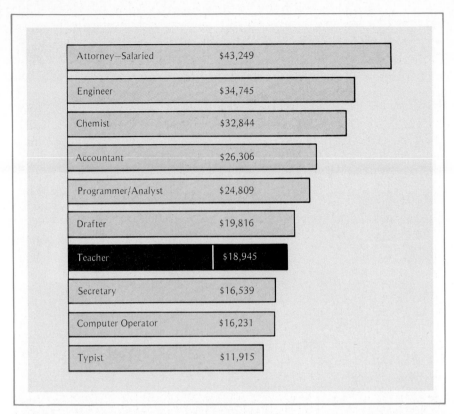

Attorney—Salaried	$43,249
Engineer	$34,745
Chemist	$32,844
Accountant	$26,306
Programmer/Analyst	$24,809
Drafter	$19,816
Teacher	$18,945
Secretary	$16,539
Computer Operator	$16,231
Typist	$11,915

FIGURE 2.5 *Teacher salaries: falling behind. The figures represent the average salaries of employees in selected white collar occupations, March 1982. (Source: AFT Annual Report,* American Federation of Teachers, Washington, D.C., p. 20. Reprinted by permission.)

of employment. In the past, career opportunities for women outside of teaching were limited. Consequently, teacher-training programs reveled in the luxury of having almost exclusive rights in educating the exceptional female brainpower on campus for careers in teaching.

As business and industry, government agencies, and other employers come to realize the availability of the exceptional talents of female graduates, many women will continue to select majors in areas other than teacher training. These career opportunities will continue to expand, thus attracting more and more of the best female students away from the teaching field.

Merit Pay—Differential Pay

School systems in a number of states are considering various forms of incentive plans as the means to reward the "best" teachers for teaching excellence and to address shortages in certain disciplines. The teacher unions

A teacher's worth can't be defined by money alone.

have been against incentive plans, claiming that they are often subject to the opinions of administrators, include questionable criteria for judging teaching excellence, and cause morale problems among teachers. On the other hand, many of the best teachers realize that the typical salary schedule rewards all teachers the same whether or not they are good or bad in the classroom. These teachers support the merit concept as a possible way to provide a differential for exceptional teaching above the provisions of the salary schedule. Previous limited attempts to utilize merit pay plans have not proved worthwhile, but ideally, basing teachers' salaries on some form of evaluation seems plausible. Consequently, it is expected that several merit plans will be developed and implemented in the 1980s.

An example of a pay incentive scheme is the Houston (Texas) school district's Second Mile Plan. The merit aspect calls for extra stipends for teachers who meet certain expectations. The differential pay aspect includes salary incentives of $2000 for mathematics, science, and special education teachers and those who teach in certain lower-income areas. The plan drew immediate fire by the Houston Teachers Association, which charges that the plan makes a shambles of the salary schedule, is subject to favoritism, and is divisive and arbitrary.

Of the several teacher incentive concepts adopted by the 1983 Florida legislature, the career ladder plan was the only one that must, by law, be carried out during the 1984–85 school year. Consequently, Florida's State Board of Education worked to implement the plan to distribute merit pay to superior teachers despite warnings from a variety of sources that the plan may be doomed to failure. About 5000 teachers identified as outstanding—4 percent of the state's teaching force—will be rewarded with $3000 bonuses. To qualify, teachers must have a master's degree in the subject they teach, four years of teaching experiences, including two in Florida, a good classroom performance evaluation, and a passing grade on a competency test in the subject they teach. They also must have no unexcused absences for two of the last three years. The teachers selected for bonuses will receive the title "associate master" and will be given the stipends for three years. At the end of that period they will be eligible to apply for "master teacher" status, which brings annual bonuses of $5000 for an additional three years. Representatives of teachers' unions have complained that the state is moving too swiftly, lured by the publicity Florida will receive if it distributes the first merit pay checks in the nation. The main point of concern is the matter of who will evaluate the teachers and how the process of evaluation will be validated.

At least the need for schools to provide additional incentive pay to attract top-notch teachers to the critical shortage areas seems without question. In the marketplace of private industry, additional pay is always used as a mechanism for attracting employees to fill critical needs. For example, though the computer science field is relatively new, the demand is very strong. Consequently, beginning salaries for graduates with bachelor's degree in computer science are already second only to those for engineering graduates. If the need for computer science graduates declines, so will the amounts paid to attract those employees.

Salary Schedules and Yearly Increments

Each board of education is an agent of the state and therefore empowered to set salary levels for employees of the school district it governs. Each school system usually has a salary schedule that outlines the minimum and maximum salary for several levels of study beyond the bachelor's degree and for each year of teaching experience. Table 2.8 is an example of a salary schedule for teachers. A beginning teacher with a bachelor's degree

TABLE 2.8 *Example of a Salary Schedule*

Years of Experience	Bachelor's Degree	Bachelor's +15 Semester Hours	Master's Degree	Master's +15 Semester Hours	Master's +30 Semester Hours
0	$14,000	$14,500	$15,000	$15,500	$16,000
1	14,400	14,900	15,400	15,900	16,400
2	14,800	15,300	15,800	16,300	16,800
3	15,200	15,700	16,200	16,700	17,200
4	15,600	16,100	16,600	17,100	17,600
5	16,000	16,500	17,000	17,500	18,000
6	16,400	16,900	17,400	17,900	18,400
7	16,800	17,300	17,800	18,300	18,800
8	17,200	17,700	18,200	18,700	19,200
9	17,600	18,100	18,600	19,100	19,600
10	18,000	18,500	19,000	19,500	20,000
11		18,900	19,400	19,900	20,400
12		19,300	19,800	20,300	20,800
13		19,700	20,200	20,700	21,200
14			20,600	21,100	21,600
15				21,500	22,000
16				21,900	22,400
17					22,800

is paid $14,000, one with a master's degree is paid $15,000, and a beginning teacher with a master's degree of 30 additional semester hours of graduate study is paid $16,000. The other columns show the increases in starting salary for additional semester hours of preparation beyond the bachelor's degree and beyond the master's degree.

The first column in the salary schedule shows the teaching year for a typical teacher. Teachers with less than a master's degree will be granted year-to-year increases for ten years, whereas teachers with preparation beyond a master's degree are granted increments for up to seventeen years. Therefore teachers are rewarded for both a maximum number of years of experience and for additional education beyond the bachelor's degree. Teachers who have reached the maximum experience level for their particular education do not receive additional raises except when all the salaries listed in the salary schedule are revised upward.

Retirement Incentives

School districts around the country are faced with the problem of aging teacher staffs. Teacher dismissals over the last few years, triggered by declining enrollments, have nearly emptied high schools of young teachers. The increased proportion of older teachers has prompted many districts to offer early retirement incentives to speed up attrition.

Early retirement (age 55–59) incentives typically offer a substantial salary increase in the last year of teaching, which results in increased pension benefits. In addition, free medical and life insurance is provided until age 65, when Medicare benefits are available. Though most administrators stress that a school needs young teachers, they also acknowledge that money is a key consideration. Younger teachers cost school districts a lot less. Many high school teachers at the typical retirement age (65) are earning $30,000 a year or more; a beginning teacher with a bachelor's degree starts at about $14,000. While it costs the district a lot of money for the early retirement benefits, most of the retiring faculty are not replaced, owing to declining enrollments. It becomes the ideal situation for the school district when young teachers are kept while salary money is actually saved by offering early retirement incentives to older faculty members.

The early retirement push has not met with favor among all teachers. Some instructors believe that they are being pushed out and resent the pressure put upon them to retire. Some of the older teachers are excellent teachers who prefer to continue in the classroom. The opportunity to enjoy other careers during the later years of their planned working life has no appeal. Perhaps for this reason, the growing emphasis on early retirement has not resulted in a mass exodus of older teachers. In Illinois, for example, original estimates that retirements might actually double with the early retirement plans have not proved true. A total of 1,946 Illinois teachers and administrators retired in 1983, compared with 1,726 in 1982 and 1,755 in 1981. Of those, only 375 were early retirees (age 55–59) in 1982 and 367 in 1981. Nonetheless, more and more school districts should offer early retirement incentives as a means of keeping young teachers while saving much-needed salary dollars.

In most states, local school districts set the amounts to be paid for the various levels of their salary schedules, such as the Table 2.8 example, with the monies coming to the local budgets from local taxes, state aid, and federal aid. In Texas, however, each district builds its salary schedule with local enrichment increments added to a standard state salary schedule. Table 2.9 is the salary schedule of a relatively stable suburban Houston independent school district; the local enrichment amounts are sizable additions. In less well-financed school districts the local enrichment amounts are much less. The pay grade categories are based only upon degrees held and do not allow for semester hours earned above any one degree. Teacher organizations in Texas not only work with the local districts for increases in the enrichment amounts, but also strongly lobby the state for increases in the state base.

Fringe Benefits, Extra Pay, and Moonlighting

Fringe benefits for teachers vary from school district to school district and from state to state. Certain fringe benefits are required by law; other benefits result from negotiations between the teachers and boards of educa-

TABLE 2.9 *Spring Branch Independent School District* 1983–84 Salary Schedule (183 days)*

Pay Grade 7 (Bachelor's Degree) Classroom Teacher, Nurse, Social Worker, Reading Specialist					Pay Grade 8 (Master's Degree) Classroom Teacher, Nurse, Social Worker, Reading Specialist					Pay Grade 9 (Doctorate) Classroom Teacher				
Years Completed	Step	State	Local Enrichment	Salary 1983–94	Years Completed	Step	State	Local Enrichment	Salary 1983–84	Years Completed	Step	State	Local Enrichment	Salary 1983–84
0	0	11,110	4,545	15,655	0	0	11,880	4,684	16,564	0	0	12,090	6,310	18,400
1	1	11,480	4,770	16,250	1	1	12,340	4,853	17,193	1	1	12,590	6,507	19,097
2	2	11,880	4,988	16,868	2	2	12,830	5,016	17,846	2	2	13,080	6,741	19,821
3	3	12,340	5,169	17,509	3	3	13,360	5,164	18,524	3	3	13,570	7,002	20,572
4	4	12,830	5,344	18,174	4	4	13,940	5,288	19,228	4	4	14,190	7,162	21,352
5	5	13,360	5,505	18,865	5	5	14,560	5,399	19,959	5	5	14,930	7,231	22,161
6	6	13,940	5,642	19,582	6	6	15,230	5,487	20,717	6	6	15,670	7,331	23,001
7	7	14,560	5,766	20,326	7	7	15,920	5,584	21,504	7	7	16,410	7,463	23,873
8	8	15,230	5,868	21,098	8	8	16,660	5,661	22,321	8	8	17,150	7,628	24,778
9	9	15,920	5,980	21,900	9	9	17,400	5,769	23,169	9	9	17,890	7,827	25,717
10	10	16,660	6,072	22,732	10	10	18,140	5,909	24,049	10	10	18,760	7,932	26,692
11	10+	16,990	6,174	23,164	11	10+	18,500	6,006	24,506	11	10+	19,130	8,068	27,198
12	11	17,400	6,204	23,604	12	11	18,880	6,092	24,972	12	11	19,620	8,093	27,713
13	11+	17,750	6,303	24,053	13	11+	19,260	6,186	25,446	13	11+	20,010	8,228	28,238
14–15	12	18,140	6,370	24,510	14–17	12	19,620	6,309	25,929	14–17	12	20,480	8,293	28,773
16–17	12+	18,500	6,476	24,976	18–19	12+	20,010	6,412	26,422	18–19	12+	20,890	8,428	29,318
18–19	13	18,880	6,571	25,451	20–21	13	20,360	6,564	26,924	20–21	13	21,350	8,524	29,874
20–22	13+	19,260	6,675	25,935	22–24	13+	20,770	6,666	27,436	22–24	13+	21,780	8,660	30,440
23+	14	19,620	6,808	26,428	25–29	14	21,100	6,887	27,957	25–29	14	22,210	8,807	31,017
					30+	14+	21,520	6,968	28,488	30+	14+	22,660	8,945	31,605

*Grateful acknowledgment is extended to the Spring Branch Independent School District, 955 Campbell Road, Houston, Texas 77024 for providing the 1983–84 salary schedule for illustrative purposes.

tion. School districts are required by law to provide teacher retirement plans and to pay for workmen's compensation, unemployment insurance coverage, and some form of sick leave provisions. Through teacher–school board negotiations, some districts provide extended health and dental insurance plans for the spouse and children of teachers, leave-of-absence provisions, extended sick leave, and payment of tuition fees for advanced study. A small proportion of school systems provide plans for sabbatical leaves, cooperative purchase programs, and extended contracts for summer employment.

Most school systems pay teachers over their scheduled salary for extra time given to coaching athletic teams and coaching speech teams, producing musicals and plays, doing yearbook and newspaper assignments, sponsoring clubs, and extra duties of various kinds. In a few cases, teachers are paid for teaching an extra class beyond the regular teaching load.

Many teachers find it necessary to work at second jobs to supplement their teaching salary. These moonlighting jobs vary from working in gas stations or selling insurance to being employed part-time by local agencies such as park boards. The summer vacation period offers many teachers opportunities for second jobs, typically at low pay and with no fringe benefits.

When considering employment in a school district, prospective teachers should carefully examine the fringe benefits and extra pay provisions in concert with the salary schedule.

Summary and Implications

Only a few aspects of teacher supply, demand, and salaries were examined in this chapter. While the general oversupply of teachers is projected to last through 1985, job prospects for new teacher graduates should improve markedly in the late 1980s. While some effects of a teacher surplus seem to indicate a rocky road to a teaching career, the long-term view suggests that a surplus could contribute to a stronger profession with better-qualified and better-paid teachers.

Enrollment declines in elementary and secondary schools will reverse in 1985, when the 5- to 17-year-old population is projected to begin increasing. In fact, the projected enrollment increases into the 1990s could result in an enrollment boom that may surpass the peak levels of 1971. Consequently, a teacher shortage is a distinct possibility in the late 1980s unless college students respond to the improved market by increasing their enrollments in teacher preparation programs.

The total number of elementary and secondary teachers in the United States increased from 1970 through 1980. During this period, additional teachers were readily available, and many were hired in order to decrease the pupil-teacher ratios from those in previously overcrowded classrooms.

As school budgets became more restricted, the local districts did not have the means to sustain such hiring practices; in fact, the rapid enrollment declines resulted in many teachers' being released. Consequently, the number of elementary teachers is now projected to stabilize through 1984 with increases to coincide with enrollment gains in the late 1980s. The number of secondary teachers will continue to decrease into the 1990s as the enrollment declines further affect the secondary student population. At the same time, shortages in selected discipline areas will become more pronounced according to the emphasis on given areas of the secondary curriculum.

During the last several years the supply of new teacher graduates has exceeded the demand for additional teachers, resulting in an oversupply of teachers. Even though secondary enrollments will decline into the 1990s, the total demand for additional teachers will be equal to the supply of new teacher graduates by 1985. The resulting job prospects for new teacher graduates will be much improved during the late 1980s. It is hoped that the decrease in pupil-teacher ratios will also continue to further increase the demand for new teachers.

New academic achievement tests that compare children in the United States to children of other countries show the United States lagging behind in all academic areas, especially in math and science. Such results, coupled with reports such as the National Commission on Excellence in Education, bring pressure on the schools to raise standards of study. Consequently, severe teacher shortages are predicted in certain academic areas. The most critical shortages are in chemistry, mathematics, physics, and data processing. Areas of surplus will continue to be art, physical education, social science, home economics, and foreign languages.

Opportunities for Americans to teach abroad are increasing. The United States Department of Defense operates a school system for the children of American men and women in the services abroad. Teacher shortages in other nations also heighten opportunities for foreign employment.

Teachers' salaries continue to be less than those of comparably prepared employees in business and industries. Even though teachers' salaries have increased considerably in recent years, teachers' buying power in actual dollars has not kept up with the cost of living. As local districts struggle to meet rising costs, teachers will find gains in salary hard to come by unless there are new sources of income.

Several school districts are attempting to devise salary incentive plans that reward the "best" teachers with additional merit pay. Another incentive would provide higher salaries for teachers in areas of short supply, such as the math and science disciplines. Even though teacher unions generally oppose such incentive plans, teachers realize that salary schedules reward all teachers equally whether or not they are good in the classroom. The general public and school boards favor merit pay for the best teachers and extra stipends to attract well-qualified teachers in critical shortage areas. The late 1980s will see more use of salary incentive plans than ever before.

Retirement incentives are being used to reduce the number of higher-salaried older teachers while keeping younger, less well-paid teachers. These retirement incentive plans have been only moderately successful to date, however. Consequently, fewer young teachers have been retained in our schools than was originally projected.

The implications of these variables for prospective teachers are straightforward. More teachers will be needed in the late 1980s than during the previous decade. In order to satisfy the clamor for improving the quality of education, more and better-prepared teachers will be needed. Further, teacher salaries will be reviewed to determine ways to upgrade salaries for those prepared to teach in the critical shortage disciplines and for those determined to be most effective in the classroom. Teacher organizations and teacher preparation schools are challenged to upgrade the competency levels of certified teachers now on the job and of students entering teacher preparation programs. Teacher tenure laws and union seniority rules are under more rigorous attack than ever before for protecting incompetent teachers. The questions of how to identify and how to remove incompetent teachers are open to much debate. The opportunity to revitalize the teaching profession is at hand. The degree to which all educators work to gain renewed faith and dignity in the profession will determine the benefits to future generations of American youth.

DISCUSSION QUESTIONS

1. How can colleges and departments of education better prepare beginning teachers so that their chances of employment in a tight job market will be enhanced?
2. Teacher shortages are reported in the subject areas of chemistry, mathematics, and physics. Are these disciplines too difficult to attract prospective teachers? What should teacher-training institutions do to meet demands for teachers in the sciences?
3. Discuss the pros and cons of the early retirement incentive plans offered by some school districts. In your response, explain your beliefs about the values of young teachers to a school; of older teachers to a school.
4. Many people believe that teachers are overpaid. As a prospective teacher, how would you respond to this charge?
5. Many young teachers work at a second job to increase their yearly income. How do you feel about teachers' holding additional jobs?

SUPPLEMENTAL ACTIVITIES

1. Invite a member of your school's placement office to class to discuss application procedures, credentials, and teacher supply and demand.
2. Invite hiring officials from nearby school districts to your class to discuss teacher supply and demand. Compare this discussion with the presentation by the placement officer.
3. Review a big-city newspaper for at least one week to obtain a selection of current discussions about education-related topics. Report your findings. Also assess trends indicated by your findings.
4. Identify several school districts that have had teacher strikes recently. Write to the teacher or-

ganizations in these districts and ask for information on the strike issues. Summarize the data obtained.

5. Invite to your class members of your graduating class who are going to work in business or industry. Why did these students choose their fields of employment? Why did they not choose teaching as a career?

NOTES

1. William S. Graybeal, *Teacher Supply and Demand in Public Schools, 1980–81* (Washington, D.C.: National Education Association, 1981).

2. *Educational and Cultural Exchange Opportunities* (Washington, D.C.: United States Department of State, Bureau of Cultural Affairs, 20520).

BIBLIOGRAPHY

Barber, Larry, and Klein, Karen. "Merit Pay and Teacher Evaluation." *Phi Delta Kappan* 65 (December 1983): 247–251.

Brandt, Norman J. "Faculty Salaries up 9.2 Percent in 1981–82." *Early Release,* National Center for Education Statistics, Washington, D.C., May 1982.

Estimates of School Statistics 1982–83. NEA Research Memo. Washington, D.C.: National Education Association, 1982.

"Gimmicks No Cure for Salary Ills." *NEA Today.* Washington, D.C.: National Education Association, (April 1983), p. 5.

Lindquist, Victor R. *The Northwestern Endicott Report.* Evanston, Ill.: Placement Center, Northwestern University, 1984.

McGrath, Ellie. "The Bold Quest for Quality." *Time* (October 10, 1983): 58–66.

Megel, Carl J. "Merit Pay is No Panacea for Schools." *American Teacher,* Washington, D.C.: American Federation of Teachers (February 1982), p. 8.

Prices, Budgets, Salaries, and Income. NEA Research Memo. Washington, D.C.: National Education Association, 1983.

Sullivan, Barbara. "Schools Luring Teachers into Early Retirement." *Chicago Tribune* (December 11, 1983), Section 4, pp. 20 and 22.

Teacher Supply/Demand in 1983. Research Report, Madison, Wis.: Association of School, College, and University Staffing (ASCUS), January 1983.

3

Legal Aspects of Teaching

Focus Questions

- Does the fact that teachers are increasingly being sued by students and parents for violations of student rights and teacher misconduct bother you? How? Why?
- How has the realm of pupil conduct been extended so that teachers have lost control? Or do teachers still have legal control of students?
- If corporal punishment were not prohibited by the school board or by state law, would you feel free to discipline students accordingly even if the parents threatened to sue you if you "touched their child"?
- What would seem to you to be the meaning of "reasonableness" when dealing with your students? What kind of teacher behavior would be unreasonable?
- What is your understanding of the concept of academic freedom? Are there limits on such freedom?

Key Terms and Concepts

Student rights
Due process
Corporal punishment
Sex discrimination
Educational malpractice

Teacher contracts
Academic freedom
Collective bargaining
Liability

What Would You Do?

Your school conducts routine student locker inspections by having all students open and stand by their lockers while the teachers inspect the locker contents. You notice a student remove a suspicious looking substance from the locker and slip it under her sweater. When you ask the student to remove the item from her sweater, she refuses, saying that you have no right to search her.

A notice is posted on the faculty bulletin board that a tennis coach is needed for the boys' team and that the position is open to present faculty only. You are qualified and become the only applicant for the job. You are then told that you will not be considered for the position, since you are a female.

The legalistic age in which we live increasingly influences education matters in general and being a teacher specifically. Not only the professional classroom practices of teachers when dealing with students are affected, but also the personal life-styles of teachers. Both controversy and interest continue to be sparked by court decisions. While actions and decisions of school boards and lower courts are of considerable local importance and provide the bases for appeal to supreme courts (state and national), the supreme court decisions have a much broader range of influence. Therefore this chapter for the most part uses supreme court decisions as references regarding the topics discussed.

Teachers are subject to the U.S. Constitution, state constitutions, statutory law, and school board policy and are protected by them when interacting with pupils, colleagues, and employers. While the federal courts have abandoned their traditional hands-off policy in cases involving local school boards, disputes involving special education, sex discrimination, school libraries, student rights, desegregation, and education for alien children all provoke dissension among the justices. It has been suggested that the division of the U.S. Supreme Court, both on legal issues in education and on court procedures, results in the Court's not providing clear leadership to the lower courts on education issues.[1] Nonetheless, the leadership of the U.S. Supreme Court is vital in resolving some of the primary legal issues in education.

School-related court cases deal with a variety of topics: student rights, teacher rights, pupil conduct, corporal punishment, academic freedom, school board rights, school records, teacher employment contracts, teachers' right to strike, and many others. Part of the preparation for teaching must concern both the relatively new concept of student rights and the responsibilities of teachers relative to certification, collective bargaining, strikes, liability, and other topics.

Student Rights and Responsibilities

Since the mid-1960s, students have had, more than ever before, a very active voice in their own education; at the same time their rights and responsibilities are being more clearly defined. Many educators and lay citizens bemoan this progress toward a clear definition of student rights and responsibilities as legal trespass on educators' power over and control of students in the school. Some claim that the dimensions of student responsibility have never been determined. However, by examining various surveys and reports on student rights and responsibilities, one can see the dual dimension of the trend. The National School Public Relations Association cites, for example, the preamble to the Baltimore County Board of Education policy statement on student rights and responsibilities:

Students have responsibilities that are inseparable from and inherent in their rights. One of the most important is the responsibility to obey a school rule or policy until such a rule is revoked. Citizens in an orderly society must accept responsibilities commensurate with their rights.[2]

Many court decisions are against students whose nonconformism seems to go beyond a reasonable norm. Often the courts support the right of the local school authority to exercise considerable control over matters that affect students. What often happens is that there is so much emotionalism that the original question of student rights and responsibilities becomes obscured.

Specific court cases are discussed briefly to illustrate some of the issues and decisions related to aspects of student rights and responsibilities. The reader is cautioned that the cases selected do not necessarily constitute the last word regarding student rights, but rather are used to provide an overview of some of the issues that have been decided in our courts. Table 3.1 summarizes the issues and decisions of the selected cases about student rights and responsibilities. This summary table is not intended to provide a complete understanding of the court decisions cited. It is necessary to read the textual narrative for a more complete understanding.

TABLE 3.1 *Summary of Selected Student Rights and Responsibility Cases*

Case	Issue	Decision
Plyler v. *Doe* (50 U.S.L.W. 4650, 1982)	Right to education of children of illegal aliens	Struck down Texas law denying a free public education to these children
Goss v. *Lopez* (U.S. Supreme Court, 1975)	Suspension of high school students without a hearing	Court ruled that students cannot be suspended without a hearing
Wood v. *Strickland* (95, S. Ct. 992, 1975)	Can school board members be sued for depriving students of their constitutional rights (suspended)?	Students could seek damages from individual school board members but not from the school district
Carey v. *Piphus* (435 U.S. 247, 1978)	Clarified *Wood* case above: what conditions for damages to be awarded students and what amount?	Student must clearly establish that an injury has occurred before damages can be collected from board members
Tinker v. *Des Moines Independent Community School District* (U.S. Supreme Court, 1969)	*In loco parentis* doctrine questioned. School denied students right to wear black armbands to protest Vietnam	Court ruled against school district—established constitutional rights of pupils

TABLE 3.1 *(Continued)*

Case	Issue	Decision
Board of Education, Inland Trees Union Free School District No. 26 v. Pico (50 U.S.L.W. 4831, 1982)	Challenged school board's decision to remove books from the school library	U.S. Supreme Court issued decision that, under certain circumstances, children may challenge board's decision to remove books
Ingraham v. *Wright* (U.S. Supreme Court, 1977)	May states authorize corporal punishment without consent of student's parent?	Yes, states may constitutionally authorize corporal punishment
Fedor v. *Mauwehu Council of Boy Scouts* (Connecticut, 1958)	Do teachers and educators have a legal privilege to administer reasonable corporal punishment?	Yes, school personnel should consider age, sex, size of pupil, and degree of punishment when determining reasonableness of punishment
Long v. *Zopp* (476 F. 2nd 180, 4th Circuit, 1973)	School's right to invoke dress code and hair length regulations	Divided opinions among courts on this issue. This case ruled the school must prove that the hair or dress interfered with students' ability to play the sport or perform the activity
Scoville v. *Board of Education* (Seventh Circuit Court of Appeals, Illinois, 1970)	Students were expelled for distributing a newspaper that criticized school officials and used vulgar language	Court ruled against school and said that students were entitled to the declaratory judgment and damage relief sought
Peter W. v. *San Francisco Unified School District* (California Courts, 1976) and *Donahue* v. *Copiague Union Free School District* (California Courts, 1978)	Former students sued for not receiving an adequate education	Courts dismissed suits by students—no way to assess the school's negligence
Hunter v. *Board of Education of Montgomery County* (425A 2d 681, 1981)	Court was asked to recognize educational malpractice as tort liability of the school district	Court rejected the request, saying that suit for educational malpractice might arise every time a child failed a grade

Student Rights to an Education

American children have a right to an education; this right is assured in many state constitutions. It has been further defined by court decisions and is now interpreted to mean that each child shall have an equal opportunity to pursue education.

The right to an education, however, is not without certain prerequisites. Citizenship alone does not guarantee a free education. Statutes that establish public school systems also generally establish how operating costs will be met. Real estate taxes are the usual source of funds, so the residence requirement is necessary for school attendance without tuition. *Residence* does not mean that the student, parent, or guardian must pay real estate taxes; it means that the student must live in the school district in which he or she wants to attend school. Residence then is a prerequisite to the right of a free public education within a specific school district.

In June 1982 the U.S. Supreme Court extended this right to include the children of undocumented illegal aliens. In *Plyler* v. *Doe* (50 U.S.L.W. 4650, 1982) the controversial five-to-four majority decision struck down a Texas law denying a free public education to these children. The majority opinion held that the Texas law "imposes a lifetime of hardship on a discrete class of children not accountable for their disabling status and promotes the creation and perpetuation of a sub-class of illiterates within our boundaries, surely adding to the problems and costs of unemployment, welfare, and crime."

Pupil Conduct

The right, or privilege, of children to attend school also depends on their compliance with the rules and regulations of the school. To ensure the day-to-day orderly operation of schools, boards of education have been given the right to establish reasonable rules and regulations controlling pupils and their conduct. In a number of instances the boards' actions have been challenged, however. Most challenges have concerned corporal punishment, rights of married students to an education, dress codes, and freedom of expression.

Goss v. *Lopez* (U.S. Supreme Court, 1975) dealt with the suspension of high school students in Columbus, Ohio. In that case the named plaintiffs alleged that they had been suspended from public high school for up to ten days without a hearing. The action was brought for deprivation of constitutional rights. Two students who were suspended for a semester brought suit charging that their due process rights were denied—because they were not present at the board meeting when the suspensions were handed out. In ruling that students cannot be suspended without some kind of hearing, the Court said:

The prospect of imposing elaborate hearing requirements in every suspension case is viewed with great concern, and many school authorities may well prefer the untrammeled power to act unilaterally, unhampered by rules about notice and hearing. But it would be a strange disciplinary system in an educational institution if no communication was sought by the disciplinarian with the student in an effort to inform him of his defalcation and to let him tell his side of the story in order to make sure than an injustice is not done. Fairness can rarely be obtained by secret, one-sided determination of the facts decisive of rights. . . . Secrecy is not congenial to truth-seeking and self-righteousness gives too slender an assurance of rightness. No better instrument has been devised for arriving at truth than to give a person in jeopardy of serious loss notice of the case against him and opportunity to meet it.

Just a month after the *Goss* v. *Lopez* decision, the U.S. Supreme Court handed down a more significant decision, which affirmed that students may sue school board members who are guilty of intentionally depriving students of their constitutional rights. In *Wood* v. *Strickland* (95, S. Ct. 992, 1975) the Supreme Court held that school officials who discipline students unfairly cannot defend themselves against civil rights suits by claiming ignorance of pupils' basic constitutional rights. As a result of this decision, Judge Paul Williams, a federal judge in Arkansas, ordered that the girls who had been suspended could seek damages from individual school board members—though not from the school district as a corporate body. The judge also ruled that the school records of the pupils must be cleared of the suspension incident. From these decisions it is apparent that the U.S. Supreme Court is taking into account the rights of students.

The Supreme Court extended and clarified its ruling in *Wood* three years later when it considered the rights of students to collect damages for having been suspended without a hearing. The case, *Carey* v. *Piphus* (435 U.S. 247, 1978), treated two issues: under what conditions damages may be awarded to students who have been deprived of their constitutional rights and the amount of damages they can receive. The Court held that a student must first clearly establish that an injury has occurred before damages can be collected. Since that condition had not been established, the Court ruled that the students were entitled only to symbolic damages of $1.00.

Efforts have been made to define student rights. One such effort, *A Bill of Rights for High School Students,* was developed by the American Civil Liberties Union of Maryland. It is based partly on court decisions and illustrates current thinking about student rights. It addresses, for example, freedom of expression, religion, and privacy and rights of equality of opportunity and due process. (The complete text is in Appendix A.)

In Loco Parentis

Historically, schools have functioned under the doctrine of *in loco parentis* (in place of a parent). This doctrine meant that schools could exercise almost complete control over students because they acted as parent substitutes. Under the doctrine of *in loco parentis* the courts usually upheld the rules and regulations of local boards of education, particularly about pupil conduct. Recently, there has been a change toward more regard for the constitutional rights of pupils; the *Tinker* case (*Tinker* v. *Des Moines Independent Community School District,* 1969) was significant. It involved a school board's attempt to keep students from wearing black armbands in a protest against hostilities in Vietnam. In 1969 the U.S. Supreme Court ruled against the Des Moines school board by a vote of seven to two. The majority opinion of the Court was that

> the wearing of armbands in the circumstances of this case was entirely divorced from actually or potentially disruptive conduct by those participating in it. It was closely akin to "pure speech" which, we have repeatedly held, is entitled to comprehensive protection, under the First Amendment. . . .
>
> First Amendment rights, applied in the light of the special characteristics of the school environment, are available to teachers and students. It can hardly be argued that either students or teachers shed their constitutional rights to freedom at the schoolhouse gate.

The Court also said, however:

> On the other hand, the Court has repeatedly emphasized the need for affirming the comprehensive authority of the States and of school officials, consistent with fundamental constitutional safeguards, to prescribe and control conduct in the schools. . . . Our problem lies in the area where students in the exercise of First Amendment rights collide with the rules of the school authorities.

The Court clearly designated what it was *not* deciding in the *Tinker* opinion:

> The problem posed by the present case does not relate to regulation of the length of skirts or the type of clothing, to hair styles, or deportment. . . . It does not concern aggressive, disruptive action or even group demonstrations. Our problem involves direct, primary First Amendment rights akin to "pure speech."

Undoubtedly, the Court's opinion in the *Tinker* case will have a long-lasting and widespread effect on the operation of schools in the United States. *It clearly said that whatever their age, students have constitutional rights.*

Another case that involved impingement upon students' First Amendment rights issued from a challenge of a school board's decision to remove books from the school library. In *Board of Education, Inland Trees Union Free School District No. 26* v. *Pico* (50 U.S.L.W. 4831, 1982) the U.S. Supreme Court issued a five-to-four fragmented decision ruling that children may, under certain circumstances, challenge the board's decision to remove the books. Three of the justices suggested that students have a "right to receive" information which is "an inherent corollary of the rights of free speech and press. . . ."

Due Process

Much of the recent involvement of the courts with student rights has concerned due process of law for pupils. Due process has two connotations—procedural and substantive. Procedural due process has to do with whether or not the procedures used in disciplinary cases are fair; substantive due process is concerned with whether or not the school authorities have deprived a student of basic substantive constitutional rights like freedom of speech or personal liberty.[3]

Procedural due process is frequently scrutinized in cases of suspension and expulsion. These most often result from disciplinary action taken by the school, which may or may not have violated a pupil's substantive constitutional right. In the *Tinker* case, in which students were suspended, the decision was made primarily on the violation of the substantive right of freedom of speech or expression.

Procedural due process cases usually involve alleged violations of the Fourteenth Amendment, which provides for the protection of specified privileges of citizens, including due process of law. They may also involve alleged violations of state constitutions or statutory law that call for specific procedures. Many states have steps for expulsion or suspension. Expulsion usually involves notifying parents or guardians in a specific way, perhaps by registered mail, and giving students the opportunity for a hearing before the board of education or a designated hearing officer. Suspension procedures are usually detailed as well, designating who has the authority to suspend and the length of time for suspension. Teachers and administrators should know due process regulations, including the specific regulations of the state where they are employed.

Corporal Punishment

In 1977 the U.S. Supreme Court ruled and finally resolved many of the issues related to corporal punishment (*Ingraham* v. *Wright,* 1977). The opinion established that states may *constitutionally* authorize corporal punishment without prior hearing or notice and without consent by the student's parents and may as a matter of policy elect to prohibit or limit the use of corporal punishment.

The common-law rule on corporal punishment prevails in most states (*Fedor* v. *Mauwehu Council of Boy Scouts,* Conn., 1958). Under that rule, teachers and educators have a legal privilege to administer *reasonable* corporal punishment. Reasonableness frequently reflects local attitudes; its definition will therefore vary from region to region. In determining whether or not to administer corporal punishment, school personnel should consider these factors: age, sex, and size of pupil; size and suitability of the instrument and force employed; and the degree of the punishment in respect to the nature of the infraction.

In response to the greater sensitivity to student rights, many school districts have adopted administrative rules and regulations to restrict the occasions, nature, and manner of administering corporal punishment. In some instances, school districts specify that corporal punishment may be administered only under the direction of the principal and in the presence of another adult.

Dress Codes and Grooming

Lower court cases dealing with grooming have been decided in some instances in favor of the board of education—in support of their rules and regulations—and in other instances in favor of the student. A general principle seems to be that if the dress and grooming do not incite or cause disruptive behavior or pose a health or safety problem, the court ruling is likely to support the student. Dress codes, once very much in vogue, are much less evident today. Although the U.S. Supreme Court has yet to consider a so-called long-hair case, federal courts in every circuit have issued rulings in such cases; half of them found such regulations unconstitutional, and half upheld them.

The courts have usually refused to uphold dress and hair-length regulations for athletic teams or extracurricular activities unless the school proves that the hair or dress interfered with a student's ability to play the sport or perform the activity, as in *Long* v. *Zopp* (476 F.2nd 180, 4th Circuit, 1973).

In the late 1970s and continuing into the 1980s, courts began to entertain fewer challenges to grooming regulations. The later decisions have continued to be consistent, however, with earlier court rulings. Courts have supported school officials who attempted to regulate student appearance if the regulation could be based on disruption, health, or safety. Presumably, the controversy over the length of a student's hair or one's grooming in general is no longer critical because officials and students have a more common ground of agreement about what is acceptable.

Sex Discrimination

Until recently, educational institutions could discriminate against females—whether they were students, staff, or faculty. In 1972 the Ninety-second Congress enacted Title IX of the Education Amendments Act to remove sex discrimination against students and employees in federally assisted programs. The key position in Title IX states: "No person in the United States shall, on the basis of sex, be excluded from participation in, be denied the benefits of, or be subjected to discrimination under any education program or activity receiving federal financial assistance." Title IX is enforced by the Office of Civil Rights of the Department of Health,

Education, and Welfare (HEW), now the Department of Education. An individual or organization can allege any policy or practice discriminatory by writing a letter of complaint to the secretary of the Department of Education.

Schools at all levels are required to comply with Title IX. The statute does exempt military schools, some religious institutions, and private undergraduate schools. After admitting students of both sexes, however, these schools cannot alter admission policy to discriminate purposely on the basis of sex.

Marriage

Courts have ruled quite consistently that marriage is not a valid reason for expulsion. They have also said that although school authorities may not bar married students from instructional classes, they may bar them from extracurricular activities. The opinions have been based on the doctrine that every child has a constitutional right to attend school. The right may be removed when a student's moral standards are proved legally to be objectionable and deleterious to other students.

School Records

14

Before November 19, 1974, the effective date of the Buckley Amendment, the law regarding the privacy of student records was extremely unclear. Many school administrators—and most parents—do not yet realize that parents now have the right to view their children's educational records. Students over the age of eighteen also have the right to see their school records for themselves. Many teachers are not yet aware that their written comments, which they submit as part of a student's record, must be shown at a parent's request, or at a student's request if the student is eighteen.

The new law (Public Law 93-380 as amended by Public Law 93-568) requires that schools receiving federal funds must comply with the privacy requirements or face loss of those funds. What must a school district do to comply? According to a 1976 clarification by HEW, the Buckley Amendment sets forth these main requirements. The school district must:

> Allow all parents, even those not having custody of their children, access to each educational record that a school district keeps on their child.
>
> Establish a district policy on how parents can go about seeing specific records.
>
> Inform all parents what rights they have under the Amendment, how they can act on these rights according to school policy, and where they can see a copy of the policy.
>
> Seek parental permission in writing before disclosing any personally identifiable record on a child to individuals other than professional personnel employed in the district (and others who meet certain specific requirements).[4]

Since the loss of federal funds could present serious problems to some school districts, the responsibility for procedures to meet the requirements of the Buckley Amendment are self-evident. Many school districts have carefully formulated procedures; others are striving to clarify such procedures in order to prevent conflicts.

Student Publications

A significant decision for student newspapers was made in *Scoville* v. *Board of Education* (1970), originating in Illinois. Students were expelled for distributing a newspaper named "Grass High," which criticized school officials and used vulgar language. The students were expelled under an Illinois statute that empowered boards of education to expel pupils guilty of gross disobedience or misconduct. The board of education was supported by a federal court in Illinois, but on appeal the Court of Appeals for the Seventh Circuit reversed the decision. The court concluded:

> . . . absent an evidentiary showing, and an appropriate balancing of the evidence by the district court to determine whether the Board was justified in a "forecast" of the disruption and interference, as required under Tinker, plaintiffs are entitled to the declaratory judgment, injunctive and damage relief sought.

In 1975 the Second Circuit Court of Appeals affirmed a lower court decision that school newspaper editors had a constitutional right to publish a sex supplement that included articles on contraception and abortion.[5] Further, the court ruled that school authorities, on the basis of their opinion that the material was not fit for high school students, could not seize nor ban its distribution. The same court in 1977 ruled that high school administrators could ban school newspaper editors from conducting and publishing a student poll that sought personal and frank information about students' sexual experiences and attitudes.[6] The court found that the state's interest in preventing psychological harm to immature students was enough to override the students' claims for license.

The issue of institutional control over publications has not yet been fully resolved. On the basis of the decisions of courts to date, a school official must be very careful in restricting the content of a school-sponsored publication unless it is clearly obscene. If the newspaper leads to disruption, school officials have a much better chance of being upheld in restricting the publication. School officials have also been protected where there is reasonable expectation of disruption or interference.

Student and Locker Searches

Most lower courts have refused to subject public school searches to the same strict Fourth Amendment standards that govern warrantless searches of criminal suspects by police and prosecutors. In general, the Fourth

Student publications can often be the focus of disputes concerning student rights and responsibilities.

Amendment protects from search without a warrant (court order). Many lower courts have decided in favor of a lenient interpretation of the Fourth Amendment in school searches. The rationale is that school authorities are obligated to maintain discipline and a sound educational environment and that, along with their *in loco parentis* powers, gives them the right to conduct searches and seize contraband upon reasonable suspicion without a judicial warrant.

School authorities do not need a warrant to search a student's locker or a student vehicle on campus. For searches of a student's person, however, courts apply a higher standard. Where reasonable suspicion exists, a school official will likely be upheld. Reasonable suspicion exists when one has information that a student is in possession of something harmful, illegal, or dangerous. The second consideration is the way in which the search of a student's person is conducted. School officials are advised to have students remove contents from their clothing rather than have a teacher or administrator do it. A further caution is not to force students to remove all their clothing or undress to their underwear. To date, courts have not upheld school officials in strip searches. These cases evoke the greatest judicial sympathy toward student damages for illegal searches.[7]

The following grounds have been held to justify a search: information from student informers, police tips, anonymous callers, unusual conduct by the searched student (secretive movements), fleeing an instructor when called, and tips from outside callers and personnel.[8]

The most recent question involving searches of students concerns the use of dogs in sniffing out narcotics. The first such case was decided in 1980, and the few cases handed down since then reveal a lack of unanimity among the courts. On the one hand, some courts have held that the use of a dog is merely preliminary to a search; others have viewed such a search as being highly invasive. Further court decisions are required to clarify this issue.

Educational Malpractice

The courts of California (*Peter W.* v. *San Francisco Unified School District,* 1976) and New York (*Donahue* v. *Copiague Union Free School District,* 1978) recently dismissed suits by former students alleging indirect injury; that is, that they did not achieve an adequate education. In the California case the student, after graduating from high school, could barely read and write. The judge in his opinion stated,

> The science of pedagogy itself is fraught with different and conflicting theories . . . and any layman might—and commonly does—have his own emphatic viewpoints on the subject. . . . The achievement of literacy in the schools, or its failure, is influenced by a host of factors . . . from outside the formal teaching process, and beyond the course of its ministers.

In essence, he said that there is no way to assess the school's negligence. In the New York case the judge said, "The failure to learn does not bespeak a failure to teach."

The *Hunter* decision of 1981 followed previous rulings, although the plaintiffs had asked the court specifically to reject the notion that public policy considerations forbade such a suit (*Hunter* v. *Board of Education of Montgomery County,* 425 A. 2d 681, 1981). The court also rejected the suggestion that it recognize a new tort, that of educational malpractice. It saw a number of problems arising from such a tort:

> It is conceivable that, if allowed, suits for educational malpractice might arise every time a child failed a grade, subject, or test, with the result that teachers could possibly spend more time in lawyers' offices and courtrooms than in the classroom. That happening could give rise to claims of educational malpractice predicted on the teacher's failure to devote sufficient time to teaching. The opposite side of the matter is that if, to avoid suits arising from a student's failing a grade, subject or test, the teacher "passed" the child, the teacher would likely find himself or herself defending a malpractice suit because the child was promoted when promotion was not warranted.

Teacher Rights and Responsibilities

[12] Teachers have the same rights as other citizens. The Fourteenth Amendment provides for substantive due process (for example, protection against the deprivation of constitutional rights such as freedom of expression) and procedural due process (procedural protection against unjustified deprivation of substantive rights). Most court cases related to teachers evolve from either liberty or property interests. Liberty interests are created by the Constitution itself, while property interests are found in some form of legal entitlement such as tenure or certification.

Teachers also have the same responsibilities as other citizens. They must abide by federal, state, and local laws and by the provisions of contracts. As professionals they must also assume the heavy responsibility of educating young people. Specific court cases are discussed briefly to illustrate some of the issues and decisions related to aspects of teacher rights and responsibilities. The reader is cautioned that the cases selected do not necessarily constitute the last word regarding teacher rights but rather are used to provide an overview of some of the issues that have been decided in our courts. Table 3.2 summarizes the issues and decisions in selected cases involving teacher rights and responsibilities. This summary table is not intended to provide a complete understanding of the court decisions cited. It is necessary to read the textual narrative for a more complete understanding.

Teacher Certification

[2] The primary purpose of teacher certification is to make sure there are qualified and competent teachers in the public schools. All states have established requirements for teacher certification. Carrying out the policies of certification is usually a function of a state certification board. The board first has to make certain that applicants meet legal requirements; it then issues the appropriate certificates. Certifying agencies may not arbitrarily refuse to issue a certificate to a qualified candidate. The courts have ruled that local boards of education may prescribe additional or higher qualifications beyond the state requirements, provided such requirements are not irrelevant, unreasonable, or arbitrary. A teaching certificate is a license or a privilege granted to practice a profession—it is not a right. Teacher certification is a property interest that cannot be revoked without constitutional due process. Certification laws usually require, in addition, that the candidate show evidence of citizenship, good moral character, and good physical health. A minimum age is frequently specified.

Teacher Employment Contracts

Usually, boards of education have the statutory authority to employ teachers. This authority includes the power to enter into contracts and to fix

TABLE 3.2 *Summary of Selected Teacher Rights and Responsibility Cases*

Case	Issue	Decision
North Haven Board of Education v. *Bell* (50 U.S.L.W. 4501, 1982)	Former women faculty members alleged sex discrimination	U.S. Supreme Court ruled that school employees as well as students are protected under Title IX
Burkey v. *Marshall County Board of Education* (513 F. Supp. 1083 W. Va., 1981)	Pay equity for female coach and male coach	Ruled that board's policy of paying female coach less than male coach violated the Equal Pay Act
Turk v. *Franklin Special School District* (640 S.W. 2d 218, Tenn., 1982)	School board dismissed tenured teacher after she was arrested for driving under the influence of alcohol	Tennessee Supreme Court ruled that before a tenured teacher can be dismissed, charges shall be made in writing specifically stating the offenses
Lucia v. *Duggan* (Massachusetts, 1969)	Is it necessary for a school district to follow due process procedures in dismissing nontenured teachers?	Court ruled that the rights of procedural due process are applicable to nontenured as well as tenured faculty.
Cooper v. *Ross* (472 F. Supp. 801 E.D. Ark., 1979)	University teacher contract not renewed because he taught classes from a Marxist view	Court ordered teacher reinstated for university's failure to advance convincing reasons related to academic freedom issue
Hillis v. *Stephen F. Austin University* (665 F. 2d 547 5th Cir., 1982)	Is awarding a course grade a right of academic freedom?	Since the university gave reasons for the nonrenewal of the instructor's contract, court ruled in favor of the university
Kingsville Independent School District v. *Cooper* (611 F. 2d 1109 5th Cir., 1980)	High school teacher's contract not renewed because simulation of rural life evoked controversy in the school and community	Court ruled that the school erred, and teacher was ordered reinstated.
Pickering v. *Board of Education* (U.S. Supreme Court, 1968)	Illinois teacher dismissed for criticizing school board and superintendent in a letter published by a local newspaper	Court upheld teacher's claim that his First and Fourteenth Amendment rights were denied

TABLE 3.2 *(Continued)*

Case	Issue	Decision
Norwalk Teachers' Association v. *Board of Education* (Connecticut Supreme Court, 1951) and *City of Manchester* v. *Manchester Teachers' Guild* (New Hampshire Supreme Court, 1957)	Do teachers have the right to strike?	Supreme courts in these two states ruled that teachers may not strike
Board of Education of City of Minneapolis v. *Public School Employees Union* (Minnesota State District Court, 1951)	Do teachers have the right to strike?	Court upheld teachers' right to strike except when denied by clear language in state law. Shortly thereafter, Minnesota legislature passed an antistrike law
Hortonville Joint School District No. 1 v. *Hortonville Education Association* (96 S. Ct. 2308, 1976)	May boards of education dismiss teachers who are striking illegally?	Court said the law gave the board power to employ and dismiss teachers as a part of the municipal labor relations balance
Mastrangelo v. *West Side Union High School District* (California, 1935)	Are a teacher and the board liable for injuries suffered in a classroom accident?	Even though the teacher was in the room and had instructed pupils regarding dangers of chemistry experiment, court held the teacher and the board of education liable
Morris v. *Douglas County School District* (Oregon, 1966)	Teacher and school liability for student injury at school	Court declared the teacher negligent for not foreseeing the possibility of injury to the students

terms of employment and compensation. In some states, only specific members of the school board may sign teacher contracts. When statutes confer the employing authority to boards of education, the authority cannot be delegated. It is usually the responsibility of the superintendent to screen and nominate candidates to the board. The board, meeting in official session, then acts officially as a group to enter into contractual agreement. Employment procedures vary from state to state, but the process is fundamentally prescribed by the legislature and must be strictly followed by local boards.

A contract usually contains elements like the following: the identification of the teacher and the board of education, a statement of the legal capacity of each party to enter into contract, a definition of the assignment specified, a statement of the salary and how it is to be paid, and a provision for signature by the teacher and by the legally authorized agents of the board. In some states, contract forms are provided by state departments of education, and these forms must be used; in others, forms are optional.

A teacher may not enter into legal contract without having a valid teaching certificate issued by the state. Funds may not be legally expended under a contract with a teacher who is not legally certified. The requirement of certification for the contract to be valid is intended to protect the public from incompetent teachers.

Often a new teacher will enter into a contract before receiving state certification, with certification scheduled before teaching duties begin. The question may be raised about whether or not such a contract is valid. The answer depends on the specific wording and interpretation of the state statute. In some states this practice is legally sanctioned. In general, "the weight of authority is that a certificate must be had at the time of making the contract unless the statutory language clearly indicates that it was the legislative intention that possession of a certificate at the time of beginning of teaching is sufficient."[9]

Teachers are responsible for making certain that they are legally qualified to enter into contractual agreements. Furthermore, they are responsible for carrying out the terms of the contract and abiding by them. In turn, under the contract they can legally expect proper treatment from an employer.

Sex Discrimination

In *North Haven Board of Eduction* v. *Bell* (50 U.S.L.W. 4501, 1982) the U.S. Supreme Court ruled that school employees as well as students are protected under Title IX. The North Haven decision involved former women faculty members who alleged sex discrimination. In upholding Title IX regulations the decision not only allows the U.S. Department of Education to investigate complaints from school employees, but also permits the department to cut off federal aid to institutions that discriminate.

Burkey v. *Marshall County Board of Education* (513 F. Supp. 1083 W.Va., 1981) was a landmark decision regarding pay equity. It ruled that the Marshall County school board's policy of paying the female coach of the girls' basketball team half the salary of the male coach of the boys' basketball team violated the Equal Pay Act, Title VII of the Civil Rights

Act of 1964, and the Constitution. The Court also ruled that the board's policy of hiring only male teachers as coaches of boys' sports constituted illegal sex discrimination.

Teacher Tenure

Teacher tenure legislation exists in most states. In many, tenure or fair dismissal laws are mandatory and apply to all school districts without exception. In other states this is not the case. The various tenure laws differ not only in extent of coverage but also in provision for coverage.

Tenure laws are intended to provide security for teachers in their positions and to prevent removal of capable teachers by capricious action or political motive. Tenure statutes generally include detailed specifications necessary for attaining tenure and for dismissing teachers who have tenure. These statutes have been upheld when attacked on constitutional grounds. The courts reason that since state legislatures create school districts, they have the right to limit their power.

A teacher becomes tenured by serving satisfactorily for a stated time. This period is referred to as the probationary period and varies in length from state to state. The actual process of acquiring tenure after serving the probationary period depends on the applicable statute. In some states the process is automatic at the satisfactory completion of the probationary period; in other states, official action by the school board is necessary.

The grounds and procedures for dismissing teachers with permanent tenure are usually spelled out as part of the tenure statute. The grounds generally include incompetency, inefficiency, insubordination, immorality, and "other good and just" causes. Generalizations cannot be made on what constitutes these grounds; the decisions are made on the merits of each case.

For example, in *Turk* v. *Franklin Special School District* (640 S.W. 2d 218 Tenn., 1982), the school board dismissed Jane Turk from her teaching position after she was arrested for driving under the influence of alcohol (DUI). Turk's appeal was upheld by the lower court judge, since there was no evidence of an adverse effect on her capacity and fitness as a teacher. The school board appealed to the Tennessee Supreme Court, which found that the school board "acted in flagrant disregard of the statutory requirement and fundamental fairness in considering matters that should have been specifically charged in writing." Tennessee law requires that before a tenured teacher can be dismissed, "the charges shall be made in writing specifically stating the offenses which are charged." Thus teacher tenure may be affected by teacher conduct outside school as well as inside. This, in a sense, deals with the personal freedom of teachers; freedom to behave as other citizens do, freedom to engage in political activities, and academic freedom in the classroom.

Tenure laws are frequently attacked by those who claim that they protect the incompetent teacher. There is undoubtedly some truth in the assertion, but it must be stated clearly and unequivocally that they also protect the competent and most able teachers. Teachers who accept the challenge of their profession and dare to use new methods, who inspire curiosity in their students, and who discuss controversial issues in their classrooms need protection from dismissal through political or capricious methods. Incompetent teachers, whether tenured or not, can be dismissed under the law by capable administrators who allow due process while evaluating teacher performance.

Although due process has been the rule for years for tenured teachers, evidence now beginning to accumulate indicates that nontenured faculty also have, or should have, procedural due process rights. In some states, complete due process procedures for nontenured faculty are spelled out in the statutes. In most states, however, provisions are only perfunctory, providing calendar dates for nonrenewal of contracts. Cases in Massachusetts (*Lucia* v. *Duggan,* 1969) and Wisconsin (*Gouge* v. *Joint School District No. 1,* 1970) point up the necessity of following due process in dismissing nontenured teachers. In the *Lucia* case the court said: "The particular circumstances of a dismissal of a public school teacher provide compelling reasons for application of a doctrine of procedural due process."[10] In the *Gouge* case the court said:

> [A] teacher in a public elementary or secondary school is protected by the due process clause of the Fourteenth Amendment against a nonrenewal decision which is wholly without basis in fact and also against a decision which is wholly unreasoned, as well as a decision which is impermissibly based.

It has become increasingly apparent that the rights of procedural due process are applicable to nontenured as well as tenured faculty.

Academic Freedom

A sensitive and vital concern to the educator is academic freedom—freedom to control what one will teach and to teach the truth as one discovers it, without fear of penalty. Academic freedom is thus essentially a pedagogical philosophy that has been applied to a variety of professional activities. A philosophical position, however, is *not necessarily* a legal right.[11] Federal judges have generally recognized certain academic protections in the college classroom while exhibiting reluctance to recognize rights for elementary and secondary school teachers.

The contract of a history teacher at the University of Arkansas—Little Rock was not renewed after he announced that he taught his classes from a Marxist point of view, since he was a communist (*Cooper* v. *Ross,* 472 F. Supp. 801 E.D. Ark., 1979). The court ordered Cooper reinstated in light of the university's failure to advance convincing reasons related to the academic freedom issue to warrant his nonrenewal. In another case (*Hillis* v. *Stephen F. Austin University,* 665 F. 2d 547 5th Cir., 1982) the instructor claimed that he was denied tenure because he refused to change a student's grade. He argued that awarding a course grade was the instructor's right of academic freedom. Since the university had given several reasons for the nonrenewal of the instructor's contract, the court did not order Hillis's reinstatement. These examples illustrate the reluctance of judges to interfere in the internal affairs of colleges and universities. The scope of a professor's right to teach is thus much more determined by the institution's own policies than by the federal courts.[12]

While federal courts generally have not recognized academic freedom for elementary and secondary school teachers, the most supportive ruling was in *Kingsville Independent School District* v. *Cooper* (611 F. 2d 1109 5th Cir., 1980), which involved a high school history teacher who used a simulation game to introduce her students to the characteristics of rural life during the post–Civil War Reconstruction era. While the role playing evoked controversy in the school and community, there was no evidence that the teacher's usefulness had been impaired. Thus the school erred in not renewing the teacher's contract, and she was ordered reinstated.

In *Pickering* v. *Board of Education* (1968), the U.S. Supreme Court dealt with academic freedom at the public school level. Pickering was a teacher in Illinois who, in a letter published by a local newspaper, was critical of the school board and the superintendent for the way they handled past proposals to raise and use new revenues for the schools. After a full hearing, the board of education terminated Pickering's employment, whereupon he brought suit under the First and Fourteenth Amendments. The Illinois courts rejected his claim. The U.S. Supreme Court, however, upheld Pickering's claim and, in its opinion, stated:

> To the extent that the Illinois Supreme Court's opinion may be read to suggest that teachers may constitutionally be compelled to relinquish the First Amendment rights they would otherwise enjoy as citizens to comment on matters of public interest in connection with the operation of the public schools in which they work, it proceeds on a premise that has been unequivocally rejected in numerous prior decisions of this Court.

The Court then addressed itself to the problem of dealing with cases involving academic freedom. It held that the problem was how to arrive at a balance between the interests of the teacher, who as citizen comments on matters of public concern, and the interests of the state, which as employer promotes the efficiency of its public services through its employees. It is difficult to define precisely the limits of academic freedom. In general, the courts strongly support it yet recognize that teachers must be professionally responsible when interacting with pupils.

Because the law regarding academic freedom is considerably unsettled, teachers should be cautious in asserting a claim to engage in classroom discussion or to choose a teaching methodology unless they are aware of supportive law in their region or are acting according to school board policy. School authorities should devote attention to developing legally sound school curriculum policies. If teachers are made aware of their class-room rights and responsibilities in advance, many potential disputes could be avoided.[13]

Right to Bargain Collectively

What are the rights of teachers to bargain collectively? This has been an active issue in recent years. In the past, teacher groups met informally with boards of education to discuss salaries and other teacher welfare provisions. Sometimes the superintendent even was the spokesperson for such teacher groups. In recent years, formal collective procedures have evolved. These procedures have been labeled collective bargaining, professional negotiation, cooperative determination, and collective negotiation. They represent a growing desire of teachers to participate officially and directly in formulating policy, particularly matters about their welfare. Teachers are demanding that the procedures of employer-employee relations be made formal by official written procedural agreements.

Collective bargaining has been defined as a way of winning improved goals and not the goal itself. A contract means that salaries, working conditions, and other matters within the scope of the collective bargaining agreement can no longer be decided unilaterally by the school administration. Instead, the contract outlines effective participation by the teachers' union and its members in formulating the school policies and programs under which they work.

The first teachers' group to bargain collectively with its local board of education was the Maywood, Illinois, Proviso Council of West Suburban Teachers, Union Local 571, in 1938. In 1957 a second local, the East St. Louis, Illinois, Federation of Teachers, was successful in negotiating a written contract. The breakthrough, however, came in December 1961, when the United Federation of Teachers, Local 2 of the American Federation of Teachers (AFT), won the right to bargain for New York City's teachers. Since then collective bargaining agreements between boards of education and teachers' groups have grown phenomenally. Both the AFT and the NEA have been active in promoting collective bargaining. Today, approximately 75 percent of the nation's teachers are covered by collective bargaining agreements.

Both the NEA and the AFT have actively proposed bargaining legislation. Many states already have collective bargaining agreements; undoubtedly, more statutes will be enacted. The details of the statutes and the proposed bills vary, but generally they include the right of public employees to organize and to bargain collectively, to determine the bargaining agent (in the case of teachers, usually either an AFT or an NEA affiliate, or a combination), to describe the scope of negotiation, and to provide an impasse procedure. In many negotiation statutes, strikes are prohibited. In some instances, when the statutes called for a single organization to represent all employees exclusively, election campaigns to select the bargaining organization have been bitterly waged. In the future we can expect that the courts and legislatures frequently will have to determine the rights of teachers and the rights of boards of education in collective bargaining.

When through unified action teachers finally get the right to help make educational policy, they must assume commensurate responsibility. Teachers share responsibility for deciding policy with boards of education and administrators who recognize a democratic principle: those affected by policy should have a voice in its determination. This participation should commit teachers to abide by these policies. Teachers, as professional educators and front-line workers dealing daily with pupils, have valuable knowledge for deciding educational policy. As specialists, they have expertise that board members often do not have and are not expected to have. Cooperative participation will benefit the schoolchildren both directly and indirectly.

Right to Strike

[12] Courts have ruled on the legality of teacher strikes. The supreme court of Connecticut (*Norwalk Teachers' Association* v. *Board of Education*, 1951) and the supreme court of New Hampshire (*City of Manchester* v. *Manchester Teachers' Guild*, 1957) ruled that teachers may not strike. The court opinion in Connecticut stated:

> Under our system, the government is established by and run for all of the people, not for the benefit of any person or group. The profit motive, inherent in the principle of free enterprise, is absent. It should be the aim of every employee of the government to do his or her part to make it function as efficiently and economically as possible. The drastic remedy or the organized strike to enforce the demands of unions of government employees is in direct contravention of this principle.

Judges generally held that public employees do not have the right to strike. A state district court in Minnesota deviated from this view when it said that to hold that a public employee has no right to strike is a personal belief that looks for legality on some tenuous theory of sovereignty or supremacy of government. The court upheld the right to strike as rooted in the freedom of men and women and was not to be denied except by clear, unequivocal language in a constitution, statute, ordinance, rule, or contract.

The decision was upheld by the supreme court of Minnesota (*Board of Education of City of Minneapolis* v. *Public School Employees Union*, 1951). Shortly thereafter, the Minnesota legislature passed an antistrike law applicable to public employees. At least seven states—Alaska, Hawaii,

The right of teachers to strike is an emotional issue.

Montana, New Hampshire, Oregon, Pennsylvania, and Vermont—permit strikes in their collective bargaining statutes. At least twenty states have statutes that prohibit strikes. Whether or not there are specific statutes prohibiting strikes, boards of education threatened by strikes usually can get a court injunction forestalling them. Both the NEA and the AFT view the strike as a last-resort technique, although justifiable in some circumstances.

In the 1960s there was a big increase in the number of teacher strikes. There were over 500 strikes during the decade, with over half a million teachers participating. The New York City teachers' strike was perhaps the most significant in that punitive action was taken against the union. The strike took place in September 1967 and lasted for eighteen days. The strike violated the state of New York's Taylor Law, which bars strikes by public employees. The United Federation of Teachers was fined $150,000, and its president was sentenced to fifteen days in jail and fined $250 for contempt of court. The board of education had obtained an injunction against the strike. The Taylor Law in this case did not prevent a strike, but it did provide the means for punitive action against the union for violating the court injunction.

Schools continued to be plagued with strikes in the 1970s at about the same level as in the 1960s. There are a number of factors interacting in the early 1980s that could have decided effects on bargaining and strikes in that decade. These include the retrenchment of public education, public support for retrenchment, an oversupply of teachers except in certain fields, and increased sophistication in collective bargaining. For the next few years, public school enrollments will continue to decline. At the same time, efforts are being made in many parts of the nation to limit local property taxes and curtail government spending. There will be increased competition for public money, resulting in tension and controversy. Many school board members are inclined to believe that the public will be squarely behind them as they fend off employee demands for wage increases. Furthermore, at least in the early 1980s, there will be a general oversupply of teachers with shortages in some specialized fields. While the sophistication of both management and labor in the bargaining process has increased, citizens continue to press for involvement in public school bargaining. Parents and taxpayers feel a sense of helplessness over critical decisions being made in which they do not feel represented by their elected school board members. Taking these facts into consideration, it is difficult to predict how prominent strikes will be in the future, but we can say quite clearly that there will be tension, controversy, competition for resources, and strife.

Recently, the U.S. Supreme Court, by a six-to-three vote, ruled that boards of education can discharge teachers who are striking illegally. Ramifications of this decision, involving a Wisconsin public school, are potentially far-reaching. The Court viewed discharge as a policy matter rather than an issue for adjudication: "What choice among the alternative responses to the teachers' strike will best serve the interests of the school system, the interests of the parents and children who depend on the system, and the interests of the citizens whose taxes support it?" The Court said that the state law in question gave the board the power to employ and dismiss teachers as a part of the balance it had struck in municipal labor relations (*Hortonville Joint School District No. 1* v. *Hortonville Education Association*, 96 S. Ct. 2308, 1976).

One can argue that strikes are unlawful when a statute is violated, that the courts in their decisions have questioned the right of public employees to strike, and that some teachers and teacher organizations consider strikes unprofessional. The question before teachers seems to be whether or not the strike is a justifiable and responsible means—after all other ways have been exhausted—of declaring abominable educational and working conditions and trying to remedy them.

Liability for Negligence

With nearly 50 million students enrolled in elementary and secondary schools, it is almost inevitable that some will be injured in educational activities. Each year some injuries will occasion lawsuits in which plaintiffs seek damages. Such suits are often brought against both the school districts and their employees. Actions seeking monetary damages for injuries are referred to as *actions in tort*. Technically, a tort is a legal wrong—an act or the omission of an act that violates the private rights of an individual. Actions in tort are generally based on alleged negligence; the basis of tort liability or legal responsibility is negligence. Understanding the concept of negligence is essential to understanding liability.

Legally, negligence is the result of a failure to exercise or practice due care. It includes a factor of foreseeability of harm. Court cases on record involving negligence are numerous and varied.

In a California high school chemistry class, pupils were injured while experimenting in the manufacture of gunpowder (*Mastrangelo* v. *West Side Union High School District*, 1935). The teacher was in the room and had supplemented the laboratory manual instructions with his own directions. Nevertheless, an explosion occurred, allegedly caused by failure of pupils to follow directions. A court held the teacher and the board of education liable. Negligence in this case meant the lack of supervision of laboratory work.

In Oregon a child was injured while on a school outing (*Morris* v. *Douglas County School District*, 1966). Children were playing on a large log in a relatively dry space on a beach. A large wave surged up onto the beach dislodging the log, which began to roll. One of the children fell seaward off the log, and the receding wave pulled the log over the child, injuring him. In the subsequent court action the teacher was declared negligent for not foreseeing the possibility of such an occurrence. The court said:

> The first proposition asks this court to hold, as a matter of fact, that unusual wave action on the shore of the Pacific Ocean is a hazard so unforeseeable that there is no duty to guard against it. On the contrary, we agree with the trial judge, who observed that it is common knowledge that accidents substantially like the one that occurred in this case have occurred at beaches along the Oregon coast. Foreseeability of such harm is not so remote as to be ruled out as a matter of law.

Although negligence is a vague concept involving due care and foreseeability, it is defined more specifically each time a court decides such a case. In each instance, somewhat reflecting past decisions, courts decide what constitutes reasonable due care and adequate foresight.

Historically, when there are no statutes imposing liability, school districts have generally been held liable for torts resulting from the negligence of their officers, agents, or employees while the school districts are acting in their governmental capacity. That concept was based on the doctrine that the state is sovereign and cannot be sued without consent. A school district, as an arm of state government, would therefore be immune from tort liability. Employees of school districts generally have not been protected by the immunity school districts enjoy; teachers may be held liable for their actions. Teachers must act as reasonable and prudent people, foreseeing dangerous situations. The degree of care that is required increases with the immaturity of the pupil. Lack of supervision and foresight form the basis of negligence charges.

There has been a trend away from governmental immunity from tort liability. As of 1976, 28 states had abrogated governmental immunity either judicially, statutorily, or through some form of legal modification; in 1958, only two states had abrogated such immunity, while nineteen maintained it.[14] There has also been an increase in the number of lawsuits. Part of this increase can be attributed to the applicaton of Section 1983 of the Civil Rights Act of 1871 as well as new federal civil rights legislation.

Many states authorize school districts to purchase insurance to protect teachers, school districts, administrators, and school board members against suits. It is important that school districts and their employees and board members be thus protected, through either school district insurance or their own personal policies. For teachers, membership in the state affiliates of the NEA and membership in the AFT permit teachers to participate in liability insurance programs sponsored by those organizations.

Summary and Implications

Court cases that deal with issues related to the rights and responsibilities of students and teachers provide the basis for more and more discussions in newsletters, newspapers, professional journals, magazines, radio, and television across our country. The range and scope of the education-related court decisions have become so broad that concentration in school law is a recognized field of preparation in the legal profession. These specialized school lawyers are in great demand to serve increasing numbers of student and teacher clients who seek court relief from what they consider abuses to their rights.

Student rights and responsibilities are being more clearly defined by both court decisions and boards of education. Court decisions have helped in interpreting the right to an education to be that each child shall have an equal opportunity to pursue education. While boards of education have the right to establish reasonable rules and regulations, most student challenges have concerned corporal punishment, rights of married students, dress codes, and freedom of expression. As more attention is given to the constitutional rights of students, the *in loco parentis* doctrine of the schools must be reasonable, rather than arbitrary, regarding student rights. Particularly in cases of suspension and expulsion, corporal punishment, dress codes, and sex discrimination, actions of school administrators and teachers may be examined regarding the due process dimensions of fairness and constitutionality. Procedures for dealing with school records, student publications, student searches, and locker searches are being studied more thoroughly to avoid conflicts, which often end up in the courts. Educational malpractice charges by students against the schools are worthy of observation during the late 1980s in light of the increased call for excellence in education.

Teachers have the same rights and responsibilities as other citizens. With the assistance of support organizations such as the American Civil Liberties Union (ACLU) and the teacher unions, more and more teachers are airing their grievances in court. The courts have said that a teaching certificate is a license to practice a profession that cannot be revoked without constitutional due process. At the same time the courts have ruled that boards of education may prescribe requirements beyond the state requirements for certification. Teachers are responsible for making certain that they are legally certified to enter into contracts. The grounds and procedures for dismissing teachers are usually spelled out as part of the tenure statute of the respective states. Teacher dismissals by capricious actions of boards of education are often taken to court for consideration of due process. The law regarding academic freedom is unsettled, especially for elementary and secondary teachers, since federal judges have been reluctant to recognize academic freedom rights at this level. The courts have clarified teachers' rights to bargain collectively and to strike (where state law permits). Court cases brought against both the school districts and their employees involving negligence are numerous and varied. Teachers should be fully aware that negligence is the result of failure to exercise or practice due care.

The implications of the actions of the courts are highly significant to the teaching profession. From the many court decisions relating to education a framework has evolved for acceptable conduct of teachers within the school setting. Today's teacher no longer can assume that personal ignorance of acceptable standards of conduct will be overlooked by the courts in adjudicating a suit brought against the teacher. (Nor should the teacher be intimidated by the courts when reasonable rules of conduct are now being evolved for the practice of pedagogy.) Courts do not start hearings on their own efforts; school boards, school employees, and teachers must be sued before a court case can develop. On the other hand, prospective teachers need to be deliberately sensitive to the legal boundaries in teaching. Although beginning teachers need not have the knowledge and expertise of a lawyer, knowing the law well as it relates to education can contribute more than incidentally to becoming a successful teacher.

DISCUSSION QUESTIONS

1. What are the legal requirements in your state with respect to teacher certification, individual teacher contracts, and teacher tenure?

2. How are the expanding legal decisions related to students' rights and responsibilities infringing on teachers' rights and responsibilities?

3. What legal considerations apply to student and locker searches by school personnel?

4. How have the courts guarded against sex discrimination in the teaching profession?

5. Students over eighteen and parents of all schoolchildren are granted the legal right to examine their personal school files. How will this affect teacher behavior?

SUPPLEMENTAL ACTIVITIES

1. Invite to your class individuals or groups who have filed legal suits against the schools. (Staff members of the American Civil Liberties Union may respond to such a request.) Consider inviting to class a lawyer who is employed by a school district to explain how he or she serves the school system.

2. Examine your local or state school code to study and evaluate certification standards, tenure legislation, and curricular requirements.

3. Form a discussion group that will report to your class on the topic "Student Rights and Responsibilities." (A.C.L.U., *The Rights of Students*, Avon Books, Chicago, 1977.)

4. Accompany a truant officer to a court hearing of a school truancy case; report the specific findings of your trip to class. Discuss the relation of the courts to the schools.

5. Invite members of nearby teacher organizations to class to discuss how teacher organizations advocate teachers' rights. Also, discuss how they protect teachers against liability suits.

NOTES

1. Thomas J. Flygare, "De Jure," *Phi Delta Kappan* 64 (December 1982): 283.

2. National School Public Relations Association, *Student Rights and Responsibilities* (Arlington, Va.: National School Public Relations Association, 1972), p. 2.

3. Lee O. Garber and Reynolds C. Seitz, *The Yearbook of School Law, 1971* (Danville, Ill.: Interstate Printers and Publishers, 1971), p. 253.

4. Lucy Knight, "Facts about Mr. Buckley's Amendment," *American Education* 13 (June 1977): 7.

5. *Bayer* v. *Kinzler*, N.Y., 1974 (affirmed Second Circuit Court, 1975).

6. *Trachtmann* v. *Anker* (Second Circuit Court, 1977).

7. William D. Valente, *Law in the Schools* (Columbus, Ohio: Charles E. Merrill, 1980), p. 282. (Copyright by Bell and Howell Company, 1980.)

8. Ibid.

9. Robert R. Hamilton and Paul R. Mort, *The Law and Public Education* (St. Paul, Minn.: Foundation Press, 1969), p. 359.

10. Haskell C. Freedman, "The Legal Rights of Untenured Teachers," *Nolpe School Law Journal* 1 (Fall 1970): 100.

11. Frank W. Kemerer, "Classroom Academic Freedom: Is It a Right?," *Kappa Delta Pi Record* 19 (Summer 1983): 101.

12. Ibid., p. 102.

13. Ibid., p. 104.

14. Wayne R. Fetter and Don C. Patton, "Liability Protection for Professional School Personnel," *Phi Delta Kappan* 60 (March 1979): 525.

BIBLIOGRAPHY

Aquila, Frank D. *Title IX: Implications for Education of Women*. Bloomington, Ind.: Phi Delta Kappa, 1980.

Bryson, Joseph E., and Bentley, Charles P. *Ability Grouping of Public School Students: Legal Aspects of Classification and Tracking Methods*. Charlottesville, Va.: Michie Company, 1980.

Bryson, Joseph E., and Detty, Elizabeth W. *Cen-*

sorship of Public School Library and Instructional Materials. Charlottesville, Va.: Michie Company, 1982.

Connors, Eugene T. *Educational Tort Liability and Malpractice.* Bloomington, Ind.: Phi Delta Kappa, 1981.

Cryan, John R., and Smith, Janie C. "The Hick'ry Stick: It's Time to Change the Tune." *Phi Delta Kappan* 62 (February 1981): 433–435.

Fisher, Louis, et al. *Teachers and the Law.* New York: Longman, 1981.

Flygare, Thomas J. "Schools and the Law." *Phi Delta Kappan.* (A regular feature in each issue of the *Phi Delta Kappan* providing timely and pertinent information.)

Gee, E. Gordon, and Sperry, David J. *Education Law and the Public Schools: A Compendium.* Boston: Allyn and Bacon, 1978.

Hudgins, H. C., Jr., and Vacca, Richard S. *Law and Education: Contemporary Issues and Court Decisions.* Charlottesville, Va.: Michie Company, 1979.

Kemerer, Frank, and Deutsch, Kenneth. *Constitutional Rights and Student Life.* St. Paul, Minn.: West Publishing Company, 1979.

Lichtenstein, Edward. "Suspension, Expulsion, and the Special Education Student." *Phi Delta Kappan* 61 (March 1980): 459–461.

McCarthy, Martha M., and Cambron, Nelda H. *Public School Law: Teachers' and Students' Rights.* Boston: Allyn and Bacon, 1981.

Moran, K. D., and McGhehey, M. A. *The Legal Aspects of School Communications.* Topeka, Kan.: National Organization on Legal Problems of Education, 1980.

Reutter, E. Edmund, Jr. *The Supreme Court's Impact on Public Education.* Bloomington, Ind.: Phi Delta Kappa and the National Organization on Legal Problems of Education, 1982.

Sergiovanni, Thomas; Burlingame, Martin; Coombs, Fred; and Thurston, Paul. *Educational Governance and Administration.* Englewood Cliffs, N.J.: Prentice-Hall, 1980.

Stelzer, Leigh, and Banthin, Joanna. *Teachers Have Rights, Too. What Educators Should Know about School Law.* Boulder, Col.: Social Science Education Consortium, 1980.

Valente, William D. *Law in the Schools.* Columbus, Ohio: Charles E. Merrill, 1980.

Teacher Organizations

Focus Questions

- How can you explain that teaching is a professional career when most teachers are members of organized teacher unions?
- Why is it necessary that local teacher groups have a single organization elected as the bargaining agent for all the teachers?
- The National Education Association (NEA) refuses to consider merging with the American Federation of Teachers (AFT) because the AFT is affiliated with organized labor. Does this make sense to you? Why or why not?

- Do you favor the payment of unified teacher organization dues that cover all levels of membership—local, state, and national? What gains arise from state and national organization membership?
- What is your opinion of teacher organizations developing political action committees? Since a large proportion of teachers identify themselves as Democrats, does this pose problems when championing selected political candidates and/or political causes?

Key Terms and Concepts

Professionalism versus unionism
Teacher power
Unified dues
National Education Association (NEA)
American Federation of Teachers (AFT)

Union merger efforts
Political action committees
World Confederation of Organizations of the Teaching Profession (WCOTP)

What Would You Do?

You receive a letter from your building principal advising you to report to an orientation workshop for new teachers before the beginning of classes. When you arrive at the building, you discover that the regular teachers are on strike, and they ask you not to cross their picket lines.

After the teacher strike is settled, you become aware that the strike has provoked considerable animosity toward teachers in the community. At a parent-teacher meeting, one of the parents refers directly to you and asks you to explain why teachers should be permitted to strike.

Teacher unionism and professionalism are not necessarily mutually exclusive. In many school districts, boards of education and school administrators resent the strength of teacher organizations, but they also realize the need to cope with teacher unionism. Although teacher organizations have strongly disagreed over the merits of allying with organized labor, they have grown as instruments of social force and are able to exert pressure on behalf of their members.

Before the 1960s, little attention was given to the activities of the various organizations; teacher organizations had not yet become the powerful groups they are today. This lack of power was not merely a matter of small membership; large numbers of teachers have always joined organizations. Mandatory membership in state education associations was a condition of teaching contracts in many if not most school districts. Teachers, like other professionals, have always wanted to belong to groups organized to serve common needs and to solve problems. Teachers usually consider the voice provided at the national level regarding teacher rights, legislation favoring education, and the development of ethical codes of teacher conduct to be of value. Similarly, political involvement, promotion of education, and lobbying the legislature are valuable at the state level. Probably the strongest factor for an individual teacher in joining a teacher organization is the support of the organization for the efforts at the local level. Local teacher organizations provide teachers with representation to the school board on matters related to working conditions such as class size, salaries, and fringe benefits. Assistance to each teacher with grievance procedures and the provision of legal services with due process rights give teachers assurances against unwarranted reprisals.

The National Education Association is by far the largest teacher organization, with over 1.6 million members, including teachers, administrators, clerical and custodial employees, and other school personnel. The American Federation of Teachers, affiliated with the AFL-CIO, has 600,000 members but does not offer membership to school administrators. These organizations are discussed in detail in this chapter.

In other large and small districts throughout the United States, teachers are members of strong local organizations that are not affiliated with national or state organizations. In New York the Federation of Catholic Teachers represents the 3000 lay teachers employed in 300 Catholic schools. Other religious teachers' organizations represent teachers in other areas. At the higher education level the American Association of Colleges of Teacher Education (AACTE) is another group that has begun to acknowledge that powerful teacher unionism and professionalism are not mutually exclusive. The result has been a continuous attempt on the part of the AACTE to consult with teacher organizations and take their recommendations seriously. On many community college, college, and university campuses, faculties are represented by chapters of the American Association of University Professors (AAUP), as well as by units affiliated with the NEA and AFT.

Beginning teachers are actively recruited for membership in teacher organizations (unions), often by competing organizations. This chapter provides a brief overview of the structure of the larger teacher unions that are most active in our public schools.

Teacher Power

For many years the large membership in teacher organizations remained a latent force; this force emerged as "teacher power" during the 1960s. As teacher power became even stronger during the 1970s, teacher organizations became more and more militant about salary issues and other concerns of teachers. As teachers worked together to identify themselves clearly as a homogeneous professional group, their most common conscious group goals were also identified. The concept of teacher power developed when the teacher groups worked to organize activities and to carry out common goals.

The main organizations that have competed for membership throughout the United States are the National Education Association (NEA) and the American Federation of Teachers (AFT). Before the teacher militancy of the 1960s, the NEA espoused nonstriking professionalism and deplored the unionistic stance of the AFT, an affiliate of the AFL-CIO. Over the years, the NEA has refused to join the AFL-CIO, which the AFT refuses to leave. At the same time, the AFT leaders oppose a union that admits principals and other supervisors, as some NEA locals do. The AFT has also stressed the need for collective bargaining contracts like those gained in Maywood, Illinois (1948); Pawtucket, Rhode Island (1951); and Butte, Montana (1953). These early contracts, as well as today's contracts, spell out the working conditions and the expectations related to each teacher's assignments. During the 1950s the rivalry between the NEA and the AFT intensified. In some school systems the NEA began to associate strongly with the union views. The first collective bargaining election between the NEA and the AFT, which took place in East St. Louis, Illinois, in 1957, was won by the AFT.

In the fall of 1961 the teachers in New York City conducted an election to determine which organization was to be the sole bargaining agent in their behalf with the Board of Education. The United Federation of Teachers (UFT), affiliated with the AFL-CIO, won the election over the Teachers' Bargaining Organization (TBO), which was supported by the NEA. This election was the first to determine a sole bargaining agent with a board of education. For this reason the 1961 New York City election is regarded as the springboard for the growth of organized power for teachers. Although such bargaining elections continued to be scarce in the early 1960s, teacher organizations have since directed much of their resources to organizing members and concentrating their combined influence for desired goals.

State and Local Teacher Organizations

While state and local units that are affiliated with a national organization operate under the umbrella of the parent national offices, these units are the power base of the organizations. The local association of teachers has the highest priority in the whole organization; however, the strength of any single local union lies in the solidarity in numbers, in resource personnel, and in services the state organization provides. In the early 1960s, teachers generally became more militant regarding salary and working conditions. Classroom teacher associations at the local level became more active in seeking assistance from state and national associations. As competition between the larger national associations grew in intensity, and continues to be intense, elections at the local level have become the procedure for gaining the bargaining representation for each district. Local elections for the role of bargaining agent among competitive teacher groups remain the most important steps in the process for organizing teachers in any district, whether or not the local classroom teacher association (CTA) is affiliated with a state or national organization.

For the most part, teachers participate directly in the affairs of local organizations. Solutions to the problems at hand are therefore primarily the concerns of local teacher groups. The influence of these groups obviously would be weakened without the support and resources of strong state and national parent organizations. At the same time, local organizations sometimes become restive about their national and state affiliation. However, leadership at the national level views the problems and differences in beliefs among the local organizations as a viable part of the democratic process rather than divisive to the groups. From the many geographic locations, grass roots views of local teacher organizations may surface through the state associations to the national level or from the local organizations directly to the national level. Decisions related to national policy are then made by majority vote with attention allowed for input from all levels—local, state, and national. There have been instances in which local organizations have severed relations with their state and national affiliates when the members felt their particular needs were not well met. Since the power of the state and national organizations is reduced somewhat each time a local organization withdraws state and national affiliation, state organizations especially are compelled to pay careful attention to the express needs of local teacher association affiliates.

Religious Education Associations

The *Education Directory* lists religious education associations of various denominations. These national and regional religious education associations are under denominational or interdenominational control and do one or more of the following: operate sectarian schools attended by students who prefer them to public or private schools, supplement the public or private school program by offering educational activities for youth and adults, operate adult educational programs open to the public, and formally promote scholarships among their members in sciences and liberal arts. Each of the religious education associations, by itself, has a very small membership compared with either the NEA or the AFT. When the memberships of the religious education associations are totaled, however, it is obvious that many teachers are members of these associations.

Dues and Services

Classroom teachers who join teacher organizations pay yearly dues that vary from $75 to over $300 for national, state, and local membership. Both the NEA and AFT incorporate a unified dues plan whereby each member pays dues covering all three levels of membership. Membership dues in the local associations are determined by each local affiliate and therefore vary. While the national organization budgets receive income from such sources as bank deposit interest and sales of publications, most of the operating income is provided by membership dues.

A wide array of professional and personal services are available to school personnel through association membership. Local organizations are buoyed in their negotiation and contract procedures by the expertise of both state and national representatives. Local associations not affiliated with state and national organizations usually have had less influence than affiliated locals when negotiating with boards of education. In addition to the counsel and training provided to local associations in negotiation and contract matters, the state and national associations make available many individual benefits. Less expensive supplemental insurance programs of all kinds are offered. Investment planning materials and workshops are provided. National legal funds are maintained to support teachers against liability suits, illegal dismissals, and other illegal sanctions. Travel planning services, as well as airfare, auto rental, and lodging discounts, are available.

Professional services provided through membership in national teacher organizations make up the most important aspect of membership. Materials dealing with teaching problems and strategies, instructional techniques, education for the handicapped, scholarships for students and teachers, newspapers and newsletters, and other topics of general importance to teachers are prepared by the research and publications departments and mailed to each member. Other professional books, documents, brochures, and research reports are price-discounted to members who order these items for their personal professional libraries.

National Education Association (NEA)

The NEA, with national headquarters located at 1201 Sixteenth Street, N.W., Washington, D.C., is headed by an executive director. The NEA is a highly developed organization with many departments, divisions, and commissions. The basic purpose of the NEA, as stated in Section 2 of the charter, is to elevate the character and advance the interests of the profession of teaching and to promote education in the United States. Figure 4.1 traces the organizational chronology of the NEA from its founding in 1857 as The National Teachers' Association (NTA). In 1870 the NTA united with the National Association of School Superintendents, organized in 1865, and the American Normal School Association, organized in 1858, to form the National Education Association. The organization was incorporated in 1886 in the District of Columbia as the National Education Association and in 1906 was chartered by act of Congress. The charter

---

National Education Association
1857–1870

The National Teachers' Association
Organized August 26, 1857, in Philadelphia, Pennsylvania.
Purpose—*To elevate the character and advance the interests of the profession of teaching and to promote the cause of popular education in the United States.*
[The word "popular" was dropped in the 1907 Act of Incorporation.]
The name of the Association was changed at Cleveland, Ohio, on August 15, 1870, to the "National Educational Association."

1870–1907

National Educational Association
Incorporated under the laws of the District of Columbia, February 24, 1886, under the name "National Education Association," which was changed to "National Educational Association," by certificate filed November 6, 1886.

1907–

National Education Association of the United States
Incorporated under a special Act of Congress, approved June 30, 1906, to succeed the "National Educational Association." The Charter was accepted and Bylaws were adopted at the Fiftieth Anniversary Convention held July 10, 1907, at Los Angeles, California.

FIGURE 4.1 *Organizational chronology of the National Education Association (NEA). (Source: NEA Handbook, 1983–84,* National Education Association, Washington, D.C., 1984, p. 138. Reprinted by permission.)

was officially adopted at the Association's annual meeting of 1907, with the name "National Education Association of the United States." The original statement of purpose of the NTA remains unchanged in the present NEA charter.

NEA Organization

The NEA organization comprises several units, including the representative assembly, board of directors, executive committee, standing committees and special committees. Figure 4.2, the organizational chart, shows the subdivisions. The councils conduct investigations, recommend standards, build supporting programs for better programs of education, and work for freedom of teaching and learning. Through the special committees, the NEA cooperates with other organizations having common interests in specific problems.

Many special needs of teachers are met through the departments, national affiliates, and associated organizations. Some of these special interest groups were originally organized as national organizations separate from the NEA, and they continue to choose their own officers and plan their own programs. Departments serve general interests such as the Association of Classroom Teachers (ACT); national affiliates represent separate disciplines like music educators; and associated organizations represent groups like the school administrators.

Figure 4.3 illustrates the membership of the NEA from 1974 to 1983. NEA membership reached an all-time high of almost 1.9 million in 1976 and has stabilized at over 1.6 million since 1980.

American Federation of Teachers (AFT)

The AFT, with national headquarters located at 11 Dupont Circle, N.W., Washington, D.C., is headed by a president. The AFT was organized on April 15, 1916, and became affiliated with the American Federation of Labor in May 1916. John Dewey held the first membership card in the AFT. Teachers' unions had existed earlier than 1916; for example, the Chicago Teachers' Federation was formed in 1897 and became affiliated with the American Federation of Labor in 1902. AFT membership grew steadily from 110,522 members in 1965 to 205,323 members in 1970—almost doubling. Membership exceeded 415,854 by 1974 and reached 573,664 in May 1983 (Figure 4.5). The AFT has local unions in the United States, Canal Zone, Guam, and the armed forces overseas schools for the dependents of military personnel. Besides the national federations, there are state federations of teachers in most states. In an effort to stabilize

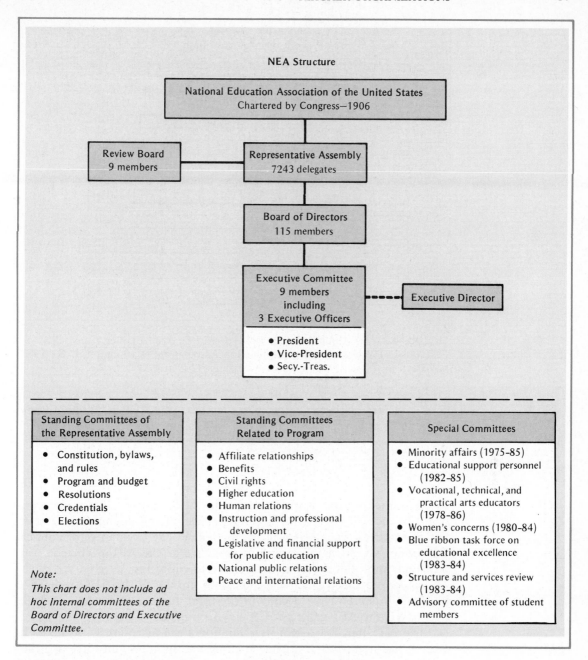

NEA Structure

National Education Association of the United States
Chartered by Congress—1906

Review Board
9 members

Representative Assembly
7243 delegates

Board of Directors
115 members

Executive Committee
9 members
including
3 Executive Officers

- President
- Vice-President
- Secy.-Treas.

Executive Director

Standing Committees of the Representative Assembly

- Constitution, bylaws, and rules
- Program and budget
- Resolutions
- Credentials
- Elections

Note:
This chart does not include ad hoc internal committees of the Board of Directors and Executive Committee.

Standing Committees Related to Program

- Affiliate relationships
- Benefits
- Civil rights
- Higher education
- Human relations
- Instruction and professional development
- Legislative and financial support for public education
- National public relations
- Peace and international relations

Special Committees

- Minority affairs (1975-85)
- Educational support personnel (1982-85)
- Vocational, technical, and practical arts educators (1978-86)
- Women's concerns (1980-84)
- Blue ribbon task force on educational excellence (1983-84)
- Structure and services review (1983-84)
- Advisory committee of student members

FIGURE 4.2 *Organization chart of the National Education Association.* (*Source: NEA Handbook, 1983–84*, National Education Association, Washington, D.C., 1984, p. 10. Reprinted by permission.)

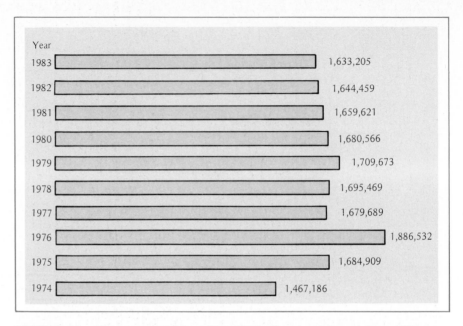

FIGURE 4.3 *NEA membership, 1974–1983.* (*Source:* Adapted from *NEA Handbook, 1983–84,* National Education Association, Washington, D.C., 1984, p. 135.)

costs and provide better services to members, the AFT is building a new building to house the national office in Washington, D.C.

AFT Organization

Figure 4.4 shows the organization of the AFT, which includes the president, 30 vice-presidents, the secretary-treasurer, an administrative staff, and eleven departments as listed in the figure. The Committee of Political Education (COPE) is becoming more active as the AFT participates increasingly in political discussions related to education.

Figure 4.5 illustrates the membership growth of the AFT from 1974 to 1983. In spite of the decline in the total number of teachers in 1983 over 1982, the AFT gained 9,329 new members.

The AFT has boasted of its affiliation since inception with the AFL-CIO. It has stressed that organized labor was an important force in establishing our system of free public schools and has actively supported school improvement programs at local, state, and national levels. Affiliation with organized labor gives the AFT the support of more than fifteen million members of the AFL-CIO. This support by local labor unions has often worked to the advantage of local AFT unions in gaining better salaries and improved fringe benefits from local boards of education.

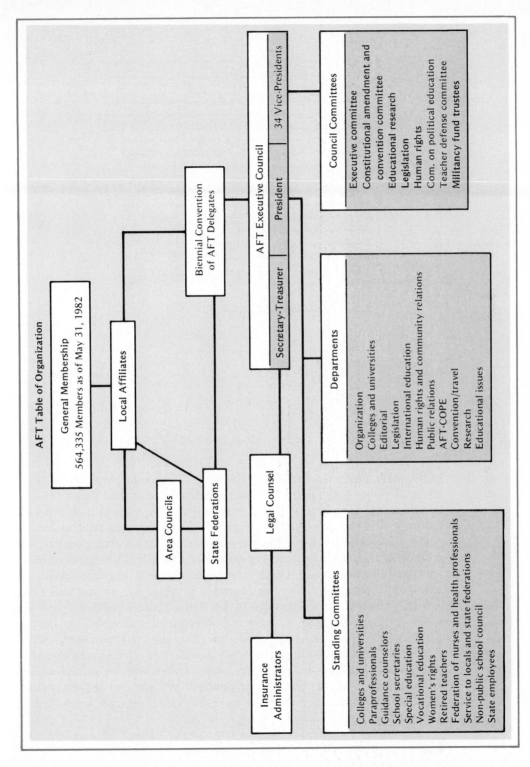

FIGURE 4.4 *Table of organization chart of the American Federation of Teachers. (Source: Constitution of the AFT, American Federation of Teachers, AFL-CIO, Washington, D.C., 1982, p. 23. Reprinted by permission.)*

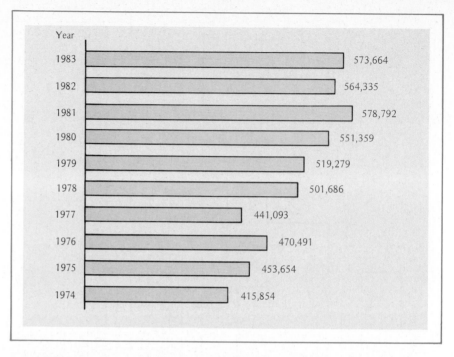

FIGURE 4.5   *AFT membership, 1974–1983. (Source: AFT Annual Report, 1982–83,* American Federation of Teachers, AFL-CIO, Washington, D.C., 1983, p. 43. Reprinted by permission.)

NEA and AFT Compared

In the early 1960s the National Education Association appealed to teachers by drawing a distinction between professionalism and unionism. As a "professional association," it claimed, only the NEA could truly represent teachers. A union like the AFT, on the other hand, was seen as beneath professionalism by the NEA leadership because of its alliance with other workers within the American Federation of Labor and Congress of Industrial Organizations (AFL-CIO). The NEA has since identified itself as a union and no longer draws lines between professionalism and unionism.

To the American Federation of Teachers, professionalism is not possible without unionism. A degree of self-control, the ability to help set professional standards, mastery of a specific body of knowledge, and the authority to define conditions of work are essential elements in the AFT's definition of professionalism. Since none of these can be gained without the kind of collective assertion of power that unionism makes possible, the AFT maintains that without unionism, teaching can never become truly professional.

During the 1960s, the AFT was generally viewed as a collection of teacher unions that would willingly, though illegally in most states, close the schools by striking to gain their demands. Many educators, NEA mem-

Teacher power represents a viable force in the process of education decision making.

bers especially, looked upon the strike as a labor union technique that should not be used by "professional" teachers. At that time the NEA used a procedure termed *sanctions*. When sanctions were imposed against a school, the professional association advertised the school district as being an unacceptable place to work and discouraged association members from taking employment in the district. Teachers completed existing contractual agreements without closing the schools. Generally, several months' notice was given before sanctions were invoked. Sanctions were applied by the NEA to local districts and also to entire states (Oklahoma and Utah). Technically, the NEA did not have a no-strike policy at that time, but such was strongly implied.

The strong competition between the AFT and the NEA for memberships and bargaining rights during the late 1960s was vocally volatile and highly intense. Teacher militancy among members of both the NEA and the AFT grew considerably. The strike tactic used by the AFT seemed to be more quickly effective than NEA sanctions. As a consequence, the NEA began to embrace the strike as a last resort rather than sanctions. The NEA also came to embrace collective bargaining, which the AFT had initiated. Thus the influences of the AFT and the NEA on each other have produced a growing convergence of philosophy and purpose. Today most teachers, administrators, and board members consider both organizations to be teacher unions using those tactics that the trade unions of organized labor have found most successful.

Toward a Single National Organization

[16] Leaders of both the NEA and AFT have, over the years, given lip service to the merits of unity. However, efforts toward a merger have been haphazard, with practically no concrete results.

In October 1968, shortly after David Selden was elected president of the AFT on a "merger" platform, the AFT invited the NEA to discuss merging. A week later the AFT invitation was declined by the NEA executive committee. Even though the first attempts at merger discussions failed to materialize at the national level, local actions toward merging began to develop. In October 1969, NEA and AFT members in Flint, Michigan, joined to form a group of 1800 members. An important merger of large urban local affiliates of the NEA and the AFT occurred in February 1970 in Los Angeles. Then in May 1973 the New York Education Association (NEA) and the Empire State Federation of Teachers (AFT) merged to form the New York State United Teachers Association, with 200,000 members. In September 1974 the Florida Education Association and the Florida AFT voted to merge. While local associations may merge to form independent organizations, the NEA expelled the Florida Teachers' Association because the proposed merger included AFL-CIO affiliation, which violates NEA policy for state affiliate organizations.

Following the annual convention of the AFT in Washington, D.C. (August 1973), the general convention felt that the NEA-AFT merger was inevitable. At the same time, David Selden, then AFT president, warned that several obstacles remained in the way of merger. Albert Shanker, then a member of the New York City AFT, now AFT president, challenged Selden's leadership. By March 1974 the merger seemed less likely. NEA President Helen Wise, following the breakoff of merger talks, stated, "NEA wants teacher unity. AFT wants AFL-CIO membership."

The annual convention in Chicago reported 1974 as a year of calm, with the possibility of merger with the AFT a faint hope. However, NEA leaders openly expressed their hostility toward both the AFT and Albert Shanker, who was swept into the AFT presidency at the union's Toronto convention. After these two conventions it was obvious that the NEA-AFT rivalry had resumed.

By the beginning of the 1977–78 school year the NEA and AFT had once again drifted apart. The 1973 New York State merged organization has since split—with the NEA and AFT again competing for dominance in numbers represented. Since national membership was declining because of declining enrollments, teacher layoffs, and school budget crises, the AFT opened membership to people outside the field, such as lawyers, who have expressed an interest in joining. The NEA views this development as unacceptable for its purposes. Seemingly, the old issues are surfacing—to delay, if not permanently set aside, further NEA-AFT merger attempts.

As the 1980s began, leaders of both the NEA and AFT editorialized in the respective official publications about the need to end organizational rivalries. Such rhetoric is similar to that of 1970 when the local affiliates of the NEA and the AFT of Los Angeles approved merger. Yet the hotly contested Spring 1980 election of the president for the United Teachers of Los Angeles (Local 1021) pointed up NEA and AFT rivalry within the Los Angeles organization.

It seems that increasing attention is again being given to local elections in which the NEA wins over the AFT or the AFT wins over the NEA to be the official representative of the teachers. The focal aspect of the NEA versus AFT competition that prevents efforts toward merger is affiliation with the American Federation of Labor and Congress of Industrial Organizations (AFL-CIO). The NEA's desire to unite all educators in a single national organization is predicated on the basic concept of no affiliation with the AFL-CIO, provision for secret ballot procedures, and minority guarantees. However, the AFT is proud of the AFL-CIO affiliation and boasts that the AFT is the fastest-growing labor union in the United States.

Political Action

An area of rapid development within teacher organizations are the political action committees. The AFT has an active Committee on Political Education (COPE). A similar NEA committee is called the Political Action Committee for Education (NEA-PAC). The NEA political action budget of

Involvement with a teacher organization need not conflict with vital classroom concerns.

over one million dollars makes it the fifth largest such committee in the United States, behind committees of the National Association of Realtors, American Medical Association, United Auto Workers, and International Association of Machinists.

One reason for this move toward the political arena is the success other unions and organizations have had through effective political action. In the past, many organizations used moral suasion, whereby delegates presented themselves to legislators or legislative committees to ask for legislation to meet organizational needs. The lessons of history show that this procedure does not work very well. Other organizations, including teacher organizations, have found a much more effective method—helping elect political candidates who are sympathetic to their particular needs. Thus the political action committees monitor elected officials' voting records on education bills and analyze the platforms of new candidates. Teacher organizations plan to support actively those candidates who will perform according to the organizations' views.

The state and national political action committees of the NEA and AFT have a common aim—to promote education by encouraging teachers to participate in the political life of their local, state, and national communities. These committees throughout the states are responsible for recommending political endorsements to their respective boards of directors. Interestingly, the NEA and AFT political action committees almost completely agreed on which candidates to endorse during the 1976–77 national elections. Both organizations have been strongly supportive of the Democratic party candidates, feeling that they would be more supportive of education at the national level.

National teacher union leaders continue to suggest that their political clout pays off for education. Regarding support of future political candidates, teacher unions remain consistent in their claims that they support those candidates who seem to favor public education. The teacher unions monitor the federal administration's actions that affect public education and have been vehement in their opposition to funding cuts in public education programs.

World Confederation of Organizations of the Teaching Profession

The aims of the World Confederation of Organizations of the Teaching Profession (WCOTP) foster a conception of education directed toward the promotion of international understanding and goodwill, with a view to safeguarding peace, freedom, and respect for human dignity. WCOTP supports efforts to improve teaching methods, educational organizations, and the academic and professional training of teachers so as to equip them better to serve the interests of youth; to defend the rights, materials, and moral interests of the teaching profession; and to promote closer relationships between teachers in the different countries.

Members of the WCOTP are from approximately 100 nations. The American Federation of Teachers, the American Teacher Association, and the National Education Association of the United States are members. In a study based on questionnaire data gathered by WCOTP, many educational problems common to all nations were identified, including lack of funds, shortage of excellent teachers, need for school buildings, and need for compulsory and free education. The WCOTP, facing these problems with determination, holds an assembly of delegates once each year. Resolutions of the assembly have ranged widely, from intensive literary programs to free education at all levels, from increased availability and status of technical education to special and adequate provision for the educational and medical needs of the physically and mentally handicapped. WCOTP also sponsors regional conferences. In the past these conferences have dealt with such topics as the status of the teaching profession in Niamey, Niger; teaching science in elementary schools in Asia; and the teacher's part in nation building. WCOTP's bulletin *Echo,* designed to promote international understanding, is published in thirteen languages. *Educational Panorama,* another WCOTP publication, is published in English, French, Spanish, Japanese, and Arabic.

Summary and Implications

This chapter presented the concept of teacher power as a viable force in the formulation of education-related decisions. Discussion of teacher power was followed by information about teacher organizations (local, state, and national), which are the vehicles through which teacher power is expressed. The National Education Association (NEA) with over 1.6 million members and the American Federation of Teachers (AFT) with approximately 600,000 members are the largest of the teacher organizations (unions). Therefore detailed attention was given to the organizational structure of both organizations, comparisons of the two, and general information about membership dues and services for members of these organizations. Mention was made of religious education associations, the erratic trends toward a single national organizaton, and a world confederation of teaching organizations. Perhaps the ultimate manifestation of teacher power comes about from the rapidly increasing development of the respective NEA and AFT political action committeees, NEA-PAC and COPE.

The implications of all this are straightforward. Prospective teachers will find concerted pressure placed on them to affiliate with the recognized teacher organizations. Each teacher must decide the advantages and disadvantages of such paid memberships. In some districts the climate of the working environment of teachers is very similar to that of trade unions. In other districts, teachers try to keep a more scholarly, professional climate analogous to that of traditional professions like law, dentistry, and medicine. How each teacher will contribute to the organizational climate associated with a particular membership must be a personal decision.

Similarly, the extent to which each teacher utilizes the professional and personal programs of teacher organizations will vary. While many teachers feel that their organizations should not engage in partisan politics, other teachers will eagerly participate in the work of political action committees at local, state, and national levels. Beginning teachers typically, and rightfully, place the highest priority on organizing and managing their classrooms for instruction. Yet as concerns related to working conditions, salaries, teaching assignments, insurance benefits, and others are defined, teachers find that their voices are best heard through the teacher organization of the district.

DISCUSSION QUESTIONS

1. Have you ever been affected by teacher strikes? Describe your reactions at that time. How do you feel about teacher strikes now?

2. Teacher organizations are increasing their activities in political action efforts to support candidates who favor increased funding of public education programs. Why are some teachers opposed to such political actions? In what ways do politicians (and politics in general) affect the teaching profession?

3. In some communities, teacher strikes seem to split the community on the strike issues. At the same time, some states are passing collective bargaining legislation for teachers that makes teacher strikes legal. List the pros and cons of the strike as a teacher strategy.

4. A lawyer for the Massachusetts Teachers Association suggests that the firing of tenured teachers is on the increase mainly because senior teachers have high salaries. "After years of good evaluations," he said, "they [school officials] evaluate your buns off for the next two, three years, and then they say you've gone downhill." What is your reaction to such a charge? Does tenure protect incompetent teachers?

5. A recent Supreme Court decision related to a Minnesota program established the constitutionality of tax deductions to help offset the cost of private school tuition. Why, in your opinion, are both the NEA and AFT bitterly opposed to such tuition tax credit programs? What are the arguments favoring tuition tax credits?

SUPPLEMENTAL ACTIVITIES

1. Write or telephone the national offices of the NEA and AFT in Washington, D.C., to solicit information about student membership. Also ask what could be gained (learned) by being a student member. Share your results with your classmates.

2. Examine a copy of a negotiated teacher contract between a teacher organization and a school district. Interview a tenured teacher and a building principal regarding the pros and cons of negotiated teacher contracts. Report the interview results to your class.

3. Invite representatives of the NEA and the AFT to class to discuss their respective organizations. Ask each representative to comment on the advantages of his or her organization over the other organization.

4. Invite a union member (or members) to discuss the strike as a power strategy for employees. Also invite a company supervisory employee to comment on the power and effect of employee strikes on company management.

5. Union leaders now agree that teachers should not obstruct reform and must improve their im-

age. What is your opinion of efforts by teacher organizations in support of higher testing standards for teachers to be certified? Also, should teachers have a larger role in getting bad teachers out of the classroom?

BIBLIOGRAPHY

AFT/NEA: The Crucial Differences. Washington, D.C.: American Federation of Teachers, AFL-CIO, 1984.

Bakalis, Michael J. "Power and Purpose in American Education." *Phi Delta Kappan* 65(1) (September 1983): 7–13.

Ching, Charles W. *Teacher Unions and the Power Structure,* Fastback No. 165, Bloomington, Ind.: Phi Delta Kappa, 1981.

Constitution of the AFT, 1984. Washington, D.C.: American Federation of Teachers, AFL-CIO, 1984.

Feistritzer, C. Emily. *The Condition of Teaching.* Princeton, N.J.: Carnegie Foundation for the Advancement of Teaching, 1983.

Kemble, Eugenia. *Teacher Unions in the USA: An Aggressive Striving for Professionalism.* Washington, D.C.: American Federation of Teachers, 1984.

NEA Handbook 1983–84. Washington, D.C.: National Education Association, 1984.

Programs and Services. Washington, D.C.: National Education Association, 1984.

Sewall, Gilbert T. "Great Expectations, Successful Schools." *Education Week* (February 29, 1984): 24.

"Sixth Circuit Rules Rights Not Violated by Teacher's Strike." *Education Week* (September 21, 1983): 4.

II

School and Society

Historically, the school has been a significant part of American culture. All cultures are identified by common customs, attitudes, and beliefs; compared with other, more homogeneous nations of the world, America remains exceptional in its diversity. Within the United States the acceptance of individuality has helped to develop a diversity of religious organization, political affiliation, and social and economic thinking.

The school has the special task of transmitting America's cultural diversity, and in doing so the school has developed relations with other institutions. The school, as an element of society, has its own culture, traditions, and customs. It deals with a constantly changing school population, rapidly developing technology, knowledge growth, and diverse expectations from parents who entrust their children to the school.

In Part II we examine the multifaceted interactions among the school, the individual, and the culture. We present the school as a social institution and investigate how it copes with social problems endemic to the American culture. In particular, we discuss the contemporary school in a rapidly changing society. Customs and values have been radically altered among both the adult and youth elements of the culture. Despite a shift in federal policies, there remain some nationwide efforts to solve social issues, and these are considered. ■

Culture, People, and the School

Focus Questions

- Why should a teacher be knowledgeable about the differences within the American culture?
- How can teachers live within and also outside the school culture?
- How do teachers decide whether to teach in an urban, suburban, or rural setting?
- What are the differences in learner and teacher roles in the school?
- How does knowledge of individual family structure help the teacher in understanding the learner?

Key Terms and Concepts

Culture
Anthropology
Sociology
Acculturation
Class structure
Social Economic Status
Mores and folkways

Mobility
Standard Metropolitan Statistical Area
Purposes of education
Values
Community school
The changing family

What Would You Do?

While attending a school play last week, you observed students "making out" in the hallways during the intermission. Some of them were really going at it. You were not on duty, but the teachers who were did not seem disturbed by the students' behavior. When you questioned one teacher, she responded, "Oh well, they do that whenever they get the chance. As long as they don't do it in my class, it's their business what they do." Since you know this behavior violates school policy, what action should you take with regard to the students' behavior and the teacher's behavior?

With a 200-year history the American school has become a recognized social institution. From a meager beginning in the original thirteen colonies, our 50-state educational program ranks as one of the best in the world. Fostering both free and private systems of education, the formal institution of school, in its many forms, has become the primary agent for

26 cultural preservation. It has gradually become responsible for many educational activities that home and church formerly provided. Although the school has become a permanent social institution in its own right, it has been continually subjected to the conflicting pressures from society. It has not had the privilege of exclusive status, as have home and church, which are relatively free to do what they want in their interactions with people, provided that they do not overtly violate constitutional or legal expectations.

Under the principle of separation of church and state, the church has not directly or significantly influenced public education in the United States. The earliest forms of education in this country, however, were affected by significant religious influences of the eighteenth and nineteenth centuries. The compulsory education laws of the twentieth century have brought about closer contacts between the school and home; these contacts have challenged the school.

26 American schools tend to remain traditional. Although many elements of society tolerate and promote change, most Americans still resist change from the norm or from the traditional. Although home living and general family structure have changed rapidly since World War II, society has

19 permitted only limited change in schooling. If the school attempts change and that change threatens the customs, traditions, and values of the home, the school will eventually revise its program. Thus the school is directed into transmitting culture. Since tradition is the dominant feature of the school, an examination and discussion of culture in general and the culture of the school in particular are pertinent.

Culture and Anthropology

Much of the knowledge about culture that concerns human development, relations between races and subgroups of races, social customs, human ways of worshiping, and human pursuits, constraints, and fears comes from the scientific study of humankind called anthropology. Anthropologists study and examine the culture of people present and past. Four specialized branches of anthropology that have special significance to the school and society are physical anthropology, archaeology, cultural anthropology, and linguistics. Although each branch may require a different method of examination, the anthropological findings are shared so that an understanding of humankind can develop. Charles Darwin's theory of evolution (1857) helped motivate a flourishing study of anthropology. As research techniques have continued to advance and as more anthropologists have been trained, a vast storehouse of findings has contributed to the current understanding of schooling as a social need.

Sociology

Sociology is the behavioral science that deals with the many aspects of a person's behavior while the person is living as a member of a group. A culture—a sociological concern—is defined as the sum total of the aspects of life of a group of people who live together or have done so in the past. Specialized areas of study in sociology are general sociology, social psychology, demography, the community, social organization, and social change. Very important to educators is general sociology, which studies how people behave while members of all sorts of groups. The school is one such group. Sociology was named by the French philosopher Auguste Comte (1798–1857). From his time on, interest in sociology has spread rapidly, and it continues to thrive today. It provides teachers and related school personnel with knowledge about the individual and personality, about the home environment and its effect on students, and about social class structure in the American culture. Further, the study of sociology helps the teacher understand how the class structure affects the school's efforts and how different value structures affect school programs.

Institutions and the Arts

All cultures have several elements in common. These may deal with material needs of people, such as food, shelter, and tools, or with nonmaterial activities, such as manners, mores, and religion. Every culture depends on common elements like the use of tools to meet daily living needs, a system of communication (language), the systems or organized group activities called institutions, and a system of expressing the desire for beauty, usually called the arts. No culture has been discovered that did not use tools for catching, growing, preparing, cooking, and eating food and for constructing houses, making clothing, and altering the physical surroundings in many ways. Every culture maintains a system of language that provides communication within the culture. Languages grow and change as needs arise within the culture or as different cultures come in contact with each other. In every culture there is a desire for beauty, expressed through a system of arts, including music, dancing, painting, sculpture, and rituals. In every culture, institutions have considerable stability, since each centers around a cultural need. An institution unites a group of people who share

The school, as one cultural institution, can expose learners to other facets of the culture.

a common need that is satisfied through that institution. The school is one of the cultural institutions.

Tools of Culture

Although cultures share many general characteristics, they also differ greatly. It is true that all cultures use tools; the kinds of tools and how they are used vary considerably. Languages are very different from one another, as are institutions and art forms. A culture that does not touch more advanced cultures may exist for hundreds of years with very little change. This can be seen in some of the more remote cultures of the world. For example, the study of Malayan tribes, isolated from much of the modern world, has revealed little change in customs and practices for hundreds of years.

One of the ways in which cultures grow and change is by borrowing from other cultures. Another way is by invention. While invention and borrowing induce cultural change, within every culture there is some inherent resistance to change. The fixed customs within a culture represent the desire to do things in the same manner and enforce conformity. For a culture to remain strong, the forces of conformity and change must balance. A reasonable amount of conformity is needed to keep groups of people working together, but growth and change are also needed for progress.

Acculturation

As a result of improved communication and rapid travel, the people of most cultures can now easily meet people of other cultures. When cultures meet, an exchange of ideas and materials results. Frequently, the people of a simple culture try to adopt a more complex culture, a process called *acculturation*. The acculturation process takes place piecemeal, and humans tend to adapt or adopt human experiences that are beneficial to them as persons or favorable to their social processes. Typically, people tend to resist learning about or adapting to a new culture; acculturation is therefore very slow. The Western world has influenced the acculturation of many non-Western peoples who have tried to learn Western culture. This influence has extended from the immediate past and still exists. Lately, a new sense of worldly consciousness has surfaced in the Western world; Western people are studying Eastern social, economic, political, and art forms. For example, in the United States, interest in the study of the Japanese theory has introduced new management and economic considerations for public and private institutions. Acculturation is worldwide.

A new type of acculturation within the United States began during the 1960s and 1970s. Seen as a new social consciousness, it has affected a growing number of minority groups. This social consciousness has fostered a different kind of acculturation, which challenges the American "melting pot" notion; this new type of acculturation is called cultural pluralism. We are trying to preserve the cultural difference of Blacks, American Indians, Spanish-speaking Americans, and others who have made unique contributions to American civilization. This movement carries with it extensive social implications for the schools.

Determinants of Class Structure

One feature of American society directly related to the school is the social class structure. Although our society does not have a rigid caste system in which no one can rise above the position he or she is born in or is placed in by religious laws, the United States is still a class society. Sociologists usually refer to five or six class divisions in the American social system: the upper-upper, the lower-upper, the upper-middle, the lower-middle, the upper-lower, and the lower-lower. A five-class division combines the two upper classes into one. The criteria usually determining social class in the United States are occupation, values, wealth, income, prestige, social contacts, and such intangibles as control over the action of others. This is often referred to as Social Economic Status (SES) and is used as a common referent for studies of schooling.

In the United States, extreme variations exist from community to community in the proportion of people within the different classes. Examples of the different types of communities that exhibit different proportions of social classes within them are metropolitan areas and small communities that are not satellites of large cities. All contain certain elements from the six class divisions, but the distributions are different.

The upper-upper and lower-upper classes consist of wealthy and socially prominent families. The distinguishing feature about these classes is that they are made up of Social Register families of long standing. Their SES is of long duration, usually inherited, and carries an "air" of aristocratic values. Members of the upper-middle class are professional workers and business people who tend to associate with the upper classes but are not as wealthy or prominent. Their SES, although sometimes comparable to the upper classes, is relatively new. In part it can be attributed to hard work, education, and the strong economic and technological growth of the United States since World War II. The lower-middle class consists of some professional workers, small business people, and white collar workers. The upper-lower class is the largest group in the American class system and consists of skilled and unskilled workers. Ironically, professional teachers, because of their SES, tend to be classified in the upper-lower class but have the practices and values of the lower-middle and upper-middle classes. The lower-lower class, often looked down on by the other classes, consists of manual laborers, migrant workers, and many unemployed.

Social Stratification

Studies have been conducted that examine social stratification, the general term that includes characteristics like hierarchy and rank within the social class structure. Although social classes may be examined as distinct groups, the various classes in American society are interrelated in a hierarchical structure. You can locate your own position in the structure by comparing your characteristics and the characteristics of your group with what the community has ascribed to the specific classes. In doing this, you identify your class rank as an individual or the class rank of your group in the community class structure. Identification of rank aids in understanding the power and prestige hierarchy of the community. Interrelation among social class groups exists with other individuals or groups having more or less influence within the same community. Studies of social stratification try to measure specific aspects of the class structure such as prestige, occupation, wealth, social interaction, class consciousness, values, and power.

Figure 5.1 shows how there can be both upward and downward social mobility in the social structure of American society. It also depicts the approximate distribution of classes in the United States. The dark, heavier arrow in the figure signifies more upward than downward mobility. Such mobility is seldom possible in a caste system. Although possible, movement from the lower-lower class to one of the upper classes is rarely, if ever, attained in one generation. After several generations, some families have moved to that extreme, however. Although the several social classes are all a part of the larger American culture, each class is a subculture, and each has characteristics somewhat different from those of the other classes. Anyone moving from one class to another—either up or down—must learn to adopt the characteristics of the subculture in order to adjust easily and to function in the new environment. Almost every school district in this nation has elements of all classes in it. Teachers who understand the characteristics of the social classes will be better able to work with students from each of the groups.

Mores and Folkways

Within each of the elements of social class structure, one can distinguish the mores and folkways of a class. *Mores* have generally been defined as

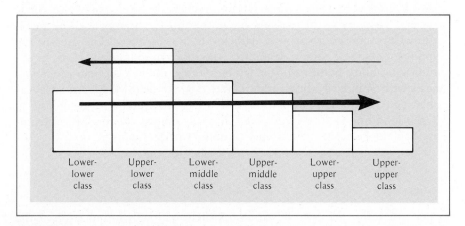

FIGURE 5.1 *Social mobility and classes. People may move freely within the social structure of the United States and usually move upward.*

rules that govern behavior. They are the morally binding customs of a particular group and tend to be classified as "good" or "bad." They are assumed to be laws of the culture, and to counter them or to violate their tenets is taboo. An example of a middle-class taboo is openly promiscuous social behavior.

Whereas mores tend to connote good or bad, *folkways* tend to be couched around "corrects" or "incorrects" of conduct, etiquette, or dress. It is not taboo to violate a folkway, but social censure may follow the challenging of a folkway. An example of such a violation is a teacher's dressing in a way that does not conform to the image of a professional in that school district. As society and the various classes with the social structure have continued to change, it has become very difficult to identify and examine mores and folkways. In addition, ethnic groups have their own mores and folkways. The exponential rate of change during the past two decades has created a cultural lag that has thoroughly shaken the confidence and comfort of the many social and ethnic groups.

Geographical Mobility

Physical movement of the population within the country is related to sex, age, occupation, economics, and education. Population mobility has typically been dominated by the male in a family, and physical movement is associated with his occupation choices. With the change in family organization and increased female economic independence, sex does not play as strong a role in mobility. Women, as economic and social heads of families, may move as freely as men. The major criterion for movement is economics. Job opportunities, low cost of living, and favorable business incentives have all helped the "sunbelt" area of the United States to attract mobile people. Young people tend to move more, whether they are single or married. A healthy national and international economy leads to increased movement among professional, technical, and other white collar workers. These types of workers move the most. The moves of all occupational groups are associated with levels of education. The greater the number of years of formal schooling, the more mobile the person. In examining mobility patterns in the United States, the U.S. Bureau of Census works with Standard Metropolitan Statistical Areas (SMSA). An SMSA is either a city of 50,000 population or a larger metropolitan-type area with 50,000 inhabitants. The larger area may encompass one or several counties. Table 5.1 shows the mobility patterns of Americans.

The School as an Institution

Every institution has an identifiable structure that helps to explain the how and what of the institution. The school is no exception. Although

TABLE 5.1 *Mobility Status of the Population by SMSA's (1982) (Residence in 1982 compared with 1975)*

Total Population of 318 SMSA's (202,216)*	Region			
	Northeast	*North Central*	*South*	*West*
Same housing units, percent of change (nonmovers)	62.1	55.2	51.0	42.5
Different housing units, percent of change (movers)	36.1	43.7	47.4	53.3
Outside SMSA	17.5	23.0	31.8	32.1

*Number in millions accounts for 88% of total U.S. population of 229,800,000.
Source: Bureau of the Census, *Statistical Abstract of the United States 1982–83*, U.S. Department of Commerce, Washington, D.C., 1982, p. 14.

difficult to understand and often criticized as being rudderless, the American school can be easily understood if its institutional structure is examined. A graphic representation of the structure of the school is shown in Figure 5.2. The dashed lines in the figure outline the structure and indicate that the school is an open system, accepting and exchanging information within its own environment. The structure has identifiable components: role, purposes, areas of emphasis, operations, organization, human and material resources, and outcomes. Besides various external social forces that affect the school, such conditions within the educational system as curricular trends and changing pupil attitudes strongly affect the school as institution. Successful performance of the institution depends wholly on how successfully all the components interact.

Role and Purposes of the School

The perceived role of the school is based on philosophical beliefs about it. A philosophical position usually encompasses national expectations, but it tends to reflect more strongly the desires of a local community. How a local school district envisions its role has significant implications for the program the school offers. Although a role for a school can be distinctly of one type, most schools tend to combine the philosophical viewpoints of three different roles: reproduction, readjustment, and reconstruction. A role of *reproduction* suggests that the school act to preserve traditions and heritage; emphasis is on the past, and decisions on what to teach are based on the customs and traditions of the past. A role of *readjustment* suggests

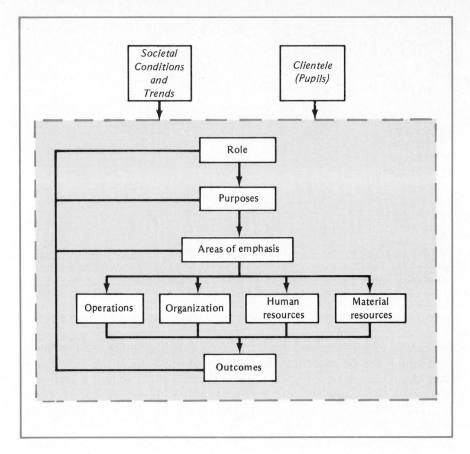

FIGURE 5.2   *The school as an open institution.* (*Source:* Adapted from Norbert J. Nelson, *The Logical Structure Theory,* Purdue University, West Lafayette, Ind.)

that the school alter its program as society indicates. Whereas change in the past was measured in periods, ages, or centuries, today—for educational purposes—it is measured in decades and years. This role requires continuous change in the school program. Emphasis on a readjustment role is judged to be utilitarian and reflects the current survival for change in society. The role of *reconstruction* suggests that the school is an agent for change in society. The school is expected to assume the major responsibility for guiding the future. In this view of the role of the school, the moral and social ills of the past and present must be remedied; therefore the school tries to reconstruct society for the future.

As today's school tries to do its job, it should attend to three especially significant purposes. These are commitments to universal education, equality of opportunity, and provision for meeting basic academic and psychological needs of learners. Compulsory attendance laws, child labor laws, and other state and national social legislation have guided this nation in its efforts toward providing universal education. The United States provides a comprehensive educational system for all of its young citizens. Despite certain critics who claim that schools no longer emphasize basics, the school has been able to provide most people with the basic tools necessary to communicate and earn a living. This is meeting a commitment to universal education. However, if the school is to keep pace with the present rate of technological change, universal education may have to be extended to include lifelong learning programs for adults.

Schools should provide programs that are worthwhile and as extensive as people want. It seems that equality of opportunity has not always had the same meaning to all people. A turning point in education came with the *Brown* v. *Board of Education* decision (1954). Continued civil rights legislation and affirmative action programs (equal rights for women and members of racial minorities) have helped the school provide equality of opportunity in education. The 1975 Public Law 94-142 addresses the national trend toward equality of opportunity, as do other national efforts in education (discussed in detail in Chapter 7).

Education should satisfy the *academic* and *psychological* needs of students. The fundamental academic needs are knowledge, understanding of choices, values, and ability to produce. The great increase in knowledge emphasizes how tools of learning are needed in the different disciplines. The nuclear age, both exciting and foreboding, calls for a keen sense of how to choose properly for shaping the future; and as our society changes, so do the mores and folkways that traditionally have aided us in developing values. As these traditional mores and folkways change, students need to perceive how the changes will affect the future. Every person needs economic productivity; one of the purposes of the school is to provide students with the proper tools for earning a living.

The psychological needs that the school tries to satisfy involve status, security, affection, independence, and achievement. Students whose needs are not satisfied become frustrated. If the teacher can help satisfy these psychological needs, the student can be more successful in concentrating on academic goals. It is realistic to realize that psychological needs are seldom fully satisfied; however, if the level of frustration can be minimized, learning will be spurred.

Areas of Emphasis

Education encompasses three broad areas: general education, exploratory education, and personal education. General education is usually considered the foundation, or core, of formal learning. Although this kind of education is present at all levels of learning from kindergarten through college, it is primarily associated with the elementary school. Exploratory education is usually a special function of the junior high school or middle school. At this level the student is exposed, at any individual rate of acceptance, to the many areas of specialization he or she may want to explore in senior high school or later. Personal education is the primary function of the senior high. It may be the student's last formal education, or it may be preparatory work for higher education.

Operations

Schools have certain formal patterns and legal obligations to meet. There are also the regular operations, including the *methodology* of teachers and the *working relation* of the four levels of rank within the institution. These four levels are the school board or the public, the administration, the teachers, and the pupils. Methodology is concerned with such matters as how mathematics or English can best be taught and what environment is conducive to the best learning. These are not the only questions to be asked, but they are typical concerns. Operational matters are important for establishing a productive theory of learning that accommodates the individual differences of all students.

Organization

Some basic aspects of the organization of school systems are *horizontal and vertical span of control, school district organization,* and *boards of education.* Teachers need to learn about the organization of the system if they are to understand their own part and be judged successful in it. The typical vertical structure of the educational system is line and staff, as in the military. A line and staff organization uses the "chain of command" principle. Teachers answer to principals, principals to superintendents, and superintendents to school boards. As teachers have become well educated and professionally competent, a definite trend has developed toward horizontal organization, in which the staff assumes wider responsibility for program development. Strong professional teacher organizations have also speeded up teacher participation in program development. It is important that the teacher understand the organization of school systems in general and how organization may differ among the many local systems. (See Part III.)

Human and Material Resources

Education would not exist without students and teachers; specialists, supervisors, administrators, and the school board are their backup. As society has become more specialized, the school staff has tried to respond to a demand for similar specialization in education. Because each member of the system is becoming more specialized, all members have to understand one another's function and cooperate to achieve school goals.

Besides the human resources, the school also needs material resources, including the physical plant, educational hardware (machines, projectors), and software (books, papers). It has become extremely important for school staffs to cooperate in planning and designing new facilities or in adapting old school buildings for maximum learning. Well-planned school buildings give teachers a chance to create a receptive learning atmosphere.

Pressures on Schools

The school as a social institution does not exist in a vacuum. Since education is still primarily a function of each state, there are 50 separate school systems in the United States. Within each of the states the schools are an integral part of each community and subject to the likes and dislikes of the community's residents. Thus no two schools are completely alike, and the beginning teacher must understand the various forces acting on what is taught in the classroom. These forces can be classified as *legal forces* and *extralegal forces,* and they exist at the local, state, regional, and national levels.

The legal forces derive from state constitutions, statutes, legal opinions, court cases, and common law. The extralegal forces have no legal origin but behave as pressure points much the same as legal forces. They mirror the society in general and constitute social pressure. Both the legal and extralegal forces directly and indirectly influence classroom instruction. At the local level the direct legal force in public education is the school board. Indirectly, the people represent the legal forces in that they elect the members of the school board.

An example of an extralegal force operating directly at the local level is the Parent-Teacher Association (PTA). In states that allow or mandate collective bargaining for teachers the influence of teachers is moving from extralegal to legal pressure on the schools. Indirectly, groups such as the local Chamber of Commerce, the Rotary Club, and taxpayers' leagues form popular opinion and thus bring pressure on the school. Figure 5.3 shows the direct and indirect influences at all levels of government.

This interplay of influence between the school system and society establishes the educational policy, affecting students and teachers. In addition to the legal and extralegal forces, local social and economic factors influence the school system. One such factor is the wealth of the community—and the availability of this wealth for education. Wealth is related to SES and the diversity of the business and industrial makeup of a community. Wealth involves not only financial ability but also, more important, financial effort—the effort made through local taxes to support the schools. In large metropolitan areas the taxes on business and industry provide considerable revenue. But since these areas must also provide other

	Legal		Extralegal	
	Direct	Indirect	Direct	Indirect
Local	Local board of education	Superintendent of local school People	PTA/PTO Local teachers' association	Local Chamber of Commerce Churches DAR ACLU
State	Legislature State school board	State courts Attorney general	State PTA State teachers' association	State Chamber of Commerce American Legion
Regional	None	None	College and university accrediting agencies	
National	None	Departments: HEW Agriculture Treasury Defense	PTA NEA AFT	U.S. Chamber of Commerce and NAM

FIGURE 5.3   *Legal and extralegal influences on the school.* (*Source:* Norbert J. Nelson, *The Logical Structure Theory,* Purdue University, West Lafayette, Ind.)

municipal services for their residents and for commuters who do not live in the area, the funds available for education are not automatically great. There is intense municipal and school government competition for the tax dollar. In middle class suburban communities with limited industry to support the tax burden, homeowners have traditionally allowed themselves to be taxed heavily to support the schools. As inflation escalated in the early 1980s while at the same time the general growth of the economy became stagnant, a demand arose for substantial increases in public taxes for continued public services. Almost uncontrolled spiraling inflation hit schools, government, and the private sector of the national economy. The problem was not unique to the United States, but was worldwide. Shrinking school enrollments, national and international comparisons of learner performance in schools, and a general public reluctance to pay higher local, state, and federal taxes led to extreme taxpayer revolts that have had a pronounced effect on local schools. The California tax revision, "Proposition 13," and the Massachusetts "Proposition 2 1/2" had immediate impact on local financial support of public schools. These laws were aimed at property taxes, the chief tax for school board budgets. In an attempt to respond to these local tax pressures, school boards began furloughing teachers, supervisors, and specialists as enrollments declined. Ironically, the fixed costs of school operations—fringe benefits for staff, heat, light, transportation, materials, and the like—have continued to escalate, and the schools have even greater competition for their share of the local tax dollar. As projected enrollment increases begin to take place in the latter half of this decade, the pressures for financial support of schools will become even greater.

Another factor affecting local influence is the social and racial composition of the community. Upper-middle class groups tend to support education more and to be more active in developing educational policy. Lower socioeconomic groups typically do not take this same interest in education. Recently, though, Blacks, Spanish-speaking Americans, and other minorities have increased their interest and participation in school concerns. However, these groups do not have the financial ability to support their desires. Somewhat trapped in a "Catch 22" situation, they seek financial redress from other sources, chiefly the federal government. A national discrepancy remains; even though the low socioeconomic groups may be in the majority, the upper-middle class still may control the school program and the school board.

A third factor is the age structure of the community. If the community is dominated by young people with children, there is usually active and enthusiastic interest in the educational program, particularly in residential suburban communities. On the other hand, if the community consists mostly of old people, the educational program may lack local support. Examples are retirement areas of Florida and Arizona.

A fourth local influence on the school system is the rate of population change within the community. Americans continue to move around a lot, and when most of the people in a community are transient, the popular interest in the schools may be low. The transient quality of a community also affects teacher attitudes; it may become difficult to hire and keep good teachers. When there is an oversupply of teachers, however, problems caused by population mobility are reduced.

Regional beliefs and attitudes also influence local school systems. The varied ways integration has been handled reflect this; many areas of the South, for example, have experienced more integration than areas of the North. In the Midwest, conservative and traditional views have dominated education. Regional beliefs have also influenced what reading materials are to be used in the classroom. For example, the problems associated with book use in Kanaha County, West Virginia, and the book-burning episode in Warsaw, Indiana, indicate regional types of religious beliefs. The so-called "moral majority" has taken on national significance and has a disproportionate influence on what shall be taught and what texts will be used. Condemnation of public schools by fundamentalist religious leaders has boosted the movement toward greater numbers of private schools. The impact of the movement has been felt differently in different parts of the country.

The school as a social institution is thus pushed this way and that. To maintain its equilibrium as an institution, it must learn to accommodate these influences, guiding them purposefully. In 1980 a ten-year history of national public opinion by the Gallup Poll identified the seven chief problems facing public schools (see Figure 5.4). Examination of these problems indicates "lack of discipline" to be the major problem as perceived by the public. It is important to note that drug problems and curriculum issues have substantially increased in importance in the eyes of the public. During the fifteen-year period, public concern over class size and integration has reduced substantially. The 1983 Poll included teachers and administrators in its sample. The predominant problem cited by the group was financial support. Thirty-five percent of the educators ranked this as the number one problem with schools. Discipline was ranked third (20 percent) on the

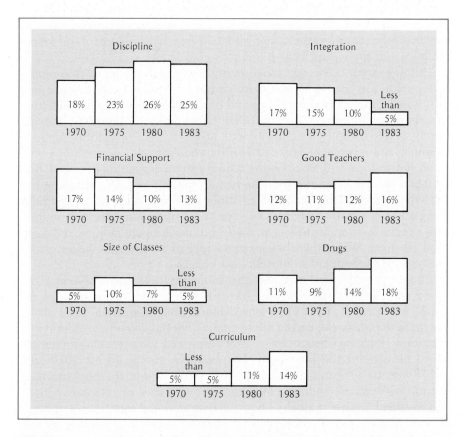

FIGURE 5.4 *Changes in public opinion about problems facing the public schools, 1970–1983.* (*Source:* Report of Gallup Poll.)

educator's list. The professional educators recognize that the public generally gets the kind of schools they are willing to pay for. Discipline problems exist but are not totally the responsibility of the school. Both the educators and general public, although citing discipline as a problem, indicated that partial responsibility also lies with the home.

As an open structure in society, the school cannot afford to resist or neglect prevailing public opinion about the school; school and society are interdependent. The school wholly depends on society for its livelihood; society likewise depends on the school to maintain and develop the culture.

Subculture of the School

Most educators agree that one of the school's functions is to transmit the prevailing culture to the child. In 1975, Havighurst and Neugarten, describing the school as a social system, wrote on the culture of the school, and their conclusions are still valid:

> The school has a subculture of its own—a complex set of beliefs, values and traditions, ways of thinking and behaving—that differentiate it from other social institutions. Education in the school, as compared with that in the family or in the peer group, goes on in relatively formal ways; and even those activities that are least formal (as in children's play at recess) are evaluated in terms of their contribution to the learning situation. Groupings are formed, not on the basis of voluntary choice, but in terms of aptitudes for learning and teaching.
>
> Differentiation develops gradually according to achivement. In the elementary school, achievement proceeds along two lines; the first is the "cognitive," or the learning of information and skills; the second is what Parsons calls "moral" or social—learning respect for the teacher, consideration of fellow-pupils, good work habits, initiative, and responsibility. In the secondary school, the emphasis is upon types, rather than levels of achievement. With its variety of subject matter, personnel, and activities, the high school offers the students a wider range of choices along both the cognitive and the social axes of achievement.[1]

Elements of the Subculture

As Havighurst and Neugarten suggest, the subculture of the school comprises many elements. In most instances the mores and folkways of the school have long persisted and directly affect school plant, personnel, students, curriculum, laws, and values. For example, although most recently built physical plants have open learning areas, the majority of school plants are still of the "egg crate" variety, with single and double corridors of classrooms. Further, teachers and other educational specialists must meet changing but long-established certification regulations that govern by credential examination persons who teach or work in the schools. Despite individual differences in ability, rate of learning, and personal interest, most students are subjected to the same type of information retrieval and processing, as determined by state curriculum regulations. The Carnegie Unit (a required time period of 20 minutes per week for 36 weeks devoted to learning) persists despite its questionable validity. Special school laws regulate fiscal practice and structure, transportation, curriculum, and social and moral behavior. The school's own system of common law regulates classroom behavior, dress code, speech behavior, and other local school board policies. Common rituals for school practice are found in athletics, clubs, promotion exercises, and a whole host of special events, usually referred to as routine school activities. The signs and emblems of the school's own culture are displayed by school songs, colors, and cheers. The culture is essentially middle class, and general values reflect that part of the society.

Formal Practices

The school operation itself embraces varied formal practices. Children are assigned to grade levels for learning on the basis of age instead of readiness, ability, or interest. Almost all children start the first grade at age six. This may vary by a year or so from state to state, but in general the practice is traditional rather than based on rational or special findings. Time modules of learning are another school formality. Class meets for certain periods each day, and all learning is concentrated in these specified time blocks. Authority is adult centered, and the learner has little or nothing to say about the lesson. Boys and girls are grouped for learning despite many findings that suggest very different maturation rates related to gender differences. The whole reporting system of educational achievement is still another example of school formality. Traditional letter grades are awarded to students in a comparative grading with other learners who have received the same type of learning stimuli. This grading system is a norm-referenced reporting system. Only recently have significant attempts been made to reduce the formalism in education by creating open-space learning centers, nongraded programs, and individualized learning packages based on readiness and interest. New grading systems judge how a child has learned by comparing individual beginning performance with what the child can do at the end of a unit. Accomplishment is referred to an established criterion, and we thus have criterion-referenced reporting systems.

To be sure, the culture of the school is not uniform. Variations may be associated with regional influences, school location (rural, urban, suburban), length of operation of the school, or social structure of the community. Regional influence may deeply influence certain athletic programs. In some regions of the Midwest, for example, basketball is generally thought to be the state sport. In one particular midwestern state it even carries a "hysteria" label. In some parts of the East this kind of fierce athletic competition is less evident, and basketball shares the arena with football, wrestling, and gymnastics. The great high school marching bands of many southern schools are a feature of the local school curriculum. Rural schools may emphasize Future Farmers of America clubs, agricultural programs, and 4-H clubs, whereas urban schools seldom sponsor such activities. A region's cohesion often shows in the school program.

Traditions

Older schools have stronger traditions than newer schools, of course, and thus variations exist even within large, growing communities. These variations can be found in feelings of pupil pride or of resignation to mediocrity. Such feelings can be carried to the adult part of the community and can affect the school positively or negatively. Local traditions can also show up in emphasis on sports or academic programs, upsetting a balance in the school program.

Undoubtedly, the culture of the school must be taken into account if its contribution to the total culture of society is to be studied. Values of students, teachers, and parents interact significantly, thereby affecting the total operation of the school and its contribution to social development.

Values

From the beginning of civilization, scholars have studied the values associated with human beings as individuals and as members of groups. *Axiology* is a branch of philosophy that describes the nature of values and their kinds and asserts the values worth holding. (Axiology is considered more fully in Chapter 16.) If personality is held to be demonstrated by behavior, we can say that behavior is largely based on the values one holds. Some personal frustration may arise from such a premise, since individual behavior is often influenced by the value structure of one's group as well as by a personal value system. We must each focus on our own values so that we can know what we hold foremost and act accordingly.

Personality and individual values are formed and affected by social class position. American schools are in turn influenced by the values of those who manage the schools and teach the pupils. Since most school board members are from the middle classes and since most American teachers have middle class backgrounds, it is natural that the public schools are predominantly influenced by middle class values. This kind of influence presents no problem as long as the students are of middle class origin. Perhaps the biggest problem facing city schools is the clash of values in institutions dominated by middle class people and attended by minority

Schools can provide a powerful socializing influence for learners.

pupils, many of whom represent a different class. For success in the class-room the beginning teacher must not only learn the values of the several social and racial classes, but also be able to teach the individual pupils who hold differing values. All too often in our schools the only attention given to value systems is in disciplining and managing pupils and guiding parents, while the school concentrates on passing along skills and knowledge.

Community Schools

The community is the dominant resource in the education of its children. In most states the local community provides the major amount of financial support for local schools. Although regulatory responsibility resides with state legislatures and federal laws promulgated for the general welfare of citizens, local communities create the kinds of schools they have. The community school concept—local control of the school program—has been carefully preserved.

There are three types of community schools that are easily identifiable with sociological patterns of population densities. They are rural, suburban, and urban. While many features of the three are similar, each has unique features peculiar to its sociological setting. It is not fair to generalize that all rural schools are the same, nor is such generalization appropriate for the suburban or urban schools. There are differences between and among schools, and there are features that are unique to different communities.

Rural Schools

Science, technology, and economics have helped to bring an end to the one-room schoolhouse of rural America. Where one-room schoolhouses exist today, they exist out of nostalgia or because some rural areas have too few children for the large geographical areas they serve. Developments in transportation and communication have helped to consolidate small rural schools into large regional rural schools. Many rural school plants in the 1980s do not appear to be any different from many urban or suburban school plants. Rural schools have been tastefully designed and reflect current thinking in the functional design of educational facilities, but their programs are often different. As a type of community school, they reflect the value structures of the rural populations they serve.

The rural sections of America have changed considerably in the past 40 years. The small operating farms that existed in great numbers through World War II have almost disappeared. In their place has grown the large-scale mechanized farm. This farm may or may not be owned by a native rural resident. While technology and science have produced modern farm machinery, crop fertilizers, land-use management procedures, and increased productivity, they have created for many rural youth different types of career patterns other than farming. It is not uncommon today for a single North Dakotan farm owner, with minimum help, to operate a 5000- to 10,000-acre farm. Since many rural communities have remained principally agricultural, however, many rural youth have migrated to the cities for employment. All this has effaced rural America as it was known before World War II. The rural school, to be effective for rural students, has had to adjust its educational program to prepare youth for other work than farming. Many consolidated schools have taken this direction and progressed rapidly.

Despite all the change that has taken place, rural America still retains its distinctive patterns. Many rural schools are the center of rural life, values tend to be conservative, and the immediate rural family tends to remain a cohesive unit. The extended family, however, has begun to disappear. Schoolchildren travel long distances to school, and social contacts at school are vital. By urban and suburban standards, rural families live long distances from one another. To the rural family, however, the distances are not great, and there is a feeling of neighborliness. This close community feeling is strongest in the rural area. The social structure is less stratified than in the most populous geographical areas, and everyone tends to know everyone else.

Since the early 1970s, more people have returned to rural living. Although employment in rural areas is scarce, increasing numbers of urban and suburban people are choosing to live in the country and commute to their employment in the more populous geographical areas. The energy situation in the 1980s may slow the migration to rural America. Those who have returned to the rural areas are generally young and well educated and are fleeing the complexities of metropolitan life to acquire what they believe is the simplicity and quiet of small rural areas. This migration is viewed as a kind of renaissance of self-reliance and confidence and a return to a healthier environment. In some instances, however, it has caused problems for the rural schools as the values of the newcomers have clashed with those of the rural community. Family living habits and expectations for school programs differ, and some newcomers demand increased social services. In many rural communities, however, it takes a considerable length of time to be accepted into the social structure, and these "new" rural people are not easily assimilated into the mainstream of rural life.

Expectations for rural teachers are different from those in urban and suburban areas. In general, rural teachers are an integral part of the rural community and are expected to behave accordingly. Patterns of dress, values, and community-school participation are expected to conform to those of the community. Rural school boards reflect these expectations. School programs are for general education, and unless specialized programs have been mandated by law, these schools tend to neglect the less able or academically talented learner. Vocational programs, with the exception of agricultural education, are often inadequate in number and type. Traveling distances and the required cooperation among school districts tend to limit vocational technical offerings. Most teachers, though as well trained as nonrural teachers, still use the single-textbook approach.

There are many exceptions to this general description of rural schools. With the increase in state and federal mandates for school improvement, more teacher organization activities, and greater education consciousness on the part of parents, many rural schools have developed fine educational programs. The rural school system of the 1980s has come a long way since 1900. However, it still has a long way to go if its students are going to continue to compete successfully with their city counterparts for college and vocational preparation.

Suburban Schools

Suburban educational systems have burgeoned with the growth of the modern American suburb. To escape the so-called evils of the big city, the large middle class continues to move to the fringe areas. They go for a variety of reasons, some to escape school integration and the financial problems of the large city school system. In suburbia they feel they can enjoy the unobstructed view of a blue sky and still be within the service area of the city. In effect, the city dweller has been transplanted to a semirural setting. The biggest growth in suburbia has come since World War II and has been concentrated around the nation's largest cities—New York, Boston, Chicago, Washington, Atlanta, and Los Angeles. This growth has brought about what demographers call the *megalopolis*. A person traveling between Washington, D.C., and Boston observes very little countryside. The same can be said for the traveler from Michigan City, Indiana, to Milwaukee, Wisconsin. California and the "sunbelt" states have experienced similar kinds of growth.

27

The key to the social pattern in suburbia has been the housing development. The city dweller has tended to be segregated by religion, nationality, or race, and the suburban dweller by income. The row houses of the city exist in kind in suburbia—but with larger lawns. What was once the retreat of the rich now welcomes the middle class leaving the city. Many of the city's problems have also moved to suburbia. Vandalism, narcotics use, and teenage pregnancy are not unique to the urban setting; they exist in suburbia in increasing numbers, although the causes of these problems may be different there. The new suburban family has in many ways turned to matriarchal supervision if the family unit is intact, since the father spends little time at home. The hours saved by a reduced workweek are used up by commuting to and from the city. When the commuting suburban father or mother is home, neither has much time for family life. In addition to weekly catch-up activities with maintenance of home, shopping, laundry, and the like, civic activities, clubs, and recreation compete for time. Suburban parents are highly organized socially and attempt to keep their children that way also. Psychologists suggest that many of the problems children bring with them to school can be traced to this changing pattern of family life. Also, suburban school districts are experiencing more single-parent families. In some school districts, 50 percent of the student body comes from single-parent families. The single parent is forced

28

to work, and the parent's absence in the home can have an effect on the child's performance in school. When these school problems occur, they are manifested by a need for psychological and social attention, which the child seeks because he or she is apparently not receiving it at home.

The suburban school is not a community school like the rural school, and recreation and social activities emanate from a variety of sources. Young people are dependent on the car and the telephone. Most suburban families have two cars and either an extension phone or a private phone for the children. Teenagers like to be on the move, and a car is considered a necessity. As the energy crisis is affecting rural life, it is also affecting suburban life but in a different way.

Suburbs have grown in number and size, and so have the schools. Most of these schools use the newest in furniture, devices, and equipment. They also try to employ the best teachers available. The programs reflect what the middle class family believes is necessary education for their children's success in life. While special programs are lacking in rural America, this is usually not the case in suburbia. Suburban schools try to provide all services for all students; one need only examine the activity program of a modern suburban high school to see this. Suburban education emphasizes college preparation, and parents have a keen interest in how the school operates. Declining enrollments and national economic problems, however, have led to a reassessment of programs and costs. More suburban districts now have fewer parents with school-age children, and public financial support has begun to be curtailed. Because of the greater pressure of college entrance requirements, the suburban school has been subjected to excessive parental influence. Parents often demand more homework for their children and insist that they be continuously challenged. Parental pressure for a return to the basics is greatest here.

With all this attention to education, suburban children appear to develop in a passive and sheltered atmosphere. Everybody wants to be like everybody else. Preparation for a secure life is the by-product of the suburban school. An inherent weakness in this kind of education is the hidden emphasis on conformity and social isolation. There are many social problems in America, and suburbanites cannot isolate themselves from these problems. Social contact is needed among all strata of society if social problems are to be solved. In our mobile society, interdependence among immediate family members (father, mother, and children) and other relatives (grandparents, aunts, uncles, cousins) has lessened. This forces the school to assume greater responsibility for transmitting the culture of all social levels of the vast middle class of suburbia.

Big-City Schools

The move to suburbia has hastened the decay of the city. City stores and recreational establishments have found it profitable to locate elaborate branches in spacious and beautifully designed shopping centers in suburbia. It is much more convenient to shop near home than to travel to the center of the city. Since wealth, or at least "credit wealth," is centered in the suburbs, business has to cater more to the people of suburbia and less to the people of the inner city.

As white city dwellers have moved to the suburbs, many people of the black, brown, and yellow races have moved into the city. These immigrants are primarily Black, Puerto Rican, Mexican-American, and American Indian. Lately, many Korean, Southeast Asian, and Cuban families have moved to the cities, too. Where the city was once a temporary domicile for the white migrant, it has become a trap for its more recent occupants. Grouped together in certain areas of the city, these new migrants find it almost impossible to move elsewhere, even if they do manage to get good jobs. The typical big-city child lives in a multifamily unit surrounded by thousands of people. The more deteriorated the slum, the more inhabitants there are. The child who lives in the center of the slum is restricted by it and has few contacts outside the area. Problems of the big city are more acute toward the city center. Here there are too few and poorly kept parks, inadequate police protection, and old, poorly maintained schools.

The multiple problems of the big city have brought about increased problems for many of our large urban school systems. Most of the problems can be traced to programs that still reflect the expectations held by whites who have moved to suburban or rural areas. The problems lie not in a clash of value structures associated with education but in different ways of providing for the needs of learners. City children need just as many skills and as much knowledge as do their suburban and rural peers, but minority customs and language barriers too often hamper efforts to provide the sound educational programs that city children need. Previously funded federal and state programs have provided day care, bilingual education, reading programs, and adult education as compensatory efforts for inner-city residents. Changes in national and state government administrations in 1981 appear to be jeopardizing these compensatory efforts. As funds for the programs are cut, the problems involved may increase substantially.

Because of the many social problems in large cities, violence and disorder have increased in the schools. In the belief that mixing children from different neighborhoods would provide better education and would mitigate the problems, the neighborhood school idea has been challenged. Nonwhite students are bused from minority attendance units to predominantly white attendance units. Some inner-city core schools have even been established to attract white children from the suburbs. Many of the busing cases of the 1960s and 1970s are being challenged again in the courts during the 1980s.

It is difficult to hire and hold high-caliber teachers for big-city schools despite the high salaries that teacher organizations have secured for all big-city teachers. Discipline problems, social class prejudice, low economic status, increased use of drugs, and deplorable living conditions all contribute to what appear to be insurmountable problems of urban education. The financial plight of the large urban areas has caused many people to declare the cities potential disaster areas. School superintendents find their jobs next to impossible and continuously request federal government aid for a massive overhaul of urban education.

The Changing Family

American families have changed dramatically during the past three decades. The following is a profile of the American family in 1981.

- Slightly more than half of the families (52 percent) have children under eighteen years of age.
- Most families with children are two-parent families (83 percent).
- There are 17 percent single-parent families with children under eighteen years of age (separated, widowed, or never married).
- Approximately 79 percent of families with children under eighteen years of age are white.
- Almost 50 percent of parents with children under eighteen years of age are 35 to 54 years old.
- The socioeconomic status of parents with children under eighteen years of age are 25 percent low, 44 percent medium, and 31 percent high socioeconomic status.
- The range of socioeconomic status for families without children is markedly different, with only 23 percent in the high socioeconomic bracket. (The largest percentage of these family members, 50 percent, however, are in the 55 years and over age group.)

The American family of the past could be described as a young couple in a home, children, room for grandparents, male-dominated, and the couple living out their years together side by side. The 1980s family, sometimes described as the nuclear family, is the same as the family of the past for some Americans but vastly different for many others. Today's family may be a couple who have never married, a couple who have had other marriages, a couple without children, a couple without extended family ties, a less male-dominated family, or a single-parent family raising children after divorce or death of a partner.

Families are smaller today, the average size, as reported in 1980 by the Bureau of the Census, being 2.73 members. It does not include the traditions of the extended family. The divorce rate among couples reached an all-time high of seven per 100 persons in 1981. However, four out of five divorced persons remarry. There is an increase in commune living, and a growing number of children are being born from these kinds of relationships.

All of these family changes have affected children. The family now has considerably less influence on family members' religious practices, education, and value structures and the general socialization of the child. Although the school has assumed many of these responsibilities, other institutions also contribute to the socialization of the child. These include peer groups; organized groups such as scouts, 4-H, and Little League; and TV, radio, newspapers, and magazines. Because of increased female influence in the family, the family is no longer patriarchal but rather has become increasingly egalitarian.

School and the Individual

The culture of the school is believed to influence the kinds of personalities that students develop. Also, the values students hold are influenced by the school. Since our society is predominantly middle class, schools are primarily oriented toward the personality development and value norms of that class. The adult culture of schools is generally in accord with this [26] middle class orientation toward personality development and values, since the adults associated with the schools are mostly from middle class environs. The peer culture of the schools does not generally agree with this single-minded school orientation, however. Many student concerns are more closely identified with individual development rather than with a middle class social philosophy. Whereas the philosophy may stress work and preparation for the future, the students' academic concerns are for instant gratification.

Personality Determinants

One's personality is the complex of characteristics that distinguishes an individual—the organization of the individual's distinguishing character traits. Social scientists have noted that people who have the same experiences in life tend to develop similar personality characteristics. On the other hand, no two personalities are exactly alike. However, personality is not fixed; rather, it continually grows and develops. Since it is flexible, teachers have a good opportunity to affect the development of their students' personalities.

Peer Influence

Although the school-age peer group reflects adult society, it has a personality of its own that rubs off on its members; it also influences adults. A school peer group is a collection of school-age children who have certain characteristics in common. These characteristics tend to guide the attitudes and actions of the group. Personality determinants such as role, values,

27 behavior, socialization concepts, status, and experiences of all kinds are learned by the child from his or her peers. The school provides prolonged contact with the peer group away from the parents. When children first make acquaintances at school, they usually respond according to the patterns they have learned at home. While early home influences are being carried along within the child as he or she develops, influences from the peer group also increasingly affect the child's personality. The satisfaction of social needs contributes to a positive personality, and strong associations with peers tend to satisfy strong social needs such as approval from others, desire for success, and yielding to the feelings of others.

The Teacher's Role

Teachers may assume many roles in the community: spouse, parent, member of a religious group, club member, and participating citizen. Teachers also have subroles in their professional capacity that are related to their behavior in the community and with their students. The beginning teacher who wants to succeed professionally must understand his or her position. Specifically, teachers should have predetermined perceptions of what their roles in society should be and should recognize that society expects certain standards from a teacher. A potential danger for the beginning teacher is a conflict in role identity. If what a community expects is different from what the teacher expects to give, tension and conflict are likely. The possibility for misunderstanding is increased when teachers live outside the community where they are employed, as is often the case in both urban and suburban areas. Sometimes it is extremely difficult for a teacher to
27 understand and appreciate a community when he or she does not live there. Teachers who live outside their school district must make a special effort to learn the composition of the community where their learners live.

The teacher is a well-educated individual, possessing many skills that the community can use profitably. At one time a primary community expectation for teachers was involvement in Sunday school activities, choir singing, or service organizations. At present it is not uncommon to find teachers active in welfare or social organizations, local government, and occasionally partisan politics; teachers serve on school boards, city councils, and state and national legislatures. Some communities still try to keep teachers from participating in community government. Generally, however, the trend is toward teacher participation in an ever-widening range of community activities. One reason for this growth is the increasing number of people from all social levels entering the teaching profession.

One of the teacher's many expected subroles is protector of morality. The level of community feeling about this depends on the particular community. On the whole, however, parents expect the teacher to be a special kind of model for their children. Although the parents' habits may be unethical and at times illegal, they do not want the teacher to exhibit such

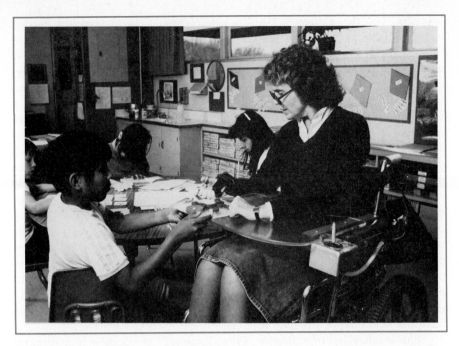

By overcoming their own handicaps, teachers serve as role models for students with other problems.

behavior. Since teacher behavior is held up for public display, teachers must use absolute discretion in their personal lives. Exemplary behavior is vital for the young teacher. Most students tend to hold their teachers in high esteem and to emulate their behavior as they do their parents'. Other subroles that the teacher may be expected to fulfill in the community are those of a cultured individual who is widely read and traveled, an explorer of knowledge who works for the continual improvement of society, a preserver of tradition and the status quo, and an expert in child growth and development. Needless to say, some of these interests conflict.

Conflict of Roles

One of the conflicts that a teacher faces relates to economics. The teacher is expected to be a model of dress and appearance, to live in a respectable house or apartment within the school community, and to participate financially in religious, social, and welfare organizations. All too often, teachers are expected to maintain a certain standard of living on salaries that are not commensurate with their needs. These community pressures have caused many teachers, especially male teachers who may be the sole source of income for their families, to get a second job, to "moonlight."

The teacher, besides being an employee of the school board, a subordinate of the principal and other superiors, and a colleague to fellow

5   teachers, also has many roles in the classroom. Teachers transmit knowledge and direct learning. They enter the classroom to teach; and if there is any role they can perform best, it should be this. They should have acquired a thorough understanding of their subject and have received special training through professional work in teaching methods, curriculum, philosophy, and psychology. The teacher has been specially trained to teach for maximum learning. Our schools have traditionally divided subject matter into courses. Teacher success is usually gauged by how successfully pupils master subject matter.

Teachers also discipline; they strive to guide children toward appropriate behavior. This guidance may be carried out in various ways. Some teachers become strict disciplinarians; some try to get students to cooperate voluntarily; still others let students be free to act as they want. Many teachers never learn to control students successfully. Discipline problems plague many beginning teachers. It is difficult to learn the techniques of disciplining students, since they cannot be specifically taught in teacher preparation programs. The public sees lack of discipline as the most urgent problem in the schools now. Teachers who have a firm background in their subjects, in educational philosophy, and in psychology of learning have the best chance for handling classroom discipline well.

The teacher is an evaluator. Like discipline, evaluation is a difficult task for a teacher. Children receive grades and are passed or held back by the decision of the teacher. Also, the teacher determines what is appropriate moral and ethical behavior for students. In many respects, teachers are entrusted with the authority of judge and jury; they need all their personal resources to evaluate each child fairly.

Often the teacher acts as a substitute for the parent. In most states the teacher stands *in loco parentis* while the child is in school. Teachers are expected not only to discipline a child as the parent might and at the same time teach, but also to help the child manage personal problems. The teacher performs a multitude of duties ranging from helping little children with their clothing to helping older students adjust to the anxieties of adolescence. Occasionally, the teacher becomes the special confidant of students—when, for example, students find it hard to tell their parents about particular personal problems.

All the foregoing does not imply that the teacher must be everything to all persons to be successful. Situations will dictate appropriate teacher response. Teachers must perceive their proper role, and they must understand the expectations and limitations that accompany that role.

Summary and Implications

Schools and society are interdependent. The diversity of our social classes, society's expectation for schooling, and the social setting of the schools add to the complexity of the school as a social institution. Cultural transmission is best protected by the school, since religious institutions and the home have continued to abandon these educative roles. School practices, programs, and traditions have not markedly changed, but learners, families, and society have. The teacher is society's model for the learner.

All of this implies that the prospective teacher must understand and appreciate the cultural diversity in which the school functions. It suggests that how well a school responds to the demands of the society may determine the future existence of the school. Teachers and administrators must educate beyond the literacy level and to the human level.

DISCUSSION QUESTIONS

1. Should the school be an instrument of change in society?
2. Have we set an unrealistic goal for the school to provide each pupil with equal opportunity when each school is directed to serving a particular student body?
3. Is the modeling expectation for the teacher appropriate when it does not mirror society as it really is?
4. How can the schools counter a fifteen-year-old public image history of ineffective discipline?
5. Urban schools need help. How can a new teacher prepare to aid in the revitalization of these schools?

SUPPLEMENTAL ACTIVITIES

1. Visit a local high school and interview a group of students about the school subculture. How is this similar to or different from your expectations?
2. Attend a PTA meeting and report your observations to your class.
3. Compare a community's expectations for an elementary teacher and for a secondary school teacher. Should they be different?
4. Interview a Chamber of Commerce member and detail his or her expectations for the community school.
5. Meet a school administrator and find out how the administrator responds to community pressures. Discuss in class.

NOTE

1. Robert J. Havighurst and Bernice L. Neugarten, *Society and Education*, 4th ed. (Boston: Allyn and Bacon, 1975), p. 139.

BIBLIOGRAPHY

A Curricular Response to Critical Realities. Washington, D.C.: Association for Supervision and Curriculum Development, 1978.

Fullan, Michael. *The Meaning of Educational Change*. New York: Teachers College Press, 1982.

Havighurst, Robert J., and Levine, Daniel. *Society and Education*. 5th ed. Boston: Allyn and Bacon, 1979.

Laska, John A. *Schooling and Education: Basic Concepts and Problems*. New York: D. Van Nostrand, 1976.

Naisbitt, John. *Megatrends: Ten New Directions Transforming Our Lives*. New York: Warner Books, 1982.

Noll, James William (editor). *Taking Sides: Clashing Views on Controversial Educational Issues*. Guilford, Conn.: The Dushkin Publishing Group, 1980.

Partners: Parents and Schools. Alexandria, Va.: Association for Supervision of Curriculum Development, 1979.

Postman, Neil. *The Disappearing Child*. New York: Delacorte Press, 1982.

Pritchard, Keith W., and Buxton, Thomas H. *Concepts and Theories in Sociology of Education*. Lincoln, Neb.: Professional Educators Publications, 1973.

Schwartz, Audrey James. *The Schools and Socialization*. New York: Harper & Row, 1975.

6

The School and Social Problems

Focus Questions

- What are the major social problems affecting today's youth?
- Should our schools help solve social problems? Why?
- How might the school reduce prejudice?
- What, if any, is the relationship between poverty and education?

Key Terms and Concepts

Poverty
Minority groups
Blacks
Spanish-speaking Americans
American Indians, Inuits, and Aleuts
Refugees
Sex discrimination
School dropouts
Juvenile delinquency

Violence and vandalism
Drugs
Alcohol
Smoking
Youth sex problems
Unemployment
Leisure
Pollution
Threat of war

What Would You Do?

You are in the middle of a lesson when there is a knock on your classroom door. You open the door to find your principal with a new student for your classroom. The new student is a recent immigrant who speaks no English. What are some of the short-range and long-range things you would do to help this new student?

Your superintendent has asked each faculty member to list ten things a teacher could do to help make the school less sexist. Your list, please!

There is a considerable amount of debate about how far the schools can and should go to help solve our country's social problems. Some people believe that our schools should be concerned only with the academic development of students. Others believe that our schools are in a unique position to help solve many of our nation's pressing social problems—and should do so. While this debate continues, social problems persist and noticeably affect our students and our schools. In this chapter we examine the relationship between our schools and some of these social problems.

Poverty

Poverty has existed since the human race appeared on earth and probably will be around as long as humans are. Poverty in the United States is complex; determining what factors contribute to poverty is difficult, if not impossible. Notions about what constitutes poverty are continually changing. One person may define poverty as physical hunger, or even starvation; another may define it as a lack of luxuries. In other words, poverty is relative. It is not merely that some people are literally starving to death in the United States that defines our poverty problem; there is also the stark contrast between those who have relatively little and those who have very much.

Most people would agree that there is less poverty today in the United States than in the past. The government's definition of poverty is based on changing economic conditions—further adjusted by such factors as family size, sex of family head, number of children, and farm or nonfarm residence. Table 6.1 presents information about the percent of families below the poverty level in the United States. This table illustrates that this problem is greater for minority families.

Slightly over 10 percent of our American families live in poverty. Although there is a higher *percentage* of nonwhite families living in poverty, *numerically* there are many more impoverished white families.

For instance, many Appalachian white families earn very little each year. Their per capita income is far less than that of the rest of the country.

TABLE 6.1 *Families Below Poverty Level*

White	8.0%
Black	28.9%
Spanish origin	23.2%
All races	10.3%

Source: Bureau of the Census, *Statistical Abstract of the United States 1982–83*, U.S. Department of Commerce, Washington, D.C.

Many Appalachian adults are unemployed, and many have very little formal schooling. The Appalachian subculture has created a way of life that keeps these mountain people impoverished. Farming and mining have traditionally furnished their livelihood; however, the mountain farms are no longer productive enough to provide a good living, and automation has largely replaced humans in the coal mines. Those who have left the mountains to go to the cities have found that their education and skills do not qualify them for desirable jobs.

In general, the amount of income that people earn is directly related to how much education they have. Figure 6.1 shows the expected lifetime earnings for people with different amounts of education. This table also shows that men earn considerably more than do women. Providing more education for the poverty stricken should help, in the long run, to reduce poverty.

Many people believe that education alone cannot solve the problem. There are immediate needs such as employment, housing, medical care,

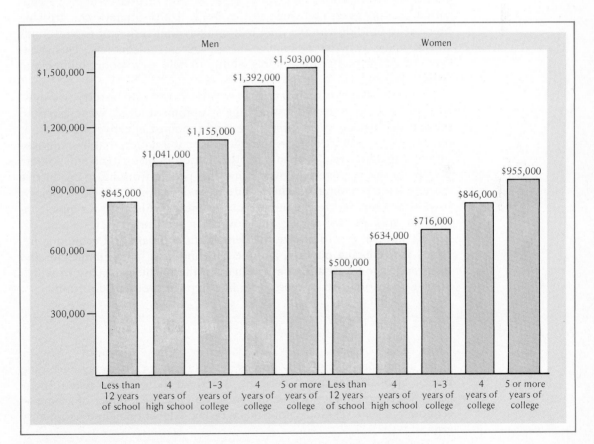

FIGURE 6.1 *Expected lifetime earnings for year-round full-time workers.*
(*Source:* U.S. Department of Education, *American Education*, June 1983, p. 59.)

and legal advice that must be met. Although immediate assistance in these areas is absolutely essential in the war on poverty, it cannot solve the long-range problem in the way that better education can.

Fortunately, our nation is concerned about poverty. Moreover, it has been postulated that tax money spent to eradicate poverty is a profitable investment. It is cheaper to help people lift themselves out of poverty than it is to pay the consequences of allowing them to remain impoverished. One need only check the cost of welfare programs and crime fighting to be convinced of this.

It is fortunate that the nation's current war on poverty is being waged partly through education. One of the many federal educational programs currently directed toward reducing poverty is the Elementary and Secondary Education Act, passed in 1965. This act has provided several billion additional dollars a year for the American school system. The purpose of the act, known as Public Law 89-10, is "to strengthen and improve educational quality and educational opportunities in the nation's elementary and secondary schools." This and other federal efforts to improve education are discussed elsewhere in this book. Unfortunately, the growing pressure to hold down taxes makes it unlikely that sufficient federal funds will be made available to finance these programs adequately. This situation will surely hinder the schools' ability to help serve poor children and reduce poverty.

It is important to realize that if we are to eradicate poverty, we must treat the disease itself and not just the symptoms. Indeed, we must try to prevent the disease in the first place, and the most effective "vaccine" at our disposal is education. It is incongruous that a nation that has amassed far more material wealth than any other nation in history can still contain pockets of severe poverty. Poverty prevents people from being productive citizens, from pursuing excellence, and from developing a sense of dignity. If we are committed to the importance of these ideals, then we must continue to work toward rooting out poverty in the United States.

We have begun to realize the democratic, human, and economic necessity for reducing poverty, and we have initiated many immediate and long-range programs aimed at eradicating the problem—many of which involve education. All of these seem like steps in the right direction.

Minority Groups

There are numerous minority groups in American society today, including Blacks, Spanish-speaking Americans, American Indians, and Asian-Americans. There are, in fact, within our society an infinite number of groups—economic, social, religious, political, agrarian, educational, and nationality groups.

Figure 6.2 shows that our country has grown rapidly over the last 50 years. The percentage of minorities in our population has also grown rap-

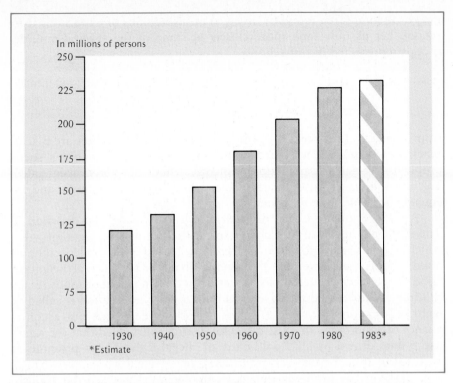

In millions of persons

FIGURE 6.2 *Population of the United States. All figures are as of April 1 except 1983, which is as of January 1.* (*Source:* Bureau of the Census, U.S. Department of Commerce, Washington, D.C.)

idly over this period of time. This increase in minorities is particularly noticeable in our schools. For instance, in 1950 only one of our nation's 25 largest school districts had more minority students than white majority students. Today, in all but two of these school districts the student bodies are made up of minority students. In fact, some states have more minority students in their entire school system than white majority students. Minority student enrollment is 57 percent in New Mexico, 52 percent in Mississippi, 46 percent in Texas, 43 percent in California and South Carolina, 33 percent in Arizona and Maryland, 32 percent in New York state, and about 35 percent in all southeastern states. The minorities are rapidly becoming the "majority" in many of our nation's school districts. It is estimated that California will have a minority of white residents by the year 2000. By that same time, almost all of our largest cities will have a "majority" of minority residents.

The challenge to our schools presented by this rising tide of minority students is indeed staggering. These minority students most often have special learning problems, often come from single-parent homes, are likely to be poor, may have trouble with the standard form of the English language, often are truant and/or involved in suspensions or expulsions from school. Let us now look more closely at some of the specific minority groups represented in our schools.

Blacks

Approximately 12 percent of all the people in the United States are Blacks. Black Americans suffer considerably from many of the nation's social problems—racial discrimination, violence, school dropouts, drugs, alcohol, unemployment, substandard housing, housing discrimination, and unequal educational opportunities.

A 1954 Supreme Court decision (*Brown* v. *Board of Education of Topeka*) made it illegal for schools to practice de jure segregation—that which is deliberate. However, nearly all school systems build neighborhood schools that serve only the children living in a particular neighborhood. Since Blacks generally live together in certain neighborhoods, Black children usually attend Black schools. This type of segregation is called de facto segregation—that which is not necessarily deliberate but a consequence of conditions. In 1961 a federal district court ruled that the attendance lines drawn by a school board are illegal if these lines promote de facto segregation (*Taylor* v. *Board of Education,* New Rochelle, New York). This decision has prompted integrationists to work toward the abolishment of de facto segregation, particularly in large northern cities. Some school systems have transported children to other neighborhood schools to try to minimize de facto segregation. Some large city school districts such as Louisville, Kentucky, reorganized with nearby suburban districts to integrate races in their schools. (More information on the legal aspects of racial desegregation of the schools is given in Chapter 8 of this book.)

Whereas Blacks once tended to live predominantly in the South, they now live throughout the country. Truly, the social problems of Black Americans pervade the entire United States and represent a challenge to all of our schools.

Spanish-speaking Americans

The 1980 census revealed that 14.5 million (6.5 percent) of the U.S. population is Spanish speaking. It is estimated that there may be as many as five million additional migrants and illegal aliens in this country who speak Spanish. Some demographers predict that Spanish-speaking Americans will surpass Blacks as the largest minority group by 1990. There are many different types of Spanish-speaking Americans, each with a different set of problems. For example, the 1980 census reported that over 1,659,000 people of Spanish origin live in the state of New York alone. Many are

Puerto Ricans, who generally pride themselves on being self-sufficient. Unfortunately, handicaps such as language barriers, poor job skills, and lack of education keep most Puerto Ricans poor. Children from these families frequently do poorly in school because of language difficulties and impoverished cultural backgrounds and because many are highly transient.

There are also numerous Mexican-Americans who live in poverty. Many have recently moved to the United States in hopes of finding a better life. The immigrants usually come from the poor sections of Mexico, and most have had little formal education or special job training. Their cultural background makes it hard for them to succeed economically in a highly technical society. Numerous Mexican-Americans live in the southwestern part of the United States; many others travel throughout the country as seasonal workers.

Migrant workers constitute a particularly difficult social problem. About a million workers and their families move about constantly, following the growing season as it progresses northward each year. Historically, the pay and the living conditions for these migrant workers have been poor. Because of constant moving, it is difficult for the migrant worker's child to attend school and to receive an adequate education. Some tangible improvements in the form of better pay and more healthful living conditions have been made for migrant workers; however, most still face an uncertain future. The migrant child moving from school to school as the parents follow their work still has serious school problems.

American Indians, Inuits, and Aleuts

Native Americans constitute still another impoverished minority of the United States population. American Indians, since losing their lands to the white people, have suffered the additional loss of their native heritage and have lived largely on government subsidies. American Indians still suffer from a lack of education and special skills that would permit them to get ahead in a technological society. Indian children have more than their share of educational problems. Many Indian children start school unable to speak English. The dropout rate is high, and the achievement level is low.

The Indian Education Act of 1972 and its 1974 amendments are designed to help Native Americans help themselves. Each year, over a quarter of a million Indian schoolchildren in over a thousand school districts now receive some benefits from the Indian Education Act. These grants are aimed at providing bilingual and bicultural enrichment activities. They also attempt to improve reading programs, guidance services, and transportation. Other grants try to involve Indian parents and Indian communities in educational activities; still other parts of the Act are aimed at training teachers for Indian schools, providing financial aid for Indian

Individual abilities are encouraged by special programs for students from various cultural backgrounds.

college students, instituting adult Indian education, and establishing tribal improvement projects. Although these recent steps are encouraging, American Indian citizens are still beset with many serious social problems.

Inuit (Eskimo) and Aleut children also have unusual educational problems. The subcultures from which they come have undergone dramatic changes over a short period of time. Many of their parents have recently received considerable money from oil and mineral rights. The children are often caught between "old" traditions and "new" educational efforts. Inuit and Aleut children will require especially responsive schools to overcome these problems.

Recent Refugees

Relatively new minority groups that constitute a social problem in the United States are the recent refugees. Growing numbers of displaced persons are immigrating, particularly from Southeast Asia, Cuba, and more recently from Poland. A high percentage of these persons do not speak English, bring few employable skills, and know very little about the American culture. Nearly one half of these refugees are school-age children, and 15 percent are illiterate in their own native language. It is estimated that by the mid-1980s the number of such recent refugees will have grown to fifteen million.

Schools throughout the country are struggling to create meaningful programs to serve the needs of these unique immigrant students. Congress provides some financial help to the schools in these efforts, through the Indochina Migration and Refugee Assistance Act (Public Law 94-23).

American Women

In 1972, Title IX of the Education Amendments was enacted, stating

> No person in the United States shall, on the basis of sex, be excluded from participation in, be denied the benefits of, or be subjected to discrimination in education, job placement, individual rights, and general status within the social structure of the nation.

Many women work out of economic necessity, others for self-fulfillment. See Table 6.2 for the percent of the U.S. labor force that is female. Over 45 million American women are now employed. Of these, 30 million are mothers who work outside the home. In all likelihood, the escalating divorce rate contributes to the large number of women in the labor force. Between 1970 and 1980 the number of one-parent families increased by 2.6 million, while the number of two-parent families decreased by one million. It is estimated that one out of every five students now comes from a home with divorced parents. These children require special understanding and skill from the teacher.

Although women may be well educated and highly qualified, they often do not enjoy equal job status with men. Except for teaching, nursing, library service, and social work, the professional and technical fields are dominated by males; discrimination against women persists in white collar and sales positions. Women tend to be concentrated in the low-skilled, poorly paying jobs of the labor market. Even when women are well represented in any given profession, they do not always receive the same pay as men.

TABLE 6.2   *Female Labor Force as Percent of Female Population*

	Single	Married, Total	Married, Husband Present	Widowed or Divorced	Total
1940	48.1	16.7	14.7	32.0	27.4
1950	50.5	24.8	23.8	36.0	31.4
1960	44.1	31.7	30.5	37.1	34.8
1970	53.0	41.4	40.8	36.2	42.6
1980	61.5	50.7	50.1	41.0	51.1

Source: Bureau of the Census, *Statistical Abstract of the United States 1982–83*, U.S. Department of Commerce, Washington, D.C.

Among a growing number of groups, the National Organization for Women (NOW) and the Women's Equity Action League (WEAL) have pressed American society for an awakening to sex discrimination. This recent movement has had an influence on American society. In addition, the feminist movement has gained national recognition with the support of a feminist press. The KNOW Press, Inc., ERIC Women Studies reports, and Betty Friedan's *The Feminine Mystique* have all questioned Whitney Darrow's children's tale:

Boys have trucks. Girls have dolls.
Boys are doctors. Girls are nurses.
Boys fix things. Girls need things fixed.
Boys build houses. Girls keep houses.[1]

Although the Civil Rights Act of 1964, Title VII, prohibited discrimination, it was not until the 1970s that women began to receive equal treatment under the law.

New federal guidelines from the Departments of Labor, Health and Human Services, and Education—and federal court cases—have helped women combat sex discrimination within all levels of society. The nation's schools are beginning to focus some attention on nonsexist education. All these steps are essential and encouraging to the cause of equal rights for women.

School Dropouts

Although high school students and college students drop out of school for different reasons, both represent a substantial loss to our society. In most states, students must attend school until they are sixteen. Thus they cannot drop out of school during the early part of high school. However, once they are past the compulsory attendance age, a disturbing percentage drops out of school. The rate of school dropouts is disturbing for many reasons. Most of these students cannot get jobs, many get into trouble with the law, and many do not qualify for military service. Most of them are not yet prepared to be productive citizens, and a large number are destined to become social liabilities.

Table 6.3 shows the percentage of seventeen-year-olds graduating from high school over the past 100 years. While considerable progress has been made over this period, there are still many American youth who drop out and do not finish high school.

There is a definite relationship between juvenile delinquency and school dropouts. A study in New York City found that 95 percent of all the seventeen-year-old juvenile delinquents were school dropouts and that 85 percent of all the sixteen-year-old juvenile delinquents were dropouts. In the District of Columbia, 57 percent of that city's criminals are high school

TABLE 6.3 *Percent of Seventeen-Year-Olds Graduating from High School*

Year	Percent
1870	2
1900	6
1930	29
1940	51
1950	59
1960	65
1970	76
1980	74

Source: Bureau of the Census, *Digest of Education Statistics 1982*, U.S. Department of Commerce, Washington, D.C., p. 65.

dropouts. Various studies of delinquency have also shown that many delinquents did failing work while in school and often were of lower intelligence than were nondelinquents. The interrelation between social class, dropping out of school, school failure, and low intelligence (as measured by existing tests) is so complex that it is difficult to assess how much each factor contributes toward juvenile delinquency.

All these data point to the desperate need for the school and society to find ways to keep children in school and to teach them at least basic life skills—not only for their own good but for the good of society. The economic cost of ignoring this problem is staggering. In other words, the money spent to keep our children in school and prevent dropouts is not really an expense but an excellent long-term investment that returns handsome dividends for our society.

The gifted high school graduate who does not go on to college represents still another kind of school dropout. Furthermore, half of the students who enter college never graduate. Although many of these students leave college for academic reasons, a lot of them have exceptional academic ability. The underdeveloped talent of these gifted students represents a substantial loss to society. Needless to say, our society and our schools have a long way to go before solving the school dropout problem.

Juvenile Delinquency and Crime

It is sad but true that many of today's dropouts will be tomorrow's criminals. Statistics on crime in the United States are staggering. Figure 6.3 shows the dramatic increase in serious crimes in recent years. To make matters worse, fewer than one in four serious crimes leads to arrest; in other words, three fourths of the people who commit serious crimes do not get caught. The President's Commission on Law Enforcement and Administration of Justice recently reported that organized crime has be-

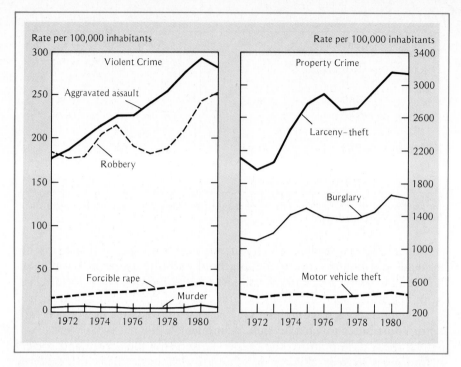

FIGURE 6.3 *Selected crime rates.* (*Source:* Bureau of the Census, *Statistical Abstract of the United States 1982–83*, U.S. Department of Commerce, Washington, D.C., p. 173.

come so great and sophisticated that it now involves narcotics, prostitution, murder, gambling, protection rackets, real estate, confidence games, politics, and the stock market—touching every American.

All of this crime costs our society an unbelievable amount of money. Table 6.4 shows the escalating cost of law enforcement. This means that law enforcement alone now costs every American man, woman, and child over $100.00 a year.

TABLE 6.4 *Public Expenditures for Law Enforcement: 1960–1979*

Year	Total Dollars
1960	$ 3,349,000,000
1970	8,571,000,000
1975	17,249,000,000
1976	19,681,000,000
1977	21,574,000,000
1978	24,132,000,000
1979	25,871,000,000

Source: Bureau of the Census, *Statistical Abstract of the United States 1982–83*, U.S. Department of Commerce, Washington, D.C., p. 183.

Violence and Vandalism in the School

The world has been vividly reminded in recent years that we live in a violent world. Such things as political assassinations, attempts to kill political and religious leaders, the terrorism in Northern Ireland and elsewhere in Europe and the Mideast, and organized crime combine to create a violent society.

Just as our whole society has become violent, so have our schools. Violence and vandalism have now become very serious problems in many schools. A U.S. Senate Committee on Delinquency has estimated that school vandalism costs our nation over $600 million each year. The National Association of School Security Directors estimates that each year there are 12,000 armed robberies, 270,000 burglaries, 204,000 aggravated assaults, and 9,000 rapes in our schools. Further, an estimated 70,000 serious physical assaults are made on teachers each year.

These statistics suggest the size of the problems of vandalism and violence faced by the schools. Unfortunately, very few solutions to these

Teachers must consider the world for which students are being prepared, and what skills are needed for success.

problems have been found. Some schools have hired police officers, adopted strict rules, expelled troublesome students, and taken a determined stance. Other schools have solicited the help of students and parents, have tried to change the curriculum to make it more appealing to students, have gone to great lengths to keep all students in school, and have generally adopted a democratic, humanistic, and sympathetic attitude.

Frankly, few schools have been successful in combating the violence—probably for two reasons. First, few schools have the financial resources to make a serious, concerted attack on the problem. Second, violence has become so prevalent in American society that some social scientists believe there is simply no way to keep it out of the schools. Violence, crime, and a general disregard and disrespect for the rights and welfare of others have become commonplace. The size and diversity of this problem can be understood only by analyzing related problems like child abuse and neglect, wife beating, juvenile delinquency, television and movie violence, illegitimate births, divorce rates, tax fraud, governmental corruption, welfare cheating, price fixing, stock manipulation, organized crime, business crime, and employee theft. Crime and violence have indeed pervaded both American life and the schools.

Drugs

One of the most tragic social problems in America today is the misuse of drugs by young people. Table 6.5 provides information on the extent of this problem in our society.

25   To counter the drug problem, many schools have embarked on a variety of programs. These programs are to provide students with information about drugs so that they realize the dangers of drug abuse and, as informed persons, will decide they are better off not using illicit drugs. Generally, the drug education programs that have been adequately funded, that involve parents and students, that are taught by well-trained teachers, and that avoid preaching and moralizing have been the most successful.

Alcohol

Student use of alcohol has risen sharply in recent years. Figure 6.4 shows the results of a recent survey that asked high school seniors to estimate the percentage of their friends who used various drugs and degree of use. It shows that alcohol was the most commonly used drug and that sizable percentages of students get drunk at least once a week. Many schools have students consuming alcohol in school buildings during the day. Medical authorities report a rapid rise in "polydrug" abuse—combining drugs and alcohol—among students. For instance, alcohol used with barbiturates,

TABLE 6.5 *Use of Drugs in the United States*

Type of Drug	Percent of Youths				Percent of Young Adults				Percent of Adults			
	Ever used		Current user		Ever used		Current user		Ever used		Current user	
	1972	1979	1972	1979	1974	1979	1974	1979	1974	1979	1974	1979
Marihuana	14.0	30.9	7.0	16.7	52.7	68.2	25.2	35.4	9.9	19.6	2.0	6.0
Inhalants	6.4	9.8	1.0	2.0	9.2	16.5	(z)	1.2	1.2	3.9	(z)	0.5
Hallucinogens	4.8	7.1	1.4	2.2	16.6	25.1	2.5	4.4	1.3	4.5	(z)	(z)
Cocaine	1.5	5.4	0.6	1.4	12.7	27.5	3.1	9.3	0.9	4.3	(z)	0.9
Heroin	0.6	0.5	(z)	(z)	4.5	3.5	(z)	(z)	0.5	1.0	(z)	(z)
Analgesics	(NA)	3.2	(NA)	0.6	(NA)	11.8	(NA)	1.0	(NA)	2.7	(NA)	(z)
Stimulants[1]	4.0	3.4	(NA)	1.2	17.0	18.2	3.7	3.5	3.0	5.8	(z)	0.5
Sedatives[1]	3.0	3.2	(NA)	1.1	15.0	17.0	1.6	2.8	2.0	3.5	(z)	(z)
Tranquilizers[1]	3.0	4.1	(NA)	0.6	10.0	15.8	1.2	2.1	2.0	3.1	(z)	(z)
Alcohol	(NA)	70.3	24.0	37.2	81.6	95.3	69.3	75.9	73.2	91.5	54.5	61.3
Cigarettes	(NA)	54.1	17.0	12.1	68.8	82.8	48.8	42.6	65.4	83.0	39.1	36.9

NA = Not available.
Z = Less than 0.5 percent.
[1]Prescription drugs.
Source: Bureau of the Census, *Statistical Abstract of the United States 1982–83*, U.S. Department of Commerce, Washington, D.C., p. 123.

147

sedatives, or tranquilizers gives a heightened effect for each substance but can cause death. Alcohol has now become the foremost drug problem for young people in America.

Smoking

19   Millions of American students regularly smoke cigarettes. The growing evidence that smoking is a serious health hazard has prompted educators to search for ways to combat this problem. Figure 6.4 shows that, in all likelihood, a very high percentage of the nation's teenagers smoke regularly.

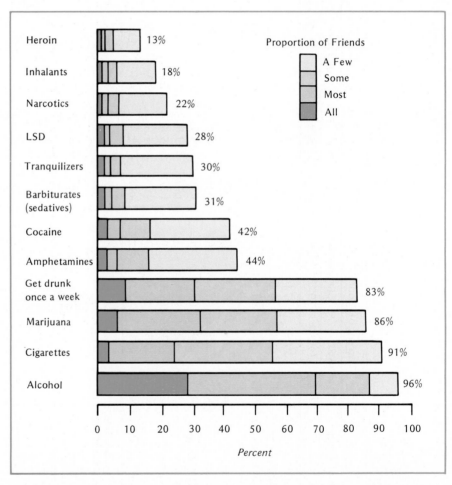

FIGURE 6.4   *Proportion of friends using each drug as estimated by high school seniors in 1980. (Source:* National Institute on Drug Abuse, *Student Drug Use in America 1975–80.)*

Most people believe the school is the only agency that has a chance to significantly reduce teenage smoking, and more and more schools are accepting the challenge. Some schools include a systematic study of the effects of smoking as part of their curriculum. The most promising approach to smoking education seems to be that in which the youngsters themselves run their own antismoking campaigns. Some schools have joined parent groups, the American Cancer Society, the American Heart Association, and the National Tuberculosis and Respiratory Diseases Association to fight teenage smoking. Unfortunately, most schools have just begun to attack this social problem.

Youth and Sexuality

Sex-related problems, including venereal diseases and unplanned pregnancies, represent yet another area of social concern for our country's youth.

A report issued jointly by the American Public Health Association, the American Social Health Association, and the Venereal Disease Association states:

> While the total number of persons in the United States reported as newly infected with gonorrhea continues to increase each year at a progressively higher rate, the number of teenagers fifteen to nineteen years old who become infected rises even more rapidly.

Syphilis, an even more medically serious venereal disease, touches the lives of many young victims. These and other less common venereal diseases, if left untreated, can cause serious health problems such as sterility, paralysis, blindness, heart disease, insanity, and death. Often, babies of infected mothers are born with mental and physical defects.

Each year, many school-age girls have unplanned and unwanted pregnancies. It is difficult to determine the exact number of such girls because authorities have no systematic way of collecting such data. Even so, authorities agree that the number is extremely high.[2]

Since abortion is now readily available, many pregnant teenagers have chosen abortion over continuing a pregnancy. Even so, an estimated 150,000 illegitimate children are born to unwed teenage girls each year. Since society does not attach the stigma to unwed motherhood that it used to, increasing numbers of unwed teenage mothers will probably choose to keep their babies in the future.

Obviously, American teenagers have many sex-related problems. Much evidence suggests that these problems are often related to ignorance or misinformation. Well-designed and well-taught sex education programs in the schools represent one promising step toward helping to reduce this social problem.

Unemployment

Table 6.6 shows the recent history of unemployment rates in the United States. The general economic condition of the country probably has more to do with unemployment than any other single factor. However, many factors influence the unemployment picture. The additional women entering the labor force, the decreased number of young people in military service, and changing trends in college enrollments all contribute to the country's unemployment rates.

Certain groups within our society are more affected by unemployment than others, as Figure 6.5 vividly points out. Although actual unemployment rates change from year to year, the relative unemployment picture for the groups represented in Figure 6.5 has remained essentially the same in recent history. Generally, nonwhites and teenagers have the highest unemployment rates.

Leisure

One outgrowth of advanced technology and increased productivity has been a decrease in the length of the workweek. In 1850 the average workweek was 66 hours; today it is fewer than 40 hours. Many predict that the workweek will continue to decrease in the future.

28   Americans spend three times as much money on leisure each year as they spend on education. This spending not only indicates the amount of leisure time these citizens enjoy, but also implies that they can afford as good an educational program as they want. Each year, millions of Americans attend sporting events, visit museums, attend live theater, collect stamps, plant gardens, carry out genealogical research, go camping, play tennis, do volunteer charitable work, and so forth.

Not only is leisure time increasing for the average American, but so is life expectancy. Life expectancy has increased from 48 years in 1900 to approximately 75 years today. The combination of the short workweek, high standard of living, long life, lack of child labor, and early retirement enables today's average American to spend more than one third of a lifetime at leisure.

TABLE 6.6   *Percent Unemployment*

	1970	1975	1980	1982*
All workers	4.9	8.5	7.1	9.5
White	4.5	7.8	6.3	8.4
Black and others	8.2	13.8	13.1	17.1

*June, seasonally adjusted
Source: Bureau of the Census, *Statistical Abstract of the United States 1982–83*, U.S. Department of Commerce, Washington, D.C., p. 392.

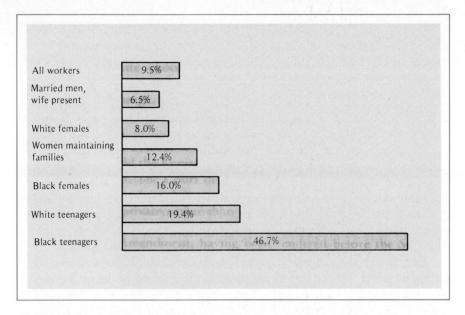

FIGURE 6.5 *Unemployment percent for selected groups.* (*Source:* Bureau of the Census, *Statistical Abstract of the United States 1982–83,* U.S. Department of Commerce, Washington, D.C., p. 392.)

This increased free time presents a challenging educational problem. In the first place, many Americans have not been "educated" to use free time purposefully. Leisure can be a burden as well as a blessing if one has not developed productive leisure interests. One out of ten Americans is so poor that he or she cannot afford the minimum essentials—much less any leisure activities. Ironically, because of unemployment, it is usually the poor who have the most leisure.

An increasing number of schools are attempting to develop programs to help people use their leisure time productively. Adult education classes throughout the country are flourishing.

Pollution

A serious problem in America is the continuing widespread pollution of the environment. Although this may well be one of the most serious problems affecting society, the public has not generally shown great concern about it. Perhaps the most promising step taken toward correcting pollution was the creation of the Environmental Education Act in 1970.

The government, as it has done so often in the past, has looked to the nation's schools to help solve a pressing social problem—this time cleaning up our badly polluted environment. The Environmental Education Act is predicated on the belief that pollution problems will be solved only when citizens are educated to the point at which they will respect the environment.

The Threat of War

A social problem of a type somewhat different from those just discussed is the constant threat to peace in the world. Most Americans worry about the threat of war, but some may not realize that the solution to this problem may depend, at least in part, upon our schools. To the extent that our schools are able to educate generations of our youth to value peace and have the wisdom and skill to achieve it, we can reduce, and perhaps even one day eliminate, the threat of war. This will require a concerted effort on the part of our schools. We must have teachers who believe in peace education and a well-developed curriculum aimed at these goals.

Even so, schools cannot accomplish this task alone. Fortunately, there are many other agencies working toward the goal of peace in the world. For instance, the United Nations represents a great effort toward international peace and understanding. Part of its charter explains this purpose:

1. To take effective collective measures for the prevention and the removal of threats to peace.
2. To develop friendly relations based on respect for the principle of equal rights and self-determination of peoples.
3. To cooperate in economic, social, cultural, and humanitarian matters and to promote respect for human rights and fundamental freedoms for all.

Numerous agencies operate under the auspices of the United Nations to foster world understanding. Some of these agencies are the World Health Organization (WHO), primarily interested in promoting personal health—mental and physical—and in developing desirable conditions of public health and sanitation; the Food and Agricultural Organization (FAO), concerned with the standard of living and with nutrition as influenced by the production of farm, forest, and fisheries; the United Nations Children's Fund (UNICEF), actively engaged in child welfare; and the International Bank for Reconstruction and Development (IBRD), also known as the World Bank, interested in international trade and foreign investments for development and reconstruction.

Summary and Implications

There are many serious social problems in the United States that have important effects on our schools. Schools cannot adequately meet the educational needs of students without considering the society from which the young people come. Our schools and our society are so intimately related that any problem affecting one affects the other; therefore the schools alone cannot solve many of the problems confronting young people. The implication here is clear. If we are serious about solving the problems facing young people, both society at large and our schools must work together purposefully—probably in a way not yet envisioned by planners. This effort would undoubtedly require that more money be spent on education than is now the case. It would require that parents work much more closely with educators than they do now. It would ask American society to make a much deeper and broader commitment to education than it has now.

DISCUSSION QUESTIONS

1. In your estimation, what still has to be done to achieve the American ideal of equality of opportunity in our public schools?
2. What are some practical solutions to our environmental pollution problem?
3. How serious do you believe alcohol and drug problems are among American youth? How can the schools help solve these problems?
4. How will current population trends in the United States affect the public school system?
5. If you had a free hand, how would you organize the schools to help people use their leisure?

SUPPLEMENTAL ACTIVITIES

1. Visit a local high school and record your impression of the socioeconomic status of the learners. Check with the teacher to see whether or not you are right.
2. Invite a law enforcement official to your class to talk about crime and juvenile delinquency.
3. Visit the schools in a poor area and compare their conditions and problems with those of a community that is wealthier.
4. Develop and carry out a class project to survey the environmental pollution in your immediate geographical area. Decide how the local public school system could use the results of your project in an environmental education program.
5. Discuss with some of your fellow students ways that teachers might develop and utilize a "peace" curriculum in their classrooms.
6. Spend a day with a local community social worker and record the cases that are investigated.

NOTES

1. Whitney Darrow, Jr., *I'm Glad I'm a Boy, I'm Glad I'm a Girl* (New York: Simon & Schuster, 1970).

2. *The Hassles of Becoming a Teenage Parent* (Washington, D.C.: U.S. Public Health Service, 1975).

BIBLIOGRAPHY

Biklen, Sari Knopp. *Women and Educational Leadership*. Lexington, Mass.: Lexington Books, 1980.

Chesler, Mark A., and Cave, William M. *A Sociology of Education*. New York: Macmillan, 1980.

Christiansen, James. *Educational and Psychological Problems of Abused Children.* Saratoga, Calif.: Century Twenty One Publishing, 1980.

Davis, V. T., and Hopkins, D. T. "Study of Family Crises Which May Relate to School Behavior." *Delta Kappa Gamma Bell* 46 (Summer 1980): 56–60.

Dotts, W. "Disaffected Youth: A Dilemma." *Education* 100 (Summer 1980): 373–376.

Filling, C. M. "Prospects for an Ethnographic Approach to Urban Education." *Urban Education* 15 (October 1980): 259–277.

Grealy, Joseph I. *School Crime and Violence: Problems and Solutions.* Fort Lauderdale, Fla.: Ferguson E. Peters. 1979.

Hogan, John C., and Schwartz, Mortimer D. *Children's Rights.* Lexington, Mass.: Lexington Books, 1980.

Ianni, F. A. J., and Reuss-Ianni, E. "Crime and Social Order in Schools." *Educational Digest* 45 (May 1980): 2–5.

King-Stoops, Joyce. *Migrant Education: Teaching the Wandering Ones,* Fastback No. 145, 44 pp. Bloomington, Ind.: Phi Delta Kappa, 1980.

Lorrance, Arleen, and Pike, Diane. *The Love Project Way.* San Diego, Calif.: L. P. Publications, 1980.

Musgrove, Frank. *School and the Social Order.* New York: Wiley, 1980.

Neill, Shirley Boes, and Vandesmyn, Gaye, eds. *Keeping Students in School: Problems and Solutions.* AASA Critical Issues Series. Arlington, Va.: American Association of School Administrators, 1970.

Ornstein, Allan C. *Introduction to the Foundations of Education.* 2d ed. Chicago: Rand McNally, 1981.

Parents, Peers, and Pot. Washington, D.C.: National Institute on Drug Abuse, 1979.

Postman, Neil. "Engaging Students in the Great Conversation." *Phi Delta Kappan* 64 (January 1983), 310–316.

Reagan, Nancy. "The First Lady Talks About Drug Abuse." *American Education* 19(1) (January/February 1983), 2–4.

Roberts, J. E. "Teenage Sexuality and Parenthood." *Journal of Home Economics* 72 (Summer 1980): 37–39.

Ross, Robert Robertson; Blum, Donna; and Blum, Frank. *Illiteracy and Crime.* Lexington, Mass.: Lexington Books, 1980.

Steiner, Elizabeth; Arnove, Robert; and McClellan, B. Edward. *Education and American Culture.* New York: Macmillan, 1980.

Taylor, Charlotte P. *Transforming Schools: A Social Perspective.* New York: St. Martin's Press, 1976.

Teaching about Drinking. Washington, D.C.: National Institute on Alcohol Abuse and Alcoholism, 1979.

Thinking about Drinking. Washington, D.C.: National Institute on Alcohol Abuse and Alcoholism, 1979.

Urman, J., and Meginnis, S. K. "Process of Problem Pregnancy Counseling." *Journal of American College Health Association* 28 (June 1980): 308–325.

Violent Schools—Safe Schools. Washington, D.C.: National Institute of Education, 1978.

7

National Directions for Education

Focus Questions

- How can the federal government have an impact on program offerings in the schools?
- What are some of the significant contributions to education that the U.S. Department of Education makes?
- Why should all teachers be knowledgeable about Public Law 94-142?
- What is the role of the teacher in providing career education opportunities for learners?
- Why should all teachers take responsibility for reading in the curriculum?

Key Terms and Concepts

Education and Improvement Act
Compensatory programs
Block grants
Direct grants
Public Law 94-142
Handicapped

Individualized Education Program (IEP)
Least restrictive environment
Mainstreaming
Due process
Career education
Bilingual-bicultural education

What Would You Do?

During a faculty meeting, several experienced tenured teachers are adamant in their negative reaction to participating in mainstreaming practices in their classrooms. As a newly hired teacher, you have just recently completed a certification program that stressed philosophical and practical compliance with P.L. 94-142. It is obvious that many on the faculty will not support working toward the development of positive learning environments for handicapped children. What is your role as a new teacher in helping your more experienced colleagues to alter their negative attitudes toward the handicapped?

Following the passage of the National Defense Education Acts, the Elementary and Secondary Education Acts, and the War on Poverty Program in the late 1950s and 1960s, the federal government liberally pumped money into compensatory programs aimed at improving school efforts and social differences in the society. Different categories of title monies abounded for a twenty-year period, and a new cabinet-level Department of Education was created in 1979. The creation of department-level status for education appeared to signal renewed federal support of education. However, federal politics took a more conservative turn with the change

28 in the national administration in 1980, and the New Federalism stressed a return to greater control, participation, and financial effort from the states rather than the federal government. The shift in federal policy has reduced compensatory welfare and education efforts in Washington and

65 increased federal spending on defense. The 1984 election is too recent to predict the direction of compensatory federal efforts during the latter half of the decade, but ongoing federal mandates of the 1970s remain to provide national direction for education. In addition, the Reagan administration initiated an effort that implies "education for defense" or "education for economic survival."

We present some of the significant federal directions that continue.

Office of Education

Created in 1979, the Department of Education is organized into six major offices, which direct federal efforts. These are the offices of Elementary and Secondary Education, Postsecondary Education, Research and Improvement, Special Education and Rehabilitation Services, Vocational and Adult Education, and Bilingual Education and Minority Languages Affairs. In addition to providing national direction for educational priorities that affect the whole country, these offices administer programs of finan-

46 cial support for those priorities. These programs span compensatory education, state and local special assistance, Indian education, migrant education, college student loans and grants, international fellowships and consultantships, higher education support programs, research and dissemination, handicapped programs, rehabilitation and vocational development, and bilingual programs. For the total expenditures on all levels of education, preprimary through graduate school, the federal government provides approximately 10 percent of the funding.

Education and Improvement Act of 1981

Before 1981, all federal support programs were administered by the federal government through a variety of agencies that had been created during the 1960s and 1970s as various educational public laws and acts were adopted. These public laws and acts were administered through a series of title regulations for each act and governed by regulatory agencies housed within and outside the Office of Education. The new cabinet-level department centralized this operation with the exception of special programs allied with other cabinet-level departments (e.g., Commerce, Interior, Agriculture).

In 1981 the Education and Improvement Act was passed, becoming effective in 1982. Two major changes to federal support were introduced with this Act. First, Chapter 1 of the Act superseded Title I of the Elementary and Secondary Education Act and extended to the states and local education agencies (LEA's) the prime responsibility for conducting the federal education program designed to meet the educational needs of disadvantaged children. Second, Chapter 2 of the Act consolidated 42 other elementary and secondary education programs into block grants for three broad purposes. These are basic skills improvement, improvement of support services, and special projects. In addition, state agencies administer Chapter 2 programs.

The granting of federal money for the various programs may be accomplished by the awarding of direct grants or entitlement (block) grants. The direct grants are monies awarded from Washington and are used for projects having national priority. Recipients of these grants, public and private, must meet federal agency criteria, which are published regularly in the Federal Register. Entitlement grants are made to the states and are based upon numbers of children or students to be served and the amounts of federal money available. Each state determines how these monies are to be distributed in keeping with intended federal priorities. These funds have been reduced yearly since 1981. Although the percentage of reduction has been small and varies by category of support, inflation has caused the decline in the real dollar value of support to be substantial. This has been particularly acute in the areas of higher education and research. The state-administered grants may be awarded with or without criteria or formulae. The intent of the 1981 Improvement Act was to shift greater financial and administrative responsibility for compensatory educational efforts to the states.

Education for Handicapped

In 1967, Congress created the Bureau of Education for the Handicapped (BEH) and began providing the states with funds to create, improve, and operate compensatory programs for the millions of handicapped children in the United States. For over eleven years (1969–1980) the federal government allocated over $200 million each year to train or retrain special education teachers and to establish research and development. All this effort was directed toward helping children handicapped by mental retardation, speech problems, emotional disorders, deafness, blindness, and other related health disabilities. The BEH programs undoubtedly improved the condition of the handicapped in the United States. Despite this national effort, substantial differences existed among the various state programs because the BEH-sponsored programs remained voluntary rather than mandatory. The mainstreaming laws of many states during the late 1970s helped to equalize compensatory efforts within individual states, but the national differences remained acute. Handicapped children in some states received better help than the handicapped in other states. Public Law 94-142 was badly needed.

Perhaps the single piece of legislation most significant for education during the 1970s was Public Law 94-142, the Education for the Handicapped Act. Congress, having ascertained that eight million handicapped children existed in the United States, passed the Act in 1975 and mandated partial operation for 1978. September 1, 1980, was established as the date for full compliance with the law. Although the bill was conceived and passed out of a desire to improve school programs for handicapped children alone, because of its due process implications it has paved the way for individualized programs for all potential learners. It has been suggested that this bill helped speed development of early childhood programs because it requires early identification of youngsters needing help. The main features of the Act are as follows:

- All handicapped learners between the ages of three and twenty-one are to be provided with a free public education.
- Each handicapped child is to have an individualized program, developed jointly by a school official, a teacher, the parents or guardian, and, if possible, the learner.
- Handicapped children are not to be grouped separately unless they are severely handicapped, in which case separate facilities and programs would be deemed more appropriate.
- Tests for identification and placement are to be free of racial and cultural bias.
- School districts are to maintain continuous efforts at identifying handicapped children.
- School districts are to establish priorities for providing educational programs in compliance with the law.
- Placement of the handicapped is to require parental approval.
- Private schools are to comply with the Act.
- Retraining or in-service training of all workers with the handicapped is required.
- Special federal grants are available for modifying school buildings.

- State departments of education are to be designated as the responsible state agencies for all programs for the handicapped.

Handicapped children are defined in the Act as those evaluated as being mentally retarded, hard of hearing, deaf, speech impaired, visually handicapped, seriously emotionally disturbed, orthopedically impaired, other health impaired, deaf-blind, multihandicapped, or having specific learning disabilities. Further, the law clearly explains least restrictive environment placement, individualized Education Programs (IEPs), due process protection, and teacher education.

Least Restrictive Environment

Least restrictive environment placement ensures that handicapped children are educated with nonhandicapped children to the maximum extent possible and that the placement of a handicapped child outside the regular classroom occurs only when the nature or severity of the handicap is such

A learner may be handicapped more by lowered expectations than by an actual disability.

that education in regular classes with the use of supplementary aids and services cannot be achieved satisfactorily.

IEP

29 An Individualized Education Program must comprise written statements developed by the public agency, the child's teacher, one or both of the child's parents, and the child when appropriate. Other specialists may be involved if the parents or public agency so desire. Each written IEP must include:

- The child's present level of educational performance.
- Annual goals, including short-term instructional objectives.
- Specific special education and related services to be provided to the child, and the extent to which the child will be able to participate in regular educational programs.
- Projected dates for initiation and anticipated duration of special services.
- Objective criteria, evaluation procedures, and schedules for determining on at least an annual basis whether or not the short-term instructional objectives are being met.

Due Process

Parents of handicapped children must be notified in writing before a public agency initiates, changes, or refuses to initiate or change the identification, evaluation, or placement of the child or the provision of a free appropriate public education to the child. This notification in the parents' native language or other mode of communication (e.g., braille, oral communication, sign language) must include:

- A full explanation of parents' due process rights.
- A description of the action proposed or refused by the agency, why the agency proposes or refuses to take the action, and a description of any options considered by the agency and reasons why they were rejected.
- A description of each evaluation procedure; that is, a test, record, or report the agency uses as a basis for the proposal or refusal.
- Any other factors relevant to the agency's proposal or refusal.

The due process concerns of this Act go to the very core of modifying education in the United States. Successful mass education has significantly raised the mean level of achievement, literacy, and school level of completion for all U.S. citizens. At the same time, however, the schools have had to resort to teaching and learning practices directed at group goals. Despite their awareness of the benefits of individualized programs for all children, the schools have been unable to develop them because of money constraints and the sheer numbers of school-age children.

A substantive due process question for educators naturally arises. If handicapped children are required to have individually tailored programs to meet their needs and interests, why not all learners? No two children are alike, and therefore each child should have his or her own program. As the constitutionality of Public Law 94-142 continues to be upheld and strengthened, the rights of all learners to have individual programs will have to be considered by the schools. Since P.L. 94-142 was conceived under the "due process" clause and since that law requires individualized programs for special learners, it seems safe to project the notion that in the future, parents may request similar treatment for their nonspecial children under the guise of due process.

Mainstreaming Practices

The Council for Exceptional Children (CEC) has since the 1960s directed its efforts for special education toward the provision of services as organized under the "Cascade model" for intervention. Basically, this model projected placement of those in need of special education either in regular classrooms with special itinerant staff or in residential settings where the learner was isolated from the mainstream. Variations from those two ex- tremes could be special classes in a regular school building or special classes in a daytime special education center. The idea was to move learners to more restrictive environments only as necessary and return them to less restrictive environments as soon as feasible. Public Law 94-142 has given the CEC opportunity for a least restrictive interpretation of the cascade of services.

Many special education services are dictated by the type of physical environment provided for the learner. Typically, regular classrooms and schools are not physically fit for many special education students; they are built for the mainstream but not the exceptional child. The "new perspective," as CEC calls it, makes regular learning areas more powerful and diverse. It allows for a broadened interpretation of the instructional cascade (Figure 7.1).

The regular classroom environment in this plan is a model of individualized instruction for all learners. Physically, learning spaces are treated better acoustically, with amplication devices and alternative treatments of illumination. Greater use of learning centers with a multiplicity of equipment and materials is provided for special needs and preferences. Collaborative teaching is expected, with special educators, other professionals, and aides working with regular teachers. Instruction is individualized for all learners. Special education students are moved out of the regular en-

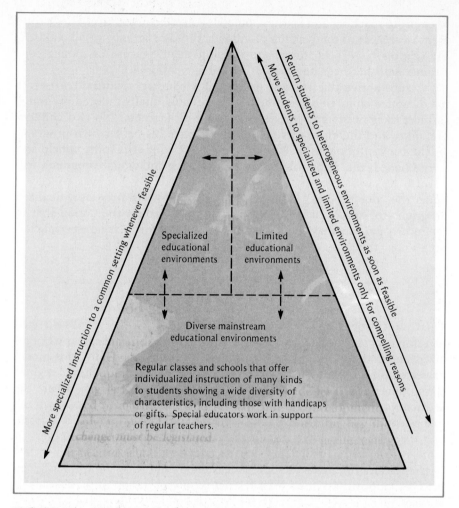

FIGURE 7.1 *The instructional cascade.* (*Source:* Jack W. Birch and Maynard C. Reynolds, *Teaching Exceptional Children in All America's Schools,* p. 47. Copyright 1982 by The Council for Exceptional Children. Reprinted with permission.)

vironment for minimal periods and only for complex individual needs. The CEC views the least restrictive environment as the new mainstream.

Career Education

During the 1970s, career education came into existence along with vocational education, and the relationship between the two areas has always been confusing. Career education is commonly understood as helping learners become familiar with the knowledge and the values of a society in which people work for a living. As learners acquire this knowledge, they can choose their life occupation wisely, knowing that society, their own leisure, and their associates are affected by this choice.

Career education should begin in the early years of a learner's life and continue into retirement. It should be related to the times before, during, and after one's life occupation. The stages of career education span one's life. These include the initial growth stage, an exploratory stage, the establishment and maintenance stages, and the final stage. The growth and exploratory stages are assigned to the elementary and secondary schools to develop. Besides learning what careers there are, the schoolchild is encouraged and helped through these two stages to choose an occupation. Experiences in careers may or may not be for pay. The differences vary by program and location. The last three stages pertain to the work market—following the career choice through and spending worthwhile retirement years.

Developed initially by the National Institute of Education (NIE), an Experienced-Based Career Education (EBCE) program has the following characteristics:

- Students move off campus for first-hand experiences in everyday community places: offices, stores, hospitals, factories, churches, government agencies, and the like.
- Off-campus sites become the setting for the curriculum rather than a brief diversion from standard lesson plans. A student who prepares and then presents a speech to a civic organization earns credit for applying those skills.
- Individual student planning of how academic and personal needs, interests, and desires will be satisfied as guided by staff members who have been trained in this new way of teaching.
- Policy directions for the programs are provided by an advisory board that includes individuals from business, labor, and other community interests (including parents and students).
- Neither students nor cooperating employers receive any payment whatsoever for the time and effort put into each learning experience.
- All learning activities lead directly to a regular high school diploma that is valid for typical postsecondary education and job-entry opportunities.[1]

It is obvious that what began as an educational need in the 1970s has been firmly established as a continuing priority during the 1980s. Although professional differences in thought between vocational and career educators will probably persist, an impressive number of school districts participate in career education programs. Efforts in career education must begin early in the elementary years and continue throughout adult education. Career education should not be remedial; it should be continuous.

Vocational Education

29   Vocational education has grown tremendously during the past twenty years. Although general enrollments in education have dropped dramatically during the past decade, the shift in enrollments to vocational education has been tremendous. These enrollment gains have increased by over 200 percent in the past fifteen years.[2]

Gene Bottoms and Patricia Copa report five types of general vocational programs and four types of occupationally specific programs.[3] The general programs are:

1. Consumer/homemaking, focusing on family life.
2. Prevocational as introductory or exploratory.

Improved vocational education programs are providing students with marketable skills in a competitive environment.

3. Prevocational basic skills.
4. Related instruction in occupational service, mathematics, and communication skills needed for specific jobs.
5. Employability skills for cooperative work programs.

The occupationally specific programs include:

1. Occupational cluster programs of comprehensive high schools.
2. Occupation-specific programs for one particular occupation.
3. Job-specific programs for an individual job within a broader cluster of occupations.
4. Employer-specific programs as needed or requested by particular employers.

The latter three specific programs are usually found in a community college or vocational/technical school.

Vocational education has traditionally been highly dependent upon federal funding since the early part of this century, and that dependence has been supported. However, the New Federalism, in keeping with its general policy toward education, has tended to shift the emphasis for financial support to state and local funding agencies. The change in philosophy for national financial support and the inflationary impact of the past five years have had a serious impact on the quality and quantity of vocational programs. Federal mandates for vocational education continue to require program improvement and addition of new technological programs, but federal financial support continues to decline. In addition to the school-age population in need of initial vocational training, there is a growing need for initial training and retraining of an older adult population. If the United States is to take any steps toward reversing the growing shortages of technically skilled workers, it seems appropriate that the federal financial role in vocational education must be bolstered.

Bilingual-Bicultural Education

The Bilingual Education Act—Title VII of the Elementary and Secondary Education Act—was enacted into law in 1968. This act and its various amendments were enacted to help with the special needs of growing numbers of American children whose first language is not English. Originally, the Act was intended to focus on low-income learners, early childhood education, adult education, dropouts, and vocational students. Funds were also provided for preservice and in-service training of teachers for these programs. [29] [30]

Bilingual-bicultural education is formal instruction for learners, using their native language for learning all subjects until second-language (English) skills have been developed. This approach increases the equal educational opportunity of minority children. The 1980 census reports that the size of the non-English-language background population in the United States is 30 million people. This is expected to increase to 39.5 million by the year 2000. People of Spanish, German, and Italian descent make up the majority of this group, with the Spanish-speaking people who have migrated from Latin America and Puerto Rico by far the largest portion. The Spanish-speaking portion will continue to grow.

Since the fall of Saigon in 1975, over 500,000 Southeast Asian refugees have entered the United States. In 1980 alone, the federal government allowed 170,000 such refugees to settle in the United States. Almost one half of these refugees are school-age children and are in need of bilingual education. It is estimated that 75 percent are illiterate in their native language. The 1980 influx of Cuban refugees has added immensely to the growing number of Spanish-speaking groups. Many of these Spanish-speaking and Asian-speaking refugees are concentrated in California, Texas, Pennsylvania, Colorado, Louisiana, Iowa, Wisconsin, Florida, and New York. In addition, the number of Native American citizens has swelled as their total population has increased. Over 30 percent of American Indians speak a tribal tongue as their first language.

English monolingual schools have helped to deny to non-English speakers equal access to education and job opportunities. Hindered by language barriers in schooling, these minority Americans have suffered from illiteracy problems. The much publicized Coleman Report (1966) showed that non-English-speaking learners were desperately behind the national achievement norms in reading, mathematics, and verbal ability. Language difficulties were cited as the source of the problem and were used to support the need for bilingual-bicultural legislation.

Three types of bilingual programs have been supported by the federal government. These are:

1. Bilingual-Bicultural Maintenance Programs. These programs are designed to teach skills needed for English that emphasize instruction in the learner's native tongue. The culture of the ethnic group receiving instruction is stressed through history, literature, and art offerings. The native language of the learner is considered an asset to society; retention of that language is a significant goal of this program.

2. Bilingual-Transitional Programs. These programs are designed to provide intensive instruction in English, yet retain support for instruction in the native language. Learners are integrated into the regular classroom as soon as they acquire sufficient skills in English. It is critical in these types of programs that the learner not be disadvantaged in expected achievement areas of the curriculum.

3. English as a Second Language (ESL). These programs provide intense study of English skills necessary to study the other subjects in the curriculum. The stress is on mastery of English grammar and

phonology. One of the major goals is to help non-English speakers acquire skills that will help them communicate with their teachers.

Bilingual-bicultural education helps learners strengthen their identities by including their own historical, literary, and cultural traditions in the regular curriculum. Children are made to feel good about themselves and their backgrounds; their successes are stressed, and they are able to adjust more readily to the new culture. Special preservice and in-service training of teachers stresses the need for positive teacher-student interaction during learning. Early studies of results of bilingual-bicultural programs report that positive self-concepts and active participation have helped non-English-speaking pupils toward better learning.

The need for bilingual-bicultural programs will continue to grow. How that need will be addressed by the federal government in the future remains a question. As social legislation continues to suffer financial cutbacks, the education efforts for non-English-speaking people will surely diminish.

Cultural diversity in our schools can enrich all students.

Reading

One of the most ambitious attacks in the war on poverty has been associated with Title 1 of the Elementary and Secondary Education Act (ESEA)—the Title 1 Reading Program for economically disadvantaged children. Nationally supported reading programs began during the 1960s, and the funding for these programs increased substantially during the 1970s. As we began the decade of the 1980s, federal funds for economically disadvantaged students constituted almost 25 percent of the total federal budget in education. Only higher education received a larger share (40 percent), and over half of this amount was higher education student assistance and educational opportunity grants.

Under the Reagan administration, reading programs continued to be administered by state departments of education. The dollar amounts have been reduced, however, and many of the funds have been allocated on a block grant basis.

Because the national economy has suffered with increased inflation, the number of children eligible for Title 1 funds has increased. Each year in which the poverty level has risen because of inflation, more compensatory reading programs have been provided, including additional reading specialists, more materials, and in many cases increased use of teacher aides. Although the national inflation rate has dropped recently, the poverty level cutoff continues to rise moderately.

Reading programs aim at "continuous progress learning." This means that the child is diagnosed at a given performance level and then moved individually through the program. This can be done within the regular program in the classroom or in special facilities for reading instruction. After a child begins to read at a given grade level, she or he is then placed in the regular reading program of the classroom. These special reading programs are meant to take care of those with the greatest need. Early intervention, it is found, leads to fewer dropouts, positive school attitudes, and reading performance that allows the child to progress normally within the regular school environment.

Summary and Implications

The federal government's activities and influence can be readily seen in education, and its participation has increased significantly during the past two decades. Many of the federal programs that were begun during the 1960s were expanded significantly and supported by increased amounts of funding during the 1970s and the beginning of the 1980s. This financial support has lessened, however, during the recent Republican administration. Spawned by the need for social and welfare changes, many of the federal efforts in education have been compensatory. The federal government has demonstrated its ability to respond more quickly to national 40 needs in education than have states and local school systems. However, federal dollars still remain a very small amount of the total dollars now spent on education. The Reagan administration has reduced that national amount of financial participation even further. Although many national commissions and studies now imply that a crisis in education exists, the federal government has generally taken the position that the individual states must address this need. Further, it seems logical to assume that "due process" and "equal opportunity" pressures will continue to expand during the remainder of the 1980s. The financial direction of the federal government seems clear. There will continue to be reduced federal financial effort in education.

DISCUSSION QUESTIONS

1. Discuss some of the due process implications of Public Law 94-142.
2. How does one solve the financial dilemma in vocational education?
3. Why should the federal government participate in a public educational program that is the responsibility of the 50 states individually?
4. Discuss the assertion that "too strong an emphasis on bicultural education will produce separatism in the United States."
5. What role should the federal government take in addressing the questions of quality in our schools that have recently been raised?

SUPPLEMENTAL ACTIVITIES

1. Investigate the day-to-day activities of a reading specialist.
2. Investigate vocational education opportunities with a high school guidance counselor.
3. Prepare a list of educational needs that the federal government might be in the best position to care for.
4. Visit a local school and prepare to report on how a handicapped learner's program is individualized.
5. Create a collage depicting the federal government's role in financing education during the last two decades.

NOTES

1. Larry McClure, ed., *Inside Experienced-based Career Education* (Washington, D.C.: National Institute of Education, 1979), p. iii.
2. *Vocational Education Data System* (Washington, D.C.: National Center for Education Statistics, 1982).

3. Gene Bottoms and Patricia Copa, "A Perspective on Vocational Education Today," *Phi Delta Kappan*, 64(5) (January 1983): 349–350.

BIBLIOGRAPHY

Council for Exceptional Children. *Teaching Exceptional Children in All America's Schools.* Reston, Va.: The Council, 1982.

Deno, Evelyn N. *Educating Children with Emotional, Learning and Behavior Problems.* Minneapolis, Minn.: National Support Systems Project, 1978.

Fullan, Michael. *The Meaning of Educational Change.* Toronto, Ontario: OISE Press, 1982.

Full Educational Opportunity Under the Law. Washington, D.C.: U.S. Department of Health, Education, and Welfare, 1975.

National Commission on Excellence in Education. *A Nation at Risk: The Imperative for Educational Reform.* Washington, D.C.: U.S. Department of Education, 1983.

Rauth, Marilyn. *A Guide to Understanding the Education for All Handicapped Children Act: P.L. 94-142.* Washington, D.C.: American Federation of Teachers, AFL-CIO, 1980.

III

Control, Organization, and Support of American Education

The control of education in the United States involves the federal, state, and local levels of government. Control at the federal level is authorized by the United States Constitution and specific federal laws relating to education. Control at the state level derives from state constitutions and laws; local boards of education, as agents of the states, function under delegated authority from the states—with some discretionary power.

Legally, under the Tenth Amendment of the U.S. Constitution, education is a function of the states, yet the schools are operated by local governments. The federal government has a strong interest in education, particularly as it relates to national security, national domestic problems, and the rights of citizens as guaranteed by the Constitution and federal laws.

The organization of education in the United States is decentralized. Local boards of education in approximately 15,500 local school districts have the responsibility, delegated to them by the states, of providing education for the citizens of the districts. The local boards must abide by the federal and state constitutions and laws, but they may with their discretionary power decide policy uniquely appropriate to their own districts. As the nation has matured from colonial days to the present, centralized control has increased proportionally. Local boards of education are generally seen as having less and less control over education. This decrease in local control is a result of federal and state legislation, court decisions, the complexities of our society, and the quest for equality of opportunity in education.

Educational activities delegated to the local, state, and federal governments have changed over the years, and it is quite likely that they will continue to change and that new patterns of governmental interrelations will be established for education.

In Part III we consider the function of each level of government in education. For each there are legal, organizational, and financial aspects. Legal, administrative, and financial decisions made at any of the three levels are likely to stimulate further interactive decisions. No matter what the decision, all citizens must be assured their inalienable rights as Americans.

The three chapters of Part III consider the legal basis for and control of education at the local, state, and federal levels. In chapter 8, attention is directed toward the current interpretations of the Constitution as they apply to the separation of church and state and to school desegregation.

The organization of education in the United States is examined in chapter 9, with particular attention paid to what is new in federal, state, regional, and local responsibilities to education. Chapter 10 covers the changing pattern of financing public education because money is important in assuring equality of educational opportunity. ∎

8

The Law and American Education

Focus Questions

- Why should you as a future teacher know about the role of law in education?
- What value is there in a teacher's knowing how policies and laws are formulated and changed?
- Why should a teacher know about the rights assured under the First and Fourteenth Amendments of the United States Constitution and the interpretations of legal cases that affect these rights, as they relate to public and private education?
- Should teachers be involved in the political process? Why? Why not?

Key Terms and Concepts

Church and state in education
Public funds and parochial education
Tuition tax credits
Child Benefit Theory

School prayer
Compulsory education
Discrimination
Desegregation and busing

What Would You Do?

A tenth-grade student in one of your classes insists on praying aloud at the beginning of your class. Reactions from other students include ridiculing the student, listening attentively to the student, and ignoring the student and visiting with nearby classmates. The general atmosphere is disruptive. In a conversation with the student you were informed that his parents feel strongly that he should pray aloud in school. What can you do to resolve this issue?

The educational systems of the United States, both public and nonpublic, are governed by law. The United States Constitution provides the law for the nation, and state constitutions provide the law for each state. Since the U.S. Constitution was created by the people, a state legislature has no right to change that Constitution. State legislatures make laws that apply to education; these laws must be in accordance with both the U.S. Constitution and the applicable state constitution. The enabling and legislative control agents of education are illustrated in the top portion of Figure 8.1. Conflicts in this system of control are not unusual. In such instances, state and federal court systems make legal interpretations that form a body of case, or common, law. The lower portion of Figure 8.1 shows interpretive and administrative agents.

The initial part of our examination of legal foundations considers how the federal government, state legislatures, and local board of education are legally empowered to control public education. It should be recognized, however, that nonpublic schools, both sectarian and secular, are also under governmental control. The rights assured to citizens of the United States by the U.S. Constitution are valid and enforceable in nonpublic and public schools. Furthermore, nonpublic schools that accept public money must abide by the requirements that accompany that acceptance. For example, they may not have racially discriminatory practices. The power of government in educational matters was made quite clear by the U.S. Supreme Court as a part of its opinion in *Pierce* v. *Society of Sisters* (1925), discussed later in this chapter. The opinion stated:

> No question is raised concerning the power of the State reasonably to regulate all schools, to inspect, supervise, and examine them, their teachers and pupils; to require that all children of proper age attend some school, that teachers shall be of good moral character and patriotic disposition, that certain studies plainly essential to good citizenship must be taught, and nothing be taught which is manifestly inimical to the public welfare.

The latter part of this chapter considers some persistent and current legal issues related to the administration of American education.

Constitutional Provisions for Education

Public schools, in contrast to nonpublic schools, are created by law, supported by general taxation, and controlled by elected officials. The U.S. Constitution does not specifically provide for public education; however, the Tenth Amendment has been interpreted as granting this power to the states. The amendment specifies that "the powers not delegated to the

176

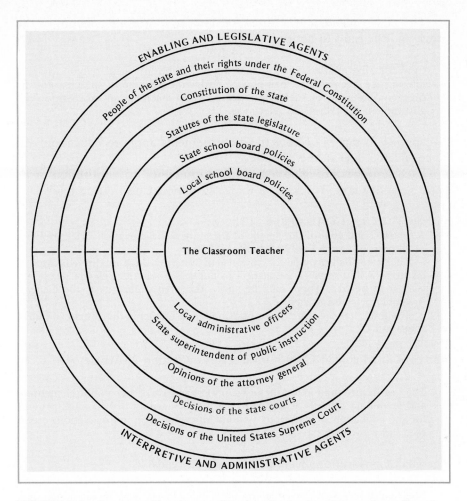

Within the concentric circles, from outermost to innermost:

ENABLING AND LEGISLATIVE AGENTS

People of the state and their rights under the Federal Constitution

Constitution of the state

Statutes of the state legislature

State school board policies

Local school board policies

The Classroom Teacher

Local administrative officers

State superintendent of public instruction

Opinions of the attorney general

Decisions of the state courts

Decisions of the United States Supreme Court

INTERPRETIVE AND ADMINISTRATIVE AGENTS

FIGURE 8.1 *Sources of legal control in American education as they affect the classroom teacher.* (*Source:* Jefferson N. Eastmond, *The Teacher and School Administration,* p. 97. Copyright © 1959 by Houghton Mifflin Company. Reprinted by permission.)

United States by the Constitution, nor prohibited by it to the states, are reserved to the states respectively, or to the people." Education is legally considered a function of the individual states but, as such, must be practiced in accordance with other provisions of the Constitution; the First and Fourteenth Amendments have been applied to the operation of education in the various states. The Fourteenth Amendment protects specified privileges of citizens. It reads in part:

> No state shall make or enforce any law which shall abrogate the privileges or immunities of citizens of the United States; nor shall any state deprive any person of life, liberty or property without due process of law; nor deny to any person within its jurisdiction the equal protection of the laws.

The First Amendment ensures freedom of speech, of religion, of the press, and the right to petition. It specifies:

> Congress shall make no law respecting an establishment of religion or prohibiting the free exercise thereof; or abridge the freedom of speech or of the press; or the right of the people peaceably to assemble and to petition the government for redress of grievances.

Specific instances of how these amendments apply to education will be considered later in this chapter.

Each state has provided for education in either its constitution or its basic statutory law. Article X of the 1970 Illinois Constitution reads:

> SECTION 1.   GOAL—FREE SCHOOLS
> A fundamental goal of the People of the State is the educational development of all persons to the limits of their capabilities.
>   The State shall provide for an efficient system of high quality educational institutions and services. Education in public schools through the secondary level shall be free. There may be such other free education as the General Assembly provides by law.
>   The State has the primary responsibility for financing the system of public education.

The current Michigan Constitution states in Section 2, Article VIII:

> The Legislature shall maintain and support a system of free public elementary and secondary schools as defined by law. Each school district shall provide for the education of its pupils without discrimination as to religion, creed, race, color, or national origin.

The Utah Constitution, Section 1, Article X, reads:

> The Legislature shall provide for the establishment and maintenance of a uniform system of public schools, which shall be open to all children of the State, and be free from sectarian control.

Through such statements the people of the various states commit themselves to a responsibility for education. The state legislatures are obliged to fulfill this commitment.

State Legislatures and Political Action

State legislatures are generally responsible for creating, operating, managing, and maintaining the state school systems. The legislators are the state policymakers for education. State departments of education are created by legislatures to serve as professional advisors and to execute state policy. State legislatures, though powerful agencies, also operate under controls. The governors of many states can veto school legislation as they can other legislation; and the attorney general and the state judiciary system, when called on, will rule on the constitutionality of educational legislation.

State legislatures make various decisions. These decisions generally concern how education is organized in the state, the certification standards and tenure rights of teachers, programs of studies, standards of building construction for health and safety, financing of schools, including tax structure and distribution, and pupil conduct and control, including compulsory attendance laws.

State legislatures, in their legislative deliberations about the schools, are continually importuned by special interest groups. These groups, realizing that the legislature is the focus of legal control of education, exert considerable influence on individual legislators. Some of the representative influential groups, as illustrated in Figure 8.2, include state teachers' as-

FIGURE 8.2 *Legislative decision making.*

sociations; state associations of school administrators; state school board associations; labor, business, professional, veterans, agricultural organizations; civil rights groups; horticultural and humane societies; taxpayers' federations; religious groups; and groups representing the handicapped.

In general, organized special interest groups, that is, formal associations and coalitions of groups, are more effective than individuals in lobbying; nevertheless, individuals can have an impact on legislation through aggressive and persistent political lobbying. Individuals can also be the catalyst in the formation of coalitions, or they can, if they are so inclined and have the time and energy, form their own special group.

It is not uncommon for over a thousand educational bills to be introduced each year in a state legislative session. Many of these bills originate with special interest groups. Throughout the nation in the past few years, state legislatures have dealt with educational proposals on a wide range of topics. These include accountability of the school, state aid, textbooks, adult basic education, negotiations, strikes, merit pay, consumer education, lotteries, education for the gifted, legal holidays, aid to parochial schools, certification of teachers, teacher tenure regulations, scholarships, sex education, fire drills, and civil and criminal liability. Many important decisions affecting education are hammered out in the political arenas of state legislatures.

Local Boards of Education

[31]
[38]
Local school boards are governmental units of the state, created by the state and responsible to it for educating pupils within specified local school districts. They have only those powers granted or implied by statute that are necessary to carry out their responsibilities. Powers usually granted to local school boards or implied include the power to:

- obtain revenue,
- maintain schools,
- purchase sites and build buildings,
- purchase materials and supplies,
- organize and provide programs of studies,
- employ necessary workers and regulate their services,
- admit and assign pupils to schools and to control their conduct.

[31]
[38]
The legal structure just outlined, under which American education functions, underlies the federal-state-local interrelations. The local operation of schools under the law must abide by the constitutional and statutory provisions of the state and at the same time assure the rights of individuals as stated in the Constitution of the United States. Conflicts arise when state constitutional and statutory provisions for education are not in accord with the U.S. Constitution, or when individuals feel that

their rights as citizens are being infringed on or are not being fully granted. From these conflicts, court cases arise; the decisions resulting from the cases produce a body of case law that further interprets constitutions and statutes. Numerous conflicts and the resultant cases have centered around the separation of church and state.

The First Amendment—Church and State

Traditionally, the United States has strongly supported separation of church and state. This basic principle, expressed in the First Amendment, was designed by our forefathers to assure each citizen freedom to practice the religion of his or her choice. Education, a governmental function necessary if an effective democracy is to survive, must be carried on so as to preserve this basic right of religious freedom. [32]

Our nation also has a strong religious heritage. In colonial times, education was primarily a religious matter; furthermore, much of this education was conducted in private religious schools. Many private schools today are still under religious sponsorship, and many students receive their education in private religiously sponsored schools. It has been estimated that approximately 11 percent of the total school population is now enrolled in nonpublic parochial and secular schools.[1]

Court cases concerned with separation of church and state most frequently involve both the First and Fourteenth Amendments of the U.S. Constitution. The First Amendment is applicable to the states by the Fourteenth Amendment. For example, a state law requiring a daily prayer to be read in classrooms throughout the state could be interpreted as establishing a religion, or at least "prohibiting the free exercise thereof." Such a law would violate the Fourteenth Amendment, since states are not permitted to make laws that abridge the privileges of citizens of the United States. The First Amendment assures the privilege of free practice of religion. [32]

Court cases related to the separation of church and state can be classified in three categories: those dealing with the use of public funds to support religious education; those dealing with the practice of religion in public schools; and those dealing with the rights of parents to provide private education for their children. In the late 1960s, 1970s, and early 1980s, renewed attention was given to the use of public funds for parochial education.

Public Funds and Parochial Education

The use of public funds to support parochial schools has been questioned on many occasions. Typically, state constitutions deny public funds to sectarian institutions or schools. However, public funds have been used to provide transportation for students to church schools and to provide textbooks for students in parochial schools. The use of funds for these [32] purposes has been challenged in many instances. See Table 8.1 for a summary of some important U.S. Supreme Court cases in this area.

The landmark case on the use of public funds to provide transportation for students to church schools was *Everson* v. *Board of Education,* ruled upon by the U.S. Supreme Court in 1947. The Court held that in using tax-raised funds to reimburse parents for bus fares expended to transport their children to church schools, a New Jersey school district did not violate the establishment clause of the First Amendment. The majority of the members of the Court viewed the New Jersey statute permitting free bus transportation to parochial school children as "public welfare legislation" to help get the children to and from school safely and expeditiously. Since the *Everson* decision, the highest courts in a number of states, under provisions in their own constitutions, have struck down enactments authorizing public funds to bus children attending denominational schools; others have upheld such enactments.

In 1975 the U.S. Supreme Court affirmed a federal district court decision in Missouri *(Luetkemeyer* v. *Kaufman)* that although a state may provide free transportation to parochial school students *(Everson* v. *Board of Education),* principles of equal protection do not require a state to do so merely because such services are provided to public school pupils.[2] It is apparent from the court decisions and legislation in the various states

TABLE 8.1   *Selected U.S. Supreme Court Cases Related to the Use of Public Funds for Private Education**

Case	Decision
Everson v. *Board of Education* (1947)	Use of tax-raised funds to reimburse parents for transportation of students to church schools did not violate the First Amendment.
Board of Education of Central School District No. 1, Towns of Greenbush, et al. v. *Allen* (1968)	Loan of public school textbooks to children in private schools did not alone demonstrate an unconstitutional degree of support for a religious institution.
Lemon v. *Kurtzman* (1971)	Pennsylvania legislation to provide direct aid for secular services including teacher salaries, textbooks, and instructional materials was ruled unconstitutional because of excessive entanglement between government and religion.
Wolman v. *Walter* (1977)	Court ruled that providing nonpublic school pupils with books, standardized testing and scoring, diagnostic services, and therapeutic and remedial services was constitutional. Provision of instructional materials and field trip services was ruled unconstitutional.
Mueller v. *Allen* (1983)	Court ruled that a Minnesota law that provided income tax deductions for parents of children in public and nonpublic schools for costs incurred up to a maximum amount for tuition, textbooks, and transportation was constitutional.

*This summary table cannot and is not intended to provide an adequate or complete understanding of the U.S. Supreme Court decisions. It is necessary to read the textual narrative for a more complete understanding.

that distinctly different opinions exist regarding the proper and valid use of public funds for private school transportation.

A similar question exists concerning the use of public funds to provide textbooks for private schools. The landmark case originated in Louisiana, where a statute provided for textbooks to be supplied to nonpublic schoolchildren free of charge. The statute had been upheld by a state court on the theory that the children, and not the nonpublic schools, were the beneficiaries.

In *Cochran* v. *Louisiana State Board of Education* (1930) the U.S. Supreme Court held the Louisiana textbook statute valid under the Fourteenth Amendment. The Court discounted the taxpayers' contention that tax-raised funds for furnishing textbooks to private school pupils constituted a tax for a private rather than a public purpose and a deprivation of taxpayers' money without due process of law. This decision did not rest on the First Amendment, having been rendered before the Supreme Court ruled that under the Fourteenth Amendment the First Amendment applies to the states.

In the later case (*Board of Education of Central School District No. 1, Towns of Greenbush et al.* v. *Allen, 1966*) the U.S. Supreme Court, on appeal (1968), upheld the constitutionality of a New York textbook statute. The New York law required boards of education, on individual request, to lend textbooks free to children in grades 7 through 12 in private schools if these schools complied with the state compulsory attendance law. The majority opinion of the Court held:

> The express purpose of Sec. 701 was stated by the New York Legislature to be furtherance of the educational opportunities available to the young. Appellants have shown us nothing about the necessary effects of the statute that is contrary to its stated purpose. The law merely makes available to all children the benefits of a general program to lend school books free of charge. Books are furnished at the request of the pupil and ownership remains, at least technically, in the State. Thus no funds or books are furnished to parochial schools, and the financial benefit is to parents and children, not to schools. Perhaps free books make it more likely that some children choose to attend a sectarian school, but that was true of the state-paid bus fares in *Everson* and does not alone demonstrate an unconstitutional degree of support for a religious institution.

"In 1974, the Missouri Supreme Court held that it was a violation of the state constitution for the state to loan textbooks free of charge to parochial school students. The U.S. Supreme Court denied review of the case, thereby preserving the state court decision, 'Thus, although a state *may* lend textbooks to parochial school students, the Court declined to *compel* a state to do so if it is supplying free books to public school pupils.' "[3]

The Supreme Court, in its decision in the *Everson* case and again in the *Allen* case, made it clear that providing transportation or textbooks per se does not violate the First Amendment.

Recently, over twenty states considered legislation providing for various forms of direct aid to nonpublic schools. In 1968, Pennsylvania enacted legislation to supply aid for the purchase of secular education services; these services were defined as consisting of courses in mathematics, modern foreign languages, physical science, and physical education. The aid embodied reimbursement for teachers' salaries, textbooks, and instructional materials. Provisions were made in the law for approval of textbooks and teachers by the superintendent of public instruction. Payments were to be made directly to the school, and school accounts were subject to audit.

In 1969, Rhode Island enacted legislation providing for salary supplements to eligible teachers in nonpublic schools. A teacher requesting supplementary salary had to satisfy certain eligibility requirements: certification, teaching only those subjects taught in public schools, and using only materials used in public schools.

Both the Pennsylvania and the Rhode Island laws were challenged, and the cases were eventually heard by the U.S. Supreme Court. The Court ruled in both the Pennsylvania case (*Lemon* v. *Kurtzman,* 1971) and the Rhode Island case (*DiCenso* v. *Robinson,* 1971) that the respective laws were unconstitutional. It envisioned excessive entanglement between government and religion in accomplishing the necessary state supervision to ensure that the state aid would support only secular education. The Court pointed out another defect of the Pennsylvania statute—it provided for the aid to be given directly to the school. In the *Everson* and *Allen* cases the aid was provided either to the student or to the student's parents, not to the church-related school.

After the Pennsylvania and the Rhode Island cases the U.S. Supreme Court in 1972 struck down an Ohio plan for direct tuition payments to parents of children in private schools. In 1973 the Court also ruled against a Pennsylvania tuition payment proposal, a New York tax credit plan, and a New York state financing plan for record keeping and testing in parochial schools.

In 1975, in *Meek* v. *Pittenger,* the Supreme Court again struck down an effort by Pennsylvania to aid its numerous parochial schools. Pennsylvania had proposed three separate aid programs: (1) providing auxiliary services like counseling, psychological services, and speech and hearing therapy by public school employees to nonpublic school pupils; (2) directly lending instructional materials and equipment to nonpublic schools; and (3) lending textbooks without charge to nonpublic school pupils. The law was drafted by the Pennsylvania legislature to avoid the pitfalls of *Lemon* v. *Kurtzman.* The Court upheld the textbook provision, basing its opinion on the *Allen* case, but struck down the provision for auxiliary services on the basis of "excessive entanglement" and the provision for instructional materials, since the materials and equipment would become subsumed in the "religious mission" of the schools.

Most recently, the U.S. Supreme Court in *Wolman* v. *Walter* (1977), a case originating in Ohio, affirmed that providing nonpublic school pupils with books, standardized testing and scoring, diagnostic services, and therapeutic and remedial services is constitutional. The proposals for instructional materials and field trip services were ruled unconstitutional.

The Court cited *Allen* and *Meek* in approving the textbook provision. Numerous cases were cited for standardized testing and scoring, diagnostic services, and therapeutic and remedial services. The Ohio law proposed "to supply for use by pupils attending nonpublic schools within the district such standardized tests and scoring services as are in use in the public schools of the state." The Court noted that (1) the tests are used to measure the progress of students in secular subjects; (2) nonpublic school personnel are not involved in either the drafting or the scoring of the tests; and (3) the statute does not authorize any payment to nonpublic school personnel for costs of administering the tests. On diagnostic services, the Court noted that (1) speech, hearing, and psychological services are to be provided within the nonpublic school; (2) personnel who perform the services (except for physicians) are employees of the local school system; (3) physicians may be hired on a contract basis; (4) the purpose of the services is to determine the pupils' deficiency or need for assistance; and (5) treatment of any defect would take place off the nonpublic school premises. The Court concluded that providing diagnostic services on nonpublic school premises would not create an impermissible risk of fostering ideological views. It foresaw no need for excessive surveillance and therefore no impermissible entanglement.

In considering therapeutic services and remedial reading, the Court noted that the Ohio proposal, in contrast to *Meek,* called for the services to be rendered in public schools, public centers, or mobile units located off nonpublic school premises. It concluded: "It can hardly be said that the supervision of public employees performing public functions on public property creates an excessive entanglement between church and state."

In reversing the Ohio district court on instructional materials the U.S. Supreme Court referred to *Meek*. Although the Ohio proposal differed from *Meek* in that it purported to provide the materials to the pupils rather than to the school, the Court reasoned: "In the view of the impossibility of separating the secular education function from the sectarian, the state aid inevitably flows, in part, in support of the religious role of the schools." Important points made by the Court in reversing the district court in the provision on field trips were (1) "Nonpublic schools control the timing of the trips, their frequency, and destination, therefore the schools rather than the children are the recipients of the service"; (2) "The field trips are an integral part of the educational experience, and where the teacher works within and for a sectarian institution, an unacceptable risk of fostering religion is an inevitable byproduct." In concluding, the Court said, "Moreover, the public school authorities will be unable adequately to insure secular use of the field trip funds without close supervision of the nonpublic teachers. This wouldcreate excessive entanglement."

In 1980 the U.S. Supreme Court, by a five-to-four vote, finally settled a ten-year dispute over a New York law that provided for reimbursement to private and parochial schools for record keeping and testing, both required by state law. The Court envisioned no excessive entanglement and voted that testing and record keeping have neither a religious purpose nor a religious effect, nor do they violate the intent of the First Amendment.

Tuition Tax Credits

Tuition tax credits have been the subject of much debate in Congress in recent years. Opponents of legislation for tuition tax credit argue that such credits represent a clear attempt to provide unconstitutional aid to parochial schools. Former President Carter held this view. In addition, opponents argue that tuition tax credit will slow progress toward desegregation (as more white persons will have easier access to private education), provide an indirect subsidy to private schools, and perhaps increase racial discrimination. Those favoring tuition tax credit legislation argue that such credit is only fair and need not involve entanglement of government with religion, advance religious causes, or disturb the First Amendment barrier between church and state. They further point out that tuition tax credit will strengthen both public and private education through competition. In addition, they predict that tuition tax credit will increase the private school enrollments of Blacks and Hispanics more than that of whites, that racial

The issue of the separation of church and state in relation to schools may never be fully resolved.

discrimination will be prohibited, and that a shift of students to lower-cost private schools can save billions of dollars for society as a whole. The Reagan administration has pledged its support for a tuition tax credit program; but as this book went to press, no legislation had been approved by Congress.

Just before it adjourned for the summer in 1983, the U.S. Supreme Court gave proponents of tuition tax deductions hope by upholding a Minnesota statute, *Mueller* v. *Allen* (1983). Unlike legislation from Pennsylvania and New York, which had been applied only to nonpublic schools, the Minnesota law covered deductions also to parents of children in public schools. Parents could deduct up to $500 per child in elementary school and $700 per child in secondary school for costs incurred for tuition, textbooks, and transportation. The Court ruled five to four that the statute was constitutional.

Justice Rehnquist's majority opinion found no conflict with the *Lemon* test. The statute had a secular legislative purpose in that parents were assisted in helping defray the costs of educating their children. The statute's effect neither advanced nor inhibited religion because the service was available to parents of children in both public and nonpublic schools. Rehnquist saw the statute as being one of many in the state that aids in some way religious interests. The statute did not foster excessive entanglement of church and state because the only involvement of the state was in screening texts to determine whether they qualified for a deduction.

Because of the narrowness of the decision, as well as the decision itself, this case will be studied very closely by legislators for its possible bearing on proposed statutes.

The issue of public aid to church-related schools is still in the process of being settled. While it is clear that aid for certain secular services (such as transportation, textbooks, and—under prescribed circumstances—testing, diagnostic, therapeutic, and remedial services) can be provided, it is [33] not yet absolutely clear what further aid will be approved. It is apparent that state legislatures are trying to find ways to provide aid to parochial schools without violating the First Amendment. It is quite probable that other laws will be developed on the basis of findings in the *Lemon* v. *Kurtzman, DiCenso* v. *Robinson, Meek* v. *Pittenger,* and *Wolman* v. *Walter* cases. It is also probable that the laws developed will be challenged and that further rulings from the courts will be forthcoming.

Child Benefit Theory

The decisions supporting use of public funds for transportation and textbooks for students in private schools have generally been based on the "child benefit theory"; the Supreme Court reasoned that transportation and books provide benefit to the children and not to the school or to a religion. Those opposed to the child benefit theory argue that aid to chil- [32]

dren receiving sectarian education instruction is effectively aiding the institution providing instruction.

The child benefit theory, as supported by the U.S. Supreme Court, has penetrated federal legislation. The Elementary and Secondary Education Act of 1965 (ESEA) and its subsequent amendments provide for assistance to both public and nonpublic school children. Title I of ESEA, which dealt with assistance for the education of children from low-income families, stated that children from families attending private schools must be provided services in proportion to their numbers.

Religion in the Public Schools

Another issue related to separation of church and state centers around religious activities in public schools. See Table 8.2 for a summary of some important U.S. Supreme Court cases in this area.

Providing "released time" for religious instruction in public schools has been challenged and acted on by the U.S. Supreme Court. In 1948 the Court held that the released-time program of the Champaign, Illinois, schools violated the principle of separation of church and state (*People of*

TABLE 8.2 *Selected U.S. Supreme Court Cases Related to the Practice of Religion in Public Schools and the Right to a Private Education* *

Case	Decision
People of the State of Illinois ex rel. McCollum v. Board of Education of School District No. 71, Champaign, Illinois (1948)	Court held that the released-time program of the Champaign schools that released pupils from their regular classes to attend religious classes in public school classrooms violated the principle of separation of church and state.
Zorach v. *Clauson* (1952)	Court upheld a New York law that provided released time to go to *religious centers* to receive religious instruction. The Champaign program used public school classrooms.
Engle v. *Vitale* (1962)	Court held that a prayer composed by the New York State Board of Regents and used as a part of the opening exercise of school violated the First Amendment.
Schempp v. *School District of Abington Township* (1963) and *Murray* v. *Curlett* (1963)	Court decision rendered on the appeals of these two lower court decisions held that reading the Bible and reciting the Lord's prayer in public schools are religious ceremonies and violate the First and Fourteenth Amendments.
Pierce v. *Society of Sisters* (1925)	An Oregon law requiring all children to attend public schools was unconstitutional in that it infringed upon the rights of parents to control their children. The Court also established that the state can regulate all schools public and private.

*This summary table cannot and is not intended to provide an adequate or complete understanding of the U.S. Supreme Court decisions. It is necessary to read the textual narrative for a more complete understanding.

the State of Illinois ex rel. McCollum v. *Board of Education of School District No. 71, Champaign, Illinois,* 1948). The program in Champaign was a cooperative program among the schools and a voluntary association of members of Jewish, Roman Catholic, and Protestant faiths. Classes were held in the public school classrooms. Pupils were released from their regular classes to attend religious classes; those who did not elect to take religious instruction were not excused from regular class duties. In its decision the Court pointed out that not only were tax-supported public school buildings being used for sectarian instruction, but also the compulsory education law was aiding religious instruction by providing pupils with released time during the school day to study religion.

A released-time program in New York was challenged a few years after the *McCollum* case; in *Zorach* v. *Clauson* (1952) the Supreme Court upheld a New York statute that provided for released time. The chief difference between the Champaign and New York cases is that in New York students were released from school to go to religious centers to receive religious instruction, whereas in Champaign the instruction was given in public school classrooms. The Court indicated that the precise type of released-time program is significant; programs differ in the extent of school cooperation and in the degree of sectarianism. It can be concluded that the concept of released time in and of itself does not necessarily violate the First Amendment.

The courts have also rendered opinions on Bible and prayer reading in the public schools. In 1962 the U.S. Supreme Court *(Engle* v. *Vitale)* [32] held that a prayer composed by the New York State Board of Regents and used as part of the opening exercises of school violated the United States Constitution. The prayer read as follows: "Almighty God, we acknowledge our dependence upon Thee, and we beg Thy blessings on us, our parents, our teachers, and our country." Pupils who objected to the prayer could be excused. The Court based its decision on the establishment clause of the First Amendment: "Congress shall make no law respecting an establishment of religion, or prohibiting the free exercise thereof." Justice Hugo Black, who wrote the decision, stated:

> The constitutional prohibition against laws respecting an establishment of religion must at least mean that . . . it is no part of the business of government to impose official prayers for any group of American people to recite as a part of a religious program carried on by the government.

In June 1963 the U.S. Supreme Court rendered a very significant decision in which it outlawed reading the Bible and reciting the Lord's Prayer in public schools. The Court indicated that these are religious ceremonies and, as such, violate the First and Fourteenth Amendments of the Constitution. The opinion emphasized that government must remain neutral in matters of religion. The Supreme Court decision resulted from appeals on two lower court decisions, one from Pennsylvania (*Schempp* v. *School*

District of Abington Township, 1963) and the other from Maryland (*Murray* v. *Curlett,* 1963), which held that reading the Bible and saying the Lord's Prayer were not illegal.

A Massachusetts school prayer law that went into effect in February 1980 was ruled unconstitutional by the Massachusetts State Supreme Court in March 1980. The law required a period of voluntary prayer each day. Each morning, teachers were to announce that prayers could be offered by students. Silent meditation was also permitted. Students not wanting to take part could wait outside their classrooms. The constitutionality of the law was challenged by the Civil Liberties Union of Massachusetts.

The rulings of the U.S. Supreme Court that forbade obligatory prayer and Bible reading have prompted attempts to amend the Constitution to permit voluntary prayer. The late Senator Everett Dirksen (R., Ill.) tried unsuccessfully in 1966 and 1967 to secure congressional approval of a prayer amendment. In 1971, Representative Chalmers P. Wylie (R., Ohio) also introduced a prayer amendment that was subsequently defeated. Since then, there have been numerous attempts to legalize prayer and Bible reading in public schools, with a strong endorsement by President Reagan.

In July 1984, President Reagan signed legislation permitting religious meetings in public schools, with some controls.

In a recent article that essentially analyzes the opinions of the U.S. Supreme Court in *Schempp* v. *School District of Abington Township* (1963), it is noted that public schools have not delineated a clear role for religion in public education that is consistent with the *Schempp* decision.[4] The author of the aforementioned article makes the following recommendations:

> The public must insist that the public schools address the religious dimension of human existence, and public educators must come to grips with the issues of curriculum, instructional materials, and methods that would support appropriate study about religion at the elementary and secondary levels. The *Schempp* decision provided a context for public education to deal with religion, but public school educators have not fully used it. Study about religion is both an opportunity and, the *Schempp* decision would suggest, a responsibility that public school educators have for too long failed to assume.[5]

Private Education: An Alternative

The court cases having to do with the right of parents to provide private education for their children are closely related to cases about compulsory education. Compulsory attendance laws appear in the statute books of all states except Mississippi. They generally require parents, or whoever has custody of a child between specific chronological ages, to cause the child to attend school. The constitutional objection raised regarding compulsory attendance laws is that they infringe on the individual liberty guaranteed by the Fourteenth Amendment. The constitutionality of compulsory education laws has been attacked in numerous cases, but the principle has been uniformly upheld. Courts have generally reasoned that education is so necessary to the welfare of our nation that compulsory school attendance laws are valid and desirable. Compulsory education does not mean compulsory public education, however.

Whether a state can compel children to attend a public school was settled in a case in Oregon (see Table 8.2 for a summary). In 1922 the legislature of Oregon passed a law requiring all children to attend public schools. The U.S. Supreme Court ruled that such a law was unconstitutional in that it infringed on the rights of parents to control the education of their children (*Pierce* v. *Society of Sisters,* 1925). This ruling established a precedent, permitting parents to have their children educated in private schools. In this same case the Court also established beyond doubt that the state may reasonably regulate all schools, public and private, and require certain subjects to be taught. It was established that private schools have a right to exist, that pupils may meet the compulsory attendance laws by attending private schools, and that private schools are subject to state regulation.

A recent case, *Kentucky State Board for Elementary and Secondary Education* v. *Rudasill* (1979), dealt with the right of the state to regulate private schools. The Kentucky State Supreme Court ruled that Kentucky cannot force private schools to meet its accreditation standards, particularly with respect to teachers, textbooks, curriculum, and attendance. Kentucky asked the U.S. Supreme Court to overturn the ruling of the State Supreme Court, but the Court did not accept the appeal.

Home Instruction

The courts have also ruled that education in a child's home can meet the requirement of compulsory education. In a case in Indiana (*State* v. *Peterman,* 1904) the court specified that a school is a place where education is imparted to the young; therefore a home can be a school if a qualified teacher is engaged in instruction as prescribed by the state. The state controls home instruction, and the instruction generally must be equivalent to what a school provides. Home instruction must be carried out in good faith and not practiced as a subterfuge to avoid sending children to school. In a court case in New Jersey (*Stephens* v. *Bongart,* 1937) regarding equivalent home instruction the opinion was rendered that the home instruction in this instance was not equivalent to the public school instruction. Most compulsory education laws provide for children who are physically or mentally unable to attend school, although the application of these laws has changed since the passage of the Education for All Handicapped Children Act in 1975.

Although the courts have generally upheld compulsory education, a decision by the U.S. Supreme Court in 1972 altered the position slightly.

In *Wisconsin* v. *Yoder* the Court ruled that the Amish religious sect is exempt from state compulsory education laws that require children to attend school beyond the eighth grade. This decision of the Court was its first in holding a religious group immune from compulsory attendance requirements. The Court held that state laws requiring children to attend school until they are sixteen years of age violate the rights of the Amish to free exercise of religion. The Court stressed the 300-year resistance of the Amish to modern influences. Justice Burger wrote:

> It cannot be overemphasized that we are not dealing with a way of life and a mode of education by a group claiming to have recently discovered some "progressive" or more enlightened process for rearing children for modern life.

In the last few years there has been a decided increase in parental requests to provide instruction in their homes for their children. Cases have been reported originating in Minnesota, Massachusetts, Maine, Virginia, Iowa, Illinois, and Washington, D.C. Many of the cases represent discontent with the public schools, mentioning that public schools are full of "drugs, sex, and Godlessness"; others claim that public schools are ineffective in dealing with gifted or handicapped children. The rulings of the state courts are individualized to each case, the guideline being whether or not the home instruction is equivalent to the instruction provided in a public school. *Yoder* is the most recent ruling of the U.S. Supreme Court relevant to home instruction.

The interpretation of compulsory education laws indicates that a reasonable balance is sought between the rights of the individual and the rights of the state. Parents who want a religious education for their children may meet the requirement of compulsory education by enrolling their children in private or parochial schools or in approved home instruction programs. At the same time the state reserves the right to reasonably regulate private education.

The Fourteenth Amendment and Desegregation

The Constitution guarantees specific rights to all citizens, and the various state constitutions provide for free educational opportunities. Under our form of government, each citizen ideally is afforded an equal opportunity to pursue education. This opportunity, or right, is not and cannot be provided, however, without commensurate citizen responsibility. The success of our decentralized educational systems with their strong local emphasis depends heavily on local support, participation, and cooperation; local citizens are responsible for assuring education of high quality. As citizens of their states and of the United States, they are responsible for providing equal opportunities for education to all children in the nation.

Local boards of education, under powers granted to them by the states, [31] may assign students to a particular grade, or classification, and to a particular school or attendance center within the school district under their jurisdiction. Courts have held that boards of education who are acting in [38] good faith must have the discretionary power of assigning pupils to maintain the orderly administration of the school system. Boards of education are expected to use this power by acting in good faith. They are responsible for ensuring, to the best of their ability, that each pupil in his or her assignment has an equal opportunity to pursue education.

Closely allied to the power of boards of education to assign pupils to schools is the issue of segregated schools. Segregation in this context refers to separating different races and peoples of a variety of descents. In recent years attention has been centered on the American Black. See Table 8.3 for a summary of some important U.S. Supreme Court cases related to desegregation.

In 1896 *(Plessy* v. *Ferguson)* the Supreme Court upheld a Louisiana law that required railway companies to provide separate but equal accommodations for the white and black races. The Court indicated in its opinion that the Fourteenth Amendment implied political, not social, equality.

TABLE 8.3   *Selected U.S. Supreme Court Cases Related to Desegregation**

Case	Decision
Brown v. *Board of Education of Topeka* (1954)	Court ruled that separate but equal education is a violation of the Fourteenth Amendment.
Swann v. *Charlotte-Mecklenburg Board of Education* (1971)	The Court ruled that "the Constitutional command to desegregate schools does not mean that every school in every community must always reflect the racial composition of the school system as a whole." It urged, however, that every effort should be made to achieve desegregation.
Milliken v. *Bradley* (1974)	A federal district judge ordered schools in Detroit and its surrounding suburbs to be desegregated. The Court overturned the lower court orders requiring cross–school district busing on the basis that "it must first be shown that there has been a constitutional violation within one district that produces a significant segregative effect in another school district."
Newburg Area Council Incorporated v. *Board of Education of Jefferson County, Kentucky* (1975)	Court decided not to hear an appeal of a ruling of the U.S. Sixth Circuit Court of Appeals that had required the Louisville city school system and the Jefferson County school districts to eliminate all vestiges of state-enforced discrimination through metropolitan integration. In this case, segregation was viewed as resulting from governmental actions by the state or school districts.
Milliken v. *Bradley II* (1977)	Court ruled that "as a part of a desegregation decree, a district court can, if the record warrants, order compensatory or remedial programs for school children who have been subjected to past acts of *de jure* segregation."

*This summary table cannot and is not intended to provide an adequate or complete understanding of the U.S. Supreme Court decisions. It is necessary to read the textual narrative for a more complete understanding.

Sometimes, change must be legislated.

This separate but equal doctrine appeared to be the rule until May 17, 1954, when the Supreme Court repudiated the separate but equal doctrine (*Brown* v. *Board of Education of Topeka*). The Court said that in education the separate but equal doctrine has no place and that separate facilities are inherently unequal. In 1955 the Court rendered the second *Brown* v. *Board of Education of Topeka* decision, requiring that the principles of the first decision be carried out.

De Jure Segregation

The *Brown* decision referred explicitly to de jure segregation—that is, segregation by law or by official action. At the time of the *Brown* decision, many southern and border states required segregated schools by law. Segregated schools also result from neighborhood housing patterns. Many neighborhoods are made up predominantly of Blacks, and their neighborhood schools have a predominantly Black enrollment. This kind of segregation, legally referred to as de facto segregation, is relatively common in most large cities in the North. The U.S. Supreme Court has never ruled specifically on de facto segregation; it has ruled only on de jure segregation.

From 1954, the time of the *Brown* decision, to 1964, little progress was made in eliminating segregated schools. On May 25, 1964, the Supreme Court, referring to a situation in Prince Edward County, Virginia, said: "There has been entirely too much deliberation and not enough speed in enforcing the constitutional rights which we held in *Brown* v. *Board of Education.*" The Civil Rights Act of 1964 added legislative power to the 1954 judicial pronouncement. The Act not only authorized the federal government to initiate court suits against school districts that were laggard in desegregating schools, but also denied federal funds for programs that discriminated by race, color, or national origin.

Many segregated school systems have tried to meet federal desegregation demands by adopting a "freedom-of-choice" or "open enrollment" plan. Under such a plan, pupils are permitted to choose the public schools they want to attend. In 1968 the U.S. Supreme Court in *Green* v. *County School Board,* a case originating in Virginia, held that a freedom-of-choice plan was not unconstitutional in and of itself but that in this case, freedom of choice was not effective in desegregating. Under the freedom-of-choice plan—after three years of operation—no white child had chosen to attend the Black school, and 85 percent of the Black children still attended the Black school. Specifically, the Court said:

> In other words, the school system remains a dual system. Rather than further dismantling of the dual system, the plan has operated simply to burden children and their parents with a responsibility which *Brown II* placed squarely on the School Board. The Board must be required to formulate a new plan, and in light of other courses which appear open to the Board, such as zoning, fashion steps which promise realistically to convert promptly to a system without a "white" school and a "Negro" school, but just schools.

A further ruling of the U.S. Supreme Court on de jure segregation resulted from a case *(Swann* v. *Charlotte-Mecklenburg Board of Education)* arising in Charlotte-Mecklenburg County, North Carolina, in April 1971. A United States district judge had ordered extensive busing of pupils to achieve integration. The goal, as expressed by the judge, was to achieve a ratio of 71 whites to 29 blacks in each school to approximate the racial ratio in the entire district. In its deliberations the Court cited four main legal questions:

1. To what extent racial balance or racial quotas may be used as a tool in a remedial order to correct a previously segregated system.
2. Whether every school that is all Black or all white must be eliminated unconditionally in remedying segregation.
3. What the limits, if any, are on rearranging school districts and attendance zones as a remedial measure.
4. What the limits, if any, are on transporting pupils in correcting state-enforced racial school segregation.

The Court said in its ruling:

> The Constitutional command to desegregate schools does not mean that every school in every community must always reflect the racial composition of the school system as a whole. . . . The use made of mathematical ratios was no more than a starting point in the process of shaping a remedy, rather than an inflexible requirement.

The Court upheld "the very limited use made of mathematical ratios" to be within the equitable remedial discretion of the district court.

About one-race schools, the Court said: "In some circumstances certain schools may remain all or largely of one race until new schools can be provided or neighborhood patterns change." Further, "the existence of some small number of one-race or virtually one-race schools within a district is not in and of itself the mark of a system which still practices segregation by law." The Court cautioned, however, that "the District judge or school authorities should make every effort to achieve the greatest possible degree of actual desegregation and will thus necessarily be concerned with the elimination of one-race schools."

About limits on the rearrangement of school districts and attendance zones, the Court emphasized that no rule by itself can adequately embrace all the difficulties. But, it noted, since there has been a history of segregation, schools of disproportionate racial composition are suspect. The Court recognized majority-to-minority optional transfers with the provision of free student transportation, remedial altering of attendance zones, and "clustering" as legitimate ways of desegregating schools. The Court stated:

> The remedy for such segregation may be administratively awkward, inconvenient, and even bizarre in some situations and may impose burdens on some; but all awkwardness and inconvenience cannot be avoided in the interim period when remedial adjustments are being made to eliminate the dual school systems.

The *Charlotte* case dealt with desegregation within a single school district. In January 1972, U.S. District Court Judge Robert R. Merhige, Jr. ordered the Richmond, Virginia, schools to be consolidated with the suburban Henrico and Chesterfield County systems. Richmond schools were approximately 70 percent Black; the schools of Henrico and Chesterfield Counties were about 90 percent white. Judge Merhige concluded that the constitutional rights of quality overrode the rights of cities and counties to establish educational boundaries. He reasoned that consolidation was the most promising remedy to integrate effectively. In June 1972 the Fourth U.S. Circuit Court of Appeals reversed the order of Judge Merhige, stating that he had exceeded his authority in ordering a merger of city and county school systems to improve racial balance.

In 1973 the Richmond metropolitan desegregation case was heard by the U.S. Supreme Court. By a four-to-four tie vote, with Justice Powell disqualifying himself, the Court upheld the Fourth U.S. Circuit Court of Appeals reversal of the metropolitan plan.

Likewise, U.S. District Judge Stephen J. Roth ordered schools in Detroit and its surrounding suburbs to be desegregated. This case *(Milliken v. Bradley)* eventually reached the U.S. Supreme Court. In July 1974 the Court in a five-to-four vote overturned lower court orders requiring the cross-busing of children between the Detroit city school system and 53 suburban school districts. Chief Justice Warren Burger delivered the opinion of the Court:

> Before the boundaries of separate and autonomous school districts may be set aside . . . it must first be shown that there has been a constitutional violation within one district that produces a significant segregative effect in another district. Specifically, it must be shown that racially discriminatory acts of the state or local school districts of a single school district have been a substantial cause of inter-district segregation. . . . Without an inner-district violation and inter-district effect, there is no constitutional wrong calling for an inter-district remedy.

The dissenting justices (Douglas, White, Brennan, and Marshall) saw the decision as a "giant step backward." Justice Douglas wrote: "When we rule against the metropolitan area remedy, we take a step that will likely put the problems of the blacks and our society back to the period that antedated the 'separate but equal' regime of *Plessy* v. *Ferguson.*" Justice Marshall noted: "The rights at issue in this case are too fundamental to be abridged on grounds as superficial as those relied on by the majority today. . . . Unless our children begin to learn together, there is little hope that our people will ever learn to live together."

Since the Detroit decision, numerous cases involving metropolitan desegregation have been heard in various courts. The most significant of these originated in Wilmington, Delaware, and Louisville, Kentucky. In the fall of 1975 the U.S. Supreme Court upheld an earlier federal court order calling for the urban-suburban desegregation of the schools in the Wilmington area. The main factor in this case, which produced a ruling that differed from that of the Detroit case, was that state school reorganization involved other school districts besides the Wilmington city district in actions that caused Blacks in Wilmington itself to be segregated. Therefore, the Court reasoned, other districts should be involved in the solution of the problem.

In the Louisville case (*Newburg Area Council Incorporated* v. *Board of Education of Jefferson County, Kentucky,* 1975) the U.S. Sixth Circuit Court of Appeals in effect required the Louisville city school system and the Jefferson County school districts to eliminate "all vestiges of state-enforced discrimination" through metropolitan integration. The appeals court determined that in Louisville, interdistrict actions had had the effect of maintaining segregated schools. In the spring of 1975 the U.S. Supreme Court decided not to review the Louisville case. In July 1975 a federal district court ordered a metropolitan plan put into action; the court ordered the Louisville city and county school systems to desegregate their schools jointly by transporting students across the lines dividing the districts. Approximately one sixth of the district's 121,000 students needed to be bused to achieve a Black enrollment of 12–40 percent in every school. Although Louisville suffered considerable turmoil in desegregating the metropolitan schools, the task was accomplished.[6] The segregation in both Wilmington and Louisville was viewed by the courts as *resulting from governmental actions* either by the state or by multiple school districts.

In June 1977 the U.S. Supreme Court, in a segregation case related to the Dayton, Ohio, public schools *(Dayton Board of Education* v. *Brinkman),* ruled that the evidence presented by the district court did not justify a systemwide remedy. A plan developed by a district court and approved by the U.S. Court of Appeals for the Sixth District as a systemwide remedy required

> beginning with the 1976–77 school year, that the racial composition of each school in the district be brought within 15 percent of Dayton's 48 percent–52 percent black-white population ratio, to be accomplished by a variety of desegregation techniques, including the "pairing" of schools, the redefinition of attendance zones, and a variety of centralized special programs and "magnet schools."

The U.S. Supreme Court, in remanding the case to the district court, pointed out that

> the finding that the pupil population in the various Dayton schools is not homogeneous, standing by itself, is not a violation of the Fourteenth Amendment absent a showing that this condition resulted from intentionally segregative actions on the part of the Board. . . . It was thus not demonstrated that the systemwide remedy, in effect imposed by the Court of Appeals, was necessary to "eliminate all vestiges of the state-imposed school segregation."

In a second significant decision, also made in June 1977 *(Milliken* v. *Bradley II),* the U.S. Supreme Court held:

> As part of a desegregation decree, a district court can, if the record warrants, order compensatory or remedial educational programs for school children who have been subjected to past acts of *de jure* segregation. Here the District Court, acting on substantial evidence in the record, did not abuse its discretion in approving a remedial plan going beyond pupil assignments and adopting specific programs that had been proposed by local school authorities.

The remedial programs included remedial reading, an in-service program for teachers and administrators, the development of an unbiased testing program, and the provision of counseling and career guidance programs for students. The costs of these programs were to be borne by the

Detroit School Board and the state. *Milliken* v. *Bradley II* (1977) was the first time the U.S. Supreme Court had directly determined whether or not federal courts could order remedial education programs as a part of a school desegregation decree.

Private Education—Fundamentalist Schools

Total enrollment in both church-related and secular schools declined approximately 28 percent between 1965 and 1975.[7] Much of this decline was due to a decrease in the number of Roman Catholic schools. Roman Catholic enrollment reached a peak of 5,600,519 in the 1964–65 academic year; it had declined to 3,289,000 in the 1977–78 school year.[8] During this period, non-Catholic nonpublic school enrollment was increasing from 615,548 in 1965 to 1,433,000 in 1975, or 134.4 percent.[9] Fundamentalist schools, defined as those belonging to the National Association of Christian Schools, the American Association of Christian Schools, the Association of Christian Schools International, and Christian Schools International, had enrollment increases from 159,916 in 1971 to 346,679 in 1977, or 118 percent.[10] In 1980, fundamentalist schools had enrollments that were 95 percent white;[11] private education in its totality was 90 percent white.[12] It is interesting to note that in the decade of the 1970s, public school enrollments declined by 10.7 percent while private school enrollments declined by only 6.4 percent.

In a recent research report the reasons given by parents for withdrawing their children from public schools were poor academic quality, perceived lack of discipline, and the fact that public schools were believed to be promulgating secular humanism, which these parents found inimical to their religious beliefs.[13] The report also stated that

> the motivation for founding and maintaining nonpublic schools appears to be more than racial prejudice. In recent decades religious influences in American public education have eroded rapidly. Many evangelical Protestants have come to believe that the public schools now espouse a philosophy that is completely secular, perhaps even antireligious.[14]

The segregation of the schools might reflect the membership of the churches. "Fundamentalist schools deny that they discriminate on the basis of race, they admit that they discriminate on the basis of religion, and feel they have a constitutional right to do so."[15]

A recent report on a study by James S. Coleman cited a finding that private high schools are, on the whole, better than public schools.[16] Furthermore, private schools provide a safer, more disciplined, and more ordered environment than public schools.[17] Most significantly, and in contrast to the 1966 Coleman report, it was reported that schools do make a different in pupil achievement.[18] Perhaps the most controversial of Cole-

33 man's conclusions are: first, that a tuition tax credit or voucher would increase the private school enrollment of Blacks and Hispanics more than that of whites and, second, that Catholic schools today more nearly approximate the common school ideal of American education than do public schools, in that the achievement levels of students from different parental educational backgrounds, of Black and white students, and of Hispanic and non-Hispanic white students, are more clearly alike in Catholic schools than in public schools.[19]

In 1983 the Supreme Court issued a ruling counter to the policy of the Reagan administration. The Court upheld a policy of the Internal Revenue Service (IRS) that denies tax-exempt status to schools that have racially discriminatory practices. The institutions that challenged this policy were a college and a private elementary and secondary school. They claimed that their policies were derived from their religious beliefs. The college admits Blacks but does not permit interracial dating and marriage. The lower school does not admit Blacks.

In upholding the IRS the Court indicated that since the *Brown* decision of 1954, racial discrimination in public education has been inconsistent with public policy. In order for an agency to qualify for the IRS exemption, the agency must serve a public purpose and must not act contrary to public policy. The two schools met the first criterion but did not meet the second one (*Goldsboro Christian Schools and Bob Jones University* v. *U.S.*, 1983).

Busing

Busing is an extremely controversial issue. Many school districts have been ordered to bus school children to end segregation, including those of Boston, Seattle, Tulsa, Oklahoma City, Louisville, Austin, Dallas, Dayton, San Francisco, Los Angeles, Pontiac, and Indianapolis. Proponents view busing as a necessary way, and sometimes the only way, to give children of all races a chance for equality of opportunity in education. They further argue that an integrated society is essential and that if people are going to live in an integrated society, preparation must begin in school. In a book by Gary Orfield,[20] it was stated that although busing is not a natural solution to segregation, it quite simply is the only solution available if there is to be substantial integration in this generation. Myths about busing must be dispelled before public support for it will occur. Orfield's research indicates that (1) busing does not adversely affect the education of white children, (2) it does not increase violence in the schools, and (3) it does not destroy the neighborhood school. It is the way in which desegregation is carried out, he says, not the act in itself that makes the difference. He notes that neighborhoods are almost as segregated as they were 30 years ago and that school integration may have to precede neighborhood integration. A positive commitment by the nation's political leaders is needed, he says, before progress can be made.[21] Opponents of busing claim that it does not improve the quality of education and that busing requires large expenditures that ought to go toward compensatory education. As indicated in the discussion of *Milliken II* (1977), the U.S. Supreme Court has recognized both compensatory education and pupil assignment (which may involve busing) programs as legitimate remedies for past acts of de jure segregation.

The *Charlotte* (1971) case, which approved busing as a segregation remedy, has been the basis for subsequent busing decisions. The Louisville and Wilmington busing orders involved metropolitan desegregation and were based on the determination that a pattern of interdistrict action had effectively maintained segregated schools.

In *Dayton I* it was held by the Court that segregation in the Dayton schools in itself was not enough evidence for a total systemwide remedy. After this decision and at the order of the Court, the district court held hearings to determine whether or not there was any evidence that the Dayton Board of Education had taken any action "which was intended to, and did in fact, discriminate against minority pupils, teachers, or staff." In the hearings the district court found that the Dayton Public Schools had "an inexcusable history of mistreatment of black students." Nevertheless, the court found that even though the Dayton schools were highly segregated, the board was not under any obligation to alleviate the condition. The case was dismissed by the district court. The district court was then reversed by the U.S. Court of Appeals. The U.S. Court of Appeals concluded that a systemwide desegregation plan was warranted. In July 1979 *(Dayton II)* the U.S. Supreme Court in a five-to-four vote upheld the systemwide desegregation plan endorsed by the U.S. Court of Appeals. In 1979 the U.S. Supreme Court also upheld an extensive busing plan for Cleveland; only three justices (Burger, Powell, and Rehnquist) voted to hear the appeal. Four votes are needed to bring about a high court review. Also in 1979, busing plans were upheld for Columbus, Ohio. In January 1980 a divided court decided not to review the Dallas desegregation plan, which utilized magnet schools. In May 1980 the U.S. Supreme Court, unable to secure the four votes necessary to review, decided not to review the Wilmington desegregation plan.

More recently, the Supreme Court of the United States delivered an opinion on busing involving the public schools of Los Angeles (*Crawford* v. *Board of City of Los Angeles,* 1982). It upheld a referendum of the city that amended the state constitution to prohibit state courts from ordering mandatory pupil busing unless a federal court did so to remedy a federal constitutional violation. Earlier, the school board had been ordered by a state court to implement a plan that included substantial busing, an order consistent with an earlier state supreme court decision that had interpreted the state constitution as requiring correction of de facto as well as de jure segregation. In its decision the U.S. Supreme Court noted that nearly 69 percent of the electorate had voted for the amendment.

31
38

The same day the Supreme Court handed down a second ruling involving busing; this time it invalidated a referendum of the city of Seattle. That law had provided that no school board could require a student to attend a school other than one of the two nearest his or her residence that offered a given course of study, nor could it employ any of seven methods of "indirect" student assignment, including redefining attendance zones and pairing of schools.

The Seattle school district had for several years been attempting to achieve a better racial balance. However, the court determined that the referendum had been proposed for racial purposes. Under its terms, persons who sought to eliminate de facto segregation must seek relief at the state level rather than at the local level. Yet the court recognized that it is at the local level where decisions involving pupil assignment are made (*Washington* v. *Seattle School Dist. No. 1, 1982*).

30

At the opening of school in the fall of 1983 the metropolitan area of St. Louis began a unique school desegregation plan based on voluntary, not mandatory, student transfers. Under the agreement, transfer students will make up at least 15 percent of the school populations in each outlying suburban school district within the next five years. The plan also permits suburban students to attend 21 specialized magnet schools in St. Louis. The voluntary plan was adopted to counter the threat of a court-ordered forced busing scheme that could have included dismantling all the suburban school districts and incorporating them along with the St. Louis schools into one metropolitan school district. A major obstacle to the success of the program centers around the estimated one million dollar cost of the program and whether the city, state, or federal government will pay the cost. The cost issue is still being studied by the courts.

37

The executive and legislative branches have also entered the debate. Presidents Nixon and Ford both spoke publicly against busing as a means of achieving racial balance. Two laws have recently been enacted to limit busing. One law states that federal agencies must try all alternative methods of desegregation before resorting to busing; the other prevents the Department of Health, Education, and Welfare from ordering a plan that requires assigning children to schools other than those nearest their homes. Antibusing amendments to the Constitution have also been proposed by Congress.

White Flight

The term "white flight," as commonly used, refers to the decline in the percentage of whites in the population of large cities or in the percentage of white enrollments in big-city school systems. There are undoubtedly many causes of white flight, and they are interrelated in complex ways; nevertheless, desegregation of schools is viewed by some authorities as

Busing evokes strong emotions, but it is an attempt to integrate school populations.

being one of the major causes. The fact that white enrollment in the Boston schools, for example, declined from 57 percent in 1973 to 39 percent after five years of busing for desegregation and that the Los Angeles schools reported a 30 percent drop in white enrollment from 1977 to 1978[22] offers some support to the contention that desegregation associated with busing is an important factor in white flight. James Coleman reported as a finding of his research that between-district segregation increased between 1968 and 1973, particularly in metropolitan areas, as whites moved to districts with fewer blacks.[23] Coleman also reported that within-system segregation had decreased in the South and the Southeast, with the chief reduction in small districts; in effect, the remaining segregation had a profile like the Northern pattern—that is, considerable segregation in large cities and little in small districts.[24]

However, there is also evidence and research to support the position that busing and desegregation are not major factors in white flight. Robert Green and Thomas Pettigrew reviewed the work of Coleman and other researchers. They found essentially that white flight would have gone on regardless of desegregation, as a response to factors such as changing neighborhoods and an eroding tax base.[25]

Resegregation

Robert Wegmann, after reviewing research findings, offered some tentative conclusions about white withdrawal and resegregation.[26] Resegregation generally means a situation wherein an integrated school population becomes an almost totally Black school population. Sometimes resegregation occurs within a school when the neighborhood from which the school's population is drawn changes from an integrated to a predominantly Black neighborhood. If the population of a city becomes predominantly Black, the schools in the city will become the same. Often, the growth of the Black population proceeds from the inner part of the city toward the outer fringe areas. Resegregation can also occur after a governmental desegregation order. In such instances, white students may withdraw or simply not reenter when the next term begins. Furthermore, white families may also move to another area not affected by the desegregation order. Wegmann concluded:

> Whites do not necessarily withdraw from desegregated schools. Some schools maintain a high level of integration for years, some change slowly, and some resegregate rapidly. Others may experience some white withdrawal followed by stability or even by white reentrance.
> Racially mixed schools located in areas bordering the inner city present some patterns of resegregation markedly different from school districts that have experienced districtwide desegregation. It is important not to extrapolate from the one situation to the other.
> In situations where there has been no governmental action to bring about desegregation, white withdrawal seems to be linked more than anything else to the underlying demographic consequences of increased minority population growth. This growth takes place primarily in neighborhoods located on the edge of the inner city as area after area "turns" from white to black. The schools "turn" more quickly than the area generally and play a significant role in making this process relatively rapid and apparently irreversible. Stable school integration seems to be a necessary, if not sufficient, precondition for stable neighborhood integration.
> Decisions on where to purchase a home or where to send one's children to school are made not only on the basis of the present situation but also on estimates of what is likely to happen in the future. The belief that presently integrated schools and neighborhoods will shortly resegregate is a major barrier to attracting whites to integrated settings.
> Little formal research has been done on the motivations behind white withdrawal from desegregated schooling. Concerns about quality of education, student safety, and social status differences may be among the chief causes. To the extent that this is true, it could be expected that—other things being equal—school integration would more likely be stable and successful (1) when combined with programs of educational improvement in settings where concerns about safety are adequately met and (2) when programs parents can be proud of are featured.
> School desegregation ordinarily creates situations that have the potential for both racial and class conflict. The expected degree of white withdrawal, when there is governmental intervention to desegregate schools, may vary

depending on the proportion of minority students being assigned to a given school and on the social-class gap between the minority and the white students.

Cost of white withdrawal from desegregated schools varies widely according to the setting. Moving to a nearby segregated suburb, moving outside a county school district, attending a parochial school, attending a private school, transferring to a segregated public school within the same system, or leaving the state are examples of options that may or may not be present in a given situation. Each of these options, if available, will have different costs for different families, just as families will have different abilities to meet these costs. As long as school desegregation is feared (or experienced) as painful, threatening, or undesirable, it can be expected that the number of families fleeing the desegregated school will be proportionate to these costs and the families' ability to pay these costs.

Although there is is a certain degree of racial mixing in many public schools, there may also be a notable lack of cross-racial friendship, understanding, and acceptance. Superintendents in desegregated districts tend to describe racial relationships as "calm" or characterized by few "incidents." Few claim they have attained anything like genuine community, nor is there much indication that extensive efforts are being made toward this end.

The issue of busing is far from being resolved. Further research and experience may help put it in perspective. The Supreme Court did give some assistance on this issue in 1976 when it ruled that once a school district has adopted a unitary—that is, an integrated—school system, annual readjustment of attendance zones is not required (*Pasadena City Bd. of Education* v. *Spangler,* 1976). That question was put to the court by the Pasadena public schools, which had taken action to ensure that no school in the district would have a majority of minority pupils enrolled in it. When this goal had been achieved, a number of people moved their residences so that resegregation actually occurred. This situation forced the school board to consider whether annual adjustment of attendance zones was required. The Supreme Court ruled that they were not. Citing Swann, the justices recognized that there are limits to the actions that a court may take in ordering the dismantling of a dual school system.

It remains to be seen whether this ruling will have general application to all school systems. Pasadena was not subject to the original *Brown* finding, and the Court may have adopted a less stringent policy here than in a school system that had at one time practiced de jure segregation.

37

De Facto Segregation

Although the Supreme Court in the *Charlotte* case again dealt only with de jure segregation, it did allude to de facto segregation. The Court said:

> We do not reach in this case the question whether a showing that school segregation is a consequence of other types of state action, without any dis-

criminatory action by the school authorities, is a constitutional violation requiring remedial action by a school-desegregation decree. This case does not
present that question and we therefore do not decide it.

Our objective in dealing with the issues presented by these cases is to see
that school authorities exclude no pupil of a racial minority from any school,
directly or indirectly, on account of race; it does not and cannot embrace all
the problems of racial prejudice, even when those problems contribute to
disproportionate racial concentrations in some schools.

Lower courts have dealt with and ruled on what has appeared to be
de facto segregation. It is difficult in practice to differentiate clearly between de jure and de facto segregation. Probably both types of segregation
are present in varying degrees in segregated schools. In June 1967 a lower
court, considering de facto segregation, made an important ruling. Judge
J. Skelly Wright of the U.S. Court of Appeals for the District of Columbia,
sitting as a district judge, ruled in *Hobson* v. *Hansen* that the segregation
of Black pupils in the District of Columbia schools that resulted from
population patterns was unconstitutional. The judge pointed out in his
ruling that Washington was formerly a de jure segregated school district.
In a four-to-three decision a court of appeals upheld many of Judge Wright's
orders. The case was complicated by the time of the appeal; the method
of selecting school board members for the District of Columbia had changed
from appointment to election. The appeals court made it clear that it did
not want to bind the new board to former plans; it preferred to leave it
to the board to evolve new programs.

A later case heard by the U.S. Supreme Court that touched on de facto
segregation was *Keys* v. *School District No. 1, Denver, Colorado.* The
Court, announcing its decision in June 1973, sent the suit back to a district
court; this court was to decide whether or not school authorities had
intentionally segregated a substantial portion of the school system. If proof
affirmed that the school district was operating a dual system (segregated)
even though there had never been any de jure or legal provisions for school
segregation, then the entire system would be required to desegregate. In
the spring of 1974, Judge William E. Doyle of the Tenth U.S. Circuit Court
of Appeals ordered integration of the city's 70,000 children. The Supreme
Court, however, had not resolved the question of de jure/de facto segregation. Justice Powell, in a separate opinion, stated: "We should abandon
a distinction which long since has outlived its time, and formulate constitutional principles of national rather than merely regional applications."
The Supreme Court did, however, change the concept of de facto segregation by turning over to federal and state trial courts the discretion to
determine, as an issue of fact and not as a question of law, whether or
not a local school board presides over a de facto or a de jure segregated
school district. In a sense, the Supreme Court broadened the concept of
de jure segregation.

While questions might be raised about whether segregated schools
31   were created by law and perpetuated by state or school board actions (de

jure) or were the result of residential population patterns (de facto), and about how far the judiciary can go in ordering the end of de facto segregation, it is clear that equality of educational opportunity is a basic right in the United States and must be attained. This right permits maximum intellectual growth and social mobility. All citizens of our democracy must have the opportunity. The Supreme Court has said basically that equality of educational opportunity cannot be provided in segregated facilities, even though the facilities appear to be equal in such tangible assets as buildings, curricula, and staffs. Boards of education must proceed with deliberation and determination to desegregate schools—a very difficult task because in many instances, residential neighborhoods are segregated. New patterns of school attendance centers must be evolved. The efforts by local boards of education to assure the constitutional right of equality of opportunity to all citizens of all races will need the strong support of local citizens. The goal will not be easily or quickly realized.

Reverse Discrimination

Discrimination can be defined as a determination that an individual or group of individuals, for example, Blacks, women, or handicapped persons, has been denied constitutional rights. In common usage the term refers to various minorities or individual members of a minority who lack rights typically accorded to the majority. The term "reverse discrimination" implies that a majority or an individual of a majority has not been accorded certain rights because of different or preferential treatment provided to a minority or an individual of a minority.

Most recently, reverse discrimination has been cited in respect to admissions to law schools and medical schools. It has also been cited in connection with affirmative action, that is, positive efforts undertaken by society to integrate the races and to assure equal opportunities. An early test case concerned Allan Bakke, a white male, who claimed that he was discriminated against when denied admission to the University of California Medical School at Davis. In the medical school's class of 100, sixteen spaces were set aside for minority applicants. The Supreme Court of California upheld Bakke's claim and ordered him admitted. Regents of the university appealed to the U.S. Supreme Court to overturn the state ruling.

In general, the arguments supporting the denial of Bakke's admission pointed out that (1) special admissions programs based on race are not quotas but goals; (2) color-sensitive admissions policies are necessary to bring minorities fully into the mainstream of American society; (3) benefits accrue to society at large from special admissions; (4) merit alone, determined by academic grades and test scores, has not been the single criterion of selection for schools; and (5) the denial did not violate the equal protection clause of the United States Constitution. The arguments supporting Bakke's admission emphasize that (1) the special admissions program was a racial quota and (2) quotas are harmful to society and are unconstitutional.

In June 1978 the U.S. Supreme Court ruled in the Bakke case. In effect, the Court ruled five to four that the University of California at Davis admissions program, which reserved sixteen places in each class for minorities, was illegal. At the same time the Court accepted minority status as a factor in admissions along with grades, test scores, and personal skills. The decision has been referred to by many legal authorities as a precedent for interpreting affirmative action in the future.

One year later the Supreme Court ruled in another significant case involving reverse discrimination (*United Steel Workers* v. *Weber* 1979). This case did not involve education directly, but it helped to clarify the Court's position on affirmative action programs. The justices upheld a plan by Kaiser Aluminum, which, under an agreement with its union, agreed to have an equal number of slots for Blacks and whites in supervisory positions until racial imbalance was corrected in its work force. Although 39 percent of its labor pool was Black, only 2 percent of the Blacks were skilled craftsmen.

The suit originated after a white worker was rejected for the supervisory program, although two Blacks with less seniority were selected for it.

The Supreme Court upheld the plan, for it saw that this program involved a voluntary agreement between private parties not subject to the equal protection clause of the Fourteenth Amendment.

Summary and Implications

The law is involved with American education, and each level of government has legal responsibilities. The U.S. Supreme Court has interpreted the Constitution in many cases related to education. Of special interest to us are those dealing with the First and Fourteenth Amendments. The First Amendment ensures freedom of speech, religion, and the press and the right to petition. Public financial support of nonpublic education and the practice of sectarian religion in public schools have persisted as issues in American education.

The Fourteenth Amendment protects specified privileges of citizens. Segregated schools existed in the United States for many years. Desegregation began in 1954 with the U.S. Supreme Court ruling on *Brown* v. *Board of Education of Topeka*. These social issues have a decided effect on how schools operate.

31   The implications of court decisions based on the First and Fourteenth Amendments are many. Local boards of education must develop and adopt

38   policies that harmonize with federal and state legislation and court decisions. The board policies guide administrators and teachers as they carry

out their responsibilities. Deciding policy on sensitive subjects like religion and desegregation is often not easy, nor is the mandated fulfillment.

In classrooms throughout the United States, teachers will need to deal with the proper relationship between religion and public education and with the diversity, potential conflict, discontinuity, and change in desegregated schools.

As was indicated earlier in this chapter, public schools have tended to avoid the topic of religion.[27] One reason given by parents for withdrawing their children from public schools was that public schools were promulgating secular humanism and ignoring religion. It is obvious that public schools cannot foster any particular religion or have religious ceremonies. They can, however, recognize the religious dimension of human existence and conduct appropriate study *about* religion. Public schools and their teachers must address rather than avoid this issue.

Hawley has observed that desegregated schools tend to be more heterogeneous academically than their racially segregated counterparts; that parents worry about the potential interracial conflict in desegregated schools; that students find themselves in environments in which the expectations they experience at home and in their neighborhoods are different from those they experience at school; and that changes brought about by desegregation often require that teachers take part in a broader range of educational programs that can greatly increase teacher workloads.[28] Teachers in desegregated schools face challenges of a greater magnitude than those in homogeneous settings. Desegregation requires changes in instruction and in professional behavior.

The rights of students as citizens must be protected; teachers should know about these rights and protect them. Teachers, because they are a primary influence in shaping the attitudes of students, ultimately have a hand in shaping society.

DISCUSSION QUESTIONS

1. Why has the federal government become stronger in education in recent years?
2. What function should the private school have in America?
3. What has been the rationale for using public money to supply transportation and textbooks to students attending private schools?
4. How has the U.S. Supreme Court influenced the operation of public education?
5. How do the court decisions and the federal legislation discussed in this chapter affect the responsibilities and behavior of classroom teachers?
6. What is the difference between de jure and de facto segregation?
7. What has been the major factor in court decisions supporting metropolitan desegregation?
8. What myths about busing did Orfield identify in his research?
9. What were the essential elements in the decision of the U.S. Supreme Court in the Bakke case?
10. What reasons did the Nordin and Taylor study identify for why parents are withdrawing their children from public schools?

SUPPLEMENTAL ACTIVITIES

1. Interview officials from private schools in your area to discuss what private education in America can do best.
2. Visit a racially integrated school and record your observations.
3. Procure and study the policy statements of a local school district; look specifically for federal or state influence.
4. Interview a public school superintendent and inquire about the effects of federal legislation and court decisions on how a local school district operates.
5. Interview the person at your college or university who is responsible for affirmative action.

NOTES

1. W. Vance Grant, *American Education* 18 (March 1982): 25.

2. Thomas J. Flygare, "State Aid to Parochial Schools: Diminished Alternatives," *Phi Delta Kappan* 57 (November 1975): 204.

3. Ibid.

4. William E. Collie, "*Schempp* Reconsidered: The Relationship between Religion and Public Education," *Phi Delta Kappan* 65 (September 1983): 59.

5. Ibid.

6. For further elaboration of this case, the reader is referred to Roger M. Williams, "What Louisville Has Taught Us About Busing," *Saturday Review* 30 (April 1977): 6.

7. Virginia Davis Nordin and William Lloyd Turner, "More Than Segregation Academies: The Growing Protestant Fundamentalist Schools," *Phi Delta Kappan* 61 (February 1980): 391.

8. Ibid.

9. Ibid.

10. Ibid.

11. Ibid., p. 392.

12. "Private School Students Are Mostly Northern, White, and Wealthy: HEW," *Phi Delta Kappan* 61 (April 1980): 515. (No author listed; appeared on a page called "Newsfront," prepared for the *Kappan* by Capitol Publications, Washington, D.C.)

13. Nordin and Turner, p. 392.

14. Ibid.

15. Ibid., p. 393.

16. James S. Coleman, Thomas Hoffer, and Sally Kilgore, *Public and Private Schools* (March 1981), p. 1. Draft report to the National Center for Educational Statistics under Contract No. 300-78-0208 by the National Opinion Research Center. Available from Educational Research Service, Inc., 1800 North Kent Street, Arlington, Va 22209.

17. Ibid., p. xxii.

18. Ibid., p. 1.

19. Ibid., pp. xxvii–xxviii.

20. Gary Orfield, *Must We Bus? Segregated Schools and National Policy* (Washington, D.C.: Brookings Institute, 1775 Massachusetts Avenue, N.W. 20036), as reported in *Education USA* 21 (October 2, 1978): 35.

21. Ibid.

22. *Education USA* 22 (September 27, 1979): 21. (National School Public Relations Association, 1801 North Moore Street, Arlington, Va.)

23. James S. Coleman, "Racial Segregation in the Schools: New Research with New Policy Implications," *Phi Delta Kappan* 57 (October 1975): 76–77.

24. Ibid.

25. Robert L. Green and Thomas F. Pettigrew, "Urban Desegregation and White Flight: A Response to Coleman," *Phi Delta Kappan* 57 (February 1976): 401–402.

26. Robert G. Wegmann, "White Flight and School Resegregation: Some Hypotheses," *Phi Delta Kappan* 58 (January 1977): 393.

27. Collie, p. 59.

28. Willis D. Hawley, "Achieving Quality Integrated Education—With or without Federal Help," *Phi Delta Kappan* 64 (January 1983): 335.

BIBLIOGRAPHY

Flygare, Thomas J. "Schools and the Law." *Phi Delta Kappan.* (A regular feature in each issue of *Phi Delta Kappan* providing timely and pertinent information.)

Hudgins, H. C., Jr., and Vacca, Richard S. *Law and Education: Contemporary Issues and Court Decisions.* Charlottesville, Va.: Michie Company, 1979.

LaMorte, Michael W. *School Law: Cases and Concepts.* Englewood Cliffs, N.J.: Prentice-Hall, 1982.

McCarthy, Martha M. *A Delicate Balance: Church, State, and the Schools.* Bloomington, Ind.: Phi Delta Kappa, 1983.

Orfield, Gary. *Must We Bus? Segregated Schools and National Policy.* Washington, D.C.: Brookings Institute, 1978.

Reutter, Edmund, Jr. *The Supreme Court's Impact on Public Education.* Bloomington, Ind.: Phi Delta Kappa and National Organization on Legal Problems in Education, 1982.

Sergiovanni, Thomas J.; Burlingame, Martin; Coombs, Fred; and Thurston, Paul. *Educational Governance and Administration.* Englewood Cliffs, N.J.: Prentice-Hall, 1980.

Thomas, Stephen B.; Cambron-McCabe, Nelda H.; and McCarthy, Martha M. *Educators and the Law: Current Trends and Issues.* Jamaica, N.Y.: Institute for the Study of School Law and School Finance, 1983.

Valente, William D. *Law in the Schools.* Columbus, Ohio: Charles E. Merrill, 1980.

Wilkinson, J. Harvie, III. *From Brown to Bakke: The Supreme Court and School Integration, 1954–1978.* New York: Oxford University Press, 1979.

9

Organizing and Administering Public Education

Focus Questions

- Why should you, as a future teacher, know or care about how schools are organized?
- How do you think changes could be brought about in the way schools operate at the local level?
- What benefits are there to you or the teaching profession by your belonging to a state and/or a national teacher association?
- Do you think teachers and parents should be active in influencing how schools are organized and operated? Why or why not?

Key Terms and Concepts

Local school district
Local board of education
Superintendent of schools
Citizen's advisory council
Local control
Teacher power
Lobbying

Public power
Neighborhood schools
State board of education
Chief state school officer
State department of education
Federal involvement in education

What Would You Do?

You are a fifth-grade teacher and have one boy in your class who is constantly disruptive. He bothers and irritates other students when they are trying to study. He is not responsive to your efforts to discipline him. Where can you go for help to begin to resolve this situation?

In discussing the legal foundations of education in Chapter 8 we examined the educational system primarily from a judicial and legislative standpoint. In this chapter we consider the organizational and administrative aspects of the educational system. Education in the United States is an immense enterprise. Currently, about 44 million students are enrolled in public and private elementary and secondary schools, and 2.4 million teachers are employed to instruct these students. Nearly one out of every four persons in the nation directly participates in education as a student, teacher, or supervisor.[1] Projections for 1993 indicate approximately 47.9 million students and 2.70 million teachers. Approximately 15,500 local school districts function under 50 state governments. How is this huge enterprise organized nationwide?

Local School Districts

A school district is a governmental unit empowered by state law to ad- minister the school system of a local community. It is controlled by a governing board composed of citizens living in the geographical area that makes up the district.

School districts have similar purposes but widely different characteristics. Some districts provide only elementary education; others provide only high school education; still others provide both elementary and secondary education. Approximately 27 percent of the districts have fewer than 300 pupils, and their total enrollments make up about 1.3 percent of the total national enrollment. Only 1.0 percent of the districts have an enrollment in excess of 25,000 students, yet these districts enroll about 26 percent of the total. Thousands of school districts have only one attendance center; a few urban districts may have as many as 500.

Local districts provide one of the few opportunities for citizens to participate directly in public decision making. Board members are local citizens, and the majority of them serve on school boards in relatively small communities in districts that enroll fewer than 1000 students. Only about 4.0 percent of board members serve in relatively large communities in districts that enroll over 10,000 students. Therefore, it is not unusual in many school districts for board members to know each other and many of their constituents by first names. The administration of local schools concerns people deeply, dealing directly as it does with their children. Local school districts also deal with local citizens' money in the form of taxation to provide funds to operate the schools. In many communities today the budget for schools is the highest of any local taxing agency. The local school district in many cases is the closest relationship citizens have with a governmental agency. Americans usually value this relation highly. Some look on the local district and its schools as a chance to determine their own destiny; others see the local district and local control as one of the few remaining opportunities to control public spending. The local district does have advantages over centralized governmental control. It permits citizens to have schools of better quality than the minimum prescribed by the state and allows them a chance to develop educational programs that meet local needs.

Local control is an important and unique feature of American education; however, its value has been challenged recently. It has been argued that the mobility of our population and the interdependence of social elements have undermined the traditional concept that local people should have a strong role in determining education. It has also been argued that our national survival requires policies and programs laid down under centralized control.

Local control, in a sense, is challenged each time a decision by a local board or a local school district is taken to the courts. Many court decisions dealing with the relationship between religion and the pubic school or with desegregation have been in response to local control. In some instances, local control, combined with the traditional system of financing education, has resulted in inequality of educational opportunity rather than equality. The alternative to local control is centralization. We have come full circle; education in large cities is already centralized, and many of these large districts are trying to solve some of their problems by decentralization. Frequently, a centralized authority does not respond well to citizens' needs and demands. Ex officio boards and councils for local community or neighborhood schools, which advise officials on large city or county boards, represent efforts to keep some form of local control in the large centralized systems.

The operational control of eduction today is still primarily local, carried out under the powers delegated by the states. Federal and state involvement, both direct, through court decisions and mandates, and indirect, through federal and state aid, has been increasing. How the local, state, and federal governments are related in their control is complicated and must be resolved. New and intricate relations keep forming.

Efforts have been made in the past to reorganize school districts for more effectiveness and more efficiency. The emphasis has been on reducing, by consolidation, the number of small rural districts. The number of school districts in the United States has decreased from approximately 100,000 in 1945 to approximately 15,500 today. California, Illinois, Nebraska, and Texas have over 1000 districts each. The progress made in consolidating districts has been slow but inevitable.

State legislatures have the power to reorganize school districts but have been reluctant to do so. Often the reorganization legislation is permissive; districts may consolidate with the blessing of the legislature, but little inducement is given. Financial incentives have been incorporated into some reorganization legislation, but still the reorganization is slow. In a few instances, school district reorganization has been mandatory. The laws usually set time limits for reorganization, provide for local community committees to study and present proposals for state review, and offer financial incentives for reorganization. Some laws have stated that if there is a public impasse or if proposals are weak, the state can intercede and effect the reorganization. Local citizens tend to resist school district reorganization because of their sentimental feelings about their school, their desire to keep control local, their failure to recognize inferior schools, their need for the school as a social and recreational facility, and their fear of potential tax increases.

A 1976 study made under a contract from the National Institute of Education raises questions about how valuable it is to consolidate small rural schools.[2] The findings of the study are still appropriate today. The researchers assert, after reviewing the literature dealing with rural consolidation, that:

1. The purported economies to be gained are frequently offset by "diseconomies," such as increased transportation costs and the cost of administering and distributing products procured through bulk purchasing.
2. Taxable wealth has not become equally spread among districts despite massive reorganization over four decades.
3. Quality of education has not improved. (The researchers base this assertion primarily on the relationship of school size to pupil achievement.)

They make three recommendations:

1. More research on small schools should be done.
2. Alternatives to consolidation and reorganization, such as regionalization, should be seriously considered.
3. Research done to demonstrate the value of proposed reforms should be scrutinized carefully.

More research is needed to verify the proclaimed benefits of consolidation and reorganization. The number and kinds of variables that must be controlled—particularly if pupil achievement is to be the measure of effectiveness of reorganization—make such research very difficult. Furthermore, school reorganization in itself is probably one of the least powerful variables affecting pupil achievement, falling far behind variables as native intellect, home environment, socioeconomic status, and motivation. Even after massive reorganization, approximately 27 percent of the school districts in the United States today still have fewer than 300 pupils, and about 54 percent have fewer than 1000 students. Regionalization as an alternative to consolidation is discussed later in this chapter.

Urban districts also present reorganization problems. Rapid growth in urban areas, combined with unplanned and indiscriminate land use, has created immense problems. Wealthy districts with few pupils adjoin poor districts with many pupils. The desires and expectations of the residents for their schools vary tremendously from district to district. Communication between the citizens and the school authorities can become distant and distorted. New York City is one place where decentralizing the large school system has been tried. The teachers' strike there in 1968 focused on this issue and illustrated the complexities that may result from urban decentralization. Improving organization is an overwhelming and complicated task.

Local Boards of Education

[31] Legal authority for operating local school systems is given to local boards of education through state statutes. The statutes prescribe specifically how school board members are to be chosen and what duties and responsibil-
[38] ities they have in office. The statutes also specify the terms of board members, procedures for selecting officers of the board, duties of the officers, procedures for filling any vacancies, and like matters. Local citizens serving as school board members are official agents of the state.

Ninety-five percent of the school boards in the United States are elected by popular vote; most members are elected in special, nonpartisan elections. About 5 percent are appointed. The percentage of appointed school boards is higher in school districts enrolling over 25,000 pupils; yet even in these large districts, about three fourths of the board members are elected. New York City and Chicago both have appointed school boards.

Citizens seeking election to school boards generally must petition for a place on the ballot. Candidates who meet the legal requirements to serve as school board members and follow proper petitioning procedures cannot be denied a place on the ballot. In some places an extralegal caucus committee approves a slate of candidates. This committee usually comprises representatives of community organizations. Members approved by a caucus committee must follow the same procedure as any other candidate placed on the ballot. The caucus process represents an attempt to nominate well-qualified candidates for board membership. This method, however, has been charged with recommending persons for board membership who would perpetuate alleged past inequities. The caucus is an extralegal procedure. A candidate on a partisan ticket is selected by the local party committee. School board members are usually elected from the district at large rather than from wards or precincts.

Appointments to boards of education (as opposed to election) are made by city councils, mayors, state legislatures, county boards, and other agencies. The most common procedure is appointment by a city council or mayor. It is not unusual for an appointing official to have an extralegal committee of citizens submit a list of persons to be considered for the vacancies. This procedure is an attempt to separate partisan politics and education and at the same time obtain highly qualified persons as board members.

Candidates for boards of education, elective or appointive, are frequently recruited from among citizens who have expressed an interest in the schools by serving on citizen advisory committees to boards of education. Local PTAs also serve as a source of potential candidates.

The members of boards of education generally come from the proprietary and professional occupations. The number of farmers serving is steadily decreasing. Board members tend to have at least a high school education; many have college educations. Board members have a higher income than average citizens and generally represent middle class society.

A study conducted in 1977 by the National School Board Association investigated board membership in the nation's 51 largest school districts. It showed:

1. In comparison with 1967, five times as many professional educators serve on school boards—and only half as many attorneys.
2. Minority representation has increased 3 percent from 1974 to 1977.
3. Sixty-nine percent of the board members are male, of an average age of 49.

It is quite likely that the percentage of male board members has decreased since this study was completed. The trend has been toward the election or appointment of more females and more members of minority groups to local school boards. (These trends may or may not prevail in small school districts.)

Teachers may not be board members in the districts where they teach; they may be board members, however, in districts where they live, while teaching in different districts. The trend in which more teachers are becoming board members most likely results from the stance that professional associations have taken to secure seats on school boards.

The powers and duties of school boards vary from state to state; the school codes of the respective states spell them out in detail. (The general powers and duties of local boards were discussed in Chapter 8.) Some duties are mandatory, others discretionary. Some duties cannot be delegated. If, for example, boards are given the power to employ teachers, the boards must be the ones to do this; the power may not be delegated even to a school superintendent. Boards can delegate much of the hiring process to administrators, however, and then act officially on administrative recommendations for employment. An illustration of a discretionary power left to the local board is a decision whether or not to participate in a nonrequired school program—for example, a program of competitive athletics. Another illustration of discretionary power is a decision to employ only teachers who exceed minimum state certification standards.

38   Powers and duties granted to boards of education are granted to the boards as a whole, not to individual members. An individual member of a board has no more authority in school matters than any other citizen of the community unless the school board legally delegates a task through official action to a specific member; in those instances, official board approval of final actions is necessary. A school board, as a corporate body, can act officially only in legally held and duly authorized board meetings, and these meetings usually must be open to the public. Executive or private sessions may be held, but ordinarily only for specified purposes such as evaluating staff members or selecting a school site. It is usually required that any official action on matters discussed in private session must be taken in an open meeting.

Superintendent of Schools

One of the primary duties of the local board is to select its executive officer, the local superintendent of schools. In Illinois the school code is specific in granting this power and in delineating the superintendent's duties and the working relationship between the board and the superintendent. The Illinois law reads that a superintendent is to be employed

School board meetings often provide a place where all parties interested in education can come together.

who shall have charge of the administration of the schools under the direction of the board of education. In addition to the administrative duties, the superintendent shall make recommendations to the board concerning the budget, building plans, and locations of sites, the selection of teachers and other employees, the selection of textbooks, instructional material, and courses of study. The superintendent shall keep or cause to be kept the records and accounts as directed and required by the board, aid in making reports required of the board, and perform such other duties as the board may delegate to him.

Many states are not as specific as Illinois. While the Illinois statute is specific for a statute, it provides only guidelines for the local policies needed in establishing further board-superintendent working relations. The cooperative development of specific policies by the board and the superintendent helps establish the roles of both the board of education and the superintendent and therefore minimizes conflict in this crucial relationship. Generally, boards are policymakers and superintendents are executive officers, but it is often very difficult to make the distinction.

The quality of the educational program of a school district is influenced strongly by the leadership the board of education and the superintendent provide. Without high expectations being communicated and supported by boards and superintendents, high-quality education is not likely to be achieved. Curriculum programs over and above state-required minimums are discretionary. Local authorities, board members, and the superintendent frequently must convince communities that specified school programs are needed.

The superintendent of schools works with a staff to carry on the program of education. The size of the staff varies with the school district, and of course some kind of organization is necessary. Many school systems use a line and staff organization like that shown in Figure 9.1. In this pattern, line officers hold the administrative power as it flows in a line from the local board of education down to the pupils. Superintendents, assistant superintendents, and principals are line officers vested with authority over the people below them on the chart. Each person is directly responsible to the official above and must work through that person in dealing with a higher official. This arrangement is frequently referred to as the "chain of command."

Administrative staff members are shown in Figure 9.1 as branching out from the direct flow of authority. Staff includes librarians, instructional supervisors, guidance officers, transportation officers, and others. They are responsible to their respective superiors, generally in an advisory capacity. Staff members usually have no authority and issue no orders. They assist and advise others from their special knowledge and abilities. Teachers are generally referred to as staff persons even though they are in the direct flow of authority. Their authority in this arrangement prevails only over pupils.

This type of strict organization has some critics who hold that it tends to stifle the teacher's potential contribution and that it goes against the

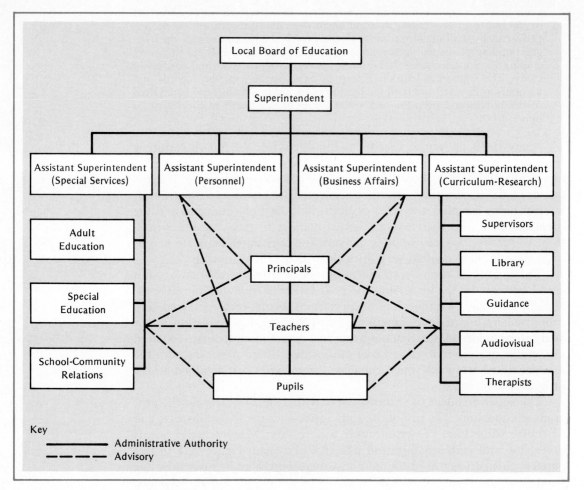

FIGURE 9.1 *Typical line and staff organization.*

idea of professional equality. Psychologists and authorities in group dynamics have indicated that a more flexible organization can be more effective in accomplishing desired goals. They suggest that a person's effectiveness is related to the satisfaction gained in employment. Teacher groups, through "teacher power" at the bargaining table, are asking for a greater say in the policies and operating procedures of school systems; in some instances these requests are granted. New structures provide for wider participation of teachers and staff in administrative matters. Figure 9.2 shows how the local educational staff can be organized to allow for wider participation in decisions.

In this structure an administrative council exists that includes not only the various assistant superintendents but also a local educational policies commission. This commission may include members from the local teach-

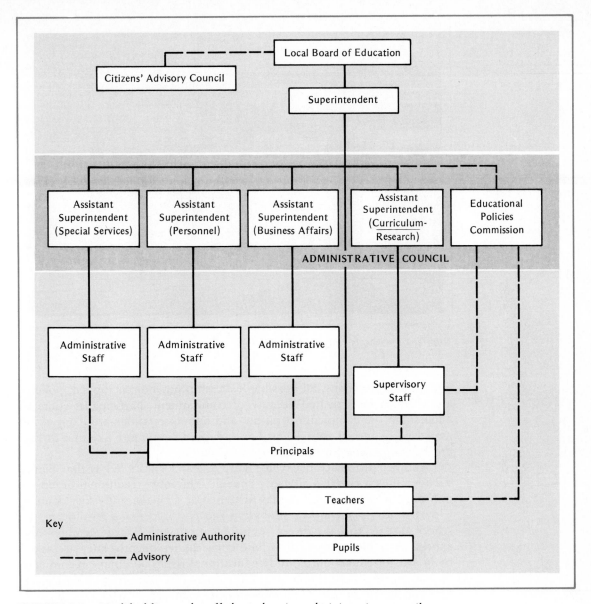

FIGURE 9.2 *Modified line and staff chart showing administrative council.*

ers' group, members from the nonteaching staff, pupils, and members from the principals' group. The commission allows for advice to be received at all levels of staff. The "line" relations are like those in Figure 9.1. For simplicity, lower-echelon central administrative workers in Figure 9.2 have been referred to as administrative staff; their relation to principals is advisory, however. Advocates of this structure cite the following advantages: wide participation allows many ideas, pooled thinking is likely to produce

Rightly or wrongly, the buck often stops with local school administrators.

high-quality decisions, all possible leadership potential is tapped, policies are likely to be activated because of commitment, participants come to understand the complete operation, and human relations are likely to be improved. Some school systems have adopted a structure like that in Figure 9.2 to provide for this wider participation.

Another difference between Figure 9.2 and Figure 9.1 is that Figure 9.2 identifies a citizen's advisory council. The more traditional organization portrayed in Figure 9.1 may also include a citizen's advisory council. Citizen's advisory councils provide a means for persons residing in the school district to have direct communication with board members and express their ideas, suggestions, and concerns. Frequently, they are asked by boards of education to study educational issues and make recommendations to the board. Of course, individuals can also attend board meetings and speak directly to members of the board.

Any organization must operate according to the law. A structure that permits wide participation in decisions must recognize that certain decisions are by law the responsibility of the board of education or perhaps the superintendent. A board or a superintendent may not shift legal authority or responsibility to another group.

The success of organizations that encourage wide participation depends largely on how committed the school board and the superintendent are to participation. They must create opportunities for participation and be willing to accept the results, if at all possible under the law. Teachers must be willing to participate in an administrative council. Citizens must also be willing to participate in a citizen's advisory council. Some teachers believe that their duties should include classroom responsibilities only and that administrative matters should be resolved by administrators. Other teachers believe strongly that their ideas should be formally negotiated and made official; they want to do more than merely advise. Wide participation requires committed participants.

Teachers who wish to express a concern should initially use the official administrative system. The first person to contact in most instances is the principal; sometimes it may be a department head. If this method fails, a teacher may continue by contacting the principal's superior—the superintendent. Another way is to file a grievance through procedures outlined in the negotiated contract given to teachers' organizations and the school district. In any instance it is wise for a beginning teacher or one new to the system to seek advice from experienced colleagues before taking action. In addition to knowing the system, one must know how the system works; colleagues can be helpful in that regard.

Local Control: A Myth?

For many years, local control was seen as the bulwark of the successful American education enterprise. To what extent does local control really exist? In recent decades, local control has been termed a myth. Those said to be in actual control included professional administrators, teachers' organizations, and state and federal legislators and courts.

A 1977 report notes four phases of control in the history of American education:[3]

Phase 1: Lay control (1835–ca. 1900)
Phase 2: Control by local professionals (1900–ca. 1968)
Phase 3: The nationalization of education (1954–1975)
Phase 4: Education and the social goal (1975–present)

Phase 1 functioned with a mandate to educators to pursue limited educational goals that would enable citizens to survive and pursue livelihoods in their own small communities. Lay boards of education, representing the community, administered the schools. During this phase the nation had over 100,000 school districts; school board members represented relatively homogeneous and unambiguous constituencies. There was ample opportunity for the citizens to interact with their board members and to hold the board accountable for its actions.

Phase 2 was ushered in during a rapid growth in school population, particularly in urban areas. Board members found that they could no longer devote enough time to administrative tasks; consequently, the position of superintendent of schools was created. During this period the responsibilities for education were shifted from lay control to local professionals, mainly administrators. This change was partly inspired by the scientific management movement then taking place and by the desire of local citizens, including board members, to reduce political influence in education. Important changes were consolidation of school districts, centralization of administration, election of fewer board members at large and more from local wards, election of board members by nonpartisan ballots, and the separation of board elections from other municipal and state elections. Phase 2 had a larger mandate than Phase 1; it called for the development of skills and values needed by a larger, homogeneous society. Phase 2 was characterized by stability, and schools were perceived as agents for transmitting knowledge, culture, and social norms.

Near the end of Phase 2, the seeds for Phase 3 were being planted. The decision in *Brown* v. *Board of Education* (1954) was an early step toward the school acting as an agent of social and economic change—the mandate of Phase 3. Subsequent court decisions, federal and state legislation, and infusion of federal and state aid (with accompanying control of the funds) have all contributed to greater control by the federal government and other nonlocal units of government. The local administrative control of Phase 2 was gradually eroded. Also contributing to the erosion was the influence gained by teachers' unions through collective bargaining.

The Ziegler study concludes that Phase 3 governance cannot achieve the Phase 3 mandate.[4] Ziegler bases this conclusion partly on (1) the research of James S. Coleman, which indicated that school quality and individual achievement are essentially unrelated; (2) the research of Christopher Jencks, who stated that school reform "cannot bring about significant social changes outside the schools"; and (3) the research of Raymond Bouden, who concluded that "educational growth as such has the effect of increasing rather than decreasing social and economic inequality, even in the case of an educational system that becomes more equalitarian."[5] In effect, the goal of Phase 3, the nationalization of education, will not be attained in Phase 4, identified with education and the social goal.

While the federal government clearly strongly encouraged, and in some instances mandated, social changes such as affirmation action, desegregation, and the rights of women and the handicapped from the early 1950s to the early 1980s, there is some evidence that economic considerations may play a more dominant role in the immediate future. Greater federal attention is likely to be given to the relationship of education both to domestic economics and to the role of the United States in worldwide economic competition.

Teacher Power

Teachers have power—power to influence the direction of American education. Collective bargaining agreements of local teacher associations—NEA or AFT affiliates—are being expanded to include not only salaries but also course content, curriculum change procedures, teacher evaluation, and teaching procedures. Teacher organizations have backed many successful candidates for political office and have recently endorsed presidential candidates. The membership of teachers on boards of education has increased fivefold in the 1970s. Teachers serve on certification boards in many states and on evaluation teams for the accreditation of teacher-education programs in colleges and universities. A federal collective bargaining bill has been proposed for the past few years by the NEA.

The nationwide public criticism of education that emerged in 1983 may provide a strong challenge to teacher power. For example, both major national teacher organizations favor salary schedules; at the same time there is a nationwide effort supported by parents, some state legislators, and persons of national prominence strongly promoting merit pay. The 15th Annual Gallup Poll of Public Attitudes toward Public Schools (1983) reveals that the general public favors merit pay by a ratio of two to one. Teacher tenure is also being challenged. Compromises and/or accommodations on these issues and others are a possibility in the near future.

Teachers have learned to make their collective influence felt through political action. The NEA and the AFT are now powerful political organizations; in the past few years they have increased their control of education at the local, state, and federal levels.

Educational Organization Lobbies

It is clear that much lobbying is directed at the policies of education at both the state and federal levels. The lobbying power of the various national educational organizations varies considerably. Among the national educational lobbying groups are:

- National Education Association (NEA)
- American Federation of Teachers (AFT)
- American Association of School Administrators (AASA)
- Council of Chief State School Officers (CCSSO)
- National Congress of Parents and Teachers (NCPT)
- National School Boards Association (NSBA)
- National Association of State Boards of Education (NASBE)
- American Association of Colleges of Teacher Education (AACTE)

All these organizations except for the CCSSO have state affiliates, and most have local affiliates, which also lobby at the state and local levels.

Often these organizations have opposing views. For example, the teacher organizations (NEA, AFT) have both supported federal bargaining legislation, whereas the AASA and the NASBE have opposed such legislation. Nevertheless, many times they do have common interests, such as adequate financial support for education. It is not unusual for these organizations to form temporary or "floating" coalitions of a few or all of the groups to achieve a desired result.

Public Power

It is clear that the American public believes in and will support public education. In answer to the question, "Would you be willing to pay more taxes to help raise the standard of education in the United States?" 58 percent of the adults nationwide responded *yes,* 70 percent of public school parents said *yes,* and 54 percent of the adults with no children in school also said *yes.*[6] Essentially, the people that make up the public can get what they want for public education if a large majority of them make their desires known strongly to the correct parties and provide the financial support necessary to accomplish their goals. Historically, the public schools have delivered what the public demanded. It is time that the public express its desire to raise standards of education by communicating it strongly to local school boards. The public can help define standards and help boards accomplish the standards by its moral, political, and fiscal support if necessary.

31

Attendance Centers—Neighborhood Schools

The school organization for pupils can be considered in two interrelated ways: grade-level grouping and attendance-center grouping. Common grade-level groupings include K8-4, K6-3-3, and K6-6. A newer type of grade grouping is K4-4-4. The rationale for grade-level grouping is presumably based primarily on child growth and on developmental and curricular considerations. (This rationale is explained further in Part VI.) Attendance-center grouping frequently is identical to grade-level grouping, although it need not be.

An attendance center is a school—within a district—to which pupils from a designated geographical area are assigned. Figure 9.3 illustrates the attendance-center concept. In this illustration there are seven attendance centers: four K–6 centers, two 7–9 centers, and one 10–12 center. The attendance area for each of the K–6 centers is approximately one fourth of the area of the school district. Their boundaries are represented by the exterior boundaries of the school district and the double dashed lines within the school district. Each 7–9 attendance center includes the area encompassed by two K–6 centers. The boundaries of the 10–12 center are the same as the district boundaries. In reality, school districts and attendance centers are not nearly so geometrically perfect. Most often, the boundaries are irregular and jagged. Occasionally, they even have long, peninsular projections extending deep into other districts. The number of attendance centers in a district may vary from one in a rural area to more than 500 in a heavily populated area.

School boards have the right to prescribe the boundaries for an attendance center. Establishing boundaries is difficult. Boards must be cautious in exercising this right, making certain that attendance areas are not de-

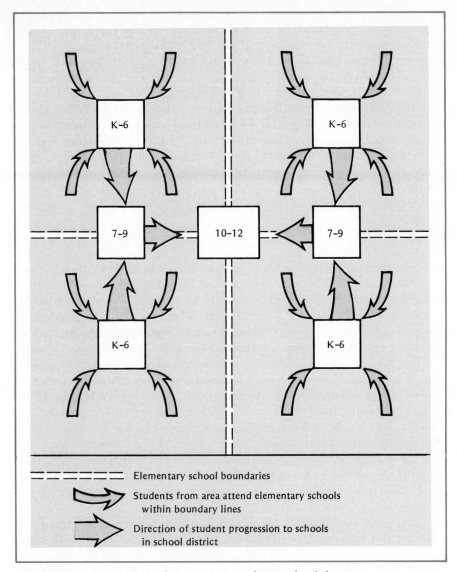

FIGURE 9.3 *School attendance centers within a school district.*

termined by race, that the distances traveled by students either walking or being transported are not unreasonable, and that the safety of youngsters is not jeopardized.

The segregation issue has further complicated attendance-area decisions. Segregation exists by race, creed, economic status, nationality, and many other characteristics. Neighborhood schools, frequently the most logical attendance centers, are under attack for perpetuating de facto segregation. No doubt the neighborhood school is often a segregated school, especially in cities. Attempts have been made to bus students from one neighborhood to another to integrate and balance the races. In other instances, voluntary transfer plans, whereby students may elect to attend schools of their choice, have been tried. Neither plan has met with much success. Recent proposals suggest educational parks, built in carefully selected locations, that would foster racial integration and would permit drawing pupils from both the city and its suburbs. The middle school, frequently composed of grades 5–8, while conceived on a curricular rationale, also can sometimes accomplish racial balance by bringing together children who were in segregated neighborhood elementary schools. These many attempts, however, seem to be chiefly stopgap and short-term solutions.

Intermediate Units

The intermediate unit of school organization, which may consist of one or more counties, functions between the state department of education and the local school districts. Historically, the intermediate unit has served as liaison between the two. In rural areas, where there is a preponderance of small schools, it has also had a direct educational function, such as providing guidance or special education services.

The fundamental purpose of the intermediate unit today is to provide two or more local districts with educational services that they cannot efficiently or economically provide individually; cooperative provisions for special education and vocational-technical education have been very successful. Area vocational-technical schools have been aided by relatively high infusions of federal money. Other services that intermediate units can provide include audiovisual libraries, centralized purchasing, in-service training for teachers and other school workers, health services, instructional materials, laboratories, legal services, and special consultant services.

According to a recent Educational Research Services study, there has been a trend toward legislature-mandated regional centers.[7] Eight states now require regional services, and four others have legislation that allows them. Many earlier intermediate units, except for county units, were voluntary consortiums. In Iowa the fifteen area-education agencies have the same boundaries as community college and vocational districts. The Pennsylvania legislature dissolved county units, which served as intermediate units, and created 29 intermediate units.

Intermediate units or regional centers are developing closer ties with higher education institutions and with other regional government subdivisions and social agencies, such as mental health agencies. The Educational Research Services study also raises some interesting questions about regional centers. Do they tend to bolster school districts that should be reorganized? How should they be financed? What kinds of governing boards should they have? Should they have the power to levy local taxes?

State Functions

The state is the governmental unit in the United States charged with the responsibility for education. State legislatures, within the limits expressed by the federal constitution and by state constitutions, are the chief policymakers for education. State legislatures grant powers to state boards of education, state departments of education, chief state school officers, and local boards of education. These groups have only the powers granted to them by the legislature, implied powers from the specific grant of power, and the necessary powers to carry out the statutory purposes. Figure 9.4 shows a typical state organization for education.

State Boards of Education

State boards of education are both regulatory and advisory. Authorities generally agree that regulation by state school boards is important primarily so that local schools will operate consistently. Some regulatory functions are establishing standards for issuing and revoking teaching certificates, establishing standards for approving and accrediting schools, and developing and enforcing a uniform system for gathering and reporting educational data. The advisory function includes considering the educational needs of the state, both long- and short-range, and recommending to the governor and the legislature ways of meeting the needs. State school boards, in studying school problems and in suggesting and analyzing proposals, can be invaluable to the legislature, especially since the legislature is under pressure to decide so many issues. A state board can provide a continuity in an educational program that ordinary legislative procedures don't allow for. A state board can also coordinate, supplement, and even replace study commissions appointed by a legislature for advising on educational matters. These commissions frequently include groups studying textbooks, finance, certification, school district reorganization, school building standards, and teacher education.

Members of state boards of education get their positions in various ways. Usually, they are appointed by the governor; they may also be elected by the people, the legislature, or local school board members in regional convention. The specific information as to how members of state boards of education in each state get these positions is in Appendix B.

In 1947, nine states were without state boards of education; by 1983, only Wisconsin was without. Iowa, New York, and Washington have elective procedures unlike those of the other states. In Iowa, conventions of delegates from areas within the state send nominations to the governor, who makes the final appointment; in New York the Board of Regents is elected by the legislature; and in Washington the state board is elected by members of boards of directors of local school districts. The terms of members are usually staggered to avoid a complete changeover at any one

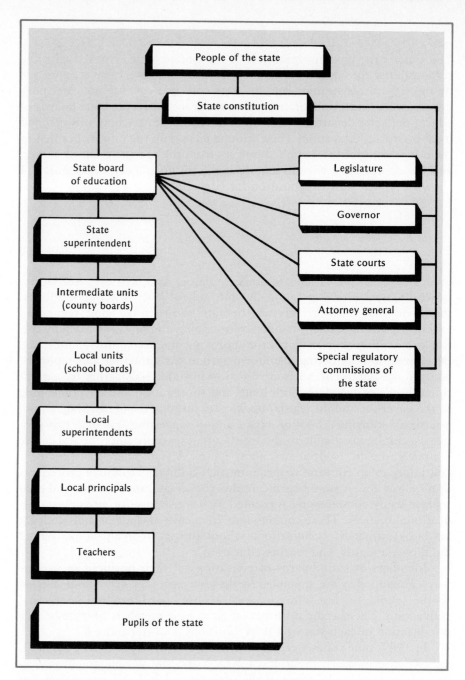

FIGURE 9.4　*Typical structure of a state school system.*

time. Members usually serve without pay but are reimbursed for expenses. The policy of nonpayment, along with the staggered terms, is considered a safeguard against political patronage.

Chief State School Officers

Every state has a chief state school officer. Currently, nineteen of these officers are elected by the people, twenty-seven are appointed by state boards of education, and four are appointed by the governor. The specific information as to how each chief state school officer gets the position is in Appendix C.

Arguments advanced for electing the chief state school officer hold that as an elected official, the person will be close to the people, responsible to them, and free from obligations to other state officials. As an elected person, he or she will also be independent of the state board of education. Opponents to the election method argue primarily that this method keeps the department of education in partisan politics, that an elected official is obligated to other members of the same political party, and that many excellent candidates prefer not to engage in political contests. Furthermore, they feel that as a matter of operating efficiency, the chief state school officer should not be chosen independently of the state board of education.

Those who advocate that the chief state school officer should be appointed by a state board of education claim that policymaking should be separated from policy execution, that educational leadership should not rest on the competence of one elected official, and that with this method recruiting and retaining qualified career workers in education would be enhanced.

Opponents of appointment by a state board of education claim mainly that the chief school officer would then not be responsible to the people. The principal objection to gubernatorial appointment is the inherent danger of the appointee's involvement in partisan politics. An elected state school officer is legally an "official" of the state, whereas an officer appointed by a state board of education is generally an "employee," not a legal official. When the chief school officer is elected, and hence is a legal official theoretically responsible to the people, the working relation between this official and the state board is not likely to be so clearly defined as when the official is appointed by the state board of education and hence is an employee of the board.

The chief state school officer can strongly influence educational ideas. This person tells the legislature, the governor, and the state board of education what he or she thinks education needs. The officer frequently reports to the legislature, perhaps suggesting legislation. Most often the chief state school officer is the executive head of the state department of education and as such, through a staff, supervises and regulates the schools. Specific duties of the office may include the following:[8]

- To serve as secretary and executive officer of the state board of education.
- To serve as executive officer of any board or council that may be established to facilitate coordination of all aspects of the educational program.
- To select competent personnel for and serve as the administrative head and professional leader of the state department of education to the end that it will contribute maximally to the improvement of education.
- To arrange for studies and organize committees and task forces as deemed necessary to identify problems and to recommend plans and provisions for effecting improvements in education.
- To recommend to the state board of education needed policies, standards, and regulations relating to public education in the state.
- To recommend improvements in educational legislation and in provisions for financing the educational program.
- To explain and interpret the school laws of the state and the regulations of the state board of education.
- To decide impartially controversies and disputes involving the administration of the public school system.
- To submit frequent reports to the public and periodic reports to the state board, to the governor, and to the legislature giving information about the accomplishments, conditions, and needs of the schools.

State Departments of Education

The state government carries on its activities in education through the state department of education, which is directed by the chief state school officer. These activities have been classified in five categories: operational, regulatory, service, developmental, and public support and cooperation activities.[9] Operational activities are those in which the state department directly administers schools and services, such as schools for the blind. Regulatory activities include overseeing that teacher certification standards are met, that school buses are safe, and that curricular requirements are fulfilled. Service activities include advising and consulting, disseminating research, and preparing materials (on state aid, for example). Developmental activities are directed to improving the department itself and include planning, staffing, and research into better performance for the operational, regulatory, and service functions. Public support and cooperation activities involve public relations, political activities with the legislature and governor, and relations with various other governmental and nongovernmental agencies.

Traditionally, state departments have not shown strong leadership. Their activities have mainly been operating and regulating. The Elementary and Secondary Education Act of 1965, under Title V, provided for funds to strengthen state departments of education. There is no question that departments have been strengthened, but the majority have not yet branched out into other activities. State departments of education, for example, have a role in the distribution of federal grants. However, their role has changed with the beginning of block grants, a concept implemented in 1981 through the Education Improvement Act by the federal government. Under the block grant concept, within their own rules and regulations, states have greater freedom to make decisions on the level of funding they wish to apply to some federal programs. The block grant is a consolidation of former categorical aid. Some specific categorical programs are continued as categorical programs with the usual restrictions on the use of the money. Since education is so closely related to the problems of society, the partners in education—federal, state, and local—must adjust their activities to meet complex needs.

Federal Involvement

It was mentioned in the introduction to this part of the book that under the Tenth Amendment to the U.S. Constitution, education is a function of the states. In effect, states have the primary responsibility for education, yet the schools are operated by local governmental units commonly called school districts. The federal government is characterized as having a strong interest in education, particularly as it relates to national security, national domestic problems, and the rights of citizens as guaranteed by the U.S. Constitution and federal laws. Illustrations of federal actions in education with respect to national security include the National Defense Act of 1958, enacted after the U.S.S.R. launched the first satellite, which provided federal money to enhance education in the sciences, mathematics, and foreign languages. In 1984, in response to lowering student achievement scores, particularly in science and mathematics, Congress was seriously considering appropriations to improve science and mathematics education, primarily in secondary schools. Chapter 6 in this book provides illustrations of federal efforts to assist in solving domestic social issues such as poverty and non-English-speaking students. The federal role in guaranteeing the rights of individuals was explained in Chapter 8.

The federal government has historically provided leadership in education in specific situations, usually in times of need or crises that could not be fully addressed by the leadership in states or local school districts. The time may be right for a more stable and consistent leadership role for the federal government, such as establishing national priorities in education similar to those issues addressed in "A Nation at Risk," the report prepared by the National Commission on Excellence in Education, published in 1983.

That report is not a mandate, nor is funding recommended, but it does provide recommendations to be seriously considered by states and local school districts. The identifying of national educational issues and the encouraging of forums on these issues at the state and local levels, along with soliciting responses, seems appropriate. Such activity could be made regular rather than sporadic. Research on significant national educational issues should be continued. The dissemination of exemplary practices should be enhanced. Leaders of education in the states should meet to provide the impetus of a coalition to implement exemplary practices. The federal government should provide leadership; priority setting, research, and dissemination are appropriate leadership areas.

The federal government also includes a Department of Education, directly operates some educational programs, and provides some financial aid to states and local school districts. (Federal aid is discussed in Chapter 10.) Most educational groups supported the creation of the department. Shirley Hufstedler, a judge, was named as secretary to the new department. She served for approximately one year and was replaced by Terrel Bell, a former Commissioner of Education of the Office of Education.

Department of Education

In October 1979, President Carter signed legislation creating a Department of Education. The Department of Education took on the functions of the U.S. Office of Education, which was created in 1953 as a unit within the Department of Health, Education, and Welfare. The first unit of education in the federal government, established in 1867 through the diligent efforts of Henry Barnard, was also called a Department of Education. Later it was called an Office of Education (1869), becoming a Bureau of Education in 1970 within the Department of the Interior. It was also called an Office of Education in 1929. In 1939 the "Office of Education" became a part of the Federal Security Agency, which in 1953 became the Department of Health, Education, and Welfare, wherein the U.S. Office of Education was assigned until the new Department was created in 1979.

The Department of Education, in contrast with the first Department of Education (1867), has potential for becoming a powerful agency. The original 1867 Department had the following stated purpose:

> To collect such statistics and facts as shall show the condition and progress of education in the several States and Territories, and to diffuse such information respecting the organization and management of schools and school systems, and methods of teaching as shall aid the People of the United States in the establishment and maintenance of efficient school systems, and otherwise promote the cause of education throughout the country.

As a U.S. Office of Education from 1953 through 1979, it had its scope of activities increased, and the office gained power, expanding in data-gathering and dissemination activities. One of its primary functions during this period was the responsibility of awarding and administering federal grants. During this period, grants increased dramatically both in numbers and in the amounts of money allocated. Many of the grants were for pilot experimental programs. The grant function, according to some authorities, permits the federal government to indirectly exercise control over education. There is no question that awarding grants is an effective way to influence the goals of education nationally. However, the block grant concept mentioned earlier will transfer some of the power to the state. On the other hand, there are persons who believe that offices of the federal government should have a strong influence on education. They maintain that the socioeconomic forces of society are not contained within local school districts or state boundaries, and therefore direct federal intervention is needed.

It is within this political educational context that the new Department of Education was created. Those who favored creating a new department felt that education was too important to be lost in the gigantic Department of Health, Education, and Welfare. Opponents took the position that a national Department of Education would result in more federal control and standardization.

Educational Programs Operated by the Federal Government

The federal government directly operates some school programs. The public school system of the District of Columbia depends on Congress for funds; for many years it was controlled by a board of education appointed by the justices of the U.S. District Court for Washington, D.C. Currently, school board members are chosen by popular election.

The Department of the Interior has the educational responsibility for children of national park employees, for Samoa (classified as an outlying possession), and for the trust territories of the Pacific, such as the Caroline Islands and the Marshall Islands. The schools on Indian reservations are financed and managed through the Bureau of Indian Affairs of the Department of the Interior.

The Department of Defense is responsible for the military academy at West Point, the naval academy at Annapolis, the Coast Guard Academy at New London, and the Air Force academy at Colorado Springs. The Department of Education will now operate a school system for the children of the military staff wherever members are stationed. The education supplied in the vocational and technical training programs of the military services has made a big contribution to the education of our nation. Many people transfer the technical and vocational skills acquired in military life to civilian occupations.

Interrelations of Governmental Educational Agencies

Federal, state, and local governments all have a part in education. The federal government has an "interest" in education, which is a state "function" and a local "operation." Each level of government has a purpose to be accomplished through education. The emphasis at each level has depended on the perspective at that level. Local school districts are concerned with immediate local educational needs, states with promoting the welfare of the state and ensuring children equal educational opportunities within the state, and the federal government with our national security, equality of opportunities, and solving national domestic problems. If local districts could and would completely meet all the needs of education—as the states and the federal government see them—then state and federal involvement would not be necessary. Federal and state involvement does seem necessary, however, so that each individual will have the right to an equal opportunity to pursue excellence in education and to achieve personal dignity. It seems likely that American public education will continue to be a local, state, and federal concern.

Summary and Implications

In summary, American education is formally organized governmentally at the local, state, and national levels. Local school boards, legislators at the state and national levels, and courts shape much of what happens in education. Lobbyists representing special interest groups affect the nature and process of education. American education is no longer operated independently by local board members in 100,000 school districts in the nation; it is an academic enterprise closely interrelated to social and economic issues, shaped in part by political processes. Professional organizations are a part of the political process.

Knowing about the formal organization of schools and the political arena in which they operate is important to those who work in schools. From initial certification, throughout daily and yearly work, and finally during retirement, teachers are affected by state regulations. Teacher organizations (NEA, AFT) are very active politically; as members of these organizations, teachers are expected to participate.

Teachers have influenced American education at local, state, and national levels and will continue to do so. At the local level this means through teaching in classrooms and through interacting with the community and the board of education. The state and national teachers' organizations gain their strength at the local level. If teachers really know how education is organized at the local level, they have an invaluable tool in shaping and working toward the goals of American education. They can then also advance the goals of the teaching profession and its members.

A knowledge of the state and national organization of education is also essential. Through political action at these levels, legislation affecting education and the teaching profession at all levels is developed. Teachers' organizations are active at the state and national levels. Members of teacher organizations who are informed about educational politics can be effective participants in determining the future of American education and the teaching profession.

DISCUSSION QUESTIONS

1. What improvements could be made in running education at the local level?
2. How can teachers affect the operation of local school districts?
3. What are the advantages and disadvantages of choosing the chief state school officers by election? by a state board of education?
4. How has local control of education been eroded? Why has this happened?
5. What arguments were used for and against the creation of the Department of Education?
6. What are the functions of state legislatures in public education in the United States and what limitations are placed upon them?
7. What are the advantages and disadvantages of school consolidation?
8. Which of the two processes for selection of local school board members, elective and appointive, do you think is not likely to result in securing effective school board members? Why?
9. What are the major functions of intermediate units? Under what circumstances could intermediate units be superior to school consolidation in providing educational services to students?
10. How have teacher associations increased their power base in American education?

SUPPLEMENTAL ACTIVITIES

1. Visit a meeting of a local board of education and write a critique of the meeting.
2. Examine and discuss educational bills considered by a recent session of a state legislature.
3. Get a copy of the school code for your state and study it.
4. Examine policy manuals from local school districts in your area, looking particularly for policies that affect what you do as a classroom teacher and policies that deal specifically with student rights.
5. Interview officers of local teachers' associations and ask their opinions on how they think they influence local educational policy.

NOTES

1. Valena White Plisko (ed.), *The Condition of Education 1984 Edition* (Washington, D.C.: National Center for Educational Statistics, 1984), pp. 3–8.
2. Jonathan P. Sher and Rachel B. Tompkins, *Economy, Efficiency and Equality: The Myths of Rural School and District Consolidation* (Washington, D.C.: National Institute of Education, U.S. Department of Health, Education, and Welfare, 1976), pp. 4–36, 40–41.
3. L. Harmon Ziegler, Harvey J. Tucker, and L. A. Wilson, "How School Control Was Wrested from the People," *Phi Delta Kappan* 58 (March 1977): 534–539.
4. Ibid., p. 539.
5. Ibid.
6. George Gallup, "The 15th Annual Gallup Poll of the Public's Attitude toward the Public Schools," *Phi Delta Kappan* 65 (September 1983): 46.
7. Robert Stephens, *Regional Educational Service Agencies* (Arlington, Va.: Educational Research Services, 1975).
8. Edgar L. Morphet, Roe L. Johns, and Theodore L. Reller, *Educational Organization and Administration: Concepts, Practices, and Issues*, 3rd ed. (Englewood Cliffs, N.J.: Prentice-Hall, 1974), p. 264.
9. Roald F. Campbell (ed.), Gerald E. Sroufe, and Donald H. Layton, *Strengthening State Departments of Education* (Chicago: University of Chicago Midwest Administration, 1967), p. 10.

BIBLIOGRAPHY

Bakalis, Michael J. "Power and Purpose in American Education." *Phi Delta Kappan* 65 (September 1983): 7–13.

Berke, Joel S., et al. *New Era of State Education Politics*. Cambridge, Mass.: Ballinger, 1977.

Donley, Marshall O., Jr. *Power to the Teacher: How America's Educators Became Militant*. Bloomington, Ind.: Indiana University Press, 1976.

Hanson, Mark E. *Educational Administration and Organizational Behavior*. Boston: Allyn and Bacon, 1978.

Monahan, William G., and Hengst, Herbert R. *Contemporary Educational Administration*. New York: Macmillan, 1982.

Park, J. Charles. "Preachers, Politics, and Public Education: A Review of Right-Wing Pressures against Public Schooling in America." *Phi Delta Kappan* 61 (May 1980): 608–611.

Sergiovanni, Thomas J.; Burlingame, Martin; Coombs, Fred; and Thurston, Paul. *Educational Governance and Administration*. Englewood Cliffs, N.J.: Prentice-Hall, 1980.

Sergiovanni, Thomas J., and Carver, Fred D. *The New School Executive: A Theory of Administration*. 2nd ed. New York: Harper & Row, 1980.

Stephens, Robert. *Regional Educational Service Agencies*. Arlington, Va.: Educational Research Services, 1975.

Thompson, John T. *Policy-making in American Public Education: A Framework for Analysis*. Englewood Cliffs, N.J.: Prentice-Hall, 1975.

Financing Public Education

Focus Questions

- Why should you as a future teacher know about how money is raised to support public schools?
- Why should it make any difference to you or the teaching profession if the expenditures per pupil differ widely from district to district and from state to state?
- Why should you be concerned about the effects of various kinds of taxes on taxpayers and the effectiveness of various kinds of taxes in producing money to operate schools?

- Do you know how states try to make certain that there is enough money provided for a basic education irrespective of the wealth of a particular school district?
- As a future teacher, do you think schools should be held fully accountable for student achievement? Why? Why not?
- Do you think students should be able to attend any school of their choice? Why? Why not?

Key Terms and Concepts

Property taxes
Planned-program budgeting
Regressive tax
State aid
Categorical aid
Foundation level
Fiscal equalization

Tax effort
Federal aid
Equality of opportunity
Equitable taxation
Accountability
Educational vouchers

What Would You Do?

The school district by which you are employed is in critical financial condition. It needs a tax referendum in order to become financially solvent. The teachers employed by the district recently went on strike, admitting publicly that they realized the poor financial condition of the school district. You were a member of the striking group. The strike ended, but the teachers were not satisfied with the settlement. The school district has now announced that it plans a tax referendum. Some members of the community plan to work to defeat the referendum because "the school board will use the funds to pay the salary demands of the strikers." Your local professional association is trying to decide whether or not to work for the passage of the referendum. What would be your position on this matter? Why?

Money to support education comes from a variety of taxes paid to local, state, and federal governments. These governments in turn distribute tax money to local school districts to operate the schools. The three principal kinds of taxes that provide revenue for schools are property taxes, sales or use taxes, and income taxes. The property tax is generally a local tax, and the sales tax a state tax; the income tax may be both a state tax and a federal one.

The percentage of total school revenue provided from federal sources steadily increased from a low of 0.3 percent in 1919 to a high of 9.8 percent in 1979.[1] It is not expected to increase further; in fact, it is likely to decrease in the next few years. The main increase occurred in 1965, when the percentage rose from 4.4 percent to 7.9 percent. This increase came primarily after the Elementary and Secondary Education Act of 1965 (ESEA) was passed.

Across the nation, school revenue from state sources has steadily increased from a low of 16.5 percent in 1919 to a current high of 48.3 percent. It is expected that as more states enact reforms in financing education, the nationwide average of state aid will increase. Revenue from local sources has steadily decreased from a high of 83.2 percent in 1919 to a low of 43.3 percent in 1981. The trend is toward decreasing federal support, accompanied by steadily increasing state support and steadily decreasing local support. This trend toward increasing state effort parallels the recommendations of many recent studies and court rulings on school finance, which are essentially directed toward equal opportunity. In some states the trend for increasing state aid was reversed in the early 1980s because of the severe economic recession.

The relative percentages of federal, state, and local revenues vary dramatically among states. As shown in Table 10.1, federal contributions vary from a high of 24.3 percent in Mississippi to a low of 5.3 percent in New Hampshire. State contributions vary from a high of 84.1 percent in Hawaii and relatively high percentages in Alaska (73.5), Kentucky (60.4), New Mexico (65.4), and Alabama (60.4) to lows of 6.1 percent in New Hampshire, 23.2 percent in Nebraska, and 27.7 percent in South Dakota. New Hampshire, Nebraska, and Connecticut have the highest percentages of local revenues; Hawaii, Alaska, Mississippi, Kentucky, and New Mexico have the lowest percentages of local revenues.[2]

Property Taxes—Local Revenue

The property tax is the primary source of local revenue for schools. It is based on the value of property, both real estate and personal. Real estate includes land holdings and buildings like homes, commercial buildings,

TABLE 10.1 *Receipts of Public Elementary and Secondary Schools by Source and by State for Selected States*

State	Percent of Receipts		
	Local	State	Federal
New Hampshire	88.6	6.1	5.3
Nebraska	68.1	23.2	8.7
Connecticut	64.4	29.4	6.2
South Dakota	59.3	27.7	13.0
Wyoming	61.3	33.2	5.5
Wisconsin	56.2	37.2	6.6
United States and D. C.	43.3	47.4	9.3
Alabama	23.0	60.4	16.6
New Mexico	19.7	65.4	15.0
Kentucky	20.0	64.0	16.0
Mississippi	19.0	56.7	24.3
Alaska	17.0	73.5	9.5
Hawaii	0.1	84.1	15.8

Source: W. Vance Grant and Thomas D. Snyder, *Digest of Educational Statistics, 1983–84,* National Center for Educational Statistics, Washington, D.C., p. 78.

and factories. Personal property consists of automobiles, machinery, livestock, and intangible property such as stocks and bonds. The property tax is an old tax, based on an agrarian economy in which the measure on one's real estate was a measure of one's wealth.

The main advantage of the property tax is its stability. Although it lags behind other changes in market values, it provides a steady, regular income. Also, property is fixed; that is, it is not easily moved to escape taxation, as income might be.

The property tax has numerous limitations. It bears heavily on housing; it tends to discourage rehabilitation and upkeep, since both of these would tend to raise the value of the property and therefore its taxes; it is often a deciding factor in locating a business or industry; and it is not likely to be applied equally on all properties.

A difficulty with the property tax lies in determining the value of property. In some areas, assessors are local people, frequently elected, with no special training in evaluating property. Their duty involves inspecting their neighbors' properties and placing values upon them. In other areas, sophisticated techniques involving expertly trained personnel are used for property appraisal. In any event, assessors are likely to be subject to political and informal pressures to keep values low. Appraisals generally take into account the location, area, and use of the property. Homes are judged by the number of rooms, facilities, type of foundation, building materials, and landscaping. In some areas, photographs of real estate are used for comparative purposes. Similar comparative scales are used to evaluate industrial and farm property. The value of real property is reviewed at regular intervals, frequently every four years, in an attempt to establish its current market value.

The assessed value of property is usually only a percentage of its market value. This percentage varies from county to county and from state to state. Attempts are made within states to equalize assessments or to make certain that the same percentage of full cash value is used in assessing property throughout the state. In recent years, attempts have been made to institute full cash value for the assessed value. For the property tax to be a fair tax, equalized assessment is a necessity.

The property tax is most generally thought of as a proportionate tax, that is, one that taxes according to ability to pay. Since assessments may be unequal and since frequently the greatest wealth is no longer related to real estate, the property tax can be regressive. Regressive taxes, like sales and use taxes, are those that affect low-income groups disproportionately. There is some evidence to support the contention that persons in the lowest-income groups pay a much higher proportion of their income in property taxes than persons in the highest-income groups.

Inequities of the Property Tax

Significant support for schools across the nation is provided by the property tax. The total value of property within a school district when related to its number of pupils is an indicator of the wealth of a school district. A school district having an assessed valuation of $30 million, for example, and responsibility for educating 1000 pupils would have $30,000 of assessed valuation per pupil. Usually, the number of pupils in average daily attendance is used as a divisor to determine assessed valuation per pupil. Since property tax rates are applied to assessed valuations, a district with a high assessed valuation per pupil is in a better position to provide quality education than one with a low assessed valuation per pupil. If school district A has an assessed valuation of $90 million and 1000 pupils, for example, and school district B has an assessed valuation of $30 million and 1000 pupils, a tax rate of $2 per $100 of assessed valuation would produce $1.8 million for education in district A and only $600,000 in district B. School district A could therefore spend $1800 per pupil, compared with $600 per pupil in school district B, with the same local tax effort.

Great differences exist in wealth per pupil from school district to school district. Concentrations of industrial developments increase valuation in one district, while a neighboring district may be almost completely residential with low valuation and many pupils.

Differences in wealth and concomitant differences in tax rates and per-pupil expenditures were most dramatically pointed out in the *Serrano* v. *Priest* (1971) decision of the Supreme Court of California.

In *Serrano* v. *Priest* the California Supreme Court was called upon to determine whether the California public school financing system, with its substantial dependence on local property taxes, violated the Fourteenth Amendment. In a six-to-one decision in August 1971 the court held that heavy reliance on unequal local property taxes "makes the quality of a child's education a function of the wealth of his parents and neighbors." Further, the court declared: "Districts with small tax bases simply cannot levy taxes at a rate sufficient to produce the revenue that more affluent districts produce with a minimum effort."

At the time of the *Serrano* v. *Priest* decision the Baldwin Park school district, for example, spent $577 per pupil, whereas the Beverly Hills school district spent $1232. Yet the tax rate in Baldwin Park of $5.48 was more than double the rate of $2.38 in Beverly Hills. The discrepancy was caused by the difference in wealth between the two districts. Beverly Hills had $50,885 of assessed valuation per child; Baldwin Park had only $3706 valuation per child—a ratio of thirteen to one. The inequities resulting from the property tax are at least twofold; the tax is oftentimes inequitably applied to the taxpayer, and in poor districts the tax frequently results in unequal opportunities for education.

Officially, the California court ruled that the system of school financing in California was unconstitutional but did not forbid the use of property taxes. Within a year of *Serrano* v. *Priest* (1971), five other courts—in Minnesota, Texas, New Jersey, Wyoming, and Arizona—ruled similarly.

In 1973 the U.S. Supreme Court consented to hear an appeal of the *San Antonio* (Texas) *Independent School District* v. *Rodriguez* case. The elements in that case were like those of the *Serrano* v. *Priest* case. The U.S. Supreme Court, in a five-to-four decision, reversed the lower court in *San Antonio Independent School District* v. *Rodriguez* and thus reaffirmed the local property tax as a basis for school financing. Justice Potter Stewart, voting with the majority, admitted that "the method of financing public schools . . . can be fairly described as chaotic and unjust." He did not, though, find it unconstitutional. The majority opinion, written by Justice Lewis F. Powell, stated: "We cannot say that such disparities are the product of a system that is so irrational as to be invidiously discriminatory." The opinion also noted that the poor are not necessarily concentrated in the poorest districts, that states must initiate fundamental reform in taxation and education, and that the extent to which quality of education varies with expenditures is inconclusive. Justice Thurgood Marshall, in the dissenting opinion, charged that the ruling "is a retreat from our historic commitment to equality of educational opportunity."

Before the *San Antonio Independent School District* v. *Rodriguez* (1973) decision, but after *Serrano* v. *Priest* (1971), the National Legislative Conference Special Commission on School Finance recommended that "states should assume responsibility for seeing that elementary and secondary schools are funded properly, and that 'equal opportunity' responsibility enunciated in *Serrano* v. *Priest* (1971) be accepted, regardless of the courts, because the Serrano principle is right."[3] Since *Rodriguez,* eleven state supreme trial courts have struck down school finance systems. Those decisions were in the states of Arkansas, California, Colorado, Connecticut, Georgia, Idaho, Maryland, New York, Ohio, Washington, and West Virginia.[4] Within nine months of *Serrano* v. *Priest,* 99 commissions or committees were organized to study the school finance systems of the 50 states.[5] Undoubtedly, changes are occurring in the state provisions for financial support for education. Since the flurry of legislation, however, the economic crunch has adversely affected what states can afford, and some states have not been able to live up to their commitments.

The property tax is only one part of the comprehensive tax system. Local financial procedures and state and federal efforts in school finance also enter the picture.

Local Planning and Budgeting

The property tax rate of a school district is determined from the monetary needs of the district as expressed in its budget. A budget encompasses the financial plan of the school district. It can be conceived of as the educational program of the school district expressed in dollars and cents. Usually, budgets are prepared on an annual basis and project the income and educational costs for a year. States generally prescribe forms and procedures to be used in preparing, administering, and adopting the school budget.

The superintendent of schools, frequently helped by a staff, usually prepares the budget. In many districts the first step is for teachers to submit budgetary requests. Usually, the school board must act officially to approve the budget and finally to adopt it. In some states, school budgets must be approved by the state. In many states a public hearing is required before the school budget can be adopted.

The classification of budgetary expenditures has been standardized largely through the efforts of the former U.S. Office of Education. Educational expenditures are classified under three headings: capital outlay, debt service, and current expenses. Capital outlay includes expenditures for land, buildings, and equipment; debt service includes the repayment of borrowed money and the interest on the debt; and current expense includes the expenditures necessary for daily operation and maintenance. The largest category of current educational expense is that of instructional expenses, which include teachers' salaries and fringe benefits. This amount frequently exceeds 70 to 85 percent of the total budget. The budget, in its final form, expresses the amount of money needed for operating the school system; hence the budget determines the tax rate.

Planned-program budgeting, a new trend in budgeting, seeks to classify expenditures by school program rather than by the traditional categories—salaries, instructional materials, and administration. A program budget, for example, would project expenditures for categories such as the elementary school reading program, the high school mathematics program, or the vocational educational program. School districts under program budgeting need to identify their programs and keep their records accordingly. An important advantage of program budgeting is accountability—the relationships between educational cost and educational accomplishment become clarified. In an accountability approach, educational records of progam accomplishment can be compared with the costs of the program. (Accountability is discussed more fully later in this chapter.)

The states usually grant by law a minimum property tax rate to cover current expenditures for local school districts. Frequently, increases in tax rate limits require voter approval. In some states there is no state limit on the school tax rate; with local approval the rate can be raised as high as desired. In other states the state establishes a maximum limit by law that cannot be exceeded, even with local approval. This maximum limit is often reached step by step with voter approval.

States usually limit how much capital outlay indebtedness a school district may incur. These limits are established in various ways. In some states the limit is an established percentage of assessed valuation; 5 to 10 percent is common. In other states no limits are set, but the legislature or the state office of public instruction must approve the indebtedness.

Limited tax rates for current expenses and limitations on indebtness point out further the significance of assessed valuation as a factor in determining the quality of an educational program. A local school district can be making the maximum effort, taxing to the limit, and still not be able to offer a program comparable to what a wealthier neighboring district offers under a medium effort. The effort made by a local school district indicates the value that the citizens place on education; yet it is obvious that equal effort does not produce equal revenue or equal opportunity.

Expenditures per pupil vary widely, partly because the districts are not equally wealthy. States also differ in wealth and correspondingly in expenditures per pupil. The current average annual expenditure per pupil in the United States is $2473. Alaska, Delaware, New Jersey, New York, and Oregon, along with the District of Columbia, all spend over $3000 per pupil; Alabama, Arkansas, Kentucky, Mississippi, Tennessee, and Utah all spend less than $1900 per pupil.[6]

Assessment practices differ from state to state; hence it is difficult to use assessed valuation per pupil as a measure in comparing the wealth of states. A more accurate index is personal income per capita. States with per capita personal income greater than $11,500 include Alaska, California, Connecticut, Illinois, Federal District of Columbia, New Jersey, Wyoming, and Nevada, whereas Alabama, Arkansas, Mississippi, South Carolina, Utah, and West Virginia all have per capita personal incomes lower than $8400.[7] In general, higher per capita personal income results in higher expenditures per pupil.

State Sources of Revenue

The main sources of tax revenue for states have been classified by the Department of Commerce in four groups: sales and gross receipts, income taxes, licenses, and miscellaneous. Sales and gross receipt taxes include taxes on general sales, motor fuels, alcohol, insurance, and amusements; income taxes include both individual and corporate; licenses include those on motor vehicles, corporations, occupations, vehicle operators, hunting, and fishing. The largest miscellaneous classification includes property taxes, severance or extraction of minerals taxes, and death and gift taxes.

The average state receives 51 percent of its tax revenue from sales and gross receipts, 36 percent from income taxes, 6.6 percent from licenses, and 6.4 percent from miscellaneous categories. Almost all states use some form of sales tax; many use individual and corporate income taxes.

Sales and Income Taxes

Sales and income taxes are lucrative sources of state revenue, and it is relatively easy to administer both. The sales tax is collected bit by bit, in a relatively painless way, by the vendor, who is responsible for keeping records. The state income tax can be withheld from wages; hence collection is eased. Some argue that this tax meets the criterion of a "good" tax because it is closely related to the ability to pay. Income taxes are referred to as progressive taxes, since they frequently are scaled to the ability of the taxpayer to pay. Sales taxes are "regressive," since they affect low-income groups disproportionately. All persons pay the sales tax at the same rate, so persons in low-income groups pay as much tax as persons in high-income groups. Part of the regression of the sales tax can be overcome by exempting food from taxation. Both sales taxes and income taxes are direct and certain; they fluctuate with the economy, and they can be regulated by the legislature that must raise the money.

State Aid

State aid to local school districts is paid out of tax revenue raised by the state; it is complicated and varies considerably among states. State aid for education exists largely for three reasons: the state has the primary responsibility for educating its citizens, the financial ability of local school districts to support education varies widely, and personal wealth is now less related to real property than it once was. We have already examined the first two reasons. The third reason relates to the property tax—the main source of local income for school districts. Since much individual wealth is not real property and since it seems reasonable that taxation should be based on ability to pay, then apparently the local property tax has serious limitations as a source of school funds. The progressive income tax seems more equitable; money so collected could be proportionately redistributed or shared by local school districts and also used to provide financial equalization for education.

State aid can be classified as having *general* or *categorical* use. General aid can be used by the recipient school district as it desires; categorical aid is earmarked for specific purposes. Categorical aid, for example, may include money for transportation, vocational education, driver education, and handicapped children. Frequently, categorical aid is given to encourage specified educational programs; in some states these aid programs are referred to as incentive programs. Categorical aid funds may be granted on a matching basis; this means that for each dollar of local effort, the state contributes a specified amount. Categorical aid has undoubtedly encouraged needed educational programs.

Historically, general aid was based on the idea that each child, regardless of place of residence or wealth of the local district, should be entitled to receive a basic education. General state aid was established on the principle of equality of opportunity and is usually administered through a foundation program. A foundation program includes determining the dollar value of the basic educational opportunities desired in a state, referred to as the foundation level; determining a minimum standard of local effort; and determining an equitable way of distributing the money to school districts, considering their local wealth. The foundation concept implies equity for taxpayers as well as equality of opportunity for students.

Figure 10.1 represents graphically how a foundation program operates. The total length of each bar represents the foundation level of edu-

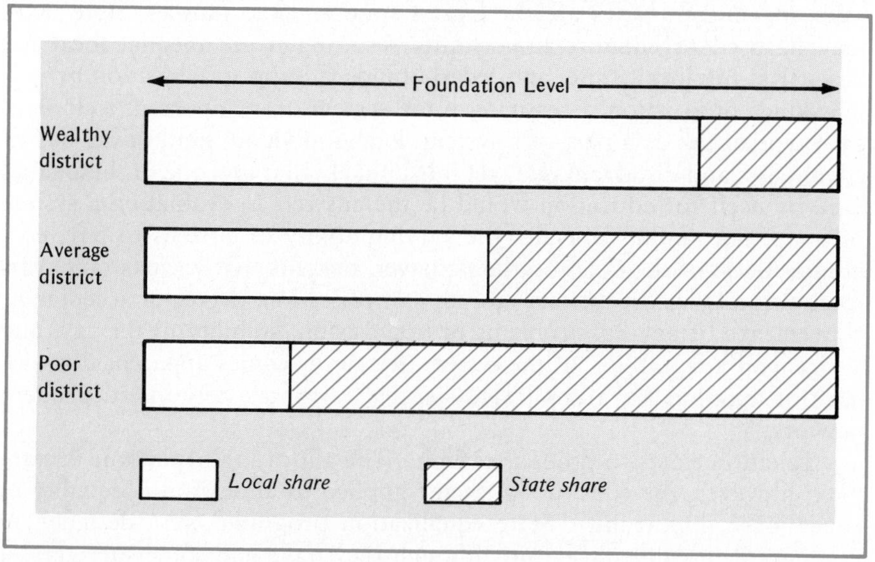

FIGURE 10.1 *Equalization and the foundation principle.*

cation required per pupil, expressed in dollars. Each school district must put forth the same minimum local effort to finance its schools; this could be a qualifying tax rate that produces the local share of the foundation level. This tax rate will produce more revenue in a wealthy district than it will in a poor district; therefore poor districts will receive more state aid than wealthy districts. Local school districts do not receive general state aid beyond that amount established as the foundation but are permitted in most instances to exceed foundation levels at their own expense.

The effectiveness of the use of various state foundation programs to achieve fiscal equalization has been limited. A major limitation is that the foundation established is frequently far below the actual expenditure or far below the level needed to provide adequate educational opportunity. For example, if a state established a per-pupil foundation level of $1200 and the average per pupil expenditure was $2000, equalization would not have occurred.

A second limitation is that most general state aid programs do not provide for the different expenditure levels for different pupil needs. Special education and vocational education, for example, both require more money to operate than the usual per-pupil expenditure for the typical elementary or secondary school pupil. These weaknesses and others—including the taxing inequities—have brought about strong and determined research efforts to find a more satisfactory and acceptable system for financing American education.

The method of distributing state aid differs from state to state. The percentage of current expenditures paid by state aid also differs from state to state, as does the ability of states to support schools.

In summary, the property tax is the largest local revenue source, and sales and income taxes are the largest state revenue sources. State taxes may be used to equalize opportunity resulting from unequal local tax bases. Raising local, state, and federal funds to support education by various kinds of taxation necessitates a tax system. It is important to look at each type of tax as a part of a system. Each individual kind of tax has its advantages and disadvantages, yet it is unlikely that any one of these taxes used by itself for education would be the answer. In evaluating a system of taxes, one should consider the varying ability of citizens to pay, economic effects of the taxes on the taxpayer, benefits that various taxpayers receive, total yield of the tax, economy of collection, degree of acceptance, convenience of paying, problems of tax evasion, stability of the tax, and the general adaptability of the system. It soon becomes apparent that systems of taxation are complicated—each is an intricately interdependent network.

Taxation exists to produce revenue. The allocation of revenue is complex; however, the educational theme applied to allocation is equality of educational opportunity. State equalization programs were designed to accomplish this objective, and although they have had some successes, it must be concluded that these successes have been limited.

Federal Aid

Many people have suggested that the logical solution to the inequities that exist in the ability of states to support education is federal aid. The United States has a history of federal aid to education, but it has been categorical and not general aid; it has been related to the needs of the nation at the time. Federal aid actually started with the Ordinance of 1785, before the U.S. Constitution was adopted, which provided land for public schools in "Western territories." Such federal aid has continued in a steady progression to the present. It has been estimated that almost 200 federal aid-to-education laws have been passed since the Northwest Ordinance.[8]

Federal activity and funding gained great momentum in the 1960s and 1970s. The Elementary and Secondary Education Act of 1965 (ESEA), approved and funded by the 89th Congress, was truly a significant act among the federal acts designed to aid education. ESEA was categorical, yet came as close to general aid to education as any federal legislation ever has. Its scope was broad, and most school districts could qualify for funds. The purpose of the Act was to equalize educational opportunities. ESEA did not operate like typical state foundation programs; it had five titles, each designed for a specific purpose. Local agencies wanting to participate had to plan and present proposals for action within the guidelines of the various titles. ESEA was amended in 1966, 1967, 1970—and then each year from 1974 to 1980. ESEA represented an extensive federal effort to improve education throughout the United States. It recognized the importance of education in a democratic government and, in so doing, sought to provide opportunities for every child to pursue educational excellence. It recognized the need for cooperative planning for education at the federal, state, and local levels.

Federal funding in recent years continued to be categorical until the passage of the Educational Improvement and Consolidation Act (EICA) in 1981. The Act consolidated 28 separate federally sponsored educational programs into one block grant. Left out of the Act were education for the handicapped; vocational, bilingual, and adult education; impact aid; ESEA Title IV civil rights programs; and the Women's Educational Equity program. ESEA Title I programs for the disadvantged were kept as the first title of the new consolidation Act. Title II of the Act consolidated the aforementioned 28 programs, providing greater discretion for state and local educational agencies as to the use of the money. Block grants are viewed by many as a threat to tightly targeted categorical programs, historically designed to provide educational assistance related to the achieving of important national goals. The trend toward block grants is an early indication of possible transformation of the federal role in education.[9]

Federal aid, while seemingly historically established, is still controversial. Advocates of federal aid point out that it is a logical answer to providing equality of educational opportunity for all children regardless of residence. They point out that federal aid to education helps the national

Cuts in programs for special needs students may deny them their full potential.

defense and general welfare ultimately and that these national concerns cannot be adequately pursued at a local or state level. Proponents of federal aid to education hold also that this help does not necessarily mean federal controls, citing the land grant acts and the National Defense Education Act of 1958 as federal aid that was not accompanied by control. They feel that federal aid, through the income tax, is the most equitable

way of paying for public education. Opponents of federal aid point out
that education is a state and a local function. They argue that variations
in fiscal ability to pay will always exist and that the distribution of federal
funds will not guarantee that whatever differences now exist will be reduced appreciably. They point out that the nation is weakened by depending on the federal government for funds, that categorical aid is federal
control, and that states can use the income tax as effectively as the federal
government.

The policies of the federal government, beginning in the early 1980s,
in respect to the federal role in education have been characterized as the
"five Ds"; diminution, deregulation, decentralization, disestablishment, and
deemphasis.[10] Clearly, diminution of federal funding has occurred along
with decentralization, manifested by the block grant and consolidation
program. Currently, education has become a campaign issue, stirred by
the publication of the National Commission on Excellence in Education
report "A Nation at Risk." In the campaign for the Presidency in 1983–
1984 the fiscal message from the incumbent administration had not
changed—state government and local school districts must fund the quest
for excellence in education.

It seems likely, nevertheless, that the federal government will continue
some financial support to American education. Interrelated domestic, social, and economic problems of national magnitude must be resolved; for
financial and other reasons these problems have not been solved, and
probably could not be, at local or state levels. The federal government has
access to funds through the most equitable kind of tax—the progressive
income tax, both personal and corporate. Personal and corporate income
now accounts for most of the national income; yet public schools in the
main are still relatively heavily supported by local revenue generated by
the property tax, which is less related to people's ability to pay. The inequality of the tax base among the states could be adjusted through federal
aid; and certainly the quality of educational opportunity is related to how
well states can support education. The principle of local support for education served well for many years, and then, because of unequal tax
bases, local communities needed the help of the state. While average state
support nationwide has increased to approximately 47 percent, further
increases are likely to be difficult to secure. There is still a fiscal role for
the federal government in education.

It is clear that the current system of school financing—with its relatively heavy reliance on local support gained from the local property tax—
cannot realize equality of educational opportunity. Further, the property
tax itself in today's economy tends to be a regressive and unfair tax. State
equalization programs have not been successful in securing equality of
opportunity, although effective steps have recently been taken in some
states. The federal effort has been feeble in terms of the total educational
expenditure, contributing only about 9.8 percent at its peak in 1979. The
question that remains debatable is what the appropriate fiscal role of the
federal government in education should be.

School Finance Issues: 1980s–1990s

The basic issue in school financing is not likely to be different in the 1980s and beyond from what it has been in the past. That issue is making an adequate education equally available to everyone, along with a system of taxation designed to be equitable—that is, a system in which taxpayers are all called upon to support education in proportion to their ability to pay. Both equal opportunity and equitable taxation are difficult to achieve, as was illustrated earlier in this chapter. The social, economic, political, and financial milieu of the 1980s and 1990s is likely to be quite different from that of the late 1960s and early 1970s, which were characterized as expansion and boom years. Some trends of the late 1970s may continue into the 1980s. Those trends include inflation, taxpayer revolt, and decreasing enrollments, which are likely to affect the adequacy of school funding and therefore further complicate the basic issue in school finance—providing an adequate education with equality of opportunity through an equitable system of taxation.

Inflation

Inflation, which increased rapidly in the late 1970s and early 1980s, affected every person and every institution. In the case of public schools, revenue simply did not keep up with expenses. The greatest effects of inflation on public schools were the dramatically increasing costs of energy and salaries. It was difficult for taxpayers to understand and accept the fact that the cost of education was increasing while enrollments were declining. The fact is that it is still costing more to educate fewer pupils, and the major culprit is inflation. Revenue coming to the schools did not increase as rapidly as inflation did. In 1983 and 1984 the rate of inflation was reduced and began to show signs of stabilizing. However, it remains to be seen whether or not inflation can be controlled.

Taxpayer Revolt

A most dramatic instance of taxpayer revolt occurred in California in June 1978 with the passage of Proposition 13, which limited by constitutional amendment the property tax as a source of revenue. Subsequent and similar propositions in other states in 1978 were not successful. Nevertheless, those efforts, along with a low rate of successful tax increase referenda nationally and the closing of school districts for periods of time because of insufficient funds to operate, indicated problems for the future funding of public schools.

Proposition 13 set a maximum tax of 1 percent on the fair market value of property, limited assessment growth to 2 percent per year, and required the state legislature to have at least a two thirds vote to substitute new taxes for lost local revenues. Proposition 2½, passed in Massachusetts in November 1980, proposed that no city or town be allowed to levy property taxes in excess of 2½ percent of the total evaluation. Furthermore, if a community taxed above this rate, Proposition 2½ called for a reduction in local property taxes by 15 percent each year until the tax floor was reached.[11] Proposition 2½ became effective on July 1, 1981. Missouri passed tax limitation legislation in 1980.[12] Other states have also placed constitutional or statutory limits on taxation or spending.

The efforts for tax reduction are not in harmony with the school finance reform that took place in many states shortly after the *Serrano* (1971) decision. School finance reform that took place during that time in at least 22 states was generally characterized by:

- Increased state aid for public schools either by tapping budget surpluses or by raising existing state taxes.
- Cutting local tax rates.
- Distributing aid increasingly on the basis of unusual educational needs or costs.
- Setting limits on local tax rates or placing ceilings on local school district expenditures.
- Creating pupil-weighting systems that provided more funding for educating children who were handicapped, who required bilingual education, or who were otherwise in need of special programs.

The tax reforms raised state expenditures for education through a leveling-up process in which most school districts received additional money in the process of establishing equity. Leveling down was a rare occurrence. Increased spending for education, be it at the state or local level, is incompatible with tax cuts. If the tax reform movement is successful in cutting taxes and if equal educational opportunity is still considered an objective to be achieved primarily with state aid, then equal educational opportunity will have to be accompanied by a leveling down rather than a leveling up, or public schools will have to become more cost effective or, more likely, will have to reduce the adequacy of education.

It is clear that property tax limitation amendments in California (Proposition 13, 1978), in Massachusetts (Proposition 2½, 1981), and in other states have had adverse effects on the services that local government agencies, including school boards, could provide. Community and educational services were cut, and alternative revenue sources, such as fees and other charges, were enacted. Some school districts filed for bankruptcy. The effect of the tax limitations was clearly differential; that is, some localities and school districts were more adversely affected than others.[13] However, it is also important to note that during the years 1978–1983 the nation first experienced high inflation that was followed by a recession, both of which had the effect of reducing fiscal resources for schools. It is also interesting to note that 30 states increased their taxes in 1983 based primarily on a weakening economy.[14]

Decreasing Enrollments

Enrollments in public schools will continue to decline in the early 1980s. Since most state aid programs are tied to enrollments, decreasing revenues are also to be expected. Furthermore, there will be an increasingly large percentage of the population over 65 years old. These facts indicate more competition for public school money.

Increasing Enrollments

It has been predicted that in the next ten to fifteen years, 1985–2000, the school population will increase by about 18 percent for the nation. The predicted increase in school population is a reversal of the 1970s and early 1980s, when the country's school age population dropped markedly.[15] Earlier, it was noted that school districts had decreasing real revenues during the decline because of inflation and the fact that many state aid programs are tied to enrollments. It has now been predicted that in the 1985–2000 period, many states will be required to increase total revenues for schools more rapidly than in the past decade in order to maintain current levels of real spending per pupil for elementary and secondary education.

Patterns: State-Local-Federal Sector Expenditures

The following quote from *Prospects for Financing Elementary and Secondary Education in the States* points out, and provides an explanation for, the steady decline of state and local support for elementary and secondary education. It also predicts a decline in federal support. The prospects for providing adequate fiscal support in the next few years with predicted expanding enrollments are quite dim.

> After a long period of expansion, state-local direct general expenditures peaked at around 18.3 percent of personal income and about 14.8 percent of Gross National Product in 1975. Since then there has been a steady decline in the relative size of the state-local public sector; state-local general expenditures as a percent of both personal income and GNP were lower in 1981 than they were in 1972. On a per capita basis, state-local expenditures rose throughout the 1970s, but real expenditures adjusted to reflect inflation have remained relatively constant since 1975. Between 1975 and 1981, real expenditures per capita rose by only about $90, or at an average annual growth rate of less than 1 percent.
>
> The major factor contributing to the decline in state-local expenditures has been a decline in fiscal effort in most states starting in the late 1970s. By 1980, all but a handful of states had levels of effort (own source revenues as a percent of personal income) below those of 1972. The steep declines in effort reflect the impact of some tax and expenditure limitations such as Prop-

osition 13 in California and numerous tax reductions enacted by state legislatures in the late 1970s. The decline in effort has been even greater if only tax revenues are considered.

Effort for education showed a similar decline. In 1972, state-local own source revenues represented 5.1 percent of personal income. By 1980, effort had dropped to 4.1 percent and by 1981 to 4.0 percent of income. . . .

Through the 1970s, federal aid grew more rapidly than state-local revenues, rising from 7.5 percent of total revenues in 1972 to 8.9 percent in 1979. Since 1979, however, there has been a steady decline in the federal share of school revenues (8.2 percent in 1981) and a decline in the real level of federal aid. With the budget cuts enacted during the 1982 fiscal year and anticipated for the 1983 fiscal year, the federal share of school revenues is likely to continue to decrease.[16]

Outlook for the 1980s

The following quote from *Prospects for Financing Elementary and Secondary Education in the States* further emphasizes the potential difficulties in providing adequate fiscal support for education in this and the next decade.

The 1980s would appear to be an especially challenging period for the finance of elementary and secondary education. Of particular significance is the reversal of the decline in school enrollments that will occur in most States by the late 1980s. With an increase in the number of children of school-age, there is likely to be a renewed demand for additional resources for public schools as well as continued pressure for greater productivity and better educational outcomes. In addition, an increasing proportion of children will come from family backgrounds associated with educational disadvantagement—poverty, minority, and non-English or limited-English-proficiency. The increased funds required for growing numbers of children will need to be further augmented to provide for more children with special educational needs.

While the demand for elementary/secondary education will be increasing, the decline in the size of the public sector—and in the level of Federal funding for education—that occurred in the late 1970s does not seem likely to be reversed. At most, the relative size of public expenditures may stabilize at the current level, but a considerable expansion similar to that of the 1960s and early 1970s is unlikely. That period may have represented an abnormal expansion of the public sector, while the last few years may represent a return to a more normal pattern.

A smaller public sector may mean several consequences for elementary/secondary school finance. First, real increases in school resources per pupil may be more difficult to achieve than they were earlier. During the late 1970s a slower growth in revenues for education did not place a severe strain on public school funding in part because of declining enrollments. Enrollment increases are, however, projected for the latter part of this decade. Secondly, large increases in non-school-age groups of the population, particularly those over 65, may result in less political support for public schools. Expansion of funding for other public services came about in the 1970s in part as a result of the decline in the proportion of expenditures devoted to schools. It is unclear whether public schools will be able to maintain their current share of total expenditures in the 1980s in the face of more intense competition from other public services, if the size of the public sector remains stable.

To return to a point made earlier in the chapter, the national economy will play an important role in shaping funding prospects for schools in the future. If the economy improves, the prospects for financing education in the future would be enhanced significantly. Many forecasts suggest an economic upturn at a time when major school enrollment increases are projected; in that case, available revenues may be sufficient to meet the anticipated demand for school resources. If the economy remains relatively stagnant or declines, school resources will be highly constrained. However, during a time of economic expansion, funding prospects are likely to differ significantly among the States.[17]

Accountability

Schools in the 1980s will continue to be called upon to be accountable. Although there are many definitions of the term "accountability," in education it means that schools must devise a way of relating the vast expenditure made available for education to the educational results. For many years the quality of education was measured by the number of dollars spent or the processes of education used. In other words, a school system that had a relatively high cost per pupil or used educational techniques judged to be effective was considered an excellent school system. Seldom was the effectiveness of school systems judged by output—the educational attainments of their students. Now attainment, and a clear record of the cost of that attainment, must be accounted for.

Accountability has its roots in two fundamental modern problems. One is the continuous escalation of educational costs. Closely related is the increasing loss of faith in educational results. The failure of the American educational system, particularly in the cities, has been accurately documented. The expectations of citizens for their children have not been met. Although the American public schools historically have done the best job of any nation in the world in providing education for all the children of all the people, they still have failed for some of their constituents. Our goals have been high, which means that the educational expectations of our citizens have also been high. We have not met the expectations, and at the same time the cost of education has gone up and up. The percentage of our gross national product that goes to education has been steadily increasing.

When the Elementary and Secondary Education Act of 1965 went into effect, the federal government called for accountability; it asked to receive documented results of educational attainment. This was the first formal call for accountability.

How can school systems become accountable? First, they must specify goals. In other words, if one goal of an elementary school is "to have pupils learn to read," then this goal must be spelled out specifically for each grade or child, whichever makes better sense, and success in meeting the goal should be measured and reported. This is the only way that results can be conveyed to the public. Many educational goals are not easily assessed, but this should not prevent educators from dealing precisely with results that do lend themselves to objective measurement. When school systems can adequately report results in "hard" data, accountability will be possible.

The second aspect, accounting for expenses related to educational results, is easier. Financial accounting systems (planning, programming, and budgeting systems) that are designed specifically to record expenditures on educational programs can effectively reveal the costs of the educational results. When costs are known, it is a simple matter to measure them against what has been accomplished in performance. Advanced computer technology has increased the sophistication of accountability reporting systems; thus better-informed educational decisions are possible, and the way is cleared for regaining the public's confidence in the educational establishment. Documented accountability may further help determine which responsibilities are clearly the schools' and which belong to other agencies.

Educational Vouchers

Use of educational vouchers represents an attempt to reform education. Under a voucher system, parents of all school-age children in a community are given vouchers roughly representing their children's share of the educational budget. A child then uses this voucher to attend any school he or she chooses, public or private, secular or parochial. Vouchers permit alternatives to the customary locked-in system of neighborhood education, [31] wherein children proceed, usually without choice, from the neighborhood elementary school to junior and senior high schools, still in the same neighborhood. The rationale of the voucher system is that it causes schools to [38] respond better to their constituencies in the face of competition. In a sense, public schools are monopolies; students cannot choose which school to attend.

Public schools do not function in a social milieu that inspires experimentation and responsiveness. They must, with rare exceptions, accept students assigned to them; the students in turn must attend these particular schools. In contrast, private schools select their students, and students, if they want and can afford private education, select their schools. The voucher plan tries to introduce the element of competition into public education; students choose the best school in the area, and the weaker schools, in theory, are forced to improve.

The idea of a voucher system has gained considerable support since it was first proposed in 1970. In 1970 a slightly higher percentage of those responding to the Gallup Poll opposed the idea than favored it. By 1981 those in favor held a slight majority over those opposed. In 1983, when asked, "Would you like to see such an idea (voucher system) adopted in this country?'', 51 percent favored the idea, and 38 percent were opposed.[18]

It is quite likely that the increasing support for the voucher system and tuition tax credit is related to the public's dissatisfaction with the educational results of the public schools. The improvement of the public schools of this nation is vital in the near future.

Summary and Implications

Education is supported from a variety of taxes paid to local, state, and federal governments. The three principle kinds of taxes that provide revenue for the schools are property taxes, sales or use taxes, and income taxes. The property tax is generally a local tax, and the sales tax a state tax; the income tax may be both a state tax and a federal tax. Historically, the property tax has provided the largest portion of local school income. State support has increased to the point that the nationwide average state share of support today is approximately 43 percent, with federal aid reaching a peak of 9.8 percent in 1979. The trend is toward increased state support and toward decreased local support along with a stable or decline in federal support.

State aid is based on the principle of equality of opportunity; that is, each child, regardless of place of residence or the wealth of the local school district, should be entitled to receive a basic education. There is wide variance in the financial capability of local school districts to support education. State aid is designed, in general, to equalize the amount of money available for education for each student in the state. Poor local school districts receive more money from the state than do wealthy ones.

The major challenge in financing schools is that of making an adequate education equally available to everyone and at the same time designing a system of taxation that is equitable—that is, a system in which taxpayers are all called upon to support education in proportion to their ability to pay. Accomplishing the goal of equality and equity is going to be increasingly difficult in the near future. Inflation, taxpayer revolt, and increasing enrollment are very likely to affect the adequacy of school funding. School districts will be expected to cut back expenditures and provide hard and convincing evidence that their students are receiving a sound basic education.

Additional funding for education is more likely to come from the states than from other sources. Other state services such as welfare, unemployment, and highway construction also need money and compete for the same, usually limited, funds. Further, legislators and governors are concerned with maintaining a fiscal balance to keep their respective states solvent. Within this milieu those fund seekers with financial and political knowledge—and with power—are likely to be the most successful.

Teacher organizations, as indicated earlier in this book, have become powerful and have been successful in shaping legislation throughout the country. Teacher organizations in the past have been politically active in seeking funding for education at the state and federal levels. They will need to continue and perhaps escalate their efforts to procure money for education in the future. Teacher organizations are known and respected for the size of their constituencies, their economic resources, their political activity, their research staffs, their legislative programs, and their lobbying efforts. Members of the profession should be familiar with the fundamentals of school finance so that they can understand the issues and be both effective and responsible in the political arena.

DISCUSSION QUESTIONS

1. What are the main advantages and disadvantages of the property tax?
2. What are the advantages of the sales and income taxes?
3. What have been some of the noticeable effects of categorical aid—both state and federal—on the curricula of the local school districts in your area?
4. How is federal aid likely to change in the next decade?
5. What are the advantages and disadvantages of the increasing level of state support for education?
6. What other factors besides equalized expenditures affect equality of opportunity?
7. What are three trends that could seriously affect the adequacy of school funding? Why?
8. What are the primary reasons behind the call for accountability and for the call for educational vouchers?

SUPPLEMENTAL ACTIVITIES

1. Study and evaluate the plan of state support of education in your state.
2. Interview members of local boards of education to determine their opinions on how schools should be financed.
3. Invite a tax assessor or supervisor of assessments to class to discuss assessing in your area.
4. Attend a budget hearing for a local school district.
5. Get a copy of a local school district budget and study it. Prepare questions about the budget and invite a local school official to class to answer your questions and explain the budgeting.

NOTES

1. W. Vance Grant and Thomas D. Snyder, *Digest of Educational Statistics 1983–84* (Washington, D.C.: National Center for Educational Statistics), p. 77.
2. Ibid.
3. Robert J. Wynkoop, "Trends in School Finance Reform," *Phi Delta Kappan* 56 (April 1975): 542.
4. David C. Long, "Rodriguez: The State Courts Respond," *Phi Delta Kappan* 64 (March 1983): 482.
5. Wynkoop, p. 543.
6. Grant and Snyder, p. 83.
7. *Rankings of the States, 1983* (Washington, D.C.: National Education Association, 1983). p. 30.
8. Committee of Finance, *Financial Status of the*

Public Schools, 1971 (Washington, D.C.: National Education Association, 1971), p. 21.

9. Joel S. Berke and Mary T. Moore, "A Developmental View of the Current Federal Government Role in Elementary and Secondary Education," *Phi Delta Kappan* 63 (January 1982): 337.

10. David L. Clark and Mary Ann Amist, "The Impact of the Reagan Administration on Federal Education Policy," *Phi Delta Kappan* 63 (December 1981): 258–262.

11. Richard A. Bumstead, "One Massachusetts School System Adapts to Proposition 2-1/2," *Phi Delta Kappan* 62 (June 1981): 722.

12. Chris Pipho, "Rich States, Poor States," *Phi Delta Kappan* 62 (June 1981): 723.

13. Lawrence Susskind (ed.), *Proposition 21-1/2: Its Impact on Massachusetts.* Prepared by IMPACT: 2-1/2 Project at the Massachusetts Institute of Technology (Cambridge, Mass.: Oelgeschlager,

Gunn, and Hain Publishers, Inc., 1983), pp. 293–319. See also Chris Pipho, "Stateline," *Phi Delta Kappan* in the January, May, and December 1983 issues.

14. Ibid.

15. *Prospects for Financing Elementary and Secondary Education in the States: Congressionally Mandated Study of School Finance,* Final Report, *Vol. I.* Report to Congress from the Secretary of Education, Preface by Donald J. Senese, Assistant Secretary, Office of Educational Research and Improvement, Washington, D.C. (December 1982): i.

16. Ibid., pp. 10–12.

17. Ibid., pp. 20–21.

18. George Gallup, "The 15th Annual Gallup Poll of the Public's Attitudes Toward the Public Schools," *Phi Delta Kappan* 65 (September 1983): 38.

BIBLIOGRAPHY

Alexander, Kern, and Jordan, K. Forbis, eds. *Educational Need in the Public Economy.* Gainesville, Fla.: University Presses of Florida, 1976.

Guthrie, James. "Funding an Adequate Education." *Phi Delta Kappan* 64 (March 1983): 471–476.

Harrison, Russell S. *Equality in Public School Finance.* Lexington, Mass.: Lexington Books, 1976.

Morgan, Edward P. "The Effects of Proposition 2-1/2 in Massachusetts." *Phi Delta Kappan* 64 (December 1982): 252–258.

National Commission on Excellence in Education. *A Nation at Risk: The Imperative for Educational Reform.* A report to the nation and the Secretary of Education by the National Commission on Excellence in Education, April 1983.

Odden, Allan. "Financing Educational Excellence." *Phi Delta Kappan* 65 (January 1984): 311–318.

Persell, Caroline H. *Education and Inequality.* New York: Free Press, 1977.

Prospects for Financing Elementary and Secondary Education in the States: Congressionally Mandated Study of School Finance. Final Report, Vol. I. Report to Congress from the Secretary of Education. Preface by Donald J. Senese, Assistant Secretary, Office of Educational Research and Improvement (Washington, D.C.: December 1982).

Puckett, John L. "Education Vouchers: Rhetoric and Reality." *Educational Forum* XLVII (Summer 1983): 467–492.

Lawrence Susskind, ed. *Proposition 2-1/2: Its Impact on Massachusetts.* Prepared by IMPACT: 2-1/2 Project at the Massachusetts Institute of Technology (Cambridge, Mass.: Oelgeschlager, Gunn, and Hain Publishers, Inc., 1983).

IV

Historical Foundations
of Education

People have tried to educate their children in one way or another since the beginning of humankind. Present-day educators can learn much from past educational efforts. Through a careful study of the history of education, educators can avoid repeating past mistakes and can capitalize on past successes.

In Part IV we first explore some of the important antecedents of American education. Many early educational practices in the American colonies were simply transplanted from Europe. Even today, many facets of our educational programs have their roots in other countries. We also examine the highlights of educational development in the United States—from colonial times to the recent past. ■

11

Antecedents of
American Education

Focus Questions

- Why do you think people created our first schools?
- How important has education been in the history of mankind?

- Is it important for teachers to understand the history of education? Why?

Key Terms and Concepts

Ancient education
Greek education
Socrates, Plato, Aristotle
Scholasticism

Renaissance
Reformation
Age of Reason
Rousseau, Pestalozzi

What Would You Do?

You are conversing with colleagues in the teachers' lounge about schools of the past. One teacher expresses the opinion that Rousseau was wrong when he suggested in the 1760s that children are born "good" and only become "bad" in the hands of men. What do you say?

The Beginning of Education (up to A.D. 476)

[42] It is generally believed that human beings have been on earth for several million years. During 99 percent of this time there was very little progress toward civilization. Not until about 10,000 years ago did people start to raise food, domesticate animals, build canoes, and live in some semblance of community life. Not until approximately 6000 years ago was a written language developed.

Once there was a written language, humans felt the need for formal education. As societies became more complex and as the body of knowledge increased, people recognized a need for schools. What they had learned composed the subject matter; the written language made it possible to record this knowledge and pass it from generation to generation.

It is impossible to determine the exact date that schools first came into existence. However, the discovery of cuneiform mathematics textbooks that have been dated to 2000 B.C. suggest that some form of school probably existed in Sumeria at that early date. There is also evidence to suggest that formal schools existed in China during the Hsia and Shang dynasties, perhaps as early as 2000 B.C. Not until about 500 B.C., however, was society sufficiently advanced to generate an organized concern for education. This happened in Greece during the Age of Pericles.

Greece consisted of a number of city-states, one of which was Sparta. Sparta was a militaristic state whose educational system was geared to support military ambitions. Infants were exposed to the elements for a stated period; if they survived the ordeal, they were adjudged sufficiently strong for soldiering or, if female, to bear healthy children. From the ages of eight to eighteen, boys were wards of the state. During this time they lived in barracks and received physical and moral training. Between eighteen and twenty, boys underwent rigorous war training; they then served in the army. All men were required to marry by the age of thirty so that they might raise healthy children to serve the state. The aims of Spartan education centered around developing such ideals as courage, patriotism, obedience, cunning, and physical strength. Plutarch (A.D. 46–120), a writer of later times, said that education of the Spartans "was calculated to make them subject to command, to endure labor, to fight, and to conquer." There was very little intellectual content in Spartan education.

In sharp contrast to Sparta was Athens, another Greek city-state, which developed an educational program that heavily stressed intellectual and aesthetic objectives. Between the ages of eight and sixteen, some Athenian boys attended a series of public schools. These schools included a grammatist school, which taught reading, writing, and counting; a gymnastics school, which taught sports and games; and a music school, which taught history, drama, poetry, speaking, and science as well as music. Because all city-states had to defend themselves against aggressors, Athenian boys received citizenship and military training between the ages of sixteen and twenty. Athenian girls were educated in the home. The aims of Athenian education stressed the development of the individual, aesthetics, and culture.

The Western World's first great philosophers came from Athens. Of the many philosophers that Greece produced, three stand out—Socrates (470–399 B.C.), Plato (427–347 B.C.), and Aristotle (384–322 B.C.).

Socrates left no writings, but we know much about him from the writings of Xenophon and Plato. Socrates developed a method of teaching that came to be known as the *Socratic method,* in which the teacher would ask a series of questions that led the student to a certain conclusion. The Socratic method is illustrated in the following account of a conversation between Socrates and city officials:

> The thirty tyrants had put many of the most distinguished citizens to death, and had encouraged others to acts of injustice. "It would surprise me," said Socrates one day, "if the keeper of a flock, who had killed one part of it and had made the other part poor, would not confess that he was a bad herdsman; but it would surprise me still more if a man standing at the head of his fellow-citizens should destroy a part of them and corrupt the rest, and were not to blush at his conduct and confess himself a bad magistrate." This remark having come to the ears of the Thirty, Critias and Charicles sent for Socrates, showed him the law, and forbade him to hold conversation with the young.
>
> Socrates inquired of them if he might be permitted to ask questions touching what might seem obscure to him in his prohibition. Upon their granting this permission: "I am prepared," he said, "to obey the laws, but that I may not violate them through ignorance, I would have you clearly inform me whether you interdict the art of speaking because it belongs to the number of things which are good, or because it belongs to the number of things which are bad. In the first case, one ought henceforth to abstain from speaking what is good; in the second, it is clear that the effort should be to speak what is right."
>
> Thereupon Charicles became angry, and said: "Since you do not understand us, we will give you something easier to comprehend; we forbid you absolutely to hold conversation with the young." "In order that it may be clearly seen," said Socrates, "whether I depart from what is enjoined, tell me at what age a youth becomes a man?" "At the time when he is eligible to the senate, for he has not acquired prudence till then; so do not speak to young men who are below the age of thirty."
>
> "But if I wish to buy something of a merchant who is below the age of thirty, may I ask him at what price he sells it?"
>
> "Certainly you may ask such a question; but you are accustomed to raise inquiries about multitudes of things which are perfectly well known to you; it is this which is forbidden."
>
> "So I must not reply to a young man who asks me where Charicles lives, or where Critias is." "You may reply to such questions," said Charicles. "But recollect, Socrates," added Critias, "you must let alone the shoemakers, and the smiths, and other artisans, for I think they must already be very much worn out by being so often in your mouth."
>
> "I must, therefore," said Socrates, "forego the illustrations I draw from these occupations relative to justice, piety, and all the virtues."[1]

Socrates traveled about Athens teaching the students who gathered about him. He was dedicated to the search for truth and at times was very critical of the existing government. Socrates was brought to trial for inciting the people against the government by his ceaseless questioning. He was found guilty and given a choice between ending his teaching or being put to death. Socrates chose death, thereby becoming a martyr for the cause of education. Socrates' fundamental principle, "Knowledge is virtue," has been adopted by countless educators and philosophers down through the ages.

Plato was a student and disciple of Socrates. In his *Republic*, Plato set forth his recommendations for the ideal society. He suggested that society should contain three classes of people: artisans, to do the manual work; soldiers, to defend the society; and philosophers, to advance knowledge and to rule the society. Plato's educational aim was to discover and develop each individual's abilities. He believed that each man's abilities should be used to serve society. Plato wrote: "I call education the virtue which is shown by children when the feelings of joy or of sorrow, of love or of hate, which arise in their souls, are made conformable to order." Concerning the goals of education, Plato wrote: "A good education is that which gives to the body and to the soul all the beauty and all the perfection of which they are capable."

Like Plato, Aristotle also believed that a person's most important purpose was to serve and improve mankind. Aristotle's educational method, however, was scientific, practical, and objective, in contrast to the philosophical methods of Socrates and Plato. Aristotle believed that the quality of a society was determined by the quality of education found in that society. His writings, which include *Lyceum, Organon, Politics, Ethics,* and *Metaphysics,* were destined to exert greater influence on humankind through the Middle Ages than the writings of any other man.

42 Insight into some of Aristotle's views concerning education can be obtained from the following passage from *Politics:*

That education should be regulated by law and should be an affair of state is not to be denied, but what should be the character of this public education, and how young persons should be educated, are questions which remain to be considered. For mankind are by no means agreed about the things to be taught, whether we look to virtue or the best life.

Neither is it clear whether education is more concerned with intellectual or with moral virtue. The existing practice is perplexing; no one knows on what principle we should proceed—should the useful in life, or should virtue, or should the higher knowledge be the aim of our training; all three opinions have been entertained. Again, about the means there is no agreement; for different persons, starting with different ideas about the nature of virtue, naturally disagree about the practice of it.

There can be no doubt that children should be taught those useful things which are really necessary, but not all things; for occupations are divided into liberal and illiberal; and to young children should be imparted only such kinds of knowledge as will be useful to them without vulgarizing them. And any occupation, art, or science, which makes the body or soul or mind of the freeman less fit for the practice or exercise of virtue, is vulgar; wherefore we call those arts vulgar which tend to deform the body, and likewise all paid employments, for they absorb and degrade the mind.[2]

The contributions that Greece made toward civilization and to education were truly outstanding.

In 146 B.C. the Romans conquered Greece, and Greek teachers and their educational system were quickly absorbed into the Roman Empire. Many of the educational and philosophical advances made by the Roman Empire after that time were actually inspired by enslaved Greeks.

Before 146 B.C., Roman children had been educated primarily in the home, though some children attended schools known as ludi, where the rudiments of reading and writing were taught. The Greek influence on Roman education became pronounced between 50 B.C. and A.D. 200. During this time an entire system of schools developed in Rome. Some children, after learning to read and write, attended a grammaticus school to study Latin, literature, history, mathematics, music, and dialectics. These Latin grammar schools were somewhat like twentieth century secondary schools in function. Students who were preparing for a career of political service received their training in a school of rhetoric. Rhetorical schools offered courses in grammar, rhetoric, dialectics, music, arithmetic, geometry, and astronomy.

The Roman Empire contained numerous institutions of higher learning that were continuations of former Greek institutions. For instance, a higher institution grew out of a library founded by Vespasian about A.D. 70. This institution, which later came to be known as the Athenaeum, eventually offered studies in law, medicine, architecture, mathematics, and mechanics.

Quintilian (A.D. 35–95) was the most influential of all Roman educators. In a set of twelve books, *The Institutes of Oratory,* he described current educational practices, recommended the type of educational system needed in Rome, and listed the great books in existence at that time.

Quintilian had considerable insight into educational psychology; concerning the punishment of students, he wrote:

> I am by no means in favor of whipping boys, though I know it to be a general practice. In the first place, whipping is unseemly, and if you suppose the boys to be somewhat grown up, it is an affront in the highest degree. In the next place, if a boy's ability is so poor as to be proof against reproach he will, like a worthless slave, become insensible to blows. Lastly, if a teacher is assiduous and careful, there is no need to use force. I shall observe further that while a boy is under the rod he experiences pain and fear. The shame of this experience dejects and discourages many pupils, makes them shun being seen, and may even weary them of their lives.[3]

Regarding the motivation of students, Quintilian stated:

Let study be made a child's diversion; let him be soothed and caressed into it; and let him sometimes test himself upon his proficiency. Sometimes enter a contest of wits with him, and let him imagine that he comes off the conqueror. Let him even be encouraged by giving him such rewards that are most appropriate to his age.[4]

These comments apply as well today as they did when Quintilian wrote them nearly 2000 years ago. Quintilian's writings were rediscovered in the 1400s and became influential in the humanistic movement in education.

The Romans had a genius for organization and for getting a job done. They made lasting contributions to architecture; many of their roads, aqueducts, and buildings remain today. This genius for organization enabled Rome to unite much of the ancient world with a common language, a religion, and a political bond—a condition that favored the spread of education and knowledge throughout the ancient world.

Education in the Middle Ages (476–1300)

[42] By A.D. 476 (the fall of the Roman Empire), the Roman Catholic Church was well on the way to becoming the greatest power in government and education. In fact, the rise of the church to a very powerful position is often cited as a main cause of the Western World's plunge into the Dark Ages. As the church stressed the importance of gaining entrance to heaven, life on earth became, in a sense, less important. Many people viewed earthly life as nothing more than a way to a life hereafter. It is easy to see that a society in which this attitude prevailed would be unlikely to make intellectual advances, except perhaps in areas tangential to religion.

One can obtain insight into how much knowledge was lost during the Dark Ages by comparing writings from that period with earlier writings. During the seventh century a Spanish bishop, Isidore of Seville, wrote an encyclopedia that supposedly contained all the knowledge in the world at that time. A map of the world, as it was then known, was included in this encyclopedia. Comparing Isidore's extremely crude map with a surprisingly accurate one drawn in the second century by Ptolemy vividly illustrates the loss of knowledge over this 500-year period.

During the Dark Ages, one of the very few bright periods for education was the reign of Charlemagne (742–814). Charlemagne realized the value of education, and as ruler of a large part of Europe, he was in a position to establish schools and encourage scholarly activity. In 800, when Charlemagne came into power, educational activity was at an extremely low ebb. The little educating that was carried on was conducted by the church, mainly to induct people into the faith and to train religious leaders. The schools in which this religious teaching took place included catechumenal schools, which taught church doctrine to new converts; catechetical schools, which at first taught the catechism but later became schools for training church leaders; and cathedral—or monastic—schools, which trained clergy.

Charlemagne sought far and wide for a talented educator who could improve education in the kingdom, finally selecting Alcuin (735–804), who had been a teacher in England. While Alcuin served as Charlemagne's chief educational adviser, he became the most famous educator of his day. His main educational writings include *On Grammar, On Orthography, On Rhetoric,* and *On Dialectics.* Alcuin, in addition to trying to improve education generally in the kingdom, headed Charlemagne's Palace School in Frankland. It is said that Charlemagne himself often would sit in the Palace School with the children, trying to further his own meager education.

At one time, Charlemagne and Alcuin issued a proclamation throughout the empire to encourage educational activity. Because this statement was one of the most important educational statements of that period and because it sheds much light on life at that time, it is reproduced here.

| 50 |

Be it known to your Devotion, pleasing to God, that we and our faithful have judged it well that, in the bishoprics and monasteries committed by Christ's favour to our charge, besides the due observance of a regular and holy life, care shall be had for the study of letters that those to whom God has given the ability to learn may receive instruction, each according to his several capacity. And this, that, just as obedience to the rule gives order and beauty to your acts, so zeal in teaching and learning may impart the like graces to your words, and thus those who seek to please God by living aright may not fail to please Him also by right speaking. For it is written "by thy words shalt thou be justified or condemned"; and though it is indeed better to do the right than to know it, yet it is needful also to know the right before we can do it. Every one, therefore, must learn what it is that he would fain accomplish, and his mind will the more fully grasp the duty which lies before him if his tongue errs not in the service of Almighty God. And, if false speaking should thus be shunned by all men, how much more must those exert themselves to shun it who have been chosen for this very purpose, to be the servants of the truth!

But in many letters received by us in recent years from divers monasteries, informing us of the prayers offered upon our behalf at their sacred services by the brethren there dwelling, we have observed that though the sentiments were good the language was uncouth, the unlettered tongue failing through ignorance to interpret aright the pious devotion of the heart.

And hence we have begun to fear that, if their skill in writing is so small, so also their power of rightly comprehending the Holy Scriptures may be far less than is befitting; and it is known to all that, if verbal errors are dangerous, errors of interpretation are still more so. We exhort you therefore, not only not to neglect the study of letters but to apply yourselves thereto with that humble perseverance which is well-pleasing to God, that so you may be able with the greater ease and accuracy to search into the mysteries of the Holy Scriptures. For, as in the sacred pages there are images and tropes and other similar figures, no one can doubt that the quickness with which the reader apprehends the spiritual sense will be proportionate to the extent of his previous instruction in letters. But let the men chosen for this task be such as are both themselves able and willing to learn and eager withal to impart their learning to others. And let the zeal with which the work is done equal the earnestness with which we now ordain it. For we desire that you may be marked, as behooves the soldiers of the Church, within by devotion, and without by wisdom—chaste in your life, learned in your speech—so that if any come to you to call upon the Divine Master, or to behold the excellence of the religious life, they may be not only edified by your aspect when they regard you, but instructed by your wisdom when they hear you read or chant, and may return home rejoicing and giving thanks to God Most High.[5]

[53] Roughly during Alcuin's time, the phrase *seven liberal arts* came into common usage to describe the curriculum that was then taught in many schools. The seven liberal arts consisted of the trivium (grammar, rhetoric, logic) and the quadrivium (arithmetic, geometry, music, astronomy). Each of these seven subjects was defined broadly, so that collectively they constituted a more comprehensive study than today's usage of the term suggests. The phrase *liberal arts* has survived time and is common now.

Despite the efforts of a few men such as Charlemagne and Alcuin, very little educational progress was made during the Dark Ages. However, between 1000 and 1300—a period frequently referred to as the *Age of the Revival of Learning*—humankind slowly regained a thirst for education. This revival of interest in learning was helped by two events; first, the rediscovery of the writings of some of the ancient philosophers—mainly Aristotle—and renewed interest in them and, second, the reconciliation of religion and philosophy. Before this time the church had denounced the study of philosophy as contradictory to the teachings of the church.

Harmonizing the doctrines of the church with the doctrines of philosophy and education was largely accomplished by Thomas Aquinas (1225–1274), himself a theologian. Aquinas formalized *scholasticism* (the logical and philosophical study of the beliefs of the church). His most important writing was *Summa Theologica,* which became the doctrinal authority of the Roman Catholic Church. The educational and philosophical views of Thomas Aquinas were made formal in the philosophy *Thomism*—a philosophy that has remained important in Roman Catholic parochial education.

The revival of learning brought about a general increase in educational activity and a growth of educational institutions, including the establishment of universities. These medieval universities, the true forerunners of our modern universities, included the University of Bologna (1158), which specialized in law; the University of Paris (1180), which specialized in theology; Oxford University (1214); and the University of Salerno (1224). By 1500, approximately 80 universities had been established in Europe.

Although it is generally true that the Middle Ages produced few educational advances in the Western World, we must remember that much of the Eastern World did not experience the Dark Ages. Mohammed (569–632) led a group of Arabs through northern Africa and into southern Spain. The Eastern learning that the Arabs brought to Spain slowly spread throughout Europe through the writings of such scholars as Avicenna (980–1037) and Averroes (1126–1198). These Eastern contributions to Western knowledge included significant advances in science and mathematics, particularly the Arabic numbering system.

Education in Transition (1300–1700)

Two very important movements took place during the Transition Period—   43
the *Renaissance* and the *Reformation*. The Renaissance represented the
protest of individuals against the dogmatic authority the church exerted
over their social and intellectual life. The Renaissance started in Italy
(around 1130), when humans reacquired the spirit of free inquiry that had
prevailed in ancient Greece. The Renaissance slowly spread throughout
Europe, resulting in a general revival of classical learning, called *humanism*. Erasmus (1466–1536) was one of the most famous humanist educators; two of his books, *The Right Method of Instruction* and *The Liberal
Education of Boys,* formed a humanistic theory of education.

Erasmus had a good deal of educational insight. Concerning the aims
of education, he wrote:

> The duty of instructing the young includes several elements, the first and also
> the chief of which is that the tender mind of the child should be instructed in
> piety; the second, that he love and learn the liberal arts; the third, that he be
> taught tact in the conduct of social life; and the fourth, that from his earliest
> age he accustom himself to good behavior, based on moral principles.[6]

His educational maxims indicated that Erasmus had much educational   42
common sense:

> We learn with great willingness from those whom we love; Parents themselves
> cannot properly bring up their children if they make themselves only to be
> feared; There are children who would be killed sooner than made better by
> blows: by mildness and kind admonitions, one may make of them whatever
> he will; Children will learn to speak their native tongue without any weari-
> ness, by usage and practice; Drill in reading and writing is a little bit tiresome,
> and the teacher will ingeniously palliate the tedium by the artifice of an at-
> tractive method; The ancients moulded toothsome dainties into the forms of
> the letters, and thus, as it were, made children swallow the alphabet; In the
> matter of grammatical rules, instruction should at the first be limited to the
> most simple; As the body in infant years is nourished by little portions dis-
> tributed at intervals, so should the mind of the child be nurtured by items of
> knowledge adapted to its weakness, and distributed little by little.[7]

The Protestant Reformation had its formal beginning in 1517, when   43
Martin Luther (1483–1546) published his 95 theses, which stated his dis-
agreement with the Roman Catholic Church. One of these disagreements
held great implications for the importance of formal education. The church
had come to feel that it was not necessary for each person to read and
interpret the Bible for himself or herself; rather, the church would pass on
its interpretation to the laity. Luther felt not only that the church had itself
misinterpreted the Bible but also that it was intended that people read and
interpret the Bible for themselves. If one accepted the church's position on
this matter, formal education remained unimportant. If one accepted Luther's position, however, education became necessary for all people so that

they might read and interpret the Bible for themselves. In a sense, education became important as a way of obtaining salvation. It is understandable that Luther and his educational co-worker, Melanchthon (1497–1560), soon came to stress universal elementary education. Melanchthon's most important educational writing was *Visitation Articles* (1528), in which he set forth his recommendations for schools. Luther and Melanchthon felt that education should be provided for all, regardless of class, and should be compulsory for both sexes. They felt also that it should be state controlled, state supported, and centered around classical languages, grammar, mathematics, science, history, music, and physical education. Luther's argument for increased governmental support for education has a familiar twentieth century ring:

> Each city is subjected to great expense every year for the construction of roads, for fortifying its ramparts, and for buying arms and equipping soldiers. Why should it not spend an equal sum for the support of one or two schoolmasters? The prosperity of a city does not depend solely on its natural riches, on the solidity of its walls, on the elegance of its mansions, and on the abundance of arms in its arsenals; but the safety and strength of a city reside above all in a good education, which furnishes it with instructed, reasonable, honorable, and well-trained citizens.[8]

To combat the Reformation movement, Ignatius of Loyola (1491–1556) organized the Society of Jesus (Jesuits) in 1540. The Jesuits worked to establish schools in which to further the cause of the Roman Catholic Church, and they tried to stem the flow of converts to the Reformation cause. Although the Jesuits' main interest was religious, they soon grew into a great teaching order and were very successful in training their own teachers. The rules by which the Jesuits conducted their schools were stated in the *Ratio Studiorum;* a revised edition still guides the Jesuit schools today. The improvement of teacher training was the Jesuits' main contribution to education.

Another Catholic teaching order, the Brothers of the Christian Schools, was organized in 1684 by Jean Baptiste de la Salle (1651–1719). Unlike the Jesuits, who were primarily interested in secondary education, de la Salle and his order were interested in elementary schools and in preparing elementary school teachers. De la Salle was probably the first educator to use student teaching in the preparation of teachers.

Many other outstanding educators existed during the Transition Period, one being Johann Amos Comenius (1592–1670). Comenius is perhaps best remembered for his many textbooks, which were among the first to contain illustrations. Concerning a school that he operated, Comenius wrote: "We pursue a general education, the teaching to all men of all the subjects of human concern."[9] Comenius advocated that an entire system of schools should be created to serve the youth. In this regard he wrote: "There should be a maternal school in each family; an elementary school in each district; a gymnasium in each city; an academy in each kingdom, or even in each considerable province."[10]

The invention and improvement of printing during the 1400s made it possible to produce books, such as those of Comenius, more rapidly and economically—a development that was essential to the growth of education. Much of the writing of Comenius reflected the increasing interest then developing in science.

Modern Period (1700–Present)

Two movements took place during the early Modern Period that influenced education. The first was a revolt of the intellectuals against the superstition and ignorance that dominated people's lives at that time. This movement has been called the *Age of Reason,* and François Marie Arouet, who wrote under the name Voltaire, was one of the leaders. Those who joined this movement became known as rationalists because of the faith they placed in human rational power. The implication for education in the rationalist movement is obvious; if one places greater emphasis on human ability to reason, then education takes on new importance as the way by which humans develop this power.

The second movement of the early Modern Period that affected education was the *emergence of common man.* Whereas the Age of Reason was a revolt of the learned for intellectual freedom, the "emergence of common man" was a revolt of common people for a better life—politically, economically, socially, and educationally. One of the leaders in this movement was Jean Jacques Rousseau (1712–1778), whose *Social Contract* (1762) became an influential book in the French Revolution. It has been suggested that *Social Contract* was also the basal doctrine of the American Declaration of Independence.[11] Rousseau was a philosopher, not an educator, but he wrote a good deal on the subject of education. His most important educational work was *Émile* (1762), in which he states his views concerning the ideal education for youth. Rousseau felt that the aim of education should be to return man to his "natural state." His view on the subject is well summed up by the opening sentence of *Émile:* "Everything is good as it comes from the hand of the author of nature; but everything degenerates in the hands of man." Rousseau's educational views came to be known as *naturalism.* Concerning the best method of teaching, Rousseau wrote:

> Do not treat the child to discourses which he cannot understand. No descriptions, no eloquence, no figures of speech. Be content to present to him appropriate objects. Let us transform our sensations into ideas. But let us not jump at once from sensible objects to intellectual objects. Let us always proceed slowly from one sensible notion to another. In general, let us never substitute the sign for the thing, except when it is impossible for us to show

the thing. . . . I have no love whatever for explanations and talk. Things! Things! I shall never tire of saying that we ascribe too much importance to words. With our babbling education we make only babblers.[12]

48   Rousseau's most important contributions to education were his belief that education must be a natural process, not an artificial one, and his compassionate, positive view of the child. Rousseau believed that children were inherently good—a belief that was in opposition to the prevailing religiously inspired belief that children were born full of sin. The contrasting implications for teaching methods suggested by these two views are self-evident, as is the educational desirability of Rousseau's view over that which prevailed at the time. Although Rousseau never taught a day of school in his life, he did more to improve education through his writing than any of his contemporaries.

Johann Heinrich Pestalozzi (1746–1827) was a Swiss educator who put Rousseau's theory into practice. Pestalozzi established two schools for boys, one at Burgdorf (1800–1804) and the other at Yverdun (1805–1825). Educators came from all over the world to view Pestalozzi's schools and to study his teaching methods. Pestalozzi enumerated his educational views in a book entitled *Leonard and Gertrude*. Unlike most educators of his time, Pestalozzi believed that a teacher should treat students with love and kindness:

> I was convinced that my heart would change the condition of my children just as promptly as the sun of spring would reanimate the earth benumbed by the winter. . . . It was necessary that my childen should observe, from dawn to evening, at every moment of the day, upon my brow and on my lips, that my affections were fixed on them, that their happiness was my happiness, and that their pleasures were my pleasures . . .
>
> I was everything to my children. I was alone with them from morning till night. . . . Their hands were in my hands. Their eyes were fixed on my eyes.[13]

Key concepts in the Pestalozzian method included an expression of love, understanding, and patience for children; a compassion for the poor; and the use of objects and sense perception as the basis for acquiring knowledge.

One of the educators who studied under Pestalozzi and was influenced by him was Johann Friedrich Herbart (1776–1841). While Pestalozzi had successfully put into practice and further developed Rousseau's educational ideas, it remained for Herbart to organize these educational views into a formal psychology of education. Herbart stressed apperception (learning by association). The Herbartian teaching method developed into five formal steps:

1. *preparation*—preparing the student to receive a new idea;
2. *presentation*—presenting the student with the new idea;

3. *association*—assimilating the new idea with old ideas;
4. *generalization*—the general idea deriving from the combination of the old and new ideas; and
5. *application*—applying the new knowledge.

Herbart's educational ideas are contained in his *Science of Education* (1806) and *Outlines of Educational Doctrine* (1835).

Friedrich Froebel (1782–1852) was another European educator who was influenced by Rousseau and Pestalozzi and who made a sizable contribution to education. Froebel's contributions included the establishment of the first kindergarten (or Kleinkinderbeschäftigungsanstalt, as he called it in 1837), an emphasis on social development, a concern for the cultivation of creativity, and the concept of learning by doing. He originated the idea that women are best suited to teach young children. Froebel wrote his main educational book, *Education of Man,* in 1826.

Two developments in the last of the 1800s were the last important European antecedents of American education: the maturing of the scientific movement, hastened by the publication of Charles Darwin's *Origin of Species* (1859), and the formulation of educational psychology near the end of the century.

It is important for the student of educational history to realize that even though many educational advances had been made by 1900, the average European received a pathetically small amount of formal education—even at that late date. Historically, education had been available only to the few who were fortunate enough to be born into the leisure class; the masses of people in the working class had received little or no education until that time. What little formal education the working person might have received was usually provided by the church for religious purposes.

Figure 11.1 lists some of the great European educators and indicates their views on several fundamental ideas concerning education.

Summary and Implications

This chapter has pointed out that the historical roots of our educational traditions can be traced to Europe. People who have helped to mold Western education include Socrates, Plato, Aristotle, Quintilian, Alcuin, Aquinas, Erasmus, Melanchthon, Rousseau, Pestalozzi, and Herbart. These and other educational pioneers labored against overwhelming odds to advance the cause of education, and many of the concepts and practices developed by them are still in use today. However, perhaps their greatest contribution was in helping humankind to discover and appreciate the potential value of education.

TEACHER	Materials adapted for children	Attention to individual differences	Discipline based on love and interest	Personal bond with pupil	Analysis of abilities	Classification of pupils	Education to be fun	Development of both mind and body	Education as guidance of native abilities	Education as a science	Emphasis upon moral growth
Socrates				✓				✓			✓
Quintilian		✓	✓	✓	✓	✓		✓	✓		✓
Origen		✓	✓	✓	✓	✓					✓
Ausonius				✓			✓				
Jerome	✓			✓					✓		✓
Alcuin	✓	✓	✓	✓	✓				✓		
Abélard				✓		✓					
Vittorino	✓	✓	✓	✓	✓	✓		✓	✓		✓
Melanchthon		✓	✓								✓
Ascham		✓	✓	✓	✓	✓		✓	✓		
Mulcaster		✓			✓	✓		✓	✓	✓	
Loyola		✓	✓	✓	✓	✓		✓	✓	✓	✓
Comenius	✓	✓	✓		✓	✓		✓	✓	✓	✓
De la Salle		✓	✓	✓					✓		
Francke		✓	✓					✓	✓		
Basedow	✓	✓		✓			✓	✓	✓	✓	✓
Pestalozzi	✓	✓	✓	✓	✓	✓		✓	✓		✓
Herbart		✓			✓	✓				✓	✓
Froebel	✓	✓	✓	✓	✓		✓	✓	✓		✓
Seguin	✓	✓		✓	✓	✓		✓		✓	
Binet	✓	✓			✓	✓				✓	
Montessori	✓	✓	✓	✓	✓	✓	✓	✓	✓	✓	✓

FIGURE 11.1 *Fundamental ideas about education. (Source:* From *A History of Education: Socrates to Montessori* by Luella Cole, Ph.D. Copyright © 1950 by Holt, Rinehart and Winston, Inc., renewed 1978 by Holt, Rinehart and Winston. Reprinted by permission of Holt, Rinehart and Winston, CBS College Publishing.)

One important implication of this chapter for current teachers is that many of our contemporary educational beliefs are very old ideas. Today's teachers also have an obligation to study the history of education so that mistakes of the past will not be repeated.

DISCUSSION QUESTIONS

1. What were the major factors that caused humans to first create schools?
2. What were the major differences between the Spartan and Athenian school systems? Why did these differences exist?
3. What factors contributed to the decline of education between 500 and 1000?
4. What were the strengths and weaknesses of Jean Jacques Rousseau's ideas about children and education?
5. Discuss the educational achievements of the Roman Empire.

SUPPLEMENTAL ACTIVITIES

1. Read and discuss Quintilian's *The Institutes of Oratory*.
2. Read and discuss Rousseau's *Émile*.
3. Read and discuss Pestalozzi's *How Gertrude Teaches Her Children*.
4. Make a chart showing the major contributions of ten of the educators discussed in this chapter.
5. Do additional library research on one of the educators discussed in this chapter.

NOTES

1. Gabriel Compayre, *History of Pedagogy*, trans. W. H. Payne (Boston: D. C. Heath, 1888), pp. 24–26.
2. Paul Monroe, *Source Book of the History of Education* (New York: Macmillan, 1901), p. 282.
3. Quintilian, *The Institutes of Oratory*, trans. W. Guthrie (London: Dewick and Clark, 1905), p. 27.
4. Ibid., p. 13.
5. C. J. B. Gaskoin, *Alcuin, His Life and Work* (London: Cambridge University Press, 1904), pp. 182–184.
6. Compayre, pp. 88–89.
7. Ibid., p. 89.
8. Ibid., p. 115.
9. Ibid., p. 128.
10. Ibid.
11. Paul Monroe, *History of Education* (New York: Macmillan, 1905), p. 283.
12. Compayre, p. 299.
13. Ibid., p. 425.

BIBLIOGRAPHY

Armytage, W. H. G. "William Byngham: A Medieval Protagonist of the Training of Teachers." *History of Education Journal* 2 (1951):107–110.
Bowen, J. "Towards an Assessment of Educational Theory: An Historical Perspective." *International Review of Education* 25 (1979):303–323.
Butts, R. Freeman. *A Cultural History of Western Education*. New York: McGraw-Hill, 1955.
Chambliss, J. J., ed. *Nobility, Tragedy and Naturalism: Education in Ancient Greece*. Minneapolis: Burgess, 1971.
Cole, Luella. *A History of Education: Socrates to*

Montessori. New York: Holt, Rinehart and Winston, 1950.

Compayre, Gabriel. *History of Pedagogy.* Translated by W. H. Payne. Boston: D. C. Heath, 1888.

Cremin, Lawrence. *American Education: The National Experience, 1783–1876.* New York: Harper, 1980.

Hillesheim, James W., and Merrill, George D., eds. *Theory and Practice in the History of American Education: A Book of Readings.* Pacific Palisades, Calif.: Goodyear, 1971.

Kaestle, Carl, and Vinovskis, Maris. *Education and Social Change in Nineteenth Century Massachusetts.* Cambridge, England: Cambridge University Press, 1980.

Lucas, Christopher J. *Our Western Educational Heritage.* New York: Macmillan, 1972.

Meyer, Adolphe. *Grandmasters of Educational Thought.* New York: McGraw-Hill, 1975.

Roper, D. "Coming Full Circle; Charity Schools in Public Education." *Social Studies* 71 (March–April 1980):90–94.

12

Early American Education

Focus Questions

- If you had been one of the early American colonists, how important would "education" have been to you? Why?
- What do you suppose life was like for the colonial schoolteacher?

- How much has education improved through the history of our country?

Key Terms and Concepts

Colonial education
Common schools
Horace Mann
Latin grammar schools
American Academy
Secondary education
Educational goals
Apprenticeship

Normal schools
The New England Primer
Blue-Backed Speller
Frederick Douglass
Emma Willard
Private education
Federal involvement in education

What Would You Do?

Recently, a small school district decided to require their teachers to use the McGuffey Eclectic Readers (written in the mid-1800s) in each elementary grade. The board of education believes that these books will be more challenging and will help children learn to be honest, patriotic, kind, punctual, and persistent. What do you think?

41 The first permanent European settlements in North America included Jamestown (1607), Plymouth (1620), Massachusetts Bay (1630), Maryland (1632), Connecticut (1635), and Providence Plantations (1636). The motives that prompted most of these settlers to move to America were religious, economic, and political. Generally, these people were not dissatisfied with education in their homelands. It is understandable, then, that nearly all educational practices and educational materials in early colonial America were simply transplanted from the Old World.

The religious motive was very strong in colonial America, and it permeated colonial education. It was generally felt that a child should learn to read so that he or she could read the Bible and thus gain salvation. Beyond this, there was no demand for mass education. Since the clergy possessed the ability to read and write, and since the ultimate utility of education was to read the Bible, it was logical for the clergy to do much of the teaching.

The early settlement of the East Coast fell into three general groups of colonies: the Southern Colonies, centered in Virginia; the Middle Colonies, centered in New York; and the Northern Colonies, centered in New England.

The Southern Colonies soon came to be made up of large tobacco plantations. Owing to the size of the plantations, people lived far apart; few towns were established until later in the colonial period. There was an immediate need for cheap labor to work on the plantations, and in 1619, only twelve years after Jamestown was settled, the first boatload of slaves was imported from Africa. Other sources of cheap labor for the Southern Colonies included white Europeans from a variety of backgrounds who purchased passage to the New World by agreeing to serve a lengthy period of indentured servitude on arrival in the colonies. There soon came to be two very distinct classes of people in the South—a few wealthy landowners and a large mass of laborers, most of whom were slaves. The educational provisions that evolved from this set of conditions were precisely what one would expect. No one was interested in providing education for the slaves, with the exception of a few missionary groups like the English Society for the Propagation of the Gospel in Foreign Parts. Such missionary groups tried to provide some education for slaves, primarily so that they could read the Bible. The wealthy landowners usually hired tutors to teach their children at home. Distances between homes and slow transportation precluded the establishment of centralized schools. When the upper class children grew old enough to attend college, they were usually sent to well-established schools in Europe.

The people who settled the Middle Colonies came from various national (Dutch, Swedes) and religious (Puritans, Mennonites, Catholics) backgrounds. This situation explains why the Middle Colonies have often been called the "melting pot" of the nation. This diversity of backgrounds made it impossible for those in the Middle Colonies to agree on a common public school system. Consequently, the respective groups established their own parochial schools. Many children received their education through an apprenticeship while learning a trade from a "master" already in that line of work. Some people even learned the art of teaching school through an apprenticeship.

The Northern Colonies were settled mainly by the Puritans. In 1630, approximately 1000 Puritans settled near Boston. Unlike the Southern Colonies, people lived close to one another in New England. Towns sprang up and soon became centers of political and social life. Shipping ports were established, and an industrial economy developed that demanded numerous skilled and semiskilled workers—a condition that created a large middle class.

These conditions of common religious views, town life, and a large middle class made it possible for the people to agree on common public schools. This agreement led to very early educational activity in the Northern Colonies. In 1642 the General Court of Massachusetts enacted a law that stated:

> This Co*t*, [Court] taking into consideration the great neglect of many parents & masters in training up their children in learning . . . do hereupon order and decree, that in euery towne y chosen men . . . take account from time to time of all parents and masters, and of their childen, concerning their . . . ability to read & understand the principles of religion & the capitall lawes of this country. . . .

This law did nothing more than encourage citizens to look after the education of children. Five years later (1647), however, another law was enacted in Massachusetts that required towns to provide education for the youth. This law stated:

> It being one chiefe proiect of y ould deluder, Satan, to keepe men from the knowledge of y Scriptures. . . . It is therefore orded [ordered], ye evy [every] towneship in this iurisdiction, aft y Lord hath increased y number to 50 houshold, shall then forthw appoint one w [with] in their towne to teach all such children as shall resort to him to write & reade . . . & it is furth ordered y where any towne shall increase to y numb [number] of 100 families or househould, they shall set up a grammar schoole, y m [aim] thereof being able to instruct youth so farr as they shall be fited for y university [Harvard] . . .

These Massachusetts school laws of 1642 and 1647 served as models for similar laws soon created in other colonies.

Several different kinds of elementary schools sprang up in the colonies. These included the dame school, which was conducted by a housewife in her home; the writing school, which taught the child to write; a variety of parochial schools; and charity, or pauper, schools taught by missionary groups.

To go back a few years, in 1635 the Latin Grammar School was established in Boston—the first permanent school of this type in what is now the United States. This school was established when the people of Boston, which had been settled only five years before, voted "that our brother Philemon Pormont, shal be intreated to become scholemaster, for the teaching and nourtering of children with us." The grammar school was a secondary school, and its function was college preparatory. The grammar school idea spread quickly to other towns. Charlestown opened its first grammar school one year later, in 1636, by contracting William Witherell "to keep a school for a twelve month." Within sixteen years after the Massachusetts Bay Colony had been founded, seven or eight towns had Latin grammar schools in operation. These schools, transplanted from Europe, where similar schools had existed for a long time, were traditional and designed to prepare children for college and "for the service of God, in church and commonwealth."

43   Harvard, the first colonial college, was established in 1636 for preparing ministers. Other early American colleges included William and Mary (1693), Yale (1701), Princeton (1746), King's College (1754), College of Philadelphia (1755), Brown (1764), Dartmouth (1769), and Queen's College (1770). The curriculum in these early colleges was traditional, with heavy emphasis on theology and the classics. An example of how far the religious motive dominated the colonial colleges can be found in one of the 1642 rules governing Harvard College, which stated: "Let every Student be plainly instructed, and earnestly pressed to consider well, the maine end of his life and studies is, to know God and Jesus Christ. . . ."

The Struggle for Universal Elementary Education

On the whole, colonial elementary schools were adaptations of schools that had existed in Europe for many years. When the colonists arrived in this country, they simply established schools like those they had known in Europe. The objectives of colonial elementary schools were purely religious. It was commonly believed that everyone needed to be able to read the Bible to receive salvation; therefore parents were eager to have their children receive some type of reading instruction.

A good idea about what a colonial elementary school was like can be gleaned from the following account of a school conducted in 1750 by Christopher Dock, a Mennonite schoolteacher in Pennsylvania:

42   The children arrive as they do because some have a great distance to school, others a short distance, so that the children cannot assemble as punctually as they can in a city. Therefore, when a few children are present, those who can read their Testament sit together on one bench; but the boys and girls occupy

separate benches. They are given a chapter which they read at sight consecutively. Meanwhile I write copies for them. Those who have read their passage of Scripture without error take their places at the table and write. Those who fail have to sit at the end of the bench, and each new arrival the same; as each one is thus released in order he takes up his slate. This process continues until they have all assembled. The last one left on the bench is a "lazy pupil."

When all are together, and examined, whether they are washed and combed, they sing a psalm or a morning hymn, and I sing and pray with them. As much as they can understand of the Lord's Prayer and the Ten Commandments (according to the gift God has given them), I exhort and admonish them accordingly. This much concerning the assembling of pupils. But regarding prayer I will add this additional explanation. Children say the prayers taught them at home half articulately, and too fast, especially the "Our Father" which the Lord Himself taught His disciples and which contains all that we need. I therefore make a practice of saying it for them kneeling, and they kneeling repeat it after me. After these devotional exercises those who can write resume their work. Those who cannot read the Testament have had time during the assemblage to study their lesson. These are heard recite immediately after prayer. Those who know their lesson receive an O on the hand, traced with crayon. This is a mark of excellence. Those who fail more than three times are sent back to study their lesson again. When all the little ones have recited, these are asked again, and any one having failed in more than three trials a second time, is called "Lazy" by the entire class and his name is written down. Whether such a child fears the rod or not, I know from experience that this denunciation of the children hurts more than if I were constantly to wield and flourish the rod. If then such a child has friends in school who are able to instruct him and desire to do so, he will visit more frequently than before. For this reason: if the pupil's name has not been erased before dismissal the pupils are at liberty to write down the names of those who have been lazy, and take them along home. But if the child learns his lesson well in the future, his name is again presented to the other pupils, and they are told that he knew his lesson well and failed in no respect. Then all the pupils call "Diligent" to him. When this has taken place his name is erased from the slate of lazy pupils, and the former transgression is forgiven.

The children who are in the spelling class are daily examined in pronunciation. In spelling, when a word has more than one syllable, they must repeat the whole word, but some, while they can say the letters, cannot pronounce the word, and so cannot be put to reading. For improvement a child must repeat the lesson, and in this way: The child gives me the book, I spell the word and he pronounces it. If he is slow, another pupil pronounces it for him, and in this way he hears how it should be done, and knows that he must follow the letters and not his own fancy.

Concerning A B C pupils, it would be best, having but one child, to let it learn one row of letters at a time, to say forward and backward. But with many, I let them learn the alphabet first, and then ask a child to point out a letter that I name. If a child is backward or ignorant, I ask another, or the whole class, and the first one that points to the right letter, I grasp his finger and hold it until I have put a mark opposite his name. I then ask for another letter, &c. Whichever child has during the day received the greatest number of marks, has pointed out the greatest number of letters. To him I owe something—a flower drawn on paper or a bird. But if several have the same number, we draw lots; this causes less annoyance. In this way not only are the very timid cured of their shyness (which is a great hindrance in learning), but a fondness for school is increased. Thus much in answer to his question, how I take the children into school, how school proceeds before and after prayers, and how the inattentive and careless are made attentive and careful, and how the timid are assisted.[1]

61   Christopher Dock's comments show the extent to which religion dominated the curriculum of colonial elementary schools. This account also points out that the curriculum of these schools was limited to the rudiments of knowledge and that instructional materials were simple and meager.

In 1805, New York City established the first monitorial school in the United States. The monitorial school, which originated in England, represented an attempt to provide mass elementary education for large numbers of children. Typically, the teacher would teach hundreds of pupils, using the better students as helpers. By 1840, nearly all monitorial schools had been closed; the children had not learned enough to justify continuance of this type of school.

Between 1820 and 1860 an "educational awakening" took place in America. This movement was strongly influenced by Horace Mann (1796–1859). As secretary of the state board of education, Mann helped to establish common elementary schools in Massachusetts. Among his many impressive educational achievements was the publication of one of the very early professional journals in this country—*The Common School Journal*. Through this journal, Mann kept educational issues before the public.

In 1852, Massachusetts passed a compulsory elementary school attendance law, the first of its kind in the country. It required all children to attend school. By 1900, thirty-two other states had passed similar compulsory school attendance laws.

Pestalozzianism and Herbartianism considerably affected elementary education when they were introduced into the United States in the late 1800s. Pestalozzianism emphasized teaching children with love, patience, and understanding. Furthermore, children should learn from objects and first-hand experiences, not from abstractions and words. Pestalozzian concepts soon spread throughout the country. Herbartianism was imported into the United States at the Bloomington Normal School in Illinois by three students who had learned about the ideas of Herbart while studying in Germany. Herbartianism represented an attempt to make a science out of teaching. The more formal system that Herbartianism brought to the often disorganized elementary teacher was badly needed at that time. Unfortunately, Herbartianism eventually contributed to an extreme formalism and rigidity that characterized many American elementary schools in the early 1900s. An example of this formalization is the school administrator who bragged that at a given moment in the school day he knew exactly what was going on in all the classrooms. One can infer from this boast that teachers often had a very strict, rigid educational program imposed on them.

If we look back at the historical development of American elementary education, it is possible to make the following generalizations.

- Until the late 1800s the motive, curriculum, and administration of elementary education were primarily religious. The point at which elementary education began to be more secular than religious was the point at which states began to pass compulsory school attendance laws.
- Discipline has traditionally been harsh and severe in elementary schools. The classical picture of a colonial schoolmaster equipped with a frown, dunce cap, stick, whip, and a variety of abusive phrases is a more accurate picture than one might expect. It is no wonder that children have historically viewed school as an unpleasant place. Pestalozzi had much to do with bringing about a gradual change in discipline when he advocated that love, not harsh punishment, should be used to motivate students.
- Elementary education has traditionally been formal and impersonal. The ideas of Rousseau, Pestalozzi, Herbart, Froebel, and Montessori helped to change this condition gradually and make elementary education more "student-centered"; this began to show about 1900.
- Elementary schools have traditionally been taught by poorly prepared teachers.
- Although the aims and methodology have varied considerably from time to time, the basic content of elementary education has historically been reading, writing, and arithmetic.

The Need for Secondary Schools

The first form of secondary school in the colonies was the *Latin grammar school* mentioned previously, first established in Boston in 1635 only five years after colonists settled in the area. The Latin grammar school was largely concerned with teaching Latin and other classical subjects and was strictly college preparatory.

[41]

Harvard was the only university in existence in the colonies at that time. The entrance requirements to Harvard stated:

> When any Scholar is able to understand Tully, or such like classicall Latine Author extempore, and make and speake true Latine in Verse and Prose, suo ut aiunt marte; and decline perfectly the Paradigms of Nounes and Verbes in the Greek tongue; let him then, and not before, be capable of admission into the college.

European colleges and later colonial colleges also demanded that students know Latin and Greek before they could be admitted. For instance, in the mid-eighteenth century, the requirements for admission to Yale stated:

> None may expect to be admitted into this College unless upon Examination of the President and Tutors, they shall be found able Extempore to Read,

Construe, and Parce Tully, Vergil and the Greek Testament; and to write true Latin in Prose and to understand the Rules of Prosodia, and Common Arithmetic, and Shal bring Sufficient Testimony of his Blameless and inoffensive Life.

Since Latin grammar schools were designed to prepare students for college, it is little wonder that the curriculum in these schools was so classical and traditional. Needless to say, a very small percentage of children attended any Latin grammar school because very few could hope to attend college. Girls did not attend; colleges at that time did not admit women. As late as 1785 there were only two Latin grammar schools in Boston, and the combined enrollment in these two schools was only 64 boys.

By the middle of the eighteenth century there was a big need for more and better-trained skilled workers. Benjamin Franklin, recognizing this need, proposed a new kind of secondary school in Pennsylvania. This proposal brought about the establishment in Philadelphia in 1751 of the first truly American educational institution—the American Academy. Franklin established this school because he thought the existing Latin grammar schools were not providing the practical secondary education needed by youth. The philosophy, curriculum, and methodology of Franklin's academy were all geared to prepare young people for employment. Similar academies were established throughout America, and these institutions eventually replaced the Latin grammar school as the predominant secondary education institution. They were usually private schools, and many of them admitted girls as well as boys. Later on, some academies even tried to train elementary school teachers.

In 1821 an English classical school (which three years later changed its name to English High School) was opened in Boston, and another distinctively American educational institution was launched. This first high school, under the direction of George B. Emerson, consisted of a three-year course in English, mathematics, science, and history. The school later added to its curriculum the philosophy of history, chemistry, intellectual philosophy, linear drawing, logic, trigonometry, French, and the United States Constitution. The school enrolled about 100 boys during its first year.

The high school was established because of a belief that the existing grammar schools were inadequate for the day and because most people could not afford to send their children to the private academies. The American high school soon replaced both the Latin grammar school and the private academy and has been with us ever since.

About 1910 the first junior high schools were established in the United States. A survey in 1916 showed 54 junior high schools existing in 36 states. One year later a survey indicated that the number had increased to about 270. More recently, some school systems have abandoned the junior high school in favor of what is called the *middle school*, which usually consists of grades 6, 7, and 8. The evolution of the American secondary school is presented schematically in Figure 12.1.

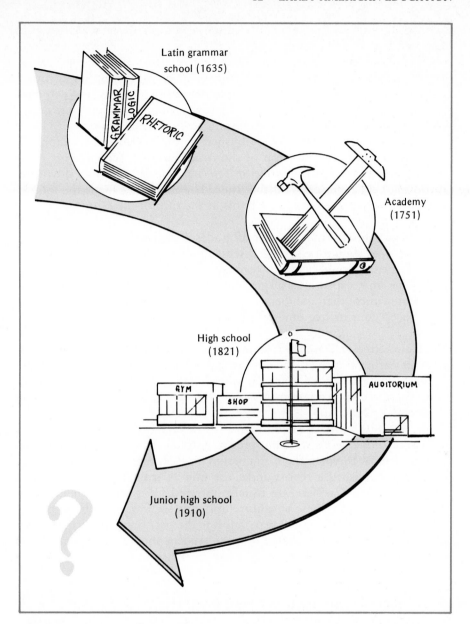

FIGURE 12.1 *Evolution of American secondary education.*

Aims of American Public Education

The aims of American public education have gradually changed over the years. During colonial times the overriding aim of education at all levels was to enable students to read and understand the Bible, to gain salvation, and to spread the gospel. Almost all historical documents preserved since colonial days reveal the dominance of the religious motive in education at that time.

After independence was won from England, educational objectives—like providing Americans with a common language, attempting to instill a sense of patriotism, developing a national feeling of unity and common purpose, and providing the technical and agricultural training our developing nation needed—became important tasks for the schools.

[61] In 1892 a committee was established by the National Education Association to study the function of the American high school. This committee, known as the *Committee of Ten,* made an effort to set down the purposes of the high school at that time. The committee made the following recommendations for high schools at the turn of the century:

- High school should consist of grades 7 through 12.
- Courses should be arranged sequentially.
- Students should be given very few electives in high school.
- One unit, called a Carnegie unit, should be awarded for each separate course that a student takes each year, provided that the course meets four or five times each week all year long.

[18] The Committee of Ten also recommended trying to graduate high school students earlier to permit them to attend college sooner. At that time the recommendation implied that high schools had a college preparatory function. These recommendations became powerful influences in the shaping of secondary education.

Before 1900, teachers had relatively little direction in their work, since most educational goals were not precisely stated. This problem was partly overcome in 1918 when the Commission on Reorganization of Secondary Education published a report under the title "Cardinal Principles of Secondary Education"; these are usually referred to as the *Seven Cardinal Principles.* In reality these constitute only one section of the basic principles discussed in the original text, but it is the part that has become more famous. These principles stated that the student should receive an education in the following fields:

1. Health
2. Command of fundamental processes
3. Worthy home membership
4. Vocation
5. Civic education
6. Worthy use of leisure
7. Ethical character

[19] In 1920 the Committee on Standards for Use in the Reorganization of Secondary School Curricula stated that the ultimate objectives of American secondary education were as follows:

1. To maintain health and physical fitness
2. To use leisure in right ways
3. To sustain successfully certain definite social relationships, civic, domestic, and community
4. To engage in vocational and exploratory vocational activities

The American Youth Commission in 1937 stated that the objectives of secondary education in modern America were to promote adequacy in the following six fields:

1. Citizenship
2. Home membership
3. Leisure life
4. Physical and mental health
5. Vocational efficiency
6. Preparation for continued learning

The following goals of education were listed by the Progressive Education Association in 1938; these "needs of youth" grew out of the Eight Year Study:

1. Physical and mental health
2. Self-assurance
3. Assurance of growth toward adult status
4. Philosophy of life
5. Wide range of personal interests
6. Esthetic appreciations
7. Intelligent self-direction
8. Progress toward maturity in social relations with age-mates and adults
9. Wise use of goods and services
10. Vocational orientation
11. Vocational competence

Also in 1938, another attempt was made to set down the goals of American education when the Educational Policies Commission of the National Education Association (NEA) set forth the "Purposes of Education in American Democracy." These objectives stated that students should receive an education in the four broad areas of self-realization, human relations, economic efficiency, and civic responsibility.

In 1944 this same commission of the NEA published another statement of educational objectives, entitled "Education for All American Youth":

Schools should be dedicated to the proposition that every youth in these United States—regardless of sex, economic status, geographic location, or race—should experience a broad and balanced education which will

1. equip him to enter an occupation suited to his abilities and offering reasonable opportunity for personal growth and social usefulness;
2. prepare him to assume full responsibilities of American citizenship;
3. give him a fair chance to exercise his right to the pursuit of happiness through the attainment and preservation of mental and physical health;
4. stimulate intellectual curiosity, engender satisfaction in intellectual achievement, and cultivate the ability to think rationally; and
5. help to develop an appreciation of the ethical values which should undergird all life in a democratic society.

28   In 1952 the Educational Policies Commission made yet another statement of educational objectives, entitled the "Imperative Needs of Youth":

1. All youth need to develop salable skills and those understandings and attitudes that make the worker an intelligent productive participant in economic life. To this end most youth need supervised work experience as well as education in the skills and knowledge of their occupations.
2. All youth need to develop and maintain good health and physical fitness.
3. All youth need to understand the rights and duties of the citizen of a democratic society, and to be diligent and competent in the performance of their obligations as members of the community and citizens of the state and nation.
4. All youth need to understand the significance of the family for the individual and society and the conditions conducive to successful family life.
5. All youth need to know how to purchase and use goods and services intelligently, understanding both the values received by the consumer and the economic consequences of their acts.
6. All youth need to understand the methods of science, the influence of science on human life, and the main scientific facts concerning the nature of the world and of man.
7. All youth need opportunities to develop their capacities to appreciate beauty in literature, art, music, and nature.
8. All youth need to be able to use their leisure time well and budget it wisely, balancing activities that yield satisfactions to the individual with those that are socially useful.
9. All youth need to develop respect for other persons, to grow in their insight into ethical values and principles, and to be able to live and work cooperatively with others.
10. All youth need to grow in their ability to think rationally, to express their thoughts clearly, and to read and listen with understanding.

A recent White House Conference on Education concluded that American youth need an education that will develop the following traits:

1. Fundamental skills of communication, arithmetic, and mathematics
2. Appreciation for our democratic heritage
3. Civic rights and responsibilities
4. Respect and appreciation for human values
5. Ability to think and evaluate constructively
6. Effective work habits and self-discipline

7. Social competency
8. Ethical behavior
9. Intellectual curiosity
10. Esthetic appreciation
11. Physical and mental health
12. Wise use of time
13. Understanding of the physical world
14. Awareness of our relationship with the world community

These various statements concerning education objectives, made over the last century, sum up fairly well the history of the aims of American public education.

Preparation of Teachers

One of the first forms of teacher training grew out of the medieval guild system, in which a young man who wished to enter a certain field of work served a lengthy period of apprenticeship with a master in the field. Some young men became teachers by serving as apprentices, sometimes for as long as seven years, to master teachers.

The first teacher-training school we have any record of was mentioned in a request to the king of England, written by William Byngham in 1438, stating that "he may yeve withouten fyn or fee (the) mansion ycalled God-deshous the which he hath made and edified in your towne of Cambridge for the free herbigage of poure scolers of Gramer. . . ."[2]

Byngham received permission and established Godshouse College on June 13, 1439. Students at this college gave demonstration lectures to fellow students as a rough way of practice teaching. Classes were conducted even during vacations so that country schoolmasters could attend. Byngham's college still exists as Christ's College of Cambridge University. At that early date of 1439, Byngham made provision for two features still considered very important in teacher education today—scheduling classes so that teachers in service may attend and providing some kind of student teaching experience. Many present-day educators would be surprised to find that these ideas are so old.

Teachers in colonial America were very poorly prepared; more often than not, they had received no special training at all. The single qualification of most of them was that they themselves had been students. Most colonial college teachers, private tutors, Latin grammar school teachers, and academy teachers had received some kind of college education, usually at one of the well-established colleges or universities in Europe. A few had received their education at a colonial American college.

Teachers in the various kinds of colonial elementary schools typically had only an elementary education, but a few had attended a Latin grammar school or a private academy. It was commonly believed that to be a teacher required only that the instructor know something about the subject matter to be taught; consequently, no teacher, regardless of the level taught, received training in the methodology of teaching.

Teaching was not considered a prestigious occupation, and the pay was poor. Consequently, many schoolteachers viewed their jobs as only temporary. For young ladies who taught elementary school, the "something better" was usually marriage. Men frequently left teaching for careers in the ministry or business. It was not uncommon to find career teachers in the colonies who were undesirable people. Records show that many teachers lost their jobs because they paid more attention to the tavern than to the school, or for stealing or swearing or other conduct unbecoming a person in such a position.

Since many colonial schools were conducted in connection with a church, the teacher was often considered an assistant to the minister. Besides teaching, other duties of some early New England teachers were "to act as court messenger, to serve summonses, to conduct certain ceremonial services of the church, to lead the Sunday choir, to ring the bell for public worship, to dig the graves, to perform other occasional duties."

It was not uncommon in the colonies to use white indentured servants as teachers; many of the people who came to America bought passage by agreeing to work for some years as indentured servants. The ship's captain would then sell the indentured servant's services, more often than not by placing an ad in a newspaper. Such an ad appeared in a May 1786 edition of the *Maryland Gazette:*

Men and Women Servants
JUST ARRIVED

In the Ship *Paca*, Robert Caulfield, Master, in five Weeks from Belfast and Cork, a number of healthy Men and Women SERVANTS.
    Among them are several valuable tradesmen, viz.
    Carpenters, Shoemakers, Coopers, Blacksmiths, Staymakers, Bookbinders, Clothiers, Diers, Butchers, Schoolmasters, Millrights, and Labourers.
    Their indentures are to be disposed of by the Subscribers,

> Brown, and Maris,
> William Wilson

Some colonial teachers learned how to keep school by serving as apprentices to schoolmasters. Court records reveal numerous such indentures of apprenticeship; the following was recorded in New York City in 1772:

This Indenture witnesseth that John Campbel Son of Robert Campbel of the City of New York with the Consent of his father and mother hath put himself and by these presents doth Voluntarily put and bind himself Apprentice to George Brownell of the Same City Schoolmaster to learn the Art Trade or Mastery—for and during the term of ten years. . . . And the said George Brownell Doth hereby Covenant and Promise to teach and instruct or Cause the said Apprentice to be taught and instructed in the Art Trade or Calling of a Schoolmaster by the best way or means he or his wife may or can.

One of Benjamin Franklin's justifications for proposing an academy in Philadelphia was that some of the graduates would make good teachers. Speculating on the need for such graduates, Franklin wrote:

> A number of the poorer sort [of academy graduates] will be hereby qualified to act as Schoolmasters in the Country, to teach children Reading, Writing, Arithmetic, and the Grammar of their Mother Tongue, and being of good morals and known character, may be recommended from the Academy to Country Schools for that purpose; the Country suffering at present very much for want of good Schoolmasters, and obliged frequently to employ in their Schools, vicious imported Servants, or concealed Papists, who by their bad Examples and Instructions often deprave the Morals and corrupt the Principles of the children under their Care.

The fact that Franklin said some of the "poorer" graduates would make suitable teachers reflects the low regard for teaching typical of the time. The academy that Franklin proposed was established in 1751 in Philadelphia, and many graduates of academies after that time did become teachers.

Many early educators recognized this country's need for better-qualified teachers; however, it was not until 1823 that the first teacher-training institution was established in the United States. This private school, called a *normal school* after its European counterpart, which had existed until the late seventeenth century, was established by the Rev. Mr. Samuel Hall in Concord, Vermont. Hall's school did not produce many teachers, but it did signal the beginning of formal teacher training in the United States. [43]

The early normal school program usually consisted of a two-year course. Students typically entered the normal school right after finishing elementary school. Most normal schools did not require high school graduation for entrance until about 1900. The curriculum was much like the curriculum of the high schools of that time. Students reviewed subjects studied in elementary school, studied high school subjects, had a course in teaching (or "pedagogy" as it was then called), and did some student teaching in a model school usually operated in conjunction with the normal school. The subjects offered by a normal school in Albany, New York, in 1845 included English grammar, English composition, history, geography, reading, writing, orthography, arithmetic, algebra, geometry, trigonometry, human physiology, surveying, natural philosophy, chemistry, intellectual philosophy, moral philosophy, government, rhetoric, theory and practice of teaching, drawing, music, astronomy, and practice teaching.

Horace Mann was instrumental in establishing the first state-supported normal school, which opened in 1839 in Lexington, Massachusetts. Other public normal schools were established shortly afterwards. They typically offered a two-year teacher-training program. Some of the students came directly from elementary school; others had completed secondary school.

Some states did not establish state-supported normal schools until the early 1900s. The dates are given in Table 12.1. They indicate the order in which each state decided that education was important—important enough to spend tax money on training better teachers.

During the early part of this century, several factors caused a significant change in normal schools. For one thing, as the population of the United States increased, so did the enrollment in elementary schools, thereby creating an ever-increasing demand for elementary teachers. Likewise, as more and more people attended high school, it created a demand for more high school teachers. To meet this demand, normal schools eventually expanded their curriculum to include secondary teacher education. The establishment of high schools also created a need for teachers highly specialized in particular academic subjects, and so normal schools established subject matter departments and developed more diversified programs. The length of the teacher-education program was expanded to two, three, and finally four years; this helped expand and diversify the normal school curriculum. The demand for teachers increased from about 20,000 in 1900 to more than 200,000 in 1930. Another factor contributed to the growth

TABLE 12.1   *The First State Normal Schools*

Massachusetts	1839	Texas	1879
New York	1844	North Dakota	1881
Connecticut	1849	South Dakota	1881
Michigan	1849	Oregon	1883
Rhode Island	1852	Virginia	1884
Iowa	1855	Louisiana	1884
New Jersey	1855	Arizona	1885
Illinois	1857	Wyoming	1886
Minnesota	1858	Florida	1887
Pennsylvania	1859	Nevada	1887
California	1862	Colorado	1889
Kansas	1863	Georgia	1889
Maine	1863	Washington	1890
Indiana	1865	Oklahoma	1891
Wisconsin	1865	Idaho	1893
Vermont	1866	Montana	1893
Delaware	1866	New Mexico	1893
Nebraska	1867	South Carolina	1895
West Virginia	1867	Maryland	1896
Utah	1869	Ohio	1900
Missouri	1870	Kentucky	1906
New Hampshire	1870	Alabama	1907
Arkansas	1872	Tennessee	1909
North Carolina	1876	Mississippi	1910

of the normal schools: the United States had advanced technologically to the point at which more college-educated citizens were needed. The normal schools assumed a responsibility to help meet this need by establishing many other academic programs in addition to teacher training. As normal schools extended their programs to four years and began granting baccalaureate degrees, they also began to call themselves *state teachers' colleges*. For most institutions the change in name took place during the 1930s.

Universities entered the teacher-preparation business on a large scale about 1900. Before then, some graduates of universities had become high school teachers or college teachers, but not until 1900 did universities establish departments of education and add teacher education to the curriculum.

Just as the normal schools expanded in size, scope, and function to the point at which they became state teachers' colleges, so did the state teachers' colleges expand to become *state colleges*. This change in name and scope took place for most institutions about 1950. The elimination of the word *teacher* really explains the story behind this transition. The new state colleges gradually expanded their programs beyond teacher education and became multipurpose institutions. One of the main reasons for this transition was that more and more students coming to the colleges demanded a more varied education. The state teachers' colleges developed diversified programs to try to meet their demands.

Many of these same state colleges have now become state universities, offering doctoral degrees in a wide range of fields. Today some of our largest and most highly regarded universities have evolved from normal schools. Figure 12.2 pictures the evolution of American teacher-preparation institutions.

This completes our review of the history of teacher education. Obviously, establishing the teaching profession has been a long and difficult task. Preparation of teachers has greatly improved since colonial times—when anyone could be a teacher—until the present, when the rigorous requirements for permanent teacher certification cannot be easily met by everyone.

Evolution of Teaching Materials

The first schools in colonial America were poorly equipped. In fact, the first elementary schools were usually conducted by housewives right in their homes. The only teaching materials likely to be found then were a Bible and perhaps one or two other religious books, a small amount of scarce paper, a few quill pens, and hornbooks. The *hornbook* was the most common teaching device in early colonial schools (Figure 12.3). Hornbooks differed widely but typically consisted of a sheet of paper showing the alphabet, covered with a thin transparent sheet of cow's horn tacked to a paddle-shaped piece of wood. A leather cord was often looped

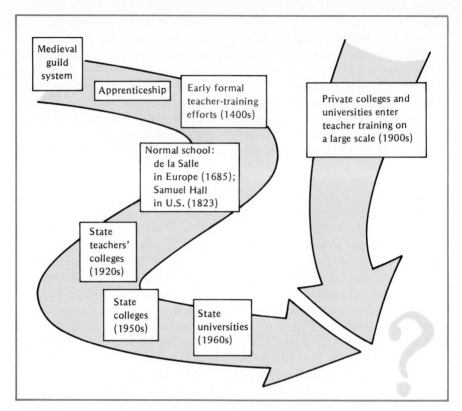

FIGURE 12.2 *Evolution of teacher-preparation institutions.*

through a hole in the paddle so that students could hang the hornbooks around their necks. Hornbooks provided students with their first reading instructions. Records indicate that hornbooks were used in Europe in the Middle Ages and were common there until about 1760.

As paper became more available, the hornbook evolved into a several-page "book" called a battledore. The battledore, printed on heavy paper, often resembled an envelope. Like the hornbook, it typically contained the alphabet and various religious prayers and/or admonitions.

The first real textbook to be used in colonial elementary schools was the *New England Primer*. Records show that the first copies of this book were printed in England in the late 1600s. Copies of the *New England Primer* were also printed as early as 1690 in the American colonies. The book was advertised in the *News from the Stars Almanac,* published in 1690 in Boston (see Figure 12.4). The oldest extant copy of the *New England Primer* is a 1727 edition, now in the Lenox Collection of the New York Public Library.

The *New England Primer* was a small book, usually about 2½ by 4½ inches, with thin wooden covers covered by paper or leather. It was from 50 to 100 pages long, depending on how many extra sections were added

FIGURE 12.3 *A hornbook.*

to each edition. The first pages contained the alphabet, vowels, and capital letters. Next came lists of words arranged from two to six syllables, followed by verses and tiny woodcut pictures for each letter in the alphabet.

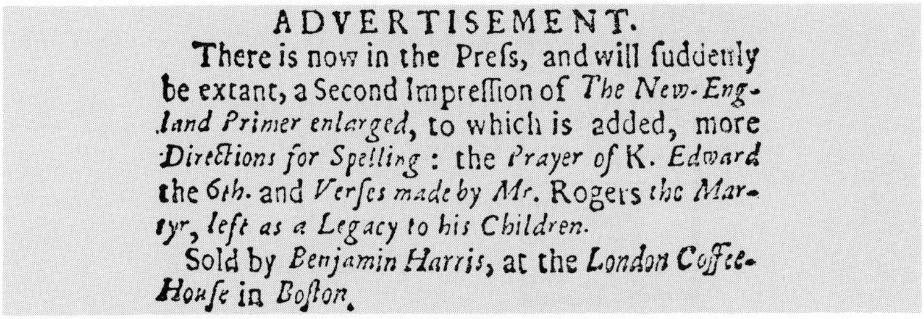

ADVERTISEMENT.
There is now in the Press, and will suddenly be extant, a Second Impreſſion of *The New-England Primer enlarged,* to which is added, more *Directions for Spelling :* the *Prayer of K. Edward the 6th.* and *Verſes made by Mr.* Rogers *the Martyr, left as a Legacy to his Children.*
Sold by *Benjamin Harris,* at the *London Coffee-House* in *Boston.*

FIGURE 12.4 *Advertisement from 1690 publication.*

A reproduction of the verses and pictures is presented in Figure 12.5. The contents of the *New England Primer* reflect the heavily religious motive in colonial education.

The primer was virtually the only reading book used in colonial schools until about 1800, when Noah Webster published *The American Spelling Book*. This book eventually became known as the *Blue-Backed Speller* because of its blue cover. It eventually replaced the *New England Primer* as the most common elementary textbook. The speller reportedly sold over 24 million copies; its royalties supported Noah Webster and his family while he prepared his still famous dictionary. The speller was approximately 4 by 6½ inches; its cover was made of thin sheets of wood covered with light blue paper. The first part of the book contained rules and instructions for using the book; next came the alphabet, syllables, and consonants. The bulk of the book was taken up with lists of words arranged according to syllables and sounds. The book also contained rules for reading and speaking, moral advice, and stories of various sorts. Figure 12.6 shows a page from a *Blue-Backed Speller* printed about 1800.

Very few textbooks were available for use in colonial Latin grammar schools, academies, and colleges, though various religious books, including the Bible, were often used. A few books dealing with history, geography, arithmetic, Latin, Greek, and certain classics were available for use in colonial secondary schools and colleges during the eighteenth century.

FIGURE 12.5 New England Primer.

OF PRONUNCIATION. 85

FABLE I. *Of the Boy that stole Apples.*

AN old Man found a rude Boy upon one of his trees stealing Apples, and desired him to come down; but the young Sauce-box told him plainly he wou'd not. Won't you? said the old Man, then I will fetch you down; so he pulled up some tufts of Grass, and threw at him; but this only made the Youngster laugh, to think the old Man should pretend to beat him out of the tree with grass only.

Well, well, said the old Man, if neither words nor grass, will do, I must try what virtue there is in Stones; so the old Man pelted him heartily with stones; which soon made the young Chap, hasten down from the tree and beg the old Man's pardon.

MORAL.

If good words and gentle means will not reclaim the wicked, they must be dealt with in a more severe manner.

FIGURE 12.6 *The* Blue-Backed Speller.

Harvard College had a large library for its day, since John Harvard, its benefactor, had bequeathed his entire library of 400 volumes to the school.

By 1800, nearly 200 years after the colonies had been established, school buildings and teaching materials were still very crude and meager. You can understand something of the physical features and equipment of an 1810 New England school by reading the following description by a teacher of that school:

41

(A) The School Building: The school house stood near the center of the district, at the junction of four roads, so near the usual track of carriages that a large stone was set up at the end of the building to defend it from injury.

Except in the dry season the ground was wet, and the soil by no means firm. The spot was particularly exposed to the bleak winds of winter; nor were there any shade trees to shelter the children from the scorching rays of the summer's sun, as they were cut down many years ago. Neither was there any such thing as an outhouse of any kind, not even a wood shed.

The size of the building was 22 × 20 feet. From the floor to the ceiling it was 7 feet. The chimney and entry took up about four feet at one end, leaving the schoolroom itself 18 × 20 feet. Around these sides of the room were connected desks, arranged so that when the pupils were sitting at them their faces were towards the instructor and their backs toward the wall. Attached to the sides of the desks nearest to the instructor were benches for small pupils. The instructor's desk and chair occupied the center. On this desk were stationed a rod, or ferule; sometimes both. These, with books, writings, inkstands, rules, and plummets, with a fire shovel, and a pair of tongs (often broken), were the principal furniture.

The windows were five in number, of twelve panes each. They were situated so low in the walls as to give full opportunity to the pupils to see every traveller as he passed, and to be easily seen. The places of the broken panes were usually supplied with hats, during school hours. A depression in the chimney, on one side of the entry, furnished a place of deposit for about half of the hats, and the spare clothes of the boys; the rest were left on the floor, often to be trampled upon. The girls generally carried their bonnets, etc., into the schoolroom. The floor and ceiling were level, and the walls were plastered.

The room was warmed by a large and deep fireplace. So large was it, and so efficacious in warming the room otherwise, that I have seen about one-eighth of a cord of good wood burning in it at a time. In severe weather it was estimated that the amount usually consumed was not far from a cord a week. . . .

The school was not infrequently broken up for a day or two for want of wood. The instructor or pupils were sometimes, however, compelled to cut or saw it to prevent the closing of the school. The wood was left in the road near the house, so that it often was buried in the snow, or wet with rain. At the best, it was usually burnt green. The fires were to be kindled about half an hour before the time of beginning the school. Often, the scholar, whose lot it was, neglected to build it. In consequence of this, the house was frequently cold and uncomfortable about half of the forenoon, when, the fire being very large, the excess of heat became equally distressing. Frequently, too, we were annoyed by smoke. The greatest amount of suffering, however, arose from excessive heat, particularly at the close of the day. The pupils being in a free perspiration when they left were very liable to take cold.

The ventilation of the schoolroom was as much neglected as its temperature; and its cleanliness, more perhaps than either. There were no arrangements for cleaning feet at the door, or for washing floors, windows, etc. In the summer the floor was washed, perhaps once in two or three weeks.

(B) The Instructors: The winter school usually opened about the first week of December, and continued twelve to sixteen weeks. The summer term commenced about the first of May. Formerly this was also continued about three or four months, but within ten years the term has been lengthened usually to twenty weeks. Males have been uniformly employed in winter, and females in summer.

The instructors have usually been changed every season, but sometimes they have been continued two successive summers or winters. A strong prejudice has always existed against employing the same instructor more than once or twice in the same district. This prejudice has yielded in one instance, so far that an instructor who had taught two successive winters, twenty-five years before, was employed another season. I have not been able to ascertain the number of instructors who have been engaged in the school during the last thirty years, but I can distinctly recollect thirty-seven. Many of them, both males and females, were from sixteen to eighteen years of age, and a few, over twenty-one.

Good moral character, and a thorough knowledge of the common branches, formerly were considered as indispensable qualifications in an instructor. The instructors were chiefly selected from the most respectable families in town. But for fifteen or twenty years, these things have not been so much regarded. They have indeed been deemed desirable; but the most common method now seems to be to ascertain, as near as possible, the dividend for that season from the public treasury, and then fix upon a teacher who will take charge of the school, three or four months, for this money. He must indeed be able to obtain a license from the Board of Visitors; but this has become nearly a matter of course, provided he can spell, read, and write. In general, the candidate is some favorite or relative of the District Committee. It gives me great pleasure, however, to say that the moral character of almost every instructor, so far as I know, has been unexceptional.

Instructors have usually boarded in the families of the pupils. Their compensation has varied from seven to eleven dollars a month for males; and from sixty-two and a half cents to one dollar a week for females. Within the past ten years, however, the price of instruction has rarely been less than nine dollars in the former case, and seventy-five cents in the latter. In the few instances in which instructors have furnished their own board the compensation has been about the same, it being assumed that they could work at some employment of their own enough to pay their board, especially the females.

(C) The Instruction: Two of the Board of Visitors usually visit the winter schools twice during the term. In the summer, their visits are often omitted. These visits usually occupy from one hour to an hour and a half. They are spent merely in hearing a few hurried lessons, and in making some remarks, general in their character. Formerly, it was customary to examine the pupils in some approved Catechism, but this practice has been omitted for twenty years.

The parents seldom visit the school, except by special invitation. The greater number pay very little attention to it at all. There are, however, a few who are gradually awakening to the importance of good instruction; but there are also a few who oppose everything which is suggested as, at the least, useless; and are scarcely willing their children should be governed in the school.

The school books have been about the same for thirty years. Webster's Spelling Book, the American Preceptor, and the New Testament, have been the principal books used. Before the appearance of the American Preceptor, Dwight's Geography was used as a reading book. A few of the Introduction to the American Orator were introduced about twelve years since, and, more recently, Jack Halyard.

Until within a few years, no studies have been permitted in the day school but spelling, reading, and writing. Arithmetic was taught by a few instructors, one or two evenings in a week, but, in spite of the most determined opposition, arithmetic is now permitted in the day school, and a few pupils study geography.[3]

About 1820 a new instructional device was introduced into American schools—the slate. These school slates were thin flat pieces of slate stone framed with wood. The pencils used to write on the slate were also made of slate and produced a light but legible line. The wooden frames of some of the slates were covered with cloth so noise would be minimized as students placed the slates on the desk. There were even double slates made by hinging two single slates together with cord or leather. Students wrote their assignments on the slates, just as today's students write on tablet paper. Later on, large pieces of slate made up the blackboards that were added to classrooms.

In the same way that Noah Webster's *Blue-Backed Speller* replaced the *New England Primer,* so did McGuffey's *Reader* eventually replace the *Blue-Backed Speller.* These readers were carefully geared to each grade and were meant to instill in children a respect for hard work, thrift, self-help, and honesty. McGuffey's *Reader* dominated the elementary school book market until approximately 1900, when they were gradually replaced by newer and improved readers written by David Tower, James Fassett, William Elson, and others. Figure 12.7 is a diagrammatic summary of the evolution of the textbook.

During the twentieth century, teachers have gradually adapted a variety of tools to assist them in educating American youth. This has come about partly through the influence of Pestalozzi, John Dewey, and others, who demonstrated that children learn best by first-hand experiences. Likewise, school buildings have become larger, more elaborate, and better designed to encourage learning. Today, many schools are equipped with an impressive array of books, laboratory equipment, movie projectors, filmstrip projectors, tape recorders, television devices, single-concept films, teaching machines, programmed materials, and learning devices of all kinds. Some of the modern school buildings are not only excellent from an educational standpoint but magnificent pieces of architecture as well. One cannot help but be awed by the contrast between American education today and its humble beginning years ago.

Education of American Blacks

In 1619, only a dozen years after Jamestown was established, the first boatload of slaves arrived in the colonies. This event was recorded for history when, in that year, John Rolfe wrote in his *Journal* that the captain of a Dutch ship "sold us twenty Negroes." These slaves were imported as a source of cheap labor for the new colonies.

The number of imported slaves steadily increased; between 1700 and 1750, thousands of Blacks were brought to the American colonies each year. By the Revolutionary War there were approximately 700,000 Blacks in the colonies; by 1860 there were about 4.5 million.

Probably the first organized attempts to educate the Blacks in colonial America were by French and Spanish missionaries.[4] These early missionary efforts set an example that influenced the education of Black people throughout the colonies. The missionaries, in their endeavors to carry out

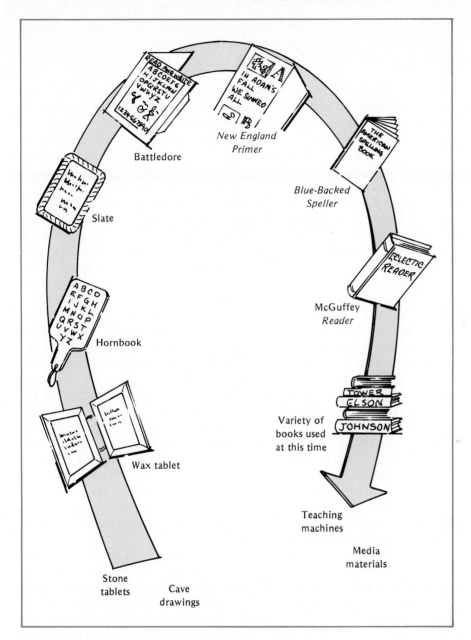

Battledore

New England
Primer

Slate

Blue-Backed
Speller

Hornbook

McGuffey
Reader

Wax tablet

Variety of
books used
at this time

Stone
tablets

Cave
drawings

Teaching
machines

Media
materials

FIGURE 12.7 *Evolution of the textbook.*

their religious missions, provided instruction for Blacks and also for the numerous offspring who were the result of mixed breeding. Educating slaves posed an interesting moral problem for the church. The English colonists had to find a way to overcome the idea that converting a slave to Christianity might logically lead to his or her freedom. The problem they faced was how to eliminate an unwritten law that a Christian should not be a slave. The church's governing bodies and the Bishop of London settled the matter by decreeing that conversion did not lead to formal emancipation.

[43] The organized church nevertheless provided the setting in which Black people were allowed to develop skills at reading, leadership, and educating their brethren. Often Blacks and whites attended church together. Eventually, some preachers, former slaves, demonstrated exceptional skill in "spreading the gospel." The Baptists in particular, by encouraging a form of self-government, allowed Blacks to become active in the church. This move fostered the growth of Black congregations; because of it, the enslaved as well as the free Black was given an opportunity for education and development not provided by many other denominations.

The efforts of the English to educate Black slaves were largely carried out by the Society for the Propagation of the Gospel in Foreign Parts. The Society was created by the Established Church of London in 1701. In 1705 the Reverend Samuel Thomas of Goose Creek Parish in South Carolina established a school fostered by the Society, enrolling 60 Black students. Nine years later the Society opened a school in New York City where 200 Black pupils were enrolled. Despite stringent opposition from many whites, who believed that educating slaves was a "dangerous business," the Society went on to establish other schools for Black people. The degree of success of these early efforts to educate Blacks varied greatly. Initially, many people were not generally opposed to educating Blacks. Education, however, seemed to make the slaves aware of their plight. In the South, much of the unrest concerning slavery was attributed to the education of slaves. Insurrections, uprisings, and threats to overseers, masters, and their families produced fear among the whites. Consequently, some states even passed legislation that eliminated any form of education for the slaves.

The Industrial Revolution in England, the invention of the cotton gin, Black insurrections, the extension of slavery into new territories, and the migration of Black people to the North were all factors that influenced our new nation's policies concerning Blacks.

The nation's leaders meeting in Philadelphia in 1775 at the First Continental Congress brazenly talked about abolishing slavery in the colonies. In the final analysis, however, southern leaders opposed these views, and the Congress compromised by not mentioning slavery in the Constitution. The Compromise of 1850, after much turmoil and debate by Henry Clay, John Calhoun, Stephen Douglas, William Seward, and Salmon Chase, consisted of the following agreements:

- California should enter the Union as a free state.
- The other territories would be organized without mention of slavery.
- Texas should cede certain lands to New Mexico and be compensated.

- Slaveholders would be better protected by a stringent fugitive slave law.
- There should be no slave trade in the District of Columbia.

The eventual migration of large numbers of Blacks from the South to the North and West held vast implications for Black education. In moving North and West, Blacks were seeking economic independence. The small number of Blacks who had previously populated the North and West did not constitute a great threat to the white worker. But large numbers of migrant Blacks, a substantial portion of whom were unskilled, threatened to replace some white workers. Retaliation took the form of rioting, and unions organized to oppose the Black worker. Some of this union opposition to Blacks on the labor front has existed to the present. This labor opposition represented yet another reason why many whites were generally reluctant to provide equal educational opportunities for Blacks.

The Blacks' individual success in acquiring education, as well as their group efforts to establish schools, was greatly enhanced by sympathetic and humanitarian white friends. John Chavis, a free Black born in 1763 in Oxford, North Carolina, was a Black who was helped by whites. Chavis became a successful teacher of aristocratic whites. His white neighbors sent him to Princeton "to see if a Negro would take a college education." His rapid advancement under Dr. Witherspoon soon indicated that the adventure was a success. He returned to Virginia and later went to North Carolina, where he preached among his own people. The success of John Chavis, even under experimental conditions, represented a small step forward in the education of American Blacks.

Phyllis Wheatley was a slave girl brought from Africa in 1761. She was placed in the service of the household of John Wheatley of Boston, and without any formal training she learned to read and speak English fluently. She eventually became well known for her poetry, which was published and read widely.

Benjamin Banneker, a distinguished Black man, was born in Baltimore County, Maryland, in 1731. Baltimore maintained a liberal policy toward educating Blacks, and this permitted Banneker to learn to read, write, and do arithmetic at a relatively early age. He became extremely well educated. In 1770, one of his first accomplishments was to manufacture the first clock made in the United States. After attracting the attention of the scientific world generally, he turned his attention specifically to astronomy. Without any instruction but with the help of books borrowed from an encouraging white inventor, Banneker soon could calculate eclipses of the sun and moon. His accuracy far excelled that of any other American. The outstanding works of this inventor aroused the curiosity of Thomas Jefferson, who in 1803 invited Banneker to his home, Monticello. The acknowledgment of a Black man's achievement by a noted American was still another milestone in the education of the Blacks and in their elevation from subservience.

Frederick Douglass, born a slave in Maryland in 1817, ran away from slavery and began talking to abolitionist groups about his experiences as a slave. He attributed his fluent speech to listening to his master talk. Douglass firmly believed that if he devoted all his efforts to improving vocational education, he could greatly improve the Blacks' plight. He thought that previous attempts by educators to combine liberal and vocational education had failed, so he emphasized vocational education solely.

One of the first northern schools regularly established for Blacks appears to have been that of Elias Neau in New York City in 1704. Neau was an agent of the Society for the Propagation of the Gospel in Foreign Parts.

In 1807, free Blacks, including George Bell, Nicholas Franklin, and Moses Liverpool, built the first schoolhouse for Blacks in the District of Columbia. Not until 1824, however, was there a Black teacher in that district—John Adams. In 1851, Washington citizens attempted to discourage Myrtilla Miner from establishing an academy for Black girls. However, after much turmoil and harassment, the white schoolmistress from New York founded her academy; it is still functioning today.

Prudence Crandall, a young Quaker, established an early boarding school at Canterbury, Connecticut. The trouble she ran into dramatizes some of the northern animosity to educating Black people then. Trouble arose when Sarah Harris, a "colored girl," asked to be admitted to the institution. After much deliberation, Miss Crandall finally consented. White parents objected to the Black girl's attending the school and withdrew their children. To keep the school open, Miss Crandall recruited Black children. The pupils were threatened with violence, local stores would not trade with her, and the school building was vandalized. The citizens of Canterbury petitioned the state legislature to enact a law that would make it illegal to educate Blacks from out of state. Miss Crandall was jailed and tried before the state supreme court in July 1834. The court never gave a final decision because defects were found in the information prepared by the attorney for the state, and the indictment was eventually dropped.

Finally, Boston, the seat of northern liberalism, established a separate school for Black children in 1798. Elisha Sylvester, a white man, was in charge. The school was founded in the home of Primus Hall, a "Negro in good standing." Two years later, 66 free Blacks petitioned the school committee for a separate school and were refused. Undaunted, the patrons of Hall's house employed two instructors from Harvard; 35 years later, the school was allowed to move to a separate building. The city of Boston opened its first primary school for the education of Black children in 1820—one more milestone in the history of Black education.

Unfortunately, despite isolated efforts like these, Blacks received pathetically little formal education until the Emancipation Proclamation issued by President Abraham Lincoln on January 1, 1863. At that time the literacy rate among Blacks was estimated at 5 percent. Sunday school represented about the only opportunity most Black people had to learn to read. In the late 1700s and early 1800s, some communities did set up separate schools for Blacks; however, only a very small percentage of Blacks ever attended the schools. A few colleges such as Oberlin, Bowdoin, Franklin, Rutland, and Harvard admitted Black students; but again, very few Blacks attended college then. There were even a few Black colleges, such as Lincoln University in Pennsylvania (1854) and Wilberforce University in Ohio (1856); however, the efforts and opportunities for the education of American Blacks were pathetically few in view of the size of the Black population.

Although there was no great rush to educate Black people, the abolishment of slavery in 1865 signaled the beginning of a slow but steady effort to improve their education. By 1890, literacy rose to 40 percent; by 1910 it was estimated that 70 percent of Black Americans had learned to read and write. These statistics showing the rapid increase in Black literacy are impressive; however, they are dampened by a report of the U.S. Commissioner of Education, which showed that by 1900, fewer than 70 out of 1000 public high schools in the South were provided for Blacks.

The most significant developments in the education of American Blacks have been in the twentieth century—mostly since 1950. These developments are discussed more fully in Parts II and III and in the next chapter.

Education of Women

Historically, women have not been afforded equal educational opportunities in the United States. Furthermore, many authorities claim that our schools have traditionally been sexist institutions. Although there is much evidence to support both these assertions, it is ironically also true that an impressive list of women have made significant contributions to our educational progress.

Colonial schools simply did not provide education for girls in any significant way. In some instances, girls were taught to read, but they were not admitted to Latin grammar schools, academies, or colleges.

One of the first early efforts to provide better education for women was that offered by Troy Female Seminary, located in New York, which was opened in 1821. Troy was founded by Emma Willard, whose lifelong goal was to further the progress of women. Many of the graduates of Troy became prominent in various fields, including education. Many other female institutions were established and became prominent during the mid- and late-1800s. These included Mary Lyon's Mount Holyoke Female Seminary; Jane Ingersoll's Seminary in Cortland, New York; Julia and Elias Mark's Southern Carolina Collegiate Institute at Barhamville—to name just a few. Unfortunately, it was not until well into the twentieth century that women were generally afforded access to higher education.

Smith College was founded under the will of Sophia Smith. Chartered in 1871, it is the largest independent college for women in the United States.

Even though women eventually could attend college, they were not given equal access to all fields of study. Although considerable progress has been made in recent years, remnants of this problem still exist today.

The fact that women have made significant contributions to our educational progress through the years has been well documented. In addition to the examples just mentioned and those discussed elsewhere in this book, we can add the following: Catherine Beecher (who founded the Hartford Female Seminary), Jane Addams (who proposed an expanded school concept as part of her new liberal social philosophy), Susan Anthony (who was a teacher in her early professional life), Mrs. Carl Schurz (who founded the first kindergarten in this country), and Mary McLeod Bethune (daughter of slave parents who became president of the American Teachers Association and founder of her own college).

Maria Montessori was still another important female educator. Born in 1870 in Italy, Montessori first became a successful physician and later a prominent educational philosopher. She developed her own theory and methods of educating young children. Her methods utilized child-size school furniture and specially designed learning materials. She emphasized independent work by children under the guidance of a trained directress. Private Montessori schools thrive in the United States today.

Private Education in America

Private education has been extremely important in the development of America. Private schools carried on most of the education in colonial America. The first colonial colleges—Harvard, William and Mary, Yale, and Princeton—were private schools. Many of the other early colonial schools were also conducted by churches, missionary societies, or private individuals.

Not until after the Revolution, when there was a strong sense of nationalism, did certain educators advocate a strong public school system for the new nation. Such recommendations, however, were not destined to be acted on for many years.

In the meantime, some of the Protestant churches continued to expand their schools during the colonial period. For instance, the Congregational, Quaker, Episcopalian, Baptist, Methodist, Presbyterian, and Reform churches all, at various times and in varying degrees, established and operated schools for their youth. It was the Roman Catholics and Lutherans, however, who eventually developed elaborate parochial school systems.

As early as 1820 there were 240 Lutheran parochial schools in Pennsylvania. Although the number of Lutheran schools in that particular state eventually dwindled, Henry Muhlenburg and other Lutheran leaders continued to establish parochial schools until the public school system became well established. The Missouri Synod Lutheran Church has continued to maintain a well-developed parochial school system right down to the present. Currently, there are approximately 1700 Lutheran elementary and secondary schools, which enroll about 200,000 pupils in the United States. Most of these schools are conducted by the Missouri Synod Lutheran Church.

The Roman Catholic parochial school system grew rapidly beginning in the 1800s. This growth continued into the twentieth century; the Roman Catholic parochial school system is now the largest private school system in the world.

History of Federal Involvement

The United States Constitution does not mention education; therefore by virtue of the Tenth Amendment, which states, "The powers not delegated to the United States by the Constitution, nor prohibited by it to the states,

42

are reserved to the states respectively, or to the people," education is a function of each state. There is some question whether the makers of the Constitution thoughtfully intended to leave education up to each state or whether they merely forgot to mention it. Some historians believe that our founding fathers wisely realized that local control of education would build a better America. Other historians believe that the framers of the Constitution were so preoccupied with what they believed were more important issues that they never thought to make national provision for education.

38

Even though the Constitution does not refer to education, the federal government has been active in educational affairs from the very beginning. In 1785 and 1787 the Continental Congress passed the Northwest Ordinance Acts. These acts provided for disposing of the Northwest Territory and encouraged the establishment of schools in the territory by stating: "Religion, morality and knowledge being necessary to good government and the happiness of mankind, schools and the means of education shall forever be encouraged." As the various states formed the Northwest Territory, they were required to set aside the sixteenth section of each township to be used for educational purposes.

In 1862 the federal government passed the Morrill Land Grant Act, when it became apparent that existing colleges were not providing the vocational programs needed. The Hatch Act of 1887 established agricultural experimental stations across the country; the Smith-Lever Agricultural Extension Act of 1914 carried the services of land grant colleges to the people through extension services. These early federal acts did much to improve agriculture and industry at a time when our rapidly developing nation badly needed such improvement.

In 1917 the federal government passed the first act providing financial aid to public schools below the college level. This was the Smith-Hughes Act, which provided for high school vocational programs in agriculture, trades and industry, and homemaking. High schools were academically oriented then, and the Smith-Hughes Act stimulated the development of badly needed vocational programs.

The 1930s were depression days, and the government was trying to solve national economic difficulties. Legislation was enacted during these years to encourage economic development, but this legislation indirectly provided financial aid to education. Five relief agencies related to education during this time included the Civilian Conservation Corps, National Youth Administration, Federal Emergency Relief Administration, Public Works Administration, and Federal Surplus Commodities Corporation.[5] These federal programs, although not sponsored primarily for education, benefited education and did so in response to the needs of the time.

The more recent involvements of the federal government, from 1940 to the present, are presented in the next chapter. Appendix D contains a chronology of these more important federal education acts.

Summary and Implications

The history of American education is filled with many messages. Some of these messages tell of successes, some of failures, others of dedicated teachers, of humble beginnings, of the individual's thirst for knowledge—even of those who have been willing to die for the truth. A chronology of these highlights of the historical development of education in the United States is presented in Appendix E.

These historical events have implications for today's educator. Teachers can learn much from our educational history if they will listen carefully to these messages from the past. In particular, they will come to realize how very important education is to the preservation and progress of our society—perhaps even more important than any other human endeavor.

DISCUSSION QUESTIONS

1. Discuss the evolution of elementary schools.
2. How did the development of public education differ in the northern, middle, and southern colonies?
3. What historical conditions led to that uniquely American institution, the comprehensive high school?
4. Discuss the role that private schools have played in American education.
5. How has the concept of the nature of humankind changed in the past 300 years? What effect has this change had on teacher education?
6. What are the highlights of the history of education of women in America?

SUPPLEMENTAL ACTIVITIES

1. Invite an elderly retired teacher to your class to discuss his or her teaching experience.
2. Invite a professor from the history department to discuss the history of education from his or her viewpoint.
3. Create several artistic displays, charts, or exhibits—using various materials—depicting significant aspects of the history of education.
4. Make a hornbook, battledore, wax tablet, or quill pen.
5. Collect some old books and other educational artifacts. Study these and then give them to your school so that future students may see and study them.

NOTES

1. Paul Monroe, *Source Book of the History of Education* (New York: Macmillan, 1901).
2. W. H. G. Armytage, "William Byngham: A Medieval Protagonist of the Training of Teachers," *History of Education Journal* 2 (Summer 1951):108.
3. Monroe, p. 282.
4. Much of the material dealing with the history of American Blacks up until the signing of the Emancipation Proclamation (1863) was taken from the doctoral dissertation of Samuel Davis, "Education, Law, and the Negro" (Urbana: University of Illinois, 1970).
5. Roe L. Johns and Edgar L. Morphet, *Financing the Public Schools* (Englewood Cliffs, N.J.: Prentice-Hall, 1960), p. 378.

BIBLIOGRAPHY

Buetow, Harold A. *Of Singular Benefit: The Story of U.S. Catholic Education.* New York: Macmillan, 1970.

Carpenter, Charles, *History of American Schoolbooks.* Philadelphia: University of Pennsylvania Press, 1963.

Church, Robert L., and Sedlak, Michael W. *Education in the United States: An Interpretive History.* New York: Macmillan, 1976.

Cohen, Sheldon S. *A History of Colonial Education 1607–1776.* New York: John Wiley, 1974.

Cordasco, Francesco, and Cremin, Lawrence. *A History of Education in American Culture.* New York: Holt, Rinehart and Winston, 1953.

Gartner, Lloyd P., ed. *Jewish Education in the United States: A Documentary History.* New York: Teachers College Press, 1970.

Griffin, Frances. *Less Time for Meddling: A History of Salem Academy and College, 1772–1866.* Winston-Salem, N.C.: Blair, 1979.

Gross, Carl H., and Chandler, Charles C. *The History of American Education through Readings.* Boston: D. C. Heath, 1964.

Herbst, J. "Beyond the Debate over Revisionism: Three Educational Pasts in Written Language." *History of Education Quarterly* 20 (Summer 1980):131–145.

Klassen, Frank. "Persistence and Change in Eighteenth-Century Colonial Education." *History of Education Quarterly* 2 (June 1962):83–99.

Maxson, M. M., and Kraus, L. L. "Curriculum Censorship in the Public School." *Educational Forum* 43 (May 1979):392–407.

Perkinson, Henry J., ed. *Two Hundred Years of American Educational Thought.* New York: McKay, 1976.

Powell, Arthur G. *The Uncertain Profession: Harvard and the Search for Educational Authority.* Cambridge, Mass.: Harvard University Press, 1980.

Rippa, Alexander S. *Education in a Free Society: An American History.* 4th ed. New York: Longman, 1980.

Travers, P. H. "Historic View of School Discipline." *Educational Horizons* 58 (Summer 1980):184–187.

Warren, Donald R., ed. *History, Education and Public Policy: Recovering the American Educational Past.* Berkeley, Calif.: McCutchan, 1978.

13

Recent Developments in Education
1940–Present

Focus Questions

- What important changes have taken place in education during your lifetime?
- In what ways, if any, should the federal government be involved in education?
- What is meant by "equal educational opportunity"?

Key Terms and Concepts

Educational growth
Federal role in education

Equal educational opportunity
Professional education

What Would You Do?

A friend of yours argues that little, if any, progress has been made over the past 50 years toward providing equal educational opportunity for all American youth. For instance, your friend points out that minorities have difficulty getting into college and that our schools are still sexist institutions. What would you say to your friend?

[38] Since World War II, education has been characterized by a great deal of growth and change: growth in terms of school enrollment, educational budgets, complexity, and federal influence; complexity in terms of court [46] decisions, proliferation of school laws, confusion about goals, school financial difficulties, struggle for control, and diversification of curricula. In this chapter we briefly highlight some of these recent major developments in education.

Perhaps the single most dramatic change that has occurred in education over the past half century is the growth of the educational enterprise. This growth took place in many ways.

Enrollment Growth

[46] Table 13.1 shows that the total number of students in the United States approximately doubled from 1940 to 1980. While part of this rapid growth in school enrollment was due to overall population growth, a good part was due to the fact that greater percentages of people were going to school. Furthermore, people were staying in school much longer, as shown in the more than sixfold increased enrollment in higher education.

Need for More Teachers

Naturally, this dramatic increase in student enrollments required many more teachers. At times our colleges simply could not produce enough additional teachers. When this happened, teacher certification requirements were lowered, sometimes to the point at which no professional education training was required at all. Over time, however, the nation seemed to meet the demand for more teachers. This increase in teachers is shown in Table 13.2

TABLE 13.1 *U.S. Total Public and Private School Enrollment 1940–1980*

Type of School	1940	1950	1960	1970	1980
Kindergarten	661,000	1,175,000	2,293,000	2,821,000	3,069,000
Grades 1–8	20,466,000	21,032,000	30,119,000	34,190,000	28,698,000
Grades 9–12	7,130,000	6,453,000	9,600,000	14,418,000	15,191,000
Higher Education	1,494,000	2,659,000	3,216,000	7,136,000	11,570,000
Total	29,751,000	31,319,000	45,228,000	58,566,000	58,529,000

Source: Bureau of the Census, *Statistical Abstract of the United States 1982–83,* U.S. Department of Commerce, Washington, D.C., p. 135.

TABLE 13.2   *U.S. Teachers: 1940–1980* (Public and Private, All Levels)

1940	1,098,000
1950	1,236,000
1960	1,831,000
1970	2,810,000
1980	3,331,000

Source: Bureau of the Census, *Digest of Education Statistics 1982,* U.S. Department of Commerce, Washington, D.C., pp. 11–12.

As one would expect, the increased numbers of students and teachers cost a great deal more money. More schools had to be built, more buses purchased, more books and other instructional materials obtained, more school personnel hired—more of everything required to provide education was needed.

School District Consolidation

The consolidation of school districts was one development that inadvertently led to increased busing costs. Table 13.3 shows that the number of separate school districts was reduced from 117,000 in 1940 to 16,000 in 1980. This table also shows the corresponding dramatic decline in the number of one-teacher schools over this same time period. These "one-room country schools" symbolized American education for millions of Americans. While school consolidation undoubtedly had many educational advantages and even saved more school dollars in some ways, it did necessitate the busing of more students over greater distances.

Growth of Busing

Table 13.4 shows the evaluation of school busing from 1940 to 1980. Both the number and percentage of students that were bused increased

TABLE 13.3   *Consolidation of Public School Districts 1940–1980*

Year	School Districts	One-Teacher Schools
1940	117,000	114,000
1950	84,000	60,000
1960	41,000	20,000
1970	18,000	2,000
1980	16,000	1,000

Source: Bureau of the Census, *Digest of Education Statistics 1982,* U.S. Department of Commerce, Washington, D.C., p. 61.

TABLE 13.4 *Public School Student Busing 1940–1980*

Year	Number of Students	Percent of Total Student Population	Total Excluding Capital Outlay	Average Cost per Pupil per Year
1940	4 million	16%	83 million	$20
1950	7 million	28%	215 million	$31
1960	12 million	38%	486 million	$40
1970	18 million	43%	1218 million	$67
1980	21 million	57%	3833 million	$175

Source: Bureau of the Census, *Digest of Education Statistics 1982,* U.S. Department of Commerce, Washington, D.C., p. 41.

considerably over this period. Likewise, the total cost and per-pupil cost rose considerably.

Bigger School Budgets

The examples of educational growth just discussed are but a few of the factors that drove the nation's public education costs to record heights. This story of increasing public school budgets is vividly told by Table 13.5. Even if corrected for inflation, public education has become considerably more expensive. (The percentage of the gross national product spent on education rose from 3.5% in 1940 to 7% in 1980.)[1]

Curricular Growth

The school curriculum also experienced considerable growth during the past 50 years. This curricular growth, like most change, was the result of an accumulation of many smaller events. One such event was the publication in 1942 of the *Eight Year Study* showing that students attending

TABLE 13.5 *Public School Budgets 1940–1980*

Year	Approximate Total Budget	Percentage Source		
		Federal	*State*	*Local*
1940	2 billion	2	30	68
1950	5 billion	3	40	57
1960	15 billion	4	39	56
1970	40 billion	8	40	52
1980	97 billion	10	47	43

Source: Bureau of the Census, *Digest of Education Statistics 1982,* U.S. Department of Commerce, Washington, D.C., p. 75.

"progressive" schools achieved as well as students at traditional schools. This report helped create a climate for more experimentation with school curriculum and teaching methodology. The publication of a series of statements on the goals of American education (the 1938 "Purposes of Education in American Democracy," the 1944 "Education for All American Youth," the 1952 "Imperative Needs of Youth") all helped to broaden our schools' curricular offerings.

Shortly after the Soviet Union launched Sputnik, the world's first artificial satellite, Congress passed the National Defense Education Act in 1958. This Act provided massive amounts of federal dollars to improve our schools' science, mathematics, engineering, and foreign language programs. Eventually, innovative curricula such as SMSG mathematics, BSCS biology, and PSCS physics grew out of these programs. Other school programs, such as guidance, were later funded through this NDEA Act. It is interesting to note that in this case the federal government called upon our schools to help solve what was perceived to be a "national defense" problem. Regardless of the motive, the NDEA represented another event that contributed to the growth of our nation's educational enterprise.

If one were to compare today's school curriculum in nearly any subject with that found in our schools 50 years ago, one would find impressive changes. The 1940 curriculum was very narrow and designed primarily for classes of college-bound students, whereas today's curriculum is very broad and designed for individual students of all abilities. Perhaps this curriculum growth is most obvious in the area of special education. Fifty years ago pathetically little special education was provided for our nation's handicapped children. Today, thanks in part to Public Law 94-142, an extensive special education program is available for each type of handicapped child. This 50-year growth in our school curriculum has come about through the dedicated work of many educators (such as Spears, Tyler, Tanner, and Goodlad) and represents one of the truly significant historical accomplishments in American education.

Increasing Federal Involvement

As was pointed out in Chapter 12, our federal government has played various important roles in our national educational programs. This federal involvement in education has gradually increased over the years and reached a crescendo during the past half century.

The 1940s saw the nation threatened by war. The Vocational Education for National Defense Act was a crash program to prepare workers needed in industry to produce goods for national defense. The program operated through state educational agencies and trained over seven million workers. In 1941 the Lanham Act provided for building, maintaining, and operating community facilities in areas where local communities had unusual burdens because of defense and war activities.

Federal involvement has been based on attempts to meet perceived national needs.

The GI Bill of 1944 provided for the education of veterans of World War II. Later, similar bills provided for veterans of the Korean conflict. It is estimated that these bills afforded education to over ten million veterans at a cost of almost $20 billion. Payments were made directly to veterans and to the colleges and schools the veterans attended. The federal government recognized a need to help young people whose careers had been interrupted by military service. In 1966 another GI Bill was passed for veterans of the war in Southeast Asia.

The National Science Foundation, established in 1950, emphasized the need for continued support of basic scientific research. It was created to "promote the progress of science; to advance the national health, prosperity, and welfare; to secure the national defense; and for other purposes." The Cooperative Research Program of 1954 authorized the U.S. Commissioner of Education to enter contracts with universities, colleges, and state education agencies to carry on educational research.

Beginning in 1957 when the first Soviet space vehicle was launched, the federal government increased its participation in education even more. The National Defense Education Act of 1958, the Vocational Education Act of 1963, the Manpower Development and Training Act of 1963, the Elementary and Secondary Education Act of 1965, and the International Education Act of 1966 are examples of recent increased federal participation in educational affairs. Federally supported educational programs such as Project Head Start, National Teacher Corps, and Upward Bound are further indications of Federal intervention in public education.

Appendix D lists some of the most important federal programs that have supported education. All these acts have involved categorical federal aid to education—that is, aid for a specific use. Some individuals believe that federal influence on education is now greater than either state or local influence. There can be no denying that through federal legislation, U.S. Supreme Court decisions, and federal administrative influence the total federal effect on education is indeed great. Indications are that this effect will become even greater in the future. It will remain for future historians to determine whether or not this is a wise trend in American education.

The Struggle for Equal Educational Opportunity

The last half century has also been characterized by an increasing struggle for equal educational opportunity for all children, regardless of race, creed, religion, or sex. This struggle was led by the Black activism movement, given additional momentum by the women's rights movement, and eventually joined by many other groups such as Spanish-speaking Americans, American Indians, and Native Alaskans. The details of this relatively recent quest for equal educational opportunity are discussed in many other parts of this book. We mention it briefly at this point simply to emphasize that the struggle for equal educational opportunity represents an important recent historical movement in education.

The Professionalization of Education

As was pointed out earlier in this book, formal teacher training is a relatively recent phenomena. Teacher training programs were developed during the first half of this century. By the midpoint of this century, each state had established requirements for a teaching certificate. Since then,

TABLE 13.6 *Average Annual Teacher Salary 1940–1980*

Year	Unadjusted	Adjusted to 1980–81 Purchasing Power
1940	1,441	8,930
1950	3,010	11,008
1960	5,174	15,251
1970	8,840	20,271
1980	16,780	18,720

Source: Bureau of the Census, *Digest of Education Statistics 1982*, U.S. Department of Commerce, Washington, D.C., p. 57.

The professionalization of education, with all its implications, has not yet been totally accepted.

during the past 40–50 years, teacher training and certification have been characterized by a "refinement" or "professionalization" movement. Table 13.6 shows that teacher salaries also improved considerably over this period of time.

In addition to teacher education, this professionalization movement touched just about all facets of education—curriculum, teaching methodology, training of school service personnel (administrators, counselors, librarians, media and other specialists), in-service teacher training, teacher organizations, and even school building construction. To clearly understand this professionalization movement, one need only compare pictures of an old one-room country school with one of our new school buildings, or read both a 1940 and a 1985 publication of the AFT or NEA, or analyze a mid–twentieth century high school curriculum with one from today, or compile a list of the teaching materials found in a 1940 school and a similar list for a typical contemporary school.

Summary and Implications

This chapter has pointed out that the past half century has been characterized by tremendous growth, increased federal involvement, a struggle for equal educational opportunity, and professionalization. Many of the specific educational events that have taken place during this time period are listed in Appendices D and E.

It is difficult to draw meaningful implications from recent events that have not yet stood the test of time. Implications of recent educational events will be found in the answers to questions such as:

1. What should the role of the federal government be in education?
2. Is there equal educational opportunity in America?
3. How professionalized do we wish our school system to be?

DISCUSSION QUESTIONS

1. Other than those mentioned in this chapter, what additional recent educational developments seem particularly important to you? Why are they important?
2. Has the increased federal involvement in education been good or bad for our schools?
3. In your opinion, how much progress have we really made in providing equal educational opportunity in the United States? Defend your answer.
4. In what respect, if any, has education become "professionalized," in your opinion?
5. What is happening in education at this very moment that is likely to be written about in future history of education books?

SUPPLEMENTAL ACTIVITIES

1. Interview a retired teacher about the educational changes that he or she witnessed over the last 50 years.
2. Scan several recently published history of education books, looking for significant recent changes in education.
3. Discuss with a fellow student who is a member of one of the minority groups mentioned in this chapter his or her views on equal educational opportunity.
4. Make a list of the ten most important federal education acts passed in the last 50 years.
5. Do a supplemental reading about an important educator in the past half century.

NOTE

1. U.S. Department of Commerce, Bureau of the Census, *Digest of Education Statistics 1982* (Washington, D.C.: U.S. Government Printing Office, 1982), p. 23.

BIBLIOGRAPHY

Avrich, Paul. *The Modern School Movement: Anarchism and Education in the United States.* Princeton, N.J.: Princeton University Press, 1980.

Conant, James B. *The American High School Today.* New York: McGraw-Hill, 1959.

Cuban, Larry. "Persistent Instruction: The High School Classroom 1900–1980." *Phi Delta Kappan* 64 (2) (October 1982):113–118.

French, William M. *American Educational Tradition: An Interpretive History.* Boston: D.C. Heath, 1964.

Krug, Edward. *The Shaping of the American High School*. New York: Harper and Row, 1964.

Lutz, J. P.; Stone, Donald O.; and Spillman, Carolyn U. "Looking Forward by Looking Backward." *Phi Delta Kappan* 64 (6) (February 1983):430–432.

Ravitch, Diane. *The Troubled Crusade: American Education 1945–1980*. New York: Basic Books, 1983.

Recognizing Sex Bias. Chicago: Illinois State Board of Education (Urban and Ethnic Education Section, 188 West Randolph Street), 1979.

Sheenhan, Patrick M. "Growing Disillusionment with Public Education: An Historical Overview." *Action in Teacher Education* (Fall 1982):1–5.

"The Negro and American Education." *Changing Education* (a Journal of the American Federation of Teachers) (Fall 1966).

Teaching Styles, Current Views, and Philosophical Concepts

The growth of the comprehensive American system of education parallels the growth of the American democratic way of life. Our democracy depends on an educated citizenry functioning under several systems of thought. The comprehensive American system of education depends on an educated faculty functioning under several systems of educational thought. Prospective teachers are urged to develop an awareness of the options available with several teaching styles/philosophies.

We hope that while you have been thinking about teaching as a career, you have also been developing a philosophy of teaching to guide your actions in given teaching situations. Your experiences with and perceptions about working with students in the classroom, your notions about presentations, and your beliefs about subject matter, testing, discipline, and school policy all contribute to your teaching philosophy. We suggest that those teachers who are at least acquainted with both the classical schools of philosophy and modern educational views will have, in addition to what they gain from daily experience, the advantage of a strong foundation on which to build an effective philosophy of teaching.

Much of what is offered in philosophy of education courses usually defines the relationship between educational philosophy and classical philosophy. Some classical philosophers label philosophy of education courses "nonsense philosophy." We make no assumptions about philosophy courses, classical or educational, the reader may have had while preparing to become a teacher. Rather, the purpose of Part V is to provide teachers with practical information that may be applied to several teaching situations.

Chapter 14 provides prospective teachers with a useful analytical tool for analyzing teacher behaviors when dealing with students, subject matter, and learning objectives in a classroom setting. The authors believe that prospective teachers are able to use this tool to assist them in formulating their preferred teaching styles, whether or not they have had any full courses in either classical or educational philosophy. Through the study and application of the analytical tool for analyzing teacher preferences, prospective teachers will at least have an enlightened feeling about various educational philosophies. Teaching style/philosophy indicators from the four questions of the analytical tool reveal the nature of the learner to be passive or active, the nature of the subject matter to be amorphous or structured, the use of the subject matter to be cognitive or affective, and the behavior trends exhibited to be toward convergent thinking or divergent thinking.

Each of the six educational philosophies (styles) considered in Chapter 15 conveys a distinct pattern of response based on these indicators. Each educational philosophy stands on its own merits for given teaching situations when specific outcomes are desired. All of these teaching styles are used in today's schools. Essentialism, perennialism, and behaviorism are three styles that favor convergent thinking. Experimentalism, reconstructionism, and existentialism favor divergent thinking. Most classroom teachers draw upon a given style as the learning needs of their students indicate. A healthy eclectic teacher is one who has knowledge about each philosophy and wisely chooses when to use a particular teaching strategy.

Most of the current views on education have roots in the classical philosophies of the past. Chapter 16 presents selected classical philosophical concepts from which the six educational philosophies presented in Chapter 15 were drawn. Any attempt to outline the many aspects of even the most well-known philosophical concepts inherently risks oversimplification. Philosophy is an academic and a comprehensive discipline. Students who want to develop a thorough knowledge of philosophy have to spend long hours studying the original works of many outstanding thinkers. We make no pretense that this part of the book is a substitute for the original works of philosophy mentioned. Part V sets the stage for one's own more extensive and profound study of philosophy. ∎

Toward a Preferred Teaching Style/Philosophy

Focus Questions

- What are you prepared to say when you are asked to state your philosophy of education during a job interview?
- How would observing another teacher's behavior permit you to understand the teacher's style? In what ways would prospective teachers benefit from observing other teachers?
- Why should a beginning teacher know about several classroom teaching styles? Wouldn't it be better to consistently follow one approach to teaching?

- What do you consider to be an authoritarian view toward teaching? What does this view have to do with the way in which learners think?
- Do you believe that students learn in similar ways, for the most part, or do learning styles vary among the students? Do you agree that teachers generally make too much out of providing for individual differences? Explain.

Key Terms and Concepts

Teaching style/philosophy
Passive learners
Active learners
Amorphous subject matter
Structured subject matter

Cognitive domain
Affective domain
Divergent thinking
Convergent thinking
Healthy eclectic

What Would You Do?

After observing the teacher to whom you have been assigned for your student teaching assignment, you are aware that you prefer to use a much different teaching style from your supervising teacher's. The students also let you know that they believe that your supervising teacher is one of the best teachers in the school.

You are assigned the task of observing three different teachers teaching the same lesson at the same grade level for the purpose of analyzing the three teaching styles. You are expected to detail the specifics of your analysis with observed teacher behaviors.

Unquestionably, teachers face many practical problems in the classroom. If one's beliefs influence one's actions, it is reasonable to suggest that an individual teacher's philosophy will help determine how he or she handles everyday problems.

A well-developed theoretical set of beliefs also provides a test of one's actual practices. Theories check practice—and vice versa. If a teacher believes in a theory of social justice, for example, and teaches in a school that practices racial segregation, the theory adhered to by the teacher is incompatible with the segregation practice. Another example is the teacher who claims to emphasize the human dignity of the pupils but in practice uses corporal punishment in the classroom. Too often teachers operate from similar hypocritical positions, professing to believe one thing but practicing something else. A suggested first step in developing your personal philosophy of education is to examine your beliefs about teaching while, at the same time, you examine the major schools of philosophical thought that have helped to shape education as we know it today. Assuming that prospective teachers are competent in their subject matter and have the ability to communicate at the relevant grade levels when entering the teaching profession, the most successful teachers will be those who have carefully identified their preferred teaching style.

Teacher's Personality and Instructional Practice

Prospective teachers are urged to develop their own personal philosophies of education. How you manage your classroom, the content, the method, and the values you stress will be based on your personal belief system—your philosophy of education. Preservice teachers should at least be aware of the options available when developing a preferred teaching style/philosophy. In teaching, one exhibits behavior that is compatible with one's personal educational view. Instructional practices must fit the teacher's personality, and the teacher must believe in the effectiveness of the practices used. Since other teaching styles might be more effective in certain situations, experienced teachers often draw from styles other than their preferred personal style. In fact, perhaps the best goal for an experienced teacher is to become a "healthy eclectic" who can comfortably use a number of teaching styles in order to meet learners' needs more completely. As long as this eclectic strategy serves the instructional purpose well, and as long as the teacher has the ability to explain to the students how they can succeed under various teaching styles, the use of various styles can be advantageous. However, if the use of various styles is merely trying technique after technique with no knowledge of how these techniques relate

330

to teaching philosophies, the result could be said to be a state of *unhealthy eclecticism,* which should be avoided.

Various state teacher certification programs include a course in the academic study of educational philosophy. When the prospective teachers enrolled in such courses have previously assessed behavioral emphases and preferences underlying a philosophical position, such courses are infinitely more valuable. While condensed explanations of teaching styles/philosophies run the inherent risks of oversimplification and of being too judgmental, our purpose is to provide prospective teachers with a working framework to help them avoid the meaningless stereotypes associated with various educational philosophies. Effective teaching is not a matter of authoritarian versus nonauthoritarian methodologies, older versus newer theories, or controlled classrooms versus noncontrolled classrooms. Rather, responsible use of any teaching style/philosophy yields benefits for learners, whereas irresponsible use of any teaching style/philosophy yields the reverse.

A useful analytical tool for studying teaching behaviors for trends and preferences was developed by Professor Lloyd Duck at George Mason University. In the following discussion of the four questions comprising the analytical tool, constructs from Duck's text (*Teaching with Charisma,* Allyn and Bacon, 1981) are utilized to provide prospective teachers with a useful process for working toward a preferred teaching philosophy, whether or not they have had a course in educational philosophy.

Classroom teachers do borrow from different philosophical systems, primarily as a means to assure variety in methods of instruction. However, a philosophical position is actually indicated by emphases and preferences that translate themselves into behavior. Thus it is the behavioral emphasis or preference that should be identified to reveal the underlying set of philosophical assumptions. Despite the tendency of many students when they have just completed an academic study of educational philosophy to rely on the term "eclectic," it seems highly unlikely that many educators are true eclectics. In fact, few, if any, teachers would apply all methodologies with equal degrees of enthusiasm. The behavioral emphases and preferences for a certain cluster of methodologies are keys to determining a philosophical position. Probably no other circumstance could exist, unless philosophical labels were viewed as indicators of separate, distinct, and mutually exclusive categories.

How to Study Teaching Behavior for Trends and Preferences[1]

To identify a series of preferences, as opposed to a set of behaviors that belong to mutually exclusive categories, any beneficial analytical tool should have more than one indicator. This analytical tool deals with the following four questions:

1. What is the nature of the learner?
2. What is the nature of the subject matter?
3. How should one use the subject matter to guide students toward meaningful learning activities?
4. What behavior trend should one exhibit in order to carry out one's philosophical position?

In this procedure for studying teaching behavior for trends and preferences, an infinite variety of answers to the first three questions exist on continua for which extremes are delineated. Where the patterns of response to the questions are illustrated for a given teacher, that teacher's style/philosophy can be associated with a particular educational philosophy. In the following, the two extremes of the continuum of answers for each question are illustrated as endpoints.

1.   What is the nature of the learner?

Passive   Active

Some teachers may feel that in particular subject areas the principal business of learners ought to be absorption because they do not bring with them into the classroom items about that subject which they can contribute to the learning environment. Such teachers may like learners immensely and may thoroughly enjoy classroom interaction. Remember that it is the extreme position regarding "absorption" of prescribed subject matter that is implied by the term *passive,* as we have used it here. The milder position of the teacher who wants youngsters to absorb knowledge about the subject matter but who finds classroom interaction very pleasantly stimulating simply belongs further down the continuum for this question about the nature of the learner.

Let us now look all the way down the continuum to the extreme that has been labeled *active.* Imagine a teacher who has so much respect for what learners can contribute to the learning environment that he or she definitely does not want them to "absorb" prescribed subject matter, as the teacher sees that subject matter. Under such circumstances, learners are viewed as the most important ingredient of the classroom environment because they teach each other and their teacher through interaction, while they are "inquiring" about problems that are meaningful to them. "Active" students provide insights that are original to them at the time such insights are offered. For example, students asked to make their own statements about life in 1908 that they can justify only from the pages of a 1908 *Sears Catalogue* reprint are expected to be "active" learners. (Please note that students could be thoroughly involved with and enjoy a competitive drill in multiplication, but they would not be "active" learners by our definition because they would not be providing original insights.)

2.   What is the nature of the subject matter?

Recently, Allen Funt, renowned for the "Candid Camera" television show, filmed a skit in which he asked primary school youngsters to explain excerpts from the "Pledge of Allegiance" to the United States' flag. The children who were interviewed and filmed had memorized the "Pledge of Allegiance" very carefully and were delighted to have an opportunity to talk about what they had learned. The answers they gave could not have been more charming and ingenuous, but none of their remarks seemed to follow logic understandable to adults. As refreshing and humorous as the youngsters' responses were, it was obvious that they had not really understood what they had memorized, although they were very successful at imitating the sounds of the "Pledge of Allegiance." It is this extreme of the continuum which has been labeled *amorphous.* This extreme denotes the ability to repeat items and details without any corresponding capacity to demonstrate insights about relationships among separate items.

The "amorphous" label has been reserved for rote learning that emphasizes that each item to be learned is equal in importance to every other item that has to be learned; hence youngsters are not encouraged to find relationships among items, and no item is seen as being more important than others. It is as if the teacher who would teach history with this approach were to assume that facts of history are always inherently good, and one must improve oneself by learning as many of these bits and pieces of information as possible. Without considering the actual effects a certain subject area can achieve, some teachers give the impression that the more bits and pieces of the subject students learn, the more benefits they will derive. In truly extreme examples of this variety of learning, the teacher may feel so satisfied to hear students recite details verbatim that there is no attempt to check their actual comprehension. . . . Use of the "amorphous" label implies that youngsters do not comprehend what they are attempting to memorize.

If we look all the way along the continuum to the extreme labeled *structured,* we may expect to find a position represented by those who have quite a realistic view of what subject matter can never accomplish for youngsters, as well as a practical assessment of its benefits. The term "structured," as used in this context, implies a view of subject matter expressed by Jerome Bruner, when he emphasized the "natural structure of a discipline." To be considered a "discipline," any subject matter should be viewed as having a natural structure, which can help to explain relationships among its components and which can also be used to find out new information within that subject matter area.

Teachers can emphasize the structure of a discipline through problem solving or through lectures. Students who are given the problem of making statements about life in 1908 that they can justify from a catalogue reprint are forced to explore relationships among components of the discipline they are using. In effect, they are asked to sort through the data from the catalogue, use facts relevant to the statements they have made, and ignore, at least for the time being, data not relevant to their statements. Another teacher might emphasize the structure of the discipline by lecturing about how mail-order businesses bridged the gap between factories and widely scattered markets. This teacher might explain facts about population density, efficiency of the postal system, and advertising techniques as they relate to the major generalization concerning factories and markets. Both teachers, however, would be emphasizing the structure of the discipline.

The continuum we have just examined concerning the subject matter embraces a broad spectrum, ranging from the position that regards subject matter as a series of items to be known (approaching the "amorphous" extreme) to the position that views subject matter as a method for finding out new things (approaching the "structured" extreme).

3.   How should one use the subject matter to guide students toward meaningful learning activities?

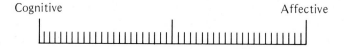

Cognitive   Affective

For this indicator's continuum the terms *cognitive* and *affective* are used as endpoints. The concepts deal not with mutually exclusive categories, but rather with matters of emphasis and preference. If cognitive learning emphasizes intellectual skills devoid of emotion and affective learning emphasizes feelings and emotions, then it is obvious that both cognitive and affective learning can be, and usually are, closely linked. Thus the decision revolves around which of the two to emphasize. Since any responsible assumption of the teacher's role involves some degree of skill development and information giving among students, the question concerns the best way to develop skills and give information—either by emphasizing the cognitive or by stressing the affective domain. Selecting between these two approaches is each teacher's personal decision.

In order to illluminate factors involved in any teacher's decision to emphasize cognitive or affective learning activities it might be helpful to consider the following addendum to our indicator for the question about the use of subject matter.

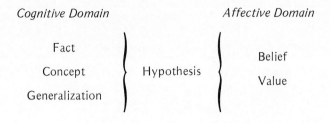

Practical Definitions

fact a verifiable truth (e.g., A certain priest sold an indulgence as indicated by church records).

concept a word or phrase containing at least one noun (e.g., indulgence, river, favorable balance of trade).

generalization a statement about facts or concepts, or both facts and concepts (e.g., Indulgences were sold in German principalities during the fifteenth century).

belief a statement that is assumed to be true, often uncritically (e.g., I believe in God [when "meaningful" others believe in God and the speaker has not examined his position critically]. I believe it is going to rain.).

value a belief about which someone cares deeply and which has been examined critically (e.g., I believe in God).

hypothesis a statement that is assumed to be true for the purpose of critical examination (e.g., any one of the following statements in which one is uncertain about their validity and wishes to examine relevant evidence: (1) Indulgences were sold in German principalities during the fifteenth century. (2) I believe it is going to rain. (3) I believe in God.).

Let us assume that all subject matter areas or disciplines are composed of three basic raw materials: facts, concepts, and generalizations. Let us also assume that youngsters bring to the classroom certain attitudes, which involve the emotions and which can be stated as beliefs and values. These beliefs and values are especially powerful in their capacities to influence the way youngsters perceive facts, concepts, and generalizations within any discipline. Some teachers see their roles as using the affective emphasis to stimulate student learning. Such teachers generally focus on personalized situations involving death, injustice, or passing time as it decreases one's power to make choices. Teachers who ask students to study inflation by having them examine the displacement of the poor as speculators renovate housing in the inner city or have students study science by asking them to measure and propose solutions for pollution in their neighborhoods are choosing to emphasize the affective. Other teachers avoid such

How teachers feel about their students will influence their teaching styles.

controversial issues and emphasize understanding economics and the phys-ical sciences through a cognitive approach. For example, inflation might be defined by such a teacher as "too much money chasing too few goods"—followed by explanations that do not highlight the social ills resulting from inflation.

Philosophical soul searching about the three questions we have just considered in our simple analytical tool has definite advantages. . . . When students are convinced that any teacher is together enough to decide what is beneficial about the subject matter he or she is selling, how he or she wants to sell it, and how he or she would like to use student contributions to the learning environment, only then will the teacher be perceived as being sincere in the desire to help students. More important, the teacher must feel secure enough to talk openly and directly with students about elements he or she considered in making decisions about these first three questions in the analytical tool.

4.   What behavior trend should one exhibit in order to carry out one's philosophical position?

Authoritarian   Nonauthoritarian
(convergent thinking)   (divergent thinking)

The question about behavior is especially critical because it is not uncommon for an observer to hear in a teacher voice one set of philosophical assumptions, yet find that the teacher's behavior seems to support an entirely different set of philosophical assumptions. This fourth question is also crucial because we must always begin with observable classroom behaviors before any answers may be inferred about a teacher's position regarding the other three questions.

The terms *authoritarian* and *non-authoritarian* have been chosen for extremes on this continuum. Although these two terms may seem to imply "strict" as opposed to "permissive" classroom management, the intention is to emphasize a more inclusive approach to classroom management than merely dealing with discipline problems. Thus it is an overall view in regard to the student and the subject matter that this indicator has been designed to examine.

For instance, suppose some teachers encourage students to view subject matter only as experts in that field might view it; these teachers habitually accept for each major question under examination only one right answer, which all students are expected to adopt and understand. In terms of analyzing classroom behaviors, such teachers would be said to encourage convergent thinking. For the purpose of our own analytical tool we shall say that such a teacher exhibits an authoritarian behavior trend by rewarding convergent thinking.

Part of this tendency toward authoritarian behavior is indicated by the subject matter with which a teacher is dealing. For instance, a chemistry teacher might set up a laboratory "experiment" in which the students are asked to determine whether Boyle's law regarding the expansion of gases still holds. In such a situation, all answers to the "experiment" should look alike, no matter which student or group of students derived them. No alternative answers would be accepted as "true" because all students are supposed to discover that, indeed, Boyle's law still holds. However,

52

there are options to the use of convergent thinking even in introductory courses in physical sciences. Suppose, for instance, that the instructor wanted students to "measure" pollution within the local school district. Some youngsters will devise means to measure pollution in the atmosphere, others may examine water pollution, and some may look at impurities in foods. Several answers to this question about pollution are possible, and the teacher would probably be expected to encourage alternative plans of action to get rid of pollutants.

This second example in which students measure pollutants would involve what Flanders has called "divergent thinking" because more than one answer is encouraged for the question at hand. For the purposes of our analytical tool we shall call this behavior trend "non-authoritarian." Although one might correctly expect the non-authoritarian trend to be most frequently associated with the humanities and the social sciences, there is some evidence of its use with the physical sciences, as the previous example from a science class points out.

Remember that the answers to our first three questions have been in the process of formulation throughout a prospective teacher's entire educational preparation. What is it that causes some prospective teachers to want to deal primarily with the physical sciences and mathematics, while others are more comfortable in dealing with the social sciences and humanities? Is it that some are more adept with convergent thinking, while others are more adept with divergent thinking? If so, we would expect these feelings, or philosophical assumptions, which have been in the process of formulation for years, to manifest themselves quite clearly in a teacher's classroom behavior.

There is only one other caveat indicated by classroom behavior trends. Do not assume that the terms "authoritarian" and "non-authoritarian," when applied to a behavior trend, connote "strictness" or "permissiveness" of classroom management. Everyone who responsibly assumes the teacher's role expects and must receive enough cooperation from students that learning can occur. This minimal amount of cooperation is necessary for every learning environment; hence a dichotomy between autocracy and chaos is definitely not the extent to which we envision the continuum for the last question in our analytical tool.

Summary and Implications

50 Prospective teachers can benefit from using the analytical tool (Figure 14.1) by first considering data regarding the last question, which deals with behavior trends. Recall the teacher behaviors that were effectively used by your former teachers; or better, observe a classroom teacher at your teaching level. Table 14.1 (field experience guidelines) lists eight items you might watch for during observation of classroom interaction. Each item is related to one or more of the questions from the analytical tool. No one would

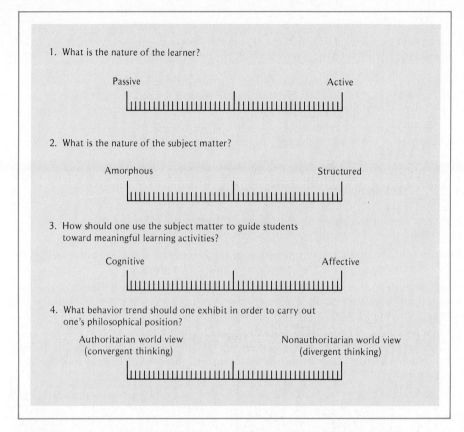

1. What is the nature of the learner?

    Passive   Active

2. What is the nature of the subject matter?

    Amorphous   Structured

3. How should one use the subject matter to guide students
   toward meaningful learning activities?

    Cognitive   Affective

4. What behavior trend should one exhibit in order to carry out
   one's philosophical position?

    Authoritarian world view   Nonauthoritarian world view
    (convergent thinking)   (divergent thinking)

FIGURE 14.1   *Analytical tool.* (*Source:* Lloyd Duck, *Teaching with Charisma*, Allyn and Bacon, Boston, 1981, p. 25. Reprinted by permission.)

be expected to see any one teacher exhibit behaviors associated with everything mentioned in these guidelines.

Record teacher behavior tendencies that you observed. Then conduct a follow-up interview with the teacher you observed and list the behaviors that the teacher believes are most effective to use. On the basis of behavior trends of the teacher, answers to the first three questions could be inferred. Identification of the behavior trend, plus the inferred answers to the first three questions, yields a total of four indicators, which, viewed as a whole, should quite accurately reveal a philosophical position.

It is a very personal matter when a teacher seeks to identify his or her teaching style preference. When one uses the analytical tool and the field experience guidelines for personal assessment, it may be difficult at first to identify your own behaviors when answering the questions. It may also be difficult to discuss with yourself the ways in which you prefer to teach, especially in light of the ways in which others teach and the ways in which you have been taught. When one considers different teaching situations,

TABLE 14.1   *Field Experience Guidelines*

The following suggested field experience activities are designed to help one prepare to analyze teaching styles and clusters of techniques which complement various teacher role models.

1.   Observe a discussion session for the kinds of student participation that occur. How often are students asked to participate in divergent thinking? How often are students asked to participate in convergent thinking? *(See the analytical tool for questions about behavior trend and the nature of the learner.)*

2.   Observe teaching techniques to determine which ones involve students in convergent thinking and which ones involve students in divergent thinking activities. *(See the analytical tool for questions about behavior trend and the nature of the learner.)*

3.   Observe a lesson and determine how many academic disciplines the teacher has decided to use in that lesson. How are these various disciplines integrated? *(See the analytical tool for the question about nature of the subject matter.)*

4.   Observe a "discovery" lesson to determine the nature of the investigation and its outcome. *(See the analytical tool for questions about behavior trend and the nature of the learner.)*

5.   Observe an "inquiry" lesson to determine the nature of the investigation and its outcomes. *(See the analytical tool for questions about behavior trend and the nature of the learner.)*

6.   Observe a lesson in which individualization of instruction is a major focus. How does the instructor plan for helping students at different skill levels improve their expertise? *(See the analytical tool for questions about nature of the subject matter and use of the subject matter.)*

7.   Talk with the cooperating teacher about the kinds of controversial issues which his or her students may be studying. Ask permission to observe a session in which a controversial issue is being examined in order to determine what the issue is and its resolution(s). *(See the analytical tool for the question about use of subject matter.)*

8.   Talk with the cooperating teacher to find out which method(s) he or she prefers to use and why: "discovery," "inquiry," problem-solving discussions, simulations, lectures, directed reading of primary sources, directed reading of secondary sources, practice exercises, learning centers, individual research, and so forth. *(A summary activity for all questions in the analytical tool.)*

Note: If you use these guidelines for personal assessment, observe your own behaviors, answer the questions as indicated, and discuss with yourself the ways you prefer to teach.
Source: Lloyd Duck, *Teaching with Charisma*, Allyn and Bacon, Boston, 1981, pp. 225, 228.

different teaching style preferences may emerge. When a teacher can effectively use each of several teaching styles in attempting to meet the needs of all learners, the teacher exhibits the potential of a *healthy eclectic* regarding his or her teaching style/philosophy. Whether one observes the classroom of a beginning teacher or an experienced healthy eclectic teacher, it is a manageable and enlightening task to analyze each lesson for teaching style and philosophical base. Additional implications that follow from analyzing teacher behaviors relate to classroom management strategies, discipline maintenance, annd other aspects of teaching.

The questions of the analytical tool and their continua of answers serve as indicators of the six teaching styles (educational philosophies) discussed in the following chapter. It is helpful to study these six teaching style choices carefully, not just for an initial awareness of the options, but also to get an idea of the potential effectiveness of the healthy eclectic teacher.

DISCUSSION QUESTIONS

1. Who was your favorite teacher? Why? Who was your best teacher? Why?
2. Experienced teachers often advise beginning teachers to be firm with the students and let them know at the beginning how you intend to teach your classes. Is this advice good or bad? Discuss the pros and cons of such procedure.
3. What is your version of democracy in the classroom? Should students be permitted to decide what they will study? When? How?
4. What is the value of observing other teachers' classrooms? Is experience a valid criterion for effective teaching? How might a beginning teacher be one of the best teachers?
5. When might a teacher focus on personalized situations involving such things as death or injustice to stimulate student learning? How would such strategy relate to the back-to-basics expectations of our schools?

SUPPLEMENTAL ACTIVITIES

1. Conduct a class discussion about the use of the analytical tool (Figure 14.1) and the field experience guidelines (Table 14.1).
2. Visit several elementary and secondary school classes for the purpose of determining the prevalent philosophy of education. Report on the practices observed. What was the teaching style of the teacher? Why do you believe the teacher style was that identified above?
3. Invite an experienced teacher to discuss effective teaching styles with you or your class. Have the teacher also discuss teacher evaluation procedures used by the school administrative staff.
4. Invite a school principal to discuss effective teaching styles with you or your class. Have the principal also discuss teacher evaluation procedures used by the school administrative staff.
5. Read Chapter Seven of *Teaching with Charisma* by Lloyd Duck (Allyn and Bacon, 1981, pp. 224–271). Then write a summary view of your philosophy and individual preference of teaching.

NOTE

1. Lloyd Duck, *Teaching with Charisma* (Boston: Allyn and Bacon, 1981), p. 2. A special note of thanks is extended to Lloyd Duck, not only for his permission to reprint excerpts of his work, but also for his careful consultation, assistance, and additional writing in structuring the format of Chapter 14. For the most part this chapter presents a digest of Chapter One, "The Heart of the Matter: An Analytical Tool," from the Duck text.

BIBLIOGRAPHY

Bloom, Benjamin, et al. *Taxonomy of Educational Objectives: Cognitive Domain.* New York: D. McKay Co., 1956.

Duck, Lloyd. *Teaching with Charisma.* Boston: Allyn and Bacon, 1981.

Illich, Ivan. *Deschooling Society.* New York: Harper and Row, 1970.

Kneller, George F. *Introduction to the Philosophy of Education.* 2nd ed. New York: John Wiley and Sons, 1971.

Knight, George R. *Issues and Alternatives in Educational Philosophy.* Berrien Springs, Mich.: Andrews University Press, 1982.

Lauderdale, William B. *Progressive Education: Lessons from Three Schools.* 59 pp. Phi Delta Kappa Fastback No. 166. Bloomington, Ind.: Phi Delta Kappa, 1981.

Rafferty, Max. "Should Gays Teach School?" *Phi Delta Kappan* 59 (October 1977):91–92.

Rubin, Louis. *Curriculum Handbook.* Boston: Allyn and Bacon, 1977.

Smith, Mortimer; Peck, Richard; and Weber,

George. *A Consumer's Guide to Educational Innovations*. Washington, D.C.: Council for Basic Education, 1972.

Wagoner, Jennings L., Jr. *Thomas Jefferson and the Education of a New Nation*. 41 pp. Phi Delta Kappa Fastback No. 73. Bloomington, Ind.: Phi Delta Kappa, 1976.

Wirsing, Marie. *Teaching and Philosophy: A Synthesis*. Boston: Houghton Mifflin, 1972.

Current Views in American Schools

Focus Questions

- How do you begin to formulate a philosophy of education if you have not had a formal course in educational philosophy? Do you agree with the notion that teachers teach the way they were taught? Explain.
- In your judgment, how do the schools (public and private) reflect the expectations of the parents and the community?
- How would you react to a critic of the schools who blames school failures on an overly permissive discipline code?

- When will you encourage your students to make their own decisions about what is to be studied? Could this be done in mathematics classes?
- Could you defend the argument that the socialization aspect of schooling is equally as valuable as subject matter content? How would the back-to-basics movement react to such an argument?

Key Terms and Concepts

Educational philosophy
Perennialism
Essentialism
Behaviorism
Experimentalism

Reconstructionism
Existentialism
Classroom management
Discipline maintenance

What Would You Do?

Your teaching objective is to introduce and demonstrate to your class a specific scientific principle. Each student should be in agreement with the scientific principle statement following your lesson.

You are interested in developing a class activity in which juvenile crime problems affect your community and the ways in which those problems may be solved. The activity needs to address itself to the individual opinions of each student.

Some classroom teachers continue to be skeptical about educational theory and those who espouse theory as a basis for practice. Yet new theories about educating children continue to proliferate, while the older beliefs remain strong in today's schools. Educators continue to hold that the purpose of education is to train pupils' minds so that they can deal better with the intellectual concepts of life; they emphasize, in addition, the mastery of facts and information. The general notion that any child can learn any subject at any level if the subject matter is properly presented remains a strong challenge to teachers to arouse motivation for subject mastery among pupils. The concept of *mastery learning* suggests that, except for the few children who are mentally, emotionally, or physically impaired, every child can master the entire curriculum of the school when adequate time is given for the slower learners to master content. Continued attention to test scores, grade level achievement, and other measures of subject matter competency reflect the importance still attached to the several views of education. School boards, parents, and the general public demand more and more often that teachers provide concrete evidence that their pupils have made progress in mastering subject matter.

On the other hand, many American teachers uphold John Dewey's view that the mind is not just a muscle to be developed. They consider as basic to teaching the notion that human beings are problem solvers who profit from experience. These educators also give credence to the existential position, which emphasizes the importance of the individual and of personal awareness. Since Dewey's philosophical views have prevailed in American teachers' colleges for the past half century, it is not surprising to find that American schools reflect this view more than do other schools throughout the world. This increasingly important experimentalist view also motivates classroom teachers. When classroom techniques are focused on student interactions rather than subject matter, some teachers find that many pupils are not interested in much of anything. In such instances, teachers are challenged to arouse student interest in inquiry, much as other teachers are challenged to arouse interest in the mastery of subject matter.

Extensive surveys of modern views of learning—as expressed in philosophy, psychology, and education journals and studies—reveal a seemingly endless and divergent range of views. Thus today's classroom teachers must identify their own beliefs about educating young people. All teachers should strive to maintain the integrity of their personal philosophies of education. While it is risky to dogmatically label the classroom practice of any one teacher, we recommend that you as a prospective teacher carefully identify a personal set of operational principles with regard to classroom techniques. Whether your operational principles are drawn from the brief descriptions of this text or elsewhere, as a classroom teacher you should strive for consistent teacher behavior within the framework of the adopted principles—your personal philosophy of education. If you diligently pursue mastery of this art, you will be more likely to succeed in a teaching career and will be more likely to find satisfaction in teaching. Further, the most successful beginning teachers will have weighed the several facets of classroom management as related to teaching style and the approaches to discipline maintenance. We hope that this chapter will serve such needs of prospective teachers.

Educational Philosophies

The six educational philosophies (styles) considered here are essentialism, perennialism, behaviorism, experimentalism, existentialism, and reconstructionism. (See Appendix F.) One can find manifestations of each of these teaching styles in today's schools. Perennialism holds that the reasoning powers of humans, along with faith, are the instruments of truly perennial knowledge. Essentialism, which stresses teaching the essentials of education, is considered to be the leading philosophy practiced in American schools.

Behaviorism supports the teaching techniques associated with essentialism and perennialism in ways that honor convergent thinking among learners. Rewards and punishments are used as the means to bring about conforming responses. Student situations are assumed to be clarified by directed rules or procedures that spell out the specified norm for all students.

Modern experimentalism and reconstructionism grew out of progressivism after the late 1950s. Experimentalism favors the scientific method of teaching and learning, drawing upon human experience as a basis for knowledge. Pupil-teacher planning is viewed as providing democracy in the classroom, which gives some freedom to students in deciding what is studied.

Reconstructionism supports the teaching techniques associated with progressivism and existentialism in ways that honor divergent thinking among learners. As the name implies, reconstructionism involves reconstructing society, which includes classroom practices. Through presenting students with dilemmas that may imply reconstructing society, the divergent views garnered are used to urge that students participate in activities that bring about social change.

It is difficult to define an educational view of existentialism. Existentialism is oriented toward individuals rather than groups and therefore cannot be wholly adapted for use in a social institution like the school. Also, it has been described as a philosophical tendency rather than a philosophy. Nonetheless, several attempts have been made to relate existentialism to education. Currently many educators are repudiating the overly social, group-oriented activities of schools and favoring instead programs that stress the individuality and personal integrity of the learners. Thus a central theme of existentialism, which places considerable emphasis on the preferences of the individual, is widely evident in the modern curriculum.

Educational trends, identified by other terms such as the "back-to-basics movement," may also be related to certain philosophies of education. The back-to-basics movement centers on subject matter and is clearly in the realms of essentialism and perennialism, whereas "free schools" and "open education" concepts are experience-based and focus on student activity as identified in experimentalism and existentialism. Figure 15.1 illustrates the association of these primary educational philosophies with the authoritarian view honoring convergent thinking and the non-authoritarian view honoring divergent thinking. The reader is again cautioned that the terms "authoritarian" and "non-authoritarian" are meant to provide an overall view in regard to the student and subject matter and not to imply strict or permissive classroom management. Since all of the ed-

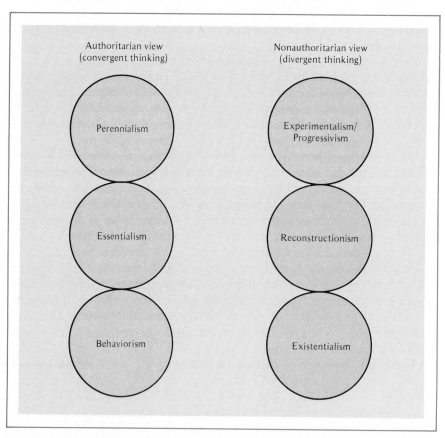

FIGURE 15.1 *Association of educational philosophies with authoritarian and nonauthoritarian views.*

ucational philosophies discussed in this text are from the Western tradition, the classroom teacher has an active role in each of them.

Perennialism

PERENNIALIST CLASS ACTIVITY

Mr. Keller's third-grade class had just had Shel Silverstein's *The Giving Tree* (New York: Harper and Row, 1964) read to them. Discussion of the story focused on questions below:

Why was it hard for the boy to be happy?
When was the boy happiest?
When was the tree happiest?
Why did the tree give so much?
Why did the tree give up even her trunk?
Is it possible to give too much? Why? Why not?
Why did the boy's ideas about having fun change?
Do people get too old to play? Why? Why not?
Does growing older mean being unhappy? Why? Why not?

This lesson follows the Great Books procedure for questioning and could therefore be considered a perennialist investigation of human nature.[1]

In this perennialist class activity the teaching style indicators from the four questions of the analytical tool are: (1) the nature of the learner is *active,* (2) the nature of the subject matter is *structured,* (3) the use of the subject matter is *cognitive,* and (4) the behavior trend is toward *convergent thinking.*

The basic educational view of perennialism is that the principles of knowledge are truly perennial. Perennialism is the parent philosophy of essentialism. The foundation of the perennialist educational view is vested in the work of Thomas Aquinas, who stressed that the rational powers of humans, along with faith, are the instruments of knowledge. Thomism recognized the importance of human daily life as well as the supernatural virtues not derived from experience; consequently, it has probably had as large a following as any Western philosophy. Nevertheless, when knowledge expanded, Thomism declined rapidly; it was difficult to fit the expanding knowledge into the confines of such a closed system of thought.

In the past few decades, perennialist philosophy has been revived under the heading "neo-Thomism." A growing number of intellectuals adhere to the idea that the beliefs and knowledge of ancient cultures can be successfully applied to our lives today. Historically, Thomism has been associated with the Roman Catholic Church, but the revival of perennialism in America is associated mainly with lay educators. When judged by religious standards, there are vast differences between the views of lay and ecclesiastical neo-Thomists. Nevertheless, Roman Catholic educators have welcomed the revival of the scholasticism of Thomas Aquinas and share many educational views with lay perennialists.

The focus of learning in perennialism lies in activities designed to discipline the mind. Subject matter of a disciplinary and spiritual nature, like mathematics, languages, logic, great books, and doctrines, must be studied. Studying these subjects disciplines the mind. The learner is assumed to be a rational and spiritual person. Difficult mental calisthenics such as reading, writing, drill, rote memory, and computations are important in training the intellect. Perennialism holds that learning to reason is also very important—an ability attained by additional mental exercises in grammar, logic, and rhetoric, as well as through use of discussion methodologies. Reasoning about human matters and about moral principles that permeate the universe is the major focus of perennialism. Such learning activities are thought to contribute to the spiritual outreaching of idealism. As the individual mind develops, the learner becomes more like the Spiritual Being. The learner is closer to ultimate knowledge when he or she gradually assumes the mind qualities of God. Idealism also includes some of the recent findings that stress the psychology of learning; in this realm it is believed the mind can combine pieces of learning into whole concepts that have meaning.

As for the school curriculum, perennialists believe that early schooling is best directed toward preparing children for maturity and emphasize the three Rs in the elementary schools. In this view, perennialism and essentialism share some thoughts. Some lay and ecclesiastical perennialists consider character training, enhanced through Bible study, to be equally as important as the three Rs at the elementary level. A perennialist program for the secondary level is directed more toward educating the intellectually elite. Perennialism favors trade and skill training for students who are not engaged in the rigors of the general education program. Perennialists generally agree that the curriculum at the secondary level should provide a general education program for the intellectually gifted and vocational training for the less gifted. However, not all perennialists agree on a curriculum design for general education. Although the Great Books program associated with Robert M. Hutchins and Mortimer Adler has brought much attention to perennialism, other leaders in this movement do not support the program. Those who endorse the Great Books program maintain that studying the works of the leading scholars of history is the best way to a general education. Perennialists who do not agree maintain that more modern sources can be used to get knowledge. The ecclesiastical perennialists insist that all programs give first importance to the study of theology.

ESSENTIALIST CLASS ACTIVITY

Students in Mr. Hardy's mathematics class were presented with pages from a 1908 *Sears Catalogue* and a current *Sears Catalogue*. From each catalogue there were pages showing the following items: watches, women's apparel, men's apparel, dining room furniture. Students were asked to calculate the percentage of increase in average prices from 1908 to today for watches, women's apparel, men's apparel, and dining room furniture, as those increases were revealed by matching appropriate pages from the two catalogues.[2]

In this essentialist class activity the teaching style indicators from the four questions of the analytical tool are: (1) the nature of the learner is *passive*, (2) the nature of the subject matter is *structured*, (3) the use of the subject matter is *cognitive*, and (4) the behavior trend is toward *convergent thinking*.

Essentialism, as a clearly defined educational philosophy, was formulated in 1938 by William C. Bagley.[3] It has dominated school practice worldwide, past and present. Although progressivism has been extremely popular in America, essentialism appears destined to continue as the dominant worldwide educational view. In the 1930s the Essentialist Committee for the Advancement of Education, led by Bagley, launched an attack on progressivism, which had gained considerable support in the 1920s. At present, educators still feel the strong influence of essentialism, even though the Essentialism Committee has been inactive since Bagley's death in 1946.

Essentialism holds that the essential elements of education should be selected from historical and modern thinking. The function of the schools is to teach the essentials of education. Essentialism includes the tenets of idealism and realism. From idealism comes the idea of viewing the mind as the central element of reality, which is significant in determining the essentials of essentialism. Realism contributes the basic view that reality is in physical things, leading to an emphasis on the quantitative aspects of education. Organization and factual mastery of content are imperative if one is to learn through observation and nature. Essentialism advocates a return to the fundamentals of learning—the three Rs.

The essentialist curriculum, as developed from the idealist point of view, contains subject matter of symbol and content. Such subject matter includes literature, history, foreign languages, and religion. Methodology requires formal discipline through emphasis on required reading, lectures, memorization, repetition, and examinations. Realist philosophers of education differ in their views on curriculum, but they generally agree about including subject matter of the physical world. Mathematics and the natural sciences are examples of subjects that contribute to the learners' knowledge of natural law. Activities that require mastering facts and information on the physical world are significant aspects of realist methodology. With truth defined as observable fact, field trips, laboratories, audiovisual materials, and nature furnish methods. Habits of intellectual discipline are considered ends in themselves. Realism advocates studying the laws of nature and the accompanying universal truths of the physical world.

Essentialism envisions subject matter as the core of education. Severe criticism has been leveled at American education by those who advocate an emphasis on basic education. Essentialism assigns to the schools the task of conserving the heritage and transmitting knowledge of the physical world. In a sense, the school is a curator of knowledge. Herein lies the chief criticism of essentialism; with the burgeoning of new knowledge, essentialism as the curator of past knowledge may be contributing to the slowness of educational change.

Perennialism and essentialism are criticized as obsolete. Such criticism implies that neither perennialism nor essentialism satisfies the twentieth century needs of our youth. The philosophers within the movement deny such criticism and claim to have incorporated modern influences in the system while maintaining academic standards.

Behaviorism

BEHAVIORIST CLASS ACTIVITY

Students in Mr. Drucker's civics class were given merit tokens for coming into the room quietly, getting into their desks, preparing notebooks and pencils for the day's lesson, and being ready to begin answering comprehension questions in their workbooks. On Fridays, students were allowed to use their tokens at an auction to buy items that Mr. Drucker knew they wanted. Sometimes, however, students had to save tokens for more than two weeks to buy what they liked best.

In this behaviorist class activity the teaching style indicators from the four questions of the analytical tool are: (1) the nature of the learner is *passive*, (2) the nature of the subject matter is *amorphous*, (3) the use of the subject matter is *cognitive or affective*, and (4) the behavior trend is toward *convergent thinking*.

---

[58] B. F. Skinner, the Harvard experimental psychologist and philosopher, is the recognized leader of the behaviorist movement. Skinner verified Pavlov's stimulus-response theory with animals and, from his research, suggested that human behavior could also be explained as responses to external

stimuli. Other behaviorists' research expanded Skinner's work in illustrating the effect of the enviroment, particularly the interpersonal environment, in shaping individual behavior.

> These writers share a common belief that a student's misbehavior can be changed and reshaped in a socially acceptable manner by directly changing the student's environment. The Behaviorist accepts the premise that students are motivated by the factor that all people will attempt to avoid experiences and stimuli that are not pleasing and will seek experiences that are pleasing and rewarding.[4]

The concept of reinforcement is very influential upon the teacher practices of behaviorists. Positive reinforcers are used to reward approved behavior with something desired by the student (praise, special privileges, higher grades, etc.). Negative reinforcers are punishment for behaviors that are not approved (reprimands, extra homework, lower grades, etc.). Behaviorists generally believe that negative reinforcement is ineffective. Further, they believe that learning takes place when approved behavior is observed and then is positively reinforced. Charles H. Wolfgang and Carl D. Glickman developed a Teacher Behavior Continuum as a construct in explaining particular teacher practices of the behaviorists. (See Figure 15.2.) They suggest that before using this construct

> the reader needs to reorient somewhat. Because the concept of reinforcement is so powerful and influential, all the other categories (visually looking on, nondirective statements, questions, and so on) are advocated as practices only when they are a form of reinforcement. In other words, the Behaviorists explain that all these practices emanate from the right hand side of our continuum.[5]

When visually looking on, a teacher may provide positive reinforcement (smiling, nodding approval, etc.) or negative reinforcement (frown-

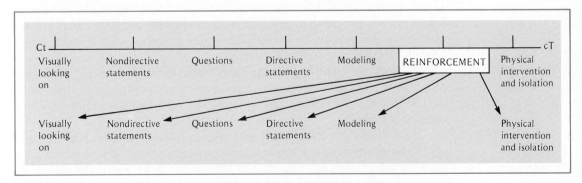

FIGURE 15.2 *Teacher behavior continuum.* (*Source:* Charles H. Wolfgang and Carl D. Glickman, *Solving Discipline Problems: Strategies for Classroom Teachers,* Allyn and Bacon, Boston, 1980, p. 122. Reprinted by permission.)

Each person's teaching style reflects his or her personal philosophy of education.

ing, shaking the head in disapproval, etc.). Similarly, nondirective statements, questions, and directive statements may be positive or negative. Both children and adults respond to the models other people (peers, adults, heroes, etc.) represent to them by imitating the model behavior. Behaviorists contend that students tend to emulate behaviors that are rewarded. In the Teacher Behavior Continuum (Figure 15.2), physical intervention and isolation refers to those times when a student, for whatever reason, does not exhibit some suitable behavior to recognize. In certain cases the teacher may physically intervene by removing the student from the classroom environment and isolating the student where reinforcement support is lacking.

The behaviorists have supplied a wealth of research that bears on the problems of attaining self-control, resisting temptation, and showing concern for others. Behaviorists do not attempt to learn about the causes of students' earlier problems. Rather, the teacher must ascertain what is happening in the classroom environment to perpetuate the child's behavior and what can be changed in the environment to "reverse the tide."[6]

Experimentalism/Progressivism

EXPERIMENTALIST CLASS ACTIVITY

Ms. Nelson's French class was given five newspaper photographs. They were asked to work in groups of three and spend 30 minutes composing, in French, a news story of no more than four paragraphs which they felt would go with the picture. After this task, students were told they would get to explain to each other how they had developed their stories and would also see the reports that had actually been published with each photograph in *Paris Match*.[7]

In this experimentalist class activity the teaching style indicators from the four questions of the analytical tool are: (1) the nature of the learner is *active*, (2) the nature of the subject matter is *structured*, (3) the use of the subject matter is *cognitive*, and (4) the behavior trend is toward *divergent thinking*.

Modern experimentalism grew out of the pragmatism of America. With the rise of democracy in the late 1800s, the expansion of modern science and technology, and the need for people to be able to adjust to change, Americans had to have a new and different approach to getting knowledge to solve problems. An American philosopher, Charles S. Peirce (1839–1914), founded the philosophical system called *pragmatism*. This philosophy held that the meaning and value of ideas could be found only in their practical results. Later, William James (1842–1910) extended Peirce's theory of meaning into a theory of truth. James went further and asserted that the satisfactory working of an idea constitutes its whole truth. Pragmatism was carried much further by John Dewey (1859–1952), who was a widely known and influential philosopher and educator. Dewey's philosophy was called experimentalism by some because he insisted that ideas must always be tested by experiment. His experimental beliefs carried over into his educational philosophy, which became the basis for what was usually described as *progressive* education.

Progressivism was a contemporary American educational philosophy. From its establishment in the mid-1920s through the mid 1950s, progressivism was the most influential educational view in America. Progressivists are basically opposed to authoritarianism and favor human experience as a basis for knowledge. Progressivists believe that all things are in a state of flux; therefore they do not stress absolute knowledge. Progressivism favors the scientific method of teaching and learning, allows for the beliefs of individuals, and stresses programs of student involvement that help students learn how to think. Progressivists believe that the school should actively prepare its students for change. Progressive schools emphasize learning *how* to think rather than *what* to think. Flexibility is important in the curriculum design, and emphasis is on *experimentation*, with no single body of content stressed more than any other. Since life experience determines curriculum content, all types of content must be permitted. Certain subjects regarded as traditional are recognized as desirable for study as well. Progressivist educators would organize scientific method-oriented learning activities around the traditional subjects. Such a curriculum is called experience-centered, or student-centered; the essentialist and perennialist curriculum is considered subject-centered. Progressivists' pupils should be brought together in heterogeneous, integrated groups so that the benefits of socialization can be incorporated as part of learning. They stress the *process* of learning rather than the end result.

Experimentalism as a contemporary teaching style has carried forth many of the tenets of progressivism since reconstructionism separated from the Progressive Education Movement in 1957. Whereas reconstructionists place increased emphasis on the ends of education, experimentalists continue to emphasize the process of democracy in the classroom. Experimentalism is more compatible with a core of problem areas across all academic disciplines than with a subject-centered approach to problem solving. It would be naive to suggest that memorization and rote practice are ruled out. However, they are not stressed as primary learning techniques. The assertion is that interest in an intellectual activity will generate all the practice needed for learning.

A tenet of experimentalism is that the school, to become an important social institution, be assigned the task of improving our way of life. To this end, experimentalism is deemed a working model of democracy. Freedom is explicit in a democracy, so it must be explicit in our schools. Certainly, freedom—rather than being a haphazard release of free will—must be organized to have meaning. Organized freedom permits each member of the school society to share in decisions, and experiences must be shared by all to ensure that the decisions are meaningful. Pupil-teacher planning is the key by which democracy in classrooms is realized and is the process that gives some freedom to students, as well as teachers, in deciding what is studied. For example, the teacher might ask students to watch a film about an issue of interest and have them list questions about the issue that were not answered by the film but that they would like to investigate. Student questions can then be analyzed by students and the teacher and refined for research. Such questions can become the basis for an inquiry and problem-solving unit of study. However, even if pupil-teacher planning is not highlighted as a specific activity, any experimentalist lesson allows students to give some of their own input in ways that influence the direction of the lesson. In that sense, experimentalist lessons always involve pupil-teacher planning, at least implicitly. For instance, asking students to make statements about life in 1908, which they justify only from catalogue reprint pages, allows students to focus on any items from the catalogue *they* choose—not items determined by the teacher.

The learner is seen as an experiencing, thinking, exploring individual. Experimentalism exposes the learner to the subject matter of social experiences, social studies, projects, problems, and experiments that, when studied by the scientific method, will result in functional knowledge from all subjects. Books are regarded as tools to be used in learning rather than as sources of indisputable knowledge.

Many believe that the socialization aspect is the most valuable aspect of the movement. Experimentalism, in this way, represents the leading edge of our culture and teaches us how to manage change. However, experimentalism is criticized for placing so much stress on the processes of education that the ends are neglected. Its severest critics contend that it has little personal commitment to anything—producing many graduates who are also uncommitted and who are content to drift through life. Experimentalism as an educational view is still relatively young and, by its principle of the scientific method, is willing to experience both trial and error. One cannot deny that its advent has given considerable excitement and impetus to the total educational movement.

51

Reconstructionism

RECONSTRUCTIONIST CLASS ACTIVITY

Mr. Ragland asked his second graders to look at a cartoon that pictured a well-dressed man and woman in an automobile pulled by a team of two horses. The highway they were traveling along passed through rolling farmland with uncrowded meadows, trees, and clear skies in the background. He led a discussion based on the following questions:

1. What is happening in this picture?
2. Do you like what is happening in the picture? Why? Why not?
3. What does it say about the way you may be living when you grow up?
4. Are you happy or unhappy about what you've described for your life as an adult?
5. How can we get people to use less gasoline now?
6. What if we could keep companies from making and selling cars that could not travel at least 40 miles on one gallon of gasoline? How could we work to get a law passed to do this?[8]

In this reconstructionist class activity the teaching style indicators from the four questions of the analytical tool are: (1) the nature of the learner is *active*, (2) the nature of the subject matter is *structured*, (3) the use of the subject matter is *affective*, and (4) the behavior trend is toward *divergent thinking*.

Theodore Brameld, a leading American philosopher of education, is regarded as the father of reconstructionism. Although reconstructionism is sometimes considered to be part of progressivism, Brameld presents reconstructionism as a separate category having something in common with essentialism, perennialism, and progressivism. "Essentialism and Perennialism, especially, will be found to share a good deal of the same philosophic, educational, and cultural outlook, as do Reconstructionism and Progressivism share theirs."[9] Figure 15.3 illustrates the position of reconstructionism in relation to the other educational views. Thus experimentalism is related to reconstructionism because they both emphasize problem solving and divergent thinking. However, reconstructionism places more emphasis on the *ends* of education than does experimentalism, since reconstructionists use affective situations to persuade their students about the wisdom of specific social reform activities. It is understood, however, that students can accept or reject the reconstructionist's persuasive arguments. Therefore divergent thinking is honored. Reconstructionism is also related to experimentalism, essentialism, and perennialism in that factual realities about the world must be investigated and learned, whatever the philosophy or teaching style. It is just that reconstructionism and experimentalism require students to engage in divergent thinking, whereas essentialism and perennialism are based on convergent thinking.

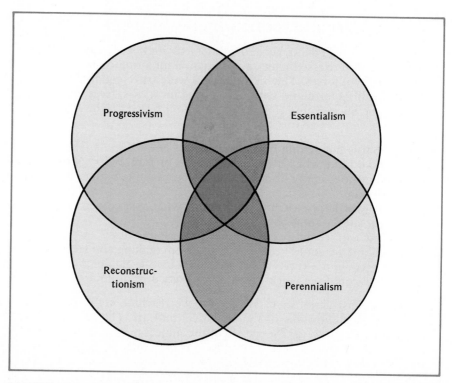

FIGURE 15.3 *Brameld's view of reconstructionism as an educational philosophy. (Source:* Theodore Brameld, *Philosophies of Education in Cultural Perspective,* Holt, Rinehart and Winston, New York, 1955, p. 77. Reprinted by permission of the author.)

A persistent theme of reconstructionism is that public education should be the direct instrument of world reformation. As a logical extension of experimentalism, reconstructionism accepts the concept that the essence of learning is the actual experience of learning. Reconstructionism espouses a theory of social welfare that can effectively prepare learners to deal with the great crises of our time—war, inflation, rapid technological changes, depression. From the experiences of World War I, the Great Depression, and World War II, reconstructionist educators believe that the total educational effort must be seen within a social context.

As was indicated earlier, John Dewey had an immense influence on progressivism. Dewey also made major contributions to reconstructionist philosophy with his efforts to define the individual as an entity within a social context. Reconstructionists go further in stressing that individuals as entities within a social context are urged to engage in specific reform activity. Classroom teachers tend to use affective emphases and moral dilemmas in directing attention toward social reform.

Existentialism

EXISTENTIALIST CLASS ACTIVITY

Mr. Sawyer had just shown his first graders the Learning Corporation of America film, *Geronimo Jones*. In the film a white man who runs a local trading post cons an Indian lad, Geronimo, out of a highly prized amulet presented to him by his grandfather. Geronimo, after much thought and after being subjected to the trader's "hard sell" tactics, gives his amulet up for a second-hand TV set. That evening, neither Geronimo nor his grandfather speaks during dinner. When Geronimo unveils the gift, which he hopes will please his grandfather, the first program to appear is an old "Western" in which "cowboys" are slaughtering "Indians." The grandfather watches in silence, but his eyes grow misty. Mr. Sawyer's discussion activity was based on the following questions:

1. How do you feel after watching this film?
2. What did you like about the story?
3. What did you not like about the story?
4. What two or three things do you think Geronimo should do now?
5. What advice would you give him about the TV set? about his grandfather?[10]

In this existentialist class activity the teaching style indicators from the four questions of the analytical tool are: (1) the nature of the learner is *active*, (2) the nature of the subject matter is *structured*, (3) the use of the subject matter is *affective*, and (4) the behavior trend is toward *divergent thinking*.

Generally, the American system of education has depended on group processes and group norms. Existentialism does not function well as a philosophy of such a group-oriented system, since it concerns individual self-fulfillment. Currently, American educators are giving a lot of attention to problems and processes concerned with individual differences. Most of their efforts are aimed at minimizing individual differences by such tactics as forming homogeneous groups for particular subject matter instruction. The rationale is that group instruction proceeds more smoothly when individuals are adjusted to the group. But, in regards to helping individuals adjust to the group, an existentialist would argue: "This we now know to be a lost cause, for studies in many fields lead us to the same conclusion, that the extent of these differences is far greater than we thought. Much injustice has been done in the process of ironing them out and many a personality violated."[11]

From the 1960s to the present, the influence of existentialism can be identified with various creative programs and written materials. A. S. Neill proposes a "radical approach to child rearing" in his book, *Summerhill*. Charles E. Silberman, in his *Crisis in the Classroom*, calls for remaking American education to provide for greater consideration of the individual. Various textbooks discuss themes like the open access curriculum, humanism in education, nongraded instruction, and multiage grouping, each of which attends to the uniqueness of the learner. Educators are now making various attempts in their school programs to individualize education. Modular scheduling permits flexibility for students to arrange classes of their choice. Free schools, storefront schools, schools without walls, and area vocational centers provide alternatives to attending traditional schools. Educational programs that treat the needs of the individual are usually more costly per pupil than the traditional group-centered programs. Consequently, as taxpayer demands for accountability mount, individualized programs are often brought under unit cost scrutiny. Nonetheless, increasing numbers of educators are willing to defend increased expenditures to meet the needs of the individual learner within the instructional programs of the schools.

Existentialism views all circumstances as they relate to the individual human being. This does not imply that emphasis given to the development of the individual has no place in the public school merely because such activity would be contrary to the group orientation of the educational system. The classroom teacher would need to function from a conceptual base that rules out time-honored conventional notions. On the existentialist view of the individual as unique and its commensurate effects on the teacher's conception of education, George Kneller writes:

> To begin, it rules out three conventional notions: that education is primarily an agency of society, set up to perpetuate a cultural heritage; that it is a pipeline of perennial truths; and that it is a means for adjusting the young to life in a democratic community. In place of these, let education exist for the individual. Let it teach him to live as his own nature bids him, spontaneously and authentically.[12]

The phrase "as his own nature bids him" illustrates the emphasis given to the affective quality of existentialist teaching. Since the values and beliefs of learners are so wide ranging, existentialists would do their problem solving for divergent solutions among their learners.

Existentialist teachers honor divergent thinking so completely that they delay giving their own personal opinions and do not attempt to persuade students to particular points of view. Even though they emphasize the affective and thereby may be supposed to make students feel a certain urgency about issues, it is always left to the individual student to decide when to take a stand, what kind of stand to take, whether a cause merits action, and, if so, what kind of action.

Classroom Management

All teachers must be able to manage the classroom environment in such ways that the environment is conducive to teaching/learning. In fact, many school principals are quick to assert that the easiest way to predict the success of a beginning teacher is to determine his or her ability to manage the classroom. A common misconception is that good classroom management means maintaining a controlled atmosphere and refusing to allow any behavior that even looks like permissiveness. Actually, classroom management is a multifaceted aspect of teaching that requires similar analysis and selection as for the identification of a preferred teaching style/philosophy.

Classroom management strategies exist on a continuum, as do teaching styles. It is not a matter of only one approach being good or bad. It is rather a question of deciding what choice(s) may be acceptable because one's personality complements a certain classroom management strategy, just as is the case with teaching styles. Classroom management deals with such facets as lesson planning, utilization of furniture and materials, evaluation of students, and grading. These facets of classroom management are important considerations for all teachers and most effectively contribute to student learning when each is consistent with the teaching style. Careful lesson planning is mandatory for effective teaching/learning to follow. However, if the learners are considered to be passive, the lesson plan may emphasize absorbing the factual content of the subject matter. Adherents of teaching styles that consider the learners as active participants would tend to emphasize processes and skills to be mastered and view the factual content of the subject matter as important but variable. Similarly, the mere arrangement of classroom furniture and the use of classroom materials may be predicated upon the passive/active perception of the learners.

In evaluating student progress and assigning grades, most teachers utilize written examinations, term papers, project reports, group discussions, and various other tools. If the subject matter is treated as amorphous, for instance, teacher-made tests would tend to seek isolated facts and concepts as "right" answers, suggesting emphasis on convergent thinking; if the subject matter is treated as structured and applicable to problem solving so as to emphasize processes and skills to arrive at several "right" answers, teacher-made tests would tend to allow for divergent thinking.

Discipline Maintenance

The attention of the national media to disruptive behavior in the classroom has rekindled the conflicting views of adherents of opposing philosophies regarding discipline. Polls of parents and teachers alike list discipline among the top issues confronting the schools. The main source of dissatisfaction for nearly two thirds of today's teachers is the inability to manage students effectively. Teachers also are concerned about the effect disrup-

Every level of the school meshes to define the context in which students may learn.

tive behavior has on learning. The discipline dilemma—stressing high teacher control in the classroom yet adhering to a more open philosophy advocating less teacher control—precludes the development of a school discipline policy that would satisfy both views. The divided views on classroom discipline have resulted in numerous books to assist teachers with discipline problems and many special courses and workshops developed to deal with classroom discipline strategies. Since beginning teachers are given little exposure to discipline strategies in teacher-preparation programs, the vast range of alternatives makes it difficult to decide on strategies for those who have yet to develop their own style.

Classroom management as an aspect of teaching has been presented as an integration of the "procedural," "physical environment," and "bookkeeping" chores with a preferred teaching style. If classroom management is viewed as merely strategies to keep down the number of problems so that learning can occur, the management strategy need not be from the same philosophical base as the teaching style. In the latter case, discipline maintenance would seem to be a more appropriate label.

Glickman and Wolfgang[13] have identified three schools of thought along a teacher-student control continuum (Figure 15.4). *Noninterventionists* represent the view that holds that teachers should not impose their own rules, since students are inherently capable of solving their own problems. *Interactionalists* suggest that students must learn that the solution to misbehavior is a reciprocal relation between student and teacher. *In-*

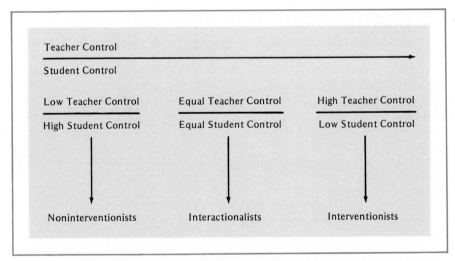

FIGURE 15.4 *Teacher-student control continuum.* (*Source:* Carl D. Glickman and Charles H. Wolfgang, "Conflict in the Classroom: An Eclectic Model of Teacher-Child Interaction," *Elementary School Guidance and Counseling* 13 (Dec. 1978). Copyright © 1978 American Association for Counseling and Development. Reprinted by permission.)

terventionists believe that teachers must set classroom standards for conduct and give little attention to input from the students.

Beginning teachers are challenged to identify their own beliefs regarding discipline in the classroom in order to keep disruptive behavior at a minimum, thus enhancing the potential for learning as well as for job satisfaction. Where discipline maintenance is the primary concern, one might choose from among the entire range of possibilities along the Wolfgang-Glickman continuum (discussed in the section on behaviorism), regardless of one's teaching style preference. Figure 15.5 illustrates how all the major theories of classroom management relate in terms of emphasis on selected references along the teacher-student control continuum given in Figure 15.4. Each of the six teaching styles/philosophies addresses in some way all seven classroom teacher behaviors on the continuum. It is the professional responsibility of each classroom teacher to understand how each behavior may be utilized to support his or her preferred teaching style. A more detailed explanation of how each behavior is portrayed within those contexts is provided in the excellent Wolfgang and Glickman text, *Solving Discipline Problems* (Allyn and Bacon, 1980).

Values Education

As the 1980s began, a vocal section of the general public in the United States was advocating a return to the traditional approaches to public edu-

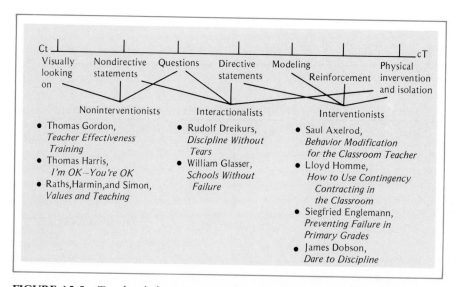

FIGURE 15.5 *Teacher behavior continuum (TBC).* (*Source:* Charles H. Wolfgang and Carl D. Glickman, *Solving Discipline Problems: Strategies for Classroom Teachers,* Allyn and Bacon, Boston, 1980, p. 18. Reprinted by permission.)

cation. The back-to-basics movement emphasizing the "three Rs" is obviously traditional with regard to curriculum. Coupled with the back-to-basics movement is a similar call for more interventionist approaches to discipline management. Today, increased attention is being directed toward the axiological (values) branch of philosophy, with particular emphasis on ethics and morals. With parents accused of yielding value development and character building to the schools, schools blamed for the misbehavior of youth, the political arena rocked by Watergate, Abscam, and other scandals, unethical business practices headlined, drugs and sex also highlighted as social issues, and racial problems spawning violence, it should not be surprising that the public is demanding that education be geared to strengthening the moral fiber of our youth.

American educators were concerned with the problem of providing moral and character education even before the days of John Dewey in the early 1900s. Some of the earlier approaches included textbooks such as the McGuffey readers that sought to instill values through the content of stories. The "bag of virtues" approach sought to obtain a cultural consensus on values to be taught in the schools. Another approach emphasized the respect for authority, while the social-adjustment approach focused on the mental health of students. During the last 50 years the continued research in psychoanalysis, behaviorism, and the humanistic and development schools of thought in American psychology has yielded information that educators and psychologists now consider when developing values education approaches in the schools. In the last decade and a half, approaches related to values education have been identified with designations such as moral development, values clarification, cognitive-developmental approach to moral judgment, behaviorism, ethics education, and self-identification.

Earlier comments about teaching styles, classroom management and method, and discipline illustrated that these continua provide a far-ranging and, in some instances, confusing array of alternatives for the classroom teacher to identify with. Approaches to values education similarly range from the behavioral approach, which emphasizes the importance of modeling behavior to be adopted by the students, to values clarification, which has the teacher guiding students in clarifying their values.

Summary and Implications

We hope that this chapter has provided prospective teachers with an overview for working toward a preferred teaching style/philosophy. While your preferred style may not be completely committed to perennialism, essentialism, behaviorism, experimentalism, reconstructionism, or existentialism, you should be able to use the analytical tool for studying teacher behavior to help you identify several preferences. Your preferences are probably compatible with, if not formulated by, your personality. The extent to which one's instructional practices fit one's personality, and vice versa, is highly related to successful teaching.

Prospective teachers, whether or not they have had educational philosophy course work in their preparation programs, should find the analytical tool to be an immediately useful way to study teaching behaviors for trends and preferences related to a teaching style/philosophy. The four questions in the analytical tool and the tendencies toward the continuum extreme responses for each question are illustrated in Figure 15.6 as associated with each of the six teaching philosophies discussed in this chapter. Perennialist, essentialist, and behaviorist teachers encourage students to view the subject matter only as experts in that field view the subject matter. Such teacher behaviors exhibit an authoritarian curriculum trend encouraging convergent thinking. Experimentalists, reconstructionists, and existentialists encourage students to use the subject matter as a means of determining more than one answer to the question at hand. This behavior could be viewed as a non-authoritarian curriculum trend encouraging divergent thinking.

When using the field experience guidelines (Table 14.1) to study teaching style preferences, it is always helpful to remember that there are no perfect teaching styles or teaching methodologies. One simply needs to

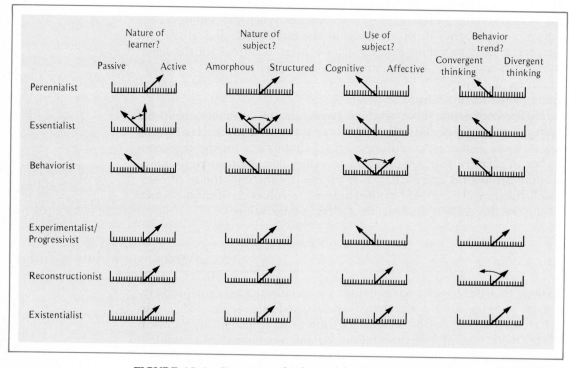

FIGURE 15.6   *Overview of role models.* (*Source:* Adapted from Lloyd Duck, *Teaching with Charisma,* Allyn and Bacon, Boston, 1981, pp. 226–227.)

know how to minimize the effects of the natural weaknesses associated with each "camp" of teaching styles. The three styles that emphasize convergent thinking tend to reward students for "reading the teacher's mind" by giving as an answer the exact phrase the teacher wants. Teachers using methods in this "camp" must be very careful with their responses, or students may receive the message that they should not risk participating in discussion unless they are absolutely certain they have the exact answer. The divergent "camp" of teaching styles may, on the other hand, require students to participate in interesting activities but not make them fully aware of why they are participating or what they are learning. If students are not required to justify the generalizations they make and are not made to see that they are learning many facts and skills, they may end up feeling that all answers are so relative that problem-solving processes are not worthwhile. Teachers who know enough about themselves and the teaching styles to show students how to succeed with both convergent thinking and divergent thinking are well on their way to reaching the ideal of being *healthy eclectics.*

When one is asked to explain one's teaching style preference or philosophy, it is also helpful to remember to follow the same order in formulating an answer that one would follow in using the field experience guidelines to study a teaching style preference. That is, always describe effective lessons first and then generalize as to whether the preference is for essentialism, experimentalism, or any of the other educational philosophies. This is a way to avoid sounding as if one is speaking in cliches. A similar procedure should be followed in studying teaching style preferences. Determine first whether convergent thinking or divergent thinking is the outcome of the lesson. Then one can make determinations about all questions in our analytical tool and apply the appropriate label. Both procedures begin with the specifics of a lesson and move to the application of the label. And remember, no one is *always* an advocate of the same teaching style for every lesson. Use of the label "experimentalism," for instance, indicates a preference for that style over others that may also be used occasionally. If no preference can be determined, then "eclectic" is the appropriate label to select.

Use of labels is not important in itself. However, knowing yourself and the options you have for teaching style choices is important. Acting on this knowledge and choosing wisely will help you to get increasingly closer to the ideal of being a healthy eclectic—that supremely effective educator who can change styles comfortably as the learning needs of youngsters might indicate. (Appendix G further illustrates two broad philosophical categories that are most easily recognizable by teaching styles and further differentiation of the six educational philosophies.)

In addition to the preferred teaching style/philosophy, all teachers must be prepared to integrate the several facets of classroom management consistent with the teaching philosophy. Strategies for discipline maintenance when necessary merely to keep down the number of problems so that learning can occur, are very important for teaching success. Discipline is maintained well where there is balancing interaction between teacher control and student control. There are times, however, when a higher degree of student control is more effective.

The implications of all this seem obvious. Teachers who enter classrooms not understanding or knowing much about their preferred teaching styles, as well as not knowing which classroom management strategies best serve their philosophies, cannot be as successful as they might otherwise be. Knowing about educational philosophies and behaviors that support each philosophy prepares prospective teachers to make professional judgments rather than merely follow prescriptions about effective classroom teaching behaviors. Likewise, knowledge about classical "root" philosophies that provide the basis for educational philosophies is important for broadening this aspect of your professional education. Chapter 16 provides an overview of selected classical philosophical concepts to consider when further studying one's preferred teaching style/philosophy.

DISCUSSION QUESTIONS

1. How do you plan to go about developing a personal philosophy of education? (a) How do you conceive your role as a teacher? (b) How do you conceive the role of the pupils? (c) How will your philosophy help to determine the methods you use as a teacher? (d) How do you intend to relate your philosophy of education to your specialization?

2. What was your biggest discipline problem during student teaching? How did you solve the problem? What did you learn from that discipline maintenance situation?

3. What specific evidence is there for the contention that essentialism has always been the predominant American philosophy of education? Are there any recent indications that this is particularly so today?

4. What are your views toward the general expectation of the public that moral and ethical values should be taught in the schools? How would you go about teaching values?

5. Should "democracy as a way of life" necessarily be an operating principle for our schools? Is American public education democratic? Do you agree that teachers must be dictatorial at times?

SUPPLEMENTAL ACTIVITIES

1. Many application forms for teaching positions ask the candidate to state briefly a philosophy of education. Write your own philosophy of education, discussing classroom management, teaching methods, discipline, and evaluation of the learner as related to a specific lesson or technique. Avoid educational jargon and cliches in your statement of philosophy. Emphasize the relationship of your philosophy to the classroom environment as much as possible.

2. Construct a teacher questionnaire that lists the

Glossary definitions of the six educational philosophies discussed in this chapter. Ask teachers which view they identify with. Ask how teachers practice their beliefs. Administer the questionnaire to the faculty of a local school and prepare a report on the results.

3. Invite a school superintendent to class to outline what is generally considered the educational philosophy of his or her school system and what is expected of beginning teachers.

4. Interview business leaders from two different

companies in order to determine the importance of ethics in the operations of the businesses. Determine the extent to which the business leaders' values were influenced by teachers. List the recommendations for teachers made by the business leaders.

5. Read from two of the following books and compare the content:

- Boyd H. Bode, *How We Learn*

- George S. Counts, *Education and American Civilization*
- John Dewey, *Democracy and Education*
- William H. Kilpatrick, *Philosophy of Education* and *Selfhood and Civilization*
- Harold Rugg, *American Life and the School Curriculum*
- Harold Taylor, *On Education and Freedom*
- V. T. Taylor, *Public Education and Its Critics*

NOTES

1. Lloyd Duck, *Instructor's Manual for Teaching with Charisma* (Boston: Allyn and Bacon, 1981), Item E, p. 41.

2. Ibid., Item G, p. 53.

3. William C. Bagley, "An Essentialist's Platform for the Advancement of American Education," *Educational Administration and Supervision* 24 (April 1938): 241–256.

4. Charles H. Wolfgang and Carl D. Glickman, *Solving Discipline Problems: Strategies for Classroom Teachers* (Boston: Allyn and Bacon, 1980), p. 121.

5. Ibid., pp. 121–122.

6. Ibid., p. 121.

7. Duck, Item K, pp. 56–57.

8. Ibid., Item N, pp. 47–48.

9. Theodore Brameld, *Patterns of Educational Philosophy* (New York: Holt, Rinehart and Winston, 1971), pp. 63–64.

10. Duck, Item F, pp. 42–43.

11. George F. Kneller, "Education, Knowledge, and the Problem of Existence," *Harvard Educational Review* 31 (Fall 1961): 430.

12. Ibid., p. 428.

13. C. Glickman and C. Wolfgang, "Conflict in the Classroom: An Eclectic Model of Teacher-Child Interaction," *Elementary School Guidance and Counseling* 13 (December 1978): 82–87.

BIBLIOGRAPHY

Bagley, William C. "An Essentialist's Platform for the Advancement of American Education." *Educational Administration and Supervision* 24 (April 1938): 241–256.

Brameld, Theodore. *Patterns of Educational Philosophy.* New York: Holt, Rinehart and Winston, 1971.

Coombs, Jerrold R., ed. *Philosophy of Education.* Proceedings of the Thirty-fifth Annual Meeting of the Philosophy of Education Society, Toronto, Canada, April 19–22, 1979.

Duck, Lloyd. *Teaching with Charisma.* Boston: Allyn and Bacon, Inc., 1981.

Goodlad, John I. "A Study of Schooling: Some Findings and Hypotheses." *Phi Delta Kappan* 64(7) (March 1983): 465–470.

Ianni, Francis A. J. "A Positive Note on Schools and Discipline." *Educational Leadership* 37 (March 1980): 457–458.

Knight, George R. *Issues and Alternatives in Educational Philosophy.* Berrien Springs, Mich.: Andrews University Press, 1982.

McGrath, Ellie. "The Bold Quest for Quality," *Time* (October 10, 1983): 58–66.

Morris, Van Cleve, and Pai, Young. *Philosophy and the American School.* 2d ed. Boston: Houghton Mifflin, 1976.

Wolfgang, Charles H., and Glickman, Carl D. *Solving Discipline Problems: Strategies for Classroom Teachers.* Boston: Allyn and Bacon, Inc., 1980.

$$\boxed{16}$$

Classical Philosophical Concepts

Focus Questions

- Why is it valuable for prospective teachers to study a classical philosophy? If you have not done so, why not?
- Are you able to identify and order your own beliefs in light of theories about reality, knowledge, or values? What is real? How do you know? What is of value to you?
- In your views about God, do you perceive God as all-good and all-powerful? Do you accept a belief in any God? Could beliefs about a Supreme Being influence your teaching? How?
- Do you believe that real learning occurs only through life's experiences? How would you justify this belief?
- Since existentialism is concerned with the emotions of individuals, of what value is this to a classroom teacher? If a teacher is more concerned with emotions than with the intellect of individuals, what would the students come away with?

Key Terms and Concepts

Metaphysics
Epistemology
Axiology
Ethics
Aesthetics

Idealism
Realism
Neo-Thomism
Experimentalism
Existentialism

What Would You Do?

In a conversation with other teachers the topic of the value of classical philosophy as a means of evaluating one's beliefs comes up. You would like to support the value of philosophy in this regard and find an unusual amount of interest in your opinion among the other teachers.

You begin to organize your teaching year by giving thought to what should be taught. While Greek thought suggests that "all men by nature desire to know," it does not specify "what" boys and girls in an American classroom desire or ought to know.

The previous chapter provided a framework for identifying a preferred teaching style/philosophy by studying teaching behavior for trends and preferences. These behavior trends and preferences may then associate a teaching style with one of several educational philosophies being practiced by teachers. While it is very important for prospective teachers to have a good understanding of what their preferred teaching philosophy means with regard to the learner, to content, and to classroom management and discipline maintenance, there is another very important dimension of the task of educational philosophy. Educators (teachers, administrators, curriculum specialists, and all others) are challenged to consider the larger questions underlying the meaning and purpose of life and education. When considering these questions, one must engage in philosophical activity dealing with such issues as the nature of reality, the meaning and source of knowledge, and the structure of values. In brief, Chapter 15 demonstrated how educational philosophies influence daily decision making about instruction. This chapter illustrates how the educational philosophies relate to classical concepts in philosophy.

If we assume that the reader may not have had a course in philosophy, it may be argued that the content of this chapter is too philosophical in the classic sense, too abstract to have meaning for the prospective teacher. Yet without a brief examination of the classic philosophical concepts upon which our educational philosophies are founded, the entire discussion of the important philosophical aspect of teaching would be short-sighted. This chapter presents an overview of selected classical concepts of philosophy for the purpose of examining the "root" structures and historical antecedents underlying current educational views and preferences.

Meaning of Philosophy

Why is it that each of several persons who share a common situation or setting will develop different beliefs? Why do individuals consider their beliefs true and others' beliefs false? Why do they value one thing as ugly while others value the same thing as beautiful? Or judge something or someone morally good or bad? Or accept something as real or not real? Why are we happy or unhappy? Can one of us contribute to the happiness of others? How do we learn to enjoy life? As we think about these kinds of questions, we are engaging in philosophical activity. This serves as the basis for formulating beliefs, a philosophy, related to the culture out of which the philosophical problems have grown. One's individual philosophy then can be defined as the organized system of convictions or beliefs adapted from this philosophical activity.

The literal meaning of philosophy is "love of wisdom." If one thinks of wisdom as "a high degree of knowledge," the extended literal meaning of philosophy becomes "love of a high degree of knowledge." On this point, Aristotle made a statement that typifies Greek thought: "All men by nature desire to know." Aristotle's statement does not specify "what" men and women desire to know. What to know as the essence of wisdom is something about which individuals disagree. Wisdom as the basis of philosophy encompasses religion, science, and art; it engages one's thinking and deals with abstract concepts and theory. One who is seeking wisdom is concerned with observations, values, mental pictures, spiritual beings, knowledge, and nature.

Philosophy is speculative in that it attempts to construct patterns from life experiences that give meaning to reality in the universe. Philosophy is prescriptive in that it evaluates facts for the purpose of recommending what *ought* to be as well as what *is*. Questions examining good or bad, right or wrong, beautiful or ugly are questions of prescriptive philosophy. Philosophy extends scientific statements of fact by considering questions that lie beyond the scope of science.

There is general agreement that there are three fundamental questions that are important in describing philosophy:

- What is real?
- How do we know?
- What is of value?

When you are able to determine your own answers to these questions, the answers will mean the most to you. Many individuals (teachers), however, borrow from existing systems of thought as they try to substantiate beliefs and discover wisdom. Classical philosophers tried to answer these basic questions; their speculations have proved of inexhaustible interest to all subsequent thinkers. Human life takes on meaning as the varied aspects of experience fall into some pattern. Philosophy tries to investigate the whole of reality by assessing experiences and then organizing those experiences in a way that is sensible to the individual. From this perspective, philosophy can be considered to be an inquiry into the whole human and cultural enterprise.

Evaluation of Beliefs

One's philosophy functions as the analysis and criticism, that is, the evaluation, of one's beliefs. A system of beliefs can be analyzed solely to review and classify beliefs so that they have meaning. If one stops at analysis, the resulting ordered view of beliefs is no more than a presentation of the dogmatic convictions of the individual. Analysis must also apply principles or standards for judging beliefs. Most of us are willing to accept the part

Each person must develop his or her own set of beliefs.

of analysis that calls for ordering our beliefs, but we are not so willing to accept the part that calls for judging our prized convictions. Perhaps we tend to be wary, fearful that judgment will show our convictions not to be valid over time. But convictions that withstand the stress of analysis and criticism will stand up over time far better than convictions based on sentiment. Finally, we should evaluate our beliefs in terms of current needs. Evaluation in this context has to do with ordering one's tested beliefs in reference to a given time. An underlying assumption is that analysis and criticism have shown the ordered beliefs to be worth keeping. Evaluation also obliges one to discard beliefs that cannot be substantiated through analysis and criticism.

Thought

Another function of philosophy is that it shows us how to think about new beliefs as they are different from existing beliefs and how they refute or support them. Each of the general questions of philosophy (What is real? How do we know? What is of value?) relates to a branch of philosophy. By considering just one of the three general questions, individual thought can be ordered at least so that that single branch of philosophy is examined for what it means. For example, individual thought geared only to what is real may generate new beliefs about reality, or it may generate beliefs that refute or support existing beliefs about reality. Similar thoughtful examination of either the branch of philosophy dealing with knowledge or the branch of philosophy dealing with values may also generate new beliefs or refute existing beliefs about knowledge and values. Philosophy functioning in this way provides an introspective examination of one's system of beliefs.

Among philosophers, Plato, Aristotle, St. Thomas Aquinas, Hegel, and Dewey are identified with elaborate systems of philosophy. To expedite understanding, a language of philosophy had to be developed. The resulting vocabulary has been mostly a straightforward development of words to identify activities or positions held within philosophy. Since most of the words have clear, straightforward meanings, confusion arises only when terms from our everyday forms of speech are loosely interpreted or carelessly used in solving philosophical problems. There are fully developed dictionaries of philosophy, but here we confine our interest to terminology identified with the three general questions of philosophy previously posed: What is real? How do we know? What is of value? *Metaphysics* (reality), *epistemology* (knowledge), and *axiology* (values) are important terms that describe these branches of philosophy.

[53]

Metaphysics

Metaphysics is the branch of philosophy that deals with various theories of reality. Metaphysics seeks to answer the first general question—What is real? Many persons have been reared according to the traditions of a Judeo-Christian culture such as that in the United States. According to them, reality depends on an ultimate being in God. Existence and God are identical. God made a perfect spiritual world, and humankind is a part of that world. Ultimate reality has been created from the Absolute Mind. Questions of reality also give rise to questions of physical existence. That is, does existence mean merely the occupation of time and space? Can we say that existence is no more than matter and physical energy? Can we say that ultimate reality is vested in the physical world? Whether ultimate reality is believed to be spiritual or physical, the reasoning behind the belief may not be philosophically valid. Why must one subscribe to the belief that existence has an ultimate quality? Perhaps a more practical approach to reality would be to accept the position that existence constantly changes. If everything constantly changes, nothing can be considered as existing in any ultimate sense. Existence, then, is of the moment and defined by the circumstances and conditions of that moment. In the future, existence will not be the same as it is for our time; nor was existence the same in the past.

Anthropologists believe that the nature of men and women is one important aspect of reality. Each of us needs to determine an acceptable belief relative to the nature of the self. In this view the self can be accepted as a spiritual, a physical, or a social phenomenon in a state of flux. Another way to deal with the nature of the self is to ask whether human beings are basically good, bad, or neutral. Many anthropological questions bear investigation so that beliefs about reality can be clarified. What is the relation of mind and body? Do mind and body interact? Is mind more fundamental than body, with body depending on mind? Or is the converse true? Consideration must also be given to the freedom of human beings. Are actions determined by forces greater than the person? Or do men and women have the power of choice through free will? Perhaps one is neither free nor determined. Teachers are obligated to identify and order their own beliefs in light of these philosophical questions about reality so that they can more completely understand their pupils.

Epistemology

Epistemology is the branch of philosophy that is concerned with theories of the nature of knowledge. Epistemology tries to answer the second general philosophical question—How do we know? One of the functions of teachers is to assemble knowledge and transmit that knowledge to students. One of the functions of epistemology is to specify the means by which knowledge is acquired. The means of acquiring knowledge vary according to the beliefs of the several schools of philosophy. Some philosophically determined beliefs about the instruments of knowledge are: (1) knowledge is gained empirically through perceptual experience; (2) knowledge is gained chiefly through reason; (3) knowledge is gained in some instances by intuition; and (4) knowledge is certified by an indisputable authority.

It can be contended that knowledge is based on experience and observation. On the other hand, some knowledge is self-evident. Certain truths have long been understood and do not require proof through observation and experimentation. Another view is that conclusive knowledge of ultimate reality is an impossibility; *agnosticism* holds to this notion. *Skepticism* holds a questioning attitude toward the possibility of gaining knowledge. You may believe that knowledge functions in situations in which it is needed. Future teachers need to be concerned with those theories about knowledge that they can accept as part of their personal philosophies.

Axiology

Axiology is the branch of philosophy that specifies the nature of values, the kinds of values, and the values worth possessing. Axiology seeks to answer the third general philosophical question—What is of value? What we desire, we value. The interest theory of value suggests that values exist only as they are supported by the interest of the valuer. A value of interest to one person may not exist at all for a second person. An opposing theory holds that values exist independently of the valuer and his or her interest. In this context, values are universal and exist for all.

Ethics is the realm of value that relates to good and bad. Ethics considers criteria of conduct in our lives and motivation of conduct. *Aesthetics* is the realm of value that searches for the principles governing the creation and appreciation of beautiful things. Other realms of value deal with religion, education, society, and utility.

In our pluralistic social world, frustration and anxiety may be induced when we behave according to the values of a group rather than as we would individually prefer to behave. By focusing on philosophical values, we can gain conscious awareness of our individually cherished values on which to base our personal behavior. Confusion about one's personal values leads to conforming behavior determined by group values for given situations. Behavior of this sort may be frustrating when the group behavior contradicts one's personally held—but not consciously identified—values.

Schools of Philosophy

Since philosophers have been unable to agree on the number of philosophies that exist, attempts to classify schools of philosophy are not very useful. The classical schools of philosophy we have chosen to examine most closely are idealism, realism, neo-Thomism, experimentalism, and existentialism. Each of the selected schools is identified and described in terms of the philosophical branches—metaphysics (reality), epistemology (knowledge), and axiology (values).

Idealism

In order to include various philosophical tenets, perhaps the term *ideaism* should be substituted for the term *idealism*. Popular confusion exists, perhaps since idealism is related to both ideas and ideals. Historically, the term *idea* has been used to mean many things: form, semblance, universal, class concepts in the human mind, subsistence in the mind of God, sense perception, faint image, and absolute. When we talk about ideas, we shall assume that activity of the mind is involved. Ideas are mental—of the mind.

Ideals are also mental—of the mind—and pertain to ideas. An ideal "something or other" is held to be perfect, judged by some standard. It can be argued that such standards are external to the mind, but when one makes a judgment relating to standards, activity of the mind is involved. Idealism embraces idea, mind, spirit, and thought.

Therefore one's "idealism" is a function of one's mind. This function of one's mind can be thought of as a conceptual process of The Ultimate Mind, in miniature, seeking reality, knowledge, and values. Idealism calls for the mind to perceive reality, knowledge, and values according to the ideal standards of perfection of The Ultimate Mind. Modern idealism strives to associate men and women with their spiritual existence.

Metaphysics of Idealism

How does *idealism* answer the question "What is real?"? What is the metaphysics of idealism? To the idealist, reality is constituted by ideas, by the mind, by the self. Reality is a world of mind; it is spiritual rather than physical. Material things are not regarded as reality, since the idealist believes that nature depends on The Universal Mind, or God. Reality can be identified essentially with subconscious spiritual principles. One of the timeworn topics of subconscious concepts of reality is the explanation of first events of nature. Any discussion almost always reaches the assertion that nature could not have brought itself into being. Consideration must then be given to what could have caused the first events of nature. Regression along a line of causes takes us back to the first cause as God. Certain theories of nature that include cause-and-effect relations suggest that the universe came to exist through the working of a creative cause. The pure idealist subscribes to the argument that the real objective existence of God is necessarily in the existence of the very idea of God and maintains that God created the universe.

Idealists hold, along with the premise of creationism, elemental conceptions about God. While it can be generally stated that God and the universe have some relation, the way in which the relation is identified may be perplexing. Is God a personal God? Is God one or more than one? Are God and the universe identical? Is God all-good and all-powerful? Or is God all-good but not necessarily all-powerful? Is God interested or not interested in the physical universe and in human beings? Pure idealism accepts the view of Christian theism that suggests that ultimate reality is a personal God who is more than the universe; the universe exists within and through God. The polytheistic doctrine that spiritual reality is plural (more than one god) could be contained within idealism. The distinguishing note is that idealism holds God or gods to be an ultimate reality that is more than the universe.

What about the nature of man or woman in relation to reality? A principle of idealism states that one has a self, which is one's soul. This soul is a spiritual being. Equating spiritual being with mind brings up how body and mind are related. Idealists usually solve this problem by purporting mind to be more fundamental than body; that is, body depends on mind. What does this mean? If one considers the mind as a miniature model of The Supreme Mind, idealism becomes deterministic. Since one's body depends on one's mind and since the mind is a working replica of The Supreme Mind, then actions are determined by forces greater than the individual. Such an analogy might be immediately countered with the suggestion that one's mind, whether or not it be considered a miniature of The Supreme Mind, works independently and interprets reality in its own right. The human mind can interpret reality, since it was given this capability by God. While these interpretations may be foreknown by God, this does not mean that actions of humans are necessarily determined by God. The deterministic quality of idealism is thus qualified.

Epistemology of Idealism

What is the epistemology of idealism? What is knowledge? How do we know? Idealists have held various theories of knowledge at various times. Today's idealists generally believe that there are other instruments of knowledge besides the scientific method. Idealism also considers faith, authoritarianism, and intuition as instruments of knowledge. It can be said that faith is a way we come to know certain things. Faith suggests that people firmly accept their beliefs as knowledge, despite arguments against them. Idealists often accept knowledge on faith. Knowledge based on faith is more than a mere belief: one believes, for example, that God exists because faith as an instrument of knowledge has enabled one to know God. Whether it be called immaterialism, mysticism, spiritualism, or something else, such belief in The Supreme Mind is a significant aspect of the epistemology of idealism. Perhaps authoritarianism and faith in God become synonymous in relation to knowledge certified to us by authorities like the Bible and the church. If so, the indisputable authority of the Bible and the church may actually be tools for formulating faith. In the absence of faith, however, important knowledge can be certified to us directly from the Bible and the church, or from any other authority, such as the state.

Intuition means to know in a direct fashion. Idealists believe that we can know some things directly without reasoning. Knowledge may come to us intuitively. One who takes an extended position on intuition as a source of knowledge would claim that all knowledge is based on intuition. Idealism includes intuition among the instruments of knowledge. Historically, in the realm of knowledge, idealists have conceived of truth as ideas. George Berkeley (1685–1753), an Anglican bishop and philosopher, was called an idealist because he believed that existence was mind dependent. For anything to exist, it must be perceived by mind, but not necessarily the human mind. Berkeley argued that things exist even when a human mind is not perceiving them because The Ultimate Mind of God is perceiving all things. Idealism is not entirely Christian thought, but as a philosophy it does concur with the philosophy of the deeply religious Berkeley in holding that ultimate existence and knowledge are perceived by The Supreme Mind.

Axiology of Idealism

What does idealism have to suggest about the most personal question of philosophy—What is of value? What are the ethics and aesthetics of idealism? Idealism has God as the standard of goodness. Moral persons seek God's principles. The inherent problem is for mortals to know the will of God. It follows that evil can be identified as action against the will of God. The assumption is that morality is based on the will of God as expressed in the Bible, in the teachings of Christ, and in the interpretations of the church. But what about the existence of evil? That has always been for idealists a most troublesome question. How can an omnipotent and benevolent God—a perfect God whose attributes of complete love, justice, and mercy cannot be expressed so as to be inconsistent with each other— allow evil to continue?

The continued existence of evil, however, can be linked to God's plan of free will for humans. If God gives free choice, there must be freedom not to choose His will and not to strive for moral perfection. The freedom not to strive for moral perfection produces evil. If God removed evil from the world, this would be inconsistent with His gift of free will because one could then choose only to follow Him. If, on the other hand, He removed all evil consequences from those seeking to follow His will and allowed evil consequences only for those who do not seek to follow Him, the freedom to choose would be meaningless. Under such conditions, free will would not operate. It would be too obvious that choosing God's will is the only way to be rewarded and choosing not to follow God's will leads to immediate punishment. God would have to keep intervening in the universe to give special protection to His followers, even in the case of natural calamities. Then choice would have little meaning, and natural laws would also not be dependable. Imagine two skiers whizzing down a hillside. One skier has been seeking God's will in his life, the other has not. Both skiers crash into trees. For one skier the tree might suddenly become like soft plastic that would not injure anyone. For the other a tree would be the same predictably hard object we know, because God is not giving this skier special protection. As C. S. Lewis has explained in *The Problem of Pain*, it might very well be that this universe, with all its evils and imperfections, is the only possible universe, since God gives humans the freedom to choose and since His other attributes will not allow Him to contradict His perfect justice and love in permitting free choice.

In the Christian view it is also not inconsistent with God's demand for justice that evil be allowed to continue. Christ's sacrificial death is seen as the act by which He suffered a just punishment for all evils past, present, and future. In that sense, any manifestation of evil has been judged, and the penalty for it has already been paid. All who believe this principle are seen as coming under its provisions and having the penalty for their evils paid by Christ's death. This principle hinges on the belief that Christ, as God in the flesh, had no inherent evil and could therefore die sacrificially for the evil choices of human beings.

Aesthetics in idealism logically grows out of the ethics in idealism. Beauty is described as the reflection of God. In other words, as people continually strive to become morally good by imitating God, they reflect God—the ideal—more and more. Such reflection of God becomes the aesthetics—the beauty—of idealism.

Realism

Realism, like naturalism, regards nature as all there is. Realism holds that objects of the external world are real in themselves. This is antithetical to idealism. Realism is not the sole antithesis of idealism: materialism and naturalism are terms that have been used interchangeably to express the antithesis of idealism. Realism, as sketched in this presentation, essentially can be interchanged with materialism and naturalism. Realism denotes the physical world as the sum total of reality. There is no dependence on a mind—human or divine—to comprehend concepts. A realist rejects the existence of anything beyond nature. Everything comes from nature and is subject to scientific laws. Naturalism has been aligned with natural science; the physical world includes only what can be scientifically investigated. Objects that science can investigate are the physical or the material. Matter is a fundamental constituent of the universe. The universe is not governed by mind, spirits, ideas, perceptions, or God as a first cause. The theory of evolution accounts for the universe and its contents by the combination of separate and diffused atoms. Plato's dualism referred to an actual world of particulars and an ideal world of pure essences. Realism as naturalism suggests that human life—physical, mental, moral, and spiritual—is an ordinary natural event attributable in all respects to the ordinary operations of nature.

Metaphysics of Realism

Realism specifies reality in things or objects. It holds that natural things have always existed, that the universe as a physical world evolved of itself naturally, as opposed to having been created by a supernatural force beyond nature. Realists consider causes of the events of nature but do not believe, as an idealist does, that the first cause is a God. A realist may hold that no ultimate reality exists behind the universe. God also may be conceived by realists as evolving with the universe. Cause-and-effect relations are viewed as governed by natural law. A realist feels that if we cannot answer a question of cause, it is because we have not learned to understand all nature. When we know all about nature, we will have answers to all questions of causes.

What about the essential nature of human beings as seen by realists? A principle of naturalism views the self as essentially the same as the body. As far as the relation of body and mind is concerned, a realist believes mind to be something new and produced by nature in the evolutionary process, neither identical with body nor wholly dependent on it. Another realist concept suggests that mind is merely a function of the brain. In this context, mind does not influence bodily activity but merely accompanies bodily activity. The stage for one's physical activity is and has been an orderly, purposeful universe. To exist in the universe is to occupy time and space as physical matter. Nature is identical with existence.

Epistemology of Realism

What are the instruments of knowledge in realism (naturalism)? What is knowledge? Realism affirms the possibility of knowledge. Truth is viewed as observable fact. Perceptual experience is the medium for gaining knowledge. Realists observe data obtained on the physical nature of the universe. From these observations, general principles are formulated to make the universe intelligible. Realism uses the inductive method of investigating nature in detecting general principles from observations. Modern naturalism adheres to the scientific method for formulating general principles of knowledge. The essence of the epistemology of realism is that knowledge is based on experience and observation. Nature contains truth, and that truth can be ascertained by investigating nature scientifically.

Axiology of Realism

Regarding the axiology of realism, values are also gotten from nature. From observing nature, one comes to know natural laws that provide the basis for ethical and aesthetical evaluations. Values will have a natural quality instead of a supernatural quality. Assuming that the universe is thus the standard of goodness, those who live in accordance with the general principles of nature are moral persons. This universe, as the standard of goodness for one's ethical structure, may also be considered the standard for determining evil; that is, evil becomes what violates one's ethical structure. Moral persons are responsible for selecting the laws of nature that denote good and then for conducting themselves by such laws. Nature provides the principles that govern appreciation of beauty; aesthetics is the reflection of nature.

Neo-Thomism

Neo means "new"; *Thomism* is the branch of Christian scholasticism associated with the work of St. Thomas Aquinas (1225–1274). Until the time of Aquinas the dualism of idealism and realism dominated philosophy. Divergence of thinking regarding supernatural and natural causes, mind and body, and physical objects and mental conceptions set the two philosophical camps apart, as shown in Figure 16.1. By the 1200s, Christian philosophers wanted to inject Christian doctrine into their systems of thought. Christian discussions were concerned with such topics as the existence of God, the nature of humankind, and faith and reason. At this time the views of Aristotle were little known, and Thomas Aquinas was instrumental in getting Aristotle's works translated from Greek into Latin. The works of Thomas Aquinas were a combination of Aristotle's thought and the thinking of church leaders at that time. Aquinas suggested that reason was the basis for universal organization; he contended that faith and reason do not conflict. St. Thomas, however, did assign preeminence to God, stating that since God cannot be at fault, any differences between conclusions based on reason and conclusions based on faith must come from faulty reasoning. In fact, scholasticism tended to emphasize deductive reasoning by beginning with principles revealed by God or the ancients and applying them to the specifics of living. This tended to minimize the chance of faulty reasoning. By contrast, realism and idealism emphasize inductive reasoning. That is, the realist looks at specific phenomena in nature and thinks of generalizations that might explain these phenomena.

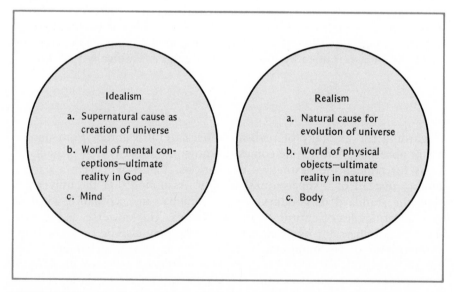

FIGURE 16.1   *Dualistic position of idealism and realism before the Middle Ages.*

Such inductive reasoning is the core of the scientific method. Plato's idealism also relied on inductive reasoning about ideas through using a process of questioning (the dialectic) to reach general truths. A famous example is from the *Meno* dialogue. In this dialogue a slave boy is being asked by his teacher if he knows the Pythagorean theorem in mathematics. Although the slave boy insists that he has never heard of the Pythagorean theorem, his teacher's skillful questions about specific triangles leads the boy to derive the theorem. After these questions the boy comes up with the general principle that the square of the hypotenuse of a right triangle is equal to the sums of the squares of the other two sides of the triangle. He is then complimented by his teacher for having really "known" the Pythagorean theorem all along. He just had to use inductive reasoning to derive and understand a principle.

Although St. Thomas had little success in solving the idealism-realism duality, his views added new perspectives to the traditional Christian doctrines and consequently generated much interest in philosophical thought. The scholarship of the Christian philosophers is referred to as *scholasticism;* Thomism is but one facet of scholasticism. Scholasticism declined as a movement by the 1400s and rose again in the early 1600s, only to decline a second time before 1700. Pope Leo III (late 1800s) adopted Thomism as the official position of the Roman Catholic Church. The version of Thomism being revived today has come to be known as neo-Thomism. There are lay groups and ecclesiastical groups (Roman Catholic) of neo-Thomists. The works of Thomas Aquinas and others have brought the philosophical positions of idealism and realism into contact with each other. Figure 16.2 shows the present relation between idealism

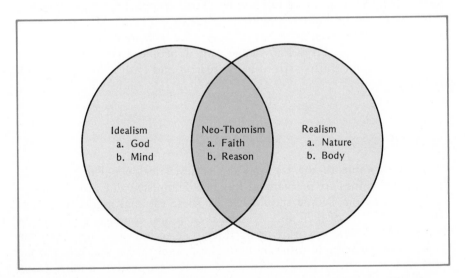

FIGURE 16.2 *Relationship of idealism, realism, and neo-Thomism after the Middle Ages.*

and realism and also shows the related position of neo-Thomism. This schema also illustrates Aquinas's contention that faith from idealism and reason from realism do not conflict.

Metaphysics of Neo-Thomism

The nature of reality in neo-Thomism is the harmony of faith and reason. Reality is proposed as a world of reason. Existence may be viewed as residing in the reasoning powers of the human mind. Ideas are real in themselves. Physical objects exist whether or not they are perceived by humans. The universe exists independent of people. However, Thomists argue, humankind, our ideas, our mind, and our spirit, as well as the physical objects in the world, have been created by God. Reality is dualistic to the Roman Catholic neo-Thomists; God and physical matter do not have a purely antithetical relation, however, since they are not in equal balance. While neo-Thomists consider both God and physical matter real, God as a perfect being is considered more important.

Epistemology of Neo-Thomism

Neo-Thomists establish knowledge through both faith and reason. The ecclesiastical group added revelation to intuition as the basis of their epistemology. Faith, by which knowledge is affirmed, develops from history, the Bible, and God's word as taught by Jesus Christ. Knowledge also comes through reason and experience. Basic knowledge, in this context, is in the realm of human thought. Empiricism (discussed below) is an instrument of knowledge wherein experience becomes the medium for gaining knowledge. From knowledge gained, people reason toward truth. The fundamental truths arrived at by reason and faith are unchangeable and dependable.

Axiology of Neo-Thomism

What is of value to the lay and the ecclesiastical neo-Thomists? Like knowledge, values are permanent. Lay neo-Thomists value moral law discerned by reason. People should live by these rational moral standards. The rational acts of men and women, their moral conduct, and their relations with others constitute their ethics. The ecclesiastical neo-Thomists go beyond reasoning to insist that God has established moral law and has provided us with the power of reason for the purpose of finding God's moral law. Thus we are bound to conduct our lives according to God's moral laws because that is God's will.

Experimentalism/Progressivism

By the beginning of the 1600s, England was rapidly growing in power and territory; consequently, a more practical approach to reality and knowledge was needed. The vast amount of new information being brought to England by merchants and scholars had to be combined with existing knowledge. Traditional beliefs and systems of thought about reality and knowledge seemed inadequate. Because of these conditions, a philosophical movement known as *empiricism* developed in England. Empiricism postulated experience to be fundamental to reality and knowledge. Through the years the term "empiricism" has been ambiguously associated with numerous positions and practices. The term "experimentalism" describes the credence English empiricists gave to experience. Although early Greek philosophers first suggested that experience was the basis of reality, experimentalism grew largely out of English empiricism and is therefore classified as a modern view. Philosophical speculations in the early 1600s centered around questions of one's acquisition of knowledge (epistemology) rather than questions of reality (metaphysics). A general premise of experimentalism, and also empiricism, is that reality and knowledge depend on one's observations and experiences.

$\boxed{51}$

Metaphysics of Experimentalism

What does reality become in this system of thought? What about causality of the universe? The metaphysics of experimentalism appears to be flexible and capable of change compared with the rigidly fixed metaphysical positions of the traditional philosophical concepts already discussed. Each of us becomes a determiner of reality through individual conceptualizations. We may choose our beliefs regarding the origin and development of the universe. We may consider the universe as coming into existence as an act of God or by natural evolution. Experimentalists consider the self as an experience in consciousness, rather than an existence in itself. Each of us exists as a social part of the universe. Our self then becomes directly observable as an appearance or action. Our mind exists as a function of the brain, so observations of activities can be pictured. From all the responses to such imaginings we draw out those responses that give direction and meaning to reality. Thus one's actions are not determined by forces greater than oneself, nor is one capable of genuine initiative, with free will or power of choice. Functioning in this manner, one becomes the determiner, or interpreter if you prefer, of numerous considerations of reality. Experimentalists see purpose in the universe as the result of one's purposeful activity and not as inherent in existence or accidental. Reality is a changing quantity consisting of numerous activities, materials, and processes; everything is in a changing state. Nothing exists in the ultimate state, that is, immune from change.

Each of us becomes a determiner of reality through individual conceptualizations.

Epistemology of Experimentalism

In what way do we come to know truth? What is knowledge? Is it possible to have ultimate knowledge when experimentalism does not allow for ultimate reality? What is the source of knowledge for the experimentalists? Questions about how we acquire knowledge are of primary concern to experimentalism. Experimentalists believe truth to be what is functional. What is necessary to solve our problems becomes the essence of our knowledge. Knowledge, although based on observation and experience, is not concluded to be final by experimentalists. Rather, knowledge is considered to be functional insofar as it can be used to solve one's problems. Knowledge can be continually added to from the observations and experiences of the individual. Thus experimentalism does not accept reality as ultimate, nor does it accept knowledge as conclusive. It is reasonable to assume that rationalism is a part of the experimentalist system of acquiring knowledge. The epistemological view of experimentalism suggests that knowledge (truth) is what we know to solve our problems.

Axiology of Experimentalism

What of values? What is the axiology of this system of thought? Experimentalists' values are relative. From what we know of the epistemology of experimentalists, it seems logical to consider their ethics as tentative. What is good or evil today may not be so valued in the future. One's moral status is largely determined by how the public accepts one's conduct. Older persons often judge younger ones to be "going to pot," which implies that a less moral system of values exists for the younger members of society. Experimentalism points to such judgments as evidence that moral standards change from generation to generation. Judgments of older generations are made from a pattern of ethics that has changed to a different pattern for younger generations. Aesthetics are determined by the public taste. Democracy as a way of life becomes a necessary ingredient of experimentalism's values. Only in a democracy is it possible for good and evil and the creation and appreciation of beautiful things to be assessed from all points of view. Ethical and aesthetical values are in continuous process. Values exist in a state of flux and are relative.

Figure 16.3 shows experimentalism in relation to the schools of philosophy previously discussed. As indicated, experimentalism overlaps idealism, neo-Thomism, and realism.

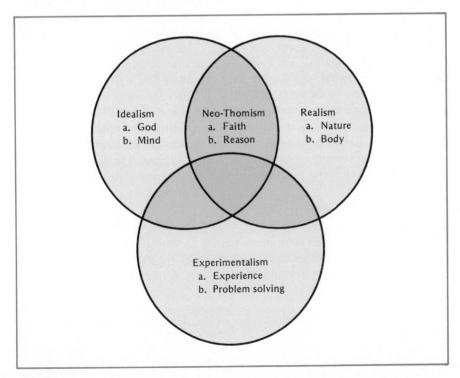

FIGURE 16.3 *Relationship of realism, idealism, neo-Thomism, and experimentalism.*

Existentialism

Existentialism is a relatively recent philosophy spawned in Europe after World War I. Actually, Danish philosopher Sören Kierkegaard (1813–1855) laid the foundation for existentialism when he wrote and taught of our inner freedom to direct our own lives. Early in the 1900s, scholars began to translate the works of Kierkegaard into German; English translations did not appear until the 1930s. As a consequence of both delayed translations of Kierkegaard and World War II, most of the development of existential philosophies has been recent. To some degree, existentialism emphasizes casting off traditional and modern philosophies. Emphasis is placed on one's responsibility for setting goals and making decisions free from group norms. The individualistic character of existentialism has often caused group-oriented societies to label existentialism as a faddish philosophy that is uninterested in morals. Such misinterpreted castigations of existentialism may be related to the popularity of the French playwright Jean-Paul Sartre. Before his death in 1980, Sartre was labeled the leader of the atheistic camp within the existentialist movement. In practice, many existentialists are strongly theistic and hold that one's desires lead to knowledge of God. Of this group, Karl Jaspers, a German, and Gabriel Marcel, a Frenchman, who are both Roman Catholics, represent the theistic segment of existentialism. American George F. Kneller suggested that one of the obstacles in trying to understand the general nature of existentialism is that it cannot be studied objectively from without, but requires that students identify themselves with its doctrines from within. Others say that existentialism is not a wholly new orientation of thought but an individualistic way of looking at other systems of thought.

Existentialism is difficult to define. By its very nature, existentialism is concerned with the emotions of individuals rather than being primarily concerned with the intellect of individuals. With the emphasis on individualism, existentialism is not regarded as a systematic philosophy regarding metaphysical, epistemological, and axiological terms. The following statements briefly sketch the positions from which existentialism speaks.

Metaphysics of Existentialism

With the inner freedom of human beings to determine existence, reality becomes one's subjective existence. As one goes through life making choices and developing preferences and dislikes, one defines who he or she is as an individual.

> Man is faced with the stark realities of life, death, and meaning, and he has the unutterable freedom of being responsible for his own essence. . . . The traditional philosophies surrender man's authenticity to a logical system, the Christian leans on God, the realist looks to nature for meaning, and the pragmatist relies on the community. All of these avenues are ways of removing man from the frightful reality of being responsible for his choices.[1]

Epistemology of Existentialism

Existentialists hold that there is no difference between one's external and internal worlds. What is true is represented by personal choice. We know ourselves as actors on life's stage and act according to individual choice. Since it is the individual who gives meaning to such things as nature, meaning and truth could not be built into the universe. Knowing is based upon the authority of the individual, who makes the ultimate decision as to what is true.

Axiology of Existentialism

The realm of axiology is central to existentialism. Existential values consist of the morality of people choosing freely. The existentialist finds beauty in one's capacity to function apart from the public norms. Each individual makes and is responsible for his or her ethical decisions and aesthetic viewpoints—no one can make such judgments for other individuals. Each of us is free to determine the nature of good conduct. Similarly, beauty is in the "eye of the beholder" rather than in public standards. What is beautiful to me is beautiful; nevertheless, existentialism stresses responsibility. While personal choice is important, once the choice is exercised, the existentialist accepts the responsibility accompanying that choice.

Summary and Implications

Systems of philosophical thought consist of three distinct branches, which deal with the questions of reality (metaphysics), knowledge and truth (epistemology), and values (axiology). This chapter presents brief sketches of these three realms as related to the classical root philosophies from which current educational philosophies are drawn. Prospective teachers may now identify the classical philosophical position that serves as the foundation of the current views in American schools discussed in Chapter 15. Any one of the six educational philosophies may then be further examined with regard to the three dimensions. Such philosophical activity serves classroom teachers in becoming familiar with and knowledgeable about these facets of philosophical systems as related to any one educational philosophy. There is no implied best quality ascribed to one philosophical position over another. Rather, it is suggested that the most successful teachers are those who are dedicated to and thoroughly understand their preferred style. Decisions about the nature of the subject matter given curricular emphasis are metaphysical commitments to reality—what is real? Classroom methods and practices aim to assist learners in acquiring knowledge and truth in the subject area. Questions related to what is true and how we know are epistemological in kind. Classroom activities that deal with what is good or bad, beauty, and character are in the realm of axiology (values). The task of the teacher is to identify a preferred style, understand that style as deeply as possible, and utilize that style with a unique group of learners seeking to accomplish reasonable educational outcomes under the leadership of the teacher.

We hope that from what has been presented so far, you will be able to work out a personal philosophy based on reality, knowledge, and value. Also, it should now be possible for you to envision how philosophical concepts carry over into and influence educational views extant in our schools. This is the theoretical, rational part of developing a personal philosophy of education. To perceive such a philosophy is one thing; to teach according to the philosophy is another. In teaching, one exhibits behavior that is compatible with a personal educational view. Most teachers find it advantageous to choose from various educational views. As long as this eclecticism serves the pedagogical purposes of the teacher and is a basis for consistent behavior by the teacher in the classroom, learning will take place. If, however, this eclecticism causes the teacher to change behavior frequently and with no apparent purpose, thus distracting pupils from learning, the teacher could better profit from subscribing to one specific educational view.

The classical philosophical concepts discussed are broad categories within the vast academic realm of philosophy. Further in-depth study would reveal many specific schools of thought for each concept briefly highlighted in this text. As with the educational philosophies, classical concepts tend toward authoritarian views, which lean to convergent thinking outcomes, and toward non-authoritarian views, which lean to divergent thinking outcomes. Table 16.1 groups the classical philosophical concepts of idealism, realism, and neo-Thomism as authoritarian views tending toward convergent thinking. Essentialism, perennialism, and behaviorism, presented in Chapter 15 as authoritarian views among educational philosophies, draw upon these classical concepts. Similarly, the classical philosophical concepts of experimentalism and existentialism are considered as non-authoritarian views tending toward divergent thinking. Experimentalism, reconstructionism, and existentialism, presented in Chapter 15 as non-authoritarian views among educational philosophies, draw upon these classical concepts.

Table 16.1 also illustrates educational implications with regard to curricular emphasis, preferred method, character education, and developing taste for each philosophical concept. As was suggested earlier, the metaphysical questions about reality in the "root" philosophy serve as the basis for the curricular emphases in current educational practices. Methodology in the classroom relates to the acquisition of knowledge, which is anchored in classic epistemological considerations. Character education (morals) and developing taste (aesthetics) are value determinants extended from the axiology branches of classic philosophies. It should be noted that since the relationships presented here are drawn from many elaborate schools and

TABLE 16.1 *Educational Implications of Authoritarian and Non-Authoritarian Views*

	Authoritarian Views (convergent thinking)			Non-Authoritarian Views (divergent thinking)	
	Idealism	Realism	Neo-Thomism	Experimentalism	Existentialism
Curricular emphasis	Subject matter of the mind: literature, intellectual history, philosophy, religion / Education should be the same for everyone / Three Rs in elementary schools	Subject matter of the physical world: mathematics, science / Initiative in education with the teacher	Subject matter of intellect and spirit, mathematics, language, and doctrine	Subject matter of social experience / Creation of a new social order	Subject matter of personal choice
Preferred method	Teaching for the handling of ideas: lecture, discussion / Preparation for life	Teaching for mastery of factual information and basic skills: demonstration, recitation / Facts help individual adjustment to life	Disciplining the mind: formal drill—readying the spirit: catechism	Problem solving: project method / Scrupulous regard for democratic procedures	Individual as entity within a social context
Character education	Imitating exemplars, heroes / Greatest aspirations in the historical record	Training in rules of conduct	Disciplining behavior to reason	Making group decisions in light of consequences / Positive modification of society	Individual responsibility for decisions and preferences
Developing taste	Studying the masterworks / Values of the past heritage	Studying design in nature	Finding beauty in reason	Participating in art projects / Based on cross-cultural and even universal values	Personal view of the world / Self-initiated activities

See Figure 16.1 and Appendix G.
Source: Adapted from Van Cleve Morris and Young Pai, *Philosophy and the American School*, p. 295. Copyright © 1976 Houghton Mifflin.

systems of philosophical thought, they are incomplete. The purpose has been to present digests of information that may serve prospective teachers in focusing attention on classroom practices that are predicated on their respective philosophies of education. Without question, additional study of philosophy, classical and educational, would serve all classroom teachers well in knowing about and utilizing the most effective ways to assist learners in accomplishing educational outcomes.

DISCUSSION QUESTIONS

1. How would an existentialist react to the aim of the American public schools—to give each student the chance to develop his or her talents to the fullest extent? How would a classroom teacher manage to give each student such chance?
2. What is your meaning of philosophy? Illustrate the extent to which individual beliefs are accounted for in your definition.
3. In your opinion, which is the most important aspect of a given philosophy (for the teacher)—the metaphysical view, the epistemological view,

or the axiological view? State the rationale for your opinion.
4. The epistemology of neo-Thomism holds that knowledge is established through both faith and reason. Discuss the implication of this statement for classroom methodology.
5. How does philosophy assist individuals in structuring their thought processes in order to refute or support their beliefs? (Extend your response to include beliefs about teaching.)

SUPPLEMENTAL ACTIVITIES

1. Argue the cases for and against the inclusion of the following offerings in a high school curriculum: driver training, home economics, vocational agriculture, physical education, athletics, electronics, computer literacy, and typing and shorthand.
2. Search the audiovisual library for tapes, slides, and films that deal with classical concepts of philosophy. Use the materials as a basis for class presentation and discussion.
3. Search the audiovisual library for tapes, slides, and films that deal with current educational philosophies. Use the materials as a basis for class presentation and discussion.
4. Visit an "open" elementary school and report to class on the educational practices in the school. Compare your observations with your own elementary school experiences. Determine how many teaching styles you see. Is this what you would expect? Why or why not?
5. Investigate the Philosophy for Children program at Montclair State College, Upper Montclair, NJ 07043, and report your findings. See Matthew Lipman, Ann Margaret Sharp, and Frederick S. O. Scanyan, *Philosophy in the Classroom* (Philadelphia: Temple University Press, 1980).

NOTE

1. George R. Knight, *Issues and Alternatives in Educational Philosophy* (Berrien Springs, Mich.: Andrews University Press, 1982), p. 72.

BIBLIOGRAPHY

Adler, Mortimer. "A Revolution in Education." *American Educator* 6(4) (Winter 1982): 20–24.

Dewey, John. *Democracy and Education*. New York: Macmillan, 1916.

Junell, Joseph S. *Matters of Feeling: Values Education Reconsidered*. Bloomington, Ind.: Phi Delta Kappa Educational Foundation, 1979.

Knight, George P. *Issues and Alternatives in Educational Philosophy*. Berrien Springs, Mich.: Andrews University Press, 1982.

Levine, Alan H., and Cary, Eve. *The Rights of Students*. New York: Avon Books, 1977.

Runes, Dagobert D. *Dictionary of Philosophy*. Totowa, N.J.: Littlefield, Adams, 1979.

Scheffler, Israel. *Conditions of Knowledge: An Introduction to Epistemology and Education*. Chicago: University of Chicago Press, 1978.

Soltis, Jonas F. *An Introduction to the Analysis of Educational Concepts*. 2d rev. ed. Reading, Mass.: Addison-Wesley, 1978.

Taylor, A. E. *Elements of Metaphysics*. 12th ed. London: Methuen, 1946.

Wingo, G. Max. *The Philosophy of American Education*. Lexington, Mass.: D.C. Heath, 1974.

VI

Program Purposes, Artifacts, and Practices

Educational programs in the United States are complex, diverse images of the society they serve. In a very real sense they reflect what the society values and what the society is willing to pay for. A nation that spends approximately ten percent of its gross national product on formal education reflects the financial priority it has for schools. The local, state, and national expectations that are verbalized by national commission studies, national pollsters, and specially anointed educational critics predominantly reflect greater expectations than what the society pays for. Despite the many cited shortcomings of the public schools of the United States, schools do a very commendable job in meeting societal demands for mass education. That they could do better, however, is not refutable. The program purposes are sound, but the artifacts and practices reflect an institutionalizing effect that tries to produce an educated citizenry without an expanding investment policy in people and programs. Thus schools reflect the real priorities of the society.

At the heart of all educational issues are the learners, who, as they are being educated, should have positive experiences that will prepare them for the future. Preparation of learners has become complicated, and scientific and technological advances have made predicting the future difficult. Because of the contradictions in our infinitely complex society, young learners question the importance of planning for the future. The contradictions abound. We can explore outer space, but we cannot keep our own environment free of pollution. Scientists are now actually capable of reproducing life on a microscopic scale, but cancer, heart disease, and other medical problems continue to baffle them. Technology now gives us comforts and goods we never had before; yet we cannot safely handle the resulting pollution. Learning materials are now quicker and easier to get than ever before, but we have not found a way to handle leisure. And finally—what is critically important for young learners—we have not learned to live with one another despite all we have enjoyed in the closing decades of this century. Fear, tension, and compe-tition continue to plague us in our quest for peace and harmony among people.

The main purpose of Part VI is to examine the organizational structure of the school's curriculum and recognize its patchwork quilt–like structure. Differing philosophical viewpoints lead to differences in the implementation of contemporary and traditional programs. The teacher in training is not expected to become a curriculum expert but is expected to become familiar with the relevant issues and purposes that direct the host of programs school systems offer.

What can be observed, touched, experienced, and collected for examination become the artifacts of the school program. These artifacts provide the operational picture of schooling and educational practices as they are perceived or experienced by learners, teachers, and other school specialists. Various kinds of administrative and space orientations promote different kinds of learning environments. The knowledge of how these different orientations affect school programs is important for new teachers to acquire. This knowledge is vital if new teachers wish to take part in creating quality learning environments for the pupils they encounter.

The key to the success of a well-designed curriculum is the way in which it is delivered to the learner. A good repertoire of instructional practices is a must for the successful teacher. Organizations, artifacts, and practices constitute the collage of the school's program; where does the teacher fit in this picture? To help create and provide educational programs, teachers are charged on the one hand with preserving American traditions and on the other with initiating social changes required by society. What does this mean for the future of educational programs? Teachers, as the mainstay of the school's curriculum, must use all their professional skills to develop teaching materials, lesson plans, evaluation devices, and a humanistic learning environment so that students will react positively to the educational program. Today's school programs are preparing youth for the twenty-first century.

Organization of the Curriculum

Focus Questions

- Why do beginning teachers need to be knowledgeable about issues that affect curriculum development?
- Why should daily lesson plans or unit plans reflect the goals and aims of a school district?
- What key questions should the teacher address before determining subject- or student-centered curricular offerings?

- Why should teachers continue to stress general education throughout the K–12 school program?
- Why should teachers be able to plan school programs that address differences among learners?

Key Terms and Concepts

Back to basics
Survival skills
Competency testing
Accountability
Reproduction
Readjustment
Reconstruction
Subject-centered curriculum

Fused curriculum
Student-centered curriculum
Core curriculum
Activity curriculum
General education
Exploratory education
Personal education
Carnegie unit

What Would You Do?

As a beginning teacher, you have been asked by your principal to join a curriculum development council that oversees the program for the school district. The council is currently engaged in the beginning efforts of a five-year long-range planning effort. During your attendance at the first meeting you are somewhat shocked to hear a growing consensus among council members that the district should abandon the current diversity in programs and institute a "no frills" basics approach with high-level minimum standards for all learners. You judge that there does not seem to be a genuine concern for differences among learners. The chairperson of the council asks you to chair a subcommittee that will prepare a draft of a basic document to be used to guide all curricular decisions for the district. Your beliefs are in conflict with those of your colleagues, but you feel obligated to accept the responsibility. How do you prepare for the first meeting with your subcommittee?

Issues for the Curriculum

Beginning teachers are expected to be knowledgeable about the critical issues associated with curriculum change and program planning. The basic purpose here is to alert the new teacher to some of these issues and the need to address them when contemplating program changes. The list is not exhaustive but is representative of the issues examined by numerous commissions, study groups, and polls by national groups.

Basic Survival Skills

60   The back-to-basics movement of the 1970s has continued to receive national attention in the 1980s. Rather than focusing on just the three Rs, however, skill development encompasses the learner as a whole person. Needed survival skills include literacy in reading, writing, speaking, computation, and computers. Other skills needed for survival are academic preparation for a career; ability to think independently, logically, and critically; respect for others; responsible self-behavior; assessment and evaluation of problems and alternatives; job placement and security; and good citizenship practice. This list of skills is by no means new but reaffirms the voluminous lists of needed learner skills that can be traced back to the Seven Cardinal Principles. What is different at this point in time is that the public has become more demanding in its expectations that these skills be developed by the schools. As elementary and secondary teachers prepare curriculum revisions and course materials, they must address the need to provide a school program that attends to basic survival skills.

Achievement Performance

National scores on the Scholastic Aptitude Test (SAT) have dropped dramatically over the past 20 years. In 1983, for the first time since the decline began, scores appeared to be leveling off somewhat, but the criticism has remained. By most measures of verbal and analytical ability, virtually every graduating class has appeared to be less able than the class before it. Some generally reported reasons for the decline include a relaxation of standards, "watered down" secondary programs used to satisfy student unrest during the 1960s and 1970s, a more diverse body of students taking the tests, poorly trained teachers with weak academic preparation, and so on. Some or all of these reasons have probably contributed to the decline. Rather than continue the debate over the causes or search for scapegoats,

64

however, the schools need to accept the reported data and take positive steps toward reversing the trend. A significant side effect to this decline has been the rise in private school enrollments. In addition, declining public school enrollments, because of lower birth rates, and increased taxpayer pressures on financing of public education have helped to create a monumental task for school program reform.

As achievement scores declined during the past two decades, grade performances in school improved. The grade inflation problem has spread from the elementary school through to the colleges and universities. Furthermore, many studies have indicated that the standardized achievement performance of U.S. students does not compare favorably with that of students in many foreign countries. Unfortunately, we may have "apple and orange" comparisons here because of the differences in students who take the tests, but the criticism remains. It is clear that as teachers revise their curricula, they need to reexamine their expectations of student performance for all kinds of students. A common expectation for all students will not address the vast differences found in any student body. These differences will always be present if the United States continues to foster mass education and equal opportunity for all. Whereas survival skills are needed by all students, higher levels of verbal and quantitative performance may be achieved only by a smaller segment of the school population. The implication for curriculum workers is that program and instruction need to become more individualized.

Competency Testing

Declining test scores, alarming rates of illiteracy among high school graduates, and demands for greater accountability for teachers all have spurred the competency testing movement. A very significant curriculum issue exists for competency testing, however. That issue is: Should the tests dictate the curriculum or should the curriculum dictate the tests? If the tests are to dictate the curriculum, then curriculum revision is more focused because the test content determines just what will be taught. On the other hand, if the curriculum dictates the tests, then local, state, and national goals need to be more narrowly defined around a general set of expected learner competencies. These goals were discussed in Part IV of this text. In either case it is a delicate issue for the curriculum. A related issue associated with competency testing is the establishment of minimal competencies. The minimal competency testing question suggests that if all learners are to be held accountable for some minimal competency performance, that performance will have to be very minimal for all learners to have any chance of meeting it.

The curriculum issue for competency testing seems clear. Goals, materials, and instructions must be common to all and endorsed uniformly by the teaching staffs. This suggests that textbooks and other materials must be prepared for the tests and periodic assessments must be made to determine progress toward the expected graduation competency. How and to what degree the teacher works in curriculum development and revision becomes wholly dependent upon the competency testing movement.

Discipline/Management

The Gallup Poll of 1983 supported the ten-year national concern over classroom discipline. Before examining this issue for effects on curriculum, the modern-day learner has to be examined. Some of the current characteristics of youth have made it extremely difficult to return, as many would like, to the disciplinary methods used in the schools 40 or more years ago. For example, youth today have greater responsibility and rights for making their own decisions. Learners do not experience the connection between today's school performance and tomorrow's reward. The future is too uncertain. Modern families are not as close as they used to be; many parents are single; and young people look to their own culture for norms rather than to the adult culture. There is greater financial dependency on parents among all youth today because of changes in our economy and technology. For increasing numbers of youth there is a cultural, political, and economic apathy. The society as they see it is not as they study it.

Teachers working in curriculum development need to explore the implications of whatever they revise or create in light of the learners who will encounter it. Classroom discipline or management cannot be improved qualitatively through fear of reprisal. The educational program must have utilitarian and affective meaning for all learners. It should not try to counter or thwart the culture of youth but find ways to utilize the youth culture meaningfully in the teaching-learning situation.

Materials Selection

All previously mentioned issues affecting the curriculum influence materials selection. Material use can be broad or narrow, depending upon the definition of basic survival skills, expected level of student achievement performances, types of testing programs and their purposes, and expectations for student personal performance and behavior in the classroom. Materials can be teacher-made or commercially prepared by companies. If materials are made or adapted by the teacher, the planned curriculum tends to direct material selection. If they are made by learning companies for exclusive use by the teachers, then the materials direct the curriculum. As was indicated earlier, the curriculum may be directed by textbooks or standardized tests for all to use. The authors of this text assert that teachers should develop and select materials if they are to provide specifically for the needs of their students.

Materials should encourage learning, not provide a substitute for it.

A key issue in curriculum development is how the curriculum is organized. Teachers need to familiarize themselves with the differences among purposes and aims of education, subject- and student-centered structures, and program requirements. Why and how new experiences are incorporated into school programing are vital questions for teachers if they want to create learning opportunities for their students. All teachers need to be aware of curriculum development—to know how to recognize and discard the poor and to adopt the good so that learners may profit.

Purposes and Aims of Education

The traditional purpose of education, which can be traced to the ancient liberal arts, stresses a selected set of learning skills and a vast store of selected information for students. Traditionalists assume that students who acquire the necessary skills and facts are "educated" and thus will behave intelligently as adults. Students are not expected or directed to use their native intelligence creatively; they are to learn passively and store knowledge for future use. Learning is the same for all; knowledge that was relevant yesterday remains so today.

The contrasting purpose of education, stressing active student involvement in learning, evolved from the work of John Dewey and his associates after 1900. This position, referred to as progressivism, has not been universally accepted in practice. It is, however, still examined and studied as a "school of thought," and as a theory it has enjoyed considerable acceptance. Ideally, progressivism, expressed vividly as "expected learner behavior," calls for students to exercise their intelligence during learning and to use their experience as a means to new learning. Intelligent adult behavior is not mystically granted at some accepted level of maturity but is acquired en route. Learning is relevant; learning is life; students learn best by participating in learning.

Curricular Role

Curriculum planners, in formulating what the school has to do, frequently find that planning is easy but realization is not. National, regional, and state commissions have all expressed their thoughts about what education should be. The school may see its job as reproduction, readjustment, or reconstruction—or a combination. In Part II we related these tasks to the school as a social institution; we examine them here as they relate to the philosophic concepts that prescribe the school and curriculum.

61

Reproduction

If the school elects merely to reproduce, then its task is to transmit simply and unquestioningly our nation's cultural heritage to its youth. Subject matter selected should be what has survived through the ages. If the school is to fulfill only the reproductive function, the teacher must consider whether the subject matter has withstood the test of time and therefore should be included in the curriculum, or whether irrelevant material may have survived along with the relevant. The teacher must also decide whether or not the relevant subject matter of yesterday is enough for today's youth. The problems associated with making this kind of decision are increased by the vast and continually growing amount of knowledge. In addition to the old knowledge that must be passed on, there is new knowledge that continues to press for its rightful place in the curriculum. How does a teacher cull the curriculum to make room for new knowledge when the school is committed to reproduction? It is obvious that a curriculum designed solely to pass on the cultural heritage is fundamentally inadequate in an age when society is constantly confronted with social change.

Readjustment

Sole attention to readjustment calls for the school to gear its curriculum to social usefulness and efficiency. A curriculum for readjustment is concerned with preparing students for present-day adult life; it stresses civic training and social responsibility. Readjustment demands that the school retain parts of the past and also suggests that the school must do a certain amount of "readjusting" to meet current needs. Concentrating purely on this function may ignore some of the principles of child development and currently accepted psychology of learning. The child's need to understand and direct personal actions, the child's need to be able to adapt and organize in the light of prior experience, and the critical need for individual attention may be neglected when the social utility theme is forced on the school. Readjustment, it if is the sole role of the school, tends to prohibit personal behavior changes necessary for adult life.

Reconstruction

The school that adopts the educational role of reconstruction favors a curriculum that moves to the forefront of current thought and practice in society—and strives to change the status quo. The school then undertakes not only to prepare young people for the future, but also to prepare the future for young people. A persistent advocate of the reconstruction role for American schools, George S. Counts, offered this challenge to education in 1932 when he introduced his controversial proposal: Dare the school build a new social order? To date, society has not completely accepted this challenge. In designing the curriculum the teacher must be aware of the pitfalls of this extreme approach and the hidden danger that past and current interests, traditions, and values may be sacrificed for the sake of change.

It is readily apparent that to overemphasize any one of the three roles for schooling—reproduction, readjustment, or reconstruction—would produce a top-heavy operational and philosophical concept inconsistent with the eclecticism needed. So that students will have the best opportunity to become self-supporting, self-respecting, and self-directing participants in American and world society, the three functions must be constantly blended.

We see blending as:

1. A systematic evaluation and reconstruction of the content of the discipline for instruction. The heritage to be preserved should be evaluated, and content considered necessary for existence in the future should be selected.
2. A reorganization of materials for instruction. This should produce not only knowledge of a variety of subjects but also a sense of direction in creating desirable attitudes and appreciations.

Schools are continually trying to adapt to the needs of various types of learners.

3. A plan for meeting the needs not only of the gifted and slow learners but of other learners as well. The average child and the mentally, emotionally, or physically handicapped learner are all too often neglected.

4. A plan for encouraging accelerated levels of personal aspiration. It is just as important to achieve excellence in the quality of personal and social life for all as it is to achieve excellence in space travel, computers, and gross national product.

Aims and Goals

Curriculum workers, in planning and stating aims and objectives of American education, must recognize at least five kinds of students who have to be accommodated:

1. Terminal—students who for various reasons drop out along the way and have to be absorbed by society. Current estimates show

the national dropout rate to be 25–30 percent, with 60 percent not uncommon in large urban areas.

2. College-bound—students preparing for higher education. Nationally, approximately 50 percent of high school graduates pursue study beyond high school. This figure is misleading, however, in that it does not account for those students who have dropped out before graduating from high school. In addition, the preparatory program for the 50 percent must be varied because of the range of post–high school educational desires and opportunities. The number of students in college has been dropping during the 1980s because of the impact of population control. The number may be reduced even further as young people find an increasingly lower correlation between college education and job placement.

3. Vocational-bound—students who are primarily preparing for jobs while in a comprehensive or vocational/technical high school. Some of these students, however, may further their education later on, on a formal or informal basis. Although the percentage of students who fall into this category varies by the criterion used, it appears to be on the increase. Data on job placement for college-trained students suggest a job shortage, whereas data for vocational/technical education suggest a much healthier job market.

4. Destination unknown—the so-called "late bloomers" or "latent students." These students have native ability but do not realize an expected level of achievement during high school.

5. Special—students who are identified as emotionally, mentally, or physically handicapped. Court decisions of the 1970s ordered that many special students be included as regular school students and accommodated by the regular curriculum. As explained earlier in the discussion of Public Law 94-142, this federal law now mandates a "least restrictive environment" for learning for exceptional children. Many of them are now being mainstreamed into the regular curriculum.

The best analysis of what currently exists as the average school curriculum suggests that the needs of the college-bound students continue to receive primary attention. If this were not the case, the national dropout rate—and especially the rate for urban areas—would probably not be so alarmingly high. Curriculum development should proceed from some special diagnostic attempts to identify the various kinds of students the curriculum is intended to serve.

As one tries to analyze aims and objectives, one must distinguish between the two as they relate to a total school program. Aims for curriculum development are considered to be the broad goals for the system as a whole. They are usually formulated by national groups who try to cater to the needs of our pluralistic society. On the other hand, objectives mean the expected learner behaviors that the curriculum is intended to produce. The history of purposes and aims was presented in Part IV of the text.

Curriculum Structure

Any school system can choose its own pattern of curriculum organization. These patterns tend to range between a subject-centered and a student-centered organization. Between the two extremes, subject-centered and student-centered, a continuum of curricular organization exists, and schools use various elements from either extreme or both. In general, curricular organization that tends to be subject centered is content oriented; if it uses a student-centered pattern, it is learner oriented.

By analyzing the curriculum continuum we can categorize those patterns that offer separate courses for the various academic disciplines and those that fuse the disciplines under the broad heading, "subject-centered patterns of curriculum organization." Correlated programs and activity programs are classified as student-centered patterns. You will recognize that often the patterns of curricular organizations used by various schools tend to be eclectic, borrowing from many sources. How a school district organizes its curriculum is related strongly to its philosophical position on the purpose of education.

Subject-centered Curriculum

The subject-centered curriculum is the oldest form and still the most widely used in schools in the United States. Its history can be traced to the liberal arts of the ancient world. The ancient trivium was composed of grammar, rhetoric, and logic; the quadrivium included arithmetic, geometry, astronomy, and music. In time, the trivium came to include history and literature, and the quadrivium expanded to include algebra, trigonometry, geography, botany, zoology, physics, and chemistry.

In the modern subject-centered curriculum, all the subjects for instruction are separated. In the extreme use of this approach, the disciplines of knowledge are taught in isolation and with no attempt at integration. The intent is to provide a discipline for students that alerts them to set classifications and to recognize arrangements of facts and ideas. An important criterion in selecting ideas for study is to choose those that have proved beneficial for solving problems of investigation in research. These are the facts and ideas that have lasted over time.

This curriculum calls for extensive explanation and oral discourse. The subject-centered curriculum uses formal step-by-step study of ideas and facts; rarely are students expected or encouraged to explore or experiment on their own. The teaching methods include extensive verbal activities—lectures, discussions, questions and answers, and written exercises such as term papers.

Often the curriculum is criticized for failure to develop critical or creative thinking. Those who decry this approach suggest that instruction is focused on absorption and memorization of the presented facts and ideas.

The subject-centered curriculum outlines in advance all the subjects everyone must take. The constant subjects (general education) usually make up most of the program, and students are not given much choice in selecting courses. Some authorities say that this curriculum alleviates the tracking system because it provides elective learning for students in various tracks. The rigid track tends to make the elective program required and constant. Within the subject-centered curriculum, however, there is some provision for individual interests and abilities. A few electives are provided for the students, and the teacher can also adjust for differences among students within the required core of subjects. This adjustment may be achieved either by ability grouping within the subject or by various special assignments designed for the many ability levels the teacher must accommodate.

The elementary teacher operating within a subject-centered curriculum may group students by subject within the self-contained classroom to provide for individual differences. A fair criticism of the subject-centered curriculum is that it tends to neglect individual differences and to establish common hurdles for all students.

One of the persistent problems with the subject-centered curriculum has been its failure to attend to recognizing and understanding current social problems. Educators tend to focus on the past rather than on the present and the future. For instance, students studying American history are not likely to study thoroughly anything beyond the Vietnam conflict, and yet most were born after that period and many are children of Vietnamese parents. Also, they may be studying and memorizing facts that probably could be stored and retrieved for better use by a computer. Although Alfred N. Whitehead made the following statement in 1929, his summation is appropriate today.

> There is only one subject-matter for education, and that is Life in all its manifestations. Instead of this single unity, we offer children—Algebra, from which nothing follows; Geometry, from which nothing follows; a couple of languages, never mastered, and lastly, most dreary of all, literature, represented by plays of Shakespeare, with philological notes and short analyses of plot and character to be in substance committed to memory. Can such a list be said to represent Life, as it is known in the midst of the living of it? The best that can be said of it is, that it is a rapid table of contents which a deity might run over in his mind while he was thinking of creating a world, and had not yet determined how to put it together.[1]

The world in which students now live and face the future is very different from the world of the past. In the teaching of literature in a subject-centered curriculum, modern writings are often neglected, as is the literature of cultures other than our own. Principles of current economics and government also seem to escape this type of curriculum, and students are passed into the adult society with little or no knowledge or appreciation of these important fields.

Those who support and defend the subject-centered curriculum argue that subjects that have withstood the test of time are the most worthy. They also argue that just because some children do not learn well in such a curriculum, it does not imply any inherent weakness in the curriculum organization. Among the many supporters of this type of curriculum are Arthur Bestor, William Bagley, James Koerner, Clifton Fadiman, and Hyman Rickover. Admiral Rickover, in his studies of American and European education, concluded that the principal task of the school is to develop the intellect of its students. When he testified before several House of Representatives committees, he elaborated on three tasks he thought the schools should accomplish. In the hearings of the Eighty-seventh Congress, he stated that the school should (1) pass on to the pupil a significant body of knowledge, (2) develop within the pupil the skill to use this knowledge intelligently in solving problems to be met during adult life, and (3) instill within the student the habit of assessing critical issues on the basis of fact and logical thinking.

Advocates of the subject-centered curriculum point out that everything cannot be studied at once, nor can any study be all-inclusive. With the rapid increase in knowledge, there simply has to be an ordered, segmented approach to study a subject effectively. The separated subjects therefore are just a convenient way to clarify all this knowledge so that it can be comprehended by students. It seems evident that the subject-centered approach to curriculum is not totally unworthy. Despite many attempts at curricular reform, the subject-centered curriculum has remained one of the most widely used curricular designs. Those who defend it point out that the subject-centered curriculum will not adequately prepare young people for the adult world they must live in.

Fused Curriculum

The fused curriculum has come about in an attempt to decrease the number of separate subjects that has been gradually brought into the subject-centered curriculum. In place of separate and isolated classes in reading, writing, spelling, grammar, speech, and literature, for example, the fused curriculum combines these subjects under English or language arts. The subject-centered curriculum remains almost intact, but students are introduced to the field as a whole rather than to bits and pieces. Subject matter goals are left whole, but the fused approach provides teachers and students more latitude within a broad subject area. The fused social studies course encompasses history, geography, economics, political science, sociology, and anthropology. Fused science programs combine botany, zoology, and geology. Mathematics fuses arithmetic, geometry, and algebra. Fusion can also take place in physical education, home economics, industrial arts, art, and music.

As an illustration of how fusion operates within the language arts, students may begin their study with a typical reading assignment. The teacher uses this basic assignment to explore principles of writing, discussion, vocabulary, and speech. The process may be reversed or arranged in any order, but the principle remains the same. Fusion tries to interrelate a core of subjects. This process is frequently called "integration of subject matter." The teacher of social studies may use an historical event to introduce principles of economics and civics. At the same time the teacher may focus attention on the geographical, sociological, and political implications of this particular historical event.

The fused, or broad-field, curriculum has enjoyed its greatest success at the elementary level. Separate subjects, once each taught for short periods during the day, are now more apt to be taught in a fused fashion over longer periods. Common fused studies in the elementary school center around language arts, social studies, general science, mathematics, art, music, and physical education and health.

In the past, junior high schools developed several variations on the fused program. Some schools combined language arts and social studies with block scheduling, thus providing a longer period for teaching these two groups of subjects. However, in recent years the movement of subject matter to lower grades has caused junior high schools to adopt the predominantly subject-centered pattern of the senior high school.

In the senior high school the fused curriculum has had relatively little success. Examples of the few high school courses that are so patterned are general science, problems of democracy in the social studies, and family living. The greatest effect the fused curriculum has had on the senior high school is probably the integration of unified areas into subject-centered courses. Many high school teachers of American history now try to interlace a certain amount of geography and political science into their history courses. Those who favor the fused curriculum offer the following advantages:

- Subject matter may be integrated more readily.
- This approach establishes a logical and useful organization for presenting knowledge.
- Students can learn with understanding and appreciation.
- Basic principles and generalizations necessary for critical thinking are emphasized more than isolated facts.

In reality, the fused curriculum has many of the advantages and disadvantages of the subject-centered curriculum. Some of the criticisms against the fused curriculum are that (1) compression of several courses into one does not guarantee integration; (2) fusion tends to result in a sketchy knowledge and a "watering down" of specific disciplines; and (3) with the emphasis on generalization rather than specifics, learning tends to be too abstract.

With a fused curriculum, students may learn with greater understanding and appreciation, but may have less specific subject knowledge.

Student-centered Curriculum

The concern for students' needs and interests has produced the student-centered curriculum. In the past, and also now to some extent, these needs have had both social and psychological interpretations. It appears that the needs of youth today are held to be what society expects of maturing young adults. Whereas in an extreme interpretation the subject-centered curriculum stresses that learning is most effective if it is rigorous and difficult, the student-centered curriculum emphasizes encouraging students' interest in learning and their appreciation for it. When the interests and needs of learners are incorporated in the curriculum, motivation tends to become intrinsic rather than extrinsic. This does not imply that the student-centered curriculum is directed by the whims of the learner but rather that learning is more successfully achieved if it is built upon the interests the learner has developed before formal learning begins. As you read about core and activity programs, compare and contrast the student-centered curriculum with the subject-centered curriculum.

Core Curriculum

The core curriculum grew out of a general dissatisfaction with the piecemeal learning promoted by the subject-centered curriculum. Proponents of the core curriculum, in trying to offer students a more enriching education, believe that subjects should be unified and new methods adopted. Since society has become increasingly fragmented, with more emphasis on science and technology, proponents feel that the only logical approach to developing social values and social vision is through a core organization. The core curriculum may have different degrees of organization and may cross broader subject lines; it places even greater stress than the fused curriculum does on the need to integrate subject matter.

The core curriculum stresses social values, and much time is given to studying the culture and its moral content. This curriculum propounds problems for solving as a learning method; within this approach, facts, descriptive principles, socioeconomic conditions, and moral rules of conduct and behavior are stressed. In its purest form the core is basically "normative" in its presentation to students. By normative we mean that concern centers around topics like "What are the social needs of today?"

A typical application of the core curriculum would be a study of the persistent themes of social living. The subject matter is not an isolated block of content; it is used to define and solve problems common to many or all students; however, student interest is not the sole criterion for selecting and organizing activities. Group processes and dynamics become the center of planned activity, and often the community becomes a resource for study.

Another special and distinguishing characteristic of the core program is the way in which students and teacher cooperate in planning learning activities. This joint planning is concerned with the "how" and the "what" to study. All students, regardless of their individual abilities, concentrate on the areas of learning that are essential to all members of society. All do not have to learn the same thing with the same degree of proficiency, but all are exposed to the common problems, and each is allowed to visualize himself or herself accepting or rejecting a particular vocation within society.

There is maximum provision in the core program for special needs and interests as they arise. Since one feature of the core curriculum is a longer block of instructional time, the classroom program is flexible and includes remedial, developmental, and accelerated activities as they fit into the study at hand. There is ample time for much-needed guidance and counseling, both individual and group. Skills are taught as needed to solve problems, and these problems are used to increase student motivation. Although it has declined in popular use, the core program still tends to be found most often in the junior high school.

A core program demands many special considerations if it is to be reasonably successful. The foremost consideration is the teacher. Core teachers need, besides a broad preparation in the liberal arts, a keen understanding of social foundations, of child and adolescent psychology, of the structure and dynamics of group processes, of guidance, and of the problem approach to learning. The lack of adequately prepared teachers has hindered the growth and acceptance of the core curriculum. Classrooms and buildings must be large and flexible to provide for group activities, and an abundance of supplementary teaching materials is essential. Schedules must include large, flexible time blocks. Also, flexible grouping of students by age and grade is necessary. Last but not least, an effective public relations program for parents and the community is vital if the core curriculum is to be understood and accepted.

Activity Curriculum

At the extreme right of a curriculum continuum is the activity curriculum (Figure 17.1). In its purest form it operates with the child as the sole center of learning. Since education is life and life is ever-changing, the activity

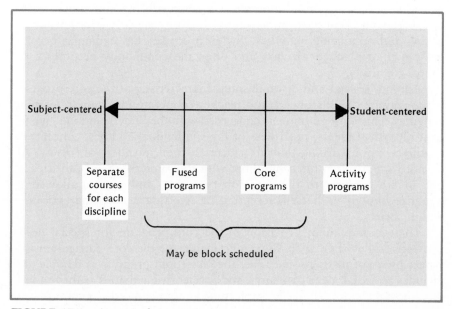

FIGURE 17.1 *A curriculum continuum.*

curriculum expects to change continually. Students' needs and interests are assessed, and the curriculum is built on that basis. The psychology of learning in this approach is based on the emotional involvement of the learner. If a child develops an interest in something and becomes emotionally involved with it, learning is enhanced according to the proponents of the activity curriculum. This curriculum, never fixed, completely crosses subject matter lines. Completely flexible, the activity for the early learner may center on such topics as pets, toys, boats, letter carriers, or police officers. Emphasis is placed on observation, play, stories, and handiwork.

The activity curriculum has not been as acceptable to the public as the subject-centered curriculum. When used, it has been most successful at the elementary level. Although it has never secured a foothold in the secondary school, the activity curriculum has had some influence on the high school program. The lack of full acceptance in the high school may be due partly to the subject orientation that secondary teachers and administrators have had. Also, the public seems to prefer the traditional organization and methodology of the subject-centered high school.

The activity curriculum has several characteristics different from all other curricular patterns. First, the interests and purposes of children determine the educational program. Second, common learning (general education) comes about as a result of individual interest. Third, this curriculum is not planned in advance, but guidelines are established to help the students choose alternatives intelligently as they progress through the program. Activities are planned cooperatively by students and teachers, and what they plan and pursue may or may not have any deliberate social direction. In the pursuit of planned goals, solving problems becomes the principal teaching method. Little or no need for extracurricular activities develops because all interests are accommodated within the regular program.

The teacher, in preparing to teach in the activity curriculum, needs all the prerequisites of the core teacher and even more. Because the activity curriculum is flexible, the need for variety in space and scheduling arrangements is paramount. Schedules using large blocks of time are necessary to afford the program its maximum potential.

Curriculum Contrasts

The subject-centered curriculum and the student-centered curriculum represent the two extremes of a curriculum continuum. The two curricula are contrasted in the following list adapted from Hopkins.[2]

Subject-centered Curriculum
1. Centered on subjects
2. Emphasis on subject matter

Student-centered Curriculum
1. Centered on learners
2. Emphasis on promoting all-around growth of learners

Subject-centered Curriculum	Student-centered Curriculum
3. Subject matter selected and organized before it is taught	3. Subject matter selected and organized cooperatively by learners during learning
4. Controlled by the teacher or someone representing authority external to the learning situation	4. Controlled and directed cooperatively by learners (pupils, teachers, parents, supervisors, principals, and others) in the learning situation
5. Emphasis on facts, information, knowledge for its own sake or for possible future use	5. Emphasis on meanings immediate to improving living
6. Emphasis on specific habits and skills as separate aspects of learning	6. Emphasis on habits and skills as integral parts of larger experiences
7. Emphasis on improving methods of teaching specific subject matter	7. Emphasis on understanding and improving through the process of learning
8. Emphasis on uniformity of exposure to learning and uniformity of learning results	8. Emphasis on variability in exposure to learning and in results expected
9. Education conforming to set patterns	9. Education aiding each child to build a socially creative individuality
10. Education considered schooling	10. Education considered a continuous intelligent process of growth

Program Requirements

Embedded in the operating program of the school are three broad academic components that constitute the function of the educational program—general education, exploratory education, and personal education. Their placement and emphasis depend wholly on the learner's needs as they relate to growth and development, the psychology of learning, instructional strategies, and various administrative arrangements.

General Education

General education is the broad area of the school program that is primarily concerned with developing common learning. Its central purpose is helping students become participating citizens and well-adjusted individuals. Although general education is concentrated mostly in the elementary school, some elements of it persist throughout the entire period of formal education. Although the other two broad areas of the school program, exploratory and personal education, contain general education outcomes, they are not organized primarily for that purpose.

The general education program concentrates on developing basic skills and introduces students to basic studies that include reading, composition, listening, speaking, and computing. Learners are expected to acquire creative and disciplined thinking skills that include different methods of inquiry and applying knowledge. General education also encompasses the humanities—an appreciation for literature, music, and the visual arts— and the social and natural sciences. Within a general education program, learners are expected to acquire the essential, adult basic performance skills needed to function successfully in society. How all this general education is accomplished varies among school districts. The identified components of common learning provide the core of general education in the elementary school and are improved and developed further throughout the total formal program of education. Figure 17.2 illustrates the general education emphasis for the formal N–12 structure.

One of the most perplexing problems facing general education planners is maintaining the placement sequence in the total scheme of education. As we have seen recently, the number of years of schooling devoted to general education is determined by changing economic factors and by society's concern with efficiency and productivity. Those who demand accountability from today's schools have joined those who call for more general education. In the very recent past the need for specialization caused a slackening of interest in general education and increased emphasis on

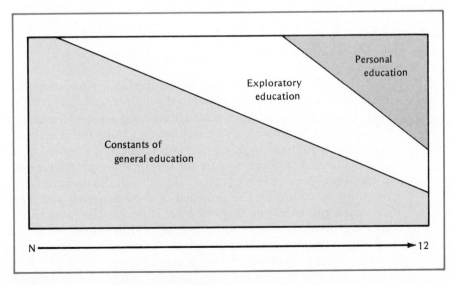

FIGURE 17.2 *Educational emphases in the N–12 program.*

specialized studies and the applied fields. It is evident that the decade of the 1980s will show more attention to the pressure for accountability in general education.

Pressures on General Education

During the 1960s and 1970s, increasing pressures caused some subjects to be presented earlier in the curriculum. Advanced skills and some special training, previously reserved for the secondary school, were introduced into the elementary school. It has become regular practice to introduce at early levels the formal teaching of foreign language, principles of economics, drug and sex education, advanced principles of mathematics, and introductory programs of vocational career choices. Although there are justifiable reasons for doing this, they do not change the nature and purpose of common learning in the elementary program. Because of this expanded common learning for younger students, educators must reassess the general education program. This may require a new definition of common learning. As preschool and early childhood education receive increased philosophical and financial support, the general education program, identified as common learning for all, should be redistributed over a broader continuum, nursery school through grade 14.

Exploratory Education

The exploratory education program is designed primarily for an organization of education unique to America—the junior high school. Depending on school district organization, the junior high—or intermediate—school continues general education and introduces students, on a limited basis, to a variety of specialized subjects. There are many reasons why the junior high school exists:

1. Junior high school provides a transitional period, easing students' transfer from the elementary school to the high school. Junior high school is designed for students who are entering early adolescence, a trying period of growth and development. Since the transition period from childhood to adulthood is so critical, the junior high school is planned to accommodate the special physical, emotional, and social problems of this age group. In general, the students have come from an administrative unit that is child centered, and they are preparing to enter one that is subject centered. The junior high school has been planned to foster a gradual development of independence in learning and self-discipline. To provide students with a "home base," block scheduling is sometimes used for the language arts–social studies program, and the teacher for this block

has a better chance to know and help the students. Junior high school students also take several courses taught by specialists; in this way they are gradually introduced to the departmentalized, more subject-centered senior high school (see Table 17.1).

2. The junior high school allows for the exploration of interest, aptitudes, and abilities, thus aiding the students in vocational and educational planning. The program introduces, in concentrated periods, such subjects as art, music, home economics, vocational education, and speech. The intention is that as the students progress toward senior high school, they will explore subjects they may specialize in later. These exploratory programs may last nine weeks or one semester and are offered on a rotating basis.

3. Junior high school students are introduced to an elaborate program of guidance and counseling that continues through senior high school. This program is intended to help students plan intelligently for adult life. By using specially trained guidance personnel, the junior high school emphasizes the development of wholesome attitudes for mental, emotional, and social growth among the student body.

4. Providing for variety in junior high helps to lower the school dropout rate. Variable programing considers the differing special abilities of youth, and its rationale stresses the important effects of the students' socioeconomic background on their interests, aptitudes, needs, and personality development.

5. Articulation of the total twelve-year school program may be stimulated by the junior high school. This administrative unit has the advantage of examining the elementary program and planning for articulation with the senior high school. Articulation is successful when all the teachers within the school system work together to understand and appreciate the special tasks each must perform.

Like the elementary school, the junior high school has had to find ways to accommodate to the continuing movement toward an earlier exposure to subjects. There is little doubt that the pressure of content requirements from the senior high school and the accompanying problems associated with Carnegie units of credits have caused the junior high school to become "a senior high school in short pants."

To return to the initial philosophy that guided the junior high school, many school districts have put the ninth grade back in the senior high school and created a new administrative organization of 5–8, 6–8, or 7–8, labeled the intermediate or middle school. Many of the early intentions of the junior high school continue for the middle school with the exception of the ninth grade. Because of societal changes, improvements in health and nutrition, and more accelerated rates of physical and social maturation, ninth graders are much more like senior high school students today than they were when the original junior high school idea was conceived.

TABLE 17.1 *A Junior High School Exploratory Program*

7th Grade		8th Grade		9th Grade	
Subjects (required)	*Periods per Week*	*Subjects (required)*	*Periods per Week*	*Subjects (required)*	*Periods per Week*
Language Arts ⎱ Social Studies ⎰ (blocked)	10	Language Arts ⎱ Social Studies ⎰ (blocked)	10	Language Arts ⎱ Social Studies ⎰ (blocked)	10
Physical education	3	Physical education	3	Physical education	3
Science	5	Science	5	General science	5
Mathematics	5	Mathematics	5	Electives	17
Practical arts	5	Electives	12		
Band or chorus	5				
Art	2				
		Electives			
Art		General business		Algebra	
Creative writing		General mathematics		Industrial arts	
Drama		Home economics		Mechanical drawing	
Foreign language		Industrial arts		Music	

416

The new middle school is intended to provide for the exploratory learning that the junior high school never quite achieved.

Personal Education

The senior high school assumes the special task of uniting the foundations of general education with the introductions to exploratory education, culminating in a rounded personal education. The senior high school will terminate formal education for many students; it will prepare others for more advanced and specialized education in college or for special post–high school training. Because a large number of high school graduates go on to college, it is tempting to overemphasize the college preparatory program. However, high school should offer programs designed to suit all students. In secondary education, Albert Oliver says that attention should be given to individual choice in establishing various programs. By this he means a "program of study in each area of curriculum specialization—professional, business, industrial, and general." Although students can register in certain programs, they may take subjects in another curriculum. Presumably, each designation refers to special interest education.[3]

As the learner progresses through the educational system, the increased personalized education should encourage an individual's intellectual curiosity and passion for knowledge. It should also provide good habits for a particular kind of inquiry. Personalized education should develop high levels of learning within the cognitive domain.

The high school, in continuing the program for general education (Figure 17.2), has an established core of general courses required for all students. These requirements usually account for seven to nine of the sixteen to twenty Carnegie units required for graduation. The arrangement varies from state to state. Generally included in the general education requirements (by state law) are English—three units; mathematics—one unit; science—one unit; social studies (American history and government)—two units; and physical education (and health history and government)—one unit. One Carnegie unit of credit is awarded for each class that meets for 200 minutes of formal instruction a week for 36 weeks in the school year. The remainder of the units required for graduation are satisfied by the elective programs for specialization and enrichment. The special programs vary in name, sequence, and scope, but the two most usual within the comprehensive senior high school are the tracking program and the constants-variable program (discussed below).

The national concern with the quality of education, as expressed in the many national commission reports, has led to an increase in the required number of general education requirements for graduation. Increasing numbers of states are now requiring four units of English instead of three, two to three units of mathematics instead of one, and two to three units of science instead of one. The mathematics and science emphasis is particularly heavy and comes at a time when the nation's most critical teacher shortage is in those disciplines.

The main difficulty with the Carnegie unit system is that it does not take into account the respected research on student learning. All students do not learn at the same rate; nor do they maintain a constant learning rate during learning. Yet the majority of American secondary schools continue to schedule students in established time modules consistent with the definition of a Carnegie unit, given for time devoted to a particular experience. School systems simply do not apply sound reasoning supported by research when they conclude that all students need 200 minutes a week of varied instruction for 36 weeks to accomplish one Carnegie unit successfully. If learning objectives are clearly specified, some students meet them in less time than others. The criterion for success should not be time or attendance; rather, it should be the successful attainment of the clearly specified learning objectives and minimum requirements. When students meet the objectives, they should be awarded the credit determined for the objectives.

Constants-Variable Program

62

Professional educators have advocated the comprehensive high school for over 30 years but have not yet achieved it. Such a school would provide a secondary program for all learners, whether academic or vocational, and maintain a continuing emphasis on general education for all except the slow or gifted students. Unfortunately, the secondary school is still primarily a preparatory school for postsecondary work, usually emphasizing college preparation.

Figure 17.3 suggests a constants-variable program advocated by the many proponents of the comprehensive senior high school. This kind of program promises more flexibility in career choices for the student and tends to thwart the rigidity that usually accompanies tracking programs. Although the constants-variable program depicted in Figure 17.3 is not all-inclusive, it suggests various elective studies that students can pursue. With more freedom in selecting courses, students may work out individualized programs according to their needs and interests. Some form of flexible scheduling and differentiated staffing to challenge the Carnegie unit system will offer teachers and learners even greater program flexibility.

The basic high school course requirements, more commonly referred to as constants, are required of all students, and many electives become required course work for a particular avenue of learning. Within the constants, however, additional provisions are made to take into account the special needs, interests, and abilities of students; for example, a high school requiring three years of English may allow its students relative freedom in

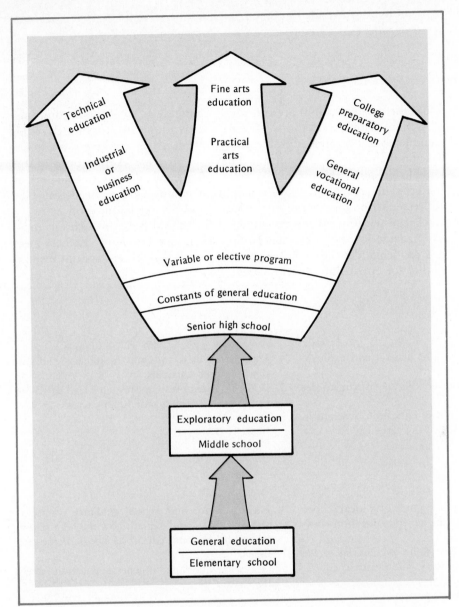

FIGURE 17.3 *The constants-variable program of the comprehensive senior high school.*

meeting this requirement. Other elective programs have, until recent years, provided this flexibility.

However, increased graduation requirements will now tend to restrict the elective flexibility of programs. If the program is too rigidly fixed within the time structure of the school day, then special elective courses may fall by the wayside. Students may no longer be able to select secondary programs that enhance vocational competence and enrichment.

Summary and Implications

Issues for the curriculum are constantly changing as society pulls and tugs the school with expectations. The teacher working in program development needs to be knowledgeable about current issues and how those issues bear on the purposes and aims of the school program. Applications of this knowledge assist the teacher in structuring curriculum with student- or subject-centered emphases. Within this structure, student needs must be addressed through general, exploratory, and personal education.

Faced with increasing demands on the school program, schools must still provide for the individual differences in learners. How teachers meet this challenge depends wholly upon how well they accept special responsibility for curriculum development.

DISCUSSION QUESTIONS

1. Contrast the purposes of general and exploratory education.
2. Why are basic survival skills so difficult to define?
3. How are general aims of education different in the 1980s from those of the early 1900s?
4. Discuss the pros and cons of subject- and student-centered curricula.
5. Will competency testing programs lead to school programs that teach only for the tests?

SUPPLEMENTAL ACTIVITIES

1. Examine the curriculum guide of a local school district and identify the general education component.
2. Study your state's curriculum regulations to see how general, exploratory, and personal educational goals are to be met.
3. Investigate your state's position on competency testing for graduation.
4. Have a senior high school guidance counselor visit your class and explain how the high school meets the personal education needs of the students.
5. Debate the question, "Is general education merely the 'basics'?"

NOTES

1. Alfred N. Whitehead, *The Aims of Education* (New York: New American Library, 1957), pp. 18–19.
2. L. Thomas Hopkins, *Interaction: A Democratic Process* (Boston: D.C. Heath, 1941).
3. Albert I. Oliver, *Curriculum Improvement: A Guide to Problems, Principles, and Process*, 2nd ed. (New York: Harper, 1977), p. 233.

BIBLIOGRAPHY

English, Fenwick W. (ed.) *Fundamental Curriculum Decisions*. 1983 Yearbook. Alexandria, Va.: Association for Supervision and Curriculum Development, 1983.

Hunkins, Francis P. *Curriculum Development: Program Planning and Improvement*. Columbus, Ohio: Charles E. Merrill, 1980.

Tanner, Daniel, and Tanner, Laurel. *Curriculum Development: Theory into Practice*. 2nd ed. New York: Macmillan, 1980.

Artifacts of Schools

Focus Questions

- What are the advantages and disadvantages of a nongraded school?
- Why is it important for teachers to plan together when developing a curriculum?
- What are some of the artifacts that teachers should look for when visiting schools?

- How is an individual teacher's philosophy related to his or her practices in grouping students for instruction?
- When should a teacher use norm-referenced tests with learners and when should he or she use criterion-referenced tests?

Key Terms and Concepts

Artifacts
Graded school
Nongraded school
Articulation
Instructional space utilization
Homogeneous grouping
Heterogeneous grouping
Tracking

Vocational education
Norm-referenced testing
Criterion-referenced testing
Team teaching
Differential staffing
Modular scheduling
Flexible scheduling
Teachers' needs

What Would You Do?

You have been assigned to teach a group of learners who have been grouped homogeneously on the bases of I.Q. and the California Achievement Test. You have not seen the recorded performance of your students on these tests but have been told that the class can be described as average. The curriculum guide that you have been given is very general but does indicate minimum levels of expected competency for all learners before they can move on to a new educational experience the next year. Your students are reasonably astute about the grouping practices in your school, and when you attempt to discuss the year's activities with them, they respond, "We know we're average and we'll do our usual average learning for you." You quickly conclude that you have an affective learning problem with them. What are some steps you could take to ease what might become a difficult and frustrating year for you?

When asked to describe an American school, one needs to create a collage that depicts the organization of space; the materials being used; the observed teacher, learner, and specialist behaviors; the grouping and teaching patterns of learners; the staffing arrangements of teachers; the pieces of written evidence that explain how things occur and what children learn; and so on. This brief list and many other pieces of observable, touchable, and experiential data constitute the artifacts of the school. Such a collage will vary from school district to school district, and various degrees of emphasis on artifacts will be found in any collection of collages. There are, however, general categories of artifacts that are found in all schools. What is different is how these categories are emphasized. This chapter examines the artifacts and discusses their impact on the program of the school.

Graded and Nongraded

The graded school is a borrowed European concept for organizing pupils in some orderly fashion by chronological age. Historically, children in the United States have usually begun formal schooling at age five or six. In almost every state of the nation, that is still true today. There are a few states that mandate age seven as the starting age for compulsory education, but most use age five or six. It became only natural that children starting their first year of formal schooling should be called "first graders." When they returned for a second year of schooling, they were called "second graders." Gradually, requirements and standards were established for each of the formal years of schooling, and the twelve-year graded school emerged. Because of the graded requirements, however, all students do not spend twelve years in graded schools. Those who fail to meet some of the graded requirements along the way must repeat a grade or several grades, and they may spend more than twelve years in school if they wish to receive a secondary school diploma. The diploma, however, indicates twelve years of successful formal education.

Most schools in the United States are graded schools. They provide organization of pupils by ages and have established standards for each grade. There are several weaknesses with this type of school organization. These are:

1. They do not account for the differences in learners as to academic readiness, social, mental, and physical maturity. For example, it does not follow that thirteen-year-old girls and boys, who are vastly different physically, mentally, and emotionally, should be grouped

423

together as seventh or eighth graders in an intermediate school. Girls are much more mature at this age than are boys, yet they are grouped with boys for learning. Additionally, all five- or six-year-olds are not very similar in maturity. Since all children usually start school in September of the year and all have been born during different months of that year, there can be a spread of up to a year in the maturation rates of each new group starting school (though in practice it is usually ten months). Ten or twelve months does not seem like a great difference, but it does account for almost one sixth of a child's life at that stage.

2. They do not account positively for what a learner has learned when the school decides that grade level requirements have not been met and the child is forced to repeat the whole grade the following year. Early failure rates among young learners helps to contribute to school dropout rates later in the graded school. Individual differences in learning rates and achievement are seldom attended to. Although many elementary schools attempt to address this problem, few secondary schools do anything about it.

3. Since most graded schools tend to use group rather than individual expectations for test performance and since so few of the tests that are used meet accepted criteria for good test making, learners who do not meet standards for grade levels are penalized in terms of the assessment of their progress.

The nongraded school, as now defined, involves a school organization that allows each child to progress through the system at an individual rate of development. The lockstep grade level concept, with its set curriculum for each grade, is abandoned in favor of an individual, flexible, and continuous educational program. Sometimes referred to as "continuous progress education," this plan introduces students to a series of stages of development geared to readiness for learning. Students are grouped flexibly according to age, ability, maturity, achievement, and other developmental factors. Within this grouping, students are encouraged to move ahead through each subject at their own speed; their grouping varies with the progress they make.

The nongraded curriculum makes the final move toward complete dissolution of the lockstep graded system. When an elementary school becomes nongraded, the kindergarten and grades 1, 2, 3, and 4 are often simply designated as the primary school. The upper elementary school, grades 5, 6, 7, and 8, becomes a new unit of organization labeled the intermediate or middle school, and the high school discards its strict traditional approach and graded pattern in favor of phases of learning and sequential development.

The nongraded school tries to minimize the shortcomings of the graded system, and the conventional grade designations of the typical American school are consequently discarded. With grade level designations gone, able students can advance at a rate commensurate with ability. Whereas in the graded system it takes five years to teach the formal learning skills expected for grades K–4, children in nongraded schools can complete this learning in four or, in some cases, three years. In addition, in the nongraded school, less able students do not have to experience psychological fear of failure or suffer the minimal learning associated with grade placement. They may take five or more years to master the necessary skills.

Most of the nongrading has appeared at the elementary level, although some high schools have attempted it. If nongrading were applied to all formal education, the curriculum could be divided into four parts—primary education, intermediate education, secondary education, and higher education. All these separate groups could be nongraded and could provide a continuous education organized around the individual progress of pupils.

Much of the adverse criticism of the nongraded school has come about because there is little or no empirical evidence showing its value over the graded school. If the nongraded school is to become popular, controlled studies must prove its worth. There are other problems with the nongraded school. One of these is associated with the growth and development of the learner. Some learners may be able to advance rapidly academically but need to be housed with learners of like social and physical development. One method of handling this problem is to establish transition-type learning environments in which the social, physical, and emotional development of more able learners can be addressed. Another problem is associated with the track-type programs of the high school. High school students tend to group themselves because of vocational direction, and learning experiences become rigidly sequenced within tracks. However, high schools could establish "schools-within-a-school" and thereby establish nongrading within tracks.

Critics of the nongraded school suggest that most of the desirable features of this type of program can be realized in the graded school. It seems fair to conclude that this eventuality would merely superimpose a nongraded organization onto the existing pattern. If the theory were then truly practiced, grade level designations would tend to disappear.

Teachers examining the artifacts of school organization should look for evidences of articulation, or interrelation, of the educational program. The most common cause of poor articulation is a lack of cooperative planning among teachers of the various academic disciplines. Too often, teachers tend to teach their own subject with little concern for what is taking place in other subjects in the same grade. Then teachers often complain that there is little if any horizontal transfer of learning. A closer examination of this problem points to a lack of cooperation among teachers. Usually, ninth-grade social studies teachers feel little obligation to correct a student's careless English in the social studies classroom. In class the social sciences are emphasized, and it is easy to ignore English. The same lack of horizontal articulation occurs between the mathematics teacher and the science teacher. The science teacher focuses on scientific inquiry and tends to slight mathematical exactness.

Just as important as horizontal articulation among subjects is articulation within each subject. In many large schools where several teachers teach the same subject at the same level, they do not try to articulate their presentations. Course guides and outlines, which theoretically could greatly improve the articulation within courses, do not even exist in many schools. Teachers tend to teach and emphasize what they want. With little or no supervision, they tend to go their own separate ways under the cloak of academic freedom. This same lack of articulation exists in large elementary schools among self-contained classrooms. Rarely do elementary teachers confer adequately with one another to correlate the educational program. Probably, any constructive move toward horizontal articulation should begin within the narrower confines of the subjects themselves before crossing subject lines for complete articulation.

Continuity within the school's curriculum refers to vertical articulation. In addition to horizontal articulation, the teacher must be concerned with the interrelation of all grade levels of the school program to provide students with continuous learning. Albert Oliver has suggested the following as a way to improve continuity in a school program:

> More comprehensive is the trend to plan continuity from kindergarten through grade 12. In some systems supervisors are given a K–12 responsibility rather than elementary or secondary. In such a plan the director of curriculum is an overseer of the total range. More effective for communication is the estab-

62

Planning is a crucial factor in the effectiveness of any curriculum plan.

lishing of committees representing all levels. Certainly schools that are being consolidated need to look at their total offerings. Related to this is the development of guides, for example, those for social studies, on a K–12 sequence, with a statement of overall objectives and philosophy. A high school that is working on its philosophy and objectives for the school as a whole should bring in representatives from levels above and below in order to effect greater understanding and continuity.[1]

Figure 18.1 suggests one means for examining the vertical articulation of the total curriculum. It applies whether the school district uses grade levels or nongraded organization. Every discipline comprises established concepts that can be identified. Because some conncepts are easier to grasp than others, some can be studied at an early stage of a learner's development, while others must be introduced at a later date. The teaching staff determines what concepts will be taught and to whom, at what stage they should be introduced, and their rate of study.

Although continuity demands the attention of all school personnel, the classroom teacher can do the most to improve vertical articulation. The teacher can improve continuity by planning lessons that take into account what a student has studied before and will study in the future. In planning for continuity, teachers must remember that learning proceeds best from the simple to the complex and from the concrete to the abstract. Teachers must also remember that students need to review a certain amount

Chronological Ages	4–8				8–12			12–15			15–18			Identified Curriculum Concepts
Grade Levels	K.	1	2	3	4	5	6	7	8	9	10	11	12	
	I	I	I	I E	E	Re	Re	E	DS	DS	DS	DS		Concept 1
		I	I	I	I	I	I	E	E	E	E	Re	Re	Concept 2
														Concept 3
	I	Re	I	I	Re	I	Re	I	I	DS	DS	DS	DS	Concept 4
														Concept K

Key: I = Introduction to concept
E = Exploratory work in the concept
Re = Reinforcement
DS = Depth study of the concept

FIGURE 18.1 *Chart showing vertical articulation in the curriculum.*

of what they learned before. Maintaining continuity is difficult and requires constant attention from educators.

Open and Fixed Space

Most school buildings have been constructed along conventional lines with
large corridors and self-contained classrooms on both sides of the corridors. Library, physical education, and other resource rooms are conveniently located for easy access to students. Use of this type of space usually
supports a grade-level type of school organization. Flexible space for instruction is usually lacking, and little or no cooperation among teachers
for teaching is apparent.

Open-space facilities tend to be larger instructional areas with movable walls, flexible learning environments, and instructional organizations
that tend to be nongraded. This type of space, however, does not automatically guarantee an instructional program developed around the philosophy of open education. What an open-space facility does imply is the
capacity for nongraded organization. Instead of corridors faced by small
classrooms—about 30 students per room—a school plant is built with
large instructional spaces that can be kept completely open for all kinds
of instruction or can be reduced to smaller areas by movable walls and
furniture. A plant like this tends to be more conducive to a variety of
instructional and grouping patterns. Although its popularity has increased
rapidly during the last 15 years, the open space facility is still found primarily at the elementary and middle school levels. One of the biggest
problems associated with the intended use of open-space facilities is the
lack of adequate preparation of teachers. When school districts contem-
plate the use of open-space facilities, they should plan for adequate in-
service staff development. If teachers learn how to be more comfortable
in open space, they will tend to use it as was intended.

With a declining school enrollment has come a decline in new school
building. If school districts are to provide open-space facilities while enrollment is declining, they must plan to renovate old buildings instead of
constructing new ones. Enrollment reductions in the 1980s may be responsible for a cutback in open-space facilities.

Grouping

The special problems of ability grouping are closely related to any examination of the artifacts of curriculum practices. Generally, ability grouping
has been defended as a way in which the teacher can provide more adequately for individual differences. Whereas the elementary school tends to
group pupils by subject areas within the self-contained classroom, the secondary school tends to group students by subject, as learners develop and

pursue special interest. The usual effects of grouping have caused special and separate classes to be established for the academically talented, the slow learners, and the average learners.

The position that school systems take on ability grouping largely depends on their conception of the individual child and of the general purpose of education. If the philosophical position of the school is focused on a predetermined curriculum, the school is more likely to support homogeneous ability grouping. On the other hand, if the school is more concerned about the personal and social development of students and believes in diversity as a technique of stimulating education, it is more likely to favor heterogeneous grouping. If ability grouping is practiced, students may be grouped through intelligence tests, achievement tests, reading levels, grades, teacher evaluation, or any combination of these measures. All too often, however, ability grouping has usually been established only from test results on intelligence and achievement. Because of the highly verbal nature of these tests, they tend not to be culture-free, placing undue restrictions and labels on minority group learners.

Despite the usual defense for ability grouping—that is, provision for individual differences—school programs still tend to be group-oriented, and individual differences are not given attention. Although ability grouping has been defended as a way to help increase learners' achievement levels, this defense is only weakly substantiated by research findings. Although many studies report positive achievement results for more able students, other studies report negative findings for less able students. One rather consistent type of research finding suggests more positive affective learning in heterogeneous grouping.

One of the chief difficulties in establishing truly homogeneous groups can be found in the lack of precision of the measurement instruments used to establish groups. Another constraint is the lack of flexible class and teaching assignments; it becomes almost impossible to select a completely homogeneous class when every class must have 30 students and when scheduling conflicts and student interests cause potentially valid diagnostic testing data to be discarded. If the school population of a school district is a sample of the total population and if that sample is a mirror of some normal curve distribution, then all class sizes cannot be the same and still be classified as homogeneous for learning purposes.

The potential for problems generated by ability grouping far outweighs the scant benefits to be gained by rigid grouping. Some of the serious problems associated with rigid homogeneous grouping are:

- Teachers tend to favor teaching average or above-average groups rather than groups of low ability.
- Students who are given labels of low ability usually perform poorly because of the teacher's low expectation of them.
- Problems associated with social class and minority group differences are usually increased with ability grouping.

- Ability grouping tends to reinforce unfavorable self-concepts among children placed in low-ability groups.
- Negative self-concepts are more severe among minority group learners when they are assigned to low-ability groups.
- For the learners, ability grouping does not enhance the value and acceptance of differences in society.
- Although academically talented students achieve better in high-ability groups, low-ability students tend to perform poorly in low-ability groups.

Despite the many negative aspects of ability grouping, the advantage of using some limited and flexible grouping pattern is that it can contribute to teachinng effectiveness. There is little doubt that the task of instruction—and the general intent to provide individualized programs—is made easier if the range of abilities and interests is reduced through grouping. If grouping remains flexible and is based on abilities, needs, interests, and social practices and if students are not locked in fixed groups, the teacher can arrange instruction to achieve a set of appropriate objectives for a particular group.

The pressures for mainstreaming suggest that all grouping be heterogeneous; mainstreaming certainly requires the teacher to expect diversity in learners. As individualized programs (IEPs) are prepared for these learners, varied types of ability grouping will be used. When a classroom atmosphere of cooperation and helping is the intent, heterogeneous grouping will be warranted. On the other hand, formal learning activities involving peer learning, cluster arrangements, or individual study will suggest flexible grouping.

The current federal mandates (P.L. 94-142) for mainstreaming require an individualized program for each exceptional child. It is not surprising that since exceptional children are getting individualized programs, parents have begun to demand due process for their "nonexceptional" children. If mainstreaming legislation is successful, it may bring individualized programs for all children. Then ability grouping, as we have known it, will pass from the public school.

Tracking

Tracking provides rigid, specified programs built on a system of prerequisite courses. A student identified with a particular high school program (college prep, business) stays "on the track" to complete the program and does not experience the flexibility associated with a constants-variable program. Rigid grouping practices are added, and the track becomes more specific. Although tracking programs were thought to provide for individual differences, they have introduced a more rigid program of constants, with little elective participation by the student. For instance, one of the

common tracks, the college preparatory program, becomes a rigorous intellectual curriculum designed to prepare the student for more advanced
learning. In so doing, it tends to limit the student's development in aesthetics and appreciation as in art and music. The typical college preparatory program requires the student to satisfy requirements of four units in
English, three in social studies, three to four in science, three to four in
mathematics, three in foreign language, and at least two units in physical
education and health. These requirements total eighteen to twenty Carnegie units; therefore very little time is available for courses in art, music,
or drama, and even less for typing or driver education. In regard to the
back-to-basics movement, tracking programs allow little room in the curriculum for basics other than the three Rs. The broader aspects of the
basic, life-coping skills, appreciations, understanding of others, and a sense
of necessity for economic productivity simply get lost in rigid tracking
programs.

Vocational Education

The narrowness of the typical track program in senior high schools has
undoubtedly contributed to the continuing shortage of high school graduates who are well prepared in the vocational-technical fields. All too
often, students drift into the vocational track because they "can't make it
academically." Apparently, educators are forgetting that this kind of training requires students who are capable of both academic and vocational-
technical work. More specifically, the constants-variable program can include training for students that has meaning for new industry and the
changing economy. Too often in the past, and even more so now, vocational-technical training has tended to be obsolescent. The constants-variable program can stress work experience and on-the-job training that relate
to school experience. A well-conceived vocational-technical program meets
the following criteria:

1. The program is directly related to employment opportunities, determined by school officials in cooperation with occupational experts and other competent individuals and groups.
2. The course content is confirmed or changed by periodic analysis
   of the occupations.
3. The courses for a specific occupation are set up and maintained
   with the advice and cooperation of the various occupational groups
   concerned.
4. The facilities and equipment used in instruction are comparable
   to what is found in the particular occupation.
5. The conditions for instruction duplicate as nearly as possible desirable conditions in the occupation itself and at the same time
   provide effective learning.

Vocational education is receiving renewed emphasis.

6. The length of teaching periods and total hours of instruction are determined by the requirements of the occupation and the needs of the students.
7. Training in a particular occupation develops marketable skills, abilities, attitudes, work habits, and appreciation to the point that enables the trainee to get and hold a job in that occupation.
8. Day and evening classes are scheduled at hours and during seasons convenient to potential students.
9. Instruction is offered only to persons who need and want it and who can profit from it occupationally.
10. The teachers are competent in the occupation and are professionally qualified for teaching.
11. Vocational guidance, including effective follow-up on all students who finish or drop out of a course, is an integral and continuing part of the program.
12. Continuous research is an integral part of the program.

This does not suggest that vocational programs should be abandoned in the senior high school; rather, they should be reorganized. Federal funds in recent years have added new dimensions to the early vocational acts of 1917. The Manpower Development and Training Act and the Vocational Acts of 1963 provided funding for a changing economy requiring new technologies, markets, materials, and occupations. These acts were strengthened by amendments in 1968 that afforded financial benefits to states that would lead in providing vocational education for the disadvantaged and physically handicapped. The whole vocational education movement now encompasses middle school and post–secondary school programs. There is doubt about how much federal support of vocational education and the emphasis on career development will continue through the 1980s.

One of the big changes associated with vocational education during the 1970s was the development of a comprehensive vocational curriculum. In this curriculum, learners are exposed to and trained in a program developed around a career cluster concept. This allows the young learner to move horizontally and vertically within the career cluster as needs and future opportunities suggest. For example, a career cluster in agriculture would encompass not only courses in farm production but also courses in agribusiness, agricultural mechanics, food processing, horticulture, and landscaping. The young learner can prepare for a variety of careers within a cluster; these clusters are developed around specific job titles.

This type of vocational training has brought about significant changes in the comprehensive high school. Since it has been extremely difficult and costly for a local school district to provide adequate vocational training in the regular high schools, programs for students from several participating school districts can provide a great variety of career clusters for vocational curricula. The area vocational-technical school can provide a far more comprehensive program than can a local high school, attempting by itself to serve the needs of all of its students. Federal funding has assisted in this type of vocational training, but not to the degree needed. As was indicated in Chapter 7, the current federal administration has not been as supportive financially as were previous administrations.

Testing in Schools

Teachers have a variety of techniques to appraise the curriculum. Using classroom tests, teachers can evaluate whether or not specific objectives set forth for a certain subject have been achieved. While test results are used primarily for teaching and for determining grades, they also aid teachers in adjusting methodology and course content. Standardized tests give the school system perspective about its relation to the state, regional, or national picture. A few words of caution are offered, however, about standardized tests: They should not be considered an effective method of evaluating teachers, and they should not be assumed to be so important that they alone determine the curriculum.

The teacher can conditionally evaluate progress toward educational objectives—associated with students' social development, educational and social interest, and values—by checklists, rating scales, inventories, and questionnaires. Teachers and guidance counselors can also assess certain kinds of curricular changes by observation, interview, anecdotal records, sociometrics, sociodrama, and student autobiographies. The school system can use opinion polls, can interview community employers, and can follow up on graduates to judge how effective the total school program is.

Norm-referenced (or normative) data—that is, data referred to local, state, or national norms—are easily obtained when teachers use standardized tests. In addition to the precautions mentioned in using standardized tests, an ever-present question is how effectively these tests measure a particular school program. These tests should be used with some degree of caution for student placement. Unless caution is exercised in identifying and interpreting student progress, these tests may be detrimental in evaluating the curriculum.

Criterion-referenced data are gathered from instruments specially designed to measure expected learning changes. These measuring instruments involve stated operational learning objectives. They do not yield test scores that indicate a percentage of achievement based on some class standards or norms; they do indicate how well a particular student has met the stated learning objectives of the teacher. If these tests are planned specifically to show minimum levels of learner competence, they can be valuable to the teacher, the student, and the parents. For instance, criterion-referenced tests not only yield total scores but also indicate how well each objective was reached. If certain objectives are not reached, the students repeat the learning activity for those objectives only and do not repeat the activities successfully completed. Instead of assigning grades for achievement, the teacher assesses pupil progress on a pass/fail basis. When these kinds of measuring instruments are used along with norm-referenced instruments, the evaluation of a curriculum, especially pupil progress, becomes much more accurate. Table 18.1 shows the difference between norm-referenced and criterion-referenced data.

Staffing and Scheduling

Although many consider team teaching to be new, it is not entirely so. It has been practiced for some time in athletics when groups of coaches—each somewhat of a specialist—work together but use the special talents of each. Team teaching has been used successfully in the military services when, in a national crisis, it becomes necessary to train masses of soldiers

TABLE 18.1 *Norm-referenced and Criterion-referenced Data Contrasts*

Norm-Referenced Data	Criterion-referenced Data
1. Are gathered from instruments established from local, state, or national norms	Gathered from instruments established from local instructional objectives
2. Indicate how a learner or a group of learners has performed in comparison with peers	Indicate to what degree a learner has achieved a particular learning objective or set of objectives
3. Tend to be valid and reliable according to some national expectations or norms	Have a high degree of validity to a set of learner objectives; reliability data, by usual measurement standards, are questionable
4. Indicate a student's overall performance, aptitude, or attitude on some broad continuum or domain—usually used for ordering pupils	Indicate a specific level of competency or development as expected by previously stated objectives; usually used for individual diagnosis and prescription

in a short time. In the nation's schools, however, team teaching on a large scale is not used to any great degree.

The needs of students are more apt to be met when students are exposed to varied learning experiences. In team teaching, learning can be most successful when large-group instruction (100–150 students), small-group instruction (8–15 students), and independent study are combined. A teaching team, organized by subject or by a combination of subjects, can provide these three kinds of experiences. The distribution of time among the large groups, the small groups, and the independent study will vary according to the subject studied. It has been suggested that, on the average, students should spend 40 percent of their time in large-group instruction, 30 percent in small-group discussion, and 30 percent in independent study.

Team teaching used in both elementary and secondary schools may take different forms, size and composition of the team may vary, and the teams may teach one subject or may cross subject lines. Some of the specific advantages offered by team teaching include:

- The specialization of teaching, whereby the particular talents of a teacher are used to the fullest.
- The improvement of supervisory arrangements, whereby team teachers criticize one another's teaching performance.
- The use of nonprofessional aides for routine duties.
- The expanded and multiple uses of many of the new mechanical teaching devices that aid the teacher.

The teaching team can be organized in two general ways. The first, a formal approach, is referred to as hierarchal team organization. This is a line-staff organization wherein a team leader heads a team made up of regular teachers and teachers' aides. Usually, there is a pay differential, and the team leader receives a higher salary than the other teachers on the team. The aides may be noncertified personnel who handle routine administrative and clerical duties formerly handled by the classroom teacher. Aides may also, under the careful supervision of the teaching team, be assigned routine instructional tasks.

The second type of organization is referred to as a collegial, or equalitarian, team. There is no formal structure to this organization; leadership is shared or exchanged voluntarily, and all teachers receive the same pay and have equal responsibility and similar duties. Team organization is binding, however, in that teachers, although enjoying a more informal organization, must work together at a common task. It is important to distinguish the collegial team from the many kinds of cooperative or joint ventures that teachers may join voluntarily and from which they may withdraw whenever they wish.

Despite the many advantages of team teaching, there are potential difficulties that may keep it from getting started or from being successful if it is already underway. First, preparation for team teaching is time consuming, and in any planning, adequate preparation time must be allotted. Second, personality clashes are always possible and should be avoided at all costs. If some teachers do not work well together, they should not be forced to be on a team. Third, there is the possibility that less attention will be given to individual students if the team teaching should degenerate into nothing more than large-group instruction or "turn-teaching." Fourth, there may be trouble in getting adequate physical facilities to enhance the success of team teaching. This is not to say that a team cannot teach well in many existing school facilities. However, if team teaching is contemplated and new or renovated facilities are needed, building should accommodate this type of teaching. Fifth, team teaching cannot and should not be forced on teachers by the administration. Teachers must want to participate, since team teaching takes maximum cooperation and effort if it is to be successful.

Differentiated staffing has added a new dimension to the pattern for team teaching. It is really a refinement of hierarchal teaching. Specifically, it establishes a career ladder that links the paraprofessional job with the superintendent's office. In one sense the director of curriculum and instruction becomes the school district program team leader. Each instructional and research staff assignment carries with it specific prerequisites for training and special instructional charges. The essential elements for differentiated staffing consist of the following:

> A minimum of three differentiated staff teaching levels are suggested: paraprofessional, staff teacher, and senior teacher.
> Salary scales for the levels should be different, but each level should specify a minimum and a maximum salary.

- Academic and professional preparation for each level should be different, with the senior teacher assuming the responsibility of staff leader.
- All levels are responsible for delivering instruction, but only the staff and the senior teacher are responsible for curricular decisions.
- All positions may be tenured, but it is recommended that the senior teacher be on a yearly contract instead.

With differentiated staffing, as with hierarchal team arrangements, one of the main deterrents has been the salary differences, usually confused with a merit pay system. Doubtless some teachers are better than others at certain tasks. If the profession is concerned about accountability and high-quality education, then it seems obvious that teachers should be placed in jobs that match their abilities. The profession desperately needs, in addition to special credentials and advanced training, valid and reliable criteria for assigning special tasks to the professional staff.

Modular and Flexible Scheduling

The two organizational terms "modular" and "flexible" refer to two different concepts in scheduling and should not be considered the same thing. Modular scheduling has existed for some time in both elementary and secondary schools. At the elementary level it has usually been associated with 30-minute time blocks (modules); at the secondary level, with 40- to 60-minute time blocks. The secondary school time blocks are tied to the instructional time allocation of the Carnegie unit. A modular schedule is just as rigid as the six- to eight-period schedule used for so many years in the secondary schools. On the other hand, a flexible schedule uses smaller time blocks (mods), but the schedule changes regularly during the school years as student needs and teaching objectives are altered for particular periods and types of instruction. Combining these two organizational concepts—modular and flexible scheduling—implies that the traditional organization for instruction can be changed to meet changing needs and concepts of learning as students pass through the school.

[62]

The regimentation of the six- or eight-period day of the typical high school does not allow enough flexibility for the best use of teacher and student resources and abilities. An increasing number of educators question the advantage of devoting the same amount of time to each subject. Some subjects can be taught best in shorter blocks of time for fewer periods a week, while others can best be taught in longer blocks.

Modular and flexible schedules have unlimited possibilities regardless of how the curriculum is organized—that is, regardless of whether it is a subject-centered curriculum or a student-centered curriculum. However, as one introduces flexibility into the pattern for instruction, a theoretical shift begins to take place; the philosophical rationale adopted for flexibility tends to direct programs toward student-centered needs rather than subject-centered goals.

A potential deterrent to adopting modular and flexible scheduling at the secondary level has been the Carnegie unit. Despite this, some high schools have worked under the newer kinds of scheduling and have managed to fulfill the cumbersome Carnegie unit requirements by allowing independent study to be counted toward the time requirement. Since the Carnegie unit seems destined to be discarded, innovative scheduling should eventually be more widely accepted.

An example of a flexible schedule is one that calls for 20- to 30-minute modules for instruction. With this kind of time allotment a schedule has a better chance of being flexible. Also, modules can be combined in various ways, and such flexibility encourages the maximum use of teacher and student talents. Some schools have adopted both modular and flexible scheduling and also teaching teams for instruction, so that the special talents of the professionals can be directed most effectively. At the same time, students may be introduced to more teachers who are specialists in one type of instruction or another.

Just as students have special needs and abilities, so do the teachers. We have continuously acknowledged the individual needs and talents of students but ignored the individual needs of teachers. Teachers who are forced to fit into the traditional schedule must also come to grips with the frustrations experienced by their students. To operate effectively, teachers need:

1. *A good opportunity to use professional skills.* Typical classroom teachers spend, in addition to 25 or 30 hours of classroom contact with pupils, many other hours in planning, grading, keeping records, collecting money, sponsoring student activities, and multitudinous other duties. Such a heavy load makes it difficult for professional teachers to keep abreast of new developments in teaching, particularly in methods of instruction and evaluation. The average teacher spends up to two thirds of the day doing nonprofessional, routine duties that could be done by others—or by machines.
2. *A suitable place to perform professional work.* The schools of tomorrow need facilities where teachers can work together to develop instructional materials. The teacher needs an office and conference rooms for individual work with students and parents.
3. *Appropriate salaries commensurate with the job.* As the school work schedule is rigid, so is the salary schedule. Regardless of performance, all teachers are paid equally. The superior teacher is seldom rewarded financially.

Teachers should not be bound to the rigid schedule of the typical K–12 school. Time should be provided during the regular school day for planning and conferring with students, other teachers, and parents. Additional time should be allotted for professional activities to aid teachers in furthering personal professional growth. Students, on the other hand, should still spend about 30 hours a week in planned school learning activities, but their time for learning experiences should be arranged so they can get the most out of school. While their interests are challenged by this multiple approach, students are still given freedom to pursue any subject as far as they like.

Summary and Implications

In examining the artifacts of the school the teacher needs to look at the program in terms of its graded or nongraded structure. Space, whether fixed or open, affects the type of operating school program. Observed grouping and teaching practices provide yet another piece of data about the school. How teachers test, the types of tests they use, and way in which they evaluate students all provide artifacts for the picture of schooling. The instructional organization of the teachers' day yields information on the operating philosophy of the school program.

Knowledge of all of these areas implies that the teacher become an evaluator of school practices. Schools exist for learners; the learning atmosphere and the artifacts of schools depict the attention given to the practice of quality learning environments.

DISCUSSION QUESTIONS

1. In what way does the nongraded plan of school organization provide for individual differences?
2. How do different teacher scheduling arrangements affect learning environments?
3. How should students be grouped for instruction?
4. Should classroom tests be criterion-based or norm-based?
5. Discuss at least three ways that teachers can improve program articulation.

SUPPLEMENTAL ACTIVITIES

1. Prepare a checklist to gather evidence of the artifacts of schools.
2. Visit a school and ask students about their perceptions of grouping practices.
3. Invite a team teacher to explain his or her role as a member of a teaching team.
4. Visit an elementary and a secondary school and write a paper contrasting the use of instructional space.
5. Compile a needed list of competencies for a teacher working in an open-space school.

NOTE

1. Albert L. Oliver, *Curriculum Improvement: A Guide to Problems, Principles, and Process*, 2nd ed. (New York: Harper, 1977), p. 229.

BIBLIOGRAPHY

Brubaker, Dale L. *Curriculum Planning: The Dynamics of Theory and Practice.* Glenview, Ill.: Scott, Foresman, 1982.

Fullan, Michael. *The Meaning of Educational Change.* Toronto: OISE Press, 1982.

McNeil, John D. *Curriculum: A Comprehensive Introduction.* 2nd ed. Boston: Little, Brown, 1981.

Squires, David A.; Huitt, William G.; and Segars, John K. *Effective Schools and Classrooms: A Research-Based Perspective.* Alexandria, Va.: Association for Supervision and Curriculum Development, 1983.

Instructional Practices

Focus Questions

- Why should a teacher be concerned about using precise learning objectives with his or her students?
- How do teachers decide what instructional practices to employ?
- Why should a teacher know the relationship between objectives and instruction?
- What criteria should teachers use to determine the type of technology they may use in instruction?
- How can computers be used effectively by learners and teachers in enhancing learning?

Key Terms and Concepts

General objectives
Specific objectives
Taxonomies of objectives
Convergent learning
Divergent learning
Lecture-recitation
Concept attainment
Inductive discovery
Group investigation
Guided discovery

Simulation/gaming
Inquiry
Mastery learning
Programmed instruction
Individualized learning
Instructional television
Computer-assisted instruction
Computer-managed instruction
Microcomputers

What Would You Do?

As a beginning teacher, you are concerned about doing a fine job in instruction and relating well to your students. You are also keenly aware that your immediate supervisor will be observing and assessing your performance for tenure decisions. You feel comfortable with the teaching strategies you acquired during preservice training but know that they need considerable practice if you are to become a competent instructor. Your supervisor is not well acquainted with a variety of teaching strategies and seems to be primarily interested in your maintaining a quiet and orderly classroom. Your teaching colleagues have shared with you their negative feelings toward all these "newfangled" teaching methods. Yet you remember the positive feelings you experienced when you tried different strategies during your preservice training. You have just learned that your supervisor is coming to visit your class. How do you plan to prepare for the supervisory visit?

The key to success for any planned curriculum is how the planned-for learning experiences are delivered to the learner. Instructional practice in the schools may vary considerably, depending upon expectations for student performance and the teacher's repertoire of instructional skills. The expectations for student performance should be based upon clusters of learning objectives by discipline, grade level, or combinations of disciplines in a nongraded school organization. Well-planned objectives assist the teacher in planning for instruction. This chapter presents a format for preparing objectives for instruction, examines a defined set of instructional strategies that all teachers should be able to use appropriately, presents different models of learning as they relate to instruction, and suggests various uses of technology appropriate for instruction.

Objectives

The broad aims that the many national committees and commissions have developed are valuable only if they have some relation to specific learning outcomes planned for the school. (These broad aims were presented in Part IV of the text.) Figure 19.1 offers a hierarchy of educational aims and objectives ranging from the general to the specific. Teachers preparing to plan the curriculum, teach the subjects therein, and evaluate the intended outcome should understand how planned-for objectives are reached. Educational goals change as the world adjusts to change, and so objectives are never final, and the curriculum is never finished. The curriculum/instruction activity is an active process.

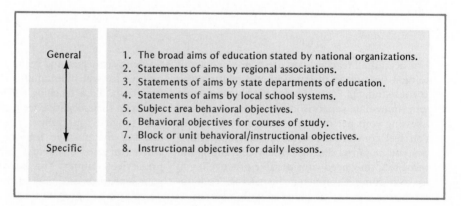

General → Specific

1. The broad aims of education stated by national organizations.
2. Statements of aims by regional associations.
3. Statements of aims by state departments of education.
4. Statements of aims by local school systems.
5. Subject area behavioral objectives.
6. Behavioral objectives for courses of study.
7. Block or unit behavioral/instructional objectives.
8. Instructional objectives for daily lessons.

FIGURE 19.1 *Hierarchy of educational aims and objectives.*

During the 1970s a monumental effort was aimed at developing criteria by which instructional objectives could be stated operationally. One has only to examine the literature cursorily to see how educators like Bloom, Mager, Popham, Glazer, Ebensen, Gagne, and many others have affected curriculum evaluation. They have tried to develop precise descriptions of how learner behavior is finally modified by instruction. They believe that if desired learner outcomes can be measured, then the goals (outcomes) of the curriculum can be measured and evaluated. These outcomes could be assessed on a pass/fail basis or on some percentage of success on cognitive tasks associated with specific goals. No preference has been reached, however, for criterion-referenced evaluation over norm-referenced evaluation. (Norm-referenced and criterion-referenced evaluations are discussed in Chapter 18). Norm-referenced evaluation judges student performance against some group, while criterion-referenced evaluation judges student performance on an individual basis against some preestablished criterion.

Specific objectives, that is, specific results from learning, consist of three explicit criteria: (1) the task confronting the learner, (2) the expected observable behavior, and (3) the minimum level of expected performance. Table 19.1 shows how a given task can be judged by a specific outcome. This format for specific objectives has become accepted use for the development of IEP's (Chapter 7).

More preservice and in-service teachers are being taught to use effectively the criteria advocated by Mager, Ebensen, and others in preparing written operational objectives. Success in this effort is the first step in developing worthy curricula. Operationally stated objectives remain descriptive. Ideally, these operational goals are derived from a stated ideological mission of a school district, state program, or national purpose.

There have been several attempts to clarify and develop educational objectives. One is the comprehensive approach of Bloom and others—the taxonomy of educational objectives. These educators classified the objectives in three groups according to the kind of learning to be produced. These groups, or domains, are described as cognitive, affective, and psychomotor.[1]

TABLE 19.1 *Criteria of a Behavioral Objective*

1.	The task confronting the learner	Given the task of matching 15 chronological events of the Vietnam War with identified incidents of social stress on the American government,
2.	The expected observable behavior	the student will identify these common events
3.	The minimum level of expected performance	with 80 percent accuracy.

1. Cognitive—objectives concerned with remembering, recognizing knowledge, and developing intellectual abilities and skills.
2. Affective—objectives concerned with interests, attitudes, opinions, appreciations, values, and emotional sets.
3. Psychomotor—objectives concerned with the development of muscular and motor skills.

These three domains are outlined in Appendix H.

Instructional Strategies

There are many strategies for instruction. In fact, instructional theorists continue to examine and experiment with different instructional behaviors and systems as allied research in learning theory creates new knowledge about how people learn. The task for the beginning teacher is to examine some of the accepted strategies and understand their use with different specific objectives and the variety of learning models, experiences, and materials available for use with learners. Figure 19.2 shows the type of relationship that should exist for the planned curriculum of a school. The

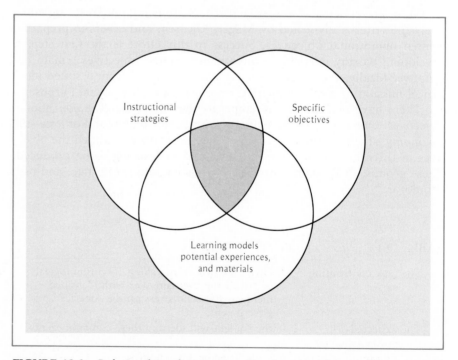

FIGURE 19.2 *Relationship of strategies, objectives, learning models, experiences, and materials.*

shaded control area of the circles depicts the interaction of the circles if there is to be a rationally planned school program.

There has been a deliberate attempt to define strategies as instructional delivery systems that are peculiar to the learning outcomes expected by teachers as they develop curriculum. Instruction is held to be directly related to the hierarchy of learning experiences between teacher and pupil. The cognitive domain of learning, developed by Bloom and his associates, ranks learning from a low order (knowledge) to a high order (evaluation). As instructional objectives are developed to enhance learning, particular teaching strategies should also be developed to give learners the best chance to meet the objectives. Thus objectives and instructional behavior are closely related. Figure 19.3 graphically presents the strategies to be examined.

Lecture-Recitation

The lecture or lecture-recitation instructional strategy is usually associated with a low order of expected learning (knowledge and comprehension). Learners are not viewed as active verbal participants in learning but are expected to digest specific knowledge for recall. Learners are viewed as receiving knowledge, and the strategy for instruction is viewed as the delivery system. This strategy requires teachers to do most of the talking. The lecture-recitation involves live teacher lecture; linear or branched programmed instruction; or special technology like television, dial-access equipment, and computers.

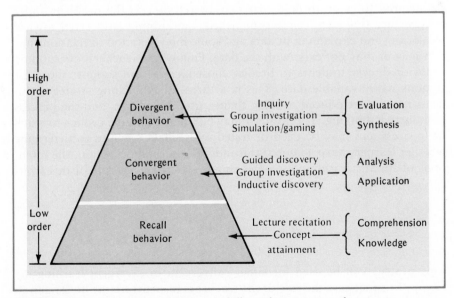

FIGURE 19.3 *Hierarchy of learning skills with instructional strategies.*

Concept Attainment

The concept attainment teaching strategy attempts to develop the thinking process of students. Developed by Jerome Bruner and his associates, the strategy uses a categorizing process to develop thinking.[2] The teacher uses a sorting process of "yes" and "no" with objects, pictures, or statements to direct a learner toward some predetermined process. This strategy can be used with objectives at the comprehension or application levels. The strategy may be used with small groups of learners or regular classroom groups. If the intended learner objective is to involve all students actively in pursuing the concept, then the learner group should be kept small. Bruner suggests that all concepts have elements of (1) name, (2) positive or negative examples, (3) attributes, (4) values, and (5) rule. Attainment of the concept is reached when all elements are understood. Teachers using this strategy need to develop good questioning skills if they wish to keep learners actively thinking while they pursue the concept.

Inductive Discovery

This teaching strategy leads to convergent learning behavior. Specific objectives eliciting this type of learning outcome are prepared for the application and/or analysis levels of the cognitive hierarchy. Again, the teacher's skill in questioning techniques is crucial for this strategy. The strategy employs a deliberate set of processes to achieve concept formation, data interpretation, and application of principles. Initially, questions involve the identification of all data that may be relevant to the problem under study. Once this has been accomplished, questioning is directed toward the sorting and explaining of data and some interpretation of relationships that may or may not exist with the data. Finally, the teacher's questioning behavior directs students to predict consequences and support those assertions with available data. This is a three-stage teaching strategy; students may be introduced to logic chains, use of matrices, and the process of inductive thinking. The strategy may be used with large groups to teach the process and may be tried or tested with smaller groups to determine whether learners have acquired this inductive technique. Again, the intentions of specific learning outcomes should determine the use of this strategy.

Group Investigation

This strategy can be used for either convergent or divergent learning behavior. In either case the role of the teacher is to structure the investigation at hand. If convergent behavior is intended, the teacher should be an active member of the group leading the group to some desired outcome. If di-

Student involvement is vital to meaningful instruction.

vergent behavior is desired, the teacher's role is minimized, and the group functions without direct teacher guidance. The learners are expected to develop their own defensible solutions to problems. In either case, students play an active role in discussing, researching, and formulating group responses to problems or issues. This strategy is best used with small groups.

Guided Discovery

This strategy is planned for application and analysis types of learning outcomes. As the teacher asks questions and students respond, the teacher's task is to use questioning techniques that are leading and thus "guide" the students to desired responses. Rather than having the students give the "answers," as in a lecture-recitation strategy, the teacher, through a series of questions, guides the students through intermediary supportive knowledge to responses and ultimate correct answers. Convergent behavior is consistent with specific objectives deemed appropriate for this level of learning. This strategy may be used with regular class-sized groups or small groups. In either case, however, the teacher is the dominant figure and handles all questions.

Simulation/Gaming

Simulation and gaming techniques have received increased attention lately as appropriate instructional strategies if the objectives call for the personal involvement of learners. These strategies are particularly well suited to the social studies curriculum but can be used in industrial arts, home economics, business, science, and communications in the elementary, junior high, and senior high schools. Under these instructional strategies the teacher places the students in planned situations with a multitude of data available to all and some data available only to a certain few. The object of the strategy is to have the learners be part of lifelike situations that they must resolve to the satisfaction of all participants. Games can be varied so that they have one best solution (convergent learner behavior) or many possible solutions (divergent learner behavior). The special task of the teacher is to see that the students use all the available data in trying to solve the problem. This strategy is a kind of learner role playing; it meets a specific need for certain instructional objectives that are planned for analysis, synthesis, and evaluation. It may be used with large groups, with small groups, or on an individual basis.

Inquiry

The goal of inquiry, as an instructional strategy, is to develop divergent thinking. This is considered the highest order of learning and is associated with synthesis and evaluation skills. There is less talk from the teacher and more from students. Through a series of questions and problems the teacher seeks assertions or hypotheses from the learners. If the teacher obtains two or more assertions from members of the group, it is the teacher's task to help the students develop support (based on logic or data) for their assertions. In this kind of teaching and learning, the teacher must encourage and expect different "right" answers to student assertions or hypotheses. Thus learning behavior planned for divergent learner responses is associated with inquiry. Figure 19.3 represents the strategies examined. If instructional objectives are planned to achieve the knowledge and comprehension levels of learning, then the lecture-recitation or concept attainment instructional strategy is appropriate. If analysis and application skills are sought for learners, then guided discovery, group investigation, or inductive discovery is appropriate for teacher and learner behaviors. As the learning behavior expected of the student moves from low order to high, the amount of teacher and student verbal output changes. At the low-order level the teacher talks most, and the students listen. As expected learner behavior moves toward higher-order learning (divergent behavior), the teacher has increasingly less to say, and the pupils have more.

Inquiry learning stresses greater student involvement.

Learning Resource Centers

Learning resource centers are valuable in any instructional strategy. This learning environment is not established to replace a school library but to enrich it. The typical verbal materials found in a library are supplemented with additional software and hardware instructional materials. With any teaching strategy the teacher uses, students may be assigned, or be free to use, a center to pursue learning on an individual basis or through small-group activities. The learning resource centers are equipped with books, programmed materials, closed-circuit television, and dial-access audiotape or videotape banks. A variety of other materials provide auditory, visual, and audiovisual learning.

Although learning centers were used initially at the elementary level, they are found increasingly in the junior and senior high school. As school districts use more varied organization and instruction, the need for learning centers becomes more apparent. The learning center has become more than an administratively planned area; it has become an adjunct classroom that the teacher can plan on for instruction. The only limitation to the learning center is the teacher's imagination as he or she develops objectives for learning experiences for children.

Models of Learning

Students are different. They learn at different rates; they have differing abilities; some are more able and some are less able; and some learn easier through some mediums of instruction while others learn easier through other mediums of instruction. Teachers should consider using appropriate models of mastery learning, programmed learning, and individualized learning in order to meet the different needs of their students.

Mastery Learning Model

This model of learning attempts to address problems of learning rate and differences in ability. Although students of differing abilities and learning rates may work with the same or similar objectives, they are all still expected to acquire mastery or satisfactory achievement of the objective. Some may be given more time than others, and some may be provided with opportunities of different levels of mastery in order to achieve the expectations. One of the keys to the success of a mastery learning model is the diagnostic and prescriptive work of the teacher. Teachers must be realistic in their expectations for learners and be reasonably confident that what they desire in learning outcomes is achievable by the students with whom they interact. If mastery learning is planned to be sequential, then the student success rate is very important. Students need to experience success in learning.

Mastery learning models are difficult to employ if the school curriculum is rigidly fixed by grade level and all students are expected to master certain objectives every year. It is used best in nongraded school programs where time (by the year) is not as crucial. These programs are more flexible, and differences in learning rates can be attended to with fewer problems. Specific objectives for learners are still used, however, and clusters of students or individual students work with those objectives.

Programmed Models

Programmed instruction can be traced to the early work of Sidney Pressy during the 1920s. Pressy was unable to promote his ideas very far during the 1930s, but B. F. Skinner presented them 30 years later. Since then, programmed instruction has gained significant acceptance. Although this model can be used, and has been, for application learning behaviors, it is perhaps best used for developing expected knowledge and comprehension.

Two approaches to programmed instruction are important for teaching. The first, linear programming, uses constructed-response frames for which the student must supply an answer. The student may receive immediate feedback to a single response or feedback only after a planned series of responses. In the second method, branch programming, the student proceeds to additional frames for learning only after correct responses. If incorrect responses are recorded, the learner is directed along an alternative route for remedial or reinforcement activities. This branching technique is designed to help the student correct and understand his or her errors before moving on to an advanced series of frames. Programmed instruction is considered to have the following advantages:

1. Students are free to learn at rates commensurate with their own abilities. Programmed instruction permits individual study.
2. Fundamental subject matter can be presented through a program; thereby the teacher gains additional time to work with pupils on an individual basis.
3. The confirmation-correction feature of the program provides reinforcement of learning and builds student interest.
4. Programs can be designed to instruct in affective as well as cognitive areas of learning.
5. Programming helps students understand a sequence of complex material and has the potential for doing this in less time than formal classroom instruction.

The primary consideration in using programmed materials is the student's reading level. Since programmed learning relies on the printed word, there may be damaging effects on the poor reader. Another consideration is that although programs can be designed for learning appreciation as well as for skills, not very much has been done for learning appreciation so far.

Individualized Models

Audiotutorial and individually prescribed instruction (IPI) models are supposed to provide for individual pacing of learning activities. Direct student-teacher contact is at a minimum except when the teacher provides remedial, developmental, or enrichment services to the learner as a result of some diagnosis. One of the chief characteristics of these strategies is test-teach-test. From predetermined instructional objectives, curricular modules for individualized instruction are developed. For each module a diagnostic test is developed to measure before instruction starts how well the learner can reach the module objectives. After diagnosis the learner proceeds through the instructional package and is retested at completion. If learners reach the expected criterion for the learning package, they go ahead at their own rate. The learning packages become individual tutors for the students. The task of the teacher is to monitor learner progress through diagnostic activities and testing.

The term "audiotutorial" refers to audiotape recorders for the instructional delivery system, whereas IPI may use a whole host of instructional delivery systems ranging from paper materials to computers. Teachers using IPI generally follow these steps:

Step 1. Administer diagnostic test for learning module and establish entering behavior.

Step 2. Have learner experience the elements of the learning module indicated by entry-level test.

Step 3. Test the learner as he or she completes the module.

Step 4. If the student attains the expected criterion for the module, move her or him to the next module and pretest.

Individually guided education (IGE) has been sponsored by the Kettering Foundation's Institute for the Development of Educational Activities (IDEA) and the Sears Roebuck Foundation. The current activities of IGE are disseminated through two major national IGE groups. One is the IGE Teacher Education Project at the University of Wisconsin, and the other is the national IGE Project operating out of IDEA in Dayton, Ohio. Where IPI takes all learners through the same preplanned program with identical objectives, IGE promotes different specific objectives for individual learners and is heavily process-oriented. Objectives are planned by the teacher and student. IGE strongly emphasizes both individualized and group learning.

There are many types of instructional models that offer variety in approaches to individualized learning. Cecil Trueblood[3] developed a model for categorizing these varieties (Figure 19.4). The model illuminates the sources of objectives and the sources of means of instruction as a classification matrix for individualized learning. Programs in which the teacher determines the objectives and means of instruction are described as category A. Programs in which the learner cooperates on either objectives or means of instruction are described as categories B and C, respectively. The most sophisticated type of individualized learning is achieved when the learner determines his or her own objectives and means of instruction, category D.

Use of Technology

Teachers must be ever alert to keep informed about the new software and hardware media. The terms "software" and "hardware" acknowledge that this is an age of "systems" and "systems development," but in their ca-

FIGURE 19.4 *Individualized learning matrix.* (*Source:* Cecil R. Trueblood, "A Model for Using Diagnosis in Individualizing Mathematics Instruction in the Elementary Classroom," *The Arithmetic Teacher,* Nov. 1971, p. 507.

pacity in education they refer to human resources and learning materials and their uses. Examples of software are books, filmstrips, audiotapes, and transparencies. Examples of hardware are projectors, television monitors, and computers. Such products have greater significance today for learning than ever before. The amount of knowledge has continued to accelerate and has greatly affected the curriculum. The American educational system has to keep finding ways to incorporate systematically this new knowledge into the planned program. American inventive genius and advanced technology have produced a vast number of devices, programs, organizations for instruction, and materials to help the teacher to do a better job. While the lay person, the educator, and the academician have recognized and clarified the disciplines of knowledge, technological genius has produced mechanical aids ranging from very simple recording equipment to complex computers. Many of the new instructional media have become part of the vast educational team that will continue to produce more advanced hardware and software materials to improve learning.

Instructional Television (ITV)

As an aid to instruction, television can be used as an open- or a closed-circuit medium. Closed-circuit units are usually used within a school build-

Instructional television can enhance both student learning and teacher instructional practices.

ing or within a district. Using closed-circuit television, school districts can create their own instructional materials as local needs dictate and provide all learners with access to the best teachers in the school system. Open-circuit units are usually those which receive television communication on a broader scale and not specific to a district. In both cases the television units use live or taped instructional packages for classroom use. The Communication Satellite System (COMSAT) has now opened new possibilities for mass education by television transmission anywhere in the United States. For formal class presentation, television has the capacity for reaching extraordinarily large groups of students.

If instructional television is to be used successfully, it should fit into the general scheme of teaching. To allow it to become dominant in instruction is to misuse the medium. If the misuse is allowed, the instructional value of television becomes as questionable as the single-textbook approach or overuse of the motion picture. Continuous evaluation of television instruction is all-important, since, as a medium of large-group instruction, its potential for misdirected learning or group indoctrination is ever present. Its primary emphasis should always be directed toward education—and not toward television for itself.

Another use of television is to help the teacher improve in instructional practices. An increasing number of teacher-training institutions have adopted television, or microteaching, techniques. If the initial endeavors of teacher training are to be successful, school districts should provide television equipment and help for teachers who are trying to improve teaching skills. Through videotapes, teachers can watch their classroom performance and thus identify and modify or eliminate teaching weaknesses. Further, television is a valuable tool for in-service training of teachers. Many outside consultants can be brought by videotape to the school district, where in-service training is most effective.

Dial-access audio and video systems provide more ways of individualizing instruction. These systems can be used either as the sole method of instruction for some parts of the curriculum or as a supplement to regular classroom instruction. Dial-access equipment was first used, on an experimental basis, in 1961 at the University of Michigan. Since then it has been used primarily for language study. Use seems to be divided evenly between teacher-mediated instruction—instruction that is part of the teacher's planned lessons—and enrichment instruction—instruction that is provided for students who complete all of the required work planned for all students.

The Coatesville Area Senior High School in Pennsylvania has been using a dial-access videotape system since 1968. Installed to aid independent study and individualized learning, the system allows students individual study in carrels that provide automated information retrieval facilities. Videotapes are prepared as teaching aids for the teacher but are not intended to replace whole units of instruction. The tapes are particularly valuable when the alternative would be difficult and costly laboratory presentations or when specialists are unavailable. The dial-access carrels are conveniently placed in the school so that students can get direct help from a teacher if it is needed. The curriculum has been built with instructional objectives, and students progress at individual rates based on diagnostic test batteries. This particular use of technology creates time for small-group learning activities with teachers; students can pursue the required common learning through individualized dial-access systems.

Another use of dial-access equipment is listening laboratories that accommodate small groups of students. These laboratories can be used with records or audiotapes. A more expanded use of existing language laboratories in many schools could provide similar instructional services.

Computer Technology

Computer-assisted instruction has opened a whole new vista for individualized learning. When a computer is used, individual learning is limited only by what the teacher can do. The established techniques of linear and branch programming can accommodate individual or small-group learning sessions in a variety of ways. The computer now acts really as a tutor in the learning environment. Through computer-assisted instruction it is now possible for a teacher to serve a large number of pupils and still have instantaneous evaluation of pupil progress readily at hand. The teacher as instructor takes on new and needed dimensions. Instead of merely dispensing knowledge, the teacher can be—with increased precision—diagnostician, prescriber of learning materials, and devotee of increased teacher-learner interaction.

Computer-assisted instruction has also proved effective in gaming and simulation. Callahan and Clark report:

> In the multitude of cases where bona fide instructional practice is prohibitively expensive or excessively dangerous to life and limb, computer simulation of real life experiences has been found to be attractive as well as effective. One such example of simulation has been in medical schools where bodies have been fitted with sensors that feed signals to a computer program. The student's diagnosis and subsequent action upon the model result in the computer assessment of the success of such action, a rapid "recovery" or the untimely "death of the patient." Another example of long-standing use is the aircraft simulator, commencing with the Link Trainer of World War II fame and advancing to today's highly technical models that are capable of simulating nearly any eventuality that could befall an aircraft.[4]

The tutorial mode of instruction can be delivered by both typewriter-type and cathode-ray typewriter computer systems. However, the new generation of computers has limited computer use in the schools; technological changes in computers make it costly for schools to keep buying new equipment. Control Data Corporation has one of the most advanced uses of computers for educational instruction with its PLATO system.

Just as the computer can deliver instruction, it can also manage the whole instructional and record-keeping program of a school district. Records of student performances and accompanying reports, use of materials, management of scheduling, and storing records of learners' progress are but a few of the possibilities of computer-managed instruction. The computer management system operating in the Admiral Peary Vocational-Technical School in Ebensburg, Pennsylvania, monitors learning progress for the teacher. As students complete prescribed tasks, modules, and units of learning, the students' progress is recorded and stored for record keeping. Upon completion of a specified vocational program the student is given, in addition to a regular high school transcript, a printout that shows the level of competency development for the whole program. This kind of information is more meaningful to prospective employers. With this kind of technology now available for use, teaching might seem to have become greatly simplified. On the contrary, teachers must now face curricular issues usually reserved for administrators and supervisors.

Micros

Microcomputers are now getting increased use in the schools. Whereas the costs associated with the huge mainframe computers made them economically unfeasible for instructional use, the economical micros have gained in popularity. The popular Apples, IBMs, Ataris, and the like, with their use of the floppy disks, are being used to answer the need for computer literacy and individualized instruction. The newer micros use less sophisticated and more easily acquired program languages for curriculum development. In addition, the computer corporations have developed a vast storehouse of academic programs for use with the computers. `61`

There are significant difficulties associated with the use of microcomputers for instruction. First, technology is expanding so rapidly in this area that the market is increasingly flooded with new, more sophisticated models of micros. The question of which one to buy is tied not only to the original cost but also to the life cycle of the model at that time. In the short span of five years the Apple computer has evolved through five models, each succeeding model more capable than its predecessor. Second, there is the problem associated with the compatibility of software among the various micros available. As the newer models emerge, there is greater compatibility of available software, but the problem still remains.

Third, and perhaps most important, instructional staffs are not trained to program or use the micros as they are intended. Teachers cannot willy-nilly buy software and inflict it upon learners. Teachers need to be retrained to evaluate software in light of planned objectives for the curriculum and learner needs.

Computer literacy for the 1980s and beyond has become a new basic skill for all learners at all levels. As we entered George Orwell's 1984, we were no longer wondering about it, we were living in the age of the computer. Every daily encounter is somehow affected by computer technology. The computer is more than just a tool for teachers to use in instruction. It is an instrument capable of mass communication and instantaneous decision making, and could—if not harnessed, understood, and utilized by all the people—be used by some to gain advantage over many.

Summary and Implications

Instructional practices involve the establishment of an orchestrated blending of specific objectives, appropriate teaching strategies, models of learning, and application of technologies. The teacher must become knowledgeable in all of these areas as they interact with learners. Without clearly stated objectives and specifically planned outcomes for learners, the school program wanders aimlessly. The curriculum issues cited earlier in this section will continue, and programs will change. So will instructional practices.

What all of this implies is that as we move toward the twenty-first century, teachers must become more professionally prepared than ever before. Education has become a sophisticated art and science. The easy way out in the machine age of Orwell is not what should be intended by society.

DISCUSSION QUESTIONS

1. Discuss the advantages of computer-assisted instruction.
2. How has technology affected instruction the most?
3. What is the value of promoting all three domains of learning?
4. Discuss some of the ways that practicing teachers can improve their instructional practice.
5. Should there be a relationship between objectives and teaching strategies? Why?

SUPPLEMENTAL ACTIVITIES

1. Write a specific learning objective in each of the three domains.
2. Prepare a one-lesson exercise to be used with a microcomputer.
3. Prepare an inquiry lesson or some high-level cognitive objective.
4. Videotape a minilesson and critique it with your instructor.
5. Visit a school for observation and report on at least three teaching strategies you observed in use.

NOTES

1. Benjamin S. Bloom, ed., *Taxonomy of Educational Objectives* (New York: Longman, Green, 1956), pp. 6–8.
2. Jerome Bruner, Jacqueline J. Goodnow, and George A. Austin, *A Study of Thinking* (New York: John Wiley, 1977).
3. Cecil R. Trueblood, "A Model for Using Diagnosis in Individualizing Mathematics Instruction in the Elementary Classroom," *The Arithmetic Teacher* (November 1971):507.
4. Joseph F. Callahan and Leonard H. Clark, *Innovations and Issues in Education: Planning for Competence* (New York: Macmillan, 1977), pp. 92–93.

BIBLIOGRAPHY

Joyce, Bruce, and Weil, Marsha. *Models of Teaching.* 2nd ed. Englewood Cliffs, N.J.: Prentice-Hall, 1980.

Kepner, Henry S., Jr. *Computers in the Classroom.* Washington, D.C.: National Education Association, 1982.

Kibler, Robert J., et al. *Objectives for Instruction and Evaluation.* 2nd ed. Boston: Allyn and Bacon, 1981.

Walker, Decker F., and Hess, Robert D. *Instructional Software.* Belmont, Calif.: Wadsworth Publishing Company, 1984.

VII

American Education and the Future

Traditionally, American education has been concerned with the past and the present. One of its important purposes has been to transmit knowledge and culture; another has been to respond to the needs of present-day society. Schools today, for example, are viewed as a primary social agency for accomplishing desegregation. But education's response has been retrospective. In other words, not until after a social problem has become apparent are the schools called upon to take part in its solution. Schools could be more effective if, instead of responding to issues retrospectively, they were to take part in creating a society deemed desirable by its members. Then schools could not only prepare young people for the future but also prepare the future for young people. Chapters 20 and 21 are devoted to considerations of the future—and the potential of American education.

Historically, all kinds of people in all walks of life have expressed concern about the future.

In recent years, deliberate concerted attempts have been made to regulate the past and present for possible future development. This new discipline is referred to as *futuristics*, futures research, policies research, or futures studies. In general, the discipline deals with forecasting and possibly determining the future.

In Chapter 20 we explore futuristics and show how the concept is used to forecast the future. Social issues like population, urbanization, the quality of life, the nature of the family, the status of women, and the status of minorities are relevant. Chapter 21 deals specifically with education in the future: the constituency likely to seek and receive formal education, the types of education and educational services that might be appropriate for this constituency, and the prospective educators needed to provide such services. We also explore the future of the teaching profession. ∎

20

Futurism and Future Society

Focus Questions

- Why should you as a future teacher know about contemporary and likely future changes in society?
- Do you think that trends in society such as environmental pollution and the aging of the population affect the role of a classroom teacher? If so, how?
- Do you believe that classroom teachers should encourage and involve their students in thinking, planning and taking action toward creating a desirable future? Why or why not?

Key Terms and Concepts

Futurism
800th lifetime
Alternative futures
Information society

Urbanization
Aging America
Divorce-extended family

What Would You Do?

Most young people are interested primarily in the present—the here and now. It is a challenge to motivate them to be concerned about societal issues with which future generations may have to cope and live. How can you as a teacher help young people to think futuristically and to decide to take what actions they can to create a desirable future both for themselves as they enter the future and for others who will follow them?

The Setting: 1980

In a recent book, *The Third Wave*,[1] Alvin Toffler analyzed the forces that are creating a new civilization. In his conceptualization the first wave was an agricultural phase that took thousands of years, lasting approximately from 8000 B.C. to around A.D. 1650–1750. The second wave, an industrial phase, began during the latter years of the first wave and dominated until about 1950, a period of about 300 years.[2] We are struggling out of the second wave and entering into the third.

> A powerful tide is surging across much of the world today, creating a new, often bizarre, environment in which to work, play, marry, raise children, or retire. In this bewildering context, businessmen swim against highly erratic economic currents; politicians see their ratings bob wildly up and down; universities, hospitals, and other institutions battle desperately against inflation. Value systems splinter and crash, while the lifeboats of family, church, and state are hurled madly about.[3]
>
> A new civilization is emerging in our lives, and blind men everywhere are trying to suppress it. This new civilization brings with it new family styles; changed ways of working, loving, and living; a new economy; new political conflicts; and beyond all this an altered consciousness as well. Pieces of this new civilization exist today. Millions are already attuning their lives to the rhythms of tomorrow. Others, terrified of the future, are engaged in a desperate futile flight into the past and are trying to restore the dying world that gave them birth.[4]

Futurism

The preceding paragraphs deal with the relationships of the past, present, and future, with a direct perspective toward the future. Futurism is concerned with forecasts, trends, and ideas; the purpose of its study is to assist policymakers in choosing wisely among alternative courses of action available to them as they look to the future. In an earlier book, Toffler stated:

> Every society faces not merely a succession of *probable* futures, but an array of *possible* futures, and a conflict over *preferable* futures. The management of change is the effort to convert certain possibles into probables, in pursuit of agreed-on preferables. Determining the probable calls for a science of futurism. Delineating the possible calls for an art of futurism. Defining the preferable calls for a politics of futurism.[5]

Futuristic research therefore includes not only studying and considering the knowledge of the past and present, but also conjuring up alternative futures. It further involves using values in choosing a desired alternative and then planning and acting to create the preferred alternative.

Our ability to forecast the future is limited, like our ability to generate possible alternative futures. Furthermore, choosing preferred alternatives from possible alternatives is likely to be more than difficult; and finally, creating or bringing about the desired state of the future may be impossible. Yet a basic assumption is that there *will* be a future that will be different from the past and the present. Can it be determined? Can the present human inhabitants of the world, with their finite wisdom and frailties, determine desirable living conditions for future inhabitants?

After extensive interviews with futurists, Harold Shane concluded that futuristic research differed from conventional planning in the following ways:

1. Futures planning is deliberately directed by the planner's examined values and is action-oriented. It emphasizes alternative avenues rather than linear projections and concentrates on relationships among probabilities, their cross-impact upon one another, and the possible implications of such influences.
2. Futures planning is designed to point to more alternative courses of action than does conventional planning; to keep good ideas from being overlooked.
3. Traditional planning has tended to be utopian, to see tomorrow merely as an improved model of the present. Futures research recognizes the need to anticipate and to plan genuinely different concepts of the future.
4. It relies more heavily on the rational study of anticipated developments and their consequences and gives less heed to statistical analysis or projection *per se*.
5. In futures planning, the focus is not on the reform of the past. Rather, it concentrates on the creation of a "probabilistic environment" in which alternative consequences and possibilities are given careful study before choices are made.[6]

Shane holds that futures planning therefore focuses on imagining and creating a better human and physical environment, first considering alternatives and their consequences before translating them into action.

Change

One certainty of the future is change. From second to second, change occurs. It occurs both imperceptibly and dramatically and slowly and rapidly. It is expected and unexpected. It is, however, inevitable.

Change has been described as a roaring current, "a current so powerful today that it overturns institutions, shifts our values, and shrivels our roots."[7] Toffler coined the term *future shock* in 1965 to describe the "dizzying disorientation brought on by the premature arrival of the future."[8] Change has at least two dimensions: direction and rate. It is important to note that the rate of change has implications different from, and sometimes more important than, the direction of change.

An illustration of the rate of change deals with "the 800th lifetime." This concept divides the last 50,000 years of human existence into lifetimes of approximately 62 years each. Of the approximately 800 lifetimes, 650 were spent in caves.

> Only during the last seventy lifetimes has it been possible to communicate effectively from one lifetime to another—as writing made it possible to do. Only during the last six lifetimes did masses of men ever see a printed word. Only during the last four has it been possible to measure time with any precision. Only in the last two has anyone anywhere used an electric motor. And the overwhelming majority of all the material goods we use in daily life today have been developed with the present, the 800th, lifetime.[9]

Although change is inevitable, its direction and rate can be somewhat under human control; futurist researchers try to forecast the direction and rate of change. They also try to decide what types of change should occur and the direction and rate at which such changes might or should occur.

Futurists' opinions on the desirability of planned intervention vary. Whether planned or not, however, intervention occurs. Present actions soon become history—but meanwhile, they do alter the future. Why do we suffer from pollution? Why is world famine a crisis? Why are we searching for new sources of energy? Daniel Bell clearly illustrates how present actions (interventions) influence the future:

> Time, said St. Augustine, is a three-fold present: the present as we experience it, the past as a present memory, and the future as a present expectation. By that criterion, the world of the year 2000 has already arrived, for in the decisions we make now, in the way we design our environment and thus sketch the lines of constraints, the future is committed. Just as the gridiron pattern of city streets in the nineteenth century shaped the linear growth of cities in the twentieth, so the new networks of radial highways, the locations of new towns, the reordering of graduate-school curricula, the decision to create or not create a computer utility as a single system, and the like will frame the tectonics of the twenty-first century. The future is not an overarching leap into the distance; it begins in the present.[10]

In summary, change is inevitable. It has two main interacting components: content, or direction, and rate. Certainly, there is little question about the desirability or need for intervention to control change in order to avert disaster. However, there is much debate about how sound any existing data would be when applied to the future, and there is no firm consensus on the kind of future environment we should create. Yet, as Daniel Bell points out, the relationship between present decisions and future events is clearly important.

From one-room schools to the electronic school.

One goal of futures research is to generate possible alternative futures. There are *probable futures*—future events that are likely if there is no intervention in present trends; *possible futures*—future events that could occur with intervention; and *preferable futures*—future events that are

68   valued and that could occur with intervention. Many forecasts of probable futures are dismal and bleak. Others—based on intervention and the premise that humans can, after a fashion, determine their own destiny— are brighter and more palatable.

Some present trends may decidedly affect the future of society and, at the same time, the future of education. We have selected a few social trends to consider. The trends are examined separately, but they are intricately interrelated.

Industrial Society—Information Society

John Naisbitt, along with other authors, including Alvin Toffler and Daniel Bell, has identified the significant role of information in the current and future societies of the world. He has written, "It always surprises me

72   that so many people passionately resist the notion of an economy built on information and, despite a wealth of evidence, deny that the industrial era is over."[11] Naisbitt maintains that we are an information society that had its beginnings in 1956 and 1957. He points out that:

> Outwardly, the United States appeared to be a thriving industrial economy, yet a little-noticed symbolic milestone heralded the end of an era: In 1956, for the first time in American history, white-collar workers in technical, managerial, and clerical positions outnumbered blue-collar workers. Industrial America was giving way to a new society, where, for the first time in history, most of us worked with information rather than producing goods.[12]

He notes a dramatic increase in the proportion of the population of the United States working in information occupations.

> In 1950, only about 17 percent of us worked in information jobs. Now more than 60 percent of us work with information as programmers, teachers, clerks, secretaries, accountants, stock brokers, managers, insurance people, bureaucrats, lawyers, bankers, and technicians. And many more workers hold information jobs within manufacturing companies. It is important to acknowledge the kind of work we do because we are what we do, and what we do shapes society.[13]

Creating, selecting, transmitting, and using information have been important to society from the beginning of time. The major differences today compared with the past are the increasingly rapid rate at which knowledge is created and the speed with which it can be transmitted. It is also much easier today to sort and classify information relevant to problem solving and decision making. High technology is the major factor that has brought these changes about.

It is clear that the information revolution is important to the world. It will affect, for example, economies, politics, government, lifestyles, learning, social structures, and work. It is important to recognize that those persons possessing information have potential power to control others—or share with others for the betterment of all. Information, in and of itself, is neither moral nor immoral. People make the decisions about how to use information.

[72]

World Population

At its current 1.7 percent annual rate of increase, the world population will double in 41 years. Forecasts for the year 2000 vary from a low of 5.9 billion to a high of 6.4 billion.[14]

The United Nations has projected a world population of about 11 billion about a century and a half from now. Another demographic forecast indicates a rapid slowdown to zero growth with a peak world population of about 8.1 billion in the year 2050. The 8.1 billion projection is based on the assumption that family planning programs will be pursued vigorously in the developing world and that steady gains in social and economic development will continue. Lester Brown, President of the Worldwatch Institute, is cited in *The Futurist* as stating that he doubts that a global population of 12 billion will ever be reached. He noted that the crucial biological systems—fisheries, forests, grasslands, and croplands—and oil resources are strained at the 4.3 billion population. Brown feels that the population must be controlled with an aim of halting population growth at 6 billion by about 2015.[15]

The highest rates of population growth are found in the less developed regions—Latin America, Africa, and Asia not including Japan. They are growing at an annual rate of 2.1 percent per year.[16] By contrast, the more developed regions of the world including the United States, Canada, Europe, the USSR, Japan, Australia, and New Zealand have an annual growth rate of 0.7 percent.[17] While the overall rate of population growth has declined, the absolute number of people needing food is still going up. Progress is being made in reducing population growth, yet food production per capita is dropping.[18]

A recent study of world fertility reported a major finding—in ten out of fifteen developing countries reporting, more than half the married women capable of having offspring said they did not want to give birth again. Furthermore, at least 75 percent in fourteen out of the fifteen countries had heard about family planning, the pill being the most widely used method in eight of the fifteen countries. In all but three of the fifteen Asian and Latin American countries studied, the number of children per woman had dropped 20–40 percent in a generation.[19]

[68]

United States Population

The population of the United States is currently about 234 million. On the basis of different fertility rates and estimated levels of net immigration, the U.S. population in 2030 could range from a low of 244.8 million, using a 1.8 fertility rate and no immigration, to 367 million, using a 2.2 fertility rate and annual net immigration rate of one million.[20] The U.S. fertility rate is currently 1.9. It has been estimated by the Population Reference Bureau, a Washington, D.C.–based research organization, that with an annual immigration rate of one million, the number of Hispanics will double by the year 2000. Hispanics historically have a higher fertility rate than whites. An increase of a few tenths of a percent in fertility rates can result in population increases of many millions of people.[21]

There is much debate about whether or not immigration policies should be changed. Legal immigration accounted for about one third of the 2.3 million increase in the U.S. population in 1981.

Other projections of interest stemming from an analysis of population data of the 1970s indicate that the migration of the 1970s to the Sunbelt will continue, but not as rapidly as in the 1970s; small towns and rural areas will continue to grow faster than cities, fostering the movement from urban areas to rural areas; and illegal immigration will continue and probably increase in the 1980s.

Urbanization

Massive urbanization of the population is one of the most pronounced trends of the twentieth century; industrialization and world trade have created our large cities. It is expected that by the year 2000 over one half of the world's population will be living in urban areas, when there will be 58 cities in the world that have more than five million people compared with 29 cities today.[22]

The population of the rural areas of the world is expected to increase by 18.6 percent between 1980 and 2000, while the number of people living in cities will increase by 77.5 percent. The largest cities in the world in the year 2000, if uncontrolled urban growth continues, will be (in millions) Mexico City (31); San Paulo, Brazil (26); Tokyo (24); Shanghai (23); Greater New York—New Jersey (23); Beijing, China (20); Calcutta (17); Greater Bombay (17); Jakarta, Indonesia (17); and Rio de Janeiro, Brazil (19). In the Third World, people are moving to cities to escape poverty and to take advantage of better medical care.[23]

The fastest-growing area in the United States is the "Sunbelt," with gains of 10–15 percent in the Southeast and over 15 percent in the Southwest and West since 1970. Declining areas are in the northeastern and north central United States. Between 1970 and 1980 the Northeast decreased in population by 0.2 percent, the northern Midwest increased by

2.4 percent, the South increased by 15 percent, and the West increased by 20.1 percent.

It has been projected that by the year 2033 the ten largest metropolitan areas in the United States and their approximate population in millions will be Los Angeles–Long Beach (10.6), New York (9.5), Chicago (9.1), Houston (8.2), Dallas–Fort Worth (7.7), Washington, D.C. (6.5), Atlanta (5.1), San Diego (5), Phoenix (4.9), and Denver–Boulder (4.8). Growth in the Southwest may be somewhat slowed by serious water shortages.[24] It is expected that people will live in regional urban centers that will sprout around the biggest cities.

The world seems destined for increased population and further urbanization. Recent trends in the United States indicate a slow growth in the established urban areas but new growth in other, more recently developed urban areas. Increased population and urbanization generate other problems, including pollution, hunger, environmental illnesses, crowding, lack of energy and water, and lack of privacy. The population of the world may be limited ultimately by a lack of natural resources, as indicated

The trend of urbanization seems destined to continue, and with it will come other problems.

earlier. One of the most favorable signs for world population control has been the sharp increase in family planning and the decrease in the overall rate of increase of the world's population.

Aging

It has been estimated that by 2033, more than one out of five Americans will be 65 years of age or older. The actual number of older Americans will more than double from 26.8 million today to 65.8 million in 2033.[25] The dramatic change in the percentage of older persons in the population has important implications for changes in social, business, economic, education, and political issues.

It is anticipated that the future older Americans will be more active physically and intellectually and better educated than earlier generations. They are likely to remain productive throughout most of their lives. Many will work until they are well into their seventies, largely because of medical advances.[26]

Business will cater to older consumers. Tomorrow's senior citizens will be a powerful force politically. Educational demands for the elderly are likely to increase, particularly with the possibilities of three or more careers in a lifetime. Social security will be strained fiscally because of a smaller percentage of contributors and a larger percentage of recipients. Housing and health care could become key issues with a large elderly population. Programs for the elderly could consume as much as 65 percent of the federal budget compared to 28 percent today.[27] Yet it is clearly expected that most senior citizens will be healthy and will prove to be both a vital resource and a challenge to the nation.

Quality of Life

It is difficult to predict *quality of life* for the future. In terms of people's basic needs, a good quality of life means at least enough to eat and adequate shelter. It may mean freedom from fear, freedom of speech, and the right to privacy. Quality of life is relative; current "haves" and "have nots" undoubtedly define freedom from hunger and adequate housing differently; and freedom from fear, freedom of speech, and the right to privacy are undoubtedly defined differently throughout the world. What lies ahead for the quality of life?

Food and Shelter

The future, with more people and less resources, with spoilage through pollution, and with diminishing water, is not bright. Earlier we noted a prediction that global population will not reach 12 billion, that crucial biological systems—fisheries, forests, grasslands, and croplands—and oil resources are strained at the 4.3 billion population level.

None of the basic resources required to expand food output—that is, land, water, energy, and fertilizer—can be considered abundant today. Urban sprawl, soil erosion, and lack of water for irrigation have reduced the acreage under production in some countries. Food production has lagged behind demand in almost every geographic region except North America. If the population had expanded as rapidly in North America as in South America, North America would be struggling for self-sufficiency rather than exporting agricultural products.

A more optimistic view on food supply is taken by Julian Simon in an article in *The Futurist*.[28] He notes that famine deaths have decreased in the past century even in absolute terms, and per person food production is up over the last 30 years.[29]

The substance that fuels the machinery to cultivate agricultural land is petroleum, but the world's oil supply is diminishing. The oceans, once considered a promising source of more food to supply an increasing population, seem at present to be yielding at their full capacity. Many marine biologists now feel that the global catch of table-grade fish is at or near the maximum sustainable level. Water pollution has affected fish production both in freshwater rivers and lakes and in the oceans.

Without some changes in existing trends the projected world population for 2000 cannot be supported by world resources. What hope is there? What are the positive signs? The greater interest in population control in underdeveloped nations is one good sign. Also, pollution control is beginning to be effective in some nations, and scientists are exploring new sources of energy. Yet an increased population may inevitably lead to a lower standard of living in some nations to permit survival in others. The standard of living in developed nations is likely to drop because of energy shortages.

Privacy

Privacy will be difficult to preserve in future years. Concentrations of people will make it increasingly difficult for a person to be alone, to commune with God, to meditate, to have a bit of private space. Andrei Sakharov has speculated on environmental alternatives to ensure an individual's privacy:

> I imagine a gradual (completed long after 2024) growth of two types of territory out of the industrial world that is overcrowded and inhospitable to human life and nature. I will conditionally term them "Work Territory" (WT) and "Preserve Territory" (PT). The PT, larger in area, will be set aside for maintaining the earth's ecological balance, for leisure activities, and for man to actively re-establish his own natural balance. The smaller and more densely populated WT will be the area where people will spend most of their time.

The WT will have intensive agriculture; nature will have been transformed completely to serve practical needs. All industry will be concentrated in giant automated and semi-automated factories. Almost all people will live in "super-cities," the centers of which will contain multi-storied apartment buildings with artificially controlled climate and lighting, with automated kitchens, landscaped walls, and so on.

But the man of the future will have the opportunity, I hope, to spend part, even though it will be the smaller part, of his time in the more natural surroundings of the PT. I predict that people will lead lives with a real social aim in the PT as well. They will not only rest but also work with their hands and their heads, read, and think. They will live in tents or in houses they have built themselves, the way their ancestors did. They will listen to the noise of a mountain stream or simply relish the silence, the wild beauty of the outdoors, the forests, the sky, and the clouds. Their basic work will be to preserve nature and themselves.[30]

Sakharov envisions WTs located in outer space: "flying cities—artificial earth satellites with important industrial functions." He also foresees a "widely developed system of subterranean cities for sleep and entertainment."[31] Perhaps such future developments would partially alleviate the individual's search and need for privacy.

The search for privacy will undoubtedly be made difficult, however, because of improved technology—more specifically, the technology of eavesdropping. Privacy can today be invaded by remote control. Interested parties can now photograph from afar, conceal microphones in tiepins, observe by closed-circuit television, tap telephone lines, pick up conversations in another room by electronic devices, and determine the content of mail without opening it.[32] There is little doubt that the technological capacity for surveillance will increase. Perhaps the solution to this dilemma lies in the individual's demand for privacy—the individual's ability to control his or her right to privacy.

Emerging Lifestyles

Lifestyles are affected by many variables, including the interrelations of culture, values, tradition, and environmental conditions. These categories in turn include population, economic circumstances, climate, and government. Lifestyles vary widely throughout the world, partly because of these variables. One's personal lifestyle might be influenced by living in a crowded apartment in a city, by being extremely poor in a climate that is hot and humid, or by living under a dictatorship. Our discussion is limited to forecasting and speculating on selected future lifestyles in the United States, judging partly from current trends.

Family

For many years the typical American family was composed of father, mother, children, and grandparents living and working together. Today, living situations are much more diverse. In the last decade there was a record high rate of divorce, with over 20 divorces for every 1000 married women, fewer live births, an increase in the number of people who live alone either by choice or because of divorce or death of a spouse, an increase in the number of unmarried people who live with a person of the opposite sex, and an increase in the number of women working outside the home. It is predicted that nonconventional living styles will become increasingly popular, as will living alone. It is also predicted that by 1990, 30 percent of the nation's households will be occupied by those living alone or by unmarried people.[33] More children will be raised in families headed by one parent, and more women will work outside the home.

Experts say that over the next five decades, society will redefine the concept of the family.

> Through the pattern of divorce and remarriage, a whole new network of kinship will arise. There will be double sets of grandparents, aunts, uncles and brothers and sisters, as well as former in-laws and ex-spouses—all of them making up the new divorce-extended family.[34]

It has been predicted that by 1990, up to 50 percent of all children will have experienced divorce and remarriage in their families. What effects will these conditions have on children and their education?

It has also been predicted that federal, state, and local government will be increasingly involved in family affairs. "In addition to fostering child care centers, government agencies will become more active in setting uniform standards for divorce settlements, providing job training for displaced homemakers, and tracking down runaway parents to collect support."[35] "With falling birth rates, some futurists foresee the day when the government will not only offer financial rewards for newborns but also encourage more births through greater use of test-tube-baby techniques and surrogate mothers."[36]

Nevertheless, it is likely that the human need for love will guarantee that the American family will survive.

Housing

The cost of housing will continue to increase, particularly the cost of single-family dwellings. Cost of labor, land, and materials will cause many young people to postpone buying homes; more people will choose condominium living. New construction in the future will use solar heat where feasible. Since old houses tend to be large and expensive to heat and maintain, they will not be suitable for those who want to live as nuclear families. Old houses may be suitable for intentional extended families or communal living.

Work

In *The Third Wave*, Alvin Toffler predicts that millions of us may soon work at home rather than in offices and factories. A return to cottage industry, but an "electronic cottage" with industry functioning from an electronic base, is plausible in the future. Such a transition would not be without difficulties—primarily people problems—because change is not easy for many of us.[37] Undoubtedly, a large share of the work force working at home would reduce transportation problems, reduce conventional fossil fuel energy consumption, and reduce pollution. "The key question is: When will the cost of installing and operating telecommunications equipment fall below the present cost of commuting?"[38]

In our discussion of the family we mentioned a number of significant trends. Those trends are basically away from the nuclear family. What about the family in the "electronic cottage" of the Third Wave, when work returns to the home? In the Third Wave "we will see a high variety of family structures. Rather than masses of people living in uniform family arrangements, we shall see people moving through the system, tracing personalized or 'customized' trajectories during the course of their lives."[39]

In a more conventional vein, it is anticipated that trends that began to escalate in the 1970s and continued through the 1980s will escalate further in the 1990s. The continuation of these trends will result in more women and nonwhites in the work force, yet neither women nor minorities will be represented in management positions in proportion to their respective proportion in the work force. Nevertheless, there will be more from both groups in management positions. Older workers may choose not to retire at the conventional age of sixty-five because of longer life expectancy, inflation, and legislation banning mandatory retirement before age seventy.

Status of Women

Clare Boothe Luce has speculated about the future of women. In respect to the "establishment," Luce stated:

> It has sprouted a heavy thicket of female twigs at its base, and many of its middling branches are covered with feminine foliage. But out of a female population of about 107 million, there are not today 100 women perched in posts of high command or in high supervisory or policymaking positions in its upper branches.[40]

Although Luce was not impressed with the progress of women up to the present, she did identify three breakthroughs that may alter the future:

1. The advance made by medical technology in giving women control over their own reproductive function.
2. The breakthrough favoring the goal of sex equality in the opening of doors of higher education to women.
3. The progress that has been made in the legal area, with women, in an organized way, taking advantage of civil rights legislation.[41]

She concludes:

> I now reach somewhat reluctantly for my crystal ball. I am sorry to say that the picture I see there is *not* one of Woman sitting in the White House in 2024. I see her playing many more roles that were once considered masculine. I see her making a little more money than she is making now. But I see her still trying to make her way up—in a man's world—and not having much more success than she is having now. There may be, and probably will be, great political and technological changes in the world in the next half century. But I venture to suggest that none of them will greatly affect the relatively inferior status of the American woman.[42]

Luce sees, as the chief inhibitor to women's upward mobility, an underlying reluctance in the American culture to allow women to have positions of authority over men.

Gloria Steinem, editor of *Ms.* magazine and a women's activist, also speculated, in an interview dealing with the future, about the future for women. When asked, "How will the lives of women change?," she responded:

> In every way. Autonomy—the ability to control our bodies and work identities and futures—is a revolution for women. We're only just beginning to understand what it might be like.
>
> Many may go on for more education. Even now, women are going back to school after they've had kids. The campus is no longer an "age ghetto" of people from 17 to 22—and that makes it possible for men to go back, too. Education may become a lifelong process for all of us, not just an intense time of preparation.
>
> Responsibility for children won't be exclusively the woman's any more, but shared equally by men—and shared by the community, too. That means that work patterns will change for both women and men, and women can enter all fields just as men can.
>
> It used to be that women couldn't succeed in work because they didn't have wives. In the future, men won't have "wives" either—not in the traditional, subservient sense.[43]

Asked if she thought there would be a woman president in the next hundred years, Ms. Steinem responded:

> I don't know. That may happen, but only after all the other male "outs" are elected—a Jewish president, a black president, a Spanish-speaking president.
>
> If we can judge from history, sex-based prejudice is the most intimate and deep-rooted; the last to go. Even now in corporate board rooms, minority men are usually invited to join the board before women of any race. White men affirm their masculinity by having a minority man on the board—providing, of course, that there are only one or two and can't outvote them. But to have a woman enjoying the same position, especially at upper levels, just devalues the work. Why should a man be honored by a job that "even a woman" can do?[44]

Sandra Day O'Connor and Geraldine Ferraro: More women will follow in their footsteps.

However, in 1984 the Democratic Party nominated Geraldine Ferraro as its candidate for the Vice President of the United States.

Without a doubt, the roles of women are changing. More women are working outside the home, and affirmative action has been effective in helping women attain executive positions in business, education, and other professions. Enforcing the regulations of Title IX will undoubtedly effect a wider scope for women in society.

Minorities

What about the present status of minorities? Documented evidence of the status of Blacks in the United States over the last twenty years reveals that the percentage of Blacks in professional and skilled work has increased, that the percentage of Blacks with high school and college educations has increased, and that striking advances have been made in the number of Blacks holding political office. If this trend continues—and it seems likely that it will—the status of Blacks and other minority groups will continue to improve gradually.

The percentage of persons of Hispanic origin has been increasing in the United States, as has the number of persons of Asian heritage. Many school systems now offer bilingual classes for Spanish- and Asian-speaking children.

Americans may be becoming more humane. Increasing tolerance for alternative lifestyles has become evident. The best hope is for human beings to continue to value all other human beings and for the new-found humanism of equal opportunity for all—women, Blacks, Hispanic minorities, Asians, American Indians—to continue to flourish.

World Governance: Twenty-first Century

How shall the world be governed? Can the world achieve peace? These are haunting questions for the future.

Kurt Waldheim, fourth secretary general of the United Nations, has observed that our future on earth depends largely on our ability to develop a new economic and social system that recognizes and balances the rights, interests, and aspirations of all peoples.[45] Waldheim calls this such a big and complex problem that we can handle it only by global cooperation far greater than anything we have hitherto achieved. He remarks how the U.N. system, through its efforts to tackle such basic matters as poverty, population, food, and the law of the sea, as well as international trade and development, the monetary system, the conservation and just apportionment of natural resources, and the preservation of the environnment, has slowly begun to take up this urgent challenge. Emmet Hughes has identified "three tolerable believable premises about global things to come":

> First, the thrust of nationalism, which so many sages thought had almost spent itself by the end of World War II, will continue to outrun all expert expectations, especially as it is reinforced by the fresh passions of the newly independent nations. Second, the force of ideology, as a guide to the conduct of nations, will continue to falter and become more feeble and irrelevant. As the dilemmas and distresses troubling the majority of peoples appear ever more insistently both practical and universal, they leave less and less place for the divisive role of the theoretical. The most inventive designs for reversing urban decay or slowing population growth—or curbing inflationary pressures or surviving energy crises—may be infinitely varied. But it will become increasingly implausible to label any of them as democratic, or communist, or fascist. Third, for these and related reasons, the line most seriously scarring the globe will be seen to run, not between East and West, but between North and South, between those societies that have perhaps enjoyed too much and those that still enjoy next to nothing, and between the most industrialized nations and the most industry-hungry nations, oddly blessed by the natural resources with which industry itself must be fed.[46]

It seems that the politics of the future will be increasingly influenced by economics, environments, energy, and the recognition of human rights—particularly the access of all people to a life of high quality.

Alvin Toffler has stated, "To build workable governments anew—and to carry out what may well be the most important political task of our lifetimes—we will have to strip away the accumulated clichés of the Second Wave era."[47] He further states,

> For today the single most important political conflict is no longer between rich and poor, between top dog and underdog ethnic groups, or even between capitalist and communist. The decisive struggle today is between those who try to prop up and preserve industrial society and those who are ready to advance beyond it.[48]

Three key governmental principles of the Second Wave will need to change to bring about a functional and desirable governance structure in the future. These principles have been classified by Toffler as minority power, semidirect democracy, and decision division.[49] It is difficult, if not impossible, today to mobilize a majority. The best that can be achieved is a coalition of minorities, which frequently is unsatisfactory to many of the subgroups. In semidirect democracy the opinions of citizens or groups of citizens are expressed by their "representatives." Without consensus, such a form of governance becomes impractical, not functional, and probably undesirable. Direct democracy, wherein each citizen could be heard, became impossible as populations increased and the world became more complex. Today's electronic age may permit increased opportunities for direct democracy in combination with representative government. Our decision structure will also need modification. Our current structure of local, state, regional, national, and transnational or global systems is ineffective for the future. The problem is to design a system in which decisions can be made at the proper level, some decisions being made concurrently at all levels.[50]

Environment and Resources

There is little doubt that people have ravaged their natural environment. Jacques Cousteau gives a succinct description:

> As far as humans are concerned, they have only very recently achieved the dominance of nature, and they suddenly realize that the long and difficult conquest of the planet and the enthusiasm of victory have spread worldwide devastation and ruin. As recently as seven or eight generations ago, Western civilization triggered various kinds of explosions: more children, more food, more tonnage of goods, more energy—which created an exhilarating climate of pride, of overconfidence. The rapture of growth. But after such a great wild party, we are just awakening with a painful hangover, and all around us our home is littered with the sad remains of the "morning after." While we are slowly and painfully attempting to clean the place and return to normal life, we realize that growth, at least in quantity, has limits, that our conventional resources can, and will soon, be exhausted, and that our very life depends on the quality of water.[51]

Advanced technology, population growth, exploitation of natural resources, urbanization, overconsumption, and innumerable other factors have contributed to our environmental problems. Toffler refers to the "industrial vomit that fills our skies and seas."[52] Harold Shane has noted that "naive use has been made of technology to the point at which many ecologists and other scientists are deeply concerned lest—within the span of the next generation—irreparable damage be done to the environment."[53] He further noted:

> Just as misuse has created many present difficulties, so the *wise* use of technological developments is needed to extricate us from the pitfalls in which we find ourselves. In the process we must be wary that we do not demonize technology. The fault is not in our skills but in ourselves, and we need to find technically sound procedures to overcome technogenic crises.[54]

A current issue that will continue to receive attention throughout the 1980s is that of our vanishing farmlands. In the past decade we have lost farmlands equivalent to the combined areas of Vermont, New Hampshire, Massachusetts, Rhode Island, Connecticut, New Jersey, and Delaware.[55] Another way to express the loss is that every day twelve square miles of farmland are converted to subdivisions, roads, and factories.[56] It is apparent that, with an increase in world population along with a decline in available land usable for agriculture, there is trouble ahead. Most countries, including the United States, do not have effective policies for preserving agricultural land. Time continues to tick away—interventions are necessary to create a desired future for all.

Many challenges must be faced in the future—we have explored just a few. These challenges are clearly interrelated; perhaps one of the most serious deals with world population and its relation to resources and environment. Clean water, clean air, and an abundant food supply are necessary for survival. Present inhabitants of the globe, learning from the past, can cooperatively resolve the issues of the future. Education will certainly play a major part in determining that future.

Summary and Implications

Futurism is a concept that deals with making forecasts on the basis of past and current trends along with ideas and imagination. It is a planning activity using data and policy analysis to develop alternative courses of action for the future. It involves not only developing alternative courses of action, but also making value judgments in choosing a desired alternative and then planning and acting to create the preferred future. Change occurs inevitably but not necessarily in a desired direction. Determining the direction and rate of change can in many instances be under human control. It is the purpose of futuristics research to assist planners in forecasting the direction and rate of change, trying to decide what types of change should occur, and then bringing about the desired changes through appropriate intervention activities.

A number of kinds of trends and forecasts were discussed, including those dealing with population, urbanization, the information age, aging and longevity of Americans, quality of life, food and shelter, privacy, life-styles, the American family, work, the status of women and minorities, world governance, and the environment. These trends and forecasts are directly related to education.

As they work with students, teachers must enlighten them about our common need to determine and to plan for a desirable future. Many subjects in the curriculum, particularly the social studies and the sciences, give teachers a good chance to emphasize the effects of continuing harmful trends—pollution and the depletion of natural resources. The effects can be speculated about in a quasi-scientific and creative way through class simulation of scenarios of life in the future. Students will need to identify their values carefully. What kind of life do they cherish? Can such a life be reached in the future if present deleterious trends continue—unless there is some sort of intervention? What kinds of intervention are possible? Without a doubt, teachers can succeed in challenging students to think about the future and perhaps to begin to act in ways that will improve the possibilities for the future.

DISCUSSION QUESTIONS

1. What does futurism entail?
2. How does futures research differ from conventional planning?
3. How can humans begin today to determine the future?
4. How does the past influence the future? Provide illustrations.
5. What kind of future world do you envision?

SUPPLEMENTAL ACTIVITIES

1. Write and enact a skit on life in future society.
2. Make a list of forecasts on future society. State the assumptions on which each forecast is based.
3. Which values would you prefer future societies to adhere to? Compare your list with other listings.
4. Interview children and older people about the future. Contrast their ideas.
5. Choose two or three aspects of the future—such as population, energy, or family life—and project two or three alternative futures based on these different premises:

Population
- Assume zero growth.
- Assume increased growth.
- Assume that there is no change in the existing trend.

Energy
- Assume total oil depletion.
- Assume new energy resources.

Family Life
- Assume that marriage disappears completely.
- Assume that single-family dwellings are no longer feasible.

NOTES

1. Alvin Toffler, *The Third Wave* (New York: Morrow, 1980. Reprinted by Bantam, 1981.)

2. Ibid., p. 30.

3. Ibid., p. 17.

4. Ibid., p. 25.

5. Alvin Toffler, *Future Shock* (New York: Bantam, 1971), p. 460.

6. Harold G. Shane, *The Educational Significance of the Future* (Bloomington, Ind.: Phi Delta Kappa, 1973), p. 2.

7. Toffler, *Future Shock*, p. 1.

8. Alvin Toffler, "The Future as a Way of Life," *Horizons* (Summer 1965): 109.

9. Toffler, *Future Shock*, p. 14.

10. Daniel Bell, "The Year 2000—The Trajectory of an Idea," in *Toward the Year 2000: Work in Progress,* ed. Daniel Bell (Boston: Houghton Mifflin, 1968), p. 1.

11. John Naisbitt, *Megatrends: Ten New Directions Transforming Our Lives* (New York: Warner Books, 1982), p. 11.

12. Ibid., p. 12.

13. Ibid., p. 14.

14. Jean van der Tak, Carl Haub, and Elaine Murphy, "A New Look at the Population Problem," *The Futurist* (April 1980): 44.

15. Ibid., pp. 44–45.

16. Ibid., p. 40.

17. Ibid.

18. "Can the U.S. Help Feed the World Much Longer?" *U.S. News & World Report* (December 24, 1979): 47–48. (Interview with Lester Brown, President, Worldwatch Institute.)

19. "Where the Population Bomb Has Stopped Ticking," *U.S. News & World Report* (November 26, 1979): 94–95.

20. Leon F. Bouvier, "The Impact of Immigration on U.S. Population Size," *Population Trends and Public Policy Series No. 1* (Washington, D.C.: Population Reference Bureau, 1981), Table 2, as reported in *The Futurist* Volume VI, No. 6 (December 1982): 72.

21. "Population Groups Question Census Bureau's ZPG Projection," *The Futurist* XVII (February 1983): 77.

22. "The New Megalopolises," *The Futurist* XVI (October 1982): 62.

23. Ibid.

24. "Goodbye Gritty City—Hello Urban Utopia," *U.S. News & World Report* 94 (May 1983): A15.

25. "If You Live to Be 100—It Won't Be Unusual," *U.S. News & World Report* 94 (May 1983): A10.

26. Ibid.

27. Ibid.

28. Julian Simon, "Life is Getting Better, Not Worse," *The Futurist* XVII (August 1983): 7–14.

29. Ibid., p. 11.

30. Andrei D. Sakharov, "Tomorrow: The View from Red Square," *Saturday Review/World* (August 24, 1974): 13–14. Copyright © 1974 by *Saturday Review/World*. Reprinted by permission.

31. Ibid., p. 14.

32. Ibid., p. 108.

33. From U.S. census data.

34. "When 'Family' Will Have a New Definition," *U.S. News & World Report* 94 (May 1983): A3–A4.

35. Ibid., p. A4.

36. Ibid.

37. Toffler, *The Third Wave*, pp. 210–223.

38. Ibid., p. 217.

39. Ibid., pp. 231–232.

40. Clare Boothe Luce, "The 21st Century Woman—Free at Last?" *Saturday Review/World* (August 24, 1974): 58.

41. Ibid., pp. 61–62.

42. Ibid., p. 62.

43. "What Kind of Future for America?" *U.S. News & World Report* (July 7, 1975): 47.

44. Ibid.

45. Kurt Waldheim, "Toward Global Interdependence," *Saturday Review/World* (August 24, 1974): 63.

46. Emmet John Hughes, "A World Atlas for 2024," *Saturday Review/World* (August 17, 1974): 26.

47. Toffler, *The Third Wave*, p. 435.

48. Ibid., p. 453.

49. Ibid., pp. 435–459.

50. Ibid. (Readers are urged to read the original source to gain a more complete understanding of the complex issues presented here in a brief summary.)

51. Jacques Cousteau, "The Perils and Potentials of a Watery Planet," *Saturday Review/World* (August 24, 1974): 41.

52. Toffler, *Future Shock*, p. 429.

53. Shane, p. 47.
54. Ibid., p. 48.
55. Peter J. Ognibene, "Vanishing Farmlands: Selling Out the Soil," *Saturday Review* 7 (May 1980), p. 29.
56. Ibid.

BIBLIOGRAPHY

Conboy, William A. *The Challenge of the Future: Visions and Versions.* Lawrence, Kan.: University of Kansas, 1979.

Counts, George S. *Dare the School Build a New Social Order?* New York: John Day, 1932. (Reprinted by Southern Illinois University Press, 1978.)

The Futurist. Washington, D.C.: World Future Society. (A bimonthly journal of forecasts, trends, and ideas for the future.)

Jennings, Lane, and Cornish, Sally, eds. *Education and the Future.* Washington, D.C.: World Future Society, 1980.

Kahn, Herman; Brown, William; and Martel, Leon. *The Next Two Hundred Years: A Scenario for America and the World.* New York: Morrow, 1976.

Naisbitt, John. *Megatrends: Ten New Directions Transforming Our Lives.* New York: Warner Books, 1982.

Olson, David H., and McCubbin, Hamilton I. *Families: What Makes Them Work.* Beverly Hills, Calif.: Sage Publications, 1983.

Toffler, Alvin. *Future Shock.* New York: Random House, 1970. (Reprinted by Bantam, 1971.)

Toffler, Alvin. *Previews and Premises.* New York: William Morrow, 1983.

Toffler, Alvin. *The Third Wave.* New York: William Morrow, 1980. (Reprinted by Bantam, 1981.)

Schools and the Future

Focus Questions

- Have you ever considered being a teacher of adults in a business or industrial setting?
- What kind of knowledge and skills do you think should be imperative for students to have for living in the year 2050?
- What would you recommend to make teaching a more attractive career?
- How do you think the duties and activities of a teacher in the year 2050 will differ from the duties and activities today?

Key Terms and Concepts

Seven Cardinal Principles
Quality-equality concern
Merit pay
Master teacher

Career ladders
Professional development
Self-renewal

What Would You Do?

You have been teaching mathematics in a high school of less than 400 students for two years. The school offers general mathematics, algebra, advanced algebra, and geometry as full-unit or two-semester courses. The state has mandated that all high school students shall have three units or six semesters of mathematics for high school graduation. It is obvious to you and your colleagues that the existing offerings are reasonable for some students but that other students with lesser capabilities are not likely to be successful in algebra, let alone advanced algebra or geometry. Because of your recent degree, you have been asked to be the leader in designing a series of mathematics courses that less capable, non-college-bound students can take and benefit from that will satisfy the three-unit mathematics mandate. How will you proceed?

The school curriculum has traditionally been oriented to transmitting culture and knowledge. Changes in school curricula most often follow changes in society. As long ago as 1932, George S. Counts, in *Dare the School Build a New Social Order?*, called for the school to become an agent for change in society. His challenge has never been completely accepted by the schools or by society. Perhaps now is the time for schools to attempt to change society, particularly to improve the quality of life in the future. Any changes made in the schools toward this new end should be carefully examined against the traditional aspects. What are some ways our schools may change in the future?

Future Education for Whom?

69 Schools are now being asked to provide formal education for a more diverse and ever-increasing proportion of the population. Whereas a few years ago, children typically started school at age six, many children now start school much earlier. The latest data available indicate that the proportion of three- to five-year-old children enrolled in preprimary education rose from 25 percent in 1964 to 52.5 percent in 1980. In 1974, approximately 20 percent of the three-year-olds were enrolled in schools, as were 38 percent of the four-year-olds and 79 percent of the five-year-olds. In 1980, approximately 27.3 percent of the three-year-olds were enrolled in school, as were 46.3 percent of the four-year-olds and 84.7 percent of the five-year-olds. Twice as many of the prekindergarten three- through five-year-olds are enrolled in nonpublic schools as are enrolled in public schools. At the kindergarten level, six times as many children are enrolled in public schools are are enrolled in nonpublic schools.[1] The trend toward increased enrollment of preprimary children is expected to continue.

Over 21 million persons participated in adult education activities in 1981, 3 million more than in 1978. Participation by all age groups grew in absolute numbers and, with the exception of the 25- to 34-year-old group, increased faster than the population. Adults, in this context, are defined as those aged seventeen and older who are not full-time students in high school or college and those over age 35 regardless of their enrollment status. There were approximately 21 million participants in adult education in 1981, compared to 17 million in 1975.[2] This trend is also expected to continue.

Participants in adult education enroll in programs sponsored by employers, two-year colleges, community organizations, trade and business schools, and union or professional organizations in addition to regular high schools and colleges. Schools provided 53.9 percent of the adult education courses; 46.1 percent of the courses are offered by nonschool organizations. The types of schools that provided the highest percentages of the adult courses were four-year institutions, with 19.2 percent, followed by the two-year institutions, with 18.8 percent. Vocational/trade schools offered 9.1 percent, and elementary and secondary schools offered 6.8 percent of the adult courses. The primary reason for taking adult education courses was to advance in a job, while the primary non-job-related reason was for personal or social purposes.[3] In a speech in 1980 at a conference of the Adult Education Association the following trends for the future were enumerated:

- Education will be increasingly competency based.
- Functional illiteracy will have to be eliminated.
- Educational resources will need to be open to more and more groups (e.g., nontraditional study, external degrees, and media).
- New institutional arrangements will be more common (e.g., educational consortiums).
- Demographic shifts to older populations will heavily influence educational programming.
- Higher education will be more adult centered.
- Adults will demand graduate credit for life experience.
- Major financial support will be provided for continuing education for adults. There will be an increased demand for career counseling.
- People will change careers up to eight times during their working lifetime.
- There will be a significant increase in understanding how adults learn.
- There will be major support to programs of education for the elderly.
- There will be new ways of serving functional work groups.[4]

A study related to adult education and early childhood education, which dealt with the future, made four pertinent points of interest to all educators: (1) a recognition of the need to make education a continuing and lifelong process, (2) the need for continuing education on a worldwide basis that would serve both mature (past age thirty) and senior (past age sixty) learners, (3) the view that problem-preventing education begun in early childhood is distinctly superior to compensatory education provided at a later time, and (4) teaching and learning should not exist only in schools.[5]

In view of these findings it seems logical to forecast that schools of the future will eventually be asked to provide varied forms of continuous education for virtually all people from the very young to the very old. How can our schools prepare to do this?

Learning is a lifelong process.

Curriculum Recommendations: 1977

In 1975, Harold Shane, in cooperation with the National Education Association, conducted a study seeking to determine the type of curriculum that would be appropriate for the twenty-first century. A distinguished panel was chosen representing students, teachers, and scholars nationwide and around the world. The panel members were asked to give their opinion on the following questions:

> 1. In broad terms, and barring such catastrophes as nuclear war, what are some of the characteristics of the most probable world you foresee by the twenty-first century?

2. In view of this image of the future, what imperative skills should education seek to develop? Also, in anticipation of the twenty-first century world, what premises should guide educational planning?
3. Have the original Seven Cardinal Principles retained their merit? If so, what are the new ways in which they should now be interpreted, amended, or applied in anticipation of the changing social, economic, and political conditions in the world community?[6]

Corollary questions were asked of student members of the panel. Interviews were conducted with each of the 46 panel members.

Characteristics of the Probable World: Twenty-first Century

Some of the issues that the panel suggested were addressed in the previous chapter. In summary they were: continued acceleration in the rate of change, greater complexity, twilight of the hydrocarbon age, reexamined concepts of growth, increased crowding, lingering hunger, continued pressure for human equity, increased demands from less-developed countries for a new economic order, troubled international waters, changing concepts of work and leisure, governmental debt and capital deficits, problems of governance, threats to freedom, and a postextravagant society.[7] It was against this background that premises, guides to action, were framed.

Guides to Curriculum Action: Premises for the Twenty-first Century

The panel was also asked: "In anticipation of the twenty-first century, what premises should guide educational planning?" Premises are viewed as guides to action rather than as goals or principles. In discussing the premises the report emphasized that education needs to be seen in a much broader context than the setting in which formal schooling currently exists.[8] Panelists further emphasized that "as we focus on the immediate *social* problems of the next two decades, we need to remember that *children now in school will not be decision-makers for nearly a generation.*"[9] Those who publish or produce books, television, and newspapers—and other potential educational media—must assume more mature responsibility for continuing education of children and adults.

The panel recommended 28 premises to guide education in the future. In their totality the premises appear to involve creating and strengthening five capacities in learners:

1. A thorough knowledge of the world and its peoples; a knowledge of realities.
2. Awareness of *alternative* solutions to problems, a requisite in a world in which compromise and persuasion must replace force.

3. Sensitivity to the consequences of one's choices.
4. Insight and values that support wise choices.
5. Skills, information, and motivation that are necessary for following through on choices.[10]

Shane concluded:

A knowledge of realities, of alternative solutions and their consequences, the ability to choose wisely and carry out ideas—these talents, acquired from warm and understanding teachers, seem to capture the spirit of the premises of both the adult and youth panelists.[11]

A third challenge was to reexamine the Seven Cardinal Principles of Education (1918).

The Seven Cardinal Principles Reexamined

Seven Cardinal Principles of Education were formulated in 1918, arising out of an NEA study by the Commission on the Reorganization of Secondary Education. They were discussed in Chapter 12. To review briefly, they were statements of educational goals that dealt with health, command of fundamental processes, worthy home membership, vocation, civic education, worthy use of leisure, and ethical character. In the previously mentioned Shane study, panelists were asked to respond to two related questions: Have the original 1918 Cardinal Principles retained their merit? If so, what are the new ways in which they now should be interpreted, amended, or applied in anticipation of changing social, economic, and political conditions in the world community? The members of the panel felt that the seven goals had retained their usefulness and importance. They did, however, propose to redefine, refine, and clarify the goals—for their applicability to and appropriateness for the future. In general they concluded that the original Cardinal Principles did not distinguish between the general responsibilities for education and those that were best assumed by or shared with agencies like the church, community, and family, nor did the original principles anticipate how much learning would be required in the future or allow for lifelong learning.[12] Furthermore, the original principles failed to distinguish the principle for the command of fundamental processes from the other six.[13]

Student Views: 1977

Ninety-five students were also interviewed separately as part of a National Education Association study Harold Shane conducted. They were asked what they thought might be done to improve their schools and their schooling.[14] Four points came through clearly: "First, in a world that youth find frustrating, distressing, and sometimes frightening, the need for coping skills and techniques was expressed." Second, "young people wanted schools that cared about them," and third, students revealed loneliness and a desire for teachers who "radiated warmth and genuine interest in students."[15] Finally, the students sought help in communicating. They sought the "opportunity to have someone to talk with, someone to whom they could listen, someone to whom and with whom they could communicate and share their feelings, hopes, and concerns."[16] The students' responses provide clues for the kind of curriculum, teachers, and instructional strategies needed now and for the future.

The Recent National Reports

The primary emphasis of Shane's study in 1977 was on the kind of education students in the twenty-first century should have to live in that period. It was strongly futuristic. The recent reports—for example, *A Nation at Risk: The Imperative for Educational Reform, Action for Excellence,* and *Twentieth Century Fund Task Force Report on Federal, Elementary and Secondary Education Policy*—tend to be less futuristic, more immediate, and more specific. (A list of the reports appears in Appendix I.) The reports seem also to have a different genesis. Harold Howe suggests they were inspired in part by (1) frustration over the diminishing capacity of the United States to compete in worldwide markets—better schools that produce better-educated workers are thought to be the way to outsell the Japanese and Germans; (2) the defense establishment, which is concerned with keeping ahead of the Soviets if their youth are better educated than ours; and (3) dissatisfaction with American education, which has coalesced because of disillusionment with the resolution of civil rights issues in the schools and because of widespread concern about declining test scores.[17]

Howe has, somewhat arbitrarily, digested the many recommendations made in the national reports into a list of ten. Though somewhat selective, his list is illlustrative of the recommendations and includes his editorial comments.

1. Achieve greater consensus on the goals of education and the priorities of those goals, as opposed to the present tendency to "do everything for everybody."
2. Focus on a "common core" of learning for all Americans, particularly in high schools.
3. Stiffen both subject-matter and skills requirements for high school graduation and college admission (with little or no comment on how to serve students rejected by this new rigor).
4. Emphasize the attracting, training, and retaining of more able people for the teaching profession, using merit pay as one strategy and providing

higher pay generally, along with more subject-matter emphasis in teacher preparation and enhanced use of testing in selecting teachers (all of this with almost no analysis of costs and how to pay them).

5. Renew the focus on basic skills, higher-order skills, and homework, and spend more time in school in order to achieve results.

6. Find ways around teacher certification to meet short-term but critical teacher shortages in mathematics, science, and computers.

7. Emphasize the selection, training, and retraining of school principals (as well as changing their role from school management to instructional and curricular leadership), and restructure the internal workings of schools to provide improved pedagogy, fewer interruptions of learning activities, more efficient use of time, and imaginative ways to enlist students in helping others to learn.

8. Define a strong federal role in education, with emphasis on such issues as math/science/computers, as well as on the primacy of the state and local roles.

9. Seek partnerships with business and higher education in working to improve the schools.

10. Emphasize a balance between quality and equality, with minimal mention of school desegregation, problems of discrimination faced by ethnic minorities and women, or the 20% of students who drop out before completing high school (40% to 45% in the inner cities).[18]

As was indicated earlier, the recommendations from the national reports are much more specific than were the premises from the Shane study. This difference is in part a function of the differing purposes of the two reports. Some congruence between the reports is also apparent. For example, in respect to the cardinal principle dealing with the command of fundamental processes, the Shane study "reaffirmed the importance of proficiency in the three Rs plus communication skills." Recent reports also recognize the importance of the basics as illustrated by their recommendations for the completion of specific courses for graduation; for example, four years of English, three years of mathematics, three years of science, three years of social studies, and half a year of computer science, along with a strong recommendation for two years of foreign language for the college bound.[19]

The recent reports have received tremendous publicity. The unanswered questions that remain are: What actions will be taken by schools and universities and state legislatures toward implementing the recommendations? What permanent change will result from the reports?

Diane Ravitch, in an historical review of American education and its capacity for change, observed, "Curiously, certain features of the U.S. school survive despite nearly unanimous condemnation by expert opinion."[20] She also noted:

What we should have learned by now is that reforms that take root are those that are limited, specific, and reasonably related to the concerns and capacities of those who must inplement them. A proposal that tells teachers that everything they have done up until now has been wrong is likely to receive a cold reception. A reform that deals contemptuously with those who must implement it is not likely to take hold. To be effective, a proposal for change must appeal to teachers' educational ideals, respect their professionalism, and build on their strengths.[21]

One must also remember that there are 50 states and approximately 15,500 school districts with great diversity that must reach conclusions on actions that are appropriate for their constituencies.

Tomorrow's Teacher

Just as future schools and curricula are destined to change, so will tomorrow's teacher also change. Tomorrow's teacher must wear the mantles of a member of the profession, an instructional leader, and a self-renewing professional.

We must never lose sight of the element of caring in education.

Member of the Profession

The American school system is a large and complex establishment. It is likely to become even more so in the future. By the year 2000 it is likely that the members of the profession will include 2,100,000 public classroom teachers, 275,000 nonpublic classroom teachers, and 700,000 faculty members in higher education. Issues that have concerned the profession in the past include (1) organizing teachers into associations or unions so as to secure power and speak with one voice concerning their collective interests, and (2) addressing issues such as salaries, fringe and retirement benefits, length of workday, tenure, participation in curricular decisions, preparation of future teachers, in-service training, academic freedom, and accountability.

A look into the future is likely to show teachers continuing to be concerned with many of the same issues. Yet these issues will be addressed in a different context. Some elements of that context previously alluded to include larger numbers of adults pursuing education, nontraditional settings such as businesses and social agencies for instruction for adults and other students, nontraditional times for instruction to accommodate students, increased use of technology in delivery systems away from schools for purposes of energy conservation and individualized learning, and perhaps smaller groups for instruction in homes and smaller schools.

What changes lie ahead for the profession in the year 2000? The following changes are likely to occur.

- Employment prospects for teachers will remain relatively poor until the late 1980s. Shortages will then tend to be widespread over many disciplines.
- The accountability trend will continue and will be accepted. However, there will also be an increasing number of questions raised about academic freedom.
- The public will have more respect for teachers as more adults return to school and as instruction becomes more individualized. Teacher-parent contact will be more frequent, which will also result in enhancing the image of the profession.
- Teacher organizations will become more politically active.
- More teachers will be employed in locations outside the traditional school and classroom and will use advanced technology as an instructional technique.
- Merit pay, master teacher plans, and career ladders will be debated seriously in the next few years. The number of school districts adopting these concepts are likely to increase.
- Teachers' salaries are likely to increase across the board.
- Both entrance and retention requirements in teacher education programs are likely to become more rigorous.

Instructional Leader

In what ways will the day-to-day work of tomorrow's teacher change? In light of the expected changes in the school curriculum, the structure of the school, the nature of the learner, and the teaching methodology already discussed, we expect that the role and behavior of teachers will change. More so than in the past, teachers are now apt to be developers of values, resource finders, learning diagnosticians, interdisciplinary specialists, human relations developers, career and leisure counselors, professional leaders, users of futuristic processes, and teaching-learning specialists.[22] These expanded and creative roles will enhance the status of the teaching profession. As those entering the teaching profession prepare to become teachers for the future, they will be challenged.

Self-renewing Professional

Self-renewal for teachers has received much attention during recent years. As the term implies, self-renewal deals with a teacher's continuous efforts to improve professional skills and to keep abreast of the most recent developments in education. Self-renewal also suggests that a teacher must be able to change constantly as society and schools change.

Concerning the future self-renewal of teachers, one might ask:

- How can our teacher-training institutions best prepare teachers for tomorrow—teachers who will be capable of continuous self-renewal?
- How important will teacher renewal be in the future? Will we be able to afford it?
- What conditions are conducive to teacher self-renewal?
- What criteria will a future teacher be able to use in determining a need for self-renewal? What standards will guide the teacher's quest for renewal?

Although these are very difficult questions, answering them will provide exciting and challenging opportunities for future educators.

The future is a paradox—frightening yet exciting, predictable yet unpredictable, inviting yet foreboding, manageable yet uncontrollable. How should educators approach the future? The following anonymous quote might provide a cue.

> You and I, since first we set out upon this strange, uncertain pilgrimage; we picked our way through the Slough of Despond and found that the bogs and quagmires were but figments of our imagination; we have visited the City of Despair and found it walled in only by its own fantasies of Space and Time; we have confronted the Lions of Automata and discovered them to be ephem-

era, the mirror image of our own minds; we have traversed the Valley of Paradise and eaten of its strange fruit, Leisure. Now, we have but a little further to go and our pilgrimage will be at an end. We must cross the Delectable Mountains. They may seem far away, shimmering there; but that is an accident of our eyesight. They really are right here under our feet, if we will but look. Like the Chinese journey of a thousand miles, we shall approach them one step at a time. Shall we go? Now?

Summary and Implications

As society changes in the future, so will its means of educating its student population. The kinds of students pursuing education, the educators, the organization, the curriculum, and instructional methods all will change.

It is clear that more children below age five and more adults will be involved in public education. These new student populations will provide teaching positions that have not existed to any great extent in the past. The positions will become available both to beginning teachers specifically trained for them and to experienced teachers who may want to prepare for them through training in service. The teacher of adult students will have a modified job, not only because of the learners themselves, but also because of the time they are in attendance. Adults, in particular, are likely to be part-time students who are not available for instruction during traditional daytime hours, when they are typically at work. It is also quite likely that the future location of the place of instruction will differ from the traditional school or classroom. Instruction will probably take place in businesses, factories, and other community facilities besides schools.

[71]   The content of the curriculum and the way that it is organized are likely to be in turmoil in the next few years and may change. The current direction of change in content is definitely toward "back to the basics" or a common core of learning, particularly in the high schools. The solid subjects of English, mathematics, science, social science, and languages will be stressed for all students if school districts take action on the recommendations of the national reports. The arts and vocational subjects are likely to suffer. In essence, a college preparatory program is advocated for all students. It will be interesting to see how school districts will make accommodations for those students who are not capable of college preparatory studies or have little interest in those courses. Will the dropout rate increase? Is that what the people of the United States want? The next few years will tell the tale.

[71]   Admission to teacher training programs will become more rigorous, as will the standards for retention. Members of the profession are likely to find their in-service activities increasing and broadening in nature with a heavier emphasis on subject matter content. Efforts will be made to implement merit pay, master teacher plans, and career ladders in some school districts. Because of these efforts the profession may change more in the next few years than it has in the past 30 years, although the changes

will be strongly resisted by the organized profession. A struggle will undoubtedly take place.

The implications for students considering education as a career and for current practitioners are many. Currently, teaching is not viewed as a desirable career because of low salaries, poor working conditions, and a general lowering of its prestige as a profession. Will raising salaries, having more rigorous preparation programs along with the enticement of merit pay, the concept of the master teacher, and the opportunity of a career ladder cause more students to enter the profession? If not, who will teach the young in the year 2000? What will the qualifications be to enter the profession?

Will the aforementioned changes entice practicing teachers to stay in the profession? Or will the younger and less experienced teachers leave the profession? At the very least, the next decade will be interesting.

DISCUSSION QUESTIONS

1. To what degree and in what ways do you feel teacher organizations, such as the NEA and the AFT, will change in the future?
2. What do you think future adult education programs will be like in America?
3. Do you believe that schools of the future should lead in social change or simply serve society by transmitting the existing culture to our children? Defend your view.
4. Discuss what important functions you feel our elementary schools should perform in the next twenty years.
5. What are the chief problems that you feel our public educational system will face by the year 2000?

SUPPLEMENTAL ACTIVITIES

1. Make a list of forecasts about future schools. State several assumptions on which you base each forecast.
2. Interview a retired teacher concerning the changes that have occurred in teaching during his or her career.
3. Discuss the future of teacher organizations with an educator who is a member of either the NEA or the AFT.
4. Compile a list of ways in which future teachers might renew their professional selves.
5. Interview a leader of a teacher organization to explore how the organization will be encouraging teacher self-renewal in the future.

NOTES

1. W. Vance Grant and Leo J. Eiden, *Digest of Educational Statistics, 1982* (Washington, D.C.: U.S. Government Printing Office, 1982), p. 45.

2. Valena White Plisko, ed., *The Condition of Education 1983 Edition*, National Center for Educational Statistics (Washington, D.C.: U.S. Government Printing Office, 1983), p. 157.

3. Ibid., pp. 168–170.

4. Speech by Malcolm S. Knowles, as reported by Paul F. Fendt, "Alternatives in Education: A Futur-

ist View," *Education Unlimited* 2 (April 1980): 12–13.

5. Harold G. Shane, "The Views of 50 Distinguished World Citizens and Educators," *The Futurist* 10 (October 1976): 255–256.

6. Harold G. Shane, *Curriculum Change toward the 21st Century* (Washington, D.C.: National Education Association, 1977), p. 8.

7. Ibid., pp. 16–26.

8. Ibid., p. 57.

9. Ibid.

10. Ibid., pp. 69–70.

11. Ibid., p. 70.

12. Ibid., pp. 42–43.

13. Ibid.

14. Ibid., p. 57.

15. Ibid.

16. Ibid.

17. Harold Howe II, "Education Moves to Center Stage: An Overview of Recent Studies," *Phi Delta Kappan* 65 (November 1983): p. 168.

18. Ibid., p. 169.

19. National Commission on Excellence, *The Nation at Risk: The Imperative for Educational Reform* (Washington, D.C.: U.S. Department of Education, 1983), p. 24.

20. Diane Ravitch, "On Thinking About the Future," *Phi Delta Kappan* 64 (January 1983): 319.

21. Ibid.

22. Joel L. Burdin, "Futurism as a Focus in Instructional Planning," *Journal of Teacher Education* 25 (Summer 1974): 146–147.

BIBLIOGRAPHY

Adler, Mortimer J. *The Paideia Proposal: An Educational Manifesto.* New York: Macmillan, 1982.

Boyer, Ernest. *High School: A Report on Secondary Education in America.* New York: Harper and Row, 1983.

Frymier, Jack, ed. *Bad Times, Good Schools.* West Lafayette, Ind.: Kappa Delta Pi, 1983.

Goodlad, John I. *A Place Called School: Prospects for the Future.* New York: McGraw-Hill, 1983.

National Commission on Excellence in Education. *A Nation at Risk: The Imperative for Educational Reform.* Washington, D.C.: U.S. Department of Education, 1983.

Phi Delta Kappan 61 (October 1980). Special Issue/ Teacher Education: Time for Reform.

Phi Delta Kappan 67 (January 1981). An issue devoted to the heritage of education and the future of education.

Shane, Harold C. *Curriculum Change toward the 21st Century.* Washington, D.C.: National Education Association, 1977.

Sizer, Theodore R. "High School Reform: The Need for Engineering." *Phi Delta Kappan* 64 (June 1983): 679–683.

Smith, B. Othanel. *A Design for a School of Pedagogy.* Washington, D.C.: U.S. Department of Education, 1980.

Appendix A

A Bill of Rights
for High School Students

Neither students nor teachers shed their constitutional rights to freedom of speech or expression at the schoolhouse gate. That has been the unmistakable holding of the Supreme Court for almost fifty years. (*Tinker v. Des Moines,* 1969)

The following statement of students' rights is intended as a guide to students, parents, teachers, and administrators who are interested in developing proper safeguards for student liberties. IT IS NOT A SUMMARY OF THE LAW, BUT SETS FORTH IN A GENERAL WAY WHAT THE ACLU THINKS *SHOULD* BE ADOPTED. . . .

ARTICLE I. Expression
  A. Students shall be free to express themselves and disseminate their views without prior restraints through speech, essays, publications, pictures, armbands, badges, and all other media of communication. Student expression may be subject to disciplinary action only in the event that such expression creates a significant physical disruption of school activities.
  B. No reporter for a student publication may be required to reveal a source of information.
  C. Students shall have the right to hear speakers and presentations representing a wide range of views and subjects in classes, clubs, and assemblies. Outside speakers and presentations may be limited only by considerations of time, space, and expense.
  D. Students shall be free to assemble, demonstrate, and picket peacefully, to petition and to organize on school grounds or in school buildings subject only to reasonable limitations on time, place, and manner designed to avoid significant physical obstruction of traffic or significant physical disruption of school activities.
  E. Students shall be free to determine their dress and grooming as they see fit, subject only to reasonable limitations designed to protect student safety or prevent significant ongoing disruption of school activities.

Source: American Civil Liberties Union of Maryland, Baltimore, Md. Reprinted by permission. (See also Alan H. Levine and Eve Cary, *The Rights of Students,* Avon Books, 224 West 57th Street, New York, NY 10019.)

F. No student shall be required to participate in any way in patriotic exercises or be penalized for refusing to participate.

ARTICLE II.   Religion

A. Students shall be free to practice their own religion or no religion.
B. There shall be no school-sanctioned religious exercises or events.
C. Religious history, ideas, institutions, and literature may be studied in the same fashion as any other academic subject.

ARTICLE III.   Privacy

A. Students should be free from undercover surveillance through the use of mechanical, electronic, or other secret methods, including undercover agents, without issuance of a warrant.
B. Students should be free from warrantless searches and seizures by school officials in their personal effects, lockers, or any other facilities assigned to their personal use. General housekeeping inspections of lockers and desks shall not occur without reasonable notice.
C. Student record files
   1. A student's permanent record file shall include only information about academic competence and notation of the fact of participation in school clubs, sports, and other such school extracurricular activities. This file shall not be disclosed to any person or agency outside the school, except to the student's parents or guardian, without the student's permission.
   2. Any other records (e.g., medical or psychological evaluations) shall be available only to the student, the student's parents or guardian, and the school staff. Such other records shall be governed by strict safeguards for confidentiality and shall not be available to others in or outside of the school even upon consent of the student.
   3. A record shall be kept, and shall be available to the student, of any consultation of the student's files, noting the date and purpose of the consultation and the name of the person who consulted the files.
   4. All records shall be open to challenge and correction by the student.
   5. A student's opinions shall not be disclosed to any outside person or agency.

ARTICLE IV.   Equality

A. No organization that officially represents the school in any capacity and no curricular or extracurricular activity organized by school authories may deny or segregate participation or award or withhold privileges on the basis of race, color, national origin, sex, religion, creed, or opinions.

ARTICLE V.   Government

A. All students may hold office and may vote in student elections. These rights shall not be denied for any reason.
B. Student government organizations and their operation, scope, and amendment procedures shall be established in a written constitution formulated with full and effective student participation.

ARTICLE VI.   Due Process

A. Regulations concerning student behavior shall be formulated with full and effective student participation. Such regulations shall be published and made available to all students. Regulations shall be fully, clearly, and precisely written.

B. No student shall be held accountable by school authorities for any behavior occurring outside the organized school day or off school property (except during school-sponsored events) unless such behavior presents a clear, present, and substantial ongoing danger to persons and property in the school.

C. There shall be no cruel, unusual, demeaning, or excessive punishments. There shall be no corporal punishment.

D. No student shall be compelled by school officials to undergo psychological therapy or use medication without that student's consent. No student may be required to participate in any psychological or personality testing, research project, or experiment without that student's written, informed, and willing consent. The nature, purposes, and possible adverse consequences of the testing, project, or experiment shall be fully explained to student.

E. A student shall have the right to due process in disciplinary and investigative proceedings. In cases that may involve serious penalties, such as suspension for more than three days, expulsion, transfer to another school, a notation on the student's record, or long-term loss of privileges:

1. A student shall be guaranteed a formal hearing before an impartial board. That student shall have the right to appeal hearing results.

2. Rules for hearings and appeals shall be written and published, and there shall be full and effective student participation in their formulation.

3. The student shall be advised in writing of any charges brought against that student.

4. The student shall have the right to present evidence and witnesses and to cross-examine adverse witnesses. The student shall have the right to have an advisor of his or her own choosing present.

5. The hearing shall be open or private as the student chooses.

6. The student shall have a reasonable time to prepare a defense.

7. A student may not be compelled to incriminate himself or herself.

8. The burden of proof, beyond a reasonable doubt, shall be upon the school.

9. A written record of all hearings and appeals shall be made available to the student, at the school's expense.

10. A student shall be free from double jeopardy.

Appendix B

Methods of Selecting
State School Board Members

State	1947 Elected by People or Representatives	1947 Appointed by Governor	1947 Other	1981 Elected by People or Representatives	1981 Appointed by Governor	1981 Other
Alabama		X		X		
Alaska		X			X	
Arizona			X		X	
Arkansas		X			X	
California		X			X	
Colorado			X	X		
Connecticut		X			X	
Delaware		X			X	
Florida			X			
Georgia		X			X	X
Hawaii		X		X		
Idaho		X			X	
Illinois	(no state board)				X	
Indiana		X			X	
Iowa	(no state board)			X		
Kansas		X		X		
Kentucky		X			X	
Louisiana	X			X		
Maine	(no state board)				X	
Maryland		X			X	
Massachusetts		X			X	
Michigan	X			X		
Minnesota		X			X	
Mississippi			X			
Missouri		X			X	
Montana		X			X	X

State	1947 Elected by People or Representatives	Appointed by Governor	Other	1981 Elected by People or Representatives	Appointed by Governor	Other
Nebraska		(no state board)		X		
Nevada	X			X		
New Hampshire		X			X	
New Jersey		X			X	
New Mexico		X		X		
New York			X	X		
North Carolina		X			X	
North Dakota		(no state board)			X	
Ohio		(no state board)		X		
Oklahoma		X			X	
Oregon		X			X	
Pennsylvania		X			X	
Rhode Island		(no state board)			X	
South Carolina		X		X		
South Dakota		(no state board)			X	
Tennessee		X			X	
Texas		X		X		
Utah			X	X		
Vermont		X			X	
Virginia		X			X	
Washington			X	X		
West Virginia		X			X	
Wisconsin		(no state board)			(no state board)	
Wyoming			X		X	
TOTALS	3	30	8	16	31	2

Source: Adapted from David E. Elder and Milburn P. Akers, "A State Board of Education," *Illinois Education* 27, January, 1965, p. 214; R. F. Will, *State Education Structure and Organizations,* U.S. Office of Education, OE-23038, Misc., No. 46, U.S. Government Printing Office, Washington, D.C., 1964; and data made available by the Council of Chief State School Officers.

Appendix C

Methods of Selecting
Chief State School Officers

State	1947 Appt. by State Board	1947 Appt. by Governor	1947 Elected by People	1981 Appt. by State Board	1981 Appt. by Governor	1981 Elected by People
Alabama			X	X		
Alaska	X			X		
Arizona			X			X
Arkansas	X			X		
California			X			X
Colorado			X	X		
Connecticut	X			X		
Delaware	X			X		
Florida			X			X
Georgia			X			X
Hawaii		X		X		
Idaho			X			X
Illinois			X	X		
Indiana			X			X
Iowa			X	X		
Kansas			X	X		
Kentucky			X			X
Louisiana			X			X
Maine		X		X		
Maryland	X			X		
Massachusetts	X			X		
Michigan			X	X		
Minnesota	X			X		
Mississippi			X			X
Missouri	X			X		
Montana			X			X
Nebraska			X	X		
Nevada			X	X		

State	1947			1981		
	Appt. by State Board	Appt. by Governor	Elected by People	Appt. by State Board	Appt. by Governor	Elected by People
New Hampshire	X			X		
New Jersey		X			X	
New Mexico			X	X		
New York	X			X		
North Carolina			X			X
North Dakota			X			X
Ohio		X		X		
Oklahoma			X			X
Oregon			X			X
Pennsylvania		X			X	
Rhode Island		X		X		
South Carolina			X			X
South Dakota			X			X
Tennessee		X			X	
Texas			X	X		
Utah			X	X		
Vermont	X			X		
Virginia		X			X	
Washington			X			X
West Virginia			X	X		
Wisconsin			X			X
Wyoming			X			X
TOTALS	11	8	31	27	4	19

Source: Adapted from David E. Elder and Milburn P. Akers, "A State Board of Education," *Illinois Education* 27, January, 1965, p. 216; R. F. Will, *State Education Structure and Organizations,* U.S. Office of Education, OE-23038, Misc., No. 46, U.S. Government Printing Office, Washington, D.C., 1964; and data made available by the Council of Chief State School Officers.

Appendix D

Federal Education Acts

1787   Northwest Ordinance
1862   First Morrill Land Grant Act
1867   Department of Education Act
1887   Hatch Act
1890   Second Morrill Land Grant Act
1911   The State Marine School Act
1914   Smith-Lever Agriculture Extension Act
1917   Smith-Hughes Vocational Act
1918   Vocational Rehabilitation Act
1919   An act to provide for further educational facilities
1920   Smith-Bankhead Act
1935   Bankhead-Jones Act
1935   Agricultural Adjustment Act
1940   Vocational Education for National Defense Act
1941   Lanham Act
1943   Vocational Rehabilitation Act
1944   GI Bill of Rights
1944   Surplus Property Act
1946   National School Lunch Act
1946   George-Barden Act
1948   United States Information and Educational Exchange Act
1949   Federal Property and Administrative Services Act
1950   National Science Foundation
1950   Financial assistance for local educational agencies affected by federal activities
1950   Housing Act
1954   Cooperative Research Act
1954   National Advisory Committee on Education Act
1954   School Milk Program Act
1956   Library Services Act
1958   National Defense Education Act
1958   Education of Mentally Retarded Children Act
1958   Captioned Films for the Deaf Act
1961   Area Redevelopment Act
1962   Manpower Development and Training Act

1962	Migration and Refugee Assistance Act of 1962
1963	Vocational Education Act
1963	Manpower Development and Training Act
1963	Higher Education Facilities Act
1964	Civil Rights Act
1964	Economic Opportunity Act
1965	Elementary and Secondary Education Act
1965	Higher Education Act
1965	Health Professions Educational Assistance Amendments
1965	National Foundation on the Arts and the Humanities Act
1965	National Technical Institute for the Deaf Act
1965	National Vocational Student Loan Insurance Act
1966	International Education Act
1966	Adult Education Act
1966	Model Secondary School for the Deaf Act
1966	Elementary and Secondary Education Amendments
1967	Education Professions Development Act
1968	Elementary and Secondary Education Amendments
1968	Handicapped Childrens' Early Education Assistance Act
1968	Vocational Education Amendments
1968	Higher Education Amendments
1970	Elementary and Secondary Education Assistance Programs
1970	National Commission on Libraries and Information Science Act
1970	Office of Education Appropriation Act
1970	Environmental Education Act
1970	Drug Abuse Education Act
1971	Comprehensive Health Manpower Training Act
1972	Title IX Education Amendment
1972	Drug Abuse Office and Treatment Act
1972	Education Amendments
1972	Indian Education Act
1973	Older Americans Comprehensive Services Amendment
1973	Comprehensive Employment and Training Act
1974	Educational Amendments
1974	Juvenile Justice and Delinquency Prevention Act
1974	White House Conference on Library and Information Services Act
1975	Education for the Handicapped Act
1975	Indian Self-Determination and Education Assistance Act
1975	Indochina Migration and Refugee Assistance Act
1976	Education Amendments
1977	Youth Employment and Demonstration Projects Act
1978	Career Education Incentive Act
1978	Tribally Controlled Community College Assistance Act
1978	Education Amendments
1978	Middle Income Student Assistance Act
1979	Department of Education Organization Act
1980	Asbestos School Hazard Protection and Control Act
1980	Amendments to the Higher Education Act of 1965
1981	Education Consolidation and Improvement Act
1983	Release of "Nation at Risk" Report by Presidential Commission

Appendix E

Important Dates in the History of Education

ca. 4000 B.C.	Written language developed
2000	First schools
1200	Trojan War
479–338	Period of Greek brilliance
445–431	Greek Age of Pericles
404	Fall of Athens
336–323	Ascendancy of Alexander the Great
303	A few private Greek teachers set up schools in Rome
167	First Greek library in Rome
146	Fall of Corinth: Greece falls to Rome
0	Christ born
A.D. 31–476	Empire of Rome
70	Destruction of Jerusalem
476	Fall of Rome in the West
800	Charlemagne crowned Emperor
1100–1300	Crusades
ca. 1150	Universities of Paris and Bologna
1209	Cambridge founded
1295	Voyage of Marco Polo
1384	Order of Brethren of the Common Life founded
ca. 1400	Thirty-eight universities; 108 by 1600
1423	Printing invented
1456	First book printed
1487	Vasco de Gama discovered African route to India
1492	Columbus lands in America
ca. 1492	Colonists begin exploiting Native Americans
ca. 1500	250 Latin grammar schools in England
1517	Luther nails theses to cathedral door; beginning of Reformation
1519–1521	Magellan first circumnavigates the globe
1534	Founding of Jesuits
1536	Sturm established his Gymnasium in Germany, the first classical secondary school
1568	Indian school established in Cuba by the Society of Jesus

1601	English Poor Law, established principle of tax-supported schools
1618	Holland had compulsory school law
1620	Plymouth Colony, Massachusetts, settled
1635	Boston Latin Grammar School founded
1636	Harvard founded
1642	Massachusetts law of 1642 compelled inspection
1647	Massachusetts law of 1647 compelled establishment of schools
1662	First newspaper in England
1672	First teacher-training class, Father Demia, France
1684	Brothers of the Christian Schools founded
1685	First normal school, de la Salle, Rheims, France
1697	First teacher training in Germany, Francke's Seminary, Halle
1723	Indian student house opened by William and Mary College
1751	Franklin established first academy in the United States
1762	Rousseau's *Émile* published
1775–1783	Revolution, United States
1789	Adoption of Constitution, United States
1798	Lancaster developed monitorial plan of education
1799–1815	Ascendancy of Napoleon, Waterloo
1804	Pestalozzi's Institute at Yverdon established
1806	First Lancastrian School in New York
1819	Dartmouth College Decision
1821	First American high school
1821	Troy Seminary for Women, Emma Willard, first higher education for women, United States
1823	First private normal school in the United States, Concord, Vermont, by Rev. Hall
1825	Labor unions come on the scene
1826	Froebel's *The Education of Man* published
1827	Massachusetts law compelled high schools
1837	Massachusetts had first state board, Horace Mann first secretary
1839	First public normal school, United States, Lexington, Massachusetts
1855	First kindergarten in United States—after German model, Mrs. Schurz
1861–1865	Civil War
1861	Oswego (New York) Normal School (Edward Sheldon)
1862	Morrill Land Grant Act: college of engineering, military science, agriculture in each state
1868	Herbartian Society founded
1872	Kalamazoo Decision, made high schools legal
1888	Teachers College, Columbia University, founded
1892	Committee of Ten established
1909–1910	The first junior high schools established at Berkeley, California, and Columbus, Ohio
ca. 1910	The first junior colleges established at Fresno, California, and Joliet, Illinois

1917	The Smith-Hughes Act, encouraged agriculture, industry, and home economics education in the United States
1932–1940	The Eight Year Study of 30 high schools completed by the Progressive Education Association; reported favorably on the modern school
1941	Japanese bomb Pearl Harbor
1941	Lanham Act
1942	The Progressive Education Association published the findings of the Eight Year Study
1944–1946	Legislation by 78th Congress provided subsistence allowance, tuition fees, and supplies for the education of veterans of World War II
1945	The United Nations Educational, Scientific, and Cultural Organization (UNESCO) initiated efforts to improve educational standards throughout the world
1946–1947	National "baby boom" eventually causing huge increase in school enrollments
1948	*McCollum* v. *Board of Education;* court ruled it illegal to release children for religious classes in public school buildings
1950	The National Science Foundation founded
1952	The GI bill's educational benefits extended to Korean veterans
1954	U.S. Supreme Court decision required eventual racial integration of public schools
1954	Cooperative Research Program
1956	The Russians launched Sputnik
1958	Federal Congress passed the National Defense Education Act
1959	James B. Conant wrote *The American High School Today*
1961	Federal court ruled de facto racial segregation illegal
1961	Peace Corps established
1961	Approximately four million college students in United States
1962	In *Engle* v. *Vitale,* court ruled compulsory prayer in public school illegal
1963	Vocational Education Act
1963	Manpower Development and Training Act
1964	The Economic Opportunity Act provided federal funds for such programs as Head Start
1964	Civil Rights Act
1965	The Elementary and Secondary Education Act allowed more federal funds for public schools
1965	Higher Education Act
1966	The GI bill's educational benefits extended to Southeast Asia war veterans
1966	One million Americans travel abroad
1948–1966	Fulbright programs in 136 nations involving 82,500 scholars
1966	U.S. International Education Act
1966	The Coleman Report suggested that racially balanced schools did not necessarily provide a better education
1967	Education Professions Development Act
1972	Indian Education Act passed, designed to help Native Americans help themselves

1972	Title IX Education Amendment outlawing discrimination on the basic of sex
1973	In *Rodriguez* v. *San Antonio Independent School,* the Supreme Court ruled that a state's system for financing schools did not violate the Constitution although there were large disparities in per-pupil expenditure
1975	Indochina Migration and Refugee Assistance Act (Public Law 94–23)
1975	Public Law 94–142, requiring local districts to provide education for special and handicapped children
1979	Department of Education Act
1980	The U.S. Secretary of Education became a cabinet post
1983	*High School: A Report on Secondary Education in America* by the Carnegie Foundation
1983	*A Nation at Risk: The Imperative for Educational Reform,* report by the National Commission on Excellence in Education
1983	Task Force on Education for Economic Growth, Action for Excellence, Education Commission of the States Report
1983	Task Force on Federal Elementary and Secondary Education Policy, Making the Grade, the Twentieth Century Fund Report
1980–1984	"Moral Majority" fundamental religious movement advocating prayer in the schools and teaching of Biblical creation story

Appendix F

Philosophical Categories Recognizable by Teaching Styles: Differentiation of Philosophies

Two Broad Philosophical Categories That Are Most Easily Recognizable by Teaching Styles

Perennialist/Essentialist → S-R Associationist Theories of Learning
Behavioral Objectives
Assumption of one right answer per problem.

Experimentalist/Existentialist → Gestalt Theories of Learning
Cognitive–Affective Objectives
Assumption of alternative appropriate answers for each problem.

Further Differentiation of Philosophies

Perennialism—emphasis on humanities as presented in great books; assumption that there are absolute truths and standards more real than the physical world.

Essentialism—emphasis on physical sciences as used by authorities; assumption that there are no absolute truths and that success is based on absorption of knowledge about the physical world.

Experimentalism—emphasis on social sciences as a framework for problem-solving; assumption that physical world is constantly changing.

Existentialism—emphasis on problem-solving about highly controversial and emotional issues in any subject matter area; assumption that learners "define" themselves and their relationships to the environment by their choices.

Reconstructionism—implies one has decided what the "perfect" form of society is and seeks to reach that society through teaching techniques associated with Experimentalism/Existentialism.

Behaviorism—implies that one has decided what the "perfect" form of society is and seeks to reach that society through teaching techniques associated with Essentialism.

Source: Lloyd Duck, *Teaching with Charisma*, Allyn and Bacon, Inc., Boston, 1981, p. 26.

Appendix G

Schematic Summary of Education Views

Comparative Philosophies

	Definition		Idealism	Realism	Neo-Thomism	Experi-mentalism	Existen-tialism
Metaphysics	The study of reality: What is real?		A world of mind	A world of things	A world of Reason and Being/God	A world of experience	A world of existing
Epistemology	The study of knowing and knowledge: What is true?		Seeing with the "mind's eye"—con-sistency of ideas	Spectator Theory: sensation and corre-spondence	Intuition, logical rea-soning, and revelation	Testing to see what works	Subjective choice, personal appropria-tion
Axiology	The study of valuing and values: What is good?	**Ethics**	The imitation of the Absolute Self	The law of nature	The rational act	The public test	The anguish of freedom
	What is beautiful?	**Aesthetics**	Reflection of the Ideal	Reflection of nature	Creative intuition	The public taste	Revolt from the public norm

Source: Van Cleve Morris and Young Pai, *Philosophy and the American School,* 2nd ed. (Boston: Houghton Mifflin, 1976), pp. 294–295. Reprinted by permission.

Educational Implications

	Idealism	Realism	Neo-Thomism	Experimentalism	Existentialism
Curricular Emphasis	Subject matter of the mind: literature, intellectual history, philosophy, religion	Subject matter of the physical world: mathematics and science	Subject matter of intellect and spirit; disciplinary subjects: mathematics and language and doctrine	Subject matter of social experience: the social studies	Subject matter of choice: art, ethics, moral philosophy, religion
Preferred Method	Teaching for the handling of ideas: lecture, discussion	Teaching for mastery of factual information and basic skills: demon-stration, recitation	Disciplining the mind: formal drill— readying the spirit: catechism	Problem solving: project method	Arousing personal response: Socratic questioning
Character Education	Imitating exemplars, heroes	Training in rules of conduct	Disciplining behavior to reason	Making group decisions in light of consequences	Awakening the self to responsibility
Developing Taste	Studying the masterworks	Studying design in nature	Finding beauty in reason	Participating in art projects	Composing a personal art work

Appendix H

Domains of Learning

The levels of cognitive learning are numerically ordered from the most superficial to the most advanced to establish a hierarchical arrangement for evaluating depth of learning.

1.00 Knowledge
    1.10 Knowledge of specifics
    1.20 Knowledge of ways and means of dealing with specifics
    1.30 Knowledge of the universals and abstractions in a field
2.00 Comprehension
    2.10 Translation
    2.20 Interpretation
    2.30 Extrapolation
3.00 Application
4.00 Analysis
    4.10 Analysis of elements
    4.20 Analysis of relationships
    4.30 Analysis of organizational principles
5.00 Synthesis
    5.10 Production of a unique communication
    5.20 Production of a plan or proposed set of operations
    5.30 Derivation of a set of abstract relations
6.00 Evaluation
    6.10 Judgments in terms of internal evidence
    6.20 Judgments in terms of external criteria

Source: Benjamin S. Bloom, ed., *Taxonomy of Educational Objectives* (New York: Longman, Green, 1956), pp. 6–8.

The taxonomy also presents the following scheme for classifying different levels of affective learning:

1.00 Receiving (attending)
    1.10 Awareness
    1.20 Willingness to receive
    1.30 Controlled or selected attention

2.00 Responding
    2.10 Acquiescence in responding
    2.20 Willingness to respond
    2.30 Satisfaction in response
3.00 Valuing
    3.10 Acceptance of a value
    3.20 Preference for a value
    3.30 Commitment
4.00 Organization
    4.10 Conceptualization of a value
    4.20 Organization of a value system
5.00 Characterization by a value or value complex
    5.10 Generalized set
    5.20 Characterization

Source: David R. Krathwohl, Benjamin S. Bloom, and Bertram B. Masia, *Taxonomy of Educational Objectives* (New York: David McKay, 1964, pp. 176–193.

The taxonomy for the psychomotor domain was presented by Anita J. Harrow in 1972. Her levels of learning for this taxonomy are as follows:

1.00 Reflex movements
    1.10 Segmental reflexes
    1.20 Intersegmental reflexes
    1.30 Suprasegmental reflexes
2.00 Basic-fundamental movements
    2.10 Locomotor movements
    2.20 Nonlocomotor movements
    2.30 Manipulative movements
3.00 Perceptual abilities
    3.10 Kinesthetic discrimination
    3.20 Visual discrimination
    3.30 Auditory discrimination
    3.40 Tactile discrimination
    3.50 Coordinated abilities
4.00 Physical abilities
    4.10 Endurance
    4.20 Strength
    4.30 Flexibility
    4.40 Agility
5.00 Skilled movements
    5.10 Simple adaptive skills
    5.20 Compound adaptive skills
    5.30 Complex adaptive skills
6.00 Nondiscursive communication
    6.10 Expressive movement
    6.20 Interpretive movement

Source: Anita J. Harrow, *A Taxonomy of the Psychomotor Domain* (New York: David McKay, 1972, pp. 1–2.

Appendix I

Selected National Education Reports 1982–1984

Adler, Mortimer H. *The Paideia Proposal*. New York: Macmillan, 1982.

American Association of Colleges for Teacher Education. *Educating a Profession: Profiles for a Beginning Teacher*. Washington, D.C.: American Association for Colleges for Teacher Education, 1983.

Boyer, Ernest. *High School: A Report on Secondary Education in America*. New York: Harper and Row, 1983.

College Board, Project Equality. *Academic Preparation for College: What Students Need to Know and Be Able to Do*. New York: College Board, 1983.

Education Commission of the States. *Action for Excellence: A Comprehensive Plan to Improve Our Nation's Schools*. Denver, Colo.: Education Commission of the States, 1983.

Goodlad, John I. *A Place Called School: Prospects for the Future*. New York: McGraw-Hill, 1983.

National Commission on Excellence in Education. *A Nation at Risk: The Imperative for Educational Reform*. Washington, D.C.: U.S. Government Printing Office, 1983.

National Education Association. *Excellence in Our Schools, Teacher Education: An Action Plan*. Washington, D.C.: National Education Association, 1982.

National Science Board Commission on Precollege Education in Mathematics, Science and Technology. *Educating Americans for the 21st Century: A Report to the American People and the National Science Board*. Washington, D.C.: National Science Board, National Science Foundation, 1983.

Sizer, Theodore. *Horace's Compromise*. Boston: Houghton Mifflin, 1984.

Southern Regional Education Board. *The Need for Quality*. Atlanta, Ga.: Southern Regional Education Board, 1983.

Twentieth Century Fund Task Force on Federal Elementary and Secondary Education Policy. *Making the Grade*. New York: Twentieth Century Fund, 1983.

Glossary

Ability grouping assigning pupils to homogeneous groups according to intellectual ability, for instruction.

Academic freedom the opportunity for a teacher to teach without coercion, censorship, or other restrictive interference.

Academic program a program of studies designed primarily to prepare students for college.

Academy an early American secondary school that stressed practical subjects.

Accelerated program the more rapid advancement of superior students through school.

Accountability holding schools and teachers responsible for what students learn.

Accreditation recognition given to an educational institution that has met accepted standards applied to it by an outside agency.

Achievement test an examination that measures the extent to which a person has acquired certain information or mastered certain skills, usually as a result of specific instruction.

Activity curriculum a curriculum design in which the interests of and learning purposes for children determine the educational program; teacher and pupils together select and plan activities.

Adult education courses and other organized educational activities taken by persons seventeen years of age and over, excluding courses taken by full-time students in programs leading toward a high school diploma or an academic degree and occupational programs of six months or more duration. It includes all courses taken for credit by part-time students. Providers of instruction include not only public and private educational institutions, but also business and industry, governmental agencies, private community organizations, and tutors.

Advanced placement programs provided by high schools, in cooperation with community colleges or universities, in which qualifying students take college-level courses.

Aesthetics referring to the nature of beauty and judgments about it.

Affective domain attitudinal and emotional areas of learning, such as values and feelings.

Affective learning the acquisition of feelings, tastes, emotions, will, and other aspects of social and psychological development gained through feeling rather than through intellectualization.

Affirmative action a plan by which personnel policies and hiring practices do not discriminate against women and members of minority groups.

Alternative education unconventional educational experiences for students inadequately taught in regular classes; alternatives include schools without walls, street academies, free schools, and second-chance schools.

Alternative school a school—private or public, innovative or fundamental—that provides options or alternatives to the regular public school.

American Federation of Teachers (AFT) a national teachers' union primarily concerned with improving educational conditions and protecting teachers' rights.

Aptitude the ability to profit from training or instruction of a specific kind.

Area vocational center a shared-time facility that provides instruction only in vocational education to students from throughout a school system or region. Students attending an area vocational center receive the academic portion of their education program in regular secondary schools or other institutions.

Articulation the relationship between the different elements of the educational program.

Associate degrees degrees and awards based on less than four years of work beyond high school.

Attendance area an administrative unit consisting of the territory from which children may legally attend a given school building.

Audiovisual material any device to encourage and facilitate the learning process through sound or sight or both.

Axiology the study of values and of value judgments.

Bachelor's or first-level degree lowest degree conferred by a college, university, or professional school requiring 4 or more years of academic work.

Back to basics a broad, largely grass roots movement evolving out of a concern for declining test scores and student incompetence in math and reading.

Behavioral objective precise statement of what the learner must do to demonstrate mastery at the end of a prescribed learning task.

Behavior modification changing behavior in a more desirable direction through the use of rewards or other reinforcement.

Behaviorism implies that one has decided what the "perfect" form of society is and seeks to reach that society through teaching techniques associated with essentialism.

Bilingual education educational program in which both English-speaking and non-English-speaking students participate in a bicultural curriculum using both languages.

Board of education agencies, constituted at the state and local levels, responsible for formulating educational policy; with members sometimes appointed but more frequently elected at the local level.

Busing a method for remedying segregation by transporting students to schools that have been racially or ethically unbalanced.

Capital outlay expenditures for land or existing buildings, improvement of grounds, construction of buildings, additions to buildings, and initial or additional equipment. Includes replacement and rehabilitation, and installment or lease payments (excluding interest) that have a terminal date and result in the acquisition of property.

Career education educational experience through which one learns about occupational opportunities and about work.

Carnegie unit a unit awarded to a student for successfully completing a high school course that meets for a minimum of 120 clock hours.

Categorical aid financial aid to local school districts from state or federal agencies for specific, limited purposes only.

Certification the act by a state department of education of officially authorizing a person to accept employment in keeping with the provisions of the credential.

Chief state school officer the executive head of a state department of education.

Child advocacy movement a movement dedicated to defining, protecting, and ensuring the rights of children.

Child-centered instruction instruction designed for the interests, abilities, and needs of individual students.

Classroom environment the physical structure, emotional climate, aesthetic characteristics, and learning resources of a classroom.

Classroom teacher a staff member assigned the professional activities of instructing students, in classroom situations, for which daily student attendance figures for the school system are kept.

Code of ethics formal statement of appropriate professional behaviors.

Cognitive domain the area of learning that involves the acquisition and utilization of knowledge.

Cognitive learning the learner's acquisition of facts, concepts, and principles through intellectualization.

Coleman Report (1981) a study comparing the effectiveness of public school and private school education.

Collective bargaining a procedure, usually specified by written agreement, for resolving disagreements on salaries, hours, and conditions of employment between employers and employees through negotiation.

Collective bargaining agent an organization such as the National Education Association, American Federation of Teachers, etc., recognized by the institution, either voluntarily or through agent elections, as representing the interests of faculty in collective bargaining.

College a postsecondary school that offers general or liberal arts education, usually leading to a first degree. Junior colleges and community colleges are included under this terminology.

Committee of Fifteen historic NEA committee that reversed the findings of the Committee of Ten (1895).

Committee of Ten historic NEA committee that studied secondary education (1893).

Common school a school open to the public and providing similar education for all social classes.

Community school a school intimately connected with the life of the community that tries to provide for the educational needs of all in the locality.

Compensatory education enriched or extended educational experiences or services made available to children of low-income families.

Competency the demonstrated ability to perform specific acts at a particular level of skill or accuracy.

Competency-based certification the general process by which the state (or agency or organization authorized by the state) provides a credential to an individual. Processes may require individuals to demonstrate a mastery of minimum essential generic and specialization competencies and other related criteria adopted by the board through a comprehensive written examination and through other procedures that may be prescribed by the board of educational examiners.

Competency-based education learning based on

highly specialized concepts, skills, and attitudes related directly to some endeavor.

Comprehensive secondary school a general secondary school offering programs in both vocational and general academic subjects, but in which the majority of the students are not enrolled in programs of vocational education.

Compulsory education school attendance required by law on the theory that it is for the benefit of the state or commonwealth to educate all the people.

Computer-assisted instruction (CAI) direct two-way teaching-learning communication between a student and programmed instructional material stored in a computer.

Computer-managed instruction (CMI) a record-keeping procedure for tracking student performance using a computer.

Consolidation the act of forming an enlarged school by uniting smaller schools.

Content subject matter.

Continuing education extended opportunity for study and training following completion of or withdrawal from full-time school and college programs.

Core curriculum curriculum design in which one subject or group of subjects becomes a center or core to which all other subjects are correlated.

Corporal punishment infliction of physical punishment on the body of a student by a school employee for disciplinary reasons.

Cost-effectiveness analysis a means of analyzing the extent to which an undertaking accomplishes its objectives in relation to its cost.

Criterion-referenced data data gathered from specially constructed instruments designed to measure expected learning changes.

Cultural bias accepting one's own cultural values as valid for all.

Cultural pluralism a way of describing a society made up of many different cultural groups coming together to form a unified whole.

Curriculum all educational experiences under supervision of the school.

Custodial student a student who is so limited in mental, social, physical, or emotional development that institutional care or constant supervision at home is required.

Dame school a low-level primary school in the colonial and other early periods, usually conducted by an untrained woman in her own home.

Day care center a place or institution charged with caring for children.

Decentralization a process whereby a higher central source of responsibility and authority assigns certain responsibility and authority to a subordinate position.

Deductive reasoning a system of logic that begins with first principles or generalizations and arrives at secondary principles or specifics.

De facto segregation the segregation of students resulting from circumstances such as housing patterns rather than from school policy or law.

De jure segregation the segregation of students on the basis of law, school policy, or a practice designed to accomplish such separation.

Desegregation the process of correcting past practices of racial or any other form of illegal segregation.

Detention keeping a student after school or in a classroom during time usually devoted to a recreation.

Developmental task a task that arises at or about a certain time in an individual's life; its successful achievement leads to the individual's happiness and success with later tasks.

Differentiated staffing educational personnel, selected, educated, and deployed so that optimum use is made of their abilities, interests, preparation, and commitments.

Doctor's degree highest academic degree conferred by a university, including Ph.D. in any field, doctor of education, doctor of juridical science, and doctor of public health (preceded by professional degree in medicine or sanitary engineering).

Dropouts persons not enrolled in school and not high school graduates.

Due process the procedural requirements that must be followed to safeguard individuals from arbitrary, capricious, or unreasonable policies, practices, or actions.

Early childhood education education for a child before the normal period of schooling begins.

Eclecticism drawing elements from several educational philosophies.

Educable child a child of moderately severe mental retardation who is capable of achieving only a limited degree of proficiency in basic learning and who usually must be instructed in a special class.

Educational park a large campuslike school plant containing several units with a variety of facilities, often including many grade levels and varied programs and often surrounded by a variety of cultural resources.

Educational television (ETV) educational programs that are telecast usually by stations outside the school system and received on standard television sets by the public.

Education major a student whose program of studies gives primary emphasis to subject matter in the area of education and who, according to his or her institutional requirements, concentrates a minimum number of courses or semester hours of college credit in the specialty of education.

Elementary school grades 1–6 inclusive; grades 1–8 inclusive in some school systems.

Emergency certificate a substandard certificate for teachers who have not met all the requirements for certification.

Endowment the portion of an institution's income derived from donations.

Enrollment the total number of entering students in a given school unit.

Environmental education the study and analysis of the conditions and causes of pollution, overpopulation, and waste of natural resources and of the ways to preserve our planet's intricate environmental balance.

Epistemology the branch of philosophy that examines the nature of knowledge and learning.

Equal educational opportunity giving every student the educational opportunity to develop fully whatever talents, interests, and abilities she or he may have without regard to race, color, national origin, sex, handicap, or economic status.

Essentialism emphasis on physical sciences as

used by authorities; assumption that there are no absolute truths and that success is based on absorption of knowledge about the physical world.

Ethics the branch of philosophy that examines values and their relation to human actions.

Evaluation testing and measurement to determine the effectiveness, quality, and progress of learning and instruction.

Exceptional learner one whose growth and development deviates from the normal so markedly that he or she cannot receive maximum benefit without modification of the regular school program.

Existentialism emphasis on problem solving about highly controversial and emotional issues in any subject matter area; assumption that learners "define" themselves and their relationships to the environment by their choices.

Expenditures per student charges incurred for a particular period of time divided by a student unit of measure, e.g., average daily attendance or average daily membership.

Experimentalism emphasis on social sciences as a framework for problem solving; assumption that the physical world is constantly changing.

Experimental schools schools in which new methods or materials are tried under controlled conditions.

Expulsion the action, taken by school authorities, compelling a student to withdraw from school for reasons such as extreme misbehavior, incorrigibility, or unsatisfactory achievement or progress in school work.

Flexible scheduling a technique for organizing time more effectively to meet the needs of instruction by dividing the school day into uniform time modules that can be combined to fit a task.

Futurism focuses not only on predicting future developments but also on formulating techniques and procedures needed for preparing for such developments.

Future shock term coined by Alvin Toffler that refers to the accelerated pace of change and to the disorientation of those unable to adapt to altered norms, institutions, and values.

General education learning that should be the common possession of all educated people.

General educational development (GED) program academic instruction to prepare persons to take the high school equivalency examination.

Gifted learner term most frequently applied to those with exceptional intellectual ability; it may also refer to learners with outstanding ability in athletics, leadership, music, creativity, and so forth.

Graded school system a division of schools into groups of students according to the curriculum or the ages of pupils, as in the six elementary grades.

Handicapped a "handicapped" person is one who has one or more of the exceptionalities defined below, whether or not he or she requires special education.

Educable mentally retarded a condition of mental retardation that includes students who are educable in the academic, social, and occupational areas even though moderate supervision may be necessary.

Trainable mentally retarded a condition of mental retardation that includes students who are capable of only very limited meaningful achievement in the traditional basic academic skills but who are capable of profiting from programs of training in self-care and simple job or vocational skills.

Hard of hearing a hearing impairment, whether permanent or fluctuating, that adversely affects a student's educational performance but that is not included under the definition of "deaf" in this section.

Deaf a hearing impairment that is so severe that the student is impaired in processing linguistic information through hearing, with or without amplification, with adverse effects on educational performance.

Speech impaired a communication disorder, such as stuttering, impaired articulation, a language impairment, or a voice impairment, that adversely affects a student's educational performance.

Visually handicapped a visual impairment that, even with correction, adversely affects a student's educational performance. The term includes both partially seeing and blind children.

Seriously emotionally disturbed a condition exhibiting one or more of the following characteristics over a long period of time and to a marked degree, that adversely affects educational performance: an inability to learn that cannot be explained by intellectual, sensory, or health factors; an inability to build or maintain satisfactory interpersonal relationships with peers and teachers; inappropriate types of behavior or feelings under normal circumstances; a general pervasive mood of unhappiness or depression; or a tendency to develop physical symptoms or fears associated with personal or school problems. The term includes children who are schizophrenic or autistic.

Orthopedically impaired a severe orthopedic impairment that adversely affects a student's educational performance. The term includes impairments caused by congenital anomaly or disease as well as those from other causes.

Other health impaired limited strength, vitality, or alertness due to chronic or acute health problems such as a heart condition, tuberculosis, rheumatic fever, nephritis, asthma, sickle cell anemia, hemophilia, epilepsy, lead poisoning, leukemia, or diabetes, that adversely affects a student's educational performance.

Specific learning disabled a disorder in one or more of the basic psychological processes involved in understanding or using language, spoken or written, which may manifest itself in an imperfect ability to listen, think, speak, read, write, spell, or do mathematical calculations. The term includes such conditions as perceptual handicaps, brain injury, minimal brain dysfunction, dyslexia, and developmental aphasia. The term does not include children who have learning problems that are primarily the result of visual, hearing, or motor handicaps, of mental retardation, or of environmental, cultural, or economic disadvantage.

Deaf-blind concomitant hearing and visual impairments, the combination of which causes such severe communication and other developmental and educational problems that they cannot be accommodated in special education programs solely for deaf or blind students.

Multihandicapped concomitant impairments (such as mentally retarded–blind, mentally retarded–orthopedically impaired, etc.), the combination of which causes such severe educational problems that they cannot be accommodated in special education programs solely for one of the impairments. The term does not include deaf-blind students. This category includes those students who are severely or profoundly mentally retarded.

Head Start program federally funded program at the preelementary school level designed to provide learning opportunities for those children who have not had access to environments and experiences conducive to academic achievement.

Herbartian method formal system of presenting subject matter to students by using the five formal steps of preparation, association, presentation, generalization, and application.

Heterogeneous grouping a group or class of students who show normal variation in ability or performance.

Homogeneous grouping the classification of pupils for the purpose of forming an instructional group with a relatively high degree of similarity in regard to certain factors that affect learning.

Hornbook a single printed page containing the alphabet, syllables, a prayer, and other simple words, used in colonial times as the beginner's first book or preprimer. Hornbooks were attached to wooden paddles for ease in carrying, each covered with a thin sheet of transparent horn.

Humanistic teacher education an approach to teacher education concerned not only with teacher candidates' cognitive development but with their emotional and attitudinal development as well.

Idealism a doctrine holding that all knowledge is derived from ideas and emphasizing moral and spiritual reality as a preeminent source of explanation.

Independent school a nonpublic school unaffiliated with any church or other agency.

Individualized Education Program (IEP) the mechanism through which a handicapped child's special needs are identified; goals, objectives, and services are outlined; and methods for evaluating progress are delineated.

Individualized instruction instruction that is particularized to the interests, needs, and achievements of individual learners.

Individually guided education (IGE) an individualized instructional program in which teachers and students plan together the learner objectives.

Individually prescribed instruction (IPI) individualized instruction in a systematic, step-by-step program based on a carefully selected sequence and a detailed listing of behaviorally stated instructional objectives.

In-service education continuing education for teachers who are actually teaching or are in service.

Institutions of higher education postsecondary institutions that are legally authorized to offer at least a one-year program of college-level studies leading toward a degree.

Instructional materials center (IMC) an area where students can use books, newspapers, pamphlets, magazines, sound tapes, slides, and films; spaces are usually provided for students to use these materials (see learning resource center).

Instructional technology the application of scientific method and knowledge to teaching and learning, either with or without machines but commonly responsive to the learning needs of individual students.

Instructional television (ITV) lessons telecast specifically for educational institutions, usually received only by special arrangement and on special equipment.

Integration the process of mixing students of different races in schools to overcome segregation.

Interest centers centers usually associated with an open classroom that provide for independent student activities related to a specific subject.

Intermediate school a synonym for middle school.

Intermediate unit (1) a division of elementary school comprising grades 4, 5, and 6; (2) a level of school organization between the state and the local district, often but not necessarily coterminous with the county.

International education the study of educational, social, political, and economic forces in international relations with special emphasis on the role and potentialities of educational forces; also includes programs to further the development of nations.

Kindergarten term coined by Froebel, who started the first schools for children aged four, five, and six.

Labeling categorizing or classifying students for the purpose of educational placement.

Laboratory school a school under the control of, or closely associated with, a teacher preparation institution whose facilities may be used for demonstration, experimentation, and student teaching.

Land grant college a college maintained to carry out the purposes of the first Morrill Act of 1862 and the supplementary legislation granting public lands to states for the establishment of colleges and to provide practical education such as agriculture and mechanical arts.

Latin Grammar School a classical secondary school with a curriculum consisting largely of Latin and Greek; its purpose was preparation for college.

Learning a change of behavior as a result of experience.

Learning disability an educationally significant discrepancy between a child's apparent capacity for language behavior and his or her actual level of language functioning.

Learning resource center a specially designed space containing a wide range of supplies and equipment for the use of individual students and small groups pursuing independent study (see instructional materials center).

Least restrictive environment the program best suited to meet a handicapped child's special needs while remaining as close as possible to the regular educational program.

Life-adjustment education experiences through which the unique and total resources of each individual are discovered and developed.

Limited-English proficient (LEP) students who have limited ability to understand, speak, or read English and who have a primary or home language other than English.

Magnet schools specialized schools open to all students in a district, sometimes on a lottery basis.

Mainstreaming a plan by which exceptional children receive special education in the regular classroom as much of the time as possible.

Marketable the ability or process of making oneself desirable to a prospective employer.

Master's degree an academic degree higher than a bachelor's but lower than a doctor's.

Mastery learning an educational practice in which an individual masters one task before moving on to the next.

Mean test score the score obtained by dividing the total sum of scores of all individuals in a group by the number of individuals in that group.

Mentally handicapped student a student whose mental powers lack maturity or are so deficient that they hinder normal achievement.

Mental retardation below average intellectual functioning.

Metaphysics the division of philosophy that examines the nature of reality.

Methodology procedure used to teach the content or discipline.

Microteaching a clinical approach to teacher training in which the teacher candidate teaches a small group of students for a brief time while concentrating on a specific teaching skill.

Middle school a type of two to four-year school organization containing various combinations of the middle grades, commonly grades 5–8, and serving as an intermediate unit between the elementary school and the high school.

Migration movement of students into or out of state to attend college. Net migration equals the number of students who come into a state minus the number of students who leave the home state to attend college.

Minicourse a short, self-contained instructional sequence.

Minimum competency testing exit level tests designed to ascertain whether or not students have achieved basic levels of performance in areas like reading, writing, and computation.

Modular scheduling arrangement of class periods in units of fifteen, twenty, thirty, or forty minutes to permit greater flexibility; sometimes called flexible scheduling.

Monitorial schools schools developed by Joseph Lancaster and Andrew Bell in which one teacher taught a number of bright students or monitors who, in turn, taught other groups of children.

Motivation impetus causing one to act.

Multipurpose high school features comprehensive, diversified offerings to meet the needs of all students regardless of their special interests, aptitudes, and capacities.

National assessment a massive national testing program that helps ascertain the effectiveness of American education and how well students have learned.

National Council for the Accreditation of Teacher Education (NCATE) an organization that evaluates teacher education programs in many colleges and universities.

National Education Association (NEA) the largest organization of educators; the NEA is concerned with the overall improvement of education and of the conditions of educators.

Nongraded school a type of school organization in which grade lines are eliminated for a sequence of two or more years.

Normal school historically, the first American institution devoted exclusively to teacher training.

Norm-referenced data data based on local, state, or national norms.

Nursery school a school that offers supervised educational experiences for prekindergarten children.

Objective purpose or goal.

Objective test a test yielding results that can be evaluated or scored by different persons with like outcomes.

Observation techniques structured methods for observing various aspects of the entire school or specific classroom environment.

Open classroom a modern educational innovation in which self-contained classrooms are replaced by an open plan with individualized instruction and freedom for the child to move about the school.

Open enrollment the practice of permitting students to attend the school of their choice within their school system.

Open space school a school building without interior walls.

Overachievement performing above the level normally expected on the basis of ability measures.

Paraprofessional one who serves as an aide, assisting the teacher in the classroom (see teacher aide).

Parochial school an institution operated and controlled by a religious denomination.

Pedagogy the science of teaching.

Perennialism emphasis on humanities as presented in great books; assumption that there are absolute truths and standards more real than the physical world.

Performance-based education learning designed to produce actual accomplishment as distinguished from knowing.

Performance contract an agreement between schools and commercial educational agencies or teachers that guarantees to produce specified educational results.

Permanent certificate certificate issued after a candidate has completed all the requirements for full recognition as a teacher.

Philosophy of education principles that guide professional educators in decision making.

Planned-Programming-Budgeting System (PPBS) an application of systems analysis to the allocation of resources to various competing educational purposes and needs through systematic planning, programming, budgeting, and evaluation.

Pragmatism a philosophy that maintains that the value and truth of ideas are tested by their practical consequences.

Primary school a separately organized and administered elementary school for students in the lower elementary grades, usually including grades 1–3 or the equivalent and sometimes including pre-primary years.

Private school a school that is controlled by an individual or by an agency other than a state, a subdivision of a state, or the federal government, usually supported primarily by other than public funds, and the operation of whose program rests with other than publicly elected or appointed officials.

Programmed learning any learning device that may be used by a student in such a way that a reaction to the student's activities is immediately supplied.

Progressive education an educational philoso-phy emphasizing democracy, the importance of creative and meaningful activity, the real needs of students, and the relationship between school and community.

Progressivism educational philosophy in which learning focuses on the experiences of the child while he or she is acquiring the content of the curriculum.

Proprietary school an educational institution that is under private control and whose profits derived from revenues are subject to taxation.

Psychomotor domain motor skill area of learning.

Psychomotor learning the acquisition of muscular development directly related to mental processes.

PTA Parent Teacher Association; officially, the National Congress of Parents and Teachers.

Public school a school operated by publicly elected or appointed school officials in which the program and activities are under the control of these officials and which is supported primarily by public funds.

Racial bias the degree to which an individual's beliefs and behavior are prejudiced on the basis of race.

Racial discrimination any action that limits or denies a person or group of persons opportunities, privileges, roles, or rewards on the basis of race.

Racial/ethnic group classification indicating general racial or ethnic heritage based on self-identification as in data collected by the Bureau of the Census or on observer identification as in data collected by the Office for Civil Rights. These categories are in accordance with the Office of Management and Budget standard classification scheme presented below:

White a person having origins in any of the original peoples of Europe, North Africa, or the Middle East.

Black a person having origins in any of the Black racial groups of Africa.

Hispanic a person of Mexican, Puerto Rican, Cuban, Central or South American, or other Spanish culture or origin, regardless of race.

Asian or Pacific Islander a person having origins in any of the original peoples of the Far East, Southeast Asia, the Indian subcontinent, or the Pacific Islands. This area includes, for example, China, India, Japan, Korea, the Philippine Islands, and Samoa.

American Indian or Alaskan Native a person having origins in any of the original peoples of North America and maintaining cultural identification through tribal affiliation or community recognition.

Racism the collection of attitudes, beliefs, and behavior that results from the assumption that one race is superior to other races.

Realism a philosophy holding that knowledge is derived from perceptual experience; it emphasizes the natural sciences in its attitude that the physical world assists a person's search for true knowledge.

Reconstructionism implies that one has decided what the "perfect" form of society is and seeks to reach that society through teaching techniques associated with experimentalism/existentialism.

Religiously affiliated school a private school over which, in most cases, a parent church group exercises some control or to which it provides some form of subsidy. Catholic schools include those affiliated with the Roman Catholic Church, including the "private" Catholic schools operated by religious orders. Other affiliation includes schools associated with other religious denominations. An unaffiliated school is usually privately operated or under control of a board of trustees or directors.

Remedial courses planned diagnostic and remedial activities for individual students or groups of students, designed to correct and prevent further learning difficulties that interfere with the student's expected progress in developing skills, understandings, and appreciations in any of several required courses.

Reorganization the act of legally changing the designation of a school district, changing the geographical area of a school district or incorporating a part or all of a school district with an adjoining district.

Resumé a written statement of qualifications prepared by an applicant for employment.

Revenues all funds received from external sources, net of refunds, and correcting transactions. Noncash transactions such as receipt of services, commodities, or other receipts "in kind" are excluded, as are funds received from the issuance of debt, liquidation of investments, and nonroutine sale of property.

Revenue sharing distribution of federal money to state and local governments to use as they wish.

Sabbatical a leave usually granted with pay after a teacher has taught for a specified period of time.

Salary the total amount regularly paid or stipulated to be paid to an individual, before deductions, for personal services rendered while on the payroll of a business or organization.

School a division of the school system consisting of students comprising one or more grade groups or other identifiable groups, organized as one unit with one or more teachers to give instruction of a defined type, and housed in a school plant of one or more buildings.

School bonds a typical method for financing a substantial, one-time educational expenditure such as a new school building.

School district an educational agency at the local level that exists primarily to operate public schools or to contract for public school services. This term is used synonymously with the terms "local basic administrative unit" and "local education agency."

School finance the ways in which monies are raised, allocated to, and handled in the schools.

School superintendent the chief administrator of a school system.

Schools without walls a type of alternative education program that stresses involving the total community as a learning resource.

Secondary school a school comprising any span of grades beginning with the next grade following an elementary or middle school and ending with or below grade 12.

Self-contained classroom a form of classroom organization in which the same teacher conducts all or nearly all the instruction in all or most subjects in the same classroom for all or most of the school day.

Self-instructional device a term used to include instructional materials that can be used by the student.

Senior high school a secondary school offering the final years of high school work necessary for graduation and invariably preceded by a junior high school.

Separate but equal a doctrine that holds that

equality of treatment is accorded when the races are provided substantially equal facilities, even though the facilities are separate.

Sexism a belief that one sex is superior to the other.

Special education direct instructional activities or special learning experiences designed primarily for students identified as having exceptionalities in one of more aspects of the cognitive process and/or as being underachievers in relation to the general level or mode of their overall abilities. Such services usually are directed at students with the following exceptionalities: (1) physically handicapped; (2) emotionally handicapped; (3) culturally different, including compensatory education; (4) mentally retarded; (5) having learning disabilities. Programs for the mentally gifted and talented are also included in some special education programs.

Standardized test an instrument presenting a uniform task or series of tasks to be performed according to specified directions and under uniform conditions so that individual performances may be compared with one another and with a reference or normative group.

State educational agency operations activities performed for the purpose of executing the responsibilities of the state educational agency, an organization established by laws for the primary purpose of carrying out at least a part of the educational responsibilities of a state.

Student an individual for whom instruction is provided in an educational program under the jurisdiction of a school, school system, or other educational institution. No distinction is made between the terms "student" and "pupil"; the term "student" is used to include individuals at all instructional levels.

Subject-centered school or curriculum a curriculum organization in which learning activities and content are planned around subject fields of knowledge, such as history and science.

Suspension temporary dismissal of a student from school by duly authorized school personnel in accordance with established regulations.

Subjective test a test that will not necessarily have the same outcome when scored by different persons.

Systems analysis a rational and systematic approach to education that analyzes objectives, then decides which resources and methods will achieve those objectives most efficiently; each step is carefully measured, tested, and controlled to make sure it moves toward the next objective.

Teacher aide a lay person who assists teachers with clerical work, library duties, housekeeping duties, noninstructional supervision, and other nonprofessional tasks (see paraprofessional).

Teacher Corps a federally funded program that gives teachers and student teachers opportunities to work with disadvantaged children in their homes and communities while attending courses and seminars on the special problems they encounter.

Teacher preparation programs departments, schools, and institutions of higher education that confer degrees in education.

Teaching center combination library, workshop, and laboratory with rich resources to help teachers solve problems and grow professionally.

Team teaching a plan by which several teachers, organized into a team with a leader, provide the instruction for a larger group of children than would usually be found in a self-contained classroom.

Tenure a system of school employment in which educators, having served a probationary period, retain their positions indefinitely unless dismissed for legally specified reasons through clearly established procedures.

Tracking the method of placing students according to their ability level in homogeneous classes or learning experiences where they all follow the same curriculum, i.e., college preparatory or vocational.

Unemployed civilians who, during a survey period, had no employment but were available for work and (1) had engaged in any specific job-seeking activity within the past four weeks or (2) were waiting to be called back to a job from which they had been laid off or (3) were waiting to report to a new wage or salary job within 30 days.

Unemployment rate the number of unemployed persons seeking employment as a percent of the civilian labor force.

Ungraded school a synonym for nongraded school.

Unit of learning a series of organized ideas and activities planned to provide worthwhile experiences for an individual or group and expected to result in a desired outcome.

Values principles that guide an individual in personal decision making.

Values clarification a model, comprised of various strategies, that encourages students to express and clarify their values on different topics.

Vocational education training that is intended to prepare the student for a particular job or to give a basic skill needed in several vocations.

Voucher plan a means of financing schooling whereby funds are allocated to students' parents who then purchase education for their children in any public or private school.

Work-study program program that combines part-time classroom study with gainful employment in industry or in the community.

Name Index

V

Vespasian, 269
Voltaire, 275

W

Waldheim, Kurt, 479
Webster, Noah, 300
Wegmann, Robert, 204
Wheatley, Phyllis, 307

Whitehead, Alfred N., 405
Willard, Emma, 309
Wolfgang, Charles H., 351, 361, 362
Wright, J. Skelly, 206

X

Xenophon, 267

Z

Ziegler, L. Harmon, 224

Subject Index